Praise for the First Edition

Each aspect is explained with numerous examples that can be applied to real-world problems right away.

—Ulf Ditmer, JavaRanch

Any developer who is making serious use of iText would be a fool not to buy this book.

—Dave Gilbert, jfree.org

Thorough and complete ... will be a long-running, valuable resource for iText and PDF.

—Alan Dennis
Software Architect, MyFamily.com

One of the best technical books I have ever read! Great work!

—Oliver Zeigermann
Technical Trainer, CoreMedia AG

I wholeheartedly recommend it.

—Doug James
eReporting Team Lead, Benefitfocus.com, Inc.

Impressive! It provides depth without all the noise.

—Justin Lee, President, Antwerkz Inc.

Valuable to any developer using PDF.

—Stuart Caborn, Consultant, Thoughtworks

iText in Action
Second Edition

BRUNO LOWAGIE

MANNING

Greenwich
(74° w. long.)

For online information and ordering of this and other Manning books, please visit www.manning.com. The publisher offers discounts on this book when ordered in quantity. For more information, please contact

Special Sales Department
Manning Publications Co.
180 Broad Street
Suite 1323
Stamford, CT 06901
Email: orders@manning.com

Manning Publications Co.   Development editor: Katharine Osborne
180 Broad Street, Suite 1323   Copyeditor: Andy Carroll
Stamford, CT 06901   Cover designer: Marija Tudor
                                         Typesetter: Gordan Salinovic

ISBN 9781935182610
Printed in the United States of America
1 2 3 4 5 6 7 8 9 10 – MAL – 15 14 13 12 11 10

To Ingeborg, Inigo, and Jago

brief contents

contents

16 *PDF streams* *526*

preface

In the summer of 2009, Manning Publications contacted me with the offer to write a revision of the first edition of *iText in Action*, published in 2007.

I initially refused, much to the surprise of the publisher. He put forward several arguments in favor of a second edition: the book had received good reviews, the first printing sold out in about a year, and the book was still selling well, in spite of the fact that it was almost three years old and that its content was probably somewhat outdated.

So I had to clarify: "I want to write a *second edition*, but I don't want it to be a *revision*." I'm always disappointed when a revised version of a book is a rehash of the first version, with only a limited amount of new material. I wanted to write a book that was valuable for developers who already owned the first edition.

I had accumulated a series of new examples, demonstrating techniques that were either presented differently, or were missing from the first edition. Moreover, I had been giving iText training sessions for different companies, and I had discovered that the order of the chapters in the first book wasn't ideal. The content needed to be reorganized, and the only good way to achieve that was to rewrite the book from scratch.

I realized that this meant more work than merely writing a revision, and although hard work doesn't scare me, I hesitated. For many companies and families, 2008 had been the year of the economic crisis, but that was the least of my concerns. For me, it was the year my twelve-year-old son was diagnosed with bone cancer. Suddenly all priorities changed.

Eighteen chemotherapy treatments later, with major surgery in between to replace his knee by a prosthesis, life wasn't the same as before. I received plenty of support from the iText community, and I want to thank everyone for being patient with me. Unfortunately, there were some who emailed me, demanding a solution for their problem for free, not realizing that I had far more important personal worries than their technical problems.

In the end, I decided to accept the offer from Manning and write a second book about iText, because it was an opportunity, and probably the best chance I would get to pick up the iText thread. There's no better way to make an inventory of a product's functionality than to write a book about it. Some new iText features were written to fill gaps I discovered while writing the book. The creative process was also very inspiring; some recently added enhancements started off as examples for the book, and eventually made it into the main iText release.

Looking back, I'm glad I took up the challenge, and I'm happy with the result. This second edition is more advanced than the first edition, aiming at the more experienced developer who wants to know more about the Portable Document Format, not just about iText. I can't hide that I'm very passionate about PDF, and I hope this book transmits this passion to as many readers as possible.

preface to the first edition

I have lost count of the number of PCs I have worn out since I started my career as a software developer—but I will never forget my first computer.

I was only 12 years old when I started programming in BASIC. I had to learn English at the same time because there simply weren't any books on computer programming in my mother tongue (Dutch). This was in 1982. Windows didn't exist yet; I worked on a TI99/4A home computer from Texas Instruments. When I told my friends at school about it, they looked at me as if I had just been beamed down from the Starship Enterprise.

Two years later, my parents bought me my first personal computer: a Tandy/Radio Shack TRS80/4P. As the P indicates, it was supposed to be a portable computer, but in reality it was bigger than my mother's sewing machine. It could be booted from a hard disk, but I didn't have one; nor did I have any software besides the TRSDOS and its BASIC interpreter. By the time I was 16, I had written my own word-processing program, an indexed flat-file database system, and a drawing program—nothing fancy, considering the low resolution of the built-in, monochrome green computer screen.

I don't remember exactly what happened to me at that age—maybe it was my delayed discovery of girls—but it suddenly struck me that I was becoming a first-class nerd. So I made a 180-degree turn, studying Latin and math in high school and taking evening classes at a local art school. I decided that I wanted to become an artist instead of going to college. As a compromise with my parents, I studied civil architectural engineering at Ghent University. In my final year, I bought myself a Compaq portable computer to write my master's thesis. It was like finding a long-lost friend!

After I earned my degree as an architect, I decided that it was time to return to the world of computers.

In 1996 I enrolled in a program that would retrain me as a software engineer. I learned and taught a brand-new programming language, Java. During my apprenticeship, I was put in charge of an experimental broadband Internet project. It was my first acquaintance with the web. This expertise resulted in different assignments for the Flemish government. One of my tasks was to write an R&D report on standard internet-intranet tools for GIS applications. That's when I wrote my first Java servlets.

I returned to Ghent University as an employee in 1998. When I published my first free/open source software library, I knew I had finally found my vocation. Now I have had the chance to write a book about it. I tried to give this book the personal touch I often miss when reading technical writings. I hope you will enjoy reading it as much as I have enjoyed writing it.

acknowledgments

I thought that writing this second edition would be easier than writing the first. I was wrong. Yes, the process of writing itself was easier because I had the experience, but I didn't take into account how little free time I have now, compared to three years ago. On top of that, different incidents have cost me handfuls of time, such as my now ex-hosting provider which caused me to lose all the data on my dedicated server.

I don't know what I would have done without the support of my wife, Ingeborg Willaert, and my children, Inigo and Jago, during those moments of despair. They always remind me of what is really important in life, and that helps when faced with problems big and small. I want to thank them for that.

iText wouldn't be iText if it weren't for the developers. In the first place, I would like to thank Paulo Soares, who started working on iText in the summer of 2000 and who has been contributing code ever since. Kudos to Xavier Le Vourch for the continuous integration server he has set up for iText, and for the many code clean-up operations. Two other developers complete the list of project members on the SourceForge pages of the iText project: Mark Storer, who was the technical editor of the first edition, and Kevin Day, who designed the functionality to extract text from PDF files. Numerous people contributed valuable code, fixed bugs, added new features, and posted useful answers on the mailing list. The list of names is too long to sum up. Thank you all for making iText the library it is today!

I want to thank Adobe's PDF technical standards evangelist Leonard Rosenthol, for sharing his insights on the PDF format; Adobe's VP of engineering Bob Wulff; and last but not least, Adobe's principal scientist Jim King, who reviewed and corrected sections 13.1 and 13.2.

Special thanks go to Andrew Binstock, Kevin Brown, and Michael Bradbury. There wouldn't be any iText business without their help. I'm also grateful to Christophe Vangeel, Evi Mellebeek, Frank Gielen, Peter Camps, Peter Myngheer, and Wouter De Stecker for helping me understand the different aspects of doing business, and I want to thank Stephan Janssen for organizing Devoxx.

A Flemish "hartelijk bedankt" goes to all of my current and former colleagues at Ghent University, especially to my fellow whiteboard artists, Johan Lauryssens, Cédric Peirsegaele, and Peter Van de Voorde; to my former bosses, professor Geert De Soete and Bernard Becue; to my current bosses, Danny Schellemans and Luc Verschraegen; and to the rector and vice-rector of the University, professor Paul Van Cauwenberghe and professor Luc Moens.

I want to take advantage of these acknowledgment pages to thank my employer for the flexibility I was offered while my son was treated for cancer.

During the year my son was in the hospital, many people gave me the courage to keep strong: William Alexander Segraves, Juancho Diaz, Ingrid Adriaens, Heidi Naeye, Marleen Depaemelaere, Ines Bruyninckx, Liesje Berteloot, Tania Bruggeman, Cathy De Kerf, Mieke Simoen, Wendy Jacobs, and many others.

The theme of this book was inspired by the friends of the film festival in Ghent, and I want to thank Wim De Witte for the excellent selection of movies presented each year, and Daniella De Decker, for helping us enjoy as many movies as possible during the festival.

I would like to thank all the people at Manning Publications for giving me the opportunity to write this book, including publisher Marjan Bace, Michael Stephens, Katharine Osborne, Andy Carroll, Elizabeth Martin, Gordan Salinovic, and Mary Piergies, as well as everyone else on the team who worked on my book.

Sincere thanks to the people who reviewed my manuscript. Their remarks and suggestions at different stages of development were invaluable to me in making this a better book: Andrew Binstock, Mark Stephens, Marc Gravell, Leonardo Padula, Jim King, Kevin Day, John S. Griffin, William A. Segraves, Alexis Pigeon, Paulo Soares, Thomas Morgner, Michael Klink, Matt Michalak, Michael Niedermair, and Saicharan Manga for completing a technical proofread of the manuscript shortly before it went to press.

Finally, I want to thank you, the people who are using iText. You are the ones who have kept me going! Many of you have sent me nice notes of appreciation. Thanks! I couldn't have written this book without your encouragement.

about this book

This book will teach you about PDF, Adobe's Portable Document Format, from a Java developer's point of view. You'll learn how to use iText in a Java/J2EE application to produce and manipulate PDF documents. Along the way, you'll become acquainted with interesting PDF features and discover e-document functionality you may not have known about before.

Who should read this book?

This book is intended for Java developers who want to enhance their projects with dynamic PDF generation or manipulation. It assumes you have some background in Java programming.

This book includes lots of ready-made solutions that can easily be adapted and integrated into larger projects. For reasons of convenience, most of the examples are constructed as standalone command-line applications. If you want to run these examples in a web application, you should know how to set up an application server, where to put the necessary Java archive files (JARs) and resources, and how to deploy a servlet.

.NET developers using iTextSharp, the C# port of iText, can also benefit from this book, but they'll have to adapt the examples.

Knowledge of the Portable Document Format isn't necessary, because this book will explain a good deal of the PDF functionality and syntax where needed. ISO-32000-1 is a good companion to this book, for those who want to know every detail about PDF internals.

How to use this book

You can read this book chronologically, starting with the part about creating PDFs, moving on to the part about manipulating documents, and then learning some essential skills in part 3. Part 4 looks under the hood and digs deeper into the PDF specification.

You can also read the book in random order or thematically, selecting specific chapters that explain how to meet your own requirements. Once you're well acquainted with iText, you'll probably use the book as a reference manual. In particular, the tables in chapter 14 are the result of my own frustration with tables that were too scattered throughout different chapters in the first edition.

What you'll be able to achieve after reading this book

The book consists of four parts:

- *Part 1*—Creating PDF documents from scratch
- *Part 2*—Manipulating existing PDF documents
- *Part 3*—Essential iText skills
- *Part 4*—Under the hood

Throughout this book, the examples use a movie database created for a (fictional) film festival. You'll access this database from a series of simple applications, creating and manipulating different PDF files that could be useful for the visitors of the imaginary film festival.

Creating PDF documents

In chapters 1 and 2 you'll create a series of PDF documents from scratch. You'll use SQL statements to query a movie database, loop over the ResultSet, and add the data from each record to a PDF document using high-level objects such as Chunks, Phrases, Paragraphs, and so on. You'll create PDF documents without having to know anything about the PDF specification.

In chapter 3, you'll learn how to draw lines, shapes, and text to create a timetable visualizing the screenings, using a different color for each festival category. To achieve this, you'll need low-level operations that demand a sound understanding of how PDF works.

In chapter 4, one of the most important chapters of the first part, you'll use the database information to create documents containing tabular data. You'll learn almost everything there is to know about the PdfPTable and PdfPCell objects.

Your knowledge about tables and cells will be completed in chapter 5, where you'll learn how to add custom behavior to a table and its cells using events. Finally, you'll also learn about page events. You'll add the finishing touch to your documents in the form of headers, footers, page numbers, and a watermark.

After reading the first part of the book, you'll be able to write a proof of concept for any project that requires you to generate PDF reports from scratch. If your project also involves existing PDF documents, you'll need to move on to part 2.

Manipulating PDF documents

Consider what you can do with paper documentation: you can bundle different articles into a book, you can cut out the pages of a large catalog to create a brochure containing only those pages that are interesting for your customers, you can fill out blanks in an exercise book, and so on.

All of this is also possible with PDF and iText. You'll use `PdfReader` to access an existing PDF file, and you'll use one or more of these document manipulation classes:

- `PdfWriter` in combination with `PdfImportedPage` objects, if you want to take "photocopies" of specific pages
- `PdfStamper`, if you want to add content to an existing PDF document
- `PdfCopy`, `PdfSmartCopy`, or `PdfCopyFields` to combine a selection of pages from different, existing documents into a new PDF document

All these classes will be explained in chapter 6.

You'll have a closer look at the `PdfStamper` class in chapter 7, where you'll use it to annotate a document.

You can interpret the word "annotate" in different ways. One special type of annotation in PDF is the interactive form field. These are used in forms using AcroForm technology. Another type of PDF form is based on the XML Forms Architecture (XFA). You'll learn about both types of interactive forms in chapter 8.

Having read parts 1 and 2, you'll have a good idea of the possibilities offered by iText, but there's more.

Essential iText skills

For the sake of simplicity, most of the examples in this book are standalone applications, but a majority of projects use iText as a PDF engine in server-side web applications. You'll certainly benefit from chapter 9 if you want to avoid the pitfalls you might encounter while integrating your iText application into a Java servlet.

Once your proof of concept is online, you'll probably be confronted with many extra user requirements:

- Can you change this or that color?
- Can you print the text in a different font?
- Can you protect the document against abuse?

Part 3 will complete your knowledge about iText.

After mastering the content of the first three parts of the book, you'll be able to meet over 90 percent of the standard requirements that have ever come up on the iText mailing list in the past 10 years. But please read on if you're hungry for more.

Under the hood

While the first three parts give you the high-level view of PDF, part 4 will focus on the lowest level of PDF creation and manipulation. You should read this part

- if you want to know what a PDF looks like under the hood
- if you need a short introduction to and a quick reference for ISO-32000-1
- if you want to learn how to tweak PDF files using iText's low-level objects and methods

In chapter 13, you'll learn that PDF has undergone many changes over the years. One of Adobe's important goals was that every new version of the specification had to be backward-compatible. This was possible thanks to the well-designed architecture of a PDF file (the *Carousel Object System*). By studying the different objects that make up a PDF document, you'll learn how iText creates a PDF file.

Chapter 14 focuses on the streams holding the content of a page in a PDF document. You'll learn all the methods for drawing lines and shapes (graphics state), and for writing letters and words (text state).

In chapter 15, you'll discover how to make content optional, and you'll also learn about structure in the content stream of a page. You'll learn how to parse content streams of existing PDF pages.

Finally, you'll get a closer look at the other streams that can be found in a PDF document: images, fonts, file attachments, and rich media.

The goal of the book

My goal for this book is for it to become a must-have reference for the many developers who are already familiar with iText. With this book, they'll have a complete overview of iText's powerful PDF capabilities. But, let's not forget the first-time users of iText. This book will lower their learning curve and inspire them to use PDF in ways they hadn't previously considered.

Code conventions

First use of technical terms is in *italic*. The same goes for emphasized terms.

Source code in listings or in text is in `fixed width font`. Some code lines are in **`bold fixed width font`** for emphasis. Java methods and parameters, XML elements and attributes, PDF operators and operands, are also presented using `fixed width font`. PDF names are preceded by a forward slash; this is a `/Name`. Methods can be recognized by the parentheses that are added: this is a `method()`. In most cases, the parameters are omitted but are explained in the text.

Occasionally, code lines that are too long for the page but that shouldn't be split on screen are broken with a code-continuation character (➡).

Code annotations accompany many of the source code listings, highlighting important concepts. Numbered annotations correspond to explanations that follow the listing.

Software requirements and downloads

iText is a free and open source library distributed by 1T3XT BVBA. You can download it from itextpdf.com or from the SourceForge site. The software is protected by the Affero General Public License (AGPL). iText requires Java 5; iTextSharp requires .NET 2.0.

All examples have been tested in a SUN Java runtime environment on Windows XP and Fedora Linux. You can download the source code, resources, and all the tools that are required to compile and run the examples from the SVN repository on SourceForge or from the publisher's website at www.manning.com/iTextinActionSecondEdition.

See appendix B.1.2 to find out how to get access to these examples.

about the title

By combining introductions, overviews, and how-to examples, the *In Action* books are designed to help with learning and remembering. According to research in cognitive science, the things people remember are things they discover during self-motivated exploration.

Although no one at Manning is a cognitive scientist, we're convinced that for learning to become permanent, it must pass through stages of exploration, play, and, interestingly, retelling of what is being learned. People understand and remember new things, which is to say they master them, only after actively exploring them. Humans learn in action. An essential part of an *In Action* book is that it is example driven. It encourages the reader to try things out, to play with new code, and to explore new ideas.

There is another, more mundane reason for the title of this book: our readers are busy. They use books to do a job or solve a problem. They need books that allow them to jump in and jump out easily and learn just what they want just when they want it. They need books that aid them in action. The books in this series are designed for such readers.

about the cover illustration

On the cover of *iText in Action, Second Edition* is "A woman from Kastela," a small town near Split in Dalmatia, Croatia. The illustration is taken from a reproduction of an album of Croatian traditional costumes from 1879 by Nikola Arsenovic, published by the Ethnographic Museum in Split. The illustrations were obtained from a helpful librarian at the Ethnographic Museum in Split, itself situated in the Roman core of the medieval center of the town: the ruins of Emperor Diocletian's retirement palace from around AD 304. The book includes finely colored illustrations of figures from different regions of Croatia, accompanied by descriptions of the costumes and of everyday life.

Kastela is a series of seven settlements located northwest of Split that developed around seven castles overlooking a large bay. The settlements are now treated as a single town with a population of 40,000. Once an ancient Greek port, a stopover point for Roman patricians and Venetian royals and a summer place for Croatian kings, Kastela today is a tourist resort, with long sandy beaches and terraces overlooking the Adriatic Sea, surrounded by pine, tamaris, and olive trees.

Dress codes and lifestyles have changed over the last 200 years, and the diversity by region, so rich at the time, has faded away. It is now hard to tell apart the inhabitants of different continents, let alone of different hamlets or towns separated by only a few miles. Perhaps we have traded cultural diversity for a more varied personal life— certainly for a more varied and fast-paced technological life.

Manning celebrates the inventiveness and initiative of the computer business with book covers based on the rich diversity of regional life of two centuries ago, brought back to life by illustrations from old books and collections like this one.

Part 1

Creating PDF documents from scratch

Part 1 shows you how to create a document from scratch. Concepts such as iText's basic building blocks and direct content will be introduced, and important objects for adding columns and tables to a document are discussed in great detail. These first five chapters also explain how to add finishing touches to your document, using page events for headers, footers, page numbers, and watermarks.

Introducing
PDF and iText

1

This chapter covers

- A summary of what will be presented in this book
- Compiling and executing your first example
- Learning the five steps in iText's PDF creation process

Call me Bruno. About ten years ago—never mind how long precisely—I thought I'd create a small PDF library in Java and publish it as free and open source software (F/OSS). Little did I know that this would lead to my writing a whale of a book about the extensive functionality that has been added over the years.

That library was iText, and the book was titled *iText in Action: Creating and Manipulating PDF* (2007). Today, iText is the world's leading F/OSS PDF library. It's released under the Affero General Public License (AGPL) and is available in two versions: the original Java version, and the C# port, iTextSharp. These libraries make it possible for you to enhance applications with dynamic PDF solutions. You can use iText to create invoices for your customers if you have a web shop, to produce tickets if you work for an airline or railway company, and so on. You can integrate iText into an application to generate PDF documents as an alternative to

3

printing on paper, to add digital signatures to a document, to split or concatenate different documents, and so forth.

In the first edition of *iText in Action*, readers learned why things work the way they do in iText, complemented with simple examples. This second edition takes you further with more real-life examples, skipping a bit on the whys, but presenting comprehensive code samples that you can use to solve everyday problems.

In this chapter, I'll give you a quick overview of the things you can do with PDF—you'll compile and execute a first "Hello World" example—and you'll learn the basics of creating PDFs with iText.

1.1   *Things you can do with PDF*

Let's start with six quick facts about PDF:

- PDF is the Portable Document Format.
- It's an open file format (ISO-32000-1), originally created by Adobe.
- It's used for documents that are independent of system software and hardware.
- PDF documents are an essential part of the web.
- Adobe Reader is the most widely used PDF viewer.
- There are a lot of free and proprietary, open and closed source, desktop and web-based software products for creating, viewing, and manipulating PDF documents.

Figure 1.1 offers an overview of the things you can do with PDF. There are tools to *create* PDF documents, there are applications to *consume* PDF documents, and there are utilities to *manipulate* existing PDF documents.

If you look at PDF creation, you'll find that graphical designers use desktop applications such as Adobe Acrobat or Adobe InDesign to create a document in a manual or semimanual process. In another context, PDF documents are created programmatically, using an API to produce PDFs directly from software applications, without—or with minimal—human intervention. Sometimes the document is created in an intermediary format first, then converted to PDF. These different approaches demand different software products. The same goes for PDF manipulation. You can update a PDF manually in Adobe Acrobat, but there are also tools that allow forms to be filled out automatically based on information from a database.

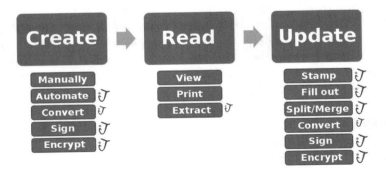

Figure 1.1   Overview of PDF-related functionality. The functionality covered by iText is marked with the iText logo.

This book will focus on the automation side of things: we'll create and manipulate PDF documents in an automated process using iText. The functionality covered by iText in figure 1.1 is marked with the iText logo. A smaller logo indicates that the functionality is only partly supported.

Typically, iText is used in projects that have one of the following requirements:

- The content isn't available in advance: it's calculated based on user input or real-time database information.
- The PDF files can't be produced manually due to the massive volume of content: a large number of pages or documents.
- Documents need to be created in unattended mode, in a batch process.
- The content needs to be customized or personalized; for instance, the name of the end user has to be stamped on a number of pages.

Often you'll encounter these requirements in web applications, where content needs to be served dynamically to a browser. Normally, you'd serve this information in the form of HTML, but for some documents, PDF is preferred over HTML for better printing quality, for identical presentation on a variety of platforms, for security reasons, or to reduce the file size. In this case, you can serve PDF on the fly.

As you read this book, you'll create and manipulate hundreds of PDF documents that demonstrate how to use a specific feature, how to solve common and less common issues, and how to build an application that involves PDF technology. We'll use iText because it's an API that was developed to allow developers to do the following (and much more):

- Generate documents and reports based on data from an XML file or a database
- Create maps and books, exploiting numerous interactive features available in PDF
- Add bookmarks, page numbers, watermarks, and other features to existing PDF documents
- Split or concatenate pages from existing PDF files
- Fill out interactive forms
- Serve dynamically generated or manipulated PDF documents to a web browser

For first-time users, this book is indispensable. Although the basic functionality of iText is easy to grasp, the first parts of this book significantly lower the learning curve and gradually offer more advanced functionality.

It's also a must-have for the many developers who are already familiar with iText. In the final chapters, many PDF secrets hidden in ISO-32000-1, the open standard that defines the Portable Document Format, will be unveiled. Even experienced iText developers will learn new ways to master the PDF specification using their favorite PDF library.

Without further ado, let's start with a simple example that explains how to compile and run the many examples that come with this book.

1.2   *Working with the examples in this book*

All the source files, as well as the resources and extra libraries necessary to run the book's examples, were uploaded to a Subversion (SVN) repository on SourceForge. If you have an SVN client, you can check out of the complete working environment at once. This way, you'll be able to get the latest updates and new examples, even after the book has been released. Please consult appendix B for the URL of this repository.

You can find more info about this on the examples page of the itextpdf.com site. That's also the place where you'll find zipped archives, in case you don't have an SVN client. You can download these archives and unzip them on your local system.

Before you start experimenting, make sure that you have a recent version of the Java Development Kit (JDK) installed. The examples won't work for versions of iText that are older than iText 5, and iText 5 is compiled with Java 5, so the minimum requirement for your JVM is Sun's JDK 1.5. You can use other JDKs, but only the JDK from Sun is supported.

Figure 1.2 shows how I compiled and executed the first example, HelloWorld, on Ubuntu Linux using OpenJDK 6. As you can see, you first change the directory to the examples folder (or whichever folder contains your copy of the project). Then you run this command:

```
javac -d bin -cp lib/iText.jar src/part1/chapter01/HelloWorld.java
```

HelloWorld.java is the source file; we'll take a close look at it in the next section. The option -d says that the compiled code should be written to the bin folder. With option -cp you define the classpath. For this simple example, you only need the iText.jar file. For other examples, you might need to add more JARs, such as a JAR with the database driver, encryption JARs, and so forth.

Once you've compiled the code, you can execute it:

```
java -cp "bin:lib/iText.jar" part1.chapter01.HelloWorld
```

If you're working on Windows, you'll need to replace the colon separating the different parts of the classpath with a semicolon:

```
java -cp "bin;lib/iText.jar" part1.chapter01.HelloWorld
```

Congratulations! You have created your first PDF file using iText. Figure 1.3 shows how everything is organized.

The source code of the examples can be found in the src folder; see, for instance, the file HelloWorld.java. The package names of the examples correspond to the part and chapter numbers of the book. In the lib directory, you'll find all the JARs you

```
File  Edit  View  Terminal  Help
bruno$ cd examples
bruno$ javac -d bin -cp lib/iText.jar src/part1/chapter01/HelloWorld.java
bruno$ java -cp "bin:lib/iText.jar" part1.chapter01.HelloWorld
bruno$ ▮
```

Figure 1.2   Compiling and running from the command line

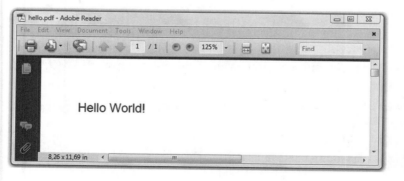

Figure 1.3   Organization of the sample files

need to compile the examples. There's also a resources folder containing all the resources you might need to run the examples: database scripts, images, special fonts, and existing PDF files, such as interactive forms.

The examples are compiled to the bin folder. The HelloWorld.class file will appear as soon as you run the `javac` command. When you execute the `java` command, you'll see the hello.pdf file appear in the results directory. Figure 1.4 shows the end result: a PDF file containing the text "Hello World!"

It's certainly possible to compile and execute all the examples from the command line, but it's more likely that you'll prefer using an integrated development environment (IDE). Figure 1.5 shows what the project looks like in Eclipse—you'll recognize the same folders. Observe that Eclipse puts the src folder on top. The bin directory is hidden; you'll find the JARs under Referenced Libraries. You can view and update the list of registered JARs by selecting Project > Properties > Java Build Path > Libraries.

**Figure 1.4
A "Hello World" PDF**

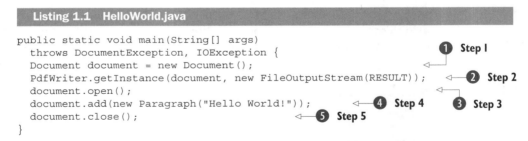

Figure 1.5   The project opened in Eclipse

Figure 1.5 already gives you a peek at the source code. The hello.pdf file is created in five steps. The next section discusses every step in detail.

1.3   *Creating a PDF document in five steps with iText*

Let's copy the content of the main method of figure 1.5, and remove the comments. The numbers to the side in this listing indicate the different steps in the PDF-creation process.

Listing 1.1   HelloWorld.java

```
public static void main(String[] args)                          ① Step 1
  throws DocumentException, IOException {
  Document document = new Document();                            ← ② Step 2
  PdfWriter.getInstance(document, new FileOutputStream(RESULT)); ←
  document.open();                                              ④ Step 4   ③ Step 3
  document.add(new Paragraph("Hello World!"));                  ←
  document.close();                                  ← ⑤ Step 5
}
```

We'll devote a separate subsection to each of these five steps:

- *Step* ①—Create a Document.
- *Step* ②—Get a PdfWriter instance.
- *Step* ③—Open the Document.
- *Step* ④—Add content.
- *Step* ⑤—Close the Document.

In each of the following subsections, we'll focus on one specific step. You'll apply small changes to step ❶ in the first subsection, to step ❷ in the second, and so on. This way, you'll create several new documents that are slightly different from the one in figure 1.4. You can hold these variations on the original hello.pdf against a strong light (literally or not) and discover the differences and similarities caused by the small code changes.

1.3.1 Creating a new Document object

`Document` is the object to which you'll add content in the form of `Chunk`, `Phrase`, `Paragraph`, and other high-level objects. These objects are often referred to as iText's basic building blocks, and they'll be discussed in chapter 2. For now, we'll only work with `Paragraph` objects.

MEASUREMENTS

Upon creating the `Document` object, you'll define the page size and the page margins of the first page. Either this happens implicitly, as is the case in step ❶ of listing 1.1; or you can define the size and margins explicitly using a `com.itextpdf.text.Rectangle` object and four `float` values for the margins as shown here.

Listing 1.2   HelloWorldNarrow.java

```
Rectangle pagesize = new Rectangle(216f, 720f);
Document document = new Document(pagesize, 36f, 72f, 108f, 180f);
```

In this example, a rectangle measuring 216 x 720 user units is created. This rectangle is used as the page size in the `Document` constructor, along with a left margin of 36 user units, a right margin of 72 user units, a top margin of 108 user units, and a bottom margin of 180 user units.

> **FAQ** *What is the measurement unit in PDF documents?* Most of the measurements in PDFs are expressed in user space units. ISO-32000-1 (section 8.3.2.3) tells us "the default for the size of the unit in default user space (1/72 inch) is approximately the same as a point (pt), a unit widely used in the printing industry. It is not exactly the same; there is no universal definition of a point." In short, 1 in. = 25.4 mm = 72 user units (which roughly corresponds to 72 pt).

If you open the document created by listing 1.2 in Adobe Reader and look at the Description tab in the Document properties dialog box (opened via File > Properties), you'll find that the document measures 3 in. x 10 in.

iText also created a left margin of 0.5 in. (36/72), a right margin of 1 in. (72/72), a top margin of 1.5 in. (108/72), and a bottom margin of 2.5 in. (180/72).

If you don't like doing all that math, there's a `Utilities` class in iText with static methods that help you switch among points, inches, and millimeters: `millimeters-ToPoints()`, `millimetersToInches()`, `pointsToMillimeters()`, `pointsToInches()`, `inchesToMillimeters()`, and `inchesToPoints()`. All these methods expect a `float` as their value.

Note that these methods refer to points, not to user units. That's because the *default* value of the user unit corresponds with a point, but it's possible to change this default.

Listing 1.3   HelloWorldMaximum.java

```
Document document = new Document(new Rectangle(14400, 14400));
PdfWriter writer
    = PdfWriter.getInstance(document, new FileOutputStream(RESULT));
writer.setUserunit(75000f);
```

Looking at the first line in this code snippet, you might expect a document with a page measuring 200 in. x 200 in., but when you look at the document properties of the resulting file, you'll see that it measures 15,000,000 in. x 15,000,000 in. That's because you've changed the user unit to 75,000 in the last line of listing 1.3. Now, one user unit corresponds with 75,000 points, and you've created a PDF document with the largest possible page size.

PAGE SIZE

Theoretically, you could create pages of any size, but the PDF specification imposes limits depending on the PDF version of the document.

Table 1.1   Minimum and maximum size of a page depending on the PDF version

PDF version	Minimum size	Maximum size
PDF 1.3 or earlier	72 x 72 units (1 in. x 1 in.)	3240 x 3240 units (45 in. x 45 in.)
PDF 1.4 and later	3 x 3 units (approximately 0.04 in. x 0.04 in.)	14,400 x 14,400 units (200 in. x 200 in.)

Changing the user unit has been possible since PDF 1.6. The minimum value of the user unit is 1 (this is the default; 1 unit = 1/72 in.); the maximum value is 75,000 points (1 unit = 1042 in.).

But enough about exotic page sizes; you're probably interested in the standard paper sizes. The default value of a page in iText, if you create a Document object without any parameters, is A4, which is the most common paper size in Europe, Asia, and Latin America. It's specified by the International Standards Organization (ISO) in ISO-216. An A4 document measures 210 mm x 297 mm, or 8.3 in. × 11.7 in., or 595 pt x 842 pt.

If you want to create a document in another standard format, take a look at the PageSize class. This class was written for your convenience, and it contains a list of static final Rectangle objects, offering a wide selection of standard paper sizes, including A0 to A10, B0 to B10, and the American standard sizes: LETTER, LEGAL, LEDGER, and TABLOID. Listing 1.4 shows how to adapt the initial HelloWorld example so that it produces a PDF document saying "Hello World!" on a page that's the American letter paper size.

Listing 1.4   HelloWorldLetter.java

```
Document document = new Document(PageSize.LETTER);
```

The orientation of most of the paper sizes defined in `PageSize` is *portrait*. You can change this to *landscape* by invoking the `rotate()` method on the `Rectangle`.

Listing 1.5   HelloWorldLandscape1.java

```
Document document = new Document(PageSize.LETTER.rotate());
```

Another way to create a `Document` in landscape orientation is to create a `Rectangle` object with a width that is greater than its height.

Listing 1.6   HelloWorldLandscape2.java

```
Document document = new Document(new Rectangle(792, 612));
```

The results of both landscape examples look exactly the same in Adobe Reader. The Reader's Description tab doesn't show any difference in size. Both PDF documents have a page size of 11 in. x 8.5 in. (instead of 8.5 in. x 11 in.), but there are subtle differences internally:

- In the first file, the page is defined with a size that has a width smaller than the height, but with a rotation of 90 degrees.
- The second file has the page size you defined without any rotation (a rotation of 0 degrees).

This difference will matter when you want to manipulate the PDF. We'll return to this issue in chapter 6.

PAGE MARGINS

In listing 1.2, you defined margins using the constructor of the `Document` object, and you added a `Paragraph` to it. In the next two examples, you'll define the page size and margins using the `setPageSize()` and `setMargins()` methods. You can use these methods at any time in the document's creation process, but be aware that the change will never affect the current page, only the next page.

In these examples, you'll add paragraphs that are aligned on both sides—justified text—so you can clearly see the left and right margins. You'll add enough paragraphs to cause a page break, so you can make sure the bottom margin is respected.

Suppose this document consists of pages that are to be printed on both sides, and bound into a book. Depending on the way the book is bound, you might want a larger or smaller margin on the inner edges of the pages: the left margin of an odd-numbered page should correspond to the right margin of an even-numbered page. The same goes for the opposite margins. In short, you want the margins to be mirrored.

Listing 1.7   HelloWorldMirroredMargins.java

```
Document document = new Document();
PdfWriter.getInstance(document, new FileOutputStream(RESULT));
```

```
document.setPageSize(PageSize.A5);
document.setMargins(36, 72, 108, 180);
document.setMarginMirroring(true);
```

Listing 1.7 assumes that the spine of the book is to the left (for Western books) or to the right (for Japanese books). But some books are bound in a completely different way, with the spine of the book at the top or bottom of the pages. In that case, you'd need to use this method.

Listing 1.8   HelloWorldMirroredMarginsTop.java

```
document.setMarginMirroringTopBottom(true);
```

Now the top and bottom margins are mirrored instead of the left and right margins.

But maybe we're getting ahead of ourselves. We're already adding content, but we haven't yet discussed step ❷ in listing 1.1 in the PDF creation process.

1.3.2   *Getting a PdfWriter instance*

PdfWriter is the class responsible for writing the PDF file. You can also add contents, such as annotations, to PdfWriter. As opposed to the high-level objects added to the Document object, manipulations on PdfWriter are often referred to as *low-level access* and *writing to the direct content.* You'll find out more about these concepts in chapter 3.

Step ❷ in listing 1.1 in the PDF creation process combines two actions:

- *It associates a* Document *with the* PdfWriter.   This writer will "listen" to the document. High-level objects, such as a Paragraph, will be translated into low-level operations. For example, iText will generate the PDF syntax that draws the textual content of a paragraph at a specific position on a page, taking into account the page size and margins.
- *It tells the* PdfWriter *to which* OutputStream *the file should be written.*   In the previous examples, you have written the content to a FileOutputStream, but you could have written to any other type of OutputStream. You could even have written the bytes of a PDF file to System.out.

In rare circumstances, creating a writer instance can cause a DocumentException.

EXCEPTIONS

DocumentException is the most general exception in iText. It can occur in step ❷ or step ❹ of listing 1.1. For example, if you try adding a Paragraph before you've done step ❸, you'll get the following error message: "The document isn't open yet; you can only add metadata information." DocumentExceptions also occur when manipulating existing documents. For instance, "Append mode requires a document without errors even if recovery was possible."

If you look at listing 1.1, you see that you can also expect an IOException. Once you start using resources such as images, fonts, or existing PDFs, this exception can occur if something goes wrong while reading from an InputStream.

In the examples we've looked at so far, the only IOException that could be thrown is a FileNotFoundException. This happens when you're trying to create a hello.pdf file, but you already have a file with that name opened—and locked—in Adobe Reader. (This happened to me all the time while writing the examples for this book.) Or maybe you're trying to create the file in the results/part1/chapter01 directory, but this directory doesn't exist on your filesystem. The empty results directories are provided with the example archives to avoid this problem.

OTHER OUTPUTSTREAMS

While you're adding content to the Document, the PdfWriter gradually writes a PDF file to the OutputStream. This PDF file will be written to a file on disk if you choose a File-OutputStream. In a web application, you'll generally prefer serving the PDF to a web browser without saving it on the server, so you could write directly to the Servlet-OutputStream, using response.getOutputStream() in your servlets. This will work with some browsers, but unfortunately not with all. Chapter 9 will explain why it's better to write the complete file to memory before transferring the bytes to the OutputStream of an HttpServletResponse object.

Here's how to write a file to memory using a ByteArrayOutputStream.

Listing 1.9 HelloWorldMemory.java

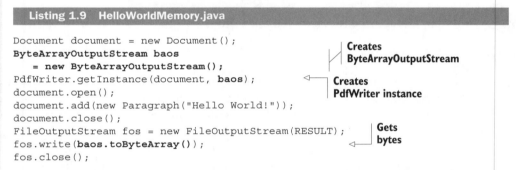

```
Document document = new Document();
ByteArrayOutputStream baos                           Creates
    = new ByteArrayOutputStream();                   ByteArrayOutputStream
PdfWriter.getInstance(document, baos);               Creates
document.open();                                     PdfWriter instance
document.add(new Paragraph("Hello World!"));
document.close();
FileOutputStream fos = new FileOutputStream(RESULT); Gets
fos.write(baos.toByteArray());                       bytes
fos.close();
```

Observe that the PDF is created in memory in the first part of this snippet; nothing is written to disk. The bytes are written to a file in the last three lines of the snippet to prove that what was generated in memory represents a valid PDF file.

Now that you have all the infrastructure in place, it's time to open the Document.

1.3.3 Opening the Document

Java programmers may not be used to having to open streams before being able to add content. When you create a new stream in Java, you can start writing bytes, chars, and Strings to it right away. With iText, it's mandatory to open the document first.

When a Document object is opened, a lot of initializations take place, and the file header is written to the OutputStream.

THE FILE HEADER AND THE PDF VERSION

Figure 1.6 shows your first PDF file, hello.pdf, opened in the Notepad++ text editor.

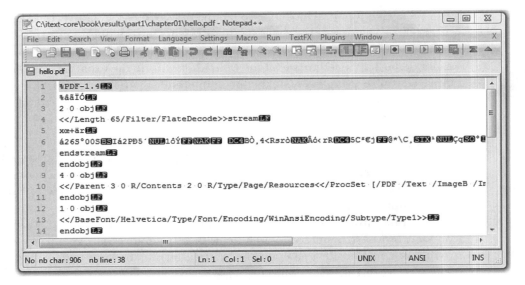

Figure 1.6   hello.pdf opened in Notepad++

As you can see, the first lines look like this:

```
%PDF-1.4
%âãÏÓ
```

This is the header of a PDF file. The structure of a PDF file, with its header, body, cross-reference table, and footer, will be discussed in great detail in chapter 13. For now, it's sufficient to know that the first line gives you an indication of the PDF version that is used.

By default, iText uses version 1.4, which was introduced in 2001. If you introduce functionality newer than what's available in PDF 1.4 after step ❸ in listing 1.1, it's your responsibility to set the correct PDF version before step ❸. Otherwise, the default version—PDF-1.4—will be written to the OutputStream, and there's no going back.

> **NOTE**   Beginning with PDF 1.4, the PDF version can also be stored elsewhere in the PDF (in the root object of the document, aka the *catalog*; see chapter 13). This implies that a file with header PDF-1.4 can be seen as a PDF 1.6 file if it's defined that way in the document root.

In some cases, iText changes the PDF version automatically. In listing 1.3, you changed the user unit, and this capability was introduced in version 1.6 of the PDF specification. Because you changed the user unit before step ❸, iText was able to update the PDF version in the header to %PDF-1.6.

It's a better practice to set the version number with PdfWriter.setPdfVersion() if you use PDF features that are newer than what was available in PDF 1.4. Here's how to change the PDF version to 1.7.

Listing 1.10   HelloWorldVersion_1_7.java

```
PdfWriter writer
  = PdfWriter.getInstance(document, new FileOutputStream(RESULT));
writer.setPdfVersion(PdfWriter.VERSION_1_7);
```

It's not forbidden for the PDF version in the header to be different from the PDF version in the catalog, but it's good practice to make setting the PDF version a part of your initializations to avoid ambiguity.

INITIALIZATIONS

`Document.open()` also performs many initializations. For instance, you can't access the outline of the bookmarks before the document has been opened (see chapter 7). If you want to create an encrypted PDF file, you must set the encryption type, strength, and permissions before step ❷ in listing 1.1 (see chapter 12).

> **FAQ**   *I have set feature X, and it doesn't work, or it doesn't work for page 1, only for the pages that follow. Why is that?* Many settings, such as the page size and margins, only go into effect on the next page. This may seem trivial, but it's a common question for new iText users. If you want the feature to work on page 1, define it before opening the document.

After step ❸, the first page of our document is available for you to add content (step ❹).

1.3.4   *Adding content*

In this section, we're creating simple Hello World PDF documents, learning the elementary mechanics of iText's PDF creation process. Once these are understood, you can start generating real-world documents containing real-world data.

To learn how to implement step ❹, you'll copy steps ❶, ❷, ❸, and ❺ from listing 1.1 into an application, then focus on step ❹: adding content to the PDF document.

There are different ways to add content. Up until now, you've been adding one or more high-level objects of type `Paragraph` to the `Document`. In the next chapter, you'll learn about other objects, such as `Chunk`, `Phrase`, `Anchor`, and `List`. You can also add content to a page using low-level methods.

DIRECT CONTENT

Listing 1.11 shows a variation on this chapter's initial "Hello World" example. Although this is a rather complex example for a first chapter about using iText, it will give you an idea of iText's internal PDF-creation process.

Listing 1.11   HelloWorldDirect.java

```
Document document = new Document();                      ← ❶ Step 1
PdfWriter writer = PdfWriter.getInstance(                    ❷ Step 2
  document, new FileOutputStream(RESULT));                       ❸ Step 3
document.open();
PdfContentByte canvas = writer.getDirectContentUnder();     ❹ Step 4
writer.setCompressionLevel(0);
```

```
canvas.saveState();                // q
canvas.beginText();                // BT
canvas.moveText(36, 788);          // 36 788 Td
canvas.setFontAndSize(
  BaseFont.createFont(), 12);      // /F1 12 Tf                    ④ Step 4
canvas.showText("Hello World");    // (Hello World)Tj
canvas.endText();                  // ET
canvas.restoreState();             // Q
document.close();                                  ←—⑤ Step 5
```

Steps ❶, ❸, and ❺ are the same as they were in listing 1.1, but you need to make a small change to step ❷. Instead of using an unnamed instance of PdfWriter, you now give it a name: writer. You need this instance because you want to grab a canvas on which you can draw lines and shapes, and, in this case, text. In listing 1.11, comment sections were added, reflecting the PDF syntax that is written by each method.

By using the setCompressionLevel() method with a parameter of 0, you avoid compressing the stream. This allows you to read the PDF syntax when opening the file in a text editor. Figure 1.7 shows the resulting PDF when opened in WordPad.

This screenshot contains less gibberish than figure 1.6, though it's showing the syntax of a similar "Hello World" PDF. You'll recognize the PDF header, followed by a PDF object with number 2: 2 0 obj. After reading part 4 of this book, you'll understand that this object is a stream object, the content stream of the first page. In figure 1.6, the content stream was compressed, but in figure 1.7, the compression is zero. You can see the syntax in clear text, although you'll need to read chapter 14 to decipher what it means.

> **NOTE** Setting the compression level to 0 can be interesting if you need to debug your PDF file, but you shouldn't change the compression level in a production environment, because the file size of the resulting PDFs will be bigger than files generated using the default compression level.

As you move on in this book, you'll find out that you'll need to add content directly to the page on different occasions, such as when adding page numbers, or when drawing

```
hello_direct.pdf - WordPad

Bestand  Bewerken  Beeld  Invoegen  Opmaak  Help

%PDF-1.4
%âãÏÓ
2 0 obj
<</Filter/FlateDecode/Length 81>>stream
xÚ F ¹ÿq
q
BT
36 788 Td
/F1 12 Tf
 (Hello World)Tj
ET
Q
```

Figure 1.7 PDF document opened in WordPad

custom borders for tables. As you might imagine, you'll need a sound understanding of the PDF reference to achieve all this.

> **FAQ** *I've added text using low-level methods and it doesn't respect the margins, nor does the text wrap at the end of the line. What is wrong?* That is expected behavior. When adding content like this, you need to do all the math necessary to split a String in different lines, and add it at the appropriate coordinates. Also, make sure that you don't add the text outside the visible area of the page; this is a common mistake when adding text to an existing PDF document.

Listing 1.11 gets increasingly complex as soon as you need to add more text. Fortunately, iText comes to the rescue: you can use convenience classes and methods that significantly reduce the complexity and the lines of code needed to work with direct content.

CONVENIENCE CLASSES AND METHODS

Listing 1.12 is identical to listing 1.11 as far as steps **1**, **2**, **3**, and **5** are concerned, but in step **4** you create a Phrase object and add this to the direct content, named canvas, using the static method ColumnText.showTextAligned(). The phrase hello will be added left aligned at coordinates (36, 788) with rotation 0.

Listing 1.12   HelloWorldColumn.java

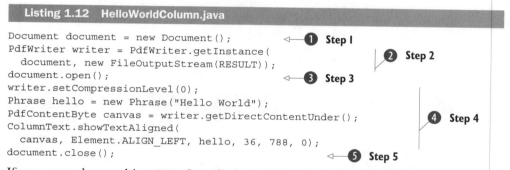

```
Document document = new Document();                          Step 1
PdfWriter writer = PdfWriter.getInstance(                    Step 2
  document, new FileOutputStream(RESULT));
document.open();                                             Step 3
writer.setCompressionLevel(0);
Phrase hello = new Phrase("Hello World");
PdfContentByte canvas = writer.getDirectContentUnder();      Step 4
ColumnText.showTextAligned(
  canvas, Element.ALIGN_LEFT, hello, 36, 788, 0);
document.close();                                            Step 5
```

If you open the resulting PDFs from listings 1.11 and 1.12 in Adobe Reader, you'll see that both documents look identical. If you open them in a text editor, you'll notice that the syntax is slightly different. There's usually more than one way to create PDF documents that look like identical twins when opened in a PDF viewer. And even if you create two identical PDF documents using the exact same code, there will be small differences between the two resulting files. That's inherent to the PDF format.

We're almost finished discussing the five steps in the PDF creation process. It's time for step 5.

1.3.5   *Closing the Document*

One of the typical uses of iText is to create documents containing many pages. For example, a financial institution uses iText to create PDFs of bank statements, consisting of 100,000 or more pages. You don't want to keep the content of that many pages in memory, and that's why iText will write content to the OutputStream as soon as possible. If a page is full, the content stream of that page will be written to the Output-Stream; if you're writing to a file, that content will be flushed from the memory.

CONTENT FLUSHED TO THE OUTPUTSTREAM VERSUS CONTENT KEPT IN MEMORY

If you return to figure 1.6 or 1.7, you'll see that object 2, the page content stream of page 1, appears as the first object in the file. Other objects will be added at a higher byte position, regardless of their object number. iText has to keep certain objects in memory because there's a chance you'll reuse them and change them during the creation process. You'll use this mechanism in section 5.4.2 to add the total number of pages—a number that is only known when the final page is reached—to all the previous pages.

Specific objects, such as the catalog and the info dictionary, will be added last by iText. They're written to the OutputStream upon closing the Document. There's also the cross-reference table, an important structure that is written immediately after the catalog and info dictionary. It contains the byte positions of the PDF objects that define the document. It's followed by the trailer, containing information that enables an application to quickly find the start of the cross-reference table, and objects such as the info dictionary. Finally, the following byte sequence will be added, indicating that the file has been completely written:

```
%EOF
```

You don't need to close the OutputStream you created in step ❷. iText will close this stream right after the end-of-file sequence.

KEEPING THE OUTPUTSTREAM OPEN

There may be occasions when you don't want the stream to be closed automatically.

Listing 1.13 HelloZip.java

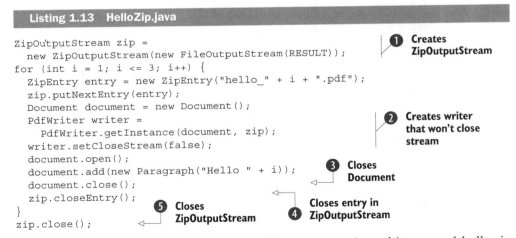

```java
ZipOutputStream zip =
  new ZipOutputStream(new FileOutputStream(RESULT));
for (int i = 1; i <= 3; i++) {
  ZipEntry entry = new ZipEntry("hello_" + i + ".pdf");
  zip.putNextEntry(entry);
  Document document = new Document();
  PdfWriter writer =
    PdfWriter.getInstance(document, zip);
  writer.setCloseStream(false);
  document.open();
  document.add(new Paragraph("Hello " + i));
  document.close();
  zip.closeEntry();
}
zip.close();
```

❶ Creates ZipOutputStream

❷ Creates writer that won't close stream

❸ Closes Document

❹ Closes entry in ZipOutputStream

❺ Closes ZipOutputStream

In ❶, you create a ZipOutputStream. It will generate a zip archive named hello.zip containing different PDF files. You use this OutputStream ❷ to create an instance of PdfWriter, but you immediately use the setCloseStream() method to tell the writer that it shouldn't close the stream. If you don't do this, the ZipOutputStream will be closed ❸, and a java.io.IOException will be thrown ❹, saying "Stream closed." You have to wait until you've closed the final entry added to the zip file, before you can close the `ZipOutputStream` ❺.

This example concludes our series of simple "Hello World" examples. You now have a solid first impression of how to use iText to create new PDF documents.

1.4 Summary

In this first introductory chapter, you've had a brief introduction to PDF, learning what is possible in PDF and what is possible with iText.

You've compiled and executed a first example, generating a simple "Hello World" PDF document. Using listings 1.1 through 1.13, you've created 15 similar files, of which three were archived in a zip file. In doing so, you've gone through the five elementary steps in iText's PDF-creation process: create a `Document`, get a `PdfWriter` instance, open the `Document`, add content, close the `Document`.

This chapter contained many forward references, and some of the examples introduced functionality that was probably too complex for a first chapter, but don't worry: every line of code will be explained further on in the book.

In the next chapter, you'll create PDFs with content that is more meaningful. I'll introduce a simple movie database and you'll use iText's high-level objects to publish the content of this database in different PDF documents.

Using iText's basic building blocks

2

This chapter covers

- An overview of the database used in the book's examples
- An overview of the basic building blocks: Chunk, Phrase, Paragraph, List, ListItem, Anchor, Chapter, Section, and Image

This chapter describes a series of high-level objects that can be used as basic building blocks. These objects allow you to generate PDF documents without having to bother with PDF syntax. Figure 2.1 is a UML diagram that serves as a visual table of contents, presenting the building blocks discussed in this chapter.

This class diagram is far from complete. All the methods, as well as a number of member variables, were omitted for the sake of clarity. The diagram will help you to understand in one glance how the interfaces and classes relate to each other.

We'll discuss a first series of objects in section 2.2: Chunk, Phrase, Paragraph, and List. In section 2.3, we'll cover a second series: Anchor, Chapter, Section, and Image. But before starting to build documents using these building blocks, let's have a look at the database you'll publish to different PDF files in the upcoming examples.

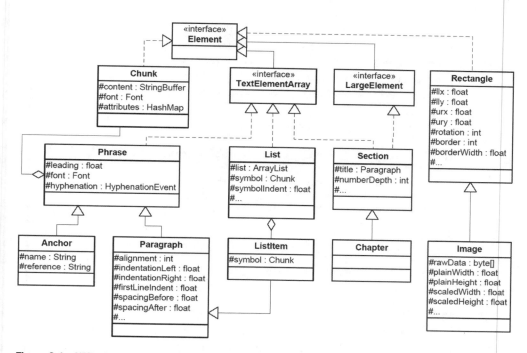

Figure 2.1 UML class diagram, presenting the building blocks that will be discussed in this chapter

2.1 *Illustrating the examples with a real-world database*

The main theme of the examples in this book is *movies*. I've made a selection of 120 movies, 80 directors, and 32 countries, and I've put all this information in a database. The entity relationship diagram (ERD) in figure 2.2 shows how the data is organized. There are three main tables, consisting of movies, directors, and countries. Furthermore, there are two tables connecting these tables.

For the examples in this book, we'll use the HSQL database engine (http://hsqldb.org/). This is a lightweight database that doesn't need to be installed. Just add hsqldb.jar to your classpath and you're set. You'll find this JAR in the lib directory. The

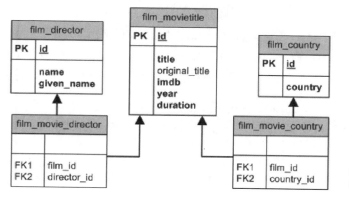

Figure 2.2 Film database entity relationship diagram

HSQL database is in the db subdirectory of the resources folder. When you execute an example using the movie database, the contents of the filmfestival.script file will be loaded into memory, and you'll see temporary files appear in the directory as soon as you start using the database.

I wrote a couple of convenience classes to hide the complexity of the database. The abstract class DatabaseConnection wraps the java.sql.Connection class, and it's extended by the HsqldbConnection class.

Listing 2.1   DatabaseTest.java

```
PrintStream out = new PrintStream(new FileOutputStream(RESULT));
DatabaseConnection connection
  = new HsqldbConnection("filmfestival");                    Creates connection
Statement stm = connection.createStatement();                to HSQL database
ResultSet rs = stm.executeQuery(
  "SELECT country FROM film_country ORDER BY country");
while (rs.next()) {
  out.println(rs.getString("country"));
}
stm.close();
connection.close();
```

This is a small standalone example to test the database connection. It writes the 32 countries from the film_country table to a file named countries.txt.

I've also created a class named PojoFactory, along with a series of plain old Java objects (POJOs), such as Movie, Director, and Country. These classes hide most of the database querying. In the examples that follow, you'll find code that looks like this:

```
List<Movie> movies = PojoFactory.getMovies(connection);
for (Movie movie : movies) {
  document.add(new Paragraph(movie.getTitle()));
}
```

Each instance of the Movie class corresponds with a record in the film_movietitle table.

In the following sections and chapters, you'll create numerous PDF files from a database, but you'll hardly ever be confronted with difficult database queries or database-related Java syntax. The database aspects of the examples won't get any more complex than in the first examples of the next section.

2.2   Adding Chunk, Phrase, Paragraph, and List objects

The general idea of step ④ in listing 1.1 in the PDF-creation process using document.add() is that you add objects implementing the Element interface to a Document object. Behind the scenes, a PdfWriter and a PdfDocument object analyze these objects and translate them into the appropriate PDF syntax, positioning the content on one or more pages, taking into account the page size and margins.

In this section, we'll explore text elements that implement the TextElementArray interface. As the name of the interface indicates, these objects will be composed of different pieces of text; most of the time, it will be text wrapped in Chunk objects.

2.2.1 *The Chunk object: a String, a Font, and some attributes*

A Chunk is the smallest significant piece of text that can be added to a Document. The Chunk object contains a StringBuffer that represents a chunk of text whose characters all have the same font, font size, font style, and font color. These properties are defined in the Font object. Other properties of the Chunk, such as the background color, the text rise—used to simulate subscript and superscript—and the underline values—used to underline text or strike a line through it—are defined as attributes. These attributes can be changed with a series of setter methods.

Listing 2.1 wrote the names of 32 countries to a text file to test the database. Here you're creating a PDF document with nothing but Chunks as building blocks.

Listing 2.2 CountryChunks.java

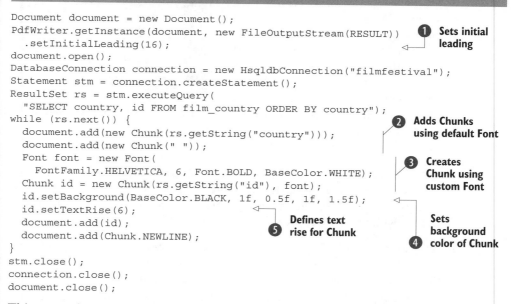

```
Document document = new Document();
PdfWriter.getInstance(document, new FileOutputStream(RESULT))
  .setInitialLeading(16);                                    ①  Sets initial
document.open();                                                   leading
DatabaseConnection connection = new HsqldbConnection("filmfestival");
Statement stm = connection.createStatement();
ResultSet rs = stm.executeQuery(
  "SELECT country, id FROM film_country ORDER BY country");
while (rs.next()) {                                          ②  Adds Chunks
  document.add(new Chunk(rs.getString("country")));             using default Font
  document.add(new Chunk(" "));
  Font font = new Font(                                     ③  Creates
    FontFamily.HELVETICA, 6, Font.BOLD, BaseColor.WHITE);      Chunk using
  Chunk id = new Chunk(rs.getString("id"), font);             custom Font
  id.setBackground(BaseColor.BLACK, 1f, 0.5f, 1f, 1.5f);
  id.setTextRise(6);                                       Sets
  document.add(id);                        Defines text   background
  document.add(Chunk.NEWLINE);          ⑤  rise for Chunk  color of Chunk ④
}
stm.close();
connection.close();
document.close();
```

This example is rather unusual: in normal circumstances you'll use Chunk objects to compose other text objects, such as Phrases and Paragraphs. Typically, you won't add Chunk objects directly to a Document, except for some special Chunks, such as Chunk.NEWLINE.

THE SPACE BETWEEN TWO LINES: LEADING

A Chunk isn't aware of the space that is needed between two lines. That's why you set the leading in ①. The word *leading* is pronounced as *ledding*, and it's derived from the word *lead* (the metal). When type was set by hand for printing presses, strips of lead were placed between lines of type to add space—the word originally referred to the thickness of these strips of lead that were placed between the lines. The PDF Reference redefined the leading as "the vertical distance between the baselines of adjacent lines of text" (ISO-32000-1, section 9.3.5). As an exercise, you could remove `setInitialLeading(16)` from line ❶. If you compile and execute the altered example, you'll find that all the text is written on the same line.

THE FONT OBJECT

Figure 2.3 shows the PDF created by listing 2.2. You can see all the fonts that are present in the document by choosing File > Properties > Fonts.

The document properties reveal that two fonts were used: Helvetica and Helvetica-Bold. These fonts weren't embedded. When I open the file on Windows, Adobe Reader replaces Helvetica with ArialMT and Helvetica-Bold with ArialBoldMT. These fonts look very similar, but nevertheless, there's a difference!

The first font in the list in figure 2.3 is the default font used for the `Chunks` created in listing 2.2 ❷.

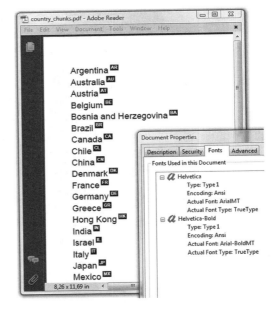

Figure 2.3   Country chunks, produced with listing 2.2

> **FAQ** *What is the default font used in iText, and can I change it?* The default font in iText is Helvetica with size 12 pt. There's no way to change this. If you need objects with another default font, just create a factory class that produces objects with the font of your choice.

In ❸, you specify a different font from the same family: Helvetica with style Bold. You define a different font size (6 pt) and set the font color to white. It would be difficult to read white text on a white page, so you also change one of the many attributes of the `Chunk` object: the background color ❹. The `setBackground()` method draws a colored rectangle behind the text contained in the `Chunk`. The extra parameters of the method define extra space (expressed in user units) to the left, bottom, right, and top of the `Chunk`. In this case, the ID of each country will be printed as white text on a black background.

You use `setTextRise()` ❺ to print the country ID in superscript. The parameter is the distance from the baseline in user units. A positive value simulates superscript; a negative value simulates subscript. You'll discover more `Chunk` attributes as you read on in the book.

Finally you add `Chunk.NEWLINE` to make sure that every country name starts on a new line. In the next subsection, we'll combine `Chunks` into a `Phrase`.

2.2.2   *The Phrase object: a List of Chunks with leading*

When I created iText, I chose the word *chunk* for the atomic text element because of its first definition in my dictionary: "a solid piece." A *phrase*, on the other hand, is defined as "a string of words." It's a composed object. Translated to iText and Java, a `Phrase` is an `ArrayList` of `Chunk` objects.

A PHRASE WITH DIFFERENT FONTS

When you create methods that compose `Phrase` objects using different `Chunks`, you'll usually create constants for the different `Fonts` you'll use.

> **Listing 2.3   DirectorPhrases1.java**

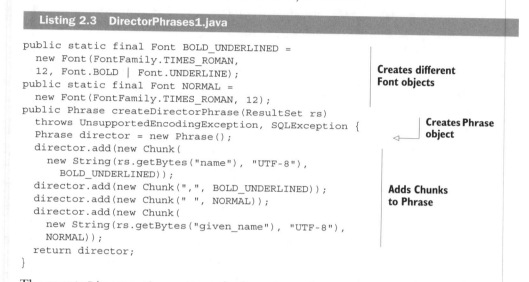

```
public static final Font BOLD_UNDERLINED =
  new Font(FontFamily.TIMES_ROMAN,
  12, Font.BOLD | Font.UNDERLINE);           Creates different
public static final Font NORMAL =            Font objects
  new Font(FontFamily.TIMES_ROMAN, 12);
public Phrase createDirectorPhrase(ResultSet rs)
  throws UnsupportedEncodingException, SQLException {   Creates Phrase
  Phrase director = new Phrase();                       object
  director.add(new Chunk(
    new String(rs.getBytes("name"), "UTF-8"),
      BOLD_UNDERLINED));
  director.add(new Chunk(",", BOLD_UNDERLINED));   Adds Chunks
  director.add(new Chunk(" ", NORMAL));            to Phrase
  director.add(new Chunk(
    new String(rs.getBytes("given_name"), "UTF-8"),
    NORMAL));
  return director;
}
```

The `createDirectorPhrase()` method produces the `Phrase` exactly the way you want it. You'll use it 80 times to list the 80 directors from the movie database. It's good practice to create a factory class containing different `createObject()` methods if you need to create `Chunk`, `Phrase`, or other objects in a standardized way.

THE LEADING OF A PHRASE

The method `createDirectorPhrase()` from listing 2.3 is used in this listing in which you're repeating the five steps in the PDF creation process.

> **Listing 2.4   DirectorPhrases1.java**

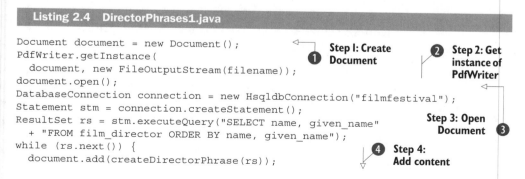

```
Document document = new Document();          Step 1: Create
PdfWriter.getInstance(                        Document      Step 2: Get
  document, new FileOutputStream(filename));                instance of
document.open();                                            PdfWriter
DatabaseConnection connection = new HsqldbConnection("filmfestival");
Statement stm = connection.createStatement();
ResultSet rs = stm.executeQuery("SELECT name, given_name"   Step 3: Open
  + "FROM film_director ORDER BY name, given_name");         Document
while (rs.next()) {
  document.add(createDirectorPhrase(rs));          Step 4:
                                                   Add content
```

```
    document.add(Chunk.NEWLINE);
}
stm.close();
connection.close();
document.close();
```

Step 4:
Add content

Step 5: Close
Document

Observe that you no longer need to set the initial leading in step ❷. Instead, the default leading is used.

> **FAQ** *What is the default leading in iText?* If you don't define a leading, iText looks at the font size of the `Phrase` or `Paragraph` that is added to the document, and multiplies it by 1.5. For instance, if you have a `Phrase` with a font of size 10, the default leading is 15. For the default font—with a default size of 12—the default leading is 18.

In the next example, you'll change the leading with the `setLeading()` method.

DATABASE ENCODING VERSUS THE DEFAULT CHARSET USED BY THE JVM

In listing 2.3, some `Strings` were created using the UTF-8 encoding explicitly:

```
new String(rs.getBytes("given_name"), "UTF-8")
```

That's because the database contains different names with special characters. If you look at the HSQL script filmfestival.script, you'll find `INSERT` statements like this:

```
INSERT INTO FILM_DIRECTOR VALUES(
    41,'I\u00c3\u00b1\u00c3\u00a1rritu','Alejandro Gonz\u00c3\u00a1lez')
```

That's the record for the director Alejandro González Iñárritu. The characters á— (char) 226—and ñ— (char) 241—can be stored as one byte each, using the ANSI character encoding, which is a superset of ISO-8859-1, aka Latin-1. HSQL stores them in Unicode using multiple bytes per character. To make sure that the `String` is created correctly, listing 2.3 uses `ResultSet.getBytes()` instead of `ResultSet.getString()`.

This isn't always necessary. In most database systems, you can define the encoding for each table or for the whole database. The JVM uses the platform's default charset, for instance, in the `new String(byte[] bytes)` constructor.

> **FAQ** *Why is the data I retrieve from my database rendered as gibberish?* This can be caused by an encoding mismatch. The records in your database are encoded using encoding *X*; but the `String` objects obtained from your `ResultSet` assume that they are encoded using your platform's charset *Y*. For instance, the name González could be rendered as GonzÃ¡lez if the Unicode characters are interpreted as ANSI characters.

Once you've created the PDF document correctly, you no longer have to worry about encodings. One of the main reasons why people prefer PDF over any other document format is because PDF, as the name tells us, is a *portable* document format. A PDF document can be viewed and printed on any platform: UNIX, Macintosh, Windows, Linux, and others, regardless of the encoding or the character set that is used.

In theory, a PDF document should look the same on any of these platforms, using any viewer available on that platform, but there's a caveat! If you take a close look at figure 2.4, you can see that this isn't always true.

FONT SUBSTITUTION FOR NONEMBEDDED FONTS

In figure 2.3, you could see that Helvetica was replaced by ArialMT. Figure 2.4 shows that the choice of the replacement font is completely up to the document viewer.

Adobe Reader on Ubuntu (see the left window in figure 2.4) replaces Helvetica with Adobe Sans MM and Times-Roman with Adobe Serif MM. The MM refers to the fact that these are *Multiple Master* fonts. Wikipedia tells us that MM fonts are "an extension to Adobe Systems' Type 1 PostScript fonts ... From one MM font, it is conceivable to create a wide gamut of typeface styles of different widths, weights and proportions, without losing the integrity or readability of the character glyphs."

Adobe Reader for Linux uses a generic font when it encounters a nonembedded font for which it can't find an exact match. Looking at the output of File > Properties > Fonts in Evince (Ubuntu's default document viewer; see the right window in figure 2.4), you might have the impression that the actual Times-Bold, Times-Roman, and Helvetica fonts are used, but that's just Evince fooling you. Helvetica and Times-Roman aren't present on my Linux distribution; Evince is using other fonts instead. On Ubuntu Linux, you can consult the configuration files in the /etc/fonts directory. I did, and I discovered that on my Linux installation, Times and Helvetica are mapped to Nimbus Roman No9 L and Nimbus Sans—free fonts that can be found in the /usr/share/fonts/type1/gsfonts directory.

Note that we are looking at the same document, on the same OS (Ubuntu Linux), yet the names of the directors in the document look slightly different because different fonts were used. We were very lucky that the names were legible.

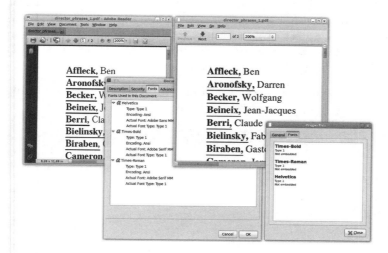

Figure 2.4   A PDF file opened in Adobe Reader and Evince on Ubuntu

FAQ   *Why are the special characters missing in my PDF document?* This isn't an iText problem. You could be using a character that has a description for the corresponding glyph on your system, but if you don't embed the font, that glyph can be missing on an end user's system. If the PDF viewer on that system can't find a substitution font, it won't be able to display the glyph. The solution is to embed the font. But even if you embed the font, some glyphs can be missing because they weren't present in the font you tried to embed. The solution here is to use a different font that does have the appropriate glyph descriptions. This will be discussed in great detail in chapter 11.

Not embedding fonts is always a risk, especially if you need special glyphs in your document. Not every font has the descriptions for every possible glyph.

NOTE   Characters in a file are rendered on screen or on paper as glyphs. ISO-32000-1, section 9.2.1, states: "A character is an abstract symbol, whereas a glyph is a specific graphical rendering of a character. For example: The glyphs A, **A**, and *A* are renderings of the abstract 'A' character. Glyphs are organized into fonts. A font defines glyphs for a particular character set."

In the next example, you'll see how to avoid possible problems caused by font substitution by embedding the font.

EMBEDDING FONTS

Up until now, you've created font objects using nothing but the Font class. The fonts available in this class are often referred to as the *standard Type 1 fonts*. These fonts aren't embedded by iText.

NOTE   The standard Type 1 fonts used to be called *built-in fonts* or *Base 14 fonts*. The font programs for fourteen fonts—four styles of Helvetica, Times-Roman, and Courier, plus Symbol and ZapfDingbats—used to be shipped with the PDF viewer. This is no longer the case; most viewers replace these fonts. It's important to understand that these fonts have no support for anything other than American/Western-European character sets. As soon as you want to add text with foreign characters, you'll need to use another font program.

The next example is a variation on the previous one. You don't have to change listing 2.4; you only have to replace listing 2.3 with this one.

Listing 2.5   DirectorPhrases2.java

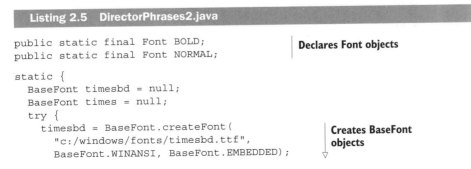

```
public static final Font BOLD;          Declares Font objects
public static final Font NORMAL;

static {
  BaseFont timesbd = null;
  BaseFont times = null;
  try {
    timesbd = BaseFont.createFont(        Creates BaseFont
      "c:/windows/fonts/timesbd.ttf",     objects
      BaseFont.WINANSI, BaseFont.EMBEDDED);
```

```
      times = BaseFont.createFont(
        "c:/windows/fonts/times.ttf",
        BaseFont.WINANSI, BaseFont.EMBEDDED);    ⟵ Creates BaseFont
    } catch (DocumentException e) {                    objects
      e.printStackTrace();
      System.exit(1);
    } catch (IOException e) {
      e.printStackTrace();
      System.exit(1);
    }
    BOLD = new Font(timesbd, 12);        ⟵ Creates Font using
    NORMAL = new Font(times, 12);             BaseFont and size
  }

  public Phrase createDirectorPhrase(ResultSet rs)
    throws UnsupportedEncodingException, SQLException {
    Phrase director = new Phrase();
    Chunk name =
      new Chunk(new String(rs.getBytes("name"), "UTF-8"), BOLD);
    name.setUnderline(0.2f, -2f);        ⟵ Underlines
    director.add(name);                       Chunk
    director.add(new Chunk(",", BOLD));
    director.add(new Chunk(" ", NORMAL));
    director.add(new Chunk(new String(
      rs.getBytes("given_name"), "UTF-8"), NORMAL));    ⟵ Defines custom
    director.setLeading(24);                                 leading
    return director;
  }
```

You tell iText where to find the font programs for Times New Roman (times.ttf) and Times New Roman Bold (timesbd.ttf) by creating a BaseFont object. You ask iText to embed the characters (BaseFont.EMBEDDED versus BaseFont.NOT_EMBEDDED) using the ANSI character set (BaseFont.WINANSI). You'll learn more about the BaseFont object in chapter 11. For now, it's sufficient to know that you can create a Font instance using a BaseFont object and a float value for the font size.

Figure 2.5 looks very similar to figure 2.4; only now the PDF file is rendered the same way in both viewers.

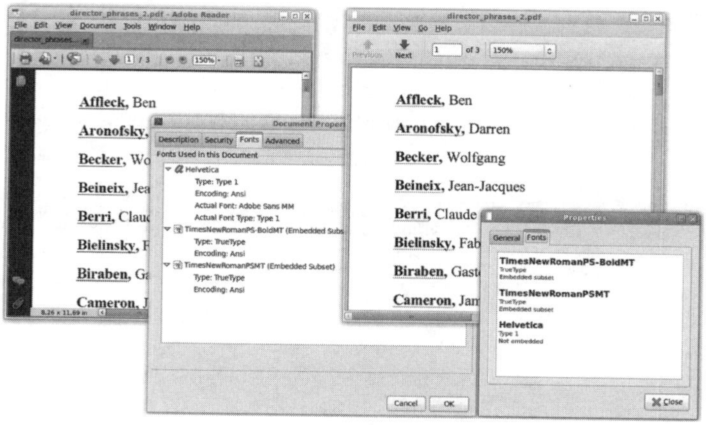

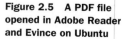

Figure 2.5   A PDF file opened in Adobe Reader and Evince on Ubuntu

Observe that there's more space between the names in this version because listing 2.5 used `setLeading()` to change the leading. The names of the directors are also underlined differently compared to the previous example, because you don't define the underlining as a property of the `Font`, but as an attribute of the `Chunk`.

With the `Chunk.setUnderline()` method, you can set the line thickness (in the example, 0.2 pt) and a *Y* position (in the example, 2 pt below the baseline). The parameter that sets the *Y* position allows you to use the same method to strike a line through a `Chunk`. There's also a variant of the method that accepts six parameters:

- A `BaseColor`, which makes the line a different color than the text.
- The absolute thickness.
- A thickness multiplication factor that will adapt the line width based on the font size.
- An absolute *Y* position.
- A position multiplication factor that will adapt the *Y* position based on the font size.
- The end line cap, defining what the extremities of the line should look like. Allowed values are `PdfContentByte.LINE_CAP_BUTT` (the default value), `PdfContentByte.LINE_CAP_ROUND`, and `PdfContentByte.LINE_CAP_PROJECTING_SQUARE`. The meaning of these options will be explained in table 14.6.

One thing may look peculiar when you look at figure 2.5. Why do both viewers still list Helvetica? You won't find any explicit reference to it in listings 2.4 and 2.5, but it's added implicitly in this line:

```
document.add(Chunk.NEWLINE);
```

`Chunk.NEWLINE` contains a newline character in the default font; and the default font is Helvetica. You could have avoided this by replacing that line with this one:

```
document.add(new Chunk("\n", NORMAL));
```

But an even better solution would be to use a `Paragraph` object instead of a `Phrase`.

2.2.3   *Paragraph object: a Phrase with extra properties and a newline*

Although the analogy isn't entirely correct, I often compare the difference between a `Phrase` and a `Paragraph` in iText with the difference between `<span>` and `<div>` in HTML. If you had used a `Paragraph` instead of a `Phrase` in the previous examples, it wouldn't have been necessary to add a newline.

Listing 2.6   MovieTitles.java

```
List<Movie> movies = PojoFactory.getMovies(connection);
for (Movie movie : movies) {
  document.add(new Paragraph(movie.getTitle()));
}
```

The `Paragraph` class is derived from the `Phrase` class. You can create instances of `Paragraph` exactly the same way as you've been creating `Phrase` objects, but there's more: you can also define the alignment of the text, different indentations, and the spacing before and after the paragraph.

EXPERIMENTING WITH PARAGRAPHS

Let's experiment with these `Paragraph` features in some examples. Listing 2.7 shows two helper methods that create `Paragraphs`:

- `createYearAndDuration()` creates a `Paragraph` that is composed of `Chunk` objects.
- `createMovieInformation()` does the same using `Phrase` objects and one `Paragraph` object that is treated as if it were a `Phrase`.

These methods are convenience methods that will be reused in different examples.

Listing 2.7 MovieParagraphs1

```
public Paragraph createYearAndDuration(Movie movie) {
  Paragraph info = new Paragraph();
  info.setFont(FilmFonts.NORMAL);
  info.add(new Chunk("Year: ", FilmFonts.BOLDITALIC));
  info.add(new Chunk(String.valueOf(movie.getYear()),
    FilmFonts.NORMAL));                                      ◁─┐
  info.add(new Chunk(" Duration: ", FilmFonts.BOLDITALIC));   │
  info.add(new Chunk(String.valueOf(movie.getDuration()),     │
    FilmFonts.NORMAL));                                     ◁─┤
  info.add(new Chunk(" minutes", FilmFonts.NORMAL));          │
  return info;                                                │
}                                                             │
                                                              │
public Paragraph createMovieInformation(Movie movie) {        │
  Paragraph p = new Paragraph();                              │
  p.setFont(FilmFonts.NORMAL);                                │
  p.add(new Phrase("Title: ", FilmFonts.BOLDITALIC));     ◁─  │
  p.add(                                                      │  ┐
    PojoToElementFactory.getMovieTitlePhrase(movie));         │  │
  p.add(" ");                                                 │  │
  if (movie.getOriginalTitle() != null) {                     │  │
    p.add(new Phrase(                                         │  │
      "Original title: ", FilmFonts.BOLDITALIC));         ◁─  │  │
    p.add(PojoToElementFactory                                │  │
      .getOriginalTitlePhrase(movie));                        │  │
    p.add(" ");              Fonts grouped in                 │  │
  }                          FilmFonts class                  │  │  get() methods
  p.add(new Phrase("Country: ", FilmFonts.BOLDITALIC));   ◁───┘  │  grouped in Pojo-
  for (Country country : movie.getCountries()) {                 │  ToElementFactory
    p.add(                                                       │
      PojoToElementFactory.getCountryPhrase(country));           │
    p.add(" ");                                                  │
  }                                                              │
  p.add(new Phrase("Director: ", FilmFonts.BOLDITALIC));  ◁──────┘
  for (Director director : movie.getDirectors()) {
```

```
    p.add(
      PojoToElementFactory.getDirectorPhrase(director));
    p.add(" ");
  }
  p.add(createYearAndDuration(movie));
  return p;
}
```

get() methods grouped
in PojoToElementFactory

Note that you're already introducing rationalizations that will keep your code maintainable as the application grows.

RATIONALIZATIONS

You're using `Font` objects that are grouped in the `FilmFonts` class. Generic names `NORMAL`, `BOLD`, `ITALIC`, and `BOLDITALIC` are chosen, so that you don't need to refactor the names if your employer doesn't like the font family you've chosen. If he wants you to switch from Helvetica to Times, you have to change your code in only one place.

The `createMovieInformation()` method from listing 2.7 is used here.

Listing 2.8   MovieParagraphs1

```
List<Movie> movies = PojoFactory.getMovies(connection);
for (Movie movie : movies) {
  Paragraph p = createMovieInformation(movie);
  p.setAlignment(Element.ALIGN_JUSTIFIED);
  p.setIndentationLeft(18);
  p.setFirstLineIndent(-18);
  document.add(p);
}
```

Next, you'll convert POJOs into `Phrase` objects using a `PojoToElementFactory`. As your application grows, you'll benefit from reusing methods such as `getMovieTitlePhrase()` and `getDirectorPhrase()` that are grouped in such a separate factory.

Listing 2.9   MovieParagraphs2

```
List<Movie> movies = PojoFactory.getMovies(connection);
for (Movie movie : movies) {
  Paragraph title = new
      Paragraph(PojoToElementFactory.getMovieTitlePhrase(movie));
  title.setAlignment(Element.ALIGN_LEFT);
  document.add(title);
  if (movie.getOriginalTitle() != null) {
    Paragraph dummy = new Paragraph("\u00a0", FilmFonts.NORMAL);
    dummy.setLeading(-18);
    document.add(dummy);
    Paragraph originalTitle = new Paragraph(
      PojoToElementFactory.getOriginalTitlePhrase(movie));
    originalTitle.setAlignment(Element.ALIGN_RIGHT);
    document.add(originalTitle);
  }
  Paragraph director;
  float indent = 20;
  for (Director pojo : movie.getDirectors()) {
    director = new Paragraph(PojoToElementFactory.getDirectorPhrase(pojo));
```

```
      director.setIndentationLeft(indent);
      document.add(director);
      indent += 20;
    }
    Paragraph country;
    indent = 20;
    for (Country pojo : movie.getCountries()) {
      country = new Paragraph(PojoToElementFactory.getCountryPhrase(pojo));
      country.setAlignment(Element.ALIGN_RIGHT);
      country.setIndentationRight(indent);
      document.add(country);
      indent += 20;
    }
    Paragraph info = createYearAndDuration(movie);
    info.setAlignment(Element.ALIGN_CENTER);
    info.setSpacingAfter(36);
    document.add(info);
  }
```

The resulting PDFs list all the movie titles in the database, including their original title (if any), director, countries where they were produced, production year, and run length. These documents probably won't win an Oscar for best layout, but the examples illustrate a series of interesting Paragraph methods.

You can tune the layout by changing several Paragraph properties.

CHANGING THE ALIGNMENT

In listing 2.8, the alignment was set to Element.ALIGN_JUSTIFIED with the setAlignment() method. This causes iText to change the spaces between words and characters— depending on the space/character ratio—in order to make the text align with both the left and right margins. Listing 2.9 shows the alternative alignments: Element.LEFT, Element.ALIGN_CENTER, and Element.RIGHT. Element.ALIGN_JUSTIFIED_ALL is similar to Element.ALIGN_JUSTIFIED; the difference is that the last line is aligned too. If you don't define an alignment, the text is left aligned.

CHANGING THE INDENTATION

There are three methods for changing the indentation:

- setIndentationLeft()—Changes the indentation to the left. A positive value will be added to the left margin of the document; a negative value will be subtracted.
- setIndentationRight()—Does the same as setIndentationLeft(), but with the right margin.
- setFirstLineIndent()—Changes the left indentation of the first line, which is interesting if you want to provide an extra visual hint to the reader that a new Paragraph has started.

In listing 2.8, a positive indentation of 18 pt (valid for the whole paragraph) was defined. The negative indentation of 18 pt for the first line will be subtracted from the left indentation, causing the first line of each paragraph to start at the left margin. Every extra line in the same Paragraph will be indented a quarter of an inch.

SPACING BETWEEN PARAGRAPHS

Another way to distinguish different paragraphs is to add extra spacing before or after the paragraph. In listing 2.9, you used `setSpacingAfter()` to separate the details of two different movies with a blank line that is half an inch high. There's also a `setSpacingBefore()` method that can produce similar results.

Finally, listing 2.9 does something it shouldn't: it uses a workaround to write the English and the original title on the same line, with the English title aligned to the left and the original title aligned to the right. It achieves this by introducing a dummy `Paragraph` with a negative leading, causing the current position on the page to move one line up. While this works out more or less fine in this example, it will fail in other examples. For instance, if the previous line causes a page break, you won't be able to move back to the previous page. Also, if the English and the original title don't fit on one line, the text will overlap. You'll learn how to fix these layout problems in section 2.2.6.

In the next section, we'll have a look at what happens when the end of a line is reached.

2.2.4   *Distributing text over different lines*

In the movie_paragraphs_1.pdf document (listing 2.8), all the information about a movie is in one `Paragraph`. For most of the movies, the content of this `Paragraph` doesn't fit on one line, and iText splits the string, distributing the content over different lines. The default behavior of iText is to put as many complete words to a line as possible. iText splits sentences when a *space* or a *hyphen* is encountered, but you can change this behavior by redefining the *split character.*

THE SPLIT CHARACTER

If you want to keep two words separated by a space character on the same line, you shouldn't use the normal space character, `(char)32`; you should use the *nonbreaking space character* `(char)160`.

Next you'll create a `StringBuffer` containing all the movies by Stanley Kubrick, and you'll concatenate them into one long `String`, separated with pipe symbols (|). In the movie titles, you'll replace the ordinary space character with a nonbreaking space character.

Listing 2.10   MovieChain.java

```
StringBuffer buf1 = new StringBuffer();
for (Movie movie : kubrick) {
  buf1.append(movie.getMovieTitle()
    .replace(' ', '\u00a0'));
  buf1.append('|');
}
Chunk chunk1 = new Chunk(buf1.toString());

Paragraph paragraph = new Paragraph("A:\u00a0");
paragraph.add(chunk1);                              Adds content without
paragraph.setAlignment(Element.ALIGN_JUSTIFIED);    SplitCharacter
document.add(paragraph);
```

```
document.add(Chunk.NEWLINE);

chunk1.setSplitCharacter(new PipeSplitCharacter());
paragraph = new Paragraph("B:\u00a0");
paragraph.add(chunk1);
paragraph.setAlignment(Element.ALIGN_JUSTIFIED);
document.add(paragraph);
document.add(Chunk.NEWLINE);
```

Adds content with SplitCharacter '|'

Because you've replaced the space characters, iText can't find any of the default split characters in chunk1. The text will be split into different lines, cutting words in two just before the first character that no longer fits on the line. Then you add the same content a second time, but you define the pipe symbol (|) as a split character.

Next is a possible implementation of the SplitCharacter interface. You can add an instance of this custom-made class to a Chunk with the method setSplitCharacter().

Listing 2.11   PipeSplitCharacter.java

```
import com.lowagie.text.SplitCharacter;
import com.lowagie.text.pdf.PdfChunk;

public class PipeSplitCharacter implements SplitCharacter {

  @Override
  public boolean isSplitCharacter(
    int start, int current, int end, char[] cc,
    PdfChunk[] ck) {
    char c;
    if (ck == null)
      c = cc[current];
    else
      c = (char)ck[Math.min(current, ck.length - 1)]
                .getUnicodeEquivalent(cc[current]);
    return (c == '|' || c <= ' ' || c == '-');
  }
}
```

The method that needs to be implemented looks complicated, but in most cases it's sufficient to copy the method shown in the previous listing and change the return line. If you're working with Asian glyphs, you may also add these ranges of Unicode characters:

```
(c >= 0x2e80 && c < 0xd7a0) || (c >= 0xf900 && c < 0xfb00)
|| (c >= 0xfe30 && c < 0xfe50)  || (c >= 0xff61 && c < 0xffa0)
```

The result is shown in the upper part of figure 2.6.

In Paragraph A, the content is split at unusual places. The word "Love" is split into "Lo" and "ve," and the final "s" in the word "Paths" is orphaned. For the Chunks in Paragraph B, a split character was defined: the pipe character (|). Paragraph C shows what the content looks like if you don't replace the normal spaces with non-breaking spaces.

Figure 2.6 Splitting paragraphs

HYPHENATION

This listing is similar to listing 2.10, except it doesn't replace the ordinary space characters. Another Chunk attribute is introduced: hyphenation.

Listing 2.12 MovieChain.java (continued)

```
StringBuffer buf2 = new StringBuffer();
for (Movie movie : kubrick) {
  buf2.append(movie.getMovieTitle());
  buf2.append('|');
}
Chunk chunk2 = new Chunk(buf2.toString());

paragraph = new Paragraph("C:\u00a0");
paragraph.add(chunk2);
paragraph.setAlignment(Element.ALIGN_JUSTIFIED);
document.add(paragraph);
document.newPage();

chunk2.setHyphenation(
  new HyphenationAuto("en", "US", 2, 2));
paragraph = new Paragraph("D:\u00a0");
paragraph.add(chunk2);
paragraph.setAlignment(Element.ALIGN_JUSTIFIED);
document.add(paragraph);
document.newPage();
```

Adds content that will split on a space

Adds content using hyphenation (American English)

```
writer.setSpaceCharRatio(PdfWriter.NO_SPACE_CHAR_RATIO);
paragraph = new Paragraph("E:\u00a0");
paragraph.add(chunk2);
paragraph.setAlignment(Element.ALIGN_JUSTIFIED);
document.add(paragraph);
```

Adds content without extra spacing between glyphs

In this listing, you create a HyphenationAuto object using four parameters. iText uses hyphenation rules found in XML files named en_US.xml, en_GB.xml, and so on. The first two parameters refer to these filenames. The third and fourth parameters specify how many characters may be orphaned at the start or at the end of a word. For instance, you wouldn't want to split the word *elephant* like this: *e-lephant.* It doesn't look right if a single letter gets cut off from the rest of the word.

> **FAQ** *I use* setHyphenation(), *but my text isn't hyphenated. Where do I find the XML file I need?* If you try the example in listing 2.12, and not one word is hyphenated, you've probably forgotten to add the itext-hyph-xml.jar to your classpath. In this JAR, you'll find files such as es.xml, fr.xml, de_DR.xml, and so on. These XML files weren't written by iText developers; they were created for Apache's Formatting Objects Processor (FOP). The XML files bundled in itext-hyph-xml.jar are a limited set, and your code won't work if you're using a language for which no XML file was provided in this JAR. In that case, you'll have to find the appropriate file on the internet and add it to a JAR in your classpath. Don't forget to read the license before you start using a hyphenation file; some of those files can't be used for free.

The hyphenated text is added twice: once with the default space/character ratio, and once with a custom space/character ratio.

THE SPACE/CHARACTER RATIO

The Paragraph objects D and E from listing 2.12, have a justified alignment. This alignment is achieved by adding extra space between the words and between the characters. In Paragraph D, you see the default spacing. The ratio is 2.5, meaning that iText has been adding 2.5 times more space between the words than between the characters to match the exact length of each line.

You can change this ratio with the PdfWriter.setSpaceCharRatio() method. This is done for Paragraph E. On the lower-right side of figure 2.6, you can see that no extra space is added between the characters, only between the words, because the ratio was changed to NO_SPACE_CHAR_RATIO (which is in reality a very high float value).

2.2.5 *The List object: a sequence of Paragraphs called ListItem*

In the previous examples, you've listed movies, directors, and countries. In the next example you'll repeat this exercise, but instead of presenting the data as an alphabetically sorted series of movie titles, you'll create a list of countries, along with the number of movies in the database that were produced in that country. You'll list those movies, and for every movie you'll list its director(s).

ORDERED AND UNORDERED LISTS

To achieve this, you'll use the List object and a number of ListItem objects. As you can see in the UML diagram (figure 2.1), ListItem extends Paragraph. The main difference is that every ListItem has an extra Chunk variable that acts as a list symbol.

A first version of this report was created using ordered and unordered lists. The list symbol for ordered lists can be numbers—which is the default—or letters. The letters can be lowercase or uppercase—uppercase is the default. The default list symbol for unordered lists is a hyphen.

Listing 2.13   MovieLists1.java

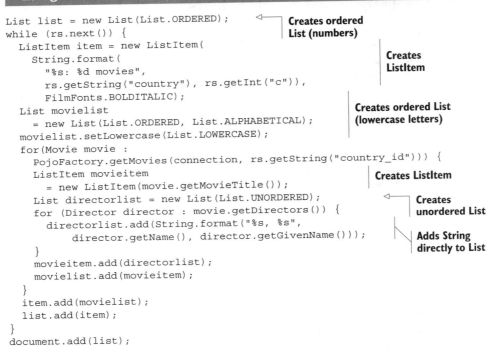

```
List list = new List(List.ORDERED);          ⟵  Creates ordered
while (rs.next()) {                               List (numbers)
  ListItem item = new ListItem(
    String.format(                                 Creates
      "%s: %d movies",                             ListItem
      rs.getString("country"), rs.getInt("c")),
      FilmFonts.BOLDITALIC);
  List movielist                                 Creates ordered List
    = new List(List.ORDERED, List.ALPHABETICAL);  (lowercase letters)
  movielist.setLowercase(List.LOWERCASE);
  for(Movie movie :
    PojoFactory.getMovies(connection, rs.getString("country_id"))) {
    ListItem movieitem                           Creates ListItem
      = new ListItem(movie.getMovieTitle());
    List directorlist = new List(List.UNORDERED); ⟵ Creates
    for (Director director : movie.getDirectors()) {  unordered List
      directorlist.add(String.format("%s, %s",
          director.getName(), director.getGivenName()));  Adds String
    }                                                      directly to List
    movieitem.add(directorlist);
    movielist.add(movieitem);
  }
  item.add(movielist);
  list.add(item);
}
document.add(list);
```

Note that it's not always necessary to create a ListItem instance. You can also add String items directly to a List; a ListItem will be created internally for you.

CHANGING THE LIST SYMBOL

Next is a variation on the same theme.

Listing 2.14   MovieLists2.java

```
List list = new List();                          Unordered List,
list.setAutoindent(false);                       fixed indentation
list.setSymbolIndent(36);
while (rs.next()) {
  ListItem item = new ListItem(String.format(    ListItem with
    "%s: %d movies",                             custom list symbol
    rs.getString("country"), rs.getInt("c")));
```

```
    item.setListSymbol(                              ⌄ ListItem with
      new Chunk(rs.getString("country_id")));        | custom list symbol
    List movielist
      = new List(List.ORDERED, List.ALPHABETICAL);    Ordered List (lowercase
    movielist.setAlignindent(false);                  letters), no realignment
    for(Movie movie :
      PojoFactory.getMovies(connection, rs.getString("country_id"))) {
      ListItem movieitem = new ListItem(movie.getMovieTitle());
      List directorlist = new List(List.ORDERED);        Ordered List
      directorlist.setPreSymbol("Director ");            with special
      directorlist.setPostSymbol(": ");                  list symbol
      for (Director director : movie.getDirectors()) {
        directorlist.add(String.format("%s, %s",         String added
          director.getName(), director.getGivenName()));  directly to List
      }
      movieitem.add(directorlist);
      movielist.add(movieitem);
    }
    item.add(movielist);
    list.add(item);
  }
document.add(list);
```

For the list with countries, you now define an indentation of half an inch for the list symbol. You also define a different list symbol for every item, namely the database ID of the country. The difference for the movie list is subtler: you tell iText that it shouldn't realign the list items. In listing 2.13, iText looks at all the items in the List and uses the maximum indentation for all the items. By adding the line `movielist.setAlignindent(false)` in listing 2.14, every list item now has its own list indentation based on the space taken by the list symbol. That is, unless you've added the line `list.setAutoindent(false)`, in which case the indentation specified with `setSymbolIndent()` is used.

As you can see in figure 2.7, a period (.) symbol is added to each list symbol for ordered lists. You can override this behavior with the methods `setPreSymbol()` and `setPostSymbol()`. In listing 2.14, the pre- and postsymbols are defined in such a way that you get "Director 1:", "Director 2:", and so on, as list symbols (shown at the top-right in figure 2.7).

SPECIAL TYPES OF LISTS

Four more variations are shown in figure 2.7. First, in listing 2.15, you'll create `List` objects of type `RomanList`, `GreekList`, and `ZapfDingbatsNumberList`. In listing 2.16, you'll create a `ZapfDingbatsList`.

Listing 2.15   MovieLists3.java

```
List list = new RomanList();
...
List movielist = new GreekList();
movielist.setLowercase(List.LOWERCASE);
..
List directorlist = new ZapfDingbatsNumberList(0);
```

Figure 2.7   `List` and `ListItem` **variations**

Be careful not to use `ZapfDingbatsNumberList` for long lists. This list variation comes in four different types defined with a parameter in the constructor that can be `0`, `1`, `2`, or `3`, corresponding to specific types of numbered bullets. Note that the output will only be correct for items 1 to 10, because there are no bullets for numbers 11 and higher in the font that is used to draw the bullets.

ZapfDingbats is one of the 14 standard Type 1 fonts. It contains a number of special symbols, such as a hand with the index finger pointing to the right: `(char)42`. This symbol is used in listing 2.16 for the director list. The special list class for this type of list is called `ZapfDingbatsList`. This is the superclass of `ZapfDingbatsNumberList`.

Listing 2.16 also shows how to change the first index of an ordered list using `setFirst()`, and how to set a custom list symbol for the entire list with `setListSymbol()`.

Listing 2.16   MovieLists4.java

```
List list = new List(List.ORDERED);
list.setFirst(9);
..
List movielist = new List();
movielist.setListSymbol(new Chunk("Movie: ", FilmFonts.BOLD));
..
List directorlist = new ZapfDingbatsList(42);
```

We'll conclude this section with a number of objects that aren't shown on the class diagram in figure 2.1: vertical position marks and separator Chunks.

2.2.6 *The DrawInterface: vertical position marks, separators, and tabs*

In section 1.3.4, you learned that there are different ways to add content to a page using iText. In this chapter, you've been using document.add(), trusting iText to put the content at the correct position in a page. But in some cases, you might want to add something extra. For instance, you might want to add a mark at the current position in the page (for example, an arrow); or you might want to draw a line from the left margin to the right margin (which is different from underlining a Chunk).

This can be achieved using DrawInterface. If you want to benefit from all the possibilities of this interface and its VerticalPositionMark implementation, you'll need some techniques that will be explained in the next chapter. For now, figure 2.8 shows classes that can be used without any further programming work.

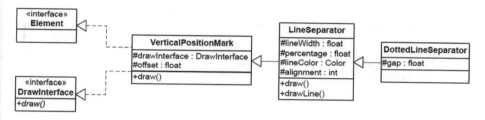

Figure 2.8   Class diagram of DrawInterface implementations

VERTICAL POSITION MARKS

Suppose that you want to create an alphabetical list of directors, and to list the movies directed by these filmmakers that are present in the database. To this list, you want to add an arrow that indicates which directors have more than two movies in the database. You also want to indicate all the movies that were made in the year 2000 or later. See figure 2.9 for an example.

director_overview_1.pdf - Adobe Reader
File Edit View Document Tools Window Help

Kelly, Richard
Donnie Darko: 2001

→ **Ki-Duk**, Kim
The Isle: 2000
Spring, Summer, Autumn, Winter... and Spring: 2003
3-Iron: 2004

→ **Kubrick**, Stanley
Killer's Kiss: 1955
The Killing: 1956
Paths of Glory: 1957

Figure 2.9   Vertical position marks

You can achieve this by subclassing VerticalPositionMark.

Listing 2.17   PositionedArrow.java

```
public class PositionedArrow extends VerticalPositionMark {

  protected boolean left;
  ...
  public static final PositionedArrow LEFT =
    new PositionedArrow(true);
  public static final PositionedArrow RIGHT =
    new PositionedArrow(false);
  ...
  public void draw(PdfContentByte canvas,
    float llx, float lly, float urx, float ury,
    float y) {
    canvas.beginText();
    canvas.setFontAndSize(zapfdingbats, 12);
    if (left) {
      canvas.showTextAligned(Element.ALIGN_CENTER,
        String.valueOf((char)220), llx - 10, y, 0);
    }
    else {
      canvas.showTextAligned(Element.ALIGN_CENTER,
        String.valueOf((char)220), urx + 10, y + 8,
        180);
    }
    canvas.endText();
  }
}
```

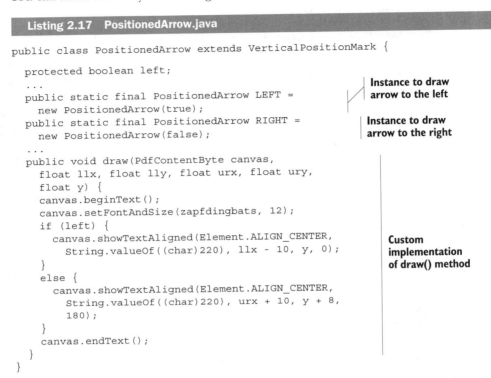

Instance to draw
arrow to the left

Instance to draw
arrow to the right

Custom
implementation
of draw() method

You could use Document.add() to add instances of this PositionedArrow class to the Document because it extends VerticalPositionMark, which means it also implements the Element interface. When this Element is encountered, the custom draw() method will be invoked, and this method has access to the canvas to which content is added. It also knows the coordinates defining the margins of the page, (llx, lly) and (urx, ury), as well as the current y position on the page. In the draw() method of the PositionedArrow class, listing 2.17 uses llx and urx to draw an arrow in the left or right margin of the page, and it uses the y value to position the arrow.

Observe that in this example PositionedArrow is not added directly to the Document.

Listing 2.18   DirectorOverview1.java

```
LineSeparator line = new LineSeparator(
  1, 100, null, Element.ALIGN_CENTER, -2);
Paragraph stars = new Paragraph(20);
stars.add(new Chunk(StarSeparator.LINE));
stars.setSpacingAfter(30);

while (rs.next()) {
  director = PojoFactory.getDirector(rs);
  Paragraph p = new Paragraph(
    PojoToElementFactory.getDirectorPhrase(director));
```

❶ Creates
LineSeparator

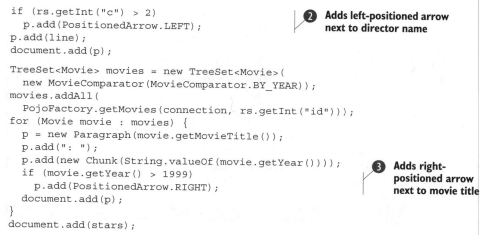

```
    if (rs.getInt("c") > 2)
      p.add(PositionedArrow.LEFT);
    p.add(line);
    document.add(p);

    TreeSet<Movie> movies = new TreeSet<Movie>(
      new MovieComparator(MovieComparator.BY_YEAR));
    movies.addAll(
      PojoFactory.getMovies(connection, rs.getInt("id")));
    for (Movie movie : movies) {
      p = new Paragraph(movie.getMovieTitle());
      p.add(": ");
      p.add(new Chunk(String.valueOf(movie.getYear())));
      if (movie.getYear() > 1999)
        p.add(PositionedArrow.RIGHT);
      document.add(p);
    }
    document.add(stars);
}
```

2 Adds left-positioned arrow next to director name

3 Adds right-positioned arrow next to movie title

The arrow refers to the content of a Paragraph, and it's better to add it to the corresponding object, as is done in **2** and **3**. Otherwise a page break could cause the text to be on one page and the arrow on the next; that could be your intention in some situations, but that's not the case here.

LINE SEPARATORS

When you need to draw a line, you want to know the current vertical position of the text of a page. In that situation, you can get a long way using the LineSeparator class. In **1** of listing 2.18, you create a line separator with the following parameters:

- *The line width*—In this case, a line with a thickness of 1 pt.
- *The percentage that needs to be covered*—In this case, 100 percent of the available width.
- *A color*—In this case, null, meaning that the default color will be used.
- *The alignment*—This only makes sense if the percentage isn't 100 percent.
- *The offset*—In this case, 2 pt below the baseline.

If this object isn't sufficient for your needs, you can write your own subclass of VerticalPositionMark, or your own (custom) implementation of the DrawInterface.

Listing 2.19   StarSeparator.java

```
public class StarSeparator implements DrawInterface {
  ...
  public void draw(PdfContentByte canvas,
    float llx, float lly, float urx, float ury, float y) {
    float middle = (llx + urx) / 2;
    canvas.beginText();
    canvas.setFontAndSize(bf, 10);
    canvas.showTextAligned(Element.ALIGN_CENTER,
      "*", middle, y, 0);
    canvas.showTextAligned(Element.ALIGN_CENTER,
      "*   *", middle, y -10, 0);
```

```
    canvas.endText();
  }
}
```

Observe that the StarSeparator object doesn't implement the Element interface. This means you can't add it directly to the Document. You need to wrap it in a Chunk object first.

SEPARATOR CHUNKS

Listing 2.9 applied a dirty hack using negative leading to create a line layout with a Paragraph to the left (the English movie title) and a Paragraph to the right (the original movie title). I told you that's not the way it's should be done. Now let's have a look at the proper way to achieve this.

Listing 2.20   DirectorOverview2.java

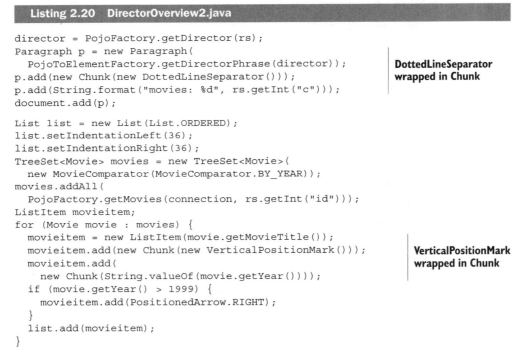

```
director = PojoFactory.getDirector(rs);
Paragraph p = new Paragraph(
  PojoToElementFactory.getDirectorPhrase(director));          DottedLineSeparator
p.add(new Chunk(new DottedLineSeparator()));                  wrapped in Chunk
p.add(String.format("movies: %d", rs.getInt("c")));
document.add(p);

List list = new List(List.ORDERED);
list.setIndentationLeft(36);
list.setIndentationRight(36);
TreeSet<Movie> movies = new TreeSet<Movie>(
  new MovieComparator(MovieComparator.BY_YEAR));
movies.addAll(
  PojoFactory.getMovies(connection, rs.getInt("id")));
ListItem movieitem;
for (Movie movie : movies) {
  movieitem = new ListItem(movie.getMovieTitle());
  movieitem.add(new Chunk(new VerticalPositionMark()));       VerticalPositionMark
  movieitem.add(                                              wrapped in Chunk
    new Chunk(String.valueOf(movie.getYear())));
  if (movie.getYear() > 1999) {
    movieitem.add(PositionedArrow.RIGHT);
  }
  list.add(movieitem);
}
document.add(list);
```

Listing 2.20 wraps a DottedLineSeparator in a Chunk and uses it to separate the name of a filmmaker from the number of movies they have directed. The DottedLineSeparator is a subclass of the LineSeparator, with the main difference being that it draws a dotted line instead of a solid line. You can also set the gap between the dots using the setGap() method.

Some of the VerticalPositionMarks in figure 2.10 act as separators to distribute content over a line. The name of the class no longer applies—you aren't adding a *mark* at a *vertical position* anymore. Instead you're using the object to separate the movie title from the year when the movie was produced. You could use multiple

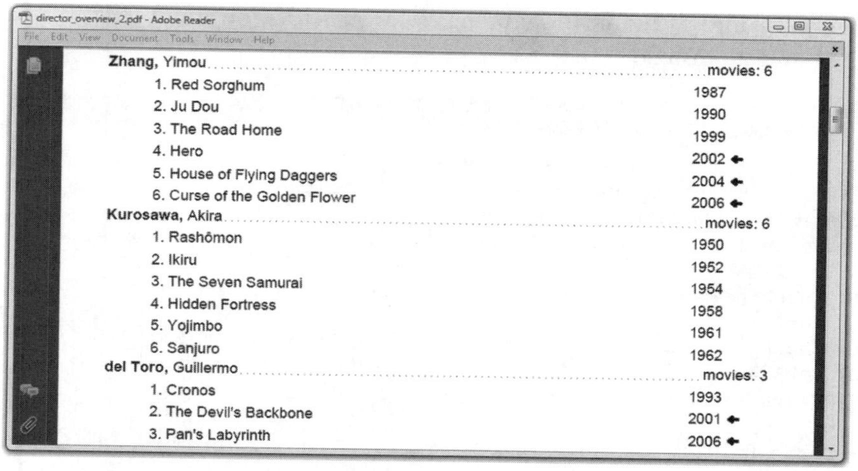

Figure 2.10 Dotted line and other separators

separators to distribute the title, the run length, and the production year: iText will look at the remaining white space for every line and distribute it equally over the number of separator Chunks.

Another way to distribute the content of a line is to use tabs.

TAB CHUNKS

Figure 2.11 shows how you can distribute the English movie title, the original title, the run length, and the year the movie was produced over one or more lines using tabs. If ordinary separator Chunks were used, the content wouldn't have been aligned in columns.

One English movie title and its corresponding original title don't fit in the available space. A new line is used because of the way you've defined the tab Chunk. If you

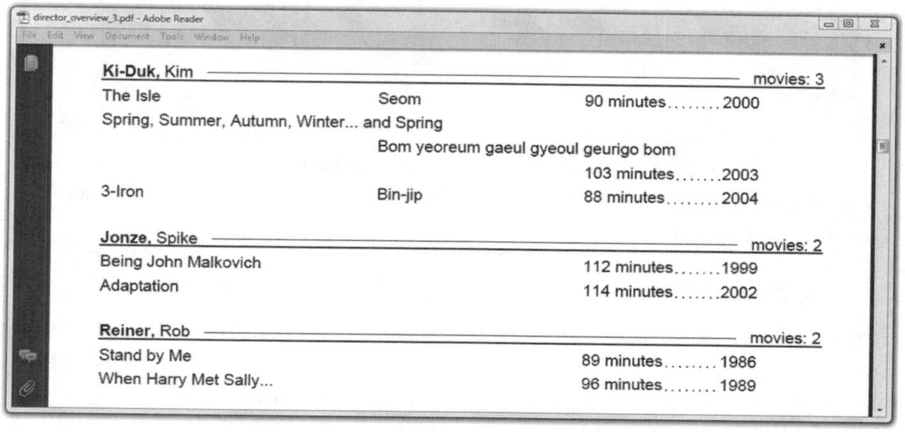

Figure 2.11 Chunks acting as tab positions

change true into false in the tab Chunk constructors, no line break will occur; the text will overlap instead.

Listing 2.21   DirectorOverview3.java

```
Chunk CONNECT = new Chunk(new LineSeparator(
  0.5f, 95, BaseColor.BLUE, Element.ALIGN_CENTER, 3.5f));
LineSeparator UNDERLINE = new LineSeparator(
  1, 100, null, Element.ALIGN_CENTER, -2);
Chunk tab1 =
  new Chunk(new VerticalPositionMark(), 200, true);
Chunk tab2 =
  new Chunk(new VerticalPositionMark(), 350, true);
Chunk tab3 =
  new Chunk(new DottedLineSeparator(), 450, true);
...
director = PojoFactory.getDirector(rs);
Paragraph p = new Paragraph(
  PojoToElementFactory.getDirectorPhrase(director));
p.add(CONNECT);
p.add(String.format("movies: %d", rs.getInt("c")));
p.add(UNDERLINE);
document.add(p);
TreeSet<Movie> movies = new TreeSet<Movie>(
  new MovieComparator(MovieComparator.BY_YEAR));
movies.addAll(
  PojoFactory.getMovies(connection, rs.getInt("id")));
for (Movie movie : movies) {
  p = new Paragraph(movie.getMovieTitle());
  p.add(new Chunk(tab1));
  if (movie.getOriginalTitle() != null)
    p.add(new Chunk(movie.getOriginalTitle()));
  p.add(new Chunk(tab2));
  p.add(new Chunk(
    String.valueOf(movie.getDuration()) + " minutes"));
  p.add(new Chunk(tab3));
  p.add(new Chunk(String.valueOf(movie.getYear())));
  document.add(p);
}
document.add(Chunk.NEWLINE);
```

Tab at position 200 for original title

Tab at position 350 for duration

Tab at position 450 for year

You can use any DrawInterface to create a separator or tab Chunk, and you can use these Chunks to separate content horizontally (within a paragraph) or vertically (lines between paragraphs). Now it's time to discuss the other building blocks shown in the class diagram in figure 2.1.

2.3   Adding Anchor, Image, Chapter, and Section objects

In the previous examples, you've used every field shown in the ERD in figure 2.2, except for one: the field named imdb. This field contains the ID for the movie on imdb.com, which is the Internet Movie Database (IMDB).

Wouldn't it be nice to link to this external site from your documents? And what kind of internal links could you add to a document? If you browse the resources that come with the book, you'll see that the imdb field is also used as part of the filename for the movie poster of each movie. The movie *Superman Returns* has the ID 0348150 at IMDB. This means that you'll find a 0348150.jpg file in the posters directory, which is a subdirectory of the resources folder.

In this section, you'll work with different types of links: internal and external. You'll create a table of contents automatically and get bookmarks for free, using the Chapter and Section objects. Finally, you'll learn how to add images.

2.3.1 *The Anchor object: internal and external links*

What would the internet be without hypertext? How would you browse the web without hyperlinks? It's almost impossible to imagine a web page without <a> tags. But what about PDF documents?

There are different ways to add a link to a PDF file using iText. In this section, you'll add references and destinations using the Anchor object, as well as by setting the reference and anchor attributes of a Chunk. You'll discover more alternatives in chapter 7.

ADDING ANCHOR OBJECTS

In listing 2.22, three Anchor objects are created. The first Anchor, with a country name as its text, will act as a destination. It's the equivalent of <a name="US"> in HTML, where US is the id of a country in the database. The third anchor, with the text "Go back to the first page." will be an internal link acting as <a href="#US">. It will allow the reader to jump to the destination with name "US" (located on the first page). iText recognizes this reference as a local destination because you're adding a number sign (#) to the name, just as you would do in HTML.

Listing 2.22 MovieLinks1.java

```
Paragraph country = new Paragraph();
Anchor dest =
  new Anchor(rs.getString("country"), FilmFonts.BOLD);      Creates named
dest.setName(rs.getString("country_id"));                   Anchor
country.add(dest);
country.add(String.format(": %d movies", rs.getInt("c")));
document.add(country);
for(Movie movie : PojoFactory.getMovies(
                connection, rs.getString("country_id"))) {
  imdb = new Anchor(movie.getMovieTitle());
  imdb.setReference(String.format(                          Creates external
    "http://www.imdb.com/title/tt%s/", movie.getImdb()));   reference
  document.add(imdb);
  document.add(Chunk.NEWLINE);
}
document.newPage();
...
Anchor toUS = new Anchor("Go to first page.");              Creates Anchor with
toUS.setReference("#US");                                   internal reference
document.add(toUS);
```

The second Anchor is a link to an external resource. In this case, to a specific page on the IMDB website. http://www.imdb.com/title/tt0348150/ refers to a page with information about the movie *Superman Returns*.

There's also another way to achieve the same result.

REMOTE GOTO, LOCAL DESTINATION, AND LOCAL GOTO CHUNKS

Listing 2.23 creates a PDF document with an opening paragraph, a list of countries, and a closing paragraph. The closing paragraph contains a link to jump to the top of the page. The other links are external.

Listing 2.23   MovieLinks2.java

```
Paragraph p = new Paragraph();
Chunk top = new Chunk("Country List", FilmFonts.BOLD);      Creates
top.setLocalDestination("top");                              destination
p.add(top);
document.add(p);

Chunk imdb =                                                 Creates
  new Chunk("Internet Movie Database", FilmFonts.ITALIC);    external link
imdb.setAnchor(new URL("http://www.imdb.com/"));
p = new Paragraph("Click on a country, and you'll get a list of movies,"
  + " containing links to the ");
p.add(imdb);
p.add(".");
document.add(p);

p = new Paragraph("This list can be found in a ");
Chunk page1 = new Chunk("separate document");               Creates link to page
page1.setRemoteGoto("movie_links_1.pdf", 1);                in another PDF
p.add(page1);
p.add(".");
document.add(p);
...
Paragraph country = new Paragraph(rs.getString("country"));
country.add(": ");
   Chunk link = new Chunk(
   String.format("%d movies", rs.getInt("c")));             Creates link to
link.setRemoteGoto(                                          destination in
   "movie_links_1.pdf", rs.getString("country_id"));        another PDF
country.add(link);
document.add(country);
...
p = new Paragraph("Go to ");
top = new Chunk("top");                                      Creates link to
top.setLocalGoto("top");                                     destination in this PDF
p.add(top);
p.add(".");
document.add(p);
```

In previous examples, you've set attributes of the Chunk object to underline text, to change the background color, and so on. You can also set attributes that provide even more functionality than the Anchor class:

- `Chunk.setLocalDestination()`—Corresponds to `Anchor.setName()`. You can use it to create a destination that can be referenced from within the document, or from another document.
- `Chunk.setLocalGoto()`—Corresponds to `Anchor.setReference()`, where the reference is a local destination. You don't need to add a # sign when using this method.
- `Chunk.setRemoteGoto()`—Can refer to any of the following:
  - *An external URL*—Defined by a `String` or a `java.net.URL` object; this corresponds to `Anchor.setReference()`.
  - *A page in another PDF document*—The document created in the `MovieLinks2` example refers to page 1 in the file movie_links_1.pdf, a file generated by `MovieLinks1`.
  - *A destination in another PDF document*—Listing 2.23 refers to the country code in movie_links_1.pdf.

You can use the movie_links_2.pdf file, which lists 32 countries, as a clickable table of contents (TOC) for the movie_links_1.pdf file, which lists the movies that were produced in these countries.

The next example will explain how to create a different type of TOC: the bookmarks panel in Adobe Reader. Note that *bookmarks* are often referred to as *outlines* in the context of PDF.

2.3.2 *Chapter and Section: get bookmarks for free*

If you scroll in the bookmarks panel shown in figure 2.12, you'll see entries numbered from 1 to 7: Forties, Fifties, Sixties, Seventies, Eighties, Nineties, and Twenty-first century. You can create these entries by organizing the content in chapters. Every `Chapter` in this PDF document contains one or more `Section` objects. In this case, years that belong to the forties, fifties, and so on. In figure 2.12, there are also subsections with titles of movies.

Let's compare listing 2.24 and figure 2.12. The chapter number is passed as a parameter when constructing the `Chapter` object. By default, a dot is added to the number, but you can change this with the `setNumberStyle()` method. `Section`s are created using the `addSection()` method. The title passed as a parameter when constructing a `Chapter` or `Section` is shown on the page and is used as the title for the bookmark. If you want to use a different title in the outline tree, you can use `setBookmarkTitle()`. You can change the indentation of a `Chapter` or `Section` by using different methods: `setIndentation()` changes the indentation of the content but doesn't affect the title; `setIndentationLeft()` and `setIndentationRight()` apply to the content and the title. Observe that the subsections aren't numbered 5.4.1., 5.4.2, 5.4.3 ... but 1., 2., 3. ... because the number depth has been reduced to 1 with `setNumberDepth()`.

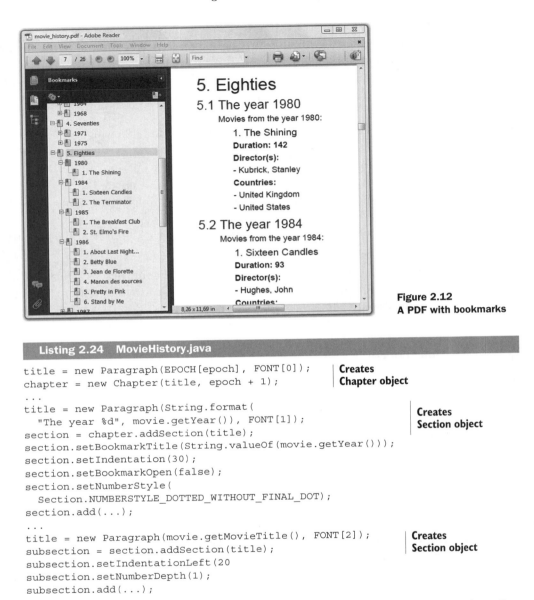

Figure 2.12
A PDF with bookmarks

Listing 2.24   MovieHistory.java

```
title = new Paragraph(EPOCH[epoch], FONT[0]);        Creates
chapter = new Chapter(title, epoch + 1);             Chapter object
...
title = new Paragraph(String.format(                 Creates
  "The year %d", movie.getYear()), FONT[1]);         Section object
section = chapter.addSection(title);
section.setBookmarkTitle(String.valueOf(movie.getYear()));
section.setIndentation(30);
section.setBookmarkOpen(false);
section.setNumberStyle(
  Section.NUMBERSTYLE_DOTTED_WITHOUT_FINAL_DOT);
section.add(...);
...
title = new Paragraph(movie.getMovieTitle(), FONT[2]);    Creates
subsection = section.addSection(title);                   Section object
subsection.setIndentationLeft(20
subsection.setNumberDepth(1);
subsection.add(...);
```

As shown in the class diagram in figure 2.1, `Section` also implements an interface named `LargeElement`. In chapter 1, you learned that iText tries to write PDF syntax to the `OutputStream`, freeing memory as soon as possible. But with objects such as `Chapter`, you're creating content in memory that can only be rendered to PDF when you add them to the `Document` object. This means that the content of several pages can be kept in memory until iText gets the chance to generate the PDF syntax.

There are two ways to work around this:

- Define the Chapter as *incomplete*, and add it to the Document in different pieces; you'll see how to do this in chapter 4, after we discuss another LargeElement, PdfPTable.
- Create the outline tree using PdfOutline instead of putting content in Chapter or Section objects. This will be discussed in chapter 7, where you'll discover that PdfOutline offers much more flexibility.

We've covered almost all the objects in the class diagram. Only two objects remain: Rectangle and Image.

2.3.3 *The Image object: adding raster format illustrations*

You created Rectangle objects in chapter 1 to define the page size, but there's very little chance you'll ever need to add a Rectangle object with Document.add(). We'll find better ways to draw shapes in chapter 3, but let's take a look at a simple example for the sake of completeness.

Listing 2.25   MoviePosters1.java

```
Rectangle rect = new Rectangle(0, 806, 36, 842);
rect.setBackgroundColor(BaseColor.RED);
document.add(rect);
```

The code draws a small red square in the upper-left corner of the first page.

ADDING AN IMAGE

To add an Image to a PDF document, do this:

Listing 2.26   MoviePosters1.java (continued)

```
document.add(new Paragraph(movie.getMovieTitle()));
document.add(
  Image.getInstance(String.format(RESOURCE, movie.getImdb())));
```

iText comes with different classes for different image types: Jpeg, PngImage, GifImage, TiffImage, and so on. All these classes are discussed in detail in chapter 10. They either extend the Image class, or they are able to create an instance of the Image class.

You could use these separate classes to create a new Image, but it's easier to let the Image class inspect the binary image and decide which class should be used, based on the contents of the file. That's one thing less to worry about.

THE IMAGE SEQUENCE

The result of the code in listing 2.26 is shown to the left in figure 2.13. Observe that the poster of the movie *Betty Blue* didn't fit on page 3. As a result, the title of the next movie, *The Breakfast Club*, is added on page 3, and the poster is added on page 4. This is the default behavior: iText tries to add as much information as possible on each page.

This may be considered undesired behavior in some projects. If that's the case, you can use this method:

**Figure 2.13
Adding images to
a PDF document**

Listing 2.27   MoviePosters2.java

```
PdfWriter.getInstance(document,
    new FileOutputStream(filename)).setStrictImageSequence(true);
```

The resulting PDF is shown on the right in figure 2.13. The method setStrictImage-
Sequence() allows you to force iText to respect the order in which content is added.

CHANGING THE IMAGE POSITION

In figure 2.14, the alignment of the image is changed so that the film information is
put next to the movie poster.

   This is done with the setAlignment() method. Possible values for this method are:

- Image.LEFT, Image.CENTER, *or* Image.RIGHT—These define the position on the
  page.
- Image.TEXTWRAP *or* Image.UNDERLYING—By default, iText doesn't wrap images.
  When you add an Image followed by text to a Document, the text will be added
  under the image, as shown in figure 2.13. With TEXTWRAP, you can add text next
  to the Image, except when you're using Image.CENTER. With UNDERLYING, the
  text will be added on top of the Image (text and image will overlap).

All of this doesn't apply if you use the method setAbsolutePosition(). With this
method, you can define coordinates (X, Y) that will be used to position the lower-left
corner of the image. The image will not follow the flow of the other objects.

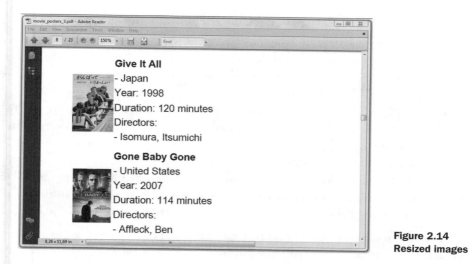

**Figure 2.14
Resized images**

CHANGING THE BORDER

The PDF shown in figure 2.14 was generated using methods that are inherited from the `Rectangle` object. Listing 2.28 shows how to define a border, and how to change its width and color.

Listing 2.28   MoviePosters3.java

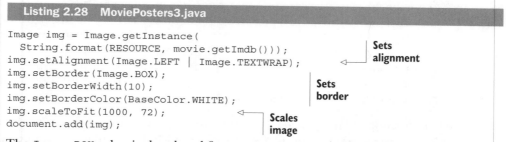

```
Image img = Image.getInstance(
  String.format(RESOURCE, movie.getImdb()));       Sets
img.setAlignment(Image.LEFT | Image.TEXTWRAP);     alignment
img.setBorder(Image.BOX);
img.setBorderWidth(10);                            Sets
img.setBorderColor(BaseColor.WHITE);               border
img.scaleToFit(1000, 72);                          Scales
document.add(img);                                 image
```

The `Image.BOX` value is shorthand for `Rectangle.LEFT | Rectangle.RIGHT | Rectangle.TOP | Rectangle.BOTTOM`, meaning that the image should have a border on all sides. You'll learn more about drawing `Rectangle` objects in chapters 3 and 14.

RESIZING IMAGES

In listing 2.28, you're also using `scaleToFit()`. You're passing an unusually high width value (1000 pt) compared to the height value (72 pt). This ensures that all the images will have a height of one inch. The width will vary depending on the aspect ratio of the image.

> **FAQ** *What is the relationship between the size and the resolution of an image in iText?* Suppose you have a paper image that measures 5 in. x 5 in. You scan this image at 300 dpi. The resulting image is 1500 pixels x 1500 pixels, so if you get an iText `Image` instance, the width and the height will be 1500 user units. Taking into account that 1 in. equals 72 user units, the image will be about 20.83 in. x 20.83 in. when added to the PDF document. If you want to display the object as an image of 5 in. x 5 in., you'll need to scale it. The best way to do this is with `scalePercent(100 * 72 / 300)`.

There are different ways to change the dimensions of an image:

- The width and height parameters of `scaleToFit()` define the maximum dimensions of the image. If the width/height ratio differs from the aspect ratio of the image, either the width, or the height, will be smaller than the corresponding parameter of this method.
- The width and height parameters will be respected when using `scaleAbsolute()`. The resulting image risks being stretched in the *X* or *Y* direction if you don't choose the parameters wisely. You can also use `scaleAbsoluteWidth()` and `scaleAbsoluteHeight()`.
- `scalePercent()` comes in two versions: one with two parameters, a percentage for the width and a percentage for the height; and another with only one parameter, a percentage that will be applied equally to the width and the height.

It's a common misconception that resizing images in iText also changes the quality of the image. It's important to understand that iText takes the image *as is*: iText doesn't change the number of pixels in the image.

> **FAQ**   *IText is adding the same image more than once to the same document. How can I avoid this?* Suppose that you have an image.jpg file with a size of 100 KB. If you create ten different `Image` objects from this file, and add these objects to your `Document`, these different instances referring to image.jpg will consume at least 1000 KB, because the image bytes will be added 10 times to the PDF file. If you create only one `Image` instance referring to image.jpg, and you add this single object 10 times to your `Document`, the image bytes will be added to the PDF file only once. In short, you can save plenty of disk space if you reuse Image objects for images that need to be repeated multiple times in your document. For example, a logo that needs to be added to the header of each page.

When creating an `Image` instance from a file, you won't always know its dimensions before or even after scaling it. You can get the width and height of the image with these methods:

- `getWidth()` and `getHeight()` are inherited from the `Rectangle` object. They return the original height and width of the image.
- `getPlainWidth()` and `getPlainHeight()` return the width and height after scaling. These are the dimensions of the image used to print it on a page.
- `getScaledWidth()` and `getScaledHeight()` return the width and height needed to print the image. These dimensions are equal to the plain width and height, except in cases where the image is rotated.

The difference between scaled width/height and plain width/height is shown in the next example.

CHANGING THE ROTATION

The rotation for images is defined counterclockwise. Listing 2.29 uses the `setRotationDegrees()` method to rotate an image –30 degrees; that's 30 degrees to the right.

Using `setRotation()` with a rotation value of `(float) -Math.PI / 6` would have had the same effect.

Listing 2.29 RiverPhoenix.java

```
Paragraph p = new Paragraph(text);
Image img = Image.getInstance(
  String.format("resources/posters/%s.jpg", imdb));
img.scaleToFit(1000, 72);
img.setRotationDegrees(-30);
p.add(new Chunk(img, 0, -15, true));
```

If you look at the poster for the movie *Stand by Me*, you'll find out that it's made up of 100 pixels x 140 pixels. These values are returned by `getWidth()` and `get-Height()`. When scaled to fit a rectangle of 1000 pixels x 72 pixels, the dimensions are changed into 51.42857 x 72—those are the values returned by `getPlainWidth()` and `getPlainHeight()`.

In figure 2.15, you can see that the image needs more space. Due to the rotation, the horizontal distance between the lower-right corner and the upper-left corner of the image is 80.53845. The vertical distance between the upper-right corner and the lower-left corner is 88.068115. These values are returned by `getScaledWidth()` and `getScaledHeight()`.

Something else is different in figure 2.15: each `Image` has been added to a `Paragraph` object, wrapped in a `Chunk`.

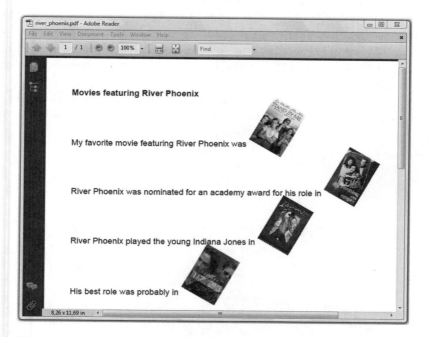

Figure 2.15   Rotated images, wrapped in `Chunk` objects

WRAPPING IMAGES IN CHUNKS

This is yet another example of setting attributes for a Chunk. By creating a Chunk using an Image as the parameter, you can add the Image to other building blocks as if it were an ordinary chunk of text. The extra parameters in this Chunk constructor define an offset in the *X* and *Y* directions. The negative value in listing 2.29 causes the image to be added 15 pt below the baseline. You can also indicate whether the leading should be adapted to accommodate the image. If you don't set the final parameter to true, the image risks overlapping with the other text (if the height of the image is greater than the leading).

This isn't a definitive overview of what you can do with images. You've learned enough to change the properties of an image, but there's more to learn about the bits and bytes of specific image types (TIFF, animated GIF, and so on), about using java.awt.Image, and about using image masks. All of this will be covered in chapter 10; now it's time to round up what we've covered in chapter 2.

2.3.4   *Summary*

We've covered a lot of ground in this chapter. You learned about Chunk objects and several—not all—of a Chunk's attributes; you'll discover more attributes as you read on in part 1 of this book. You've worked with Phrases and Paragraphs, and you've been introduced to the Font and BaseFont classes. You've made Lists containing List-Items, and you've discovered different ways to use separator Chunks.

With the Anchor object and its alternatives, you've created internal and external links and destinations. The Chapter and Section classes were used to create bookmarks, but you'll learn more about the outline tree and the LargeElement object in the chapters that follow. That's also true for the Image object: you've learned how to use the most common methods, but you'll learn more about the bits and bytes of images in chapter 10.

Up until now, you've worked with the building blocks of iText, which are often referred to as high-level objects. In the next chapter, you'll discover the world of low-level PDF creation.

Adding content
at absolute positions

This chapter covers

- Low-level access to page content, aka direct content
- Convenience methods for writing direct content
- Using the `ColumnText` object
- Reusing content with the `PdfTemplate` object

In chapter 1, you learned that there are different ways to add content to a document when generating a PDF file from scratch. In chapter 2, you learned to add high-level objects to a `Document`. Now you're going to learn an approach that's totally different: you'll add content to a page using methods that are referred to as *low-level operations* because they write PDF syntax directly to the content stream of the page.

A complete overview of the PDF operators and operands will follow in chapter 14. This chapter will cover the basics, but will quickly move on to convenience methods that hide some of the complexity of PDF. We'll also unleash the power of the `ColumnText` object, an object that allows you to add basic building blocks at absolute positions.

We'll start with an example that mixes the high-level and low-level approaches.

3.1   *Introducing the concept of direct content*

As a first example, you'll use high-level objects to create a postcard inviting people to the movie that will open the Foobar Film Festival; then you'll add extra content at absolute positions in the document using low-level methods.

The page to the left in figure 3.1 is created by adding a Paragraph with the text "Foobar Film Festival" and an Image of the poster of *Lawrence of Arabia*. The Image was positioned using the setAbsolutePositions() method. The order in which these Elements were added doesn't matter; document.add() always adds images to the image layer *under* the text layer.

To the right is another page with the same Paragraph and Image, but now with a colored rectangle added *under* the image layer, and the text "SOLD OUT" added *over* the text layer. This can be achieved by writing to the *direct content*.

Figure 3.1   Adding content using low-level methods to a page created with high-level objects

3.1.1   *Direct content layers*

Here is the source code used to create the PDF shown in figure 3.1.

Listing 3.1 FestivalOpening.java

```
Paragraph p = new Paragraph("Foobar Film Festival",
  new Font(FontFamily.HELVETICA, 24));
p.setAlignment(Element.ALIGN_CENTER);
document.add(p);
Image img = Image.getInstance(RESOURCE);
img.setAbsolutePosition(
  (PageSize.POSTCARD.getWidth()
    - img.getScaledWidth()) / 2,
  (PageSize.POSTCARD.getHeight()
    - img.getScaledHeight()) / 2);
document.add(img);
document.newPage();
document.add(p);
document.add(img);
PdfContentByte over = writer.getDirectContent();
over.saveState();
float sinus = (float)Math.sin(Math.PI / 60);
float cosinus = (float)Math.cos(Math.PI / 60);
BaseFont bf = BaseFont.createFont();
over.beginText();
over.setTextRenderingMode(
  PdfContentByte.TEXT_RENDER_MODE_FILL_STROKE);
over.setLineWidth(1.5f);
over.setRGBColorStroke(0xFF, 0x00, 0x00);
over.setRGBColorFill(0xFF, 0xFF, 0xFF);
over.setFontAndSize(bf, 36);
over.setTextMatrix(
  cosinus, sinus, -sinus, cosinus, 50, 324);
over.showText("SOLD OUT");
over.endText();
over.restoreState();
PdfContentByte under = writer.getDirectContentUnder();
under.saveState();
under.setRGBColorFill(0xFF, 0xD7, 0x00);
under.rectangle(5, 5, PageSize.POSTCARD.getWidth() - 10,
  PageSize.POSTCARD.getHeight() - 10);
under.fill();
under.restoreState();
```

Adds Paragraph with Document.add()

Adds Image with Document.add()

Adds text on top of other content

Adds rectangle under other content

How does this work? When you add content to a page—be it with `Document.add()` or otherwise—iText writes PDF syntax to a `ByteBuffer` that is wrapped in a `PdfContentByte` object. When a page is full, these buffers are added to the PDF file in a specific order. Each buffer can be seen as a separate *layer*, and iText draws these layers in the sequence indicated in figure 3.2.

When a page is initialized, two `PdfContentByte` objects are created for the basic building blocks:

❸ A `PdfContentByte` *object for text*—The content of `Chunks`, `Phrases`, `Paragraphs`, and so on

❷ A `PdfContentByte` *for graphics*—The background of a `Chunk`, `Images`, the borders of a `PdfPCell`, and so forth

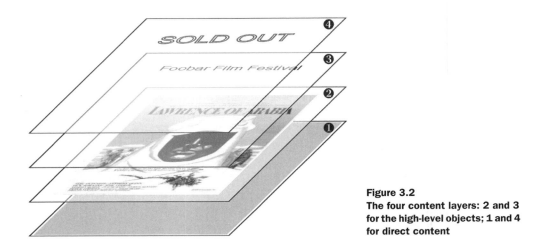

Figure 3.2
The four content layers: 2 and 3
for the high-level objects; 1 and 4
for direct content

You can't access the `PdfContentByte` objects of layers ❷ and ❸ directly—these layers are managed by iText internally. But there are two extra `PdfContentByte` objects: layers ❹ and ❶.

❹ *A layer that goes on top of the text and graphics*—You can get an instance of this upper layer with the method `PdfWriter.getDirectContent()`.

❶ *A layer that goes under the text and graphics*—You can get access to this lower layer with the method `PdfWriter.getDirectContentUnder()`.

In iText terminology, adding content to these extra layers is called *writing to the direct content*, or *low-level access* because you're performing low-level operations on a `PdfContentByte` object, as shown in listing 3.1. You're also going to change the *state*, draw lines and shapes, and add text at absolute positions. But before you can do any of that, you need to know what the PDF reference says about the graphics state.

3.1.2 *Graphics state and text state*

The graphics state stack is defined in ISO-32000-1, section 8.4.2, as follows:

> *A PDF document typically contains many graphical elements that are independent of each other and nested to multiple levels. The graphics state stack allows these elements to make local changes to the graphics state without disturbing the graphics state of the surrounding environment. The stack is a LIFO (last in, first out) data structure in which the contents of the graphics state may be saved and later restored.*

Let's analyze this by means of a simple example.

GRAPHICS STATE

In listing 3.1 you constructed a rectangle to be drawn under the existing content using the `rectangle()` method. This rectangle is a graphical element, and you'll add five of them in the next example. See figure 3.3 and the next listing.

Here you'll change the way the graphical objects are rendered by changing the graphics state. In between, you'll also save or restore the previous state.

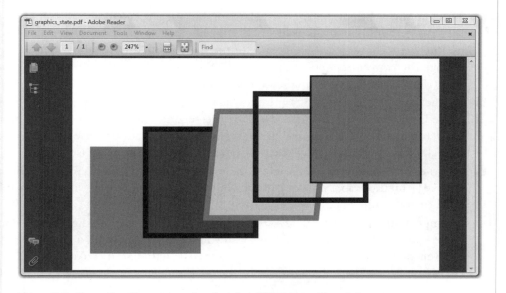

Figure 3.3   Repeating the same rectangle using different graphics states

Listing 3.2   GraphicsStateStack.java

```
canvas.setRGBColorFill(0xFF, 0x45, 0x00);
canvas.rectangle(10, 10, 60, 60);                         ❶  Original state 0
canvas.fill();
canvas.saveState();
canvas.setLineWidth(3);
canvas.setRGBColorFill(0x8B, 0x00, 0x00);
canvas.rectangle(40, 20, 60, 60);                         ❷  New state 1
canvas.fillStroke();
canvas.saveState();
canvas.concatCTM(1, 0, 0.1f, 1, 0, 0);
canvas.setRGBColorStroke(0xFF, 0x45, 0x00);
canvas.setRGBColorFill(0xFF, 0xD7, 0x00);                 ❸  New state 2
canvas.rectangle(70, 30, 60, 60);
canvas.fillStroke();
canvas.restoreState();
canvas.rectangle(100, 40, 60, 60);                        ❹  Restored state 1
canvas.stroke();
canvas.restoreState();
canvas.rectangle(130, 50, 60, 60);                        ❺  Restored state 0
canvas.fillStroke();
```

This is how the code should be interpreted:

❶ The first element is a rectangle measuring 60 by 60 user units—a square with sides of 60 pt. The square doesn't have a border; it's filled with the color orange, because you use the fill() method after changing the fill color to orange (#FF4500).

❷ The second square is colored dark red (#8B0000). It has a border in the default line color—black—because you use the fillStroke() method. Note that the border is 3 pt thick because you change the line width with the setLineWidth() method.

③ This line width is kept for the third element, but the stroke color is changed to orange (#FF4500). The fill color is gold (#FFD700), but the shape is no longer a square. You use the same `rectangle()` method with the same width and height as before, but you change the *current transformation matrix* (CTM) in such a way that the square is skewed. The CTM will be discussed in detail in section 14.3.3.

④ All the changes made to the graphics state to draw the third element are now discarded, and the graphics state used for the second element is restored. You might expect a square that is identical to the second element, but because you use `stroke()` instead of `fillStroke()` only the border is drawn, and the shape isn't filled.

⑤ For the final element, the original graphics state is restored. You use the `fillStroke()` method, so a border is drawn in the default line color, with the default line width: 1 user unit.

It's important that the `saveState()` and `restoreState()` methods are balanced in your code. You can't invoke `restoreState()` if you haven't performed a `saveState()` first; for every `saveState()`, you need a `restoreState()`. If they aren't balanced, an `IllegalPdfSyntaxException` will be thrown by the `PdfContentByte.sanityCheck()` method.

> **NOTE** In this chapter, you're adding content at absolute positions. These absolute positions are defined with (x,y) coordinates with the lower-left corner of the page as the origin of the coordinate system.

The graphics state stack also applies to text.

TEXT STATE

Text state is a subset of graphics state. In section 2.2, you learned that a computer font is a program that knows how to draw glyphs. These glyphs are shapes that are filled with a fill color. No borders are drawn unless you change the text-rendering mode with `setTextRenderingMode()`. You used this text state operator in listing 3.1 to draw the words "SOLD OUT" in white letters with a red border. You also used `setFontAndSize()` to choose a font and a font size, `setTextMatrix()` to change the text matrix, and `showText()` to draw the glyphs. You'll find an overview of all the possible graphics state and text state operators in section 14.4.

In the next section, you'll add three tables to the film database and use the content of those tables to create a real-world example involving direct content.

3.1.3 *A real-world database: three more tables*

Figure 3.4 shows the ERD diagram of a film festival database. You'll recognize one table: film_movietitle. That's the same table you used in chapter 2. It is now connected to three new tables with a "festival_" prefix. These tables contain extra information about a movie in the Foobar Film Festival.

The festival_entry table will help you find the movies that are shown at a certain edition of the film festival. Currently, the database only contains entries for the 2011 edition of the Foobar Film Festival, but you could easily add entries for other years. Every festival entry also refers to a category.

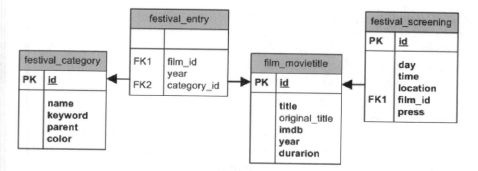

Figure 3.4   Festival database entity relationship diagram

All the categories are described in the festival_category table. Categories have a name, a short keyword, possibly a parent—because there's a hierarchy in the categories—and a color code that will be used when drawing movies on a timetable.

Every movie can have multiple screenings, listed in the festival_screening table. A screening is defined by a day, a time, and a place. Some screenings are reserved for the press only.

CREATING A TIMETABLE

The Foobar Film Festival involves three movie theaters: Cinema Paradiso, Googolplex, and The Majestic. Any resemblance to theaters in movies, or to the favorite multiplex cinema in *The Simpsons,* is purely coincidental.

In the examples that follow, you'll create a timetable that looks like figure 3.5.

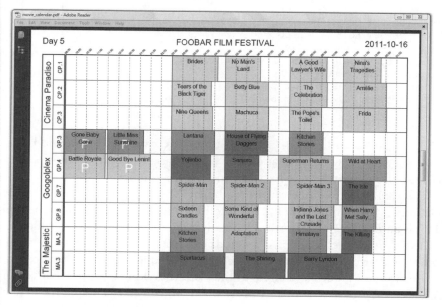

Figure 3.5   Film festival timetable

Observe that three screens are reserved for the festival at Cinema Paradiso: CP.1, CP.2, and CP.3; four screens at the Googolplex: GP.3, GP.4, GP.7, and GP.8; and two at The Majestic: MA.2 and MA.3. During the film festival, different movies will be projected on these screens between 9:30 a.m. and 1:30 a.m. the next day.

You'll start by drawing the grid with the different locations and time slots, using a series of graphics state operators and operands.

DRAWING THE GRID

In listing 3.2, you drew rectangles using the rectangle() method. Now you'll use a sequence of moveTo(), lineTo(), and closePath() operators to construct a path that will be drawn with the stroke() method.

Listing 3.3   MovieTimeTable.java

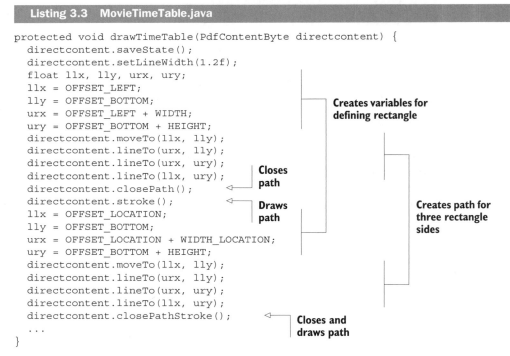

```
protected void drawTimeTable(PdfContentByte directcontent) {
    directcontent.saveState();
    directcontent.setLineWidth(1.2f);
    float llx, lly, urx, ury;
    llx = OFFSET_LEFT;
    lly = OFFSET_BOTTOM;                          Creates variables for
    urx = OFFSET_LEFT + WIDTH;                    defining rectangle
    ury = OFFSET_BOTTOM + HEIGHT;
    directcontent.moveTo(llx, lly);
    directcontent.lineTo(urx, lly);
    directcontent.lineTo(urx, ury);
    directcontent.lineTo(llx, ury);      Closes
    directcontent.closePath();        ← path
    directcontent.stroke();           ← Draws                 Creates path for
    llx = OFFSET_LOCATION;               path                 three rectangle
    lly = OFFSET_BOTTOM;                                      sides
    urx = OFFSET_LOCATION + WIDTH_LOCATION;
    ury = OFFSET_BOTTOM + HEIGHT;
    directcontent.moveTo(llx, lly);
    directcontent.lineTo(urx, lly);
    directcontent.lineTo(urx, ury);
    directcontent.lineTo(llx, ury);
    directcontent.closePathStroke();    ←    Closes and
    ...                                       draws path
}
```

In this case, it would have been simpler to use the rectangle() method, but as soon as you need to draw other shapes, you'll use these methods to draw straight lines. You'll use the different curveTo() methods to draw curves.

Listing 3.3 also shows that you can combine closePath() and stroke() in one close-PathStroke() method. Or, in PDF syntax, the h and the S operators can be replaced by s. This is an example of a shorthand notation inherent to the PDF specification.

iText also offers convenience methods that combine operators to compensate for operations that can't be done with only one PDF operator. For instance, there's no operator to draw an arc or a circle in the PDF syntax. In iText, you can use the methods arc(), ellipse(), and circle(), which will invoke a sequence of curveTo() methods to draw the desired shape.

Next you need to draw the dashed lines for the time slots. The width of each time slot, defined in the constant `WIDTH_TIMESLOT`, corresponds to half an hour.

Listing 3.4   MovieTimeTable.java (continued)

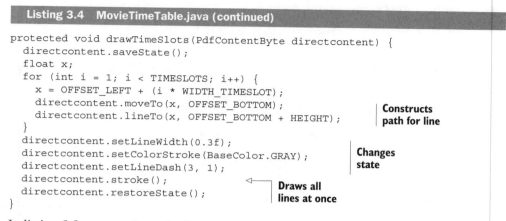

```
protected void drawTimeSlots(PdfContentByte directcontent) {
  directcontent.saveState();
  float x;
  for (int i = 1; i < TIMESLOTS; i++) {
    x = OFFSET_LEFT + (i * WIDTH_TIMESLOT);
    directcontent.moveTo(x, OFFSET_BOTTOM);                        Constructs
    directcontent.lineTo(x, OFFSET_BOTTOM + HEIGHT);               path for line
  }
  directcontent.setLineWidth(0.3f);
  directcontent.setColorStroke(BaseColor.GRAY);                    Changes
  directcontent.setLineDash(3, 1);                                 state
  directcontent.stroke();                           Draws all
  directcontent.restoreState();                     lines at once
}
```

In listing 3.3, you used `stroke()` or `closePathStroke()` after drawing every shape, but that wasn't really necessary. You can postpone changing the state until after you've constructed all the paths. When you call `stroke()` in listing 3.4, the lines are drawn as 0.3 pt thick, gray dashed lines.

You've constructed the grid using the methods `drawTimeTable()` and `draw-TimeSlots()`; now it's time to add screenings to the grid.

DRAWING TIME BLOCKS

Just like you did on many occasions in chapter 2, you can let the `PojoFactory` query the database for you. Besides `Movie`, `Director`, and `Country` objects, the `PojoFactory` can create collections of `Category`, `Entry`, and `Screening` POJOs. Here you'll use a method that returns a `List` of locations (`String` objects) and festival days (`java.sql.Date`).

Listing 3.5   MovieTimeBlocks.java

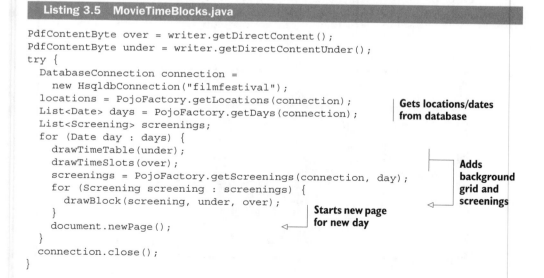

```
PdfContentByte over = writer.getDirectContent();
PdfContentByte under = writer.getDirectContentUnder();
try {
  DatabaseConnection connection =
    new HsqldbConnection("filmfestival");
  locations = PojoFactory.getLocations(connection);        Gets locations/dates
  List<Date> days = PojoFactory.getDays(connection);       from database
  List<Screening> screenings;
  for (Date day : days) {
    drawTimeTable(under);
    drawTimeSlots(over);                                              Adds
    screenings = PojoFactory.getScreenings(connection, day);         background
    for (Screening screening : screenings) {                         grid and
      drawBlock(screening, under, over);                             screenings
    }
    document.newPage();                      Starts new page
  }                                          for new day
  connection.close();
}
```

You reuse the `drawTimeTable()` method from listing 3.3 to draw the table to the lowest direct content layer, and the `drawTimeSlots()` method to draw dashed lines to the upper direct content layer.

The `drawBlock()` method that is called for every screening shouldn't hold too many secrets for you.

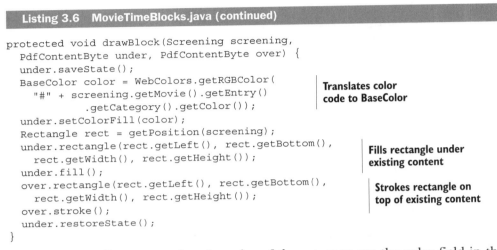

Listing 3.6   MovieTimeBlocks.java (continued)

```java
protected void drawBlock(Screening screening,
    PdfContentByte under, PdfContentByte over) {
  under.saveState();
  BaseColor color = WebColors.getRGBColor(          Translates color
    "#" + screening.getMovie().getEntry()            code to BaseColor
         .getCategory().getColor());
  under.setColorFill(color);
  Rectangle rect = getPosition(screening);
  under.rectangle(rect.getLeft(), rect.getBottom(),  Fills rectangle under
    rect.getWidth(), rect.getHeight());              existing content
  under.fill();
  over.rectangle(rect.getLeft(), rect.getBottom(),   Strokes rectangle on
    rect.getWidth(), rect.getHeight());              top of existing content
  over.stroke();
  under.restoreState();
}
```

The fill color will correspond to the color of the category; see the color field in the festival_category table. The position, a `Rectangle` object, will be calculated based on the location and time stored in the festival_screening table. The "paint" of the rectangle will be added to the lower direct content layer. The border will be drawn in the default state (black, 1 pt thick) to the upper direct content layer. This means that the border will cover some of the dashed lines of the time slots, but the dashed lines will cover the colored rectangle. That way, you'll be able to estimate the run length of each movie, based on the number of time slots intersecting with the rectangle. Figure 3.6 shows the results so far.

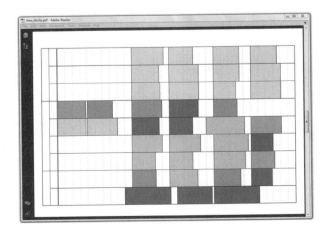

Figure 3.6
Timetable with movie time blocks

This timetable isn't very useful because you haven't yet added any text. You'll do this in the next section, using the convenience methods available to add text to the direct content.

3.2 Adding text at absolute positions

In listing 3.1, you wrote "SOLD OUT" on top of a poster of the movie that is opening the film festival. You used methods such as setTextRenderingMode(), setTextMatrix(), and so on, but it's not easy to create a complete document using these low-level methods. It's easier to use convenience methods that do part of the work for you. They'll demand fewer lines and reduce the complexity of your code.

3.2.1 Convenience method: PdfContentByte.showTextAligned()

There was a lot of math involved when you added the words "SOLD OUT" in listing 3.1. You had to calculate the sine and the cosine of the rotation angle. You had to measure the length of the String "SOLD OUT" to determine the (x,y) coordinates so that the text was more or less centered. This length doesn't depend solely on the characters in the String; you also needed to know which font was used to render it. The words "SOLD OUT" will have a different length in Helvetica than the same String in Times-Roman, even if the same font size is used.

MEASURING A STRING

You can calculate the length of a String if you have an instance of the BaseFont class that will be used to draw the glyphs. In listing 3.7, you'll measure the length of the String "Foobar Film Festival" using the getWidthPoint() method. This will return a width in points. For example, when you use the getWidthPoint() method with the font Helvetica and a font size of 12 pt, the resulting length is 108.684 pt. When you use the font program times.ttf with the same font size, the result is 100.572 pt. That's a difference of 0.11 in.

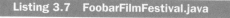

Listing 3.7   FoobarFilmFestival.java

```java
Chunk c;
String foobar = "Foobar Film Festival";

Font helvetica = new Font(FontFamily.HELVETICA, 12);
BaseFont bf_helv
  = helvetica.getCalculatedBaseFont(false);
float width_helv = bf_helv.getWidthPoint(foobar, 12);
c = new Chunk(foobar + ": " + width_helv, helvetica);
document.add(new Paragraph(c));
document.add(new Paragraph(String.format(
  "Chunk width: %f", c.getWidthPoint())));

BaseFont bf_times = BaseFont.createFont(
  "c:/windows/fonts/times.ttf",
  BaseFont.WINANSI, BaseFont.EMBEDDED);
Font times = new Font(bf_times, 12);
float width_times = bf_times.getWidthPoint(foobar, 12);
c = new Chunk(foobar + ": " + width_times, times);
```

Creates BaseFont from Font object

Creates BaseFont object directly

Creates corresponding Font object

```
document.add(new Paragraph(c));
document.add(new Paragraph(String.format(
  "Chunk width: %f", c.getWidthPoint())));
```

Note that the `Chunk` object also has a `getWidthPoint()` method. You could use it to measure the width of a `Chunk` in points. While you're at it, you could also measure the ascent and descent of the `String`.

ASCENT AND DESCENT OF THE STRING

The ascent is the space needed by a glyph above the baseline, and the descent is the space below the baseline. In listing 3.8, you'll calculate the ascent and descent of the font Helvetica using the `getAscentPoint()` and `getDescentPoint()` methods.

> **Listing 3.8**   **FoobarFilmFestival.java (continued)**

```
document.add(new Paragraph("Ascent Helvetica: "
  + bf_helv.getAscentPoint(foobar, 12)));
document.add(new Paragraph("Descent Helvetica: "
  + bf_helv.getDescentPoint(foobar, 12)));
```

You can calculate the height of a `String` by subtracting the descent from the ascent.

> **NOTE**   The font size isn't the height of any specific glyph; it's an indication of the vertical space used by a line of text.

Looking at figure 3.7, you might assume that the font size is about 9 pt, but you would be wrong. The ascent for the `String` in Helvetica is 8.328. You need to add the

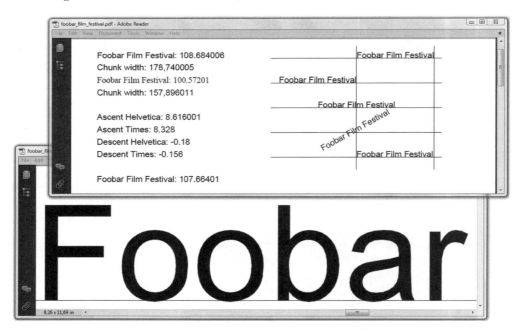

Figure 3.7   **Measuring and positioning text: width, ascent, and descent of a `String`**

descent to the ascent, but the value of the descent is unusually low in this example because it doesn't include glyphs like "g", "j", "p", "q", or "y", which have a descent that exceeds –0.18.

The word "Foobar" is magnified so you can see the descent caused by the rounding of the glyphs "o", "b", and "a". In the same screenshot, you can see that the same String was added a couple of times more, at absolute positions relative to a grid of lines.

POSITIONING A STRING

Now that you know how to measure the length of a String, you can compute the (x,y) coordinates and use them to change the text matrix so that the text is right aligned or centered (listing 3.9). Fortunately, there's an easier way to achieve this. You can use the setTextAligned() method, which will act as a shorthand notation for two types of transformations: a translation and a rotation. You've already seen the result in figure 3.7.

Listing 3.9 FoobarFilmFestival.java (continued)

```
canvas.beginText();
canvas.setFontAndSize(bf_helv, 12);
canvas.showTextAligned(Element.ALIGN_LEFT, foobar, 400, 788, 0);      ❶
canvas.showTextAligned(Element.ALIGN_RIGHT, foobar, 400, 752, 0);     ❷
canvas.showTextAligned(Element.ALIGN_CENTER, foobar, 400, 716, 0);    ❸
canvas.showTextAligned(Element.ALIGN_CENTER, foobar, 400, 680, 30);   ❹
canvas.showTextAlignedKerned(Element.ALIGN_LEFT, foobar, 400, 644, 0);
canvas.endText();
```

❶ The text starts at position x = 400; the baseline y = 788.

❷ The text ends at position x = 400; the baseline y = 752.

❸ The text is centered at position x = 400, y = 716.

❹ The text is centered at position x = 400, y = 680, and rotated 30 degrees.

The showTextAlignedKerned() method in listing 3.9 shows the same String, but it takes into account the kerning of the glyphs that were used.

KERNING

Kerning is the process of adjusting the space between the glyphs in a proportional font. When taking advantage of kerning, you can save some space between a series of specific glyph combinations. For instance, you can move the glyphs of the word "AWAY" closer to each other, due to the shapes of the A and the W. In listing 3.9, the kerned version of the String "Foobar Film Festival" is only slightly shorter than the nonkerned version. Here you compute the width of this String measured in points.

Listing 3.10 FoobarFilmFestival.java (continued)

```
width_helv = bf_helv.getWidthPointKerned(foobar, 12);
c = new Chunk(foobar + ": " + width_helv, helvetica);
document.add(new Paragraph(c));
```

The result indicates that the kerned version measures 107.664 pt; the String without kerning measures 108.684 pt.

ADDING TEXT TO THE TIMETABLE

Returning to the film festival timetable, you can now add the names of the movie theaters and the screens, the time slot information, and the information about the day and date. For instance, you can add the text "Day 5" and "2011-10-16" shown in figure 3.5.

Listing 3.11   MovieTextInfo.java

```
protected void drawDateInfo(Date day, int d,
  PdfContentByte directcontent) {
  directcontent.beginText();
  directcontent.setFontAndSize(bf, 18);
  float x, y;
  x = OFFSET_LOCATION;
  y = OFFSET_BOTTOM + HEIGHT + 24;
  directcontent.showTextAligned(Element.ALIGN_LEFT,
    "Day " + d, x, y, 0);
  x = OFFSET_LEFT + WIDTH;
  directcontent.showTextAligned(Element.ALIGN_RIGHT,
    day.toString(), x, y, 0);
  directcontent.endText();
}
```

Note that the sanityCheck() method mentioned in section 3.1.2 that checks for unbalanced saveState() and restoreState() sequences also looks for possible problems related to text state:

- Unbalanced beginText() and endText() combinations
- Text state operators outside a beginText() and endText() sequence
- Text for which you forgot to set a font and size

The showTextAligned() examples you've worked with so far have been very straightforward, but wouldn't it be nice if you could create a Phrase object, and add that object at an absolute position? That's what you'll do in the next section with the showTextAligned() method of the ColumnText object.

3.2.2   *Convenience method: ColumnText.showTextAligned()*

Next, instead of adding a String after selecting a BaseFont object and a font size, as you did in listing 3.9, you create a Phrase containing text in a certain Font.

Listing 3.12   FoobarFilmFestival.java (continued)

```
Phrase phrase = new Phrase(foobar, times);
ColumnText.showTextAligned(canvas,
  Element.ALIGN_LEFT, phrase, 200, 572, 0);
ColumnText.showTextAligned(canvas,
  Element.ALIGN_RIGHT, phrase, 200, 536, 0);
ColumnText.showTextAligned(canvas,
  Element.ALIGN_CENTER, phrase, 200, 500, 0);
ColumnText.showTextAligned(canvas,
  Element.ALIGN_CENTER, phrase, 200, 464, 30);
ColumnText.showTextAligned(canvas,
  Element.ALIGN_CENTER, phrase, 200, 428, -30);
```

Apart from the fact that you no longer need beginText() and endText() sequences, there seems to be little difference, but you'll need fewer lines of code and less math for more complex Phrases.

POSITIONING A PHRASE

A Phrase can be composed of a series of Chunk objects. By adding a Phrase at an absolute position, you can easily switch fonts, font sizes, and font colors. iText will calculate the offset of every Chunk inside the Phrase, and change the text state accordingly for you.

In the next step, you draw a big "P" with a white font color on top of all the colored rectangles that represent preview screenings that are reserved for the press.

Listing 3.13 MovieTextInfo.java (continued)

```
Font f = new Font(bf, HEIGHT_LOCATION / 2);
f.setColor(BaseColor.white);
press = new Phrase("P", f);
...
protected void drawMovieInfo(Screening screening,
  PdfContentByte directcontent)
  throws DocumentException {
  if (screening.isPress()) {
    Rectangle rect = getPosition(screening);
    ColumnText.showTextAligned(directcontent,
      Element.ALIGN_CENTER, press,
      (rect.getLeft() + rect.getRight()) / 2,
      rect.getBottom() + rect.getHeight() / 4, 0);
  }
}
```

Although you're working with high-level objects here, it's possible to change their text state by setting Chunk attributes that we haven't discussed yet.

CHUNKS: SCALING, SKEWING, RENDERING MODE

On the left side in figure 3.8, you can see the result of listing 3.12: the String "Foobar Film Festival" is added at an absolute position using different alignment options and different angles.

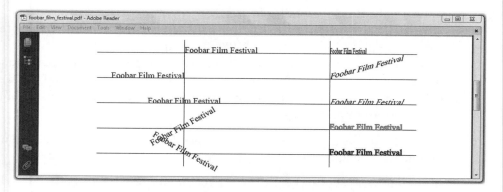

Figure 3.8 Adding text with ColumnText.showTextAligned()

On the right side of figure 3.8, the same `String` is added left aligned, but the text is scaled or skewed, or the rendering mode was changed.

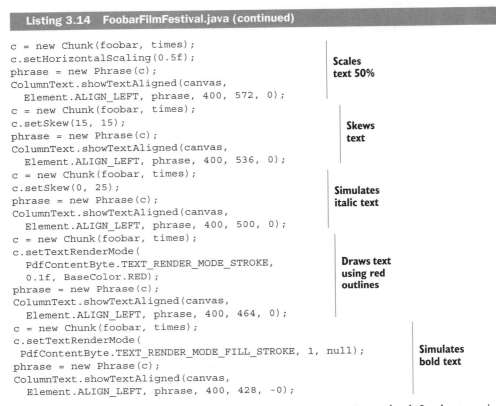

Listing 3.14 FoobarFilmFestival.java (continued)

```
c = new Chunk(foobar, times);
c.setHorizontalScaling(0.5f);                           Scales
phrase = new Phrase(c);                                 text 50%
ColumnText.showTextAligned(canvas,
   Element.ALIGN_LEFT, phrase, 400, 572, 0);
c = new Chunk(foobar, times);
c.setSkew(15, 15);                                      Skews
phrase = new Phrase(c);                                 text
ColumnText.showTextAligned(canvas,
   Element.ALIGN_LEFT, phrase, 400, 536, 0);
c = new Chunk(foobar, times);
c.setSkew(0, 25);                                       Simulates
phrase = new Phrase(c);                                 italic text
ColumnText.showTextAligned(canvas,
   Element.ALIGN_LEFT, phrase, 400, 500, 0);
c = new Chunk(foobar, times);
c.setTextRenderMode(
   PdfContentByte.TEXT_RENDER_MODE_STROKE,              Draws text
   0.1f, BaseColor.RED);                                using red
phrase = new Phrase(c);                                 outlines
ColumnText.showTextAligned(canvas,
   Element.ALIGN_LEFT, phrase, 400, 464, 0);
c = new Chunk(foobar, times);
c.setTextRenderMode(
   PdfContentByte.TEXT_RENDER_MODE_FILL_STROKE, 1, null);   Simulates
phrase = new Phrase(c);                                     bold text
ColumnText.showTextAligned(canvas,
   Element.ALIGN_LEFT, phrase, 400, 428, -0);
```

You can change the width of a `Chunk` with the `setScaling()` method. In the top right of figure 3.8, the words "Foobar Film Festival" are scaled to 50 percent of their width, but the height of the glyphs is preserved. This means that the aspect ratio of the letters is changed. You have to be careful not to exaggerate the scaling. At some point, your text will become almost illegible.

The `setSkew()` method expects two parameters. With the first parameter, you change the angle of the baseline. That's what happened in the second line on the right side of figure 3.8: the angle of the baseline is changed to 15 degrees. The second parameter can be used to define the angle between the characters and the baseline. The third line on the right in figure 3.8 looks as if an italic font were used. In reality, the glyphs were skewed 25 degrees.

> **NOTE** If you have to use a font for which you can't find the corresponding font with italic or oblique style, you can use `setSkew(0, 25)` to simulate italics.

Finally, there's the `setTextRenderMode()` method. These are possible values for the first parameter:

- `PdfContentByte.TEXT_RENDER_MODE_FILL`—This is the default rendering mode; the glyph shapes are filled, not stroked.
- `PdfContentByte.TEXT_RENDER_MODE_STROKE`—This causes the glyphs to be stroked, not filled. This is shown in figure 3.8: the letters are hollow.
- `PdfContentByte.TEXT_RENDER_MODE_FILL_STROKE`—This changes the text state so that the glyphs are filled and stroked. This state was used in figure 3.1 to cover existing content with the words "SOLD OUT" in white letters with red contours.
- `PdfContentByte.TEXT_RENDER_MODE_INVISIBLE`—This will make all the text that is added invisible. The text will be there, but it won't be visible.

Two extra parameters define the line width and the color that will be used to stroke the glyph. If you pass a `null` value for the stroke color, the fill color (defined in the Chunk's Font object) will be used. The final line in figure 3.8 looks as if a bold font were used.

> **TIP** If you have to use a font for which you can't find the corresponding font with bold style, you could use `setTextRenderMode(PdfContentByte .TEXT_ RENDER_MODE_FILL_STROKE, 0.5f, null)` to simulate bold.

These attributes also work if you're adding Chunks with `document.add()`.

The timetable for the film festival is almost finished, as you can see in figure 3.9.

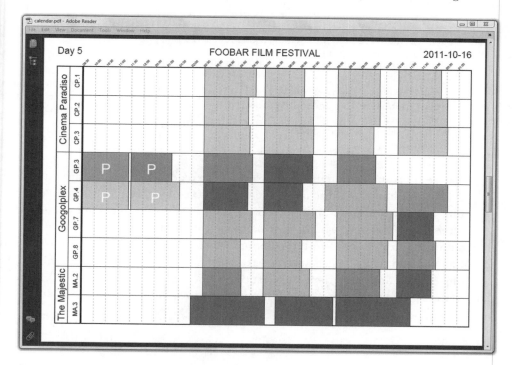

Figure 3.9 Timetable without movie titles

The only bits of information missing in the figure are the movie titles. It would be nice if you could add the text to the rectangles without having to scale the text or downsize the font size if the title is too long to fit the width of the rectangle. This can't be done with the showTextAligned() method, to which you only pass a single set of (x,y) coordinates; you need an instance of the ColumnText object instead.

3.3   *Working with the ColumnText object*

In this section, you'll learn about the different ways to use the ColumnText object: *text mode* if you only use Chunks and Phrases, *composite mode* if you want to use other types of high-level objects as well.

In listing 3.13, you wrote a showMovieInfo() method. If a screening was reserved for the press, you marked the corresponding time block of the movie with a white, uppercase "P". You could try adding the movie title the same way, but the showText-Aligned() method isn't able to wrap text. You also can't use newlines in Strings or Chunks using any version of this method.

Let's extend the previous example and reuse almost all of its methods. The only change involves the drawMovieInfo() method.

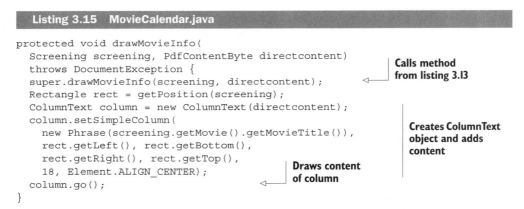

```
Listing 3.15   MovieCalendar.java

protected void drawMovieInfo(
  Screening screening, PdfContentByte directcontent)
  throws DocumentException {
  super.drawMovieInfo(screening, directcontent);         ⟵ Calls method from listing 3.13
  Rectangle rect = getPosition(screening);
  ColumnText column = new ColumnText(directcontent);
  column.setSimpleColumn(                                 ⟵ Creates ColumnText object and adds content
    new Phrase(screening.getMovie().getMovieTitle()),
    rect.getLeft(), rect.getBottom(),
    rect.getRight(), rect.getTop(),
    18, Element.ALIGN_CENTER);                            ⟵ Draws content of column
  column.go();
}
```

The result is shown in figure 3.10. Now you're ready to go to the film festival!

We aren't finished discussing the ColumnText object yet. This example worked out fine because you were able to fit the content inside the rectangles reserved for the screenings. But what would have happened if the text didn't fit? Also, you've been adding a Phrase object to the column to display its contents at an absolute position. Can you add other objects such as Paragraphs, Lists, and Images with the ColumnText object? The answer to the first question will be explained in section 3.3.1; the answer to the second question is "yes," but not in *text mode*, only in *composite mode*.

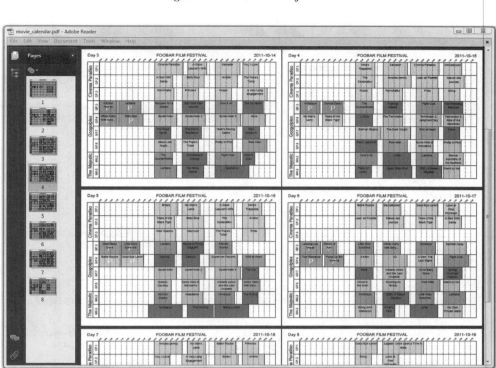

Figure 3.10   The finished timetable, now with the movie titles

3.3.1   *Using ColumnText in text mode*

In section 2.3.3, you created PDF documents with movie information that was organized in `Paragraphs`. Suppose you want to repeat this exercise, but now you want to organize the same information in columns, as is shown in figure 3.11.

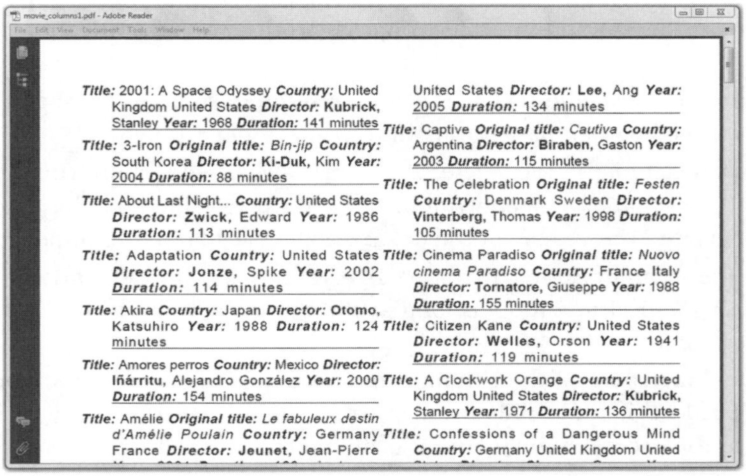

Figure 3.11
Movie information,
organized in columns

Instead of the setSimpleColumn() method from listing 3.15, which can be used for a single Phrase, you'll use addText() to add a series of Phrases and Chunks.

ADDING CONTENT WITH ADDTEXT()

Take a look at the code used to produce the columns shown in figure 3.11.

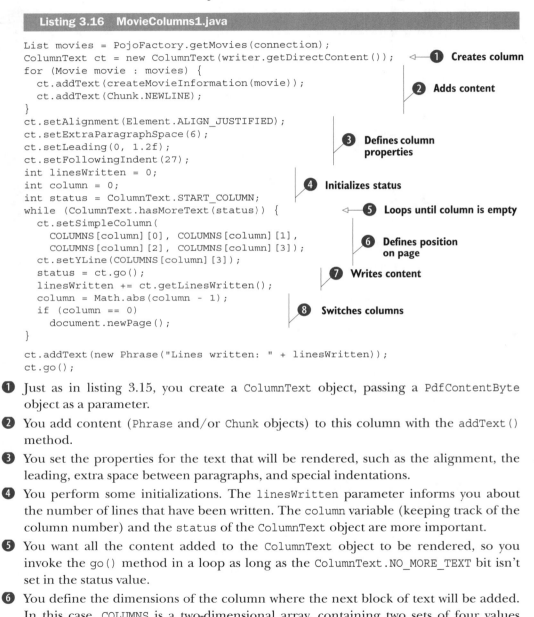

Listing 3.16   MovieColumns1.java

```
List movies = PojoFactory.getMovies(connection);
ColumnText ct = new ColumnText(writer.getDirectContent());      ← 1 Creates column
for (Movie movie : movies) {
  ct.addText(createMovieInformation(movie));                      2 Adds content
  ct.addText(Chunk.NEWLINE);
}
ct.setAlignment(Element.ALIGN_JUSTIFIED);
ct.setExtraParagraphSpace(6);
ct.setLeading(0, 1.2f);                                           3 Defines column
ct.setFollowingIndent(27);                                          properties
int linesWritten = 0;
int column = 0;                                                   4 Initializes status
int status = ColumnText.START_COLUMN;
while (ColumnText.hasMoreText(status)) {                          ← 5 Loops until column is empty
  ct.setSimpleColumn(
    COLUMNS[column][0], COLUMNS[column][1],                       6 Defines position
    COLUMNS[column][2], COLUMNS[column][3]);                        on page
  ct.setYLine(COLUMNS[column][3]);
  status = ct.go();                                               7 Writes content
  linesWritten += ct.getLinesWritten();
  column = Math.abs(column - 1);
  if (column == 0)                                                8 Switches columns
    document.newPage();
}
ct.addText(new Phrase("Lines written: " + linesWritten));
ct.go();
```

1 Just as in listing 3.15, you create a ColumnText object, passing a PdfContentByte object as a parameter.

2 You add content (Phrase and/or Chunk objects) to this column with the addText() method.

3 You set the properties for the text that will be rendered, such as the alignment, the leading, extra space between paragraphs, and special indentations.

4 You perform some initializations. The linesWritten parameter informs you about the number of lines that have been written. The column variable (keeping track of the column number) and the status of the ColumnText object are more important.

5 You want all the content added to the ColumnText object to be rendered, so you invoke the go() method in a loop as long as the ColumnText.NO_MORE_TEXT bit isn't set in the status value.

6 You define the dimensions of the column where the next block of text will be added. In this case, COLUMNS is a two-dimensional array, containing two sets of four values (one rectangle for each column). You also define the Y position; that's the vertical start position of the text in the column.

❼ Lines of text are written as soon as you invoke the `go()` method. Text that didn't fit the current column remains in the `ColumnText` object. The content that was rendered is consumed; it's no longer present in the `ColumnText` object.

❽ Each time a column is written, you have to switch to the next column. If there are no more columns on the current page, you have to go to a `newPage()`.

In this example, you're changing the properties of the text. The `setAlignment()` method is similar to the `Paragraph` method with the same name. It takes the same parameters: `Element.ALIGN_LEFT`, `Element.ALIGN_RIGHT`, `Element.ALIGN_JUSTIFIED`, and `Element.ALIGN_JUSTIFIED_ALL`. The `setLeading()` method comes in two flavors: in listing 3.16, you define an absolute leading of 0 pt and a relative leading of 1.2. The resulting leading will be 0 + 1.2 x 12 pt (the font size) = 14.4 pt. In listing 3.17, you'll use the other `setLeading()` method to define a leading of 14 pt.

Let's examine the properties that can be set for the text that has to be rendered.

COLUMNTEXT PROPERTIES

Although you aren't using `Paragraph` objects here (when in text mode, `Paragraphs` are treated as `Phrase` objects) the `setExtraParagraphSpace()` method gives you a means to help the reader distinguish different paragraphs in a visual way. In listing 3.16, you tell iText to add 6 pt whenever a new portion of text is started on a new line. Another visual aid can be provided with the `setFollowingIndent()` method—this sets the left indentation of the lines that follow the first line. Listing 3.17 shows its counterpart: `setIndent()` can be used to change the indentation of the first line. There's also a `setRightIndent()` method.

In section 2.2.4, you learned how to change the character/space ratio at the `PdfWriter` level for all the basic building blocks at once. With `ColumnText`, it's possible to change the character/space ratio in a more fine-grained way. See the `setSpaceCharRatio()` method in listing 3.17.

ADDING CONTENT IN SMALL PORTIONS

In listing 3.16, you filled a `ColumnText` object with all the movie information that is present in the movie database. Then you rendered all that content until the `ColumnText` object had no more data.

There are 120 movies in the database, so at some point you have a `ColumnText` object that contains 120 `Phrase` objects. Maybe it's better to invoke `go()` more frequently to avoid the memory building up in the `ColumnText` object.

Listing 3.17   MovieColumns2.java

```
List movies = PojoFactory.getMovies(connection);
ColumnText ct = new ColumnText(writer.getDirectContent());
ct.setAlignment(Element.ALIGN_JUSTIFIED);
ct.setExtraParagraphSpace(6);
ct.setLeading(14);
ct.setIndent(10);                                        Sets column
ct.setRightIndent(3);                                    properties
ct.setSpaceCharRatio(PdfWriter.NO_SPACE_CHAR_RATIO);
int column = 0;
```

```
int status = ColumnText.START_COLUMN;
ct.setSimpleColumn(
  COLUMNS[column][0], COLUMNS[column][1],
  COLUMNS[column][2], COLUMNS[column][3]);
for (Movie movie : movies) {
  ct.addText(createMovieInformation(movie));
  status = ct.go();
  if (ColumnText.hasMoreText(status)) {
    column = Math.abs(column - 1);
    if (column == 0)
      document.newPage();
    ct.setSimpleColumn(
      COLUMNS[column][0], COLUMNS[column][1],
      COLUMNS[column][2], COLUMNS[column][3]);
    ct.setYLine(COLUMNS[column][3]);
    status = ct.go();
  }
}
```

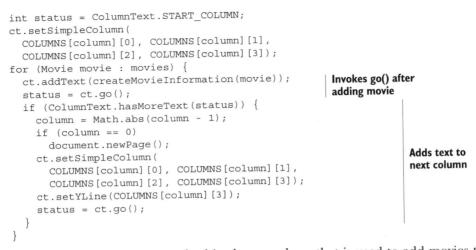

Invokes go() after adding movie

Adds text to next column

You now invoke the `go()` method in the same loop that is used to add movies to the `ColumnText` object. The content is consumed immediately; if it doesn't fit the current column, it's added to the next one.

This brings us to the next question: what if you want to keep all the information about a specific movie together in one column? What if you don't want the information to be split into two parts?

ADDING CONTENT IN SIMULATION MODE

To answer the previous questions, you use a special `go()` method introduced here.

Listing 3.18   MovieColumns3.java

```
List movies = PojoFactory.getMovies(connection);
ColumnText ct = new ColumnText(writer.getDirectContent());
int column = 0;
ct.setSimpleColumn(
  COLUMNS[column][0], COLUMNS[column][1],
  COLUMNS[column][2], COLUMNS[column][3]);
int status = ColumnText.START_COLUMN;
Phrase p;
float y;
for (Movie movie : movies) {
  y = ct.getYLine();
  p = createMovieInformation(movie);
  ct.addText(p);
  status = ct.go(true);
  if (ColumnText.hasMoreText(status)) {
    column = Math.abs(column - 1);
    if (column == 0)
      document.newPage();
    ct.setSimpleColumn(
      COLUMNS[column][0], COLUMNS[column][1],
      COLUMNS[column][2], COLUMNS[column][3]);
    y = COLUMNS[column][3];
```

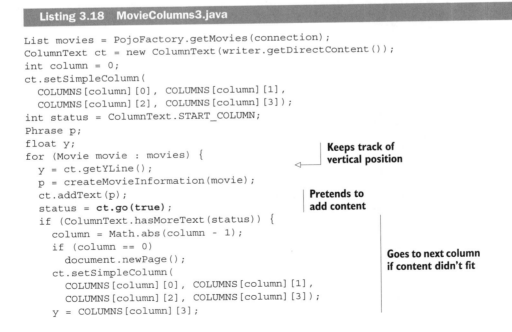

Keeps track of vertical position

Pretends to add content

Goes to next column if content didn't fit

```
    }
    ct.setYLine(y);                         Resets vertical
                                            position
    ct.setText(p);
    status = ct.go(false);                  Adds content
                                            for real
}
```

Listing 3.18 is almost identical to listing 3.17, except that you now invoke the go()
method twice. The first time go() is simulated: nothing is added for real, but the
content is consumed. If all the content of the column is gone, you need to go back to
the initial *Y* position obtained with the getYLine() method, fill the column a second
time, and then perform go() for real. If the content wasn't entirely consumed,
you have to switch to the next column and add the entire portion of movie information there.

> **NOTE** The getYLine() method returns the *Y* position on the page after
> the last line was written, either for real or in simulation mode. You can use
> this method to find out the height that is needed to show the content,
> given a certain column width. If you want to center text vertically inside a
> column, you can add the text in simulation mode first to determine the
> height that is needed; then you can compute the offset like this: *(available
> height – needed height) / 2.* You can use this offset when adding the column
> for real.

It's important to notice that you don't use addText() just before the second go().
Instead you use setText(). The setText() method removes all the unconsumed text
that may still be present in the column; otherwise you'd add portions of the movie
information twice.

> **NOTE** The basic building blocks discussed in chapter 2 can be reused. They
> can be added more than once to the same, or to a different, document. This
> isn't true for the ColumnText object. Each ColumnText object belongs to a spe-
> cific PdfWriter, and it can't be used more than once; the go() method con-
> sumes its content.

This technique is also used in the PDF shown in figure 3.12. There was space available
in the first column of the page to the right, but the content was added to the second
column to keep it together.

This screenshot also demonstrates another feature that is available when in text
mode: irregular columns. As you can see, the columns in figure 3.12 are no longer
rectangular. The border of each column is defined as a polygon, resulting in an irregular shape, so the text flows around the boxes.

IRREGULAR COLUMNS

Setting irregular columns is possible by using a variation on the original example in
listing 3.16.

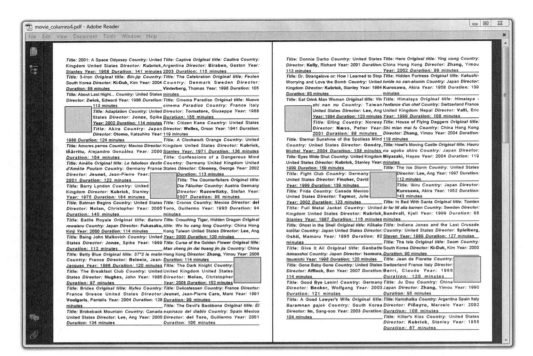

Figure 3.12   Irregular columns

Listing 3.19   MovieColumns4.java

```
PdfContentByte canvas = writer.getDirectContent();
drawRectangles(canvas);                                    ◁─── Draws three
List movies = PojoFactory.getMovies(connection);                rectangles
ColumnText ct = new ColumnText(canvas);
ct.setAlignment(Element.ALIGN_JUSTIFIED);                       Defines right and
ct.setLeading(14);                                              left borders of
int column = 0;                                                 irregular column
ct.setColumns(LEFT[column], RIGHT[column]);                ◁───
int status = ColumnText.START_COLUMN;
Phrase p;
float y;
for (Movie movie : movies) {
  y = ct.getYLine();
  p = createMovieInformation(movie);
  ct.addText(p);
  status = ct.go(true);
  if (ColumnText.hasMoreText(status)) {
    column = Math.abs(column - 1);
    if (column == 0) {
      document.newPage();                       Draws three
      drawRectangles(canvas);          ◁───     rectangles           Defines right and
    }                                                                left borders of
    ct.setColumns(LEFT[column], RIGHT[column]);                 ◁─── irregular column
    y = 806;
```

```
    }
    ct.setYLine(y);
    ct.setText(p);
    status = ct.go();
}
```

The `drawRectangles()` method draws the squares that are shown in figure 3.12. This example is almost identical to the previous one, except that you no longer use the `setSimpleColumn()` method, but `setColumns()`. The parameters `RIGHT` and `LEFT` look like this:

```
public static final float[][] LEFT =
    { { 36,806, 36,670, 108,670, 108,596, 36,596, 36,36 },
      { 299,806, 299,484, 336,484, 336,410, 299,410, 299,36 } };
public static final float[][] RIGHT =
    { { 296,806, 296,484, 259,484, 259,410, 296,410, 296,36 },
      { 559,806, 559,246, 487,246, 487,172, 559,172, 559,36 } };
```

`LEFT` contains the coordinates of the line that is used for the left border of the two columns. `RIGHT` defines the right borders.

Using irregular columns isn't allowed in composite mode.

3.3.2 Using ColumnText in composite mode

So far, you've only used `Phrase` and `Chunk` objects and added them to a `ColumnText` object using the methods `addText()` and `setText()`. In this section, you'll add other building blocks using the `addElement()` method. Invoking the `addElement()` method on the `ColumnText` object automatically switches you from text mode to composite mode.

ADDING CONTENT WITH ADDELEMENT()

Figure 3.13 shows a page in landscape format with four columns defined. `Image`, `Paragraph`, `List`, and `Chunk` objects have been added to it.

Figure 3.13   Columns in composite mode

Listing 3.20 shows how the content was added to the ColumnText object.

Listing 3.20   ColumnsMovies1.java

```java
public void addContent(ColumnText ct, Movie movie, Image img) {
  ct.addElement(img);
  ct.addElement(new Paragraph(movie.getTitle(), FilmFonts.BOLD));
  if (movie.getOriginalTitle() != null) {
    ct.addElement(
      new Paragraph(movie.getOriginalTitle(), FilmFonts.ITALIC));
  }
  ct.addElement(PojoToElementFactory.getDirectorList(movie));
  ct.addElement(PojoToElementFactory.getYearPhrase(movie));
  ct.addElement(PojoToElementFactory.getDurationPhrase(movie));
  ct.addElement(PojoToElementFactory.getCountryList(movie));
  ct.addElement(Chunk.NEWLINE);
}
```

This addContent() method is used in this bit of code ❶ which doesn't differ that much from the listings in the previous section demonstrating text mode.

Listing 3.21   ColumnsMovies1.java (continued)

```java
List movies = PojoFactory.getMovies(connection);
ColumnText ct = new ColumnText(writer.getDirectContent());
int column = 0;
ct.setSimpleColumn(
  COLUMNS[column][0], COLUMNS[column][1],
  COLUMNS[column][2], COLUMNS[column][3]);
int status = ColumnText.START_COLUMN;
float y;
Image img;
for (Movie movie : movies) {
  y = ct.getYLine();
  img = Image.getInstance(String.format(RESOURCE, movie.getImdb()));
  img.scaleToFit(80, 1000);
  addContent(ct, movie, img);                    ◁ ─── ❶ Adds content to ColumnText          ┐ Creates and
  status = ct.go(true);                                                                       │ scales movie
  if (ColumnText.hasMoreText(status)) {                                                       │ poster
    column = (column + 1) % 4;                                                                ┘
    if (column == 0)
      document.newPage();
    ct.setSimpleColumn(
      COLUMNS[column][0], COLUMNS[column][1],
      COLUMNS[column][2], COLUMNS[column][3]);
    y = COLUMNS[column][3];
  }
  ct.setYLine(y);                    ◁ ─┐ ❷ Clears
  ct.setText(null);                     ┘   content!
  addContent(ct, movie, img);                    ◁ ─── ❶ Adds content to ColumnText
  status = ct.go();
}
```

Again, you're using the go() method twice—once in simulation mode, and once for real—to keep the information about a movie together in the same column. Line ❷ is important because it makes sure the content is added only once! Omit this line, and you'll notice that part of the content is added twice.

PROPERTIES OF THE COLUMNTEXT OBJECT VERSUS ELEMENT PROPERTIES

As soon as you start using `addElement()`, all the content that was added in text mode previously and that hasn't been rendered yet will be cleared. `ColumnText` properties, such as the leading and the alignment, will be ignored. Instead, the properties of the `Elements` that were added will be used.

Figure 3.14 shows four columns with `Paragraphs` that are centered, right-aligned, and justified.

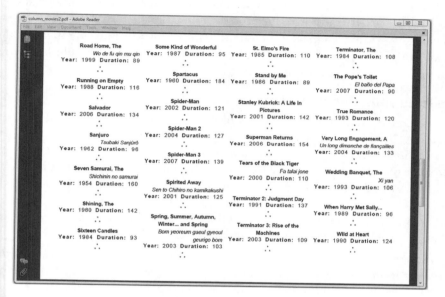

Figure 3.14   Alignment in composite mode

You can reuse listing 3.21 to create the result in figure 3.14 by just changing the `add-Content()` method from listing 3.20 to what is shown next.

Listing 3.22   ColumnsMovies2.java

```
public void addContent(ColumnText ct, Movie movie) {
  Paragraph p;
  p = new Paragraph(new Paragraph(movie.getTitle(), FilmFonts.BOLD));
  p.setAlignment(Element.ALIGN_CENTER);
  p.setSpacingBefore(16);
  ct.addElement(p);
  if (movie.getOriginalTitle() != null) {
    p = new Paragraph(movie.getOriginalTitle(), FilmFonts.ITALIC);
    p.setAlignment(Element.ALIGN_RIGHT);
    ct.addElement(p);
  }
  p = new Paragraph();
  p.add(PojoToElementFactory.getYearPhrase(movie));
  p.add(" ");
  p.add(PojoToElementFactory.getDurationPhrase(movie));
  p.setAlignment(Element.ALIGN_JUSTIFIED_ALL);
  ct.addElement(p);
```

```
    p = new Paragraph(new Chunk(new StarSeparator()));
    p.setSpacingAfter(12);
    ct.addElement(p);
}
```

It's not possible to create irregular columns in composite mode, but you could work around this by adding the content in small portions, changing the column definition after every go().

The difference between text mode and composite mode will also matter in the next chapter when you create PdfPCell objects, but first we'll return to the movie timetable. We won't change the content. The result will look identical to the PDF shown in figures 3.5 and 3.10, but you'll learn how to reduce the file size by reusing data that is added multiple times.

3.4   *Creating reusable content*

In this section, we'll discuss two types of reusable content: Images and PdfTemplate objects.

Do you remember section 2.3.3 about the Image object? In an FAQ, I explained that you can add the same image to a document more than once, but that you should reuse the same Image instance if you want to avoid the image bytes being added more than once. In normal circumstances, the bits and bytes of an image are stored in separate stream objects in the PDF file. Pages that contain such an image refer to this external object. Such an object is also known as an XObject.

> *An external object (XObject) is an object defined (in ISO-32000-1, section 8.2) outside the content stream and referenced as a named resource. The interpretation of an XObject depends on its type. An image XObject defines a rectangular array of color samples to be painted; a form XObject is an entire content stream to be treated as a single graphics object.*

There are other types of XObjects, but image and form XObjects are the most important ones.

3.4.1   *Image XObjects*

You've already worked with image XObjects when you added Images to a Document. In figure 3.2, you saw that iText adds these images under the text objects for which you've used document.add(). But what if you want to add an image on top of the text?

ADDING AN IMAGE TO THE TOP LAYER

Figure 3.15 shows a PDF document that resembles the one shown in figure 3.1. The code to create it is in listing 3.23. The Paragraph "Foobar Film Festival" was added to the Document, but the text is covered by an Image. Note that the text is present in the content stream: if you look closely at figure 3.15, you can see that I was able to select the text. If I copied the content to the clipboard, it would read: "Foobar Film Festival". Adobe Reader also offers to look up the word "Foobar".

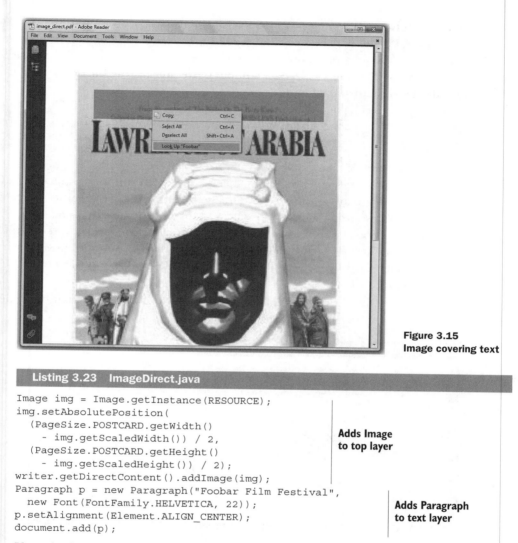

Figure 3.15
Image covering text

Listing 3.23   ImageDirect.java

```java
Image img = Image.getInstance(RESOURCE);
img.setAbsolutePosition(
  (PageSize.POSTCARD.getWidth()
    - img.getScaledWidth()) / 2,
  (PageSize.POSTCARD.getHeight()
    - img.getScaledHeight()) / 2);
writer.getDirectContent().addImage(img);
Paragraph p = new Paragraph("Foobar Film Festival",
  new Font(FontFamily.HELVETICA, 22));
p.setAlignment(Element.ALIGN_CENTER);
document.add(p);
```

Adds Image to top layer

Adds Paragraph to text layer

If you look inside the PDF, you'll see the following PDF syntax:

```
q
BT
30 386 Td
11.87 -33 Td
/F1 22 Tf
(Foobar Film Festival)Tj
-11.87 0 Td
ET
Q
q 232 0 0 362 25.5 27 cm /img0 Do Q
```

The part between the first q/Q sequence is responsible for drawing the words "Foobar Film Festival". The part between the second q/Q changes the current transformation matrix (CTM). Using the Do operator, you add an image of 232 by 362 user space units at position x = 25.5 and y = 27. The content of the image (the bits and bytes) are kept outside the content stream.

Each page has a page dictionary with numerous key-value pairs. The value corresponding to the /Resources key will tell you where to find the resources that are used in the page:

```
/Resources<</XObject<</img0 1 0 R>> ... >>
```

As you can see, there's an entry for XObjects, and it tells you that /img0 can be found in object 1: the stream containing the image bytes. Note that I omitted some of the other types of resources, such as references to the fonts that were used.

In the previous chapter, you learned how to translate, scale, and rotate Image objects, but adding an image to the direct content gives you more power: using the CTM, you can create any two-dimensional transformation you want.

SKEWING IMAGES

If you want to know how I created figure 3.2, you should take a look at the code used to create figure 3.16, shown in listing 3.24.

Figure 3.16   Skewing an image

There's plenty of algebra involved in this skewing transformation. The details will be explained in section 14.3.3.

Listing 3.24   ImageSkew.java

```
Image img = Image.getInstance(RESOURCE);
writer.getDirectContent().addImage(img,
  img.getWidth(), 0,
  0.35f * img.getHeight(), 0.65f * img.getHeight(), 30, 30);
```

The extra parameters passed to the addImage() method in listing 3.24 are reflected in the PDF syntax.

```
q 232 0 126.7 235.3 30 30 cm /img0 Do Q
```

If you want to prevent the creation of an image XObject, you can add the image as an inline object.

INLINE IMAGES

An image is considered *inline* when its bits and bytes are part of the content stream.

Listing 3.25 ImageInline.java

```
Image img = Image.getInstance(RESOURCE);
img.setAbsolutePosition(
  (PageSize.POSTCARD.getWidth() - img.getScaledWidth()) / 2,
  (PageSize.POSTCARD.getHeight() - img.getScaledHeight()) / 2);
writer.getDirectContent().addImage(img, true);
```

Now if you look at the PDF syntax in the content stream of the page, you'll see information about the image between the operators BI—begin image—and EI—end image. To keep this code to a reasonable length, I replaced the bits and bytes of the image with an ellipsis.

```
q 232 0 0 362 25.5 27 cm
BI
/CS /DeviceRGB
/BPC 8
/W 232
/H 362
/F /DCTDecode
ID                          Bits and bytes
...                  <────┘  of image
EI
Q
```

It should be evident that inline image data can't be reused, so this is probably not the best way for you to add images. It's better to use an image XObject.

Another important type of XObject is a *form XObject*. This is an entire content stream that is treated as a single graphics object.

3.4.2 *The PdfTemplate object*

The use of the word *form* may be confusing in this context: we aren't talking about forms that can be filled in. To avoid confusion with AcroForm and XFA forms, the iText object corresponding to a form XObject is called PdfTemplate.

PDFTEMPLATE: ANOTHER NAME FOR FORM XOBJECT

A PdfTemplate is a PDF content stream that is a self-contained description of any sequence of graphics objects. PdfTemplate extends PdfContentByte and inherits all its methods. A PdfTemplate is a kind of extra *template layer* with custom dimensions that can be used for different purposes.

Suppose that you would like to present all the posters of the movies in your film database on one page. As an extra visual element, you'd like to draw different strips of film, so that it looks as if the posters were photographed or filmed. See figure 3.17 for an example.

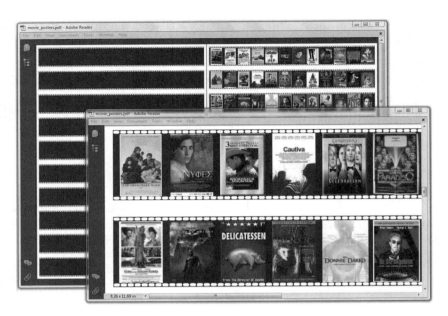

Figure 3.17   Mimicking strips of film using a `PdfTemplate`

There are 120 movie titles in the movie database, so if you put 12 movies on one strip, you'd need a page with 10 strips. You only need to create the strip once.

Listing 3.26   MoviePosters.java

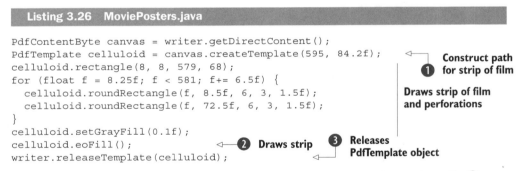

```
PdfContentByte canvas = writer.getDirectContent();
PdfTemplate celluloid = canvas.createTemplate(595, 84.2f);     ◁────  Construct path
celluloid.rectangle(8, 8, 579, 68);                                 ❶  for strip of film
for (float f = 8.25f; f < 581; f+= 6.5f) {
  celluloid.roundRectangle(f, 8.5f, 6, 3, 1.5f);              Draws strip of film
  celluloid.roundRectangle(f, 72.5f, 6, 3, 1.5f);            and perforations
}
celluloid.setGrayFill(0.1f);
celluloid.eoFill();            ◁─❷  Draws strip  ❸  Releases
writer.releaseTemplate(celluloid);        ◁────────     PdfTemplate object
```

You create a `PdfTemplate` for a specific content layer, passing its dimensions. In ❶, you create a layer that will have the same width as the page, and one tenth of the height of the page. You draw one large rectangle and a series of small rounded rectangles representing the perforations. Line ❷ is special. You probably expected `celluloid.fill()`, but that would also fill the perforations using the fill color. By using `eoFill()`, the shape is filled using the *even odd rule*; `fill()` uses the *nonzero winding number rule*. If you're not familiar with these rules, they'll be explained in detail in section 14.2.2.

The most important thing to know is that the XObject stream is stored in a separate object:

```
1 0 obj
<</Length 153/Filter/FlateDecode>>stream
8 8 579 68 re
...
581.75 72.5 m
584.75 72.5 l
585.58 72.5 586.25 73.17 586.25 74 c
586.25 74 l
586.25 74.83 585.58 75.5 584.75 75.5 c
581.75 75.5 l
580.92 75.5 580.25 74.83 580.25 74 c
580.25 74 l
580.25 73.17 580.92 72.5 581.75 72.5 c
0.1 g
f*
endstream
```

Omits l593 lines
of PDF syntax

The complete stream is much longer than the snippet. If you look at the complete file, you'll see that the XObject is the first object in the file, both logically—the object number is 1—and physically—the object starts on the 15th byte. This isn't standard behavior in iText. Normally `PdfTemplate` objects are kept in memory until you invoke `Document.close()`, unless you explicitly use `writer.releaseTemplate()` as is done in line ❸. This is done on purpose—you'll find out the benefits of keeping form XObjects in memory in chapter 5.

ADDING PDFTEMPLATE OBJECTS

Instead of adding this long sequence of PDF syntax 10 times to the content stream of the page, you refer to it like this:

```
q 1 0 0 1 0 0 cm /Xf1 Do Q
q 1 0 0 1 0 84.2 cm /Xf1 Do Q
q 1 0 0 1 0 168.4 cm /Xf1 Do Q
q 1 0 0 1 0 252.6 cm /Xf1 Do Q
q 1 0 0 1 0 336.8 cm /Xf1 Do Q
q 1 0 0 1 0 421 cm /Xf1 Do Q
q 1 0 0 1 0 505.2 cm /Xf1 Do Q
q 1 0 0 1 0 589.4 cm /Xf1 Do Q
q 1 0 0 1 0 673.6 cm /Xf1 Do Q
q 1 0 0 1 0 757.8 cm /Xf1 Do Q
```

This snippet of PDF syntax is easy to interpret: the form XObject /Xf1 is added in its original size at position (0,Y) with Y being a value going from 0 to 757.8 in steps of 84.2 user units.

Here's how you first add the strips of film, followed by the images. The method `addTemplate()` is used to add the `PdfTemplate` object celluloid at a specific x,y position.

Listing 3.27   MoviePosters.java (continued)

```
for (int i = 0; i < 10; i++) {
  canvas.addTemplate(celluloid, 0, i * 84.2f);
}
```

```
List movies = PojoFactory.getMovies(connection);
Image img;
float x = 11.5f;
float y = 769.7f;
for (Movie movie : movies) {
  img = Image.getInstance(String.format(RESOURCE, movie.getImdb()));
  img.scaleToFit(1000, 60);
  img.setAbsolutePosition(x + (45 - img.getScaledWidth()) / 2, y);
  canvas.addImage(img);
  x += 48;
  if (x > 578) {
    x = 11.5f;
    y -= 84.2f;
  }
}
```

Figure 3.18 demonstrates the use of another version of the `addTemplate()` method.

Figure 3.18 Adding the same `PdfTemplate` object using different transformations

In figure 3.18, the strip of film is added four times, but it's translated, scaled, skewed, and rotated.

Listing 3.28   MoviePosters.java (continued)

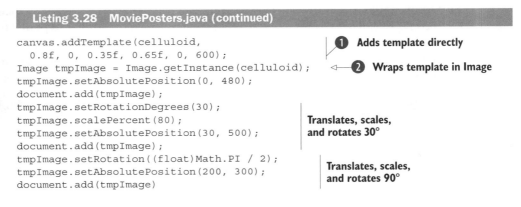

```
canvas.addTemplate(celluloid,
  0.8f, 0, 0.35f, 0.65f, 0, 600);                    ①  Adds template directly
Image tmpImage = Image.getInstance(celluloid);   ←── ②  Wraps template in Image
tmpImage.setAbsolutePosition(0, 480);
document.add(tmpImage);
tmpImage.setRotationDegrees(30);
tmpImage.scalePercent(80);                           Translates, scales,
tmpImage.setAbsolutePosition(30, 500);               and rotates 30°
document.add(tmpImage);
tmpImage.setRotation((float)Math.PI / 2);            Translates, scales,
tmpImage.setAbsolutePosition(200, 300);              and rotates 90°
document.add(tmpImage)
```

The extra parameters of the addTemplate() method ❶ are elements of the current transformation matrix, as discussed briefly in the previous subsection. You can use this method to compose complex transformations.

If you only need to move, scale, or rotate the template, you can improve the readability of your code by wrapping the PdfTemplate in an Image object ❷.

WRAPPING A PDFTEMPLATE INSIDE AN IMAGE

The syntax generated using addTemplate() looks like this:

```
q 0.8 0 0.35 0.65 0 600 cm /Xf1 Do Q
```

You'll recognize the elements from the transformation matrix.

The syntax generated for the templates wrapped in an Image object looks like this:

```
q 1 0 0 1 0 480 cm /Xf1 Do Q
q 0.69282 0.4 -0.4 0.69282 63.68 500 cm /Xf1 Do Q
q 0 0.8 -0.8 0 267.36 300 cm /Xf1 Do Q
```

As you can see, the object is still treated as a form XObject; it's not converted into an image XObject, nor is it rasterized. Wrapping a PdfTemplate inside an Image is an elegant way to avoid having to calculate the transformation matrix yourself.

To conclude this chapter, we'll reduce the file size of the film festival's timetable—as promised.

ADAPTING THE TIMETABLE EXAMPLE

In section 3.1.3, you added a grid with locations and time slots to every page of your timetable document. It would have been a better idea to draw the grid with the locations to one PdfTemplate object, and the grid with the time slots to another.

Listing 3.29 MovieTemplates.java

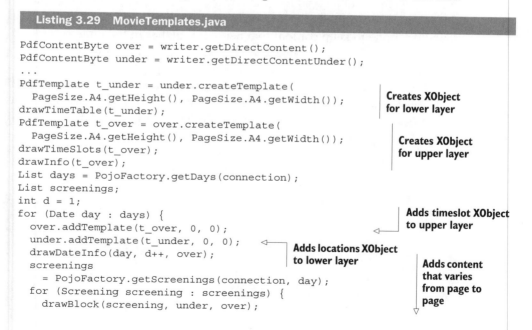

```
PdfContentByte over = writer.getDirectContent();
PdfContentByte under = writer.getDirectContentUnder();
...
PdfTemplate t_under = under.createTemplate(
  PageSize.A4.getHeight(), PageSize.A4.getWidth());
drawTimeTable(t_under);
PdfTemplate t_over = over.createTemplate(
  PageSize.A4.getHeight(), PageSize.A4.getWidth());
drawTimeSlots(t_over);
drawInfo(t_over);
List days = PojoFactory.getDays(connection);
List screenings;
int d = 1;
for (Date day : days) {
  over.addTemplate(t_over, 0, 0);
  under.addTemplate(t_under, 0, 0);
  drawDateInfo(day, d++, over);
  screenings
    = PojoFactory.getScreenings(connection, day);
  for (Screening screening : screenings) {
    drawBlock(screening, under, over);
```

Creates XObject for lower layer

Creates XObject for upper layer

Adds timeslot XObject to upper layer

Adds locations XObject to lower layer

Adds content that varies from page to page

```
        drawMovieInfo(screening, over);
    }
    document.newPage();
}
```

↑ **Adds content that varies from page to page**

The MovieTemplates example (listing 3.29) extends MovieCalendar (listing 3.15) so that methods such as drawTimeTable() and drawTimeSlots() can be reused. If you open both PDFs in Adobe Reader, you'll see no difference at all between them, except when you go to File > Properties > Description. The PDF generated with MovieCalendar has a size of 18.82 KB; the one generated with MovieTemplates has a size of 14.29 KB. This means we've saved almost 25 percent in file size by using form XObjects in this example. Isn't that a nice way to conclude chapter 3?

3.5   *Summary*

In the first section of this chapter, you learned how iText adds content to a page. High-level objects are written to two layers in the middle. You have low-level access to an extra level on top of these layers and an extra level below. Low-level access means that you can change the graphics state to fill and stroke lines and shapes; you change the text state to draw glyphs.

You used this knowledge to make a visual representation of the data in the film festival database. You drew a grid with locations and time slots, on which you added blocks representing movie screenings. Movie titles were added with the ColumnText object. This object forms a bridge between the high-level objects and low-level access. You added content in columns, and you experienced the difference between text mode (Chunk and Phrase objects added with addText()) and composite mode (implementations of the Element interface added with addElement()). You also used ColumnText in simulation mode to keep content that belongs together in the same column.

Finally, the PdfTemplate object was introduced, allowing you to create extra layers that can be reused on the same page or on different pages.

In the next chapter, you'll learn how to organize the information about the film festival movies in tabular form using PdfPTable and PdfPCell. You'll learn that each PdfPCell uses a ColumnText internally to draw the content of a cell at the correct position.

Organizing
content in tables

4

This chapter covers

- Constructing a `PdfPTable` object
- Exploring the properties of a `PdfPCell` object
- Adding tables to the `Document` object

iText has existed for more than ten years now. If you were to ask me which objects have been the most important in the iText-related projects I've done in all those years, I wouldn't have to think twice about the answer. Most of my assignments have consisted of creating reports that render the content of a database to a PDF document. This content had to be organized in tabular form. This can be achieved using two classes that are important enough to be the focus of an entire chapter: `PdfPTable` and `PdfPCell`.

We'll start with simple examples, then move on to more complex tables using the data from the movie database.

4.1   *Constructing tables*

iText's table functionality has evolved from a very low-level class in the early versions of iText to the twin classes `Table` and `PdfTable` in iText 0.30 (2000). These classes were useful, but they had some flaws. It was hard to fine-tune them due to design decisions made by the iText developers; that is, by me. Developers wanted to define how to split the table upon a page break, to control the way borders are drawn, and so on. The `PdfPTable` class, introduced by the codeveloper of iText, Paulo Soares, solved this problem.

The `Table` and `PdfTable` classes were removed in iText 5 (2009). So were `SimpleTable` and `SimpleCell`, two other table classes discussed in the first edition of *iText in Action*. Only `PdfPTable` and `PdfPCell` remain. They will be discussed in this chapter.

4.1.1   *Your first PdfPTable*

Suppose that you need to create a simple table that looks like figure 4.1. The code to generate this kind of table is pretty simple.

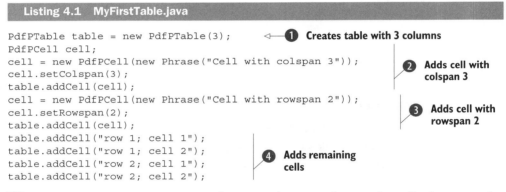

Listing 4.1   MyFirstTable.java

```java
PdfPTable table = new PdfPTable(3);        ⟵—❶ Creates table with 3 columns
PdfPCell cell;
cell = new PdfPCell(new Phrase("Cell with colspan 3"));
cell.setColspan(3);                                    ❷ Adds cell with
table.addCell(cell);                                      colspan 3
cell = new PdfPCell(new Phrase("Cell with rowspan 2"));
cell.setRowspan(2);                                    ❸ Adds cell with
table.addCell(cell);                                      rowspan 2
table.addCell("row 1; cell 1");
table.addCell("row 1; cell 2");
table.addCell("row 2; cell 1");    ❹ Adds remaining
table.addCell("row 2; cell 2");       cells
```

When you create a `PdfPTable`, you always need to pass the number of columns to the constructor. Creating a table with zero columns results in a `RuntimeException`. You can add different objects to a `PdfPTable` object using the `addCell()` method.

AUTOMATIC CREATION OF ROWS

There's a `PdfPRow` object in the `com.itextpdf.text.pdf` package, but you aren't supposed to address it directly. iText uses this class internally to store the cells that belong to the same row.

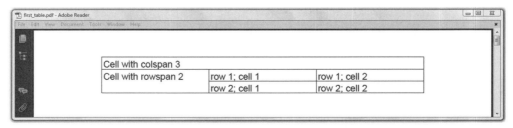

Figure 4.1   Your first `PdfPTable`

In listing 4.1, the table has three columns ❶. After adding the first cell with column span 3 ❷, the first row is full. The next cell is added to a second row that is created automatically by iText. This cell has to span 2 rows ❸, so a third row is created, of which the first cell is reserved. Four more cells are then added ❹; the first pair completes the second row; the second pair completes the third row.

> **NOTE** When you add a PdfPTable to a Document, only complete rows are added. If you have a table with three columns and your final row has only two cells, the row won't be added unless you use the method PdfPTable. completeRow().

You don't have to worry about creating rows; iText creates them for you. Just make sure you're adding the correct number of cells.

4.1.2 PdfPTable properties

We'll talk about cells and cell properties such as text alignment, spacing, and borders in the next section. First, let's take a look at the properties of the table: the width of the table and its columns, the spacing before and after the table, and the alignment of the table.

The default width of a table is 80 percent of the available width. Let's do the math for the table created by listing 4.1. The width of the page is 595 pt minus the margins, which are 36 pt. Eighty percent of this width is $(595 - (2 * 36)) * 0.80$, which amounts to 418.4 pt.

TABLE WIDTH

Each PdfPTable keeps two values for the width:

- widthPercentage—A percentage of the available width
- totalWidth—The absolute width expressed in user space units

When you add a PdfPTable to a Document, iText looks at one of these values, ignoring the other, depending on the value of lockedWidth. If this value is true, the table will have a fixed width, as defined by the totalWidth variable. By default, the value is false, and the exact width of the table will depend on the width available on the page or the width of the ColumnText object to which it's added. The default width of the columns is equal to the width of the table divided by the number of columns.

> **FAQ** *Is it possible to have the column width change dynamically based on the content of the cells?* PDF isn't HTML, and a PdfPTable is completely different from an HTML table rendered in a browser; iText can't calculate column widths based on the content of the columns. The result would depend on too many design decisions and wouldn't always correspond to what a developer expects. It's better to have the developer define the widths.

You could say that each column has a relative width equal to 1. You can change this by defining new relative widths, or by setting absolute widths for the columns.

RELATIVE COLUMN WIDTHS

Figure 4.2 shows five tables that look identical, but the widths of the table and columns were changed in five different ways.

In the first three tables you define the column widths using relative values: new int[] {2, 1, 1} or new float{2, 1, 1}. This means that you want to divide the width of the table into four parts (2 + 1 + 1): two parts for the first column, one part for columns two and three.

Listing 4.2   ColumnWidths.java

```java
public static PdfPTable createTable1() throws DocumentException {
  PdfPTable table = new PdfPTable(3);
  table.setWidthPercentage(288 / 5.23f);          // Changes width percentage
  table.setWidths(new int[]{2, 1, 1});            // Defines relative column widths
  ...
  return table;
}

public static PdfPTable createTable2() throws DocumentException {
  PdfPTable table = new PdfPTable(3);
  table.setTotalWidth(288);
  table.setLockedWidth(true);                     // Changes total width
  table.setWidths(new float[]{2, 1, 1});          // Defines relative column widths
  ...
  return table;
}

public static PdfPTable createTable3() throws DocumentException {
  PdfPTable table =
    new PdfPTable(new float[]{ 2, 1, 1 });        // Defines relative column widths in constructor
  table.setWidthPercentage(55.067f);
  ...
  return table;
}
```

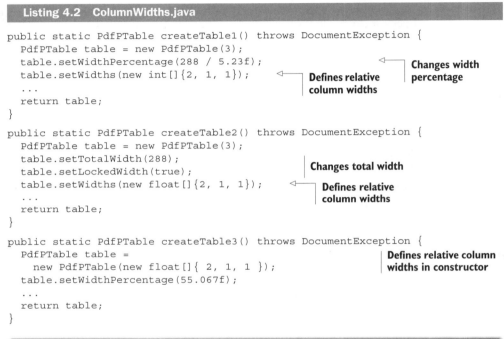

Figure 4.2   Changing the widths of tables and columns

Suppose you want a table with a width of 288 pt instead of 523 pt. You could compute the width percentage like this: (288 / 523) * 100 = 55.067. Or you could use the methods setTotalWidth() and setLockedWidth() instead of setWidthPercentage(), which is easier, because you can avoid the math. Listing 4.2 also demonstrates the use of an alternative constructor: instead of creating a PdfPTable with an int defining the number of columns, you pass the widths array as a parameter for the constructor.

ABSOLUTE COLUMN WIDTHS

The last two tables in figure 4.2 are created by code which defines absolute widths for the columns instead of for the whole table. This can be done in two different ways, both shown in this listing.

Listing 4.3 ColumnWidths.java (continued)

```
public static PdfPTable createTable4() throws DocumentException {
  PdfPTable table = new PdfPTable(3);
  Rectangle rect = new Rectangle(523, 770);
  table.setWidthPercentage(                         Computes width
    new float[]{ 144, 72, 72 }, rect);              percentage
  ...
  return table;
}

public static PdfPTable createTable5() throws DocumentException {
  PdfPTable table = new PdfPTable(3);
  table.setTotalWidth(new float[]{ 144, 72, 72 });     Sets locked
  table.setLockedWidth(true);                          width
  ...
  return table;
}
```

The first method—computing the width percentages—isn't ideal. It will only work if you know the available width in advance. In listing 4.3, you pass a Rectangle object that represents the page size minus the margins.

It's better to use setTotalWidth() with an array of float values as the parameter, then set the locked width to true.

SPACING BEFORE AND AFTER A PDFPTABLE

The five tables from listings 4.2 and 4.3 are added to the Document using this code.

Listing 4.4 ColumnWidths.java (continued)

```
PdfPTable table = createTable1();
document.add(table);
table = createTable2();
table.setSpacingBefore(5);                Extra space before
table.setSpacingAfter(5);                 and after table 2
document.add(table);
table = createTable3();
document.add(table);
table = createTable4();
table.setSpacingBefore(5);                Extra space before
table.setSpacingAfter(5);                 and after table 4
```

```
document.add(table);
table = createTable5();
document.add(table);
```

If you don't provide any extra spacing, it's hard to distinguish the different tables. This can be an advantage! You can create a structure that looks as if it's one big table by adding a series of smaller, separate tables that are glued to each other.

TABLE ALIGNMENT

In figure 4.3, three tables were added after each other without extra spacing, but the alignment of the tables was changed in between.

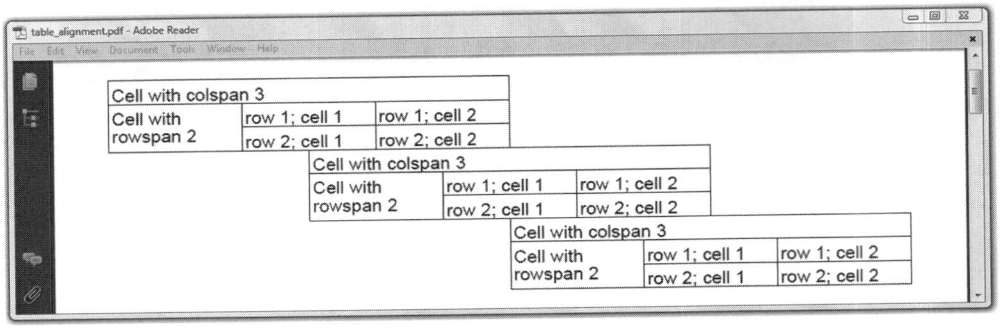

Figure 4.3   Three tables with different alignments

The tables in figures 4.1 and 4.2 were centered; that's the default alignment. You can change the alignment with the setHorizontalAlignment() method.

Listing 4.5   TableAlignment.java

```
PdfPTable table = createFirstTable();
table.setWidthPercentage(50);
table.setHorizontalAlignment(Element.ALIGN_LEFT);
document.add(table);
table.setHorizontalAlignment(Element.ALIGN_CENTER);
document.add(table);
table.setHorizontalAlignment(Element.ALIGN_RIGHT);
document.add(table);
```

You've now played around with your first table; it's time to pick up the thread started in the previous examples and return to the movie database.

4.2   *Changing the properties of a cell*

PdfPCell extends Rectangle, inheriting a plethora of methods to change the way borders are drawn and backgrounds are painted. We'll discuss these methods later on. First, we'll focus on the content of a PdfPCell.

Internally, PdfPCell content is kept inside a ColumnText object. The mechanics of a PdfPCell are easy to understand if you know how the ColumnText object works. If you skipped chapter 3 because you were eager to know more about tables, please return to section 3.3 before reading about adding cells in text or composite mode.

4.2.1 PdfPCell in text mode

In this subsection, you're going to create tables with content that can be expressed as `Chunk` or `Phrase` objects. An example of such a table is shown in figure 4.4.

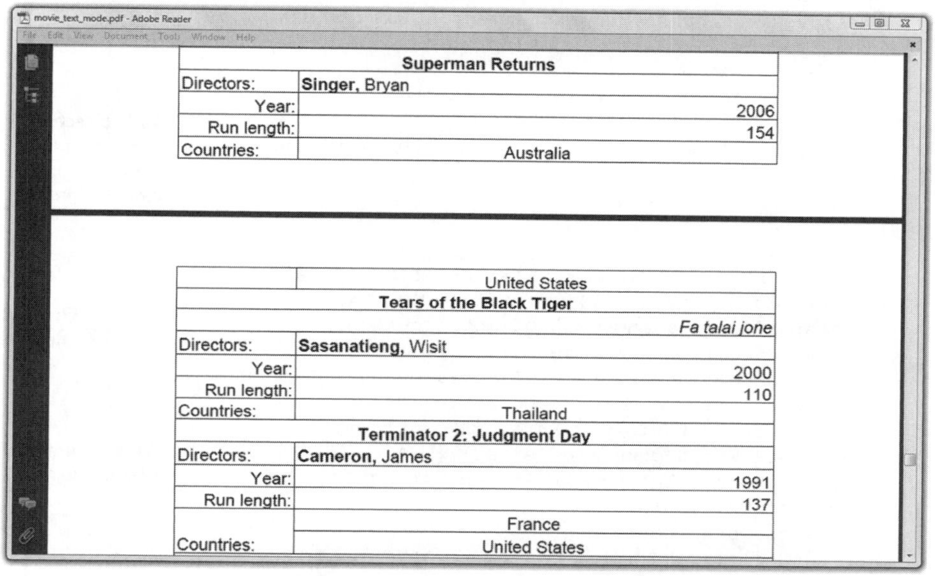

Figure 4.4   Cells in text mode

You won't use any `Paragraph`, `List`, or `Image` objects here. You'll work in text mode, and therefore define the alignment and leading of the text using methods of the `Pdf-PCell` class.

COLSPAN, ROWSPAN, AND THE ALIGNMENT OF A CELL

You can experiment with colspan, rowspan, and different alignment methods.

Listing 4.6   MovieTextMode.java

```
List movies = PojoFactory.getMovies(connection);
for (Movie movie : movies) {
  PdfPTable table = new PdfPTable(2);
  table.setWidths(new int[]{1, 4});
  PdfPCell cell;
  cell = new PdfPCell(
    new Phrase(movie.getTitle(), FilmFonts.BOLD));
  cell.setHorizontalAlignment(Element.ALIGN_CENTER);
  cell.setColspan(2);
  table.addCell(cell);
  if (movie.getOriginalTitle() != null) {
```

Adds content with different alignments

```
    cell = new PdfPCell(PojoToElementFactory
      .getOriginalTitlePhrase(movie));
    cell.setColspan(2);
    cell.setHorizontalAlignment(Element.ALIGN_RIGHT);
    table.addCell(cell);
  }
  List directors = movie.getDirectors();
  cell = new PdfPCell(new Phrase("Directors:"));
  cell.setRowspan(directors.size());
  cell.setVerticalAlignment(Element.ALIGN_MIDDLE);
  table.addCell(cell);
  int count = 0;
  for (Director pojo : directors) {
    cell = new PdfPCell(
      PojoToElementFactory.getDirectorPhrase(pojo));
    cell.setIndent(10 * count++);
    table.addCell(cell);
  }
  table.getDefaultCell()
    .setHorizontalAlignment(Element.ALIGN_RIGHT);
  table.addCell("Year:");
  table.addCell(String.valueOf(movie.getYear()));
  table.addCell("Run length:");
  table.addCell(String.valueOf(movie.getDuration()));
  List countries = movie.getCountries();
  cell = new PdfPCell(new Phrase("Countries:"));
  cell.setRowspan(countries.size());
  cell.setVerticalAlignment(Element.ALIGN_BOTTOM);
  table.addCell(cell);
  table.getDefaultCell()
    .setHorizontalAlignment(Element.ALIGN_CENTER);
  for (Country country : countries) {
    table.addCell(country.getCountry());
  }
  document.add(table);
}
```

Adds content with different alignments

Adds director name with variable indentation

Changes the default cell

Adds "Countries:" bottom-aligned

Adds horizontally centered countries

In listing 4.6, cells are added to the table in two ways.

- *With a* PdfPCell *object*—You create a PdfPCell using a Phrase as a parameter, and add it to the table with the addCell() method. Before adding the cell, you use methods such as setHorizontalAlignment(), setVerticalAlignment(), and so on, to change the properties of the PdfPCell.

- *Without a* PdfPCell *object*—You add a String or a Phrase object straight to the table with addCell(), using the properties of the *default cell*. The default cell is a special PdfPCell instance owned by the PdfPTable object. It can be accessed with the getDefaultCell() method.

The possible values for the setHorizontalAlignment() method are the same ones you used to set the alignment of the ColumnText object in the previous chapter. The possible values for setVerticalAlignment() are Element.ALIGN_TOP, Element. ALIGN_MIDDLE, and Element.ALIGN_BOTTOM.

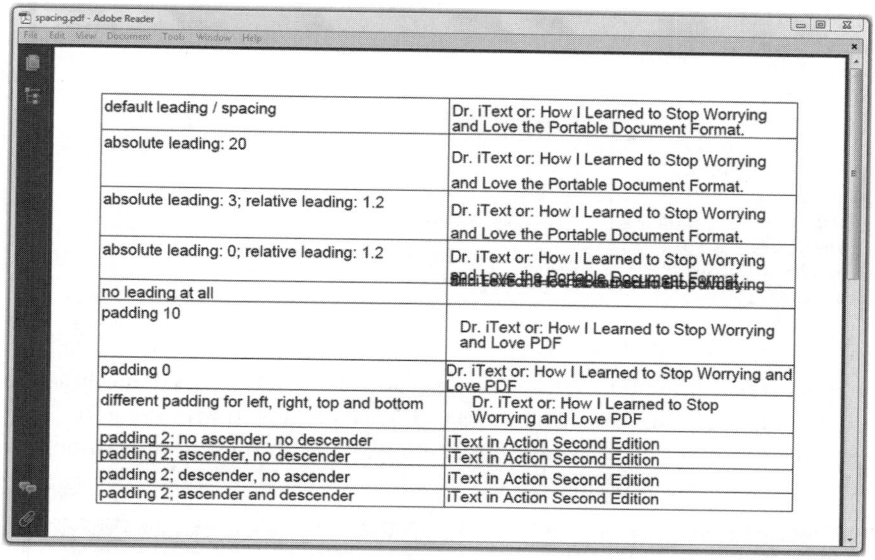

Figure 4.5   Different spacing in cells

Just as with `ColumnText`, you can use the `setIndent()` method to define an indentation for the first line of a paragraph in the cell, `setFollowingIndent()` to specify the indentation of the first line of the paragraphs following the first paragraph, and `setRightIndent()` to change the indentation to the right. Finally, there's also a `setSpaceCharRatio()` to change the ratio of the word spacing if you set the alignment to `Element.ALIGN_JUSTIFIED`.

In the next example, you'll experiment with the leading and the padding of a cell.

SPACING IN CELLS

The cells in the right column of the table shown in figure 4.5 have different leading or padding. Observe that the default leading of the content of a cell in text mode is equal to the font size. Internally, the leading is set like this:

```
setLeading(0, 1);
```

This is different from the default leading of a `Phrase` object outside a `PdfPCell`.

You can change the leading with the same `setLeading()` methods you've used for `ColumnText`; listing 4.7 is the code that produced the first five rows in figure 4.5. Note that setting the leading to 0 isn't advised! The text will be added outside the cell, and if the content is split into multiple lines, they will overlap, resulting in illegible gibberish.

Listing 4.7   Spacing.java

```
PdfPCell cell = new PdfPCell(p);
table.addCell("default leading / spacing");       Row I in figure 4.5
table.addCell(cell);
```

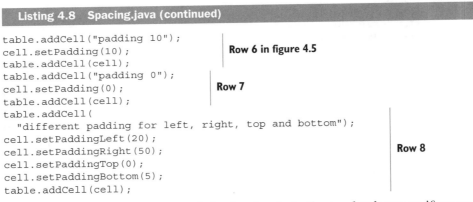

```
table.addCell("absolute leading: 20");
cell.setLeading(20f, 0f);                          Row 2
table.addCell(cell);
table.addCell(
  "absolute leading: 3; relative leading: 1.2");   Row 3
cell.setLeading(3f, 1.2f);
table.addCell(cell);
table.addCell(
  "absolute leading: 0; relative leading: 1.2");   Row 4
cell.setLeading(0f, 1.2f);
table.addCell(cell);
table.addCell("no leading at all");
cell.setLeading(0f, 0f);                            Row 5
table.addCell(cell);
```

The default padding of a PdfPCell is 2 pt, and the setPadding() method can be used to change the default. Rows 6-8 in figure 4.5 are produced with the code in the following listing. Observe that you can differentiate: you can set different values for the top, bottom, left, and right padding.

Listing 4.8   Spacing.java (continued)

```
table.addCell("padding 10");
cell.setPadding(10);                       Row 6 in figure 4.5
table.addCell(cell);
table.addCell("padding 0");
cell.setPadding(0);                        Row 7
table.addCell(cell);
table.addCell(
  "different padding for left, right, top and bottom");
cell.setPaddingLeft(20);
cell.setPaddingRight(50);                   Row 8
cell.setPaddingTop(0);
cell.setPaddingBottom(5);
table.addCell(cell);
```

Note that setPadding() creates a behavior that is similar to what happens if you use the cellpadding attribute of a <table> tag in an HTML table. There is no equivalent of the cellspacing attribute, but in chapter 5 you'll mimic that behavior using cell events.

You can adjust the padding depending on the ascender of the first line in the cell. The bottom padding can be adapted to the descender of the last line. By tweaking the boolean values of the setUseAscender() and setUseDescender() methods, you can create rows 9 to 12 in figure 4.5. This listing refers only to row 12.

Listing 4.9   Spacing.java (continued)

```
table.getDefaultCell().setUseAscender(true);
table.getDefaultCell().setUseDescender(true);
table.addCell("padding 2; ascender and descender");   Row 12
cell.setPadding(2);
```

Remember that you have measured text in the previous chapter: the ascender was the space needed above the baseline; the descender was the space needed below the baseline.

Changing the leading and padding and using the ascender and descender have an impact on the height of a cell and, by extension, on the height of a row.

ROW HEIGHT

The height of a row is a value that needs to be computed, but iText doesn't always have sufficient data to do the math.

Listing 4.10   TableHeight.java

```
PdfPTable table = createFirstTable();
document.add(new Paragraph(String.format(
  "Table height before document.add(): %f",
  table.getTotalHeight())));              ◁── Returns 0
document.add(new Paragraph(
  String.format("Height of the first row: %f",
    table.getRowHeight(0))));             ◁── Returns 0
document.add(table);
document.add(new Paragraph(
  String.format("Table height after document.add(): %f",
  table.getTotalHeight())));              ◁── Returns 48
document.add(new Paragraph(
  String.format("Height of the first row: %f",
    table.getRowHeight(0))));             ◁── Returns 16
 table = createFirstTable();
document.add(new Paragraph(String.format(
  "Table height before setTotalWidth(): %f",
  table.getTotalHeight())));              ◁── Returns 0
document.add(new Paragraph(
  String.format("Height of the first row: %f",
    table.getRowHeight(0))));             ◁── Returns 0
table.setTotalWidth(50);
table.setLockedWidth(true);
document.add(new Paragraph(String.format(
  "Table height after setTotalWidth(): %f",
  table.getTotalHeight())));              ◁── Returns 192
document.add(new Paragraph(
  String.format("Height of the first row: %f",
    table.getRowHeight(0))));             ◁── Returns 40
document.add(table);
```

In this example, the height of the table is 0 pt *before* and 48 pt *after* you add it to the Document. That's normal: the height of a table can't be computed before iText knows its width. The same table with a fixed width of 50 pt has a height of 192 pt. Due to this fixed width, which is much smaller than 80 percent of the available page width, the content in the cells has to be wrapped. This results in a larger table and cell height.

You could tell iText not to wrap the content with the setNoWrap(true) method, but I wouldn't advise this. Unwrapped text risks exceeding the borders of the table and overlapping with the content of the next cell, or even, as shown in figure 4.6, going outside the page boundaries.

If you don't like the calculated height, you can use setFixedHeight() to define the height yourself. Rows 3–6 in figure 4.6 are created with listing 4.11. Paragraph p

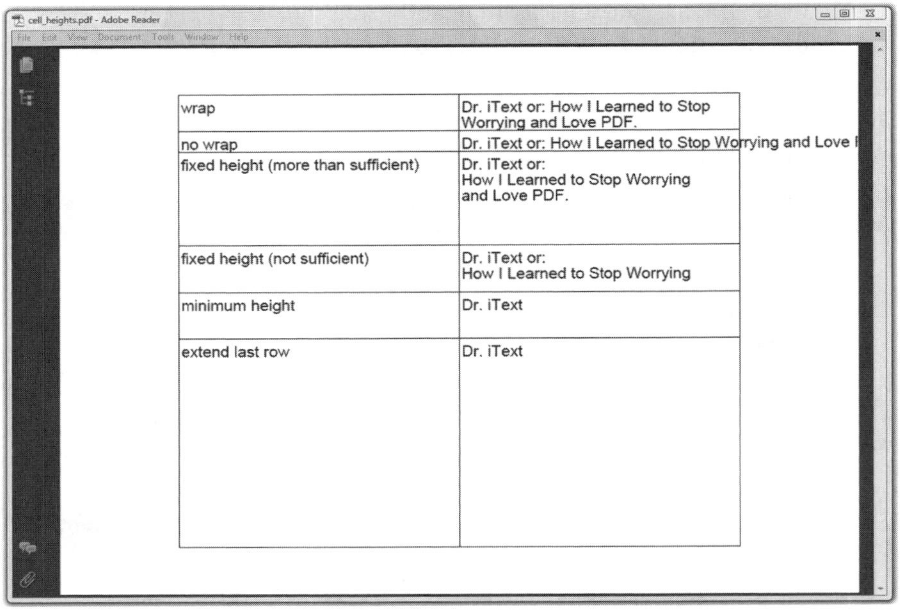

Figure 4.6   Different row height methods for cells and tables

contains the `String` "Dr. iText or: How I Learned to Stop Worrying and Love PDF." It is added to the table twice: once to a cell with a fixed height of 72 pt, and once to a cell with a fixed height of 36 pt.

A height of 36 pt isn't enough, and the words "and Love PDF" aren't shown. To put it in the terminology we used in chapter 3, the `go()` method of the internal `Column-Text` method was invoked, and the content didn't fit the rectangle. That content is never added to the table! Use this method only if you know for sure the content will fit the cell, or if it's OK for your application to reduce the lines that are printed.

To assure a certain cell height, without losing any content, you can use the `setMin-imumHeight()` method. If the text fits the rectangle, the height will be equal to the desired height; if the text doesn't fit, it will be larger.

Listing 4.11   CellHeights.java

```
cell = new PdfPCell(p);
table.addCell("fixed height (more than sufficient)");
cell.setFixedHeight(72f);
table.addCell(cell);
table.addCell("fixed height (not sufficient)");
cell.setFixedHeight(36f);
table.addCell(cell);
table.addCell("minimum height");
cell = new PdfPCell(new Phrase("Dr. iText"));
cell.setMinimumHeight(36f);
```

```
table.addCell(cell);
table.setExtendLastRow(true);
table.addCell("extend last row");
table.addCell(cell);
document.add(table);
```

Note that the height of the final row is extended to the bottom margin of the page in figure 4.6. This isn't a cell property; it's something that has to be defined at the table level with the setExtendLastRow() method.

> **NOTE** The setExtendLastRow() method exists in two versions. In listing 4.11, you use one Boolean to tell iText whether the row should be extended (true) or not (false). With a second Boolean, you can indicate whether the final row of the table has to be extended if the table is split and distributed over different pages.

So far, you've been working in text mode, but except for the leading, the horizontal alignment, and the indentation, the cell properties we've discussed are also valid in composite mode: cell height, padding, and so on. The same goes for the properties that are inherited from the Rectangle class.

ROTATION, BACKGROUND COLOR, BORDERS, AND BORDER COLORS

You can rotate the content of a cell with the setRotation() method. Just like with images, the rotation is defined counterclockwise. The answer to the questions, "What is horizontal?" and "What is vertical?" is affected by the rotation angle. This matters when setting the alignment. The word "GRAY" in the second row of figure 4.7 is centered horizontally, but not using the setHorizontalAlignment() method. Instead, it's done by using setVerticalAlignment() with the parameter Element.ALIGN_MIDDLE.

The first thing that jumps to the eye when looking at figure 4.7 is the fact that it's more colorful than the previous table examples. The background color of the cells in the first row is changed with the setBackground() method. The setGrayFill() method changed the backgrounds of the cells in the second row. Note that the borders are different because the setBorder() method was used. Take a look at the next bit of code, which created some of the cells in figure 4.7, to discover more new Rectangle methods that can be used to change the properties of a cell.

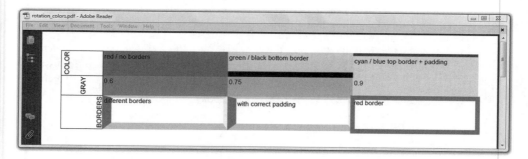

Figure 4.7 Cells and rotation, background color, borders, and border colors

Listing 4.12   RotationAndColors.java

```
PdfPCell cell;
...
cell = new PdfPCell(new Phrase("red / no borders"));
cell.setBorder(Rectangle.NO_BORDER);
cell.setBackgroundColor(BaseColor.RED);
table.addCell(cell);
...
cell = new PdfPCell(new Phrase(
  "cyan / blue top border + padding"));
cell.setBorder(Rectangle.TOP);
cell.setUseBorderPadding(true);
cell.setBorderWidthTop(5f);
cell.setBorderColorTop(BaseColor.BLUE);
cell.setBackgroundColor(BaseColor.CYAN);
table.addCell(cell);
...
cell = new PdfPCell(new Phrase("0.6"));
cell.setBorder(Rectangle.NO_BORDER);
cell.setGrayFill(0.6f);
table.addCell(cell);
```

Sets red
background,
no borders

❶ Adapts padding

Sets cyan
background, blue
5 pt top border

Sets gray
background,
no borders

Rectangle.NO_BORDER (which removes the border) is one possible value that can be used for the setBorder() method. To define a top, bottom, left, and right borders, you need Rectangle.TOP, Rectangle.BOTTOM, Rectangle.LEFT, and Rectangle.RIGHT. You'll probably remember from chapter 2, when we discussed the borders of the Image objects, that Rectangle.BOX is shorthand for the combination of the four borders. Rectangle.BOX is the default value for cell borders.

In listing 4.12, you use setUseBorderPadding(true) ❶. This adapts the padding to take the border width into account. Otherwise the border could overlap the content of the cell. This problem is demonstrated in the second cell of row 3 in figure 4.7.

The border width can be set with the setBorderWidth() method, but there are variations for every side of the border. The same goes for the setBorderColor() method. This is demonstrated in the next listing, which is responsible for drawing two more cells in figure 4.7.

Listing 4.13   RotationAndColors.java (continued)

```
cell = new PdfPCell(new Phrase("different borders"));
cell.setBorderWidthLeft(16f);
cell.setBorderWidthBottom(12f);
cell.setBorderWidthRight(8f);
cell.setBorderWidthTop(4f);
cell.setBorderColorLeft(BaseColor.RED);
cell.setBorderColorBottom(BaseColor.ORANGE);
cell.setBorderColorRight(BaseColor.YELLOW);
cell.setBorderColorTop(BaseColor.GREEN);
table.addCell(cell);
...
cell = new PdfPCell(new Phrase("red border"));
cell.setBorderWidth(8f);
cell.setBorderColor(BaseColor.RED);
```

❶ Variable borders

❷ Uniform borders

There's a subtle difference between the row with the variable borders ❶ (cell 2 in row 3 of figure 4.7) and the row with the uniform borders ❷. Whenever you use a method that changes a property of a single border, the `setUseVariableBorders(true)` method is invoked. This will cause the borders to be drawn within the cell boundaries and the different parts to be miter joined. You can also invoke this method youself on a cell with uniform borders. Because you didn't use this method in ❷, the final cell looks slightly bigger than the others: the thickness of the border is distributed equally inside and outside the cell dimensions.

And now it's time to switch to composite mode.

4.2.2 *PdfPCell in composite mode*

Text mode is meant for `Chunk` and `Phrase` objects. As soon as you need `Paragraphs`, `Lists`, or `Images`, you have to work in composite mode. There's a huge difference between

```
PdfPCell cell = new PdfPCell(new Paragraph("some text"));
```

and

```
PdfPCell cell = new PdfPCell();
cell.addElement(new Paragraph("some text"));
```

In the first code line, the `Paragraph` is treated in text mode: `Paragraph`-specific properties, such as the leading and the alignment, are ignored. Instead, the corresponding properties of the `PdfPCell` are used.

In the last two lines, you switch to composite mode by using `addElement()`. All the content that was previously inside the cell in text mode is discarded. Now the leading, alignment, and indentation set for the cell are ignored in favor of the properties of the elements that are added. This is exactly the same mechanism we discussed in the previous chapter when we talked about the `ColumnText` object..

MOVIE LIST

You can now create a table of movie information and introduce `Paragraph`, `List`, and `Image` objects. See figure 4.8.

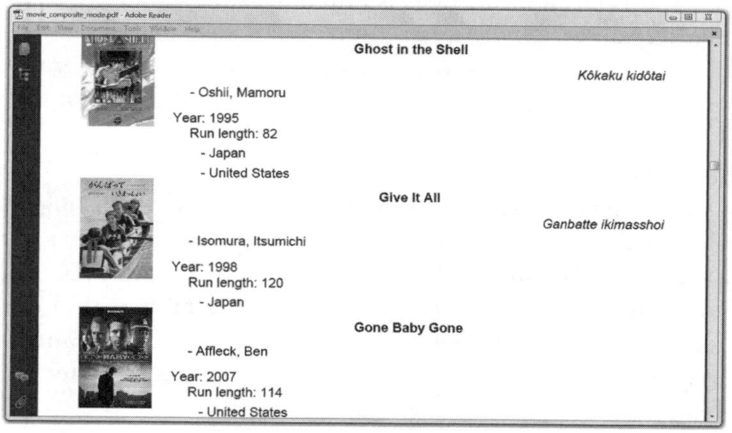

Figure 4.8 Cells in composite mode

Each movie in the next listing takes only two cells: one with the movie poster ❶, another one with information about the movie ❷.

Listing 4.14   MovieCompositeMode.java

```
cell = new PdfPCell(
  Image.getInstance(String.format(RESOURCE, movie.getImdb())), true);    ❶
cell.setBorder(PdfPCell.NO_BORDER);
table.addCell(cell);
cell = new PdfPCell();
Paragraph p = new Paragraph(movie.getTitle(), FilmFonts.BOLD);
p.setAlignment(Element.ALIGN_CENTER);
p.setSpacingBefore(5);
p.setSpacingAfter(5);
cell.addElement(p);
cell.setBorder(PdfPCell.NO_BORDER);
if (movie.getOriginalTitle() != null) {
  p = new Paragraph(movie.getOriginalTitle(), FilmFonts.ITALIC);
  p.setAlignment(Element.ALIGN_RIGHT);
  cell.addElement(p);
}
list = PojoToElementFactory.getDirectorList(movie);
list.setIndentationLeft(30);
cell.addElement(list);                                                    ❷
p = new Paragraph(
  String.format("Year: %d", movie.getYear()), FilmFonts.NORMAL);
p.setIndentationLeft(15);
p.setLeading(24);
cell.addElement(p);
p = new Paragraph(String.format(
  "Run length: %d", movie.getDuration()), FilmFonts.NORMAL);
p.setLeading(14);
p.setIndentationLeft(30);
cell.addElement(p);
list = PojoToElementFactory.getCountryList(movie);
list.setIndentationLeft(40);
cell.addElement(list);
able.addCell(cell);
```

Cell 2 consists of `Paragraph` and `List` objects with different alignments, leading, spacing, and indentation values ❷. Because you're using the `addElement()` method, you're working in composite mode, and all the properties that are set for these different `Elements` are preserved. For `Images`, you can specify whether or not they have to be scaled.

ADDING IMAGES TO A TABLE

Figure 4.9 shows four movie posters added in four different ways. Listing 4.15 shows that the posters of the first two X-Men movies (directed by Bryan Singer) were added using a special `PdfPCell` constructor. The poster of the final part in the X-Men trilogy (directed by Brett Ratner) was added straight to the table with `addCell()`. A fourth poster was added to a cell with `addElement()`. (FYI: Bryan Singer stepped down as director of *X-Men 3* in favor of *Superman Returns*; he has regretted his mistake ever since.)

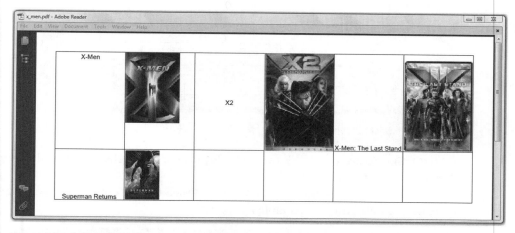

Figure 4.9 Cells and images

Listing 4.15 XMen.java

```
table.addCell("X-Men");
PdfPCell cell = new PdfPCell(img[0]);                               ❶
table.addCell(cell);
table.getDefaultCell().setVerticalAlignment(Element.ALIGN_MIDDLE);
table.addCell("X2");
cell = new PdfPCell(img[1], true);                                  ❷
table.addCell(cell);
table.getDefaultCell().setVerticalAlignment(Element.ALIGN_BOTTOM);
table.addCell("X-Men: The Last Stand");
table.addCell(img[2]);                          ❸
table.addCell("Superman Returns");
cell = new PdfPCell();
img[3].setWidthPercentage(50);              ❹
cell.addElement(img[3]);
table.addCell(cell);
```

When you create a `PdfPCell` with an `Image` as a parameter, the default padding is 0 pt instead of 2 pt. With an extra parameter of type `boolean`, you can ask iText to scale the image so that it fits the width of the cell ❷. By default, the value of this `boolean` is `false` and the image isn't scaled ❶. This is a risk; if the image doesn't fit within the borders of the cell, it will exceed them and overlap other cells.

Adding an `Image` with `addCell()` will scale it, but the properties of the default cell will be used ❸: the third poster in image 4.9 has a padding of 2 pt, and it's bottom-aligned.

Finally, you can add an image as an element ❹. The `Image` is scaled so that it fills 100 percent of the cell width, unless you change the width percentage with the `setWidth-Percentage()` method.

Another special object that can be added to a cell is `PdfPTable`: tables can be nested!

NESTED TABLES

There was a time when rowspan wasn't supported for `PdfPCells`. The only way to work around this was to use nested tables. Cells 1.1 and 1.2 in figure 4.10 are part of a

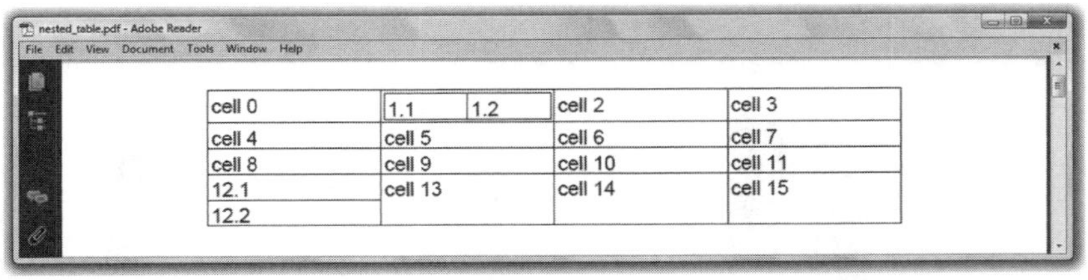

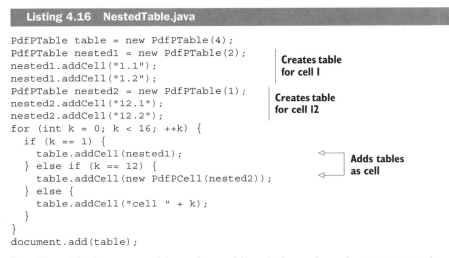

Figure 4.10   Nested tables

nested table. So are cells 12.1 and 12.2. Because of this, cells 13, 14, and 15 look as if they have their rowspan set to 2.

Looking at next listing, you'll immediately see the difference between the nested table in cell 1 and the nested table in cell 12.

Listing 4.16   NestedTable.java

```
PdfPTable table = new PdfPTable(4);
PdfPTable nested1 = new PdfPTable(2);        Creates table
nested1.addCell("1.1");                      for cell I
nested1.addCell("1.2");
PdfPTable nested2 = new PdfPTable(1);        Creates table
nested2.addCell("12.1");                     for cell I2
nested2.addCell("12.2");
for (int k = 0; k < 16; ++k) {
  if (k == 1) {
    table.addCell(nested1);                  Adds tables
  } else if (k == 12) {                      as cell
    table.addCell(new PdfPCell(nested2));
  } else {
    table.addCell("cell " + k);
  }
}
document.add(table);
```

Just like with the Image object, the padding is 2 pt when the PdfPTable is added with addCell() directly. The padding is 0 pt when you wrap the table in a PdfPCell first.

COMPLEX TABLE LAYOUTS

You can use nested tables to create layouts that are tabular, but that don't fit in a traditional grid. Figure 4.11 is an example of such a layout.

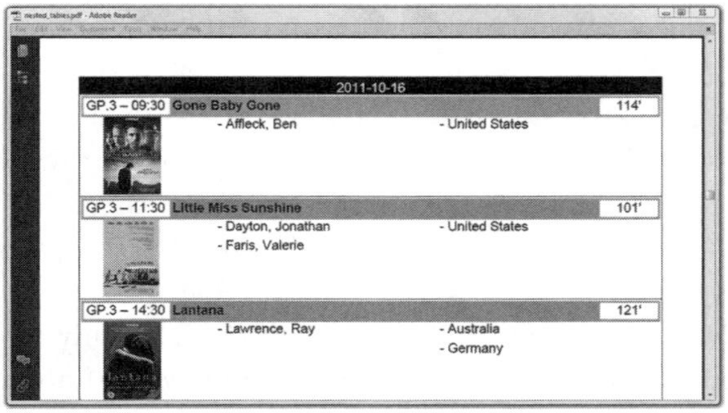

**Figure 4.11
Nesting tables for complex layouts**

This layout is created using the next listing, which is an example of deep nesting. A table is nested inside a nested table.

Listing 4.17   NestedTables.java

```
public void createPdf(String filename)
  throws SQLException, DocumentException, IOException {
  DatabaseConnection connection = new HsqldbConnection("filmfestival");
  Document document = new Document();
  PdfWriter.getInstance(document, new FileOutputStream(filename));
  document.open();
    List days = PojoFactory.getDays(connection);
      for (Date day : days) {
        document.add(getTable(connection, day));
        document.newPage();
    }
    document.close();
    connection.close();
}
public PdfPTable getTable(
  DatabaseConnection connection, Date day)
  throws SQLException, DocumentException, IOException {       Master
  PdfPTable table = new PdfPTable(1);                         table
  ...
  List screenings
    = PojoFactory.getScreenings(connection, day);
  for (Screening screening : screenings) {
    table.addCell(getTable(connection, screening));
  }
  return table;
}
private PdfPTable getTable(
  DatabaseConnection connection, Screening screening)
  throws DocumentException, IOException {
  PdfPTable table = new PdfPTable(4);
  ...
  Movie movie = screening.getMovie();                        Table nested
  PdfPCell cell = new PdfPCell();                            inside master
  cell.addElement(fullTitle(screening));                     table
  ...
  table.addCell(cell);
  ...
  return table;
}
private static PdfPTable fullTitle(Screening screening)
  throws DocumentException {
  PdfPTable table = new PdfPTable(3);                        Deep nested
  ...                                                        table
  return table;
}
```

The table created with the fullTitle() method was added with the addElement() method. The effect is different from adding a PdfPTable as a parameter of the addCell() method or the PdfPCell constructor. With addElement(), the table is added to the `ColumnText` object of the cell, and you can add other elements to the same cell.

You've now worked with some small, almost academic, table examples to demonstrate the properties of tables and cells, but once you start working with real-world examples, tables can get really large. In the next section, we'll discuss tips and tricks that are important as soon as a table spans multiple pages.

4.3 Dealing with large tables

The table in figure 4.11 has a header with a date. If you download the example and generate the PDF on your own computer, you'll see that the table with all the movies spans more than one page for most of the days. The table is nicely split, but unfortunately the header isn't repeated. In this section, you'll fix this, and also add a footer while you're at it.

4.3.1 Repeating headers and footers

Figure 4.12 is another overview of movie screenings on a specific day. The date is shown in the first row. The second row consists of headers that describe the content of the columns: Location, Time, Run Length, Title, and so on. The same information is also added as a footer.

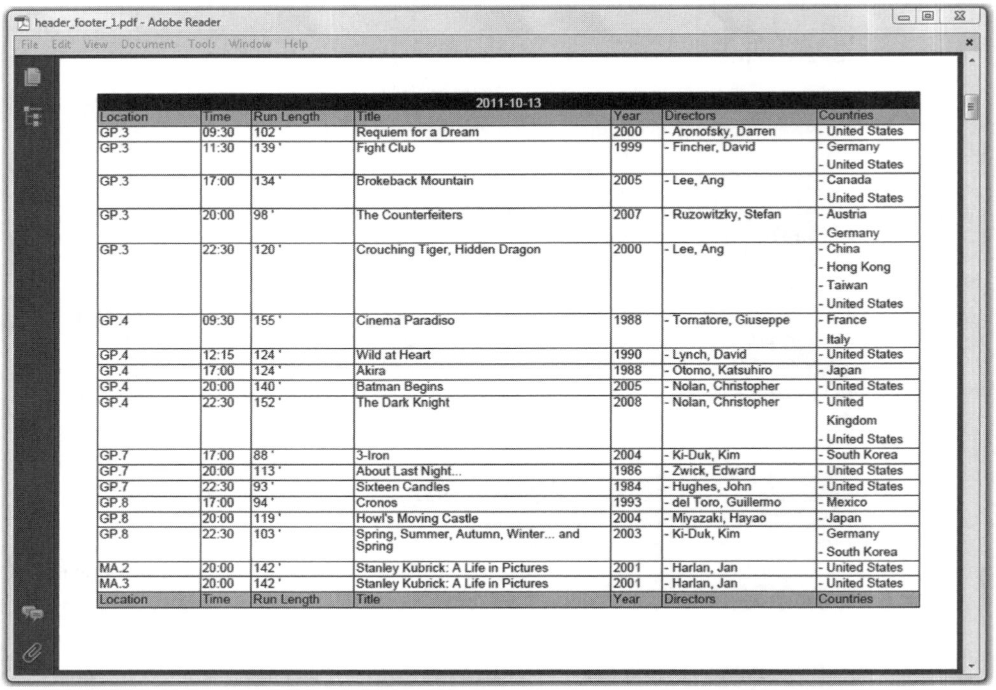

2011-10-13						
Location	Time	Run Length	Title	Year	Directors	Countries
GP.3	09:30	102 '	Requiem for a Dream	2000	- Aronofsky, Darren	- United States
GP.3	11:30	139 '	Fight Club	1999	- Fincher, David	- Germany - United States
GP.3	17:00	134 '	Brokeback Mountain	2005	- Lee, Ang	- Canada - United States
GP.3	20:00	98 '	The Counterfeiters	2007	- Ruzowitzky, Stefan	- Austria - Germany
GP.3	22:30	120 '	Crouching Tiger, Hidden Dragon	2000	- Lee, Ang	- China - Hong Kong - Taiwan - United States
GP.4	09:30	155 '	Cinema Paradiso	1988	- Tornatore, Giuseppe	- France - Italy
GP.4	12:15	124 '	Wild at Heart	1990	- Lynch, David	- United States
GP.4	17:00	124 '	Akira	1988	- Otomo, Katsuhiro	- Japan
GP.4	20:00	140 '	Batman Begins	2005	- Nolan, Christopher	- United States
GP.4	22:30	152 '	The Dark Knight	2008	- Nolan, Christopher	- United Kingdom - United States
GP.7	17:00	88 '	3-Iron	2004	- Ki-Duk, Kim	- South Korea
GP.7	20:00	113 '	About Last Night...	1986	- Zwick, Edward	- United States
GP.7	22:30	93 '	Sixteen Candles	1984	- Hughes, John	- United States
GP.8	17:00	94 '	Cronos	1993	- del Toro, Guillermo	- Mexico
GP.8	20:00	119 '	Howl's Moving Castle	2004	- Miyazaki, Hayao	- Japan
GP.8	22:30	103 '	Spring, Summer, Autumn, Winter... and Spring	2003	- Ki-Duk, Kim	- Germany - South Korea
MA.2	20:00	142 '	Stanley Kubrick: A Life in Pictures	2001	- Harlan, Jan	- United States
MA.3	20:00	142 '	Stanley Kubrick: A Life in Pictures	2001	- Harlan, Jan	- United States
Location	Time	Run Length	Title	Year	Directors	Countries

Figure 4.12 Repeating headers and footers

To get the effect in figure 4.12, you add three rows: a black row with the date ❶, then a light gray row twice ❷ (once for the header and once for the footer).

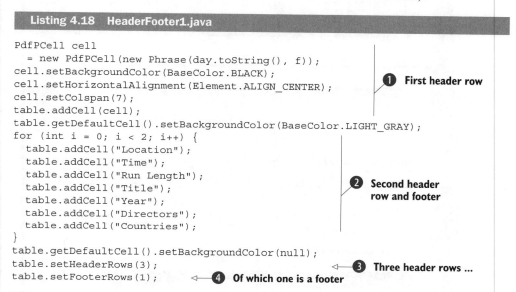

Listing 4.18 HeaderFooter1.java

```
PdfPCell cell
  = new PdfPCell(new Phrase(day.toString(), f));
cell.setBackgroundColor(BaseColor.BLACK);
cell.setHorizontalAlignment(Element.ALIGN_CENTER);
cell.setColspan(7);
table.addCell(cell);
table.getDefaultCell().setBackgroundColor(BaseColor.LIGHT_GRAY);
for (int i = 0; i < 2; i++) {
  table.addCell("Location");
  table.addCell("Time");
  table.addCell("Run Length");
  table.addCell("Title");
  table.addCell("Year");
  table.addCell("Directors");
  table.addCell("Countries");
}
table.getDefaultCell().setBackgroundColor(null);
table.setHeaderRows(3);
table.setFooterRows(1);
```

❶ First header row

❷ Second header row and footer

❸ Three header rows ...

❹ Of which one is a footer

This may seem strange, adding the footer before you start adding any other content, but this is the twist: first you use the `setHeaderRows()` method to tell iText how many rows are part of the header, and you add the row count of the footer. In listing 4.18, you set the value to 3 ❸. Then you use the `setFooterRows()` method to tell iText how many of the header rows are actually footer rows. If there are none, there's no need to do this, but in this example you set the value to 1 ❹.

The result is that the first two rows will be added first, followed by the real content of the table. When a new page is necessary, or when there's no more real data, the third row—the footer row—will be added. If the table continues on another page, the header is repeated. And so is the footer at the end of the table, unless you've used `setSkipLastFooter(true)`. This method is useful if you want to add a footer saying, "This table continues on the next page." It's obvious that you don't want to add this text if there is no more data in the table. There's also a `setSkipFirstHeader()` method for a similar reason: if you want the header to say something like, "This is the continuation of the table on the previous page."

All the screenshots so far have showed only one page, or part of a page. But how does iText split a table that runs over to a new page?

4.3.2 Splitting tables

What do you want iText to do if a row doesn't fit on the page? Do you want iText to start the row on a new page? Or do you want iText to add as much data from that row on the current page, and add the rest to the next page? Both options are possible, and they're demonstrated in figure 4.13.

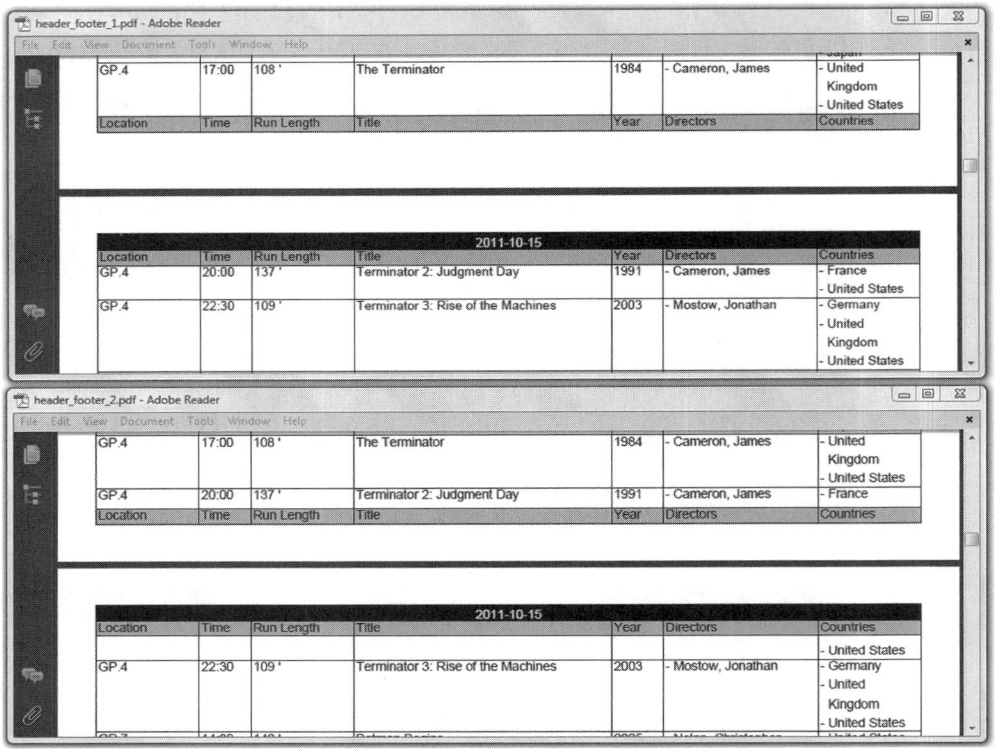

Figure 4.13   Different ways to split a table

In the first example, the second Terminator movie doesn't fit on the upper page. The complete row is forwarded to the next page. This is the default behavior of iText.

In the lower example, most of the data is added to the current page, but one country is printed on the next page.

Listing 4.19   HeaderFooter2.java

```
PdfPTable table = getTable(connection, day);
table.setSplitLate(false);
document.add(table);
```

The `HeaderFooter2` example extends the `HeaderFooter1` example, and it reuses the `getTable()` method, so the table is constructed in exactly the same way. But with the `setSplitLate()` method, you decide whether iText should wait to split the cells of the first row that doesn't fit the page.

By default, iText only splits rows that are forwarded to the next page but that still don't fit because the row height exceeds the available page height. You can avoid this by using the following line of code:

```
table.setSplitRows(false);
```

This is a dangerous line, because now *not one row* will be split. Rows that are too high to fit on a page will be *dropped from the table*!

Dealing with large tables isn't only about repeating headers and footers, or about splitting tables. It's also about managing the memory that is used by a table, making sure that you don't consume more memory than is available in the Java Virtual Machine (JVM).

4.3.3 Memory management for LargeElement implementations

In chapter 2, you learned that the Chapter and Section objects implement the LargeElement interface. Just like PdfPTable, you risk consuming a lot of memory adding many Elements to a LargeElement before adding the LargeElement to a Document.

When an object is added to a Document, you can decide to make it eligible for garbage collection (removal from memory). The problem with objects such as PdfPTable and Chapter is that you can't add the object to the Document until you've completed it; or can you? In section 3.2, you constructed a large table that consisted of several small tables that were glued to each other, but that doesn't work if you want repeating headers and footers that are drawn in the correct place automatically. What you need is to write part of the table to the PdfWriter and its corresponding OutputStream, then find a way to flush that part from memory. You should be able to do this without unwanted side effects affecting the headers, footers, and, in the case of chapters, indentations, titles, and so on.

The LargeElement interface was created to help you solve this problem. Classes implementing this interface need to implement three methods: setComplete(), isComplete(), and flushContent(). The isComplete() and flushContent() methods are used by iText internally. The only method that is important for you is the set-Complete() method.

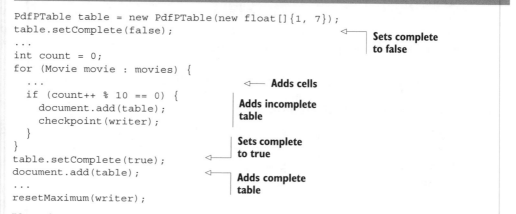

Listing 4.20 MemoryTests.java

```
PdfPTable table = new PdfPTable(new float[]{1, 7});
table.setComplete(false);                          ⟵——— Sets complete
...                                                       to false
int count = 0;
for (Movie movie : movies) {
  ...                            ⟵——— Adds cells
  if (count++ % 10 == 0) {
    document.add(table);         Adds incomplete
    checkpoint(writer);          table
  }
}
table.setComplete(true);         Sets complete
document.add(table);     ⟵———    to true
...                              Adds complete
resetMaximum(writer);            table
```

If you know you'll be adding a LargeElement, and you don't plan to reuse it, you have to inform iText that you haven't finished adding content. In listing 4.20, you're adding the table to the document every ten movies, but you've told iText that it isn't complete yet. Internally, iText will use the method isComplete(). If this method returns true, the flushContent() method will be called.

In previous examples, all the rows were added to the table and they were kept in memory until the table was added to the document. In listing 4.20, rows are written to the PdfWriter at an earlier stage. Once the cell and row objects are rendered to PDF, they're deleted, so that the JVM can remove them from the memory. Once you've finished adding rows, you flag the table as completed, and you add the remaining rows to the document.

The checkpoint() and resetMaximum() methods in listing 4.20 write information about the memory use to a text file. By inspecting this file, you can discover that a table with the information and posters for 120 movies consumes about 4 MB. If you add the table to the document before it's completed (for instance, every 10 movies), the maximum memory needed by the JVM amounts to about 160 KB. This is a huge difference; using the LargeElement interface can help you fine-tune your application if you're dealing with a large volume of data.

The setComplete() method is only useful if you're adding the table with the Document.add() method. In the next section, you'll add a PdfPTable to the direct content. This will give you more power, but also more responsibility: you'll need to tell iText where you want to position every part of the table.

4.4 *Adding a table at an absolute position*

In chapter 2, you created high-level objects, and you let iText decide where they had to be put on the page. In chapter 3, you learned about writing to the direct content, and you discovered how to combine high-level objects with low-level access using the ColumnText object.

Up until now, you've used the PdfPTable class as a high-level object. When added to the Document, iText writes the textual content of the cells to the text layer, and all the borders, background colors, and images are written to the layer just beneath. It's also possible to write a PdfPTable to one of the direct content layers on top of or under the text and graphics layers. See figure 3.2 and read section 3.1.1 for a more elaborate description.

In the next section, you'll discover that a table also has different layers.

4.4.1 *Working with writeSelectedRows()*

Figure 4.14 shows a calendar I made for 2011. In the background, you can see a picture taken by one of the editors of the book; in the foreground, you can see a table that was added at an absolute position.

Listing 4.21 shows how it's done.

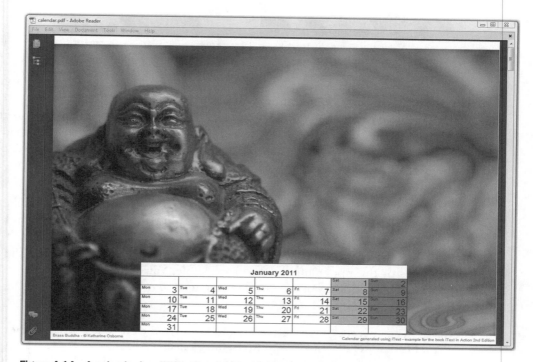

Figure 4.14 A calendar in a PDF with a table added at an absolute position

Listing 4.21   PdfCalendar.java

```
PdfPTable table;
Calendar calendar;
PdfContentByte canvas = writer.getDirectContent();
for (int month = 0; month < 12; month++) {
  calendar = new GregorianCalendar(year, month, 1);
  drawImageAndText(canvas, calendar);
  table = new PdfPTable(7);
  table.setTotalWidth(504);                                    ① Sets width
  table.getDefaultCell().setBackgroundColor(BaseColor.WHITE);      of table
  table.addCell(getMonthCell(calendar, locale));               ◁── Adds table
  int daysInMonth =                                                  caption
    calendar.getActualMaximum(Calendar.DAY_OF_MONTH);
  int day = 1;
  int position = 2;
  while (
    position != calendar.get(Calendar.DAY_OF_WEEK)) {
    position = (position % 7) + 1;                             Adds empty
    table.addCell("");                                         cells first row
  }
  while (day <= daysInMonth) {
    calendar
      = new GregorianCalendar(year, month, day++);            Adds days
    table.addCell(getDayCell(calendar, locale));              of month
  }
```

```
    table.completeRow();
    table.writeSelectedRows(0, -1,
      169, table.getTotalHeight() + 18, canvas);
    document.newPage();
}
```

❷ **Adds table
to canvas**

**Adds empty
cells last row**

Note that you always have to set the total width ❶ if you intend to add the PdfPTable at an absolute position. You don't have to lock the width, because iText will ignore the width percentage anyway; that width only makes sense when using document.add().

The table is added to a PdfContentByte object using the writeSelectedRows() method ❷. Let's take a look at the parameters.

SELECTING THE ROWS AND THE TABLE POSITION

With the first two parameters, you can define the start and the end of the table rows. In listing 4.21, all the rows are added, because you use 0 as the starting row and –1 as end row. The value –1 means, "show all the remaining rows."

The next two parameters of the writeSelectedRows() method define the (x,y) coordinates of the upper-left corner of the table. You want the table to end 18 pt above the lower boundary of the page, so you need to calculate the height of the table and add 18 to that value.

> **NOTE**   The writeSelectedRows() method returns the current *Y* position after the table is added. If you were to wrap line ❷ inside a System.out.println() statement in listing 4.21, you'd see that every table returns the value 18.

The final parameter is the PdfContentByte object to which you want to add the table.

CONTENT CANVASES

Instead of a single PdfContentByte object, you could pass an array of four PdfContentByte objects as the final parameter of the writeSelectedRow() method. These represent four direct content layers (aka, canvases). Each canvas has a specific name and purpose:

- PdfPtable.BASECANVAS—Anything placed here will be under the table.
- PdfPtable.BACKGROUNDCANVAS—This is the layer where the backgrounds are drawn.
- PdfPtable.LINECANVAS—This is the layer where the lines are drawn.
- PdfPtable.TEXTCANVAS—This is the layer where the text goes. Anything placed here will cover the table.

If you only pass one PdfContentByte object, text will cover lines, lines will cover backgrounds, and backgrounds will cover anything added to the base canvas. Note that iText never adds content to the base canvas. It's there in case you want to add something that goes under all the other content in a table or a cell event; see chapter 5 for examples.

SPLITTING A PDFPTABLE VERTICALLY

Suppose that a table has so many columns that it doesn't fit the width of a page. In that case, your only option is to split it vertically. This is demonstrated in figure 4.15.

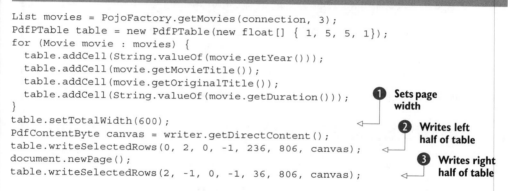

Figure 4.15   Splitting a table vertically

This is a single table listing the movies directed by Zhang Yimou. The total width is set
to 600 pt in listing 4.22 ❶, but the width of a page is only 595 pt.

In this example the `writeSelectedRows()` method was used twice, with two extra
parameters to select the columns.

Listing 4.22   Zhang.java

```
List movies = PojoFactory.getMovies(connection, 3);
PdfPTable table = new PdfPTable(new float[] { 1, 5, 5, 1});
for (Movie movie : movies) {
  table.addCell(String.valueOf(movie.getYear()));
  table.addCell(movie.getMovieTitle());
  table.addCell(movie.getOriginalTitle());
  table.addCell(String.valueOf(movie.getDuration()));    ❶ Sets page
}                                                              width
table.setTotalWidth(600);
PdfContentByte canvas = writer.getDirectContent();         ❷ Writes left
table.writeSelectedRows(0, 2, 0, -1, 236, 806, canvas);       half of table
document.newPage();
table.writeSelectedRows(2, -1, 0, -1, 36, 806, canvas);    ❸ Writes right
                                                              half of table
```

Columns 0 to 2 (2 not included) are added at position (236, 806) ❷ on one page.
Column 2 and all the remaining columns (–1 is used instead of the real number of
columns) are added at position (36, 806) on the next page ❸.

This is one way to add a `PdfPTable` at an absolute position. The other way is to
wrap a `PdfPTable` object inside a `ColumnText` object.

4.4.2   *Wrapping tables in columns*

Figure 4.16 shows a table with a header and footer that were added at absolute positions in two separate columns on the same page.

In listing 4.23, you use the `ColumnText` mechanism from chapter 3 in combination
with the `PdfPTable` functionality that repeats headers and footers (explained in section 4.3.1).

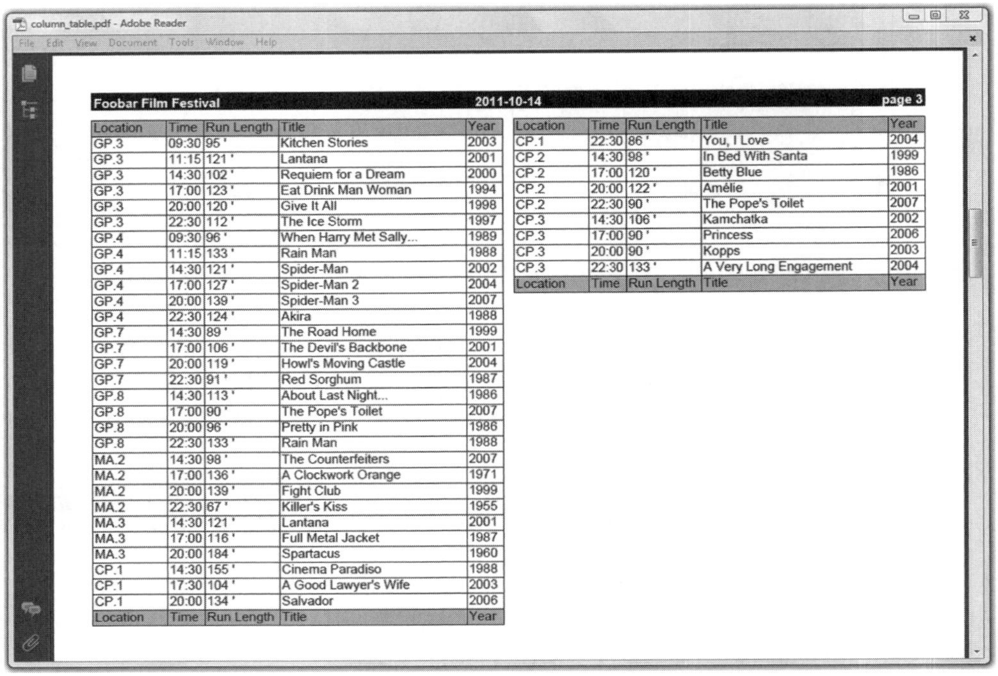

Figure 4.16 A `PdfPTable` rendered in two columns

Listing 4.23   ColumnTable.java

```
ColumnText column = new ColumnText(writer.getDirectContent());
List days = PojoFactory.getDays(connection);
float[][] x = {
  { document.left(), document.left() + 380 },
  { document.right() - 380, document.right() }
};
for (Date day : days) {
  column.addElement(getTable(connection, day));
  int count = 0;
  float height = 0;
  int status = ColumnText.START_COLUMN;
  while (ColumnText.hasMoreText(status)) {
    if (count == 0) {
      height = addHeaderTable(document,
        day, writer.getPageNumber());
    }
    column.setSimpleColumn(
      x[count][0], document.bottom(),
      x[count][1], document.top() - height - 10);
    status = column.go();
    if (++count > 1) {
      count = 0;
      document.newPage();
```

Annotations:
- **Defines column borders**
- **Adds table with screenings**
- **Adds extra header table**

```
        }
      }
    document.newPage();
}
```

This section introduced some low-level functionality of the high-level table object. In the next chapter, we'll return to the PdfPTable and PdfPCell objects, and you'll use low-level methods to draw tables and cells with rounded corners and other fancy layout features. But first, let's look back on what you've learned in this chapter.

4.5   *Summary*

This chapter was dedicated entirely to tables. You learned how to create PdfPTable and PdfPCell objects. You were made aware of the PdfPRow class, but you know that you shouldn't worry about it: rows are created behind the scenes by iText.

You learned how to define the width, alignment, and spacing of the complete table and its columns, and you discovered that cells are very similar to the ColumnText object that was discussed in the previous chapter. You've worked with cells in text mode and in composite mode. In the subsection about text mode, you learned more about the properties of a cell. The section with the examples in composite mode focused on special types of cells: cells with images, and cells containing other tables (nested tables).

As soon as you have a table that spans multiple pages, you need to pay special attention to headers and footers if you want them to repeat on every page. You also have to choose whether you want to split the cells of a row if they don't fit on the current page, or if you want to forward them to the next page. You also learned about the implications on your JVM of having a large table; you learned how to reduce the maximum amount of memory needed when dealing with a large table.

Finally, you added a PdfPTable at absolute coordinates in two different ways: with the writeSelectedRows() method, and by wrapping the table inside a ColumnText object.

In the next chapter, you'll learn how to fine-tune the layout by using table and cell events.

5

Table, cell, and page events

This chapter covers

- Cell and table events
- Events for Chunks, Paragraphs, Chapters, and Sections
- Page boundaries
- Adding headers, footers, and watermarks using page events

In chapters 2 and 4, you added content to a document using a plethora of objects and methods available in iText. When adding a Chunk, you were able to use methods to add lines and a background color. When creating a PdfPTable, you could define borders and backgrounds. But what if all of this isn't sufficient? What if you don't want a rectangular background for a Chunk, but a custom shape instead, such as an ellipse? What if you want the borders of a PdfPCell to have rounded corners? This chapter explains how to write custom functionality for Chunk, Paragraph, Chapter, Section, PdfPTable, and PdfPCell objects.

122

In previous examples involving these objects, you've seen that iText takes responsibility for creating a new page whenever the content doesn't fit the current page. You may want to automatically add artifacts with meta-content to each page—perhaps a running head with a title, a footer with the page number, or a watermark. This can be done using *page events*.

All of this will be covered in this chapter, but let's first continue with more table examples, and find out how to create *table and cell events*.

5.1 Decorating tables using table and cell events

Two methods that are present in the API documentation for `PdfPTable` and `PdfPCell` were overlooked in chapter 4: `PdfPTable.setTableEvent()` and `PdfPCell.setCellEvent()`. The former method expects an implementation of the `PdfPTableEvent` interface as its parameter; the latter expects a `PdfPCellEvent` implementation. These interfaces can be used to define a custom layout for tables and cells; for instance, a custom background or custom borders for a table and its cells. You'll use these events on a table you created in the previous chapter.

5.1.1 Implementing the PdfPTableEvent interface

Suppose you want to add a background color to every other row of a table, as shown in figure 5.1.

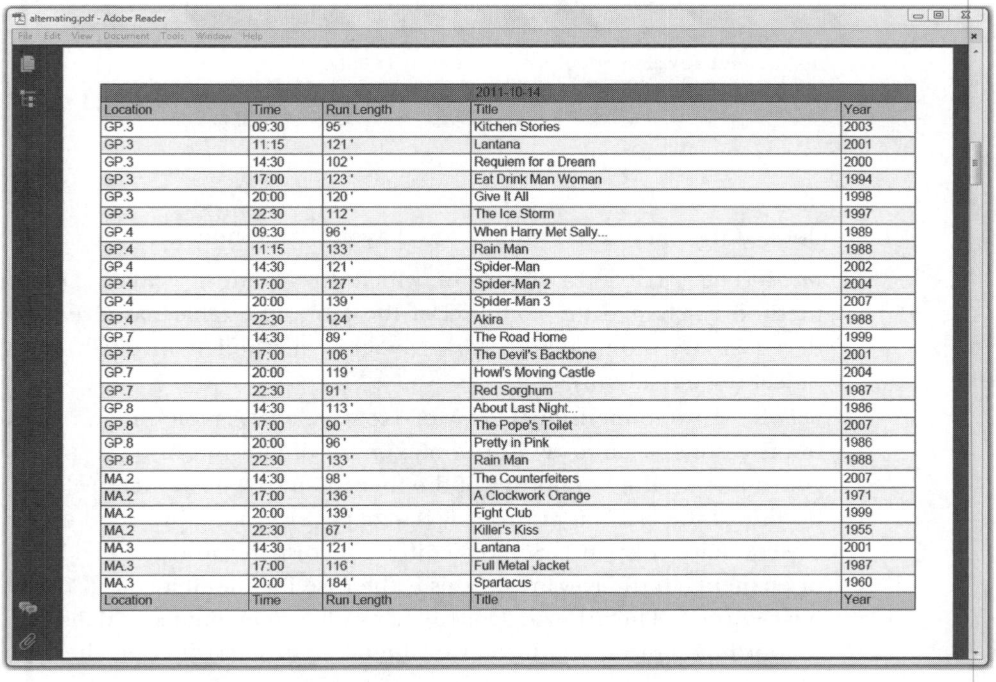

2011-10-14				
Location	Time	Run Length	Title	Year
GP.3	09:30	95 '	Kitchen Stories	2003
GP.3	11:15	121 '	Lantana	2001
GP.3	14:30	102 '	Requiem for a Dream	2000
GP.3	17:00	123 '	Eat Drink Man Woman	1994
GP.3	20:00	120 '	Give It All	1998
GP.3	22:30	112 '	The Ice Storm	1997
GP.4	09:30	96 '	When Harry Met Sally...	1989
GP.4	11:15	133 '	Rain Man	1988
GP.4	14:30	121 '	Spider-Man	2002
GP.4	17:00	127 '	Spider-Man 2	2004
GP.4	20:00	139 '	Spider-Man 3	2007
GP.4	22:30	124 '	Akira	1988
GP.7	14:30	89 '	The Road Home	1999
GP.7	17:00	106 '	The Devil's Backbone	2001
GP.7	20:00	119 '	Howl's Moving Castle	2004
GP.7	22:30	91 '	Red Sorghum	1987
GP.8	14:30	113 '	About Last Night...	1986
GP.8	17:00	90 '	The Pope's Toilet	2007
GP.8	20:00	96 '	Pretty in Pink	1986
GP.8	22:30	133 '	Rain Man	1988
MA.2	14:30	98 '	The Counterfeiters	2007
MA.2	17:00	136 '	A Clockwork Orange	1971
MA.2	20:00	139 '	Fight Club	1999
MA.2	22:30	67 '	Killer's Kiss	1955
MA.3	14:30	121 '	Lantana	2001
MA.3	17:00	116 '	Full Metal Jacket	1987
MA.3	20:00	184 '	Spartacus	1960
Location	Time	Run Length	Title	Year

Figure 5.1 Table with alternating row backgrounds

One way to achieve this would be to change the background color of the default cell for each row so that odd rows don't have a background color, and the background of even rows is yellow. This would work, but you must consider a possible side effect. If you look at figure 5.1, you'll see that you're able to fit 27 rows on one page, not including header and footer rows. The table continues on the next page. If you alternate the background color of the default cell, the background of row 28 in the table (an even row) will be colored, in spite of the fact that it's row 1 on the next page (an odd row). Maybe you don't want this—maybe you want the first row after the header to be a row without a background color. If that's the case, you should implement the `tableLay-out()` method and use a table event.

Listing 5.1   AlternatingBackground.java

```
Public class AlternatingBackground implements PdfPTableEvent {
  public void tableLayout(PdfPTable table,
    float[][] widths, float[] heights,
    int headerRows, int rowStart, PdfContentByte[] canvases) {
    int columns;
    Rectangle rect;
    int footer = widths.length - table.getFooterRows();
    int header
      = table.getHeaderRows() - table.getFooterRows() + 1;
    for (int row = header; row < footer; row += 2) {
      columns = widths[row].length - 1;
      rect = new Rectangle(widths[row][0], heights[row],
        widths[row][columns], heights[row + 1]);
      rect.setBackgroundColor(BaseColor.YELLOW);
      rect.setBorder(Rectangle.NO_BORDER);
      canvases[PdfPTable.BASECANVAS].rectangle(rect);
    }
  }
}
```

1 Use this instead of headerRows parameter

Take a look at the parameters of the `tableLayout()` method:

- *table*—The `PdfPTable` object to which the event is added. Don't use this method to change the contents of the table; the table has already been rendered at the moment the `tableLayout()` method is invoked. Consider this object to be read-only.

- *widths*—A two-dimensional array of `float` values. A table with m rows and n columns results in an array with a maximum dimension of m x (n + 1). The *X* coordinate of the left border of the first cell in row *r* is `widths[r][0]`; the right border of the last cell in this row is `widths[r][n + 1]`, provided that all cells in the row have colspan 1. Setting a different colspan can result in a lower number of elements in the row array. This is the case for the first row in figure 5.1 (the header row). The array `widths[0]` has only two elements: `widths[0][0]` is the *X* coordinate of the left border of the table; `widths[0][1]` is the *X* coordinate of the right border.

- *heights*—An array with float values. You can see 30 rows in figure 5.1. The heights array passed to the table event when this part of the table is drawn will contain 31 values. These values are the *Y* coordinates of the borders of the rows: heights[0] is the *Y* coordinate of the upper border of the table; heights[30] is the *Y* coordinate of the lower border.
- *headerRows*—An int with the same value as table.getHeaderRows(). If you also have footer rows, you should use ❶ to retrieve the correct number of header and footer rows. This parameter dates from the time when the footer row functionality wasn't available yet.
- *rowStart*—This int value will always be 0 if you add the table with document.add(). If you use writeSelectedRows(), it will be identical to the parameter with the same name passed to this method: the row number of the first row that is drawn.
- *canvases*—An array of PdfContentByte objects. There are four of them, and you encountered them in section 4.4.1: PdfPtable.BASECANVAS, PdfPtable.BACKGROUNDCANVAS, PdfPtable.LINECANVAS, and PdfPtable.TEXTCANVAS.

In listing 5.1 you loop over the rows, starting with the second row after the header, in steps of two rows. Every row can have a different number of columns. Using the widths and the heights arrays, you define a rectangle encompassing the complete row. Finally, you draw a yellow rectangle to the BASECANVAS. You chose the base canvas because you don't want to cover background colors that may be defined for some cells. There aren't any cells with backgrounds in this example, except in the header and footer rows, but this way you can easily reuse this code for other tables.

For the event to take effect, you need to use the setTableEvent() method.

Listing 5.2 AlternatingBackground.java (continued)

```
List days = PojoFactory.getDays(connection);
PdfPTableEvent event = new AlternatingBackground();
for (Date day : days) {
  PdfPTable table = getTable(connection, day);
  table.setTableEvent(event);
  document.add(table);
  document.newPage();
}
```

Thanks to the information that is passed to the tableLayout() method, you can write text and shapes to the direct content to change the appearance of a table and its cells. A similar mechanism exists for PdfPCell objects.

5.1.2 Implementing the PdfPCellEvent interface

In figure 5.1, you list a number of screenings and include the run length of each movie. Suppose you wanted to add visual information that is identical to the textual info, but that can be read in a glance. This is done in figure 5.2: by looking at the

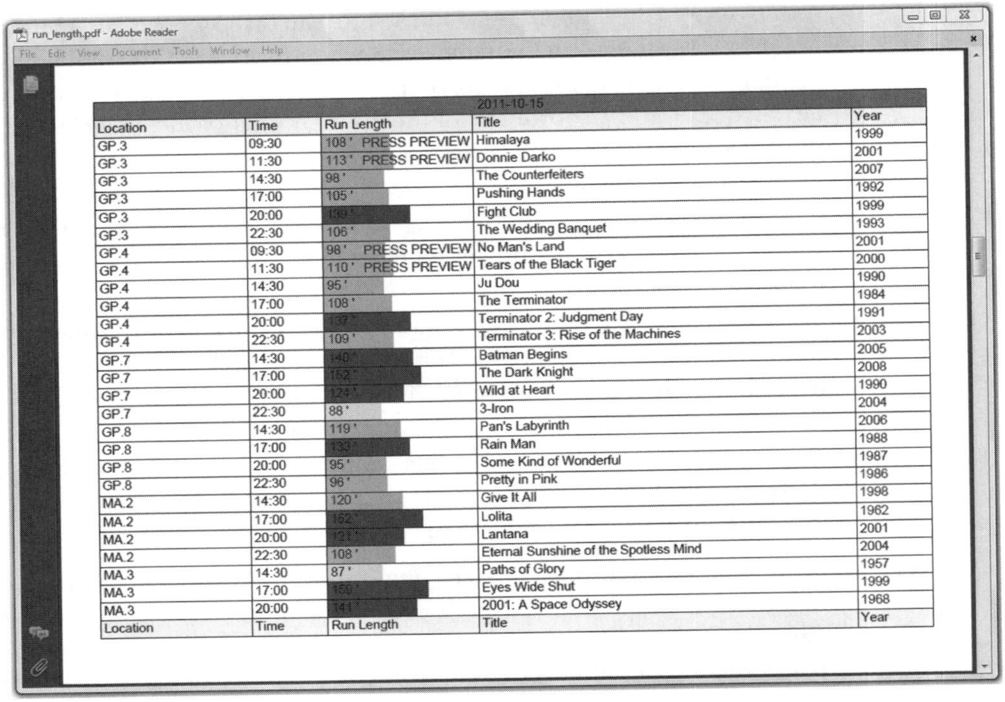

2011-10-15				
Location	Time	Run Length	Title	Year
GP.3	09:30	108 ' PRESS PREVIEW	Himalaya	1999
GP.3	11:30	113 ' PRESS PREVIEW	Donnie Darko	2001
GP.3	14:30	98 '	The Counterfeiters	2007
GP.3	17:00	105 '	Pushing Hands	1992
GP.3	20:00	139 '	Fight Club	1999
GP.3	22:30	106 '	The Wedding Banquet	1993
GP.4	09:30	98 ' PRESS PREVIEW	No Man's Land	2001
GP.4	11:30	110 ' PRESS PREVIEW	Tears of the Black Tiger	2000
GP.4	14:30	95 '	Ju Dou	1990
GP.4	17:00	108 '	The Terminator	1984
GP.4	20:00	137 '	Terminator 2: Judgment Day	1991
GP.4	22:30	109 '	Terminator 3: Rise of the Machines	2003
GP.7	14:30	140 '	Batman Begins	2005
GP.7	17:00	152 '	The Dark Knight	2008
GP.7	20:00	124 '	Wild at Heart	1990
GP.7	22:30	88 '	3-Iron	2004
GP.8	14:30	119 '	Pan's Labyrinth	2006
GP.8	17:00	133 '	Rain Man	1988
GP.8	20:00	95 '	Some Kind of Wonderful	1987
GP.8	22:30	96 '	Pretty in Pink	1986
MA.2	14:30	120 '	Give It All	1998
MA.2	17:00	152 '	Lolita	1962
MA.2	20:00	121 '	Lantana	2001
MA.2	22:30	108 '	Eternal Sunshine of the Spotless Mind	2004
MA.3	14:30	87 '	Paths of Glory	1957
MA.3	17:00	159 '	Eyes Wide Shut	1999
MA.3	20:00	141 '	2001: A Space Odyssey	1968
Location	Time	Run Length	Title	Year

Figure 5.2 Cells with custom background and extra info added using cell events

background of the cell with the duration, you immediately get an indication of the run length of the movie.

The width of column 3 in figure 5.2 corresponds to 240 minutes. That's 100 percent. For a two-hour movie (50 percent of four hours), you draw a rectangle in the background that takes half the width of that cell. If a movie has a duration less than 90 minutes, you draw a green rectangle. Movies with a duration greater than 120 minutes are drawn in dark red. Movies with a run length between 90 and 120 minutes get an orange rectangle. All of this is done in the `cellLayout()` implementation.

Listing 5.3 RunLengthEvent.java

```
class RunLength implements PdfPCellEvent {
  public int duration;
  public RunLength(int duration) {
    this.duration = duration;
  }

  public void cellLayout(PdfPCell cell, Rectangle rect,
    PdfContentByte[] canvas) {
    PdfContentByte cb = canvas[PdfPTable.BACKGROUNDCANVAS];
    cb.saveState();
    if (duration < 90) {
```

```
      cb.setRGBColorFill(0x7C, 0xFC, 0x00);
    }
    else if (duration > 120) {
      cb.setRGBColorFill(0x8B, 0x00, 0x00);
    }
    else {
      cb.setRGBColorFill(0xFF, 0xA5, 0x00);
    }
    cb.rectangle(rect.getLeft(), rect.getBottom(),
      rect.getWidth() * duration / 240, rect.getHeight());
    cb.fill();
    cb.restoreState();
  }
}
```

Observe that the cellLayout() method is a lot easier to understand than the table-Layout() method. There are only three parameters:

- *cell*—The PdfPCell object to which the event is added. This is just for read-only purposes! Do not try to change the content of this cell—it won't have any effect. Once the method of the cell event is triggered, the cell has already been rendered.
- *rect*—The Rectangle object defining the borders of the cell.
- *canvas*—An array of PdfContentByte objects with the same elements as described in sections 4.4.1 and 5.1.1.

Suppose you're planning to project the extended version of the *Lord of the Rings* trilogy. The run length of part 3 is 250 minutes, pauses not included, so the background of the duration cell for *The Return of the King* will exceed the cell borders. By using cell events, you can extend the background color beyond the cell borders.

NOTE   The layout methods give you access to direct content layers of the complete page, along with coordinates that are helpful if you want to know the position of the table or cell that was added. It's up to you to use these coordinates, or not. You can't change the content and the appearance defined for the original table or cell objects. These objects are already rendered to the page when the layout method is called.

Cell events are declared to a PdfPCell using the setCellEvent() method.

> **Listing 5.4   RunLengthEvent.java (continued)**

```
PdfPCell runLength = new PdfPCell(table.getDefaultCell());
runLength.setPhrase(
  new Phrase(String.format("%d '", movie.getDuration())));
runLength.setCellEvent(new RunLength(movie.getDuration()));
if (screening.isPress()) {
  runLength.setCellEvent(press);
}
table.addCell(runLength);
```

In listing 5.4, you use the copy constructor of PdfPCell to create a new cell with the same characteristics as the default cell of the table. You use the setPhrase() method to add content in text mode—this corresponds to the ColumnText.setText() method. Before you add the cell to the table, you add the cell events. First the Run-Length event, with the behavior explained in listing 5.3, then an event named press. This is an instance of PressPreview, a cell event that adds the words "PRESS PREVIEW" if the screening is a press preview.

> **NOTE** Events are cumulative. The PressPreview event doesn't replace the RunLength event. The layout methods of both classes will be called if the screening is a press preview. If you want to replace an existing cell event by a new one, you need to remove the old event first. This can be done by setting the event to null, like this: cell.setCellEvent(null);.

Here is the PressPreview class.

Listing 5.5 RunLengthEvent.java (continued)

```java
class PressPreview implements PdfPCellEvent {

  public BaseFont bf;
  public PressPreview() throws DocumentException, IOException {
    bf = BaseFont.createFont();
  }

  public void cellLayout(PdfPCell cell, Rectangle rect,
    PdfContentByte[] canvas) {
    PdfContentByte cb = canvas[PdfPTable.TEXTCANVAS];
    cb.beginText();
    cb.setFontAndSize(bf, 12);
    cb.showTextAligned(Element.ALIGN_RIGHT, "PRESS PREVIEW",
      rect.getRight() - 3, rect.getBottom() + 4.5f, 0);
    cb.endText();
  }
}
```

Many things that can be done with table events can be done in an easier way with cell events. But cell events can never replace all the table events you need. Usually, you'll combine the power of table events with the ease of use of cell events.

5.1.3 Combining table and cell events

The table in figure 5.3 mimics the cell spacing you get from using the HTML cellspacing attribute for the <table> tag. There's more than one way to achieve this look.

You need a table event to draw the outer border of the complete table, but you can choose what type of event to use to draw the cell borders.

MIMICKING HTML CELL SPACING

You can either use the widths and heights arrays from the tableLayout() method to draw these inner borders. Or you can use a cell event for each cell, in which case you

Location	Date/Time	Run Length	Title	Year
GP.3	2011-10-12 09:30	98 '	The Counterfeiters	2007
GP.3	2011-10-12 11:30	120 '	Give It All	1998
GP.3	2011-10-12 14:30	102 '	Moscou, Belgium	2008
GP.4	2011-10-13 09:30	155 '	Cinema Paradiso	1988
GP.3	2011-10-13 09:30	102 '	Requiem for a Dream	2000
GP.3	2011-10-13 11:30	139 '	Fight Club	1999
GP.4	2011-10-13 12:15	124 '	Wild at Heart	1990
GP.4	2011-10-14 09:30	96 '	When Harry Met Sally...	1989
GP.3	2011-10-14 09:30	95 '	Kitchen Stories	2003
GP.4	2011-10-14 11:15	133 '	Rain Man	1988
GP.3	2011-10-14 11:15	121 '	Lantana	2001
GP.4	2011-10-15 09:30	98 '	No Man's Land	2001
GP.3	2011-10-15 09:30	108 '	Himalaya	1999
GP.4	2011-10-15 11:30	110 '	Tears of the Black Tiger	2000
GP.3	2011-10-15 11:30	113 '	Donnie Darko	2001
GP.4	2011-10-16 09:30	114 '	Battle Royale	2000
GP.3	2011-10-16 09:30	114 '	Gone Baby Gone	2007
GP.4	2011-10-16 11:30	121 '	Good Bye Lenin!	2003
GP.3	2011-10-16 11:30	101 '	Little Miss Sunshine	2006
GP.4	2011-10-17 09:30	120 '	True Romance	1993
GP.3	2011-10-17 09:30	111 '	Leaving Las Vegas	1995
Location	Date/Time	Run Length	Title	Year

Figure 5.3 Mimicking cell spacing using cell and table events

get the coordinates of the border as a `Rectangle` object. Listing 5.6 combines table and cell events.

Listing 5.6 PressPreviews.java

```java
public class PressPreviews implements PdfPCellEvent, PdfPTableEvent {
  public void tableLayout(PdfPTable table,
    float[][] width, float[] height,
    int headerRows, int rowStart,
    PdfContentByte[] canvas) {
    float widths[] = width[0];
    float x1 = widths[0];
    float x2 = widths[widths.length - 1];       Implements table
    float y1 = height[0];                        event method
    float y2 = height[height.length - 1];
    PdfContentByte cb = canvas[PdfPTable.LINECANVAS];
    cb.rectangle(x1, y1, x2 - x1, y2 - y1);
    cb.stroke();
    cb.resetRGBColorStroke();
  }

  public void cellLayout(
    PdfPCell cell, Rectangle position,          Implements cell
    PdfContentByte[] canvases) {                 event method
    float x1 = position.getLeft() + 2;
```

```
      float x2 = position.getRight() - 2;
      float y1 = position.getTop() - 2;
      float y2 = position.getBottom() + 2;
      PdfContentByte canvas                              Implements cell
         = canvases[PdfPTable.LINECANVAS];               event method
      canvas.rectangle(x1, y1, x2 - x1, y2 - y1);
      canvas.stroke();
      canvas.resetRGBColorStroke();
   }

   ...

  public PdfPTable getTable(DatabaseConnection connection)
     throws SQLException, DocumentException, IOException {
     PdfPTable table = new PdfPTable(new float[] { 1, 2, 2, 5, 1 });
     table.setTableEvent(new PressPreviews());              Sets table
     table.setWidthPercentage(100f);                        event
     table.getDefaultCell().setPadding(5);
     table.getDefaultCell().setBorder(PdfPCell.NO_BORDER);
     table.getDefaultCell()                              Sets cell event
       .setCellEvent(new PressPreviews());
     ...
     List screenings = PojoFactory.getPressPreviews(connection);
     Movie movie;
     for (Screening screening : screenings) {
       movie = screening.getMovie();
       table.addCell(screening.getLocation());
       table.addCell(String.format("%s    %2$tH:%2$tM",
         screening.getDate().toString(), screening.getTime()));
       table.addCell(String.format("%d '", movie.getDuration()));
       table.addCell(movie.getMovieTitle());
       table.addCell(String.valueOf(movie.getYear()));
     }
     return table;
   }
}
```

Note that you're setting the cell event for the default cell so the behavior is valid for all the cells of the table in this particular case.

In the examples so far in this chapter, you've used table and cell events for PdfPTable objects that were added with document.add(). This functionality also works if you write a table to the direct content using the writeSelectedRows() method.

TABLE AND CELL EVENTS AND WRITESELECTEDROWS()
Figure 5.4 shows a calendar sheet created in almost the same way as the calendar you made in the previous chapter (see figure 4.14). The PdfPTable with the information about the month was added at an absolute position.

The only difference between the two examples is the style used for the table and its cells. In the previous chapter, you used standard PdfPTable and PdfPCell methods. In this example, you'll use table and cell events to obtain special effects, such as rounded corners. You'll use TableBackground, CellBackground, and RoundRectangle.

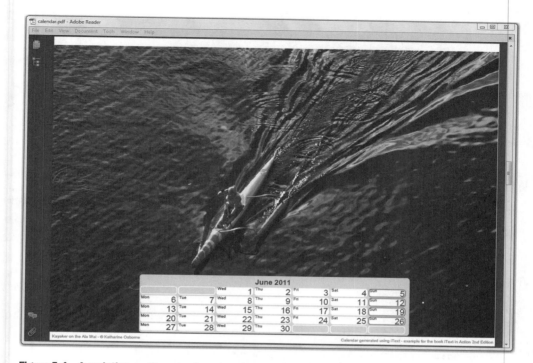

Figure 5.4 A variation on the calendar example, now with rounded corners

---

Listing 5.7   PdfCalendar.java

```
class TableBackground implements PdfPTableEvent {
  public void tableLayout(PdfPTable table,
    float[][] width, float[] height,
    int headerRows, int rowStart,
    PdfContentByte[] canvas) {
    PdfContentByte background
      = canvas[PdfPTable.BASECANVAS];
    background.saveState();
    background.setCMYKColorFill(0x00, 0x00, 0xFF, 0x0F);
    background.roundRectangle(
      width[0][0], height[height.length - 1] - 2,
      width[0][1] - width[0][0] + 6,
      height[0] - height[height.length - 1] - 4, 4);
    background.fill();
    background.restoreState();
  }
}

class CellBackground implements PdfPCellEvent {
  public void cellLayout(PdfPCell cell, Rectangle rect,
    PdfContentByte[] canvas) {
    PdfContentByte cb
      = canvas[PdfPTable.BACKGROUNDCANVAS];
    b.roundRectangle(
```

Specifies yellow
background,
rounded corners

Specifies white
background,
rounded corners

```
            rect.getLeft() + 1.5f, rect.getBottom() + 1.5f,
            rect.getWidth() - 3, rect.getHeight() - 3, 4);
        cb.setCMYKColorFill(0x00, 0x00, 0x00, 0x00);
        cb.fill();
      }
    }
    class RoundRectangle implements PdfPCellEvent {
      protected int[] color;
      public RoundRectangle(int[] color) {
        this.color = color;
      }
      public void cellLayout(PdfPCell cell, Rectangle rect,
        PdfContentByte[] canvas) {
        PdfContentByte cb = canvas[PdfPTable.LINECANVAS];
        cb.roundRectangle(
          rect.getLeft() + 1.5f, rect.getBottom() + 1.5f,
          rect.getWidth() - 3, rect.getHeight() - 3, 4);
        cb.setLineWidth(1.5f);
        cb.setCMYKColorStrokeF(
          color[0], color[1], color[2], color[3]);
        cb.stroke();
      }
    }

    ...

    public void createPdf(String filename, Locale locale, int year)
      throws IOException, DocumentException {
      Document document = new Document(PageSize.A4.rotate());
      PdfWriter writer =
        PdfWriter.getInstance(document, new FileOutputStream(RESULT));
      document.open();
      PdfPTable table;
      Calendar calendar;
      PdfContentByte canvas = writer.getDirectContent();
      for (int month = 0; month < 12; month++) {
        calendar = new GregorianCalendar(year, month, 1);
        drawImageAndText(canvas, calendar);
        table = new PdfPTable(7);
        table.setTableEvent(tableBackground);
        table.setTotalWidth(504);
        table.setLockedWidth(true);
        table.getDefaultCell().setBorder(PdfPCell.NO_BORDER);
        table.getDefaultCell().setCellEvent(whiteRectangle);
        table.addCell(getMonthCell(calendar, locale));
        int daysInMonth = calendar.getActualMaximum(Calendar.DAY_OF_MONTH);
        int day = 1;
        int position = 2;
        while (position != calendar.get(Calendar.DAY_OF_WEEK)) {
          position = (position % 7) + 1;
          table.addCell("");
        }
        while (day <= daysInMonth) {
          calendar = new GregorianCalendar(year, month, day++);
          table.addCell(getDayCell(calendar, locale));
```

Specifies white background, rounded corners

Specifies colored rectangle, rounded corners

Sets table event

❶ Specifies cell default: white border, rounded corners

Formats month cell ❷

```
      }
      table.completeRow();
      table.writeSelectedRows(
        0, -1, 169, table.getTotalHeight() + 20, canvas);
      document.newPage();
    }
    document.close();
  }

  public PdfPCell getMonthCell(Calendar calendar, Locale locale) {
    PdfPCell cell = new PdfPCell();
    cell.setColspan(7);
    cell.setBorder(PdfPCell.NO_BORDER);
    cell.setUseDescender(true);
    Paragraph p = new Paragraph(
      String.format(locale, "%1$tB %1$tY", calendar), bold);
    p.setAlignment(Element.ALIGN_CENTER);
    cell.addElement(p);
    return cell;
  }

  public PdfPCell getDayCell(Calendar calendar, Locale locale) {
    PdfPCell cell = new PdfPCell();
    cell.setCellEvent(cellBackground);
    if (isSunday(calendar) || isSpecialDay(calendar))
      cell.setCellEvent(roundRectangle);
    cell.setPadding(3);
    cell.setBorder(PdfPCell.NO_BORDER);
    Chunk chunk = new Chunk(
      String.format(locale, "%1$ta", calendar), small);
    chunk.setTextRise(8);
    Paragraph p = new Paragraph(chunk);
    p.add(new Chunk(new VerticalPositionMark()));
    p.add(new Chunk(String.format(locale, "%1$te", calendar), normal));
    cell.addElement(p);
    return cell;
  }
```

❸ **Formats day cells**

❹ **Formats special day cells**

After creating the table, you set the table event to draw the background of the table, and you make sure the default cells get a rounded rectangle as their border. ❶ doesn't apply to the cell with the month ❷. The getMonthCell() method returns a PdfPCell object with the name of the month. ❶ also doesn't apply to the cells created with getDayCell(). These cells get a white background with rounded corners ❸. Sundays and special days (holidays) get a colored border ❹.

There's a similar mechanism that allows you to write custom functionality for Chunk, Paragraph, and Chapter and Section objects. The layout methods to achieve this are bundled in the PdfPageEvent interface.

5.2   *Events for basic building blocks*

When you add a basic building block to a Document instance, it's translated into PDF syntax and written to a PDF file by a PdfWriter object. In this process, there's an important class you'll hardly ever need to address directly: PdfDocument. This class is responsible for examining the high-level objects. It's the invisible rope tying the document to the writer.

The `PdfDocument` class is also responsible for firing the page events defined by the `PdfPageEvent` interface. This interface has 11 methods that can be divided into two groups:

- *Methods that involve basic building blocks*—These are similar to the `tableLayout()` and `cellLayout()` methods discussed in the previous section, but instead of tables, they involve Chunks, Paragraphs, Chapters, and Sections. These methods will be discussed in this section.
- *Methods that involve the document and its pages*—These are called when the document is opened or closed, or when a page starts or ends. We'll discuss these methods in section 5.4.

The `onGenericTag()` method is without any doubt the most powerful method in the first category.

5.2.1 *Generic Chunk functionality*

When we discussed the Chunk object in section 2.2.1, there was an example (shown in figure 2.3) where we displayed country codes using a white font on a black background. This example demonstrated the `setBackground()` method. Figure 5.5 does something similar, but instead of a rectangular background, you draw a filmstrip for the year, and a blue ellipse for the link to the IMDB.

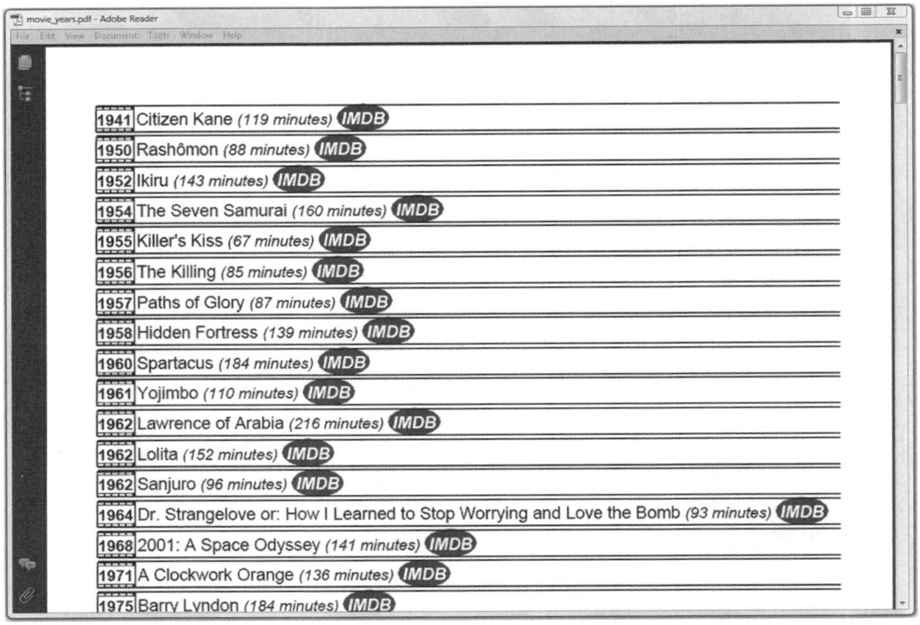

Figure 5.5   Page events for `Chunks` and `Paragraphs`

There are no standard methods to draw special backgrounds for Chunks, but you can write your own custom Chunk functionality by implementing the onGenericTag() method of the PdfPageEvent interface.

Listing 5.8   MovieYears.java

```
class GenericTags extends PdfPageEventHelper {          ◄── ❶ PdfPageEventHelper
  public void onGenericTag(                                    implements PdfPageEvent
    PdfWriter writer, Document pdfDocument,
    Rectangle rect, String text) {
    if ("strip".equals(text))
      strip(writer.getDirectContent(), rect);
    else if ("ellipse".equals(text))
      ellipse(writer.getDirectContentUnder(), rect);
    else
      countYear(text);
  }

  public void strip(
    PdfContentByte content, Rectangle rect) {
    content.rectangle(
      rect.getLeft() - 1, rect.getBottom() - 5f,
      rect.getWidth(), rect.getHeight() + 8);
    content.rectangle(
      rect.getLeft(), rect.getBottom() - 2,
      rect.getWidth() - 2, rect.getHeight() + 2);
    float y1 = rect.getTop() + 0.5f;
    float y2 = rect.getBottom() - 4;                           Draws
    for (float f = rect.getLeft();                             filmstrip
      f < rect.getRight() - 4; f += 5) {
      content.rectangle(f, y1, 4f, 1.5f);
      content.rectangle(f, y2, 4f, 1.5f);
    }
    content.eoFill();
  }

  public void ellipse(
    PdfContentByte content, Rectangle rect) {
    content.saveState();
    content.setRGBColorFill(0x00, 0x00, 0xFF);
    content.ellipse(                                           Draws
      rect.getLeft() - 3f, rect.getBottom() - 5f,              ellipse
      rect.getRight() + 3f, rect.getTop() + 3f);
    content.fill();
    content.restoreState();
  }

  TreeMap<String, Integer> years
    = new TreeMap<String, Integer>();
  public void countYear(String text) {
    Integer count = years.get(text);                           Tracks years
    if (count == null) {                                       in TreeMap
      years.put(text, 1);
    }
    else {
```

```
        years.put(text, count + 1);                    ↑  Tracks years
    }                                                   │  in TreeMap
  }
}
```

Instead of ❶, you could have written GenericTags implements PdfPageEvent, but then you'd need to implement all the methods defined in the PdfPageEvent interface. Here you're only interested in the onGenericTag() method, so it's easier to extend the PdfPageEventHelper class. This class contains nothing but empty implementations of the interface's methods. In this example, you override one specific method, and you can safely ignore the other methods.

The code in listing 5.8 won't be executed unless you declare the event to a writer. The onGenericTag() method will never be invoked if you don't define generic tags for Chunks.

Listing 5.9   MovieYears.java (continued)

```
Document document = new Document();
PdfWriter writer = PdfWriter.getInstance(                   │ Creates instance
  document, new FileOutputStream(filename));   ◀──          │ of event
GenericTags event = new GenericTags();
writer.setPageEvent(event);                    ◀──    Declares event
...                                                   to writer
document.open();
...
Paragraph p;
Chunk c;
...
p = new Paragraph(22);
c = new Chunk(String.format("%d ", movie.getYear()), bold);  │ Sets "strip"
c.setGenericTag("strip");                                    │ as generic tag
p.add(c);
c = new Chunk(movie.getMovieTitle());                        │ Sets year as
c.setGenericTag(String.valueOf(movie.getYear()));            │ generic tag
p.add(c);
c = new Chunk(
  String.format(" (%d minutes)  ", movie.getDuration()), italic);
p.add(c);
c = new Chunk("IMDB", white);                                │ Sets "ellipse"
c.setAnchor("http://www.imdb.com/title/tt" + movie.getImdb());│ as generic tag
c.setGenericTag("ellipse");
p.add(c);
document.add(p);
...
document.close();
```

Before we study the mechanisms used in this code, let's look at the parameters passed to the onGenericTag() method:

- writer—The PdfWriter object to which the event is added.
- pdfDocument—*Not* the Document object to which the Paragraph is added. This is a PdfDocument that is created internally when you create a PdfWriter instance. Use this object just for read-only purposes!

- rect—Rectangle defining the boundaries of the Chunk for which a generic tag is set.
- text—The String passed to the Chunk with the setGenericTag() method.

In listing 5.9 you're tagging the Chunks representing the year with a generic tag named "strip". When the content is written to the page, the onGenericTag() method is invoked. In the page event implementation, the onGenericTag() method looks at the text, and calls the strip() method to draw a filmstrip over the year.

NOTE If a Chunk is split over multiple lines, the onGenericTag() method will be invoked as many times as there are lines. Every line will have its own Rectangle.

The same happens for the IMDB links: the text "ellipse" corresponds with the ellipse() method. You're using this page event to achieve more or less the same goals as with table and cell events: to add special shapes. But there's more.

In listing 5.8, you'll also find a countYear() method. This method is invoked because you're setting the year as a generic tag for the movie titles. A list of these years and the number of times each year occurs is kept in the member variable years. Here is what you can do with this TreeMap.

Listing 5.10   MovieYears.java (continued)

```
document.newPage();
writer.setPageEvent(null);
for (Map.Entry entry : event.years.entrySet()) {
  p = new Paragraph(String.format("%s: %d movie(s)",
    entry.getKey(), entry.getValue()));
  document.add(p);
}
```

You start a new page and remove the page events from the writer by setting the page events to null. You don't want any of the page events to be active, and figure 5.5 shows that GenericTags wasn't the only event used in this example—you also used a Paragraph event to draw extra lines. You don't want these lines to appear when you create an overview of the years for which you have a film in the database, along with the number of times each year occurs. This overview is shown in figure 5.6.

Listing 5.9 was far from complete—the lines in figure 5.5 were added using another type of page event. The following line actually came right after GenericTags was set:

```
writer.setPageEvent(new ParagraphPositions());
```

ParagraphPositions is an example of how to create events for Paragraph objects.

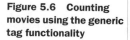

Figure 5.6   Counting movies using the generic tag functionality

5.2.2   *Paragraph events*

The `ParagraphPositions` class creates Paragraph events.

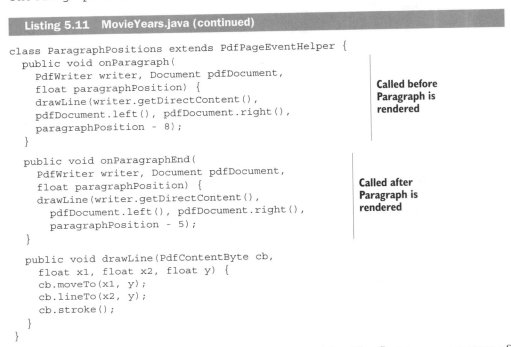

Listing 5.11   MovieYears.java (continued)

```
class ParagraphPositions extends PdfPageEventHelper {
  public void onParagraph(
    PdfWriter writer, Document pdfDocument,
    float paragraphPosition) {
    drawLine(writer.getDirectContent(),
    pdfDocument.left(), pdfDocument.right(),
    paragraphPosition - 8);
  }
  public void onParagraphEnd(
    PdfWriter writer, Document pdfDocument,
    float paragraphPosition) {
    drawLine(writer.getDirectContent(),
      pdfDocument.left(), pdfDocument.right(),
      paragraphPosition - 5);
  }
  public void drawLine(PdfContentByte cb,
    float x1, float x2, float y) {
    cb.moveTo(x1, y);
    cb.lineTo(x2, y);
    cb.stroke();
  }
}
```

Called before Paragraph is rendered

Called after Paragraph is rendered

There are two page event methods involving paragraphs. The first two parameters of these methods, `writer` and `pdfDocument`, have the same meaning as the `onGeneric-Tag()` parameters with the same names. I repeat: use `pdfDocument` for read-only purposes. In this example, you use `pdfDocument` to get the values of the left and right margins of the page. An extra parameter named `paragraphPosition` gives you access to a *Y* coordinate.

These are the two page event methods:

- `onParagraph()`—Called before a `Paragraph` is rendered. The `paragraphPosition` passed to the method is the *Y* coordinate of the baseline of the first line of the `Paragraph`, augmented with its leading.
- `onParagraphEnd()`—Called after a `Paragraph` is rendered. The `paragraphPosition` is the *Y* coordinate of the baseline of the last line of the `Paragraph`.

There are also page events involving `Chapter` and `Section`.

5.2.3   *Chapter and Section events*

You can use `Chapter` and `Section` events for the same reasons you use `Paragraph` events: to retrieve a *Y* position and use that coordinate to draw lines or shapes. This is what's done in figure 5.7.

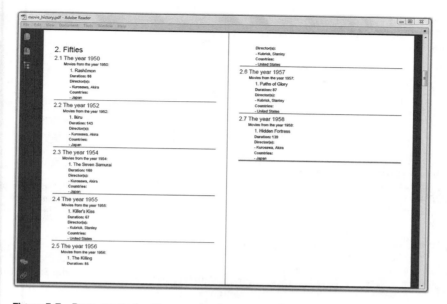

Figure 5.7 Page events for `Chapters` and `Sections`

As you know, using `Chapter` and `Section` automatically creates an outline tree, visible in the bookmarks pane of Adobe Reader. In the next example, you'll use page events to create a table of contents that can be printed. See figure 5.8.

Next, you'll reuse the example from section 2.3.2, but add a page event implementation for events that are triggered when a `Chapter`, a `Section`, or both, starts or ends.

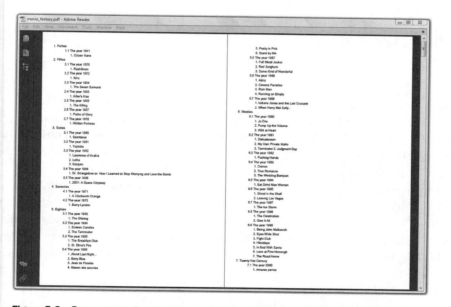

Figure 5.8 Page events for `Chapters` and `Sections`: reordering pages

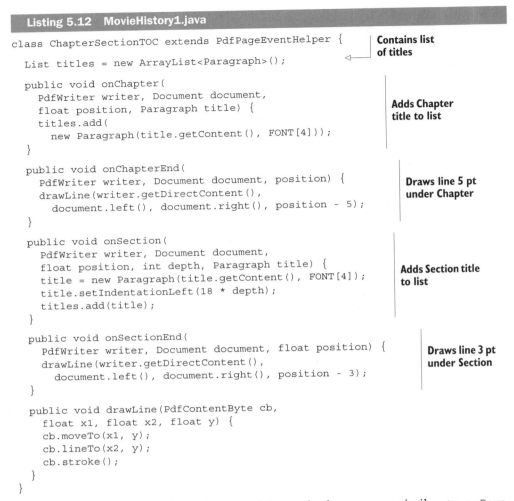

Listing 5.12   MovieHistory1.java

```java
class ChapterSectionTOC extends PdfPageEventHelper {          Contains list
                                                              of titles
  List titles = new ArrayList<Paragraph>();

  public void onChapter(
    PdfWriter writer, Document document,                      Adds Chapter
    float position, Paragraph title) {                        title to list
    titles.add(
      new Paragraph(title.getContent(), FONT[4]));
  }

  public void onChapterEnd(
    PdfWriter writer, Document document, position) {          Draws line 5 pt
    drawLine(writer.getDirectContent(),                       under Chapter
      document.left(), document.right(), position - 5);
  }

  public void onSection(
    PdfWriter writer, Document document,
    float position, int depth, Paragraph title) {            Adds Section title
    title = new Paragraph(title.getContent(), FONT[4]);        to list
    title.setIndentationLeft(18 * depth);
    titles.add(title);
  }

  public void onSectionEnd(
    PdfWriter writer, Document document, float position) {    Draws line 3 pt
    drawLine(writer.getDirectContent(),                       under Section
      document.left(), document.right(), position - 3);
  }

  public void drawLine(PdfContentByte cb,
    float x1, float x2, float y) {
    cb.moveTo(x1, y);
    cb.lineTo(x2, y);
    cb.stroke();
  }
}
```

The onChapterEnd() and onSectionEnd() methods are very similar to onPara-graphEnd(). The onChapter() and onSection() methods are similar to onPara-graph(), but they have extra parameters. The title parameter contains the title you've defined for the Chapter or Section; depth tells you how deep the Section can be found in the outline tree.

In this example, you're adding Paragraphs with the content of the Chapter and Section titles to a list, and you're using the depth of the Sections to define an indentation. You can create a table of contents if you add all the Paragraphs in this list to the Document. You'll find this table of contents (TOC) on the last pages of the document. The TOC entries are stored only after Chapters and Sections are rendered. You can't add the TOC up front.

If you want the document to start with the TOC on the first page, you'll need to find a way to reorder the pages before the Document is closed.

5.2.4 *Page order and blank pages*

Before we look at the code to reorder pages, you have to know that pages in a PDF document are usually organized in a page tree with different branches and leaves.

LINEAR PAGE MODE

By default, iText creates a balanced tree, because using such a tree optimizes the performance of viewer applications. The simplest page tree structure consists of a single node that references all of the document's page objects directly.

Reordering pages with iText is only possible if you tell `PdfWriter` to create this simple structure. To do so, you need to add the following line before opening the document:

```
writer.setLinearPageMode();
```

After opening the document, you add all the content. In this case, the content consists of a series of chapters.

REORDERING PAGES

Once the content is added, you can reorder the pages.

> **Listing 5.13 MovieHistory1.java (continued)**

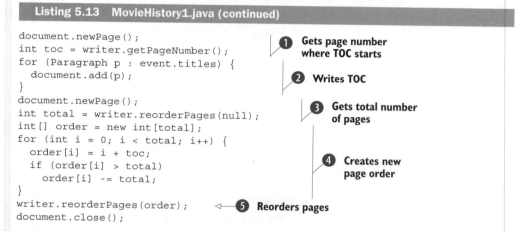

```
document.newPage();
int toc = writer.getPageNumber();          ❶ Gets page number
for (Paragraph p : event.titles) {            where TOC starts
  document.add(p);
}                                           ❷ Writes TOC
document.newPage();
int total = writer.reorderPages(null);     ❸ Gets total number
int[] order = new int[total];                 of pages
for (int i = 0; i < total; i++) {
  order[i] = i + toc;
  if (order[i] > total)                     ❹ Creates new
    order[i] -= total;                         page order
}
writer.reorderPages(order);   ◀—❺ Reorders pages
document.close();
```

Let's examine this code step by step.

❶ You start on a new page, and you store the current page number. That's where the table of contents starts *before* reordering the pages. In this example, the TOC starts on page 27.

❷ You add the TOC. That's the list of `Paragraph`s you've created in the page event.

❸ You need to start a new page before you can count the number of pages that need to be reordered. You obtain this value by calling the `reorderPages()` method a first time with `null` as the parameter. In this example, the total number of pages is 30.

❹ You create an array of `int` values that will be used to map the new page index to the old page number. The new page with index 0—the new page 1—will be the old page with number `toc`. In this example, the first page will be the old page 27. The TOC consists of 4 pages. The new page with index 4—that is, page 5—was originally page 1. Creating the new order is a matter of doing some simple math.

 Once this mapping is done, you invoke `reorderPages()` a second time with the new order as the parameter.

You could replace the two lines marked with ❸ with the following line:

```
int total = writer.getPageNumber();
```

But experience has taught me that this can cause exceptions if the current page is empty.

You may wonder if using `document.newPage()` won't result in an unnecessary extra blank page at the end of the document. The answer is no: iText ignores `document.newPage()` if the current page is empty. iText never adds a blank page to a document unintentionally.

ADDING A BLANK PAGE

If adding a blank page is a requirement, you have to tell iText explicitly about this.

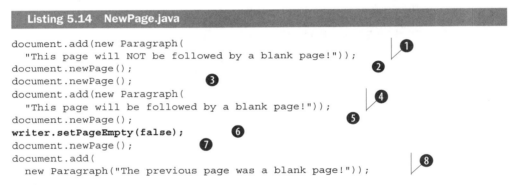

Listing 5.14   NewPage.java

```
document.add(new Paragraph(
  "This page will NOT be followed by a blank page!"));    ❶
document.newPage();                                        ❷
document.newPage();                          ❸
document.add(new Paragraph(
  "This page will be followed by a blank page!"));         ❹
document.newPage();                                        ❺
writer.setPageEmpty(false);          ❻
document.newPage();                  ❼
document.add(
  new Paragraph("The previous page was a blank page!"));   ❽
```

In ❶, you add a `Paragraph` to page 1.

With `document.newPage()` ❷, you go to page 2, but you don't add anything to this page: you immediately ask for another new page. Since nothing was added to page 2, ❸ will be ignored: the second `Paragraph` ❹ will be added on page 2.

Page 2 is no longer empty, so ❺ will take you to page 3. You don't add any content to page 3, but with ❻ you tell iText that the current page should not be treated as an empty page.

❼ takes you to page 4, and that's where the third `Paragraph` ❽ will be added.

The example about creating a TOC using `Chapter` and `Section` events led us somewhat astray and resulted in a discussion about pages. We'll talk about the second category of page events in section 5.4, but first we'll take a closer look at the boundaries of a page.

5.3   *Overview of the page boundaries*

Up until now, you've defined the page size using a `Rectangle` as the value of one of the five different page boundaries that can exist for a page in a PDF document. You'll learn more about these boundaries in this section, and you'll work through an example that demonstrates the difference between the two most important page boundaries.

Suppose that I wanted to avoid being accused of false modesty. I could try to print a poster measuring one square meter, featuring myself in a Superman outfit. Seriously! The famous commercial artist Dick Kline once made such a drawing. It was sent to me as a gift by Bill Segraves, a long-time iText user.

The drawing isn't a raster image. It consists of a sequence of Bézier curves that I've copied into a text file named hero.txt. To do this, you'd create a `PdfTemplate` from such a text file.

Listing 5.15   Hero1.java

```
public PdfTemplate createTemplate(PdfContentByte content, Rectangle rect,
  int factor) throws IOException {
  PdfTemplate template = content.createTemplate(
    rect.getWidth(), rect.getHeight());
  template.concatCTM(factor, 0, 0, factor, 0, 0);
  FileReader reader = new FileReader(RESOURCE);
  int c;
  while ((c = reader.read()) > -1) {
    template.setLiteral((char)c);
  }
  return template;
}
```

As you can see, you can write literal PDF syntax to the direct content using the `setLiteral()` method. It accepts a `char`, a `float`, or a `String` value.

> **WARNING**   Incorrect use of this method can result in seriously damaged PDF files. Please don't use it before you've read chapter 14. In the next chapter, we'll return to this example and find a much better way to reuse existing content.

The original drawing is intended to be added on an A4 page, but I want to put it on an A0 document, so I have to scale it with a factor 4 (see ISO-216). I could create a `Document` with `PageSize.A0` like this:

```
Document document = new Document(PageSize.A0);
```

This line defines the *media box* of the first page in the document.

5.3.1   *The media box*

So far, you've been creating documents with only one type of boundary: the media box.

> *The media box defines the boundaries of the physical medium on which the page is to be printed. It may include any extended area surrounding the finished page for bleed, printing marks, or other such purposes. It may also include areas close to the edges of the medium that cannot be marked because of physical limitations of the output device. Content falling outside this boundary may safely be discarded without affecting the meaning of the PDF file.*
>
> —ISO-32000-1:2008, section 14.1.2

The A0 rectangle used in the code line at the end of the previous section is defined like this:

```
public static final Rectangle A0 = new RectangleReadOnly(2384,3370);
```

This corresponds to a physical medium measuring 2384 pt x 3370 pt (or 84.10 cm x 118.89 cm, or 33.11 in x 46.81 in).

> **NOTE** The values 2384 and 3370 in this constructor match the width and height of the page, but they really form the coordinates of the upper-right corner of a rectangle. The values for the coordinate of the lower-left corner are omitted because they are zero: the lower-left coordinates are (0,0).

When you learned how to add lines, shapes, and text at absolute positions in chapter 3, you assumed that the origin of the coordinate system coincided with the lower-left corner of the page. This assumption is correct as long as the media box is defined with (0,0) as the coordinate for its lower-left corner, but that's not mandatory. It's perfectly OK for an application to create a media box with a different origin. It might be interesting to have the origin of the coordinate system in the upper-left corner of the page. Or you could place the origin in the middle of a page, so that you can distinguish four quadrants for your drawing operations. That's what I did when I created my Superman poster in PDF.

Figure 5.9   A PDF with a different origin

The cross that is drawn in figure 5.9 (close to my navel) marks the origin of the coordinate system.

Listing 5.16   Hero1.java (continued)

```
Rectangle rect = new Rectangle(-1192, -1685, 1192, 1685);          Specifies page size
Document document = new Document(rect);                            with negative origin
PdfWriter writer =
  PdfWriter.getInstance(document, new FileOutputStream(filename));
document.open();

PdfContentByte content = writer.getDirectContent();
PdfTemplate template = createTemplate(content, rect, 4);          Adds template with
content.addTemplate(template, -1195, -1685);                      negative offset
content.moveTo(-595, 0);                        Draws line from
content.lineTo(595, 0);                         negative to positive X
content.moveTo(0, -842);        Draws line from
content.lineTo(0, 842);         negative to position Y
content.stroke();

document.close();
```

If you look at all the PDFs that can be found in the wild, you'll discover that the lower-left corner is the origin of the coordinate system for most PDF documents. This example proves that you shouldn't assume that this is true for every possible PDF. Knowing this will be important when you start manipulating existing PDFs in the next chapter. When you add content at an absolute position, you'll need to take the (x,y) value of the origin into account if it's different from (0,0). Otherwise, you risk adding content in the wrong place, maybe even outside the visible area of the page.

You also have to make sure not to add anything outside the *crop box* of the page.

5.3.2   The crop box

The crop box is another type of boundary that can be defined as a rectangle that differs from the media box.

> *The crop box defines the region to which the contents of the page shall be clipped (cropped) when displayed or printed. Unlike the other boxes, the crop box has no defined meaning in terms of physical page geometry or intended use; it merely imposes clipping on the page contents. However, in the absence of additional information ..., the crop box determines how the page's contents shall be positioned on the output medium. The default value is the page's media box.*
>
> —ISO-32000-1:2008, section 14.1.2

Suppose I want to print my A0 Superman poster, but I have a printer that is only able to print A4 pages. As defined in ISO-216, an A4 page can be obtained by folding an A0 page 4 times. My printing problem could be solved if I manage to split the single page shown in figure 5.9 into 16 smaller pages. See figure 5.10 for the result.

Now I can print the A0 as 16 separate pages, and I can start gluing them together into one large page. To achieve this, I'll specify a media box with size A0, but I'll use the setCropBox() method to define a crop box with size A4.

Figure 5.10   An A0 sized page divided into 16 A4 pages

Listing 5.17   Hero2.java

```
float w = PageSize.A4.getWidth();
float h = PageSize.A4.getHeight();
Rectangle rect = new Rectangle(-2*w, -2*h, 2*w, 2*h);
Rectangle crop = new Rectangle(-2*w, h, -w, 2*h);
Document document = new Document(rect);
PdfWriter writer =
  PdfWriter.getInstance(document, new FileOutputStream(filename));
writer.setCropBoxSize(crop);
document.open();
PdfContentByte content = writer.getDirectContent();
PdfTemplate template = createTemplate(content, rect, 4);
float adjust;
while(true) {
  content.addTemplate(template, -2*w, -2*h);
  adjust = crop.getRight() + w;
  if (adjust > 2 * w) {
    adjust = crop.getBottom() - h;
    if (adjust < - 2 * h)
      break;
    crop = new Rectangle(
      -2*w, adjust, -w, crop.getBottom());
  }
  else {
    crop = new Rectangle(
      crop.getRight(), crop.getBottom(),
      adjust, crop.getTop());
  }
  writer.setCropBoxSize(crop);
  document.newPage();
}
document.close();
```

① Defines MediaBox size

② Defines CropBox size

③ Sets CropBox size

④ Adds template

⑤ Defines new CropBox size

⑥ Sets new CropBox size

This code snippet crops the large image into smaller parts, sixteen times in a row. First I create a `Rectangle` that is about the size of an A0 page ❶. I'll use this object as the media box. Note that this line defines an origin with a negative *X* and *Y,* just like in the previous example. Then I create a page that's the size of an A4 page ❷. Compared to the `Rectangle` defined in ❶, it's positioned in the top-left corner of the media box. I'll use this second rectangle as the crop box ❸.

Next, I add the Superman template multiple times to the document in a loop ❹. Because of the crop box, the first page will be blank. The visible area on the A0 poster is cropped to the size of an A4 page in the upper-left corner. For the next pages, I redefine the crop box ❺. I continue with the next A4 rectangle that fits inside the A0 page to the right of the previous page. If that's not possible, I start with the first A4 rectangle on the next row. As long as I can create valid A4 pages, I use these rectangles to set a new crop box value that will be valid for the next page ❻.

The result will be a PDF document with 16 pages, each page clipped to an A4 that reveals part of the complete A0 poster.

But suppose that I don't want to print the poster myself. Instead I want to send the PDF to a graphical designer, asking them to add a nice caption, some publicity for this book, and so on. However, I don't want the image altered or overwritten, so I need to define a region that is preserved for the Superman drawing. I could use an *art box* to pass this information to a third party. That's one of the three remaining page boundaries discussed in the next section.

5.3.3 *Other page boundaries*

You can set the media box in the `Document` constructor, or with the `setPageSize()` method. You can define a crop box with the `setCropBox()` method, but there's also a `setBoxSize(String boxName, Rectangle size)` method that's more generic. Allowed names for `boxName` are `crop`, `bleed`, `trim`, and `art`.

> *The bleed box defines the region to which the contents of the page shall be clipped when output in a production environment. This may include any extra bleed area needed to accommodate the physical limitations of cutting, folding, and trimming equipment. The actual printed page may include printing marks that fall outside the bleed box. The default value is the page's crop box.*
>
> *The trim box defines the intended dimensions of the finished page after trimming. It may be smaller than the media box to allow for production-related content, such as printing instructions, cut marks, or color bars. The default value is the page's crop box.*
>
> *The art box defines the extent of the page's meaningful content (including potential white space) as intended by the page's creator. The default value is the page's crop box.*
>
> —ISO-32000-1:2008, section 14.1.2

Note that the crop, bleed, trim, and art boxes shouldn't extend beyond the boundaries of the media box. If they do, they are reduced to their intersection with the media box.

These values are important primarily for the PDF consumer. Setting these boundaries doesn't have any effect on the way iText creates the document. For instance, setting the art box doesn't affect the page margins.

Listing 5.18   Hero3.java

```
Document document = new Document(PageSize.A4);
PdfWriter writer =
   PdfWriter.getInstance(document, new FileOutputStream(filename));
Rectangle art = new Rectangle(50, 50, 545, 792);
writer.setBoxSize("art", art);
document.open();
PdfContentByte content = writer.getDirectContent();
PdfTemplate template = createTemplate(content, PageSize.A4, 1);
content.addTemplate(template, 0, 0);
document.close();
```

In the first example of the next section, you'll use the art box to retrieve information that can be used to add a header and footer.

5.4   *Adding page events to PdfWriter*

After the intermezzo about page boundaries, containing some self-glorifying examples, it's time to return to the real topic of this chapter: page events. We have already discussed seven methods of the PdfPageEvent interface; four more methods involving the document and its pages remain:

- onOpenDocument()—Triggered when a document is opened. This is a good place to initialize variables that will be needed throughout the document.
- onStartPage()—Triggered when a new page is started. Use this method for initializing variables or for setting parameters that are page-specific. Do not use this method to add content.
- onEndPage()—Triggered just before starting a new page and before closing the document. This is the best place to add a header, a footer, a watermark, and so on.
- onCloseDocument()—Triggered just before the document is closed. This is the ideal place for any finalizations and to release resources (if necessary).

Let's use these methods to solve common issues that are often mentioned in mailing-list questions. For instance, how can you add a page header while creating a PDF document.

5.4.1   *Adding a header and a footer*

Let's return to the Chapter and Section example from section 2.3.2. You'll make two small changes: you'll define an art box, and you'll add an event to the writer. This event, an instance of the HeaderFooter class, will add a header and a footer to the document as shown in figure 5.11.

First, take a look at the footer: you want to add page numbers that start with "page 1" every time a new chapter begins. The text should be put under the actual content of the

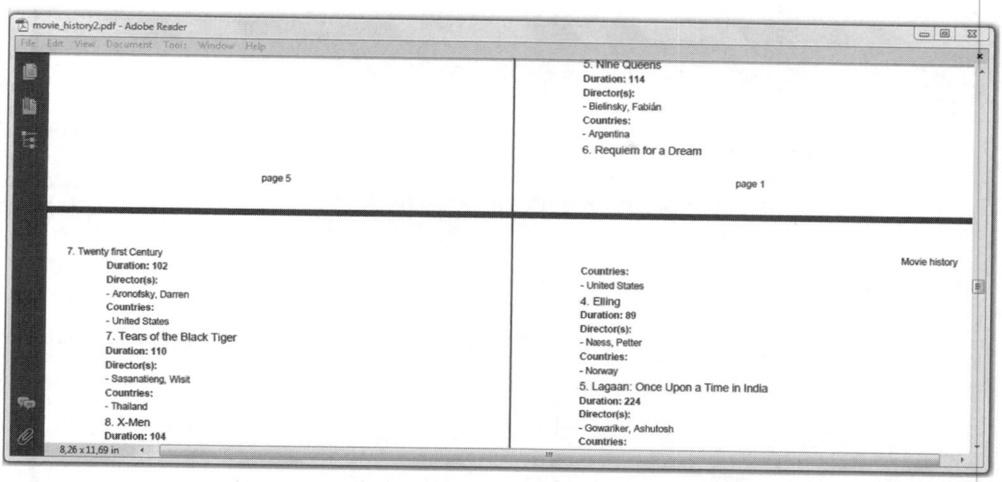

Figure 5.11   Adding headers and footers using page events

page, as a centered String. As for the header, you want it to alternate between the chapter title aligned to the left, and the String "Movie history" aligned to the right. The following implementation of the PdfPageEvent interface meets these requirements.

Listing 5.19   MovieHistory2.java

```java
class HeaderFooter extends PdfPageEventHelper {

  Phrase[] header = new Phrase[2];
  int pagenumber;

  public void onOpenDocument(PdfWriter writer, Document document) {
    header[0] = new Phrase("Movie history");
  }

  public void onChapter(PdfWriter writer, Document document,
    float paragraphPosition, Paragraph title) {
    header[1] = new Phrase(title.getContent());
    pagenumber = 1;
  }

  public void onStartPage(PdfWriter writer, Document document) {
    pagenumber++;
  }

  public void onEndPage(PdfWriter writer, Document document) {
    Rectangle rect = writer.getBoxSize("art");
    switch(writer.getPageNumber() % 2) {
      case 0:
        ColumnText.showTextAligned(writer.getDirectContent(),
          Element.ALIGN_RIGHT, header[0],
          rect.getRight(), rect.getTop(), 0);
        break;
      case 1:
```

Adds header for even pages

```
        ColumnText.showTextAligned(writer.getDirectContent(),
          Element.ALIGN_LEFT, header[1],
          rect.getLeft(), rect.getTop(), 0);
        break;
    }
    ColumnText.showTextAligned(writer.getDirectContent(),
    Element.ALIGN_CENTER, new Phrase(
      String.format("page %d", pagenumber)),
      (rect.getLeft() + rect.getRight()) / 2,
      rect.getBottom() - 18, 0);
  }
}
```

> **Adds header for odd pages**

> **Adds footer with page number**

There are no surprises in this code sample. You define two member variables:

- *header*—An array with two `Phrase` objects. One is set in `onOpenDocument()`, and it's valid for the full document. The other varies depending on the current chapter. It's set in the `onChapter()` method.
- `pagenumber`—A custom page number that is reset to 1 every time a new chapter starts. It's augmented in the `onStartPage()` method.

No content is added in the page event until a page has been completed. The header and footer are written to the direct content in the `onEndPage()` method. The parameters `writer` and `document` are to be used in the same way as done in section 5.2.

Note that you ask the writer for the art box rectangle using the `getBoxSize()` method. You use this rectangle to position the header and the footer. This will only work if you've defined that specific page boundary between steps 2 and 3 in the PDF creation process. Otherwise, the `getBoxSize()` method will return `null`.

> **FAQ** *Why is it not advised to add content in the* `onStartPage()` *method?* You'll remember from section 5.2.4 that iText ignores `newPage()` calls when the current page is empty. This method is executed—or ignored—when you call it explicitly from your code, but it's also invoked implicitly from within iText on multiple occasions. It's important that it's ignored for empty pages; otherwise you'd end up with plenty of unwanted new pages that are unintentionally left blank. If you add content in an `onStartPage()` method, there's always a risk of having unwanted pages. Consider it more safe to reserve the `onEndPage()` method for adding content.

In the next example, you'll put the page number in the header, and you'll add the total number of pages.

5.4.2   *Solving the "page X of Y" problem*

An example of a "page *X* of *Y*" header is shown in figure 5.12.

Retrieving the value of *X* is easy. You have access to the `PdfWriter` object in the `onEndPage()` method, so you can get the page number with `getPageNumber()`. But how can you retrieve the value for *Y*? There's no way of knowing the total number of pages when the headers for the first pages are written. You only know the value of *Y* for sure when iText has finished writing the last page.

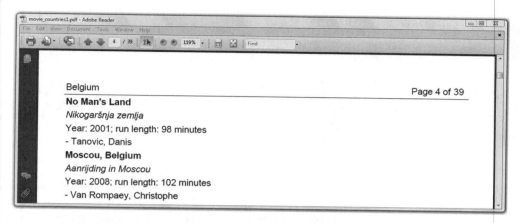

Figure 5.12   Solving the page X of Y problem with page events

There are two ways to solve this problem. One solution will be discussed in the next chapter. It involves creating the PDF in two passes. You add the content in the first pass and the header or footer in a second pass. The other solution involves a PdfTemplate object and page events.

When we discussed form XObjects in section 3.4.2, I explained that iText only writes a PdfTemplate to the OutputStream when you explicitly use the releaseTemplate() method. Otherwise the object is kept in memory until you close the Document. This opens possibilities: you can add a template to page 1, and wait until the final page to write content to this template. Even if the content stream of the first page has already been sent to the OutputStream, the content added to the template afterwards will still be shown on the first page.

Listing 5.20   MovieCountries1.java

```java
class TableHeader extends PdfPageEventHelper {
  String header;
  PdfTemplate total;

  public void setHeader(String header) {
    this.header = header;
  }

  public void onOpenDocument(PdfWriter writer, Document document) {
    total = writer.getDirectContent().createTemplate(30, 16);
  }

  public void onEndPage(PdfWriter writer, Document document) {
    PdfPTable table = new PdfPTable(3);
    try {
      table.setWidths(new int[]{24, 24, 2});
      table.setTotalWidth(527);
      table.setLockedWidth(true);
      table.getDefaultCell().setFixedHeight(20);
      table.getDefaultCell().setBorder(Rectangle.BOTTOM);
```

Creates empty template ❶

```
        table.addCell(header);
        table.getDefaultCell().setHorizontalAlignment(
          Element.ALIGN_RIGHT);
        table.addCell(
          String.format("Page %d of", writer.getPageNumber()));
        PdfPCell cell = new PdfPCell(Image.getInstance(total));
        cell.setBorder(Rectangle.BOTTOM);
        table.addCell(cell);
        table.writeSelectedRows(0, -1,
          34, 803, writer.getDirectContent());
      }
    catch(DocumentException de) {
      throw new ExceptionConverter(de);
    }
  }
  public void onCloseDocument(PdfWriter writer, Document document) {
    ColumnText.showTextAligned(total, Element.ALIGN_LEFT,
      new Phrase(String.valueOf(writer.getPageNumber() - 1)), 2, 2, 0);
  }
}
```

Adds empty template wrapped in Image ❷

Fills out template ❸

When the document is opened, you create a template with a size of 30 pt x 16 pt ❶. This time, you use a table with one row and three columns to draw the header. In the first cell, you add the text for the header. In this example, you're listing movies by country, so you'll let the header reflect the name of the country. This name is set using the setHeader() setter method.

In the second cell, you add "page *X* of" where *X* is the value returned by writer.get-PageNumber(). The third cell is special: you add the template created in the onOpen-Document() method, wrapped in an Image ❷. No content has been added to this template yet—it's just an empty canvas. It isn't until the onCloseDocument() method is invoked that you add the page number of the final page to this small canvas ❸.

> **NOTE**   When the document is closed, the newPage() method is triggered to perform finalizations on the current page. When newPage() is called, the page number is augmented, so you need to use (writer.getPageNumber() - 1) if you want to add the total number of pages in the onCloseDocument() method.

In the previous example, you added a header and footer with the showTextAligned() method. This example demonstrates that it's sometimes more interesting to use PdfPTable and writeSelectedRows(). You can define a bottom border for each cell so that the header is underlined. This is the most elegant way to add headers and footers, because the table mechanism allows you to position and align lines, images, and text.

Another common requirement when creating documents is to add a watermark.

5.4.3   *Adding a watermark*

The next example extends the previous one. The main difference is one extra feature, demonstrated in figure 5.13: we've added a watermark.

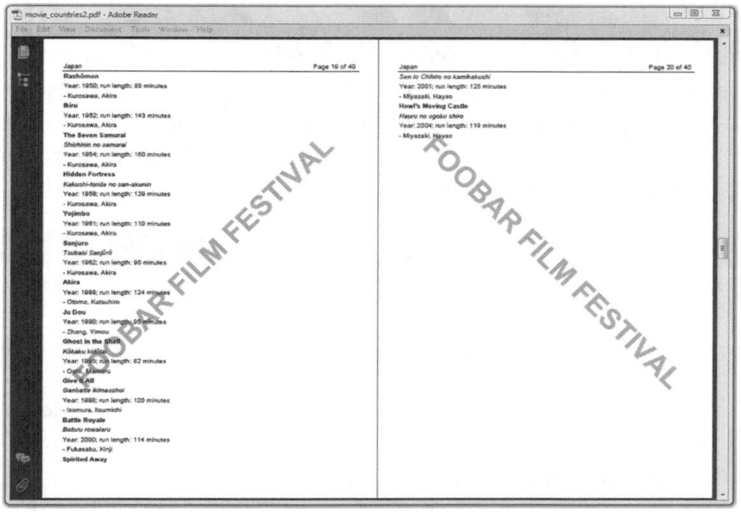

Figure 5.13 Adding a watermark using page events

The code to create this document is almost identical to the code used in the previous example. You only need to add one extra page event, the `Watermark` class.

Listing 5.21 MovieCountries2.java

```
class Watermark extends PdfPageEventHelper {
  Font FONT =
    new Font(FontFamily.HELVETICA, 52, Font.BOLD, new GrayColor(0.75f));
  public void onEndPage(PdfWriter writer, Document document) {
    ColumnText.showTextAligned(writer.getDirectContentUnder(),
      Element.ALIGN_CENTER, new Phrase("FOOBAR FILM FESTIVAL", FONT),
      297.5f, 421, writer.getPageNumber() % 2 == 1 ? 45 : -45);
  }
}
```

If your watermark is an image, you have options: you can add it with the `PdfContentByte.addImage()` method, or you can wrap it in a `ColumnText` object, or you can put it inside a cell in a table.

NOTE If you add an `Image` in a page event, be sure you create the `Image` object only once, such as in the event's constructor or in the `onOpenDocument()` method. If you create the `Image` object in `onStartPage()` or `onEndPage()`, your PDF will become bloated: you risk adding the same byte sequence over and over again. This will cost you not only in performance, but also in file size.

We'll conclude this chapter with one more example, introducing functionality that creates a document that can be displayed as a presentation, similar to a PowerPoint presentation.

5.4.4   *Creating a slideshow*

When you read a PDF document on screen, you usually hit a key, click a button, or use a scrollbar to go to the next page. But you can also let the viewer go to the next page automatically after a number of seconds, define a transition, or both.

In the example, you'll set the viewer preferences to "Full Screen" mode ❶, because you want to use the PDF as a presentation.

Listing 5.22   MovieSlideShow.java

```
class TransitionDuration extends PdfPageEventHelper {
  public void onStartPage(PdfWriter writer, Document document) {
    writer.setTransition(new PdfTransition(PdfTransition.DISSOLVE, 3));   ◄
    writer.setDuration(5);   ◄
  }
}
public void createPdf(String filename)
  throws IOException, DocumentException, SQLException {
  DatabaseConnection connection = new HsqldbConnection("filmfestival");
  Document document = new Document(PageSize.A5.rotate());
  PdfWriter writer =
    PdfWriter.getInstance(document, new FileOutputStream(filename));
  writer.setPdfVersion(PdfWriter.VERSION_1_5);
  writer.setViewerPreferences(PdfWriter.PageModeFullScreen);   ◄
  writer.setPageEvent(new TransitionDuration());   ◄
  document.open();
  List movies = PojoFactory.getMovies(connection);
  Image img;
  PdfPCell cell;
  PdfPTable table = new PdfPTable(6);
  for (Movie movie : movies) {
    img = Image.getInstance(String.format(RESOURCE, movie.getImdb()));
    cell = new PdfPCell(img, true);
    cell.setBorder(PdfPCell.NO_BORDER);
    table.addCell(cell);
  }
  document.add(table);
  document.close();
  connection.close();
}
```

Sets duration for new page

Sets transition for new page

Sets event

Changes page mode to Full Screen ❶

There are two new special methods in onStartPage():

- setDuration()—This method's parameter defines for how many seconds the page is shown. If no duration is defined, user input is expected to go to the next page.
- setTransition()—This method expects a Transition object. The main constructor of this class takes two parameters: a transition type and a value for the duration of the transition. Don't confuse this with the value for the page duration.

There are different groups of transition types:

- *Dissolve*—The old page gradually dissolves to reveal a new one (DISSOLVE).
- *Glitter*—Similar to dissolve, except that the effect sweeps across the page in a wide band: diagonally (DGLITTER), from top to bottom (TBGLITTER), or from left to right (LRGLITTER).
- *Box*—A rectangular box sweeps inward from the edges (INBOX) or outward from the center (OUTBOX).
- *Split*—The lines sweep across the screen horizontally or vertically, depending on the value that was passed: SPLITHIN, SPLITHOUT, SPLITVIN, or SPLITVOUT.
- *Blinds*—Multiple lines, evenly spaced across the screen, sweep in the same direction to reveal the new page horizontally (BLINDH) or vertically (BLINDV).
- *Wipe*—A single line sweeps across the screen from one edge to the other: from top to bottom (TWIPE), from bottom to top (BWIPE), from right to left (RLWIPE), or from left to right (LRWIPE).

If you don't specify a type, BLINDH is used. The default duration of a transition is 1 second. This is a nice example showing how onStartPage() can be used to set page parameters, because you need to set the transition and duration for every page.

With this example, we've covered all the methods of the PdfPageEvent interface. It's high time for a short summary of this chapter, and of part 1 as a whole.

5.5 *Summary*

After a short introduction to what you can do with PDF, we started with the basic mechanics of iText's PDF creation process. You created several "Hello World" examples that demonstrated the famous "five steps" that were used in every example of part 1.

Two chapters dealt with building blocks offered by iText, allowing you to create PDF documents using high-level concepts. In chapter 2, you learned about Chunks, Phrases, Paragraphs, Lists, ListItems, Anchors, Images, Chapters, and Sections. Chapter 4 was dedicated entirely to the PdfPTable and PdfPCell objects.

Chapter 3 explained how to add content at a lower level: you added lines, shapes, and text to different direct content layers. You also discovered two other important objects: using the ColumnText object, you added high-level objects at absolute positions; with PdfTemplate you learned how to reuse content as an XObject.

You've made good use of that knowledge in this chapter. First you found a way to extend the functionality of PdfPTable and PdfPCell using table and cell events. Then you learned how to use the PdfPageEvent interface. Initially you added custom features to Chunk, Paragraph, Chapter, and Section objects. After an intermezzo about pagination, involving reordering pages, adding blank pages, and defining page boundaries, you used a second series of page events to solve a number of common issues: adding headers and footers, adding "page *X* of *Y*" to every page, adding watermarks, and even defining a duration and a transition for each page.

Now that you've finished part 1, you're ready to start writing a prototype application that creates PDF documents from scratch. If you need to integrate this prototype into a web application, you'll have to read further in part 3. That's where you'll learn how to generate a PDF document using Java servlet technology. Also, when you want to make your application production-ready, you'll probably want to know more about using special fonts, about protecting your documents, and so on. Part 3 will teach you these essential iText skills.

But first, we'll take a look at another aspect of iText programming. In part 2, you'll learn how to manipulate existing PDF documents: how to import pages from one PDF document into another, how to stamp content on an existing PDF document, how to split one PDF into smaller PDFs, how to combine different PDFs into one large document, and so on. You'll also learn how to fill out interactive forms using iText.

Part 2

Manipulating existing PDF documents

Part 2 deals with existing PDF files, be they documents created with iText as discussed in part 1, or PDFs created with Adobe Acrobat, Open Office, or any other PDF producer. You'll learn different ways to copy, stamp, split, and merge documents. You'll add actions and JavaScript, and you'll learn all about filling out interactive forms.

Working with existing PDFs

6

When I wrote the first book about iText, the publisher didn't like the subtitle "Creating and *Manipulating* PDF." He didn't like the word *manipulating* because of some of its pejorative meanings. If you consult the dictionary on *Yahoo! education*, you'll find the following definitions:

- To influence or manage shrewdly or deviously
- To tamper with or falsify for personal gain

Obviously, that's not what the book is about. The publisher suggested "Creating and *Editing* PDF" as a better subtitle. I explained that PDF isn't a document format well suited for editing. PDF is an end product. It's a *display* format. It's *not* a *word processing* format.

In a word processing format, the content is distributed over different pages when you open the document in an application, not earlier. This has some disadvantages: if you open the same document in different applications, you can end up with a different page count. The same text snippet can be on page *X* when looked at in Microsoft Word, and on page *Y* when viewed in Open Office. That's exactly the kind of problem you want to avoid by choosing PDF.

In a PDF document, every character or glyph on a PDF page has its fixed position, regardless of the application that's used to view the document. This is an advantage, but it also comes with a disadvantage. Suppose you want to replace the word "edit" with the word "manipulate" in a sentence, you'd have to *reflow* the text. You'd have to reposition all the characters that follow that word. Maybe you'd even have to move a portion of the text to the next page. That's not trivial, if not impossible.

If you want to "edit" a PDF, it's advised that you change the original source of the document and remake the PDF. If the original document was written using Microsoft Word, change the Word document, and make the PDF from the new version of the Word document. Don't expect any tool to be able to edit a PDF file the same way you'd edit a Word document.

This being said, the verb "to manipulate" also means

- To move, arrange, operate, or control by the hands or by mechanical means, especially in a skillful manner

That's exactly what you're going to do in this chapter. Using iText, you're going to manipulate the pages of a PDF file in a skillful manner. You're going to treat a PDF document as if it were made of digital paper.

But before you can take copies of pages or add new content, you'll need an object that can "read" an existing PDF document.

6.1 Accessing an existing PDF with PdfReader

First, we'll look at how you can retrieve information about the document you're going to manipulate. For instance, how many pages does the original document have? Which page size is used? All of this is done with a `PdfReader` object.

6.1.1 Retrieving information about the document and its pages

In this first example, we'll inspect some of the PDF documents you created in part 1. You can query a `PdfReader` instance to get the number of pages in the document, the rectangle defining the media box, the rotation of the page, and so on.

Listing 6.1 PageInformation.java

```
public static void inspect(PrintWriter writer, String filename)
  throws IOException {
  PdfReader reader = new PdfReader(filename);
  writer.println(filename);
  writer.print("Number of pages: ");
  writer.println(reader.getNumberOfPages());
```

```
    Rectangle mediabox = reader.getPageSize(1);
    writer.print("Size of page 1: [");
    writer.print(mediabox.getLeft());
    writer.print(',');
    writer.print(mediabox.getBottom());
    writer.print(',');
    writer.print(mediabox.getRight());
    writer.print(',');
    writer.print(mediabox.getTop());
    writer.println("]");
    writer.print("Rotation of page 1: ");
    writer.println(reader.getPageRotation(1));
    writer.print("Page size with rotation of page 1: ");
    writer.println(reader.getPageSizeWithRotation(1));
    writer.print("File length: ");
    writer.println(reader.getFileLength());
    writer.print("Is rebuilt? ");
    writer.println(reader.isRebuilt());
    writer.print("Is encrypted? ");
    writer.println(reader.isEncrypted());
    writer.println();
    writer.flush();
}
```

The following output was obtained while inspecting some of the PDFs from chapters 1 ❶ and ❷, 3 ❸, and 5 ❹.

```
results/part1/chapter01/hello_landscape1.pdf
Number of pages: 1
Size of page 1: [0.0,0.0,612.0,792.0]
Rotation of page 1: 90
Page size with rotation of page 1:
  Rectangle: 792.0x612.0 (rot: 90 degrees)
Is rebuilt? false
Is encrypted? false
```

**Output from PDF
in chapter 1**

```
results/part1/chapter01/hello_landscape2.pdf
Number of pages: 1
Size of page 1: [0.0,0.0,792.0,612.0]
Rotation of page 1: 0
Page size with rotation of page 1:
  Rectangle: 792.0x612.0 (rot: 0 degrees)
Is rebuilt? false
Is encrypted? false
```

**Output from PDF
in chapter 1**

```
results/part1/chapter03/movie_templates.pdf
Number of pages: 8
Size of page 1: [0.0,0.0,595.0,842.0]
Rotation of page 1: 90
Page size with rotation of page 1:
  Rectangle: 842.0x595.0 (rot: 90 degrees)
Is rebuilt? false
Is encrypted? false
```

**Output from PDF
in chapter 3**

```
results/part1/chapter05/hero1.pdf
Number of pages: 1
```

**Output from PDF
in chapter 5**

```
Size of page 1: [-1192.0,-1685.0,1192.0,1685.0]
Rotation of page 1: 0
Page size with rotation of page 1:
  Rectangle: 2384.0x3370.0 (rot: 0 degrees)
Is rebuilt? false
Is encrypted? false
```

**Output from PDF
in chapter 5**

The most important `PdfReader` methods you'll use in this chapter are `getNumberOf-Pages()` and `getPageSizeWithRotation()`. The former method will be used to loop over all the pages of the existing document; the latter is a combination of the methods `getPageSize()` and `getPageRotation()`.

PAGE SIZE

The first two examples show the difference between creating a document with landscape orientation using

```
Document document = new Document(PageSize.LETTER.rotate());
```

and a document created using

```
Document document = new Document(new Rectangle(792, 612));
```

This difference will matter when you import a page or when you stamp extra content on the page. Observe that in example ❹ of the earlier output, the coordinates of the lower-left corner are different from (0,0) because that's how I defined the media box in section 5.3.1.

BROKEN PDFS

When you open a corrupt PDF file in Adobe Reader, you can expect the message, "There was an error opening this document. The file is damaged and could not be repaired." `PdfReader` will also throw an exception when you try to read such a file. You can get an `InvalidPdfException` with the following message: "Rebuild failed: trailer not found; original message: PDF startxref not found." If that happens, iText can't do anything about it: the file *is* damaged, and it *can't* be repaired. You'll have to contact the person who created the document, and ask him or her to create a version of the document that's a valid PDF file.

In other cases, for example if a rogue application added unwanted carriage return characters, Adobe Reader will open the document and either ignore the fact that the PDF isn't syntactically correct, or will show the warning "The file is damaged but is being repaired" very briefly. `PdfReader` can also overcome small damages like this. No alert box is shown, because iText isn't necessarily used in an environment with a GUI. You can use the method `isRebuilt()` to check whether or not a PDF needed repairing.

You may also have difficulties trying to read encrypted PDF files.

ENCRYPTED PDFS

PDF files can be protected by two passwords: a user password and an owner password. If a PDF is protected with a user password, you'll have to enter this password before you can open the document in Adobe Reader. If a document has an owner password, you must provide the password along with the constructor when creating a `PdfReader` instance, or a BadPasswordException will be thrown. More details about the different ways you can encrypt a PDF document, and about the different permissions you can set, will follow in chapter 12.

6.1.2 *Reducing the memory use of PdfReader*

In most of this book's examples, you'll create an instance of PdfReader using a String representing the path to the existing PDF file. Using this constructor will cause PdfReader to load plenty of PDF objects (from the file) into Java objects (in memory). This can be overkill for large documents, especially if you're only interested in part of the document. If that's the case, you can choose to read the PDF only partially.

PARTIAL READS

Suppose you have a document with 1000 pages. PdfReader will do a full read of these pages, even if you're only interested in page 1. You can avoid this by using another constructor. You can compare the memory used by different PdfReader instances created to read the timetable PDF from chapter 3:

Listing 6.2   MemoryInfo.java

```
public static void main(String[] args) throws IOException {
  MovieTemplates.main(args);
  PrintWriter writer = new PrintWriter(new FileOutputStream(RESULT));
  fullRead(writer, MovieTemplates.RESULT);
  partialRead(writer, MovieTemplates.RESULT);
  writer.close();
}
public static void fullRead(PrintWriter writer, String filename)
  throws IOException {
  long before = getMemoryUse();
  PdfReader reader = new PdfReader(filename);
  reader.getNumberOfPages();
  writer.println(String.format("Memory used by full read: %d",
    getMemoryUse() - before));
  writer.flush();
}
public static void partialRead(PrintWriter writer, String filename)
  throws IOException {
  long before = getMemoryUse();
  PdfReader reader = new PdfReader(
    new RandomAccessFileOrArray(filename), null);
  reader.getNumberOfPages();
  writer.println(String.format("Memory used by partial read: %d",
    getMemoryUse() - before));
  writer.flush();
}
```

The file size of the timetable document from chapter 3 is 15 KB. The memory used by a full read is about 35 KB, but a partial read needs only 4 KB. This is a significant difference. When reading a file partially, more memory will be used as soon as you start working with the reader object, but PdfReader won't cache unnecessary objects. That also makes a huge difference, so if you're dealing with large documents, consider using `PdfReader` with a `RandomAccessFileOrArray` parameter constructed with a path to a file.

> **NOTE** In part 4, you'll see how to manipulate a PDF at the lowest level. You'll change PDF objects in `PdfReader` and then save the altered PDF. For this to work, the modified objects need to be cached. Depending on the changes you want to apply, using a `PdfReader` instance created with a `RandomAccessFile-OrArray` may not be an option.

Another way to reduce the memory usage of `PdfReader` up front is to reduce the number of pages before you start working with it.

SELECTING PAGES

Next, you'll read the timetable from example 3 once again, but you'll immediately tell `PdfReader` that you're only interested in pages 4 to 8.

Listing 6.3   SelectPages.java

```
PdfReader reader = new PdfReader(MovieTemplates.RESULT);
reader.selectPages("4-8");
```

The general syntax for the range that's used in the `selectPages()` method looks like this:

```
[!] [o] [odd] [e] [even] start [-end]
```

You can have multiple ranges separated by commas, and the ! modifier removes pages from what is already selected. The range changes are incremental; numbers are added or deleted as the range appears. The `start` or the `end` can be omitted; if you omit both, you need at least o (odd; selects all odd pages) or e (even; selects all even pages).

If you ask the reader object for the number of pages *before* `selectPages()` in listing 6.3, it will tell you that the document has 8 pages. If you do the same *after* making the page selection, it will tell you that there are only 5 pages: pages 4, 5, 6, 7, and 8. The old page 4 will be the new page 1. Be careful not to try getting information about pages that are outside the new range. Don't add the following line to listing 6.3:

```
reader.getPageSize(6);
```

This line will throw a `NullPointerException` because there are no longer 6 pages in the reader object.

Now that you've had a short introduction to `PdfReader`, you're ready to start manipulating existing PDF documents.

6.2   *Copying pages from existing PDF documents*

You probably remember the Superman PDF from chapter 5. The `Hero` example imported a plain text file containing PDF syntax into the direct content. I explained that this wasn't standard practice. If you want to reuse existing content, it's dangerous to copy and paste PDF syntax like I did in listing 5.14. There are safer ways to import existing content, as you'll find out in the next example.

In this section, you'll use an object named `PdfImportedPage` to copy the content from an existing PDF opened with `PdfReader` into a new `Document` written by `PdfWriter`.

6.2.1 Importing pages

Let's continue working with the timetable from chapter 3. Suppose you want to reuse the pages of this document and treat them as if every page were an image. Figure 6.1 shows how you could organize these imported pages into a `PdfPTable`. The document in the front of figure 6.1 is created with the code in listing 6.4.

Listing 6.4   ImportingPages1.java

```java
Document document = new Document();                          ←— Step 1
PdfWriter writer = PdfWriter.getInstance(
  document, new FileOutputStream(RESULT));       Step 2
document.open();                                            ←— Step 3
PdfPTable table = new PdfPTable(2);
PdfReader reader = new PdfReader(MovieTemplates.RESULT);
int n = reader.getNumberOfPages();
PdfImportedPage page;
for (int i = 1; i <= n; i++) {
  page = writer.getImportedPage(reader, i);
  table.addCell(Image.getInstance(page));
}
document.add(table);                             ←— Step 4
document.close();                    ←— Step 5
```

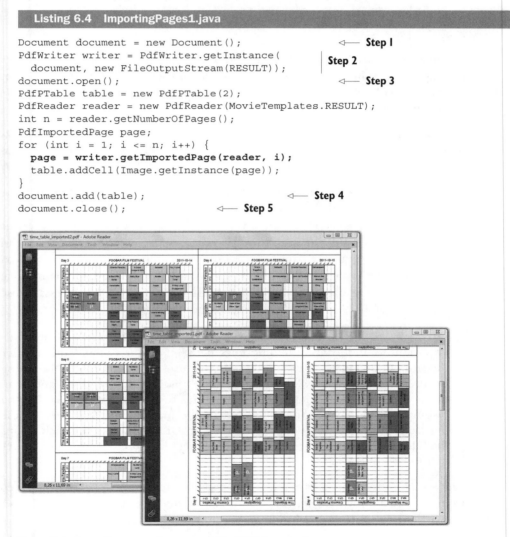

Figure 6.1   Importing pages from an existing PDF document

You'll recognize the five steps in the PDF creation process discussed in part 1. Now you're also creating a `PdfReader` object and looping over all the pages, getting `PdfImportedPage` instances with the `getImportedPage()` method (as highlighted in bold). What does this method do?

PAGE CONTENT AND RESOURCES

If you browse the API of the `PdfReader` class, you'll discover the `getPageContent()` method, which returns the content stream of a page. This content stream is very similar to what's inside the hero.txt file. In general, such a content stream contains references to external objects, images, and fonts.

In section 3.4.1, for instance, we examined the PDF syntax needed to draw a raster image:

```
q 232 0 0 362 25.5 27 cm /img0 Do Q
```

In this snippet, `/img0` referred to a key in the `/Resources` dictionary of the page. The corresponding value was a reference to a stream object containing the bits and bytes of the image. Without the bits and bytes of the image, the PDF syntax referring to `/img0` is meaningless.

> **WARNING** It doesn't make sense to get the content stream of a page from one PDF document, and copy that stream into another PDF *without* copying all the resources that are needed.

The `Hero` example was an exception: the syntax to draw the vector image of Superman was self-contained, and this is very unusual. As soon as there's text involved, you'll have at least a reference to a font. If you don't copy that font, you'll get warnings or errors, such as "Could not find a font in the Resources dictionary." That's why it's never advisable to extract a page from `PdfReader` directly. Instead, you should pass the reader object to the writer class, and ask the writer (not the reader!) to import a page. A `PdfImportedPage` object is returned. Behind the scenes, all the necessary resources (such as images and fonts) are retrieved and copied to the writer.

> **FAQ** *Why are all my links lost when I copy a page with* `PdfImportedPage`*?* It's important to understand the difference between resources needed to render the content of a page and the interactive features of a page. In general, these features are called *annotations*. They include links, text annotations, and form fields. Annotations aren't part of the content stream. They aren't listed in the resources dictionary of the page, but in the annotation dictionary. These interactive features aren't copied when using `PdfImportedPage`, which means that all interactivity is lost when copying a page with the `getImportedPage()` method of the `PdfWriter` class.

The `PdfImportedPage` class extends `PdfTemplate`, but you can't add any new content to it. It's a read-only XObject you can reuse in a document with the method `addTemplate()`; or you can wrap it inside an `Image`. You've already used these techniques in section 3.4. The original dimensions of each imported page are the same as the original media box, but in this example, the PdfImportedPages are scaled to fit inside a table. Note that the rotation of the original page isn't taken into account. If that's a problem, you'll have to apply the rotation.

Listing 6.5 ImportingPages2.java

```
PdfPTable table = new PdfPTable(2);
for (int i = 1; i <= n; i++) {
  page = writer.getImportedPage(reader, i);
  table.getDefaultCell().setRotation(-reader.getPageRotation(i));
  table.addCell(Image.getInstance(page));
}
```

You can see the result in figure 6.1 (the figure in the back). Observe that cell and image rotations go counterclockwise. In the next example, we'll look at how to apply more transformations.

6.2.2 Scaling and superimposing pages

You can transform pages in iText, just like you can transform images. Do you remember figure 3.2? That was the image I used to explain the different content layers used by iText. I created this image by generating a document with four pages, and then importing those pages into a new one; see figure 6.2.

The imported pages are added to the new PDF document using addTemplate(). The parameters are calculated so that each page is scaled and skewed.

Figure 6.2   Scaling and skewing pages from an existing PDF

Listing 6.6   Layers.java

```
PdfContentByte canvas = writer.getDirectContent();
PdfImportedPage page;
BaseFont bf = BaseFont.createFont(BaseFont.ZAPFDINGBATS, "",
    BaseFont.EMBEDDED);
for (int i = 0; i < reader.getNumberOfPages(); ) {
  page = writer.getImportedPage(reader, ++i);
  canvas.addTemplate(page, 1f, 0, 0.4f, 0.4f, 72, 50 * i);
  canvas.beginText();
  canvas.setFontAndSize(bf, 20);
  canvas.showTextAligned(Element.ALIGN_CENTER,
    String.valueOf((char)(181 + i)), 496, 150 + 50 * i, 0);
  canvas.endText();
}
```

A common technique used with PDF files is called *superimposing*.

SUPERIMPOSING PDF PAGES

Superimposing means that you add different PDF pages on top of each other on the same page. You could do this with the four pages shown to the left in figure 6.2 to obtain the PDF shown in figure 6.3.

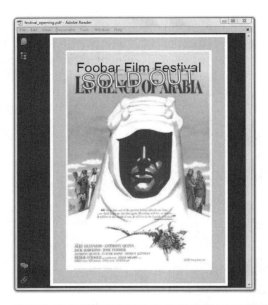

Figure 6.3   PDF created by superimposing four different pages

Listing 6.7   Superimposing.java

```
PdfReader reader = new PdfReader(SOURCE);
Document document = new Document(PageSize.POSTCARD);
PdfWriter writer = PdfWriter.getInstance(document,
    new FileOutputStream(RESULT));
document.open();
PdfContentByte canvas = writer.getDirectContent();
PdfImportedPage page;
```

```
for (int i = 1; i <= reader.getNumberOfPages(); i++) {
  page = writer.getImportedPage(reader, i);
  canvas.addTemplate(page, 1f, 0, 0, 1, 0, 0);
}
document.close();
```

Superimposing is often used to create documents with a standard header and footer.

IMPORTING COMPANY STATIONERY

Suppose your company has preprinted paper containing the company name and logo in the letterhead, and maybe also a watermark. All letters are printed on this company stationery. You can achieve something similar with PDF, as shown in figure 6.4.

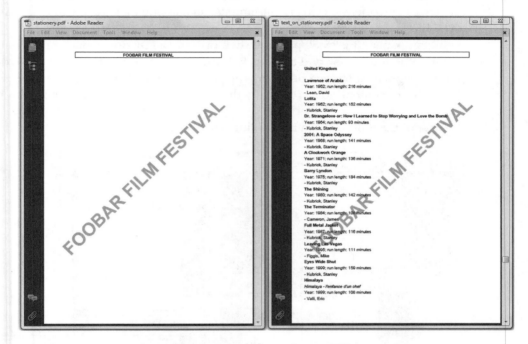

Figure 6.4   Using an existing PDF as background image for new PDFs

In figure 6.4, the PDF to the left is the equivalent of the preprinted paper. When creating a new document, as shown to the right, the template page is imported and added to the background of each new page using a page event.

Listing 6.8   Stationery.java

```
public class Stationery extends PdfPageEventHelper {
  protected PdfImportedPage page;

  public void useStationary(PdfWriter writer) throws IOException {
    writer.setPageEvent(this);
    PdfReader reader = new PdfReader(STATIONERY);
    page = writer.getImportedPage(reader, 1);
```

```
  }
  public void onEndPage(PdfWriter writer, Document document) {
    writer.getDirectContentUnder().addTemplate(page, 0, 0);
  }
}
```

We'll conclude the series of PdfImportedPage examples by introducing two more concepts.

6.2.3   *N-up copying and tiling PDF documents*

When searching for PDF tools on the internet, you'll find numerous small tools that are designed to meet specific requirements, such as one that creates an *N*-up layout in a PDF file.

To cut paper costs by 50 percent when printing a PDF document, you can copy an existing PDF into a new one that has half the number of pages. All you have to do is put two pages next to each other on one page. This is called 2-up copying. Figure 6.5 shows the document you created in the previous example in its 2-up, 4-up, 8-up, and 16-up forms.

Most of the tools you can find online have iText on the inside.

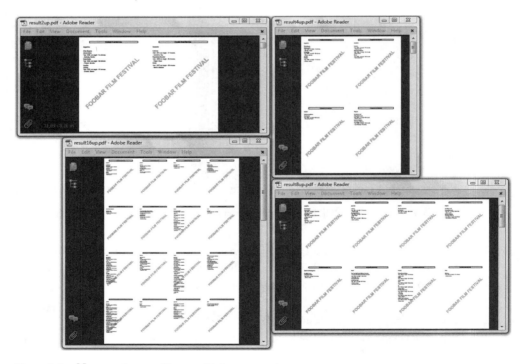

Figure 6.5   *N*-up copying combines multiple pages onto one page

Listing 6.9 NUp.java

```java
public void manipulatePdf(String src, String dest, int pow)
  throws IOException, DocumentException {
  PdfReader reader = new PdfReader(src);
  Rectangle pageSize = reader.getPageSize(1);
  Rectangle newSize = (pow % 2) == 0 ?
    new Rectangle(
      pageSize.getWidth(), pageSize.getHeight()) :
    new Rectangle(
      pageSize.getHeight(), pageSize.getWidth());
  Rectangle unitSize = new Rectangle(
    pageSize.getWidth(), pageSize.getHeight());
  for (int i = 0; i < pow; i++) {
    unitSize = new Rectangle(
      unitSize.getHeight() / 2, unitSize.getWidth());
  }
  int n = (int)Math.pow(2, pow);
  int r = (int)Math.pow(2, pow / 2);
  int c = n / r;

  Document document = new Document(newSize, 0, 0, 0, 0);
  PdfWriter writer = PdfWriter.getInstance(document,
    new FileOutputStream(String.format(dest, n)));
  document.open();
  PdfContentByte cb = writer.getDirectContent();
  PdfImportedPage page;
  Rectangle currentSize;
  float offsetX, offsetY, factor;
  int total = reader.getNumberOfPages();
  for (int i = 0; i < total; ) {
    if (i % n == 0) {
      document.newPage();
    }
    currentSize = reader.getPageSize(++i);
    factor = Math.min(
      unitSize.getWidth() / currentSize.getWidth(),
      unitSize.getHeight() / currentSize.getHeight());
    offsetX = unitSize.getWidth() * ((i % n) % c)
      +(unitSize.getWidth()
      - (currentSize.getWidth() * factor))/2f;
    offsetY = newSize.getHeight()
      - (unitSize.getHeight() * (((i % n) / c) + 1))
      + (unitSize.getHeight()
      - (currentSize.getHeight() * factor))/2f;
    page = writer.getImportedPage(reader, i);
    cb.addTemplate(page,
      factor, 0, 0, factor, offsetX, offsetY);
  }
  document.close();
}
```

Annotations:
- Gets original page size
- Sets page size of new document
- Calculates page size of unit
- Calculates helper variables
- Calculates scale factor
- Calculates offset
- Scales and positions page

Figure 6.6   Scaling and tiling a PDF file

The opposite of *N*-up copying a PDF file is when you have one page, and you want to print it on different pages; see figure 6.6. We already looked at this in chapter 5, but now you'll do the exercise again using PdfImportedPage.

The next bit of code takes one page from a PDF document and scales it so that the one page is "tiled" over 16 pages.

Listing 6.10   TilingHero.java

```
public void manipulatePdf(String src, String dest)
  throws IOException, DocumentException {
  PdfReader reader = new PdfReader(src);
  Rectangle pagesize = reader.getPageSizeWithRotation(1);
  Document document = new Document(pagesize);
  PdfWriter writer =
    PdfWriter.getInstance(document, new FileOutputStream(dest));
  document.open();
  PdfContentByte content = writer.getDirectContent();
  PdfImportedPage page = writer.getImportedPage(reader, 1);
  float x, y;
  for (int i = 0; i < 16; i++) {
    x = -pagesize.getWidth() * (i % 4);
    y = pagesize.getHeight() * (i / 4 - 3);
    content.addTemplate(page, 4, 0, 0, 4, x, y);
    document.newPage();
  }
  document.close();
}
```

In this section, we've been reusing content from existing PDF documents in a new document. You can take digital photocopies of existing pages, scale them up or down, and use them as if they were an image or an XObject.

In the next section, we're going to take an existing PDF and add extra content.

6.3 *Adding content with PdfStamper*

Up until now, we've created new documents using the five steps in the iText document-creation process. In this chapter we'll add content to an existing document using `PdfStamper`.

`PdfStamper` uses a different mechanism, as demonstrated in the `manipulateWith-Stamper()` method.

Listing 6.11   SelectPages.java

```
public static void main(String[] args)
  throws IOException, DocumentException {
  new MovieTemplates().createPdf(MovieTemplates.RESULT);
  PdfReader reader = new PdfReader(MovieTemplates.RESULT);    ❶
  reader.selectPages("4-8");
  manipulateWithStamper(reader);
  ...
}
private static void manipulateWithStamper(PdfReader reader)
  throws IOException, DocumentException {
  PdfStamper stamper =
    new PdfStamper(reader, new FileOutputStream(RESULT1));     ❷
  stamper.close();
}
```

You've already seen part of this example in listing 6.3. It's an example that creates a new PDF document containing only a selection of pages from the original document. In ❶, you create a `PdfReader` that will read the 8 pages of the timetable PDF, but you immediately tell the reader that you're only interested in pages 4 to 8. In ❷, you create a `PdfStamper` object. As soon as you close the stamper, a new document will be created. It will contain only 5 pages. You can add content between the constructor and the `close()` method.

6.3.1 *Adding content at absolute positions*

Let's start with the "Hello World" examples with paper size Letter in landscape format from chapter 1. There were two versions of this example. Let's add the words "Hello people!"

Listing 6.12   StampText.java

```
PdfReader reader = new PdfReader(src);
PdfStamper stamper = new PdfStamper(reader, new FileOutputStream(dest));
PdfContentByte canvas = stamper.getOverContent(1);
ColumnText.showTextAligned(canvas,
  Element.ALIGN_LEFT, new Phrase("Hello people!"), 36, 540, 0);
stamper.close();
```

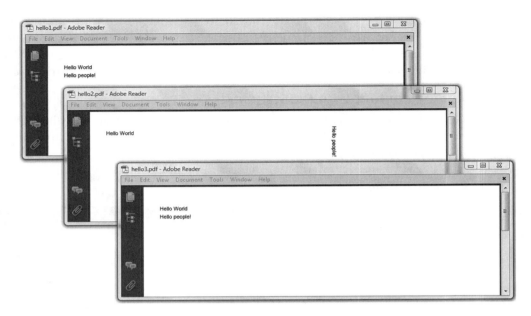

Figure 6.7   Adding text to an existing document

The getOverContent() method is similar to the getDirectContent() method discussed in chapter 3. It returns a PdfContentByte object that allows you to write to a new layer that goes on top of the existing content of the page you choose. There's also a getUnderContent() method, which is the equivalent of getDirectContentUnder().

> **NOTE**   The methods getOverContent() and getUnderContent() give you the option to write to the direct content on a layer that goes on top of or below the existing content. They don't give you access to the layer with the existing content. You can't use these methods to replace existing content, nor to complete it. It's not possible to say: "I want to add the words 'Hello people!' after the words 'Hello World'." You can only add those words to the layer above or below the existing content at an absolute position whose coordinates you know.

The media box of the file that was used as the basis for hello3.pdf was 792 pt x 612 pt. I've added the extra text at the coordinates (36,540). That's near the top-left corner. The file used as the basis for hello1.pdf had a media box measuring 612 pt x 792 pt, but the page had a rotation of 90 degrees. The difference between these two ways of creating a page in landscape is made transparent: iText took the rotation into account and rotated the coordinate system. If you don't want this, you can tell iText to ignore the fact that the page is rotated. That's what happened with hello2.pdf in figure 6.7.

In the next code snippet, the extra text was added at the same coordinates as in listing 6.12, but the rotation of the page isn't taken into account. This is prevented with the setRotateContents() method.

Listing 6.13 StampText.java (continued)

```
PdfReader reader = new PdfReader(src);
PdfStamper stamper = new PdfStamper(reader, new FileOutputStream(dest));
stamper.setRotateContents(false);
PdfContentByte canvas = stamper.getOverContent(1);
ColumnText.showTextAligned(canvas,
  Element.ALIGN_LEFT, new Phrase("Hello people!"), 36, 540, 0);
stamper.close();
```

We could now repeat everything that we covered in chapter 3, and explain how to draw lines, shapes, and text to the PdfContentByte layers obtained with getOverContent() and getUnderContent(), but it's a better idea to look at practical examples.

6.3.2 *Creating a PDF in multiple passes*

In section 5.4.2, we solved the "page *X* of *Y*" problem by using page events and a PdfTemplate object. One of the problems inherent to this solution is that you don't know the number of pages when you create and position the placeholder. You create a small canvas up front, but you can only add the page number once the document is completely finished. You don't know in advance how much space will be needed to draw this number. Will the document eventually have 9 pages or 9999? You could guess the number of digits beforehand and reserve enough space for them accordingly, but you won't always be able to make the right guess.

That's why you might consider an alternative way to add page numbers. The document shown in figure 6.8 is made in two passes.

In the first pass, the document is created without a header. The header, and—if necessary—a footer and a watermark, can be added in a second pass. Note that it isn't necessary to create two files on disk. If the file size isn't huge, and the memory available in your JVM allows it, you can easily keep the file created during the first pass in memory.

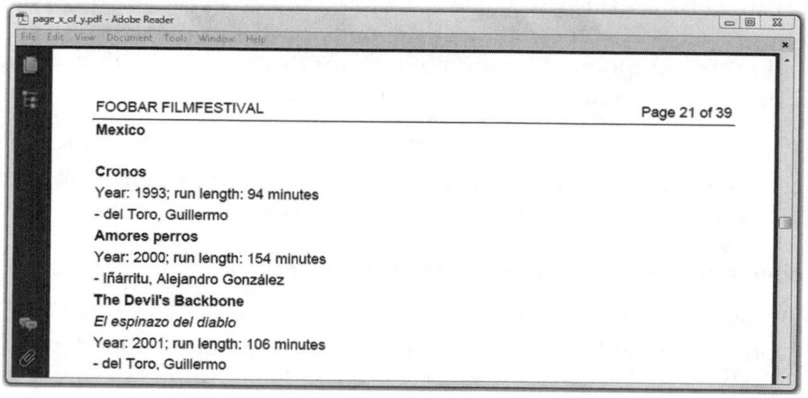

Figure 6.8 Adding a page *X* of *Y* header to an existing document

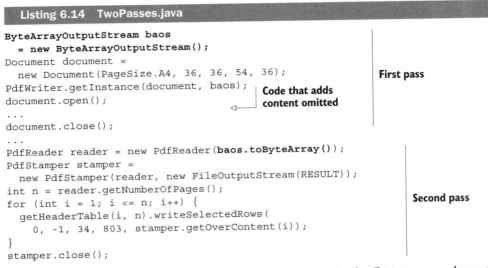

Listing 6.14 TwoPasses.java

```
ByteArrayOutputStream baos
  = new ByteArrayOutputStream();
Document document =
  new Document(PageSize.A4, 36, 36, 54, 36);
PdfWriter.getInstance(document, baos);
document.open();
...
document.close();
...
PdfReader reader = new PdfReader(baos.toByteArray());
PdfStamper stamper =
  new PdfStamper(reader, new FileOutputStream(RESULT));
int n = reader.getNumberOfPages();
for (int i = 1; i <= n; i++) {
  getHeaderTable(i, n).writeSelectedRows(
    0, -1, 34, 803, stamper.getOverContent(i));
}
stamper.close();
```

First pass

Code that adds
content omitted

Second pass

Instead of writing the document to a `FileOutputStream` in the first pass, you keep the file in memory using a `ByteArrayOutputStream` (see section 1.3.2). In the second pass, you use the bytes from this `OutputStream` to create a `PdfReader` instance.

> **FAQ** `PdfStamper` *always creates a new PDF file, but how can I manipulate the existing file?* You can't use the same physical file used by `PdfReader` to create a `FileOutputStream` for `PdfStamper`. Common sense tells us that changing a file while you're still reading it risks corrupting the file. There are different ways to work around this. Some applications read a file into memory before changing it; you could read the original file into a byte array and create a `PdfReader` object as demonstrated in listing 6.13. Other applications work with temporary files; once you've finished "stamping," you could replace the original file with the new one. Finally, you could also create the new file in memory using a `ByteArrayOutputStream`, and then overwrite the original file using these bytes. The "best choice" depends on the context. As a rule of thumb, I prefer temporary files for applications that run on the desktop; in a web environment, I create all files in memory.

In section 6.2, you added an existing PDF as the background of a newly created PDF using page events. But suppose you're given an existing PDF, and you need to add company stationery after the fact. That's what the next example is about.

6.3.3 *Adding company stationery to an existing document*

Figure 6.9 looks very similar to figure 6.4, but now you have an existing file, original.pdf, to which you want to add the file stationary.pdf, with the file stamped_stationery.pdf being the result.

To achieve this, you need to import a page from one PDF and add it as the background to another PDF.

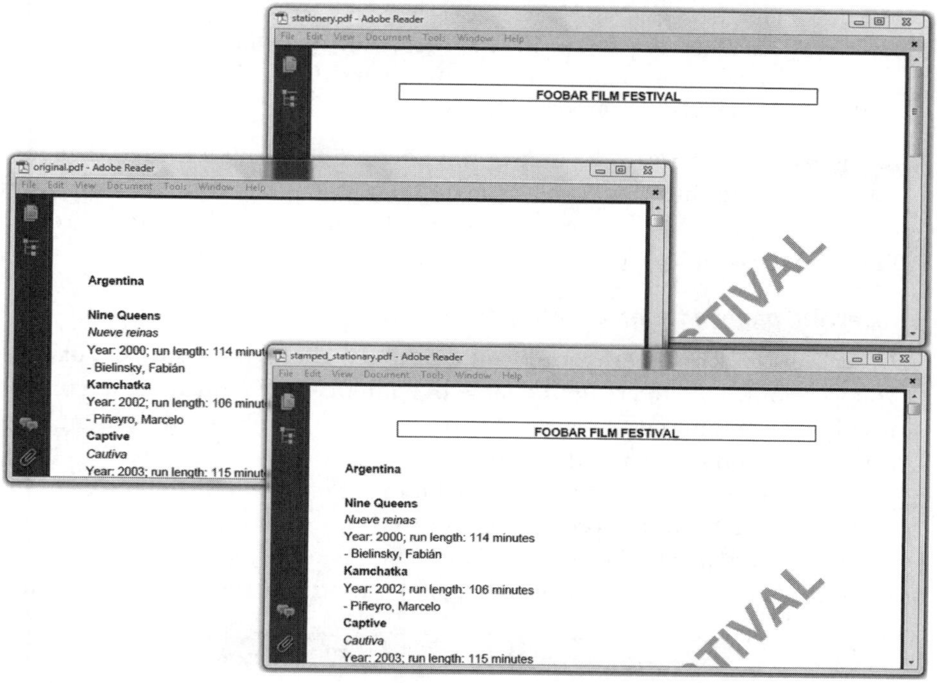

Figure 6.9 Adding stationery to an existing document

Listing 6.15 StampStationery.java

```
PdfReader reader = new PdfReader(src);
PdfReader s_reader = new PdfReader(stationery);
PdfStamper stamper =
  new PdfStamper(reader, new FileOutputStream(dest));
PdfImportedPage page = stamper.getImportedPage(s_reader, 1);
int n = reader.getNumberOfPages();
PdfContentByte background;
for (int i = 1; i <= n; i++) {
  background = stamper.getUnderContent(i);
  background.addTemplate(page, 0, 0);
}
stamper.close();
```

Here you obtain a `PdfImportedPage` object from `PdfStamper` with the `getImported-Page()` method. This method writes the resources necessary to render the imported page to the writer associated with the stamper.

This technique is often used to add watermarks to existing document. You can easily adapt the example to add an `Image` with the `addImage()` method instead of an imported page. All the methods from chapter 3 are at your disposal.

> **NOTE** This example combines `PdfStamper` with `PdfImportedPage`. All the interactive features present in the document that's being manipulated with `PdfStamper` are preserved, but the interactive features that were present on the page that's being imported are lost.

As discussed in the introduction of this chapter, PDF isn't a format that can be used for word processing. You can't insert a couple of lines between two existing paragraphs on a page. You can only insert complete pages. That's what you're going to do in the next example.

6.3.4   *Inserting pages into an existing document*

In section 5.2.4, you were faced with a problem concerning the TOC of a document. You were only able to create the table of contents (TOC) once the document was finished. But you wanted to display the TOC before the rest of the content, not after. In listing 5.12, you reordered the pages.

Listing 6.16 offers an alternative solution: you could create the PDF in two passes and add the TOC in the second pass by inserting extra pages. You could, for instance, create a `ColumnText` object containing a series of `Paragraphs`, then you add these `Paragraphs` to a number of pages that are inserted into the existing document.

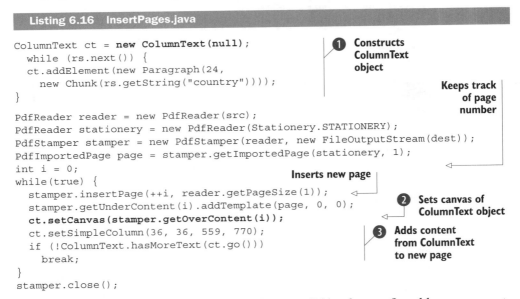

Listing 6.16   InsertPages.java

```
ColumnText ct = new ColumnText(null);            ❶ Constructs
   while (rs.next()) {                              ColumnText
   ct.addElement(new Paragraph(24,                  object
     new Chunk(rs.getString("country"))));
}
                                                    Keeps track
                                                    of page
                                                    number
PdfReader reader = new PdfReader(src);
PdfReader stationery = new PdfReader(Stationery.STATIONERY);
PdfStamper stamper = new PdfStamper(reader, new FileOutputStream(dest));
PdfImportedPage page = stamper.getImportedPage(stationery, 1);
int i = 0;                            Inserts new page
while(true) {
   stamper.insertPage(++i, reader.getPageSize(1));
   stamper.getUnderContent(i).addTemplate(page, 0, 0);    ❷ Sets canvas of
   ct.setCanvas(stamper.getOverContent(i));                  ColumnText object
   ct.setSimpleColumn(36, 36, 559, 770);               ❸ Adds content
   if (!ColumnText.hasMoreText(ct.go()))                   from ColumnText
     break;                                                to new page
}
stamper.close();
```

There's a significant difference between what you did in chapter 3 and how you create the `ColumnText` object here in ❶. Normally, you have to pass a `PdfContentByte` object with the constructor. In this case, you don't have a reference to the direct content yet: you use `null` as the parameter. You wait to set the canvas until ❷. In ❸ you try to fit the content inside a rectangle. If the content doesn't fit on page one, you insert a second page, and so on.

In the previous example, the TOC consists of only two pages; the actual content consists of 39 pages. What if you want to reorder the pages?

Listing 6.17   InsertPages.java (continued)

```
PdfReader reader = new PdfReader(RESULT1);
reader.selectPages("3-41,1-2");
PdfStamper stamper =
  new PdfStamper(reader, new FileOutputStream(RESULT2));
stamper.close();
```

There's nothing new in the listing. It's almost identical to what you did in listing 6.11, but now you're using `selectPages()` to reorder the pages. The document created by `PdfStamper` will start on page 3 of the original document, go on until page 41, and then add pages 1 and 2 at the end of the document.

These are practical examples that can be used to solve common problems with the help of `PdfStamper`, and using the concept of writing to the direct content as discussed in chapter 3. In the next section, we'll look at a totally different concept. We'll talk about interactive forms.

6.3.5   *Filling out a PDF form*

There are different flavors of forms in PDF. We'll discuss the details in chapter 8, where we'll create forms using iText. For now, we're going to use another tool to create an interactive PDF form.

CREATING A FORM WITH OPEN OFFICE

Figure 6.10 shows how you can use Open Office to create an XML form document. Using the Form Controls toolbar, you can add different kinds of form fields. Figure 6.11 shows a Film Data Sheet. It has text fields for the title, director, year, and duration. It has check boxes for the locations, because one movie can be screened in different movie theaters during the film festival. Finally, it has radio buttons for the

Figure 6.10   Creating an XML form document with Open Office Writer

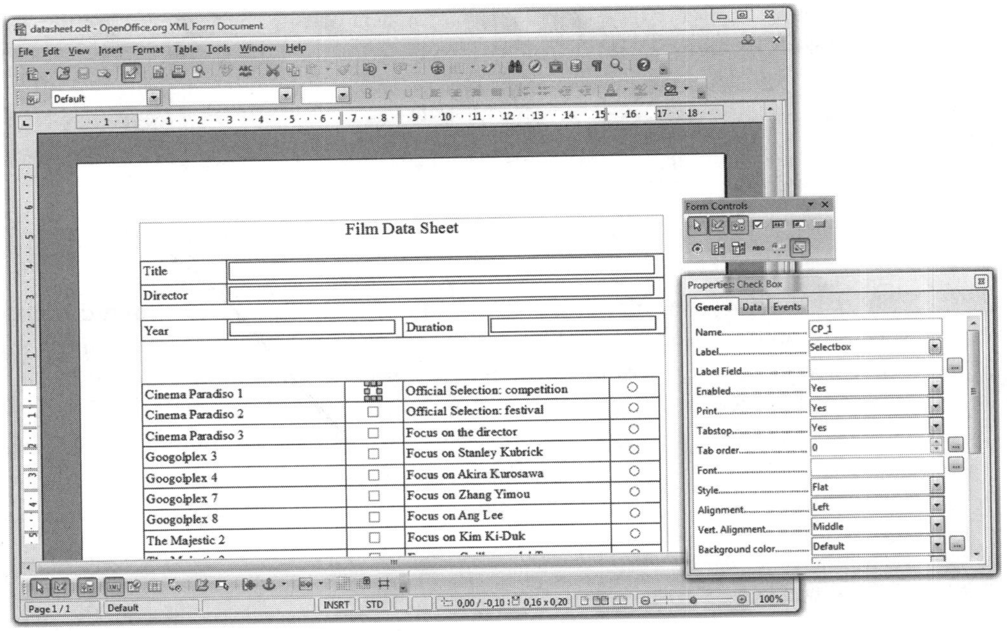

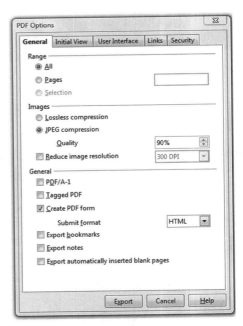

Figure 6.11   Creating fields in an Open Office document

category, because each film in the selection belongs to only one category. The properties for each of these fields—name, possible values, and so on—are set in a separate Properties dialog box.

When you create such a document, you may want to save it as an ODT file first. This will allow you to edit the document afterwards, in case something has to be changed. Then choose File > Export as PDF to open the PDF Options dialog box shown in figure 6.12.

Make sure that the check box next to Create PDF Form is checked. The resulting PDF document will be a form, as shown in figure 6.13.

This is an interactive form. You can start entering data manually into the fields you defined. However, when using Adobe Reader, you'll get a message saying, "You cannot save data typed into this form." In section 9.2, you'll see how data entered in a

Figure 6.12   Exporting an Open Office document as a PDF form

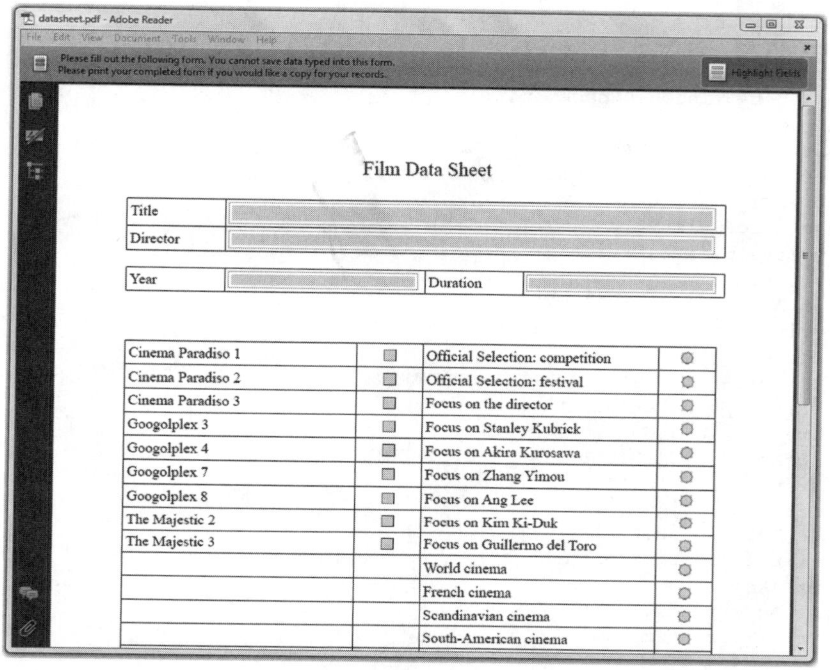

Figure 6.13   A form created with Open Office Writer

form that has a Submit button can be posted to a server, but the film data sheet you're using in this chapter was created for a different purpose: you're going to fill it out programmatically, using iText and `PdfStamper`. That is, after you've learned how to inspect the form.

INSPECTING THE FORM AND ITS FIELDS

If you want to fill out the form using iText, you need to know the name of each field you want to fill out. In the case of check boxes and radio buttons, you also need to know the different values that can be chosen. You know these names and values if you've created the form yourself, but in most cases the form will be created by a graphical designer. As a developer, you'll have to inspect the form to find out which names were used.

Listing 6.18 shows the different types of fields you can encounter. These types will be discussed in detail in chapter 8, except for signature fields, which will be discussed in chapter 12.

Listing 6.18   FormInformation.java

```
PdfReader reader = new PdfReader(DATASHEET);          Gets read-only
AcroFields form = reader.getAcroFields();             AcroFields instance
Set<String> fields = form.getFields().keySet();
for (String key : fields) {                           Gets all field names
```

```
      writer.print(key + ": ");
      switch (form.getFieldType(key)) {
        case AcroFields.FIELD_TYPE_CHECKBOX:
          writer.println("Checkbox");
          break;
        case AcroFields.FIELD_TYPE_COMBO:
          writer.println("Combobox");
          break;
        case AcroFields.FIELD_TYPE_LIST:
          writer.println("List");
          break;
        case AcroFields.FIELD_TYPE_NONE:
          writer.println("None");
          break;
        case AcroFields.FIELD_TYPE_PUSHBUTTON:
          writer.println("Pushbutton");
          break;
        case AcroFields.FIELD_TYPE_RADIOBUTTON:
          writer.println("Radiobutton");
          break;
        case AcroFields.FIELD_TYPE_SIGNATURE:
          writer.println("Signature");
          break;
        case AcroFields.FIELD_TYPE_TEXT:
          writer.println("Text");
          break;
        default:
          writer.println("?");
      }
    }
    writer.println("Possible values for CP_1:");
    String[] states = form.getAppearanceStates("CP_1");
    for (int i = 0; i < states.length; i++) {
      writer.print(" - ");
      writer.println(states[i]);
    }
    writer.println("Possible values for category:");
    states = form.getAppearanceStates("category");
    for (int i = 0; i < states.length - 1; i++) {
      writer.print(states[i]);
      writer.print(", ");
    }
    writer.println(states[states.length - 1]);
```

**Checks
field type**

**Gets different values
for check box CP_1**

**Gets different values for
radio group category**

The result when executing this code for the form shown in figure 6.13 looks like this:

```
MA_2: Checkbox
GP_8: Checkbox
GP_7: Checkbox
director: Text
CP_1: Checkbox
MA_3: Checkbox
CP_2: Checkbox
CP_3: Checkbox
title: Text
```

```
duration: Text
category: Radiobutton
GP_3: Checkbox
GP_4: Checkbox
year: Text
Possible values for CP_1:
 - Off
 - Yes
Possible values for category:
spec, toro, anim, comp, hero, Off, worl, rive, teen, kim,
kauf, zha, fest, s-am, fdir, lee, kubr, kuro, fran, scan
```

Note that the movie theaters are stored in the database like this: CP.1, GP.3, MA.3, ... But when you define the check boxes using Open Office (as in figure 6.11), you replace the dot with an underscore character because the dot character is forbidden in field names.

A check box has two possible values that correspond with an *appearance state*. In the case of the locations, the value can be Off—the check box isn't checked—or Yes—the check box is checked. These values can vary from PDF to PDF, so it's important to check the possible states before you start filling out the form. The possible values for the group of radio buttons is either Off—no radio button is selected—or a code that corresponds with the keyword field in the festival_category table (see figure 3.4).

Now that you've inspected the form, you have enough information to fill it out using iText.

FILLING OUT THE FORM

Filling out forms programmatically is usually done for two reasons: prefilling data in an editable form, and presenting information in a standard layout.

Imagine an online insurance company. When a customer wants to report an incident, they can log in, and choose among a number of PDF forms. These forms contain a number of standard fields with content that's already present in the company's database: name, address, and so on. When the customer logs in, the application could have access to this information, so why require the customer to enter all this information manually? Wouldn't it be better to take the blank form and prefill part of the information to save time for the customer?

That's what's done in figure 6.14. The film data sheet is filled with data from the database, but the data is still editable. In the context of an insurance company, the customer's phone number could be filled in, but the customer could still change it in case his number has changed.

Another typical use of PDF forms is when you want to use the form as a standard template. You don't really need a form to communicate with an end user. You just want to create documents that share the same structure, but with differing content.

The PDF shown in figure 6.15 was made using the Film Data Sheet form, but it's no longer interactive. The form has disappeared. The fields were only used as placeholders for the film title, director, and so on.

The process of keeping the data but removing the form is called *flattening*, and there are different possibilities in-between. You can choose to flatten only specific

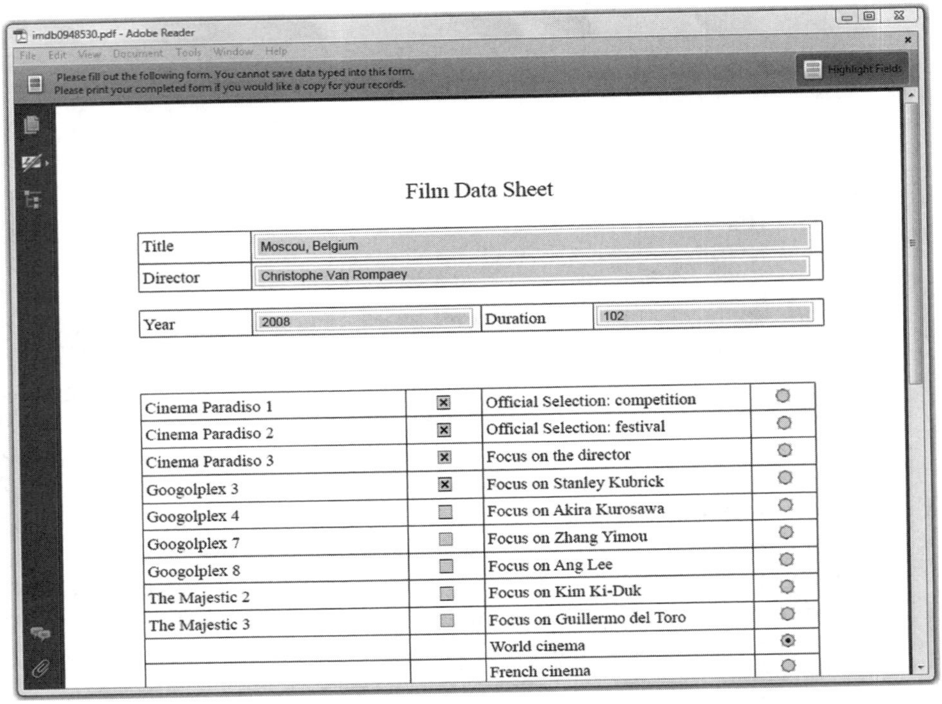

Figure 6.14   A form filled out using iText

fields, or you can change the status of specific fields to read-only. For instance, a customer of an insurance company is allowed to change their telephone number on the prefilled form, but not their name. Flattening will be discussed in chapter 8; in this chapter, you'll only use the basic mechanism of form filling.

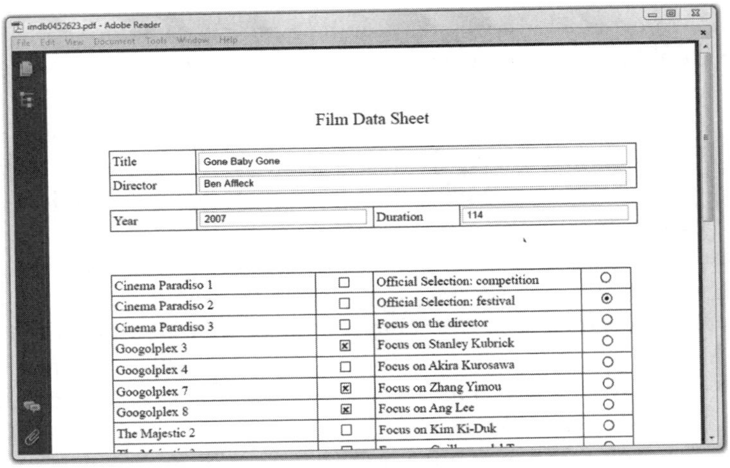

Figure 6.15   A form filled out and flattened using iText

Listing 6.19 FillDataSheet.java

```java
public static void main(String[] args)
  throws SQLException, IOException, DocumentException {
  DatabaseConnection connection = new HsqldbConnection("filmfestival");
  List movies = PojoFactory.getMovies(connection);
  PdfReader reader;
  PdfStamper stamper;
  for (Movie movie : movies) {
    if (movie.getYear() < 2007)
      continue;
    reader = new PdfReader(DATASHEET);
    stamper = new PdfStamper(reader,
      new FileOutputStream(
        String.format(RESULT, movie.getImdb())));
    fill(stamper.getAcroFields(), movie);
    if (movie.getYear() == 2007)
      stamper.setFormFlattening(true);
    stamper.close();
  }
  connection.close();
}

public static void fill(AcroFields form, Movie movie)
  throws IOException, DocumentException {
  form.setField("title", movie.getMovieTitle());
  form.setField("director", getDirectors(movie));
  form.setField("year",
    String.valueOf(movie.getYear()));
  form.setField("duration",
    String.valueOf(movie.getDuration()));
  form.setField("category",
    movie.getEntry().getCategory().getKeyword());
  for (Screening screening :
    movie.getEntry().getScreenings()) {
    form.setField(
      screening.getLocation().replace('.', '_'), "Yes");
  }
}
```

Annotations:
- **Gets AcroFields instance from stamper**
- **Creates reader and stamper**
- **1 Flattens forms for movies in 2007**
- **Closes stamper**
- **Fills out fields**

In this listing, you're creating a separate document for every movie in the database that was made after 2006. The new reader instance is created *inside* the loop.

FAQ *Why do I get a* DocumentException *saying "The original document was reused. Read it again from file."?* Every PdfReader object can be used for one and only one PdfStamper object. Looking at the example in listing 6.19, you might argue that new PdfReader(DATASHEET) could be moved outside the loop, because it's the same for all the PdfStamper objects, but that won't work. As soon as you use a PdfReader object to create a PdfStamper, the reader object is *tampered*. You can check this by adding the line reader.isTampered();. If this method returns true, you can't use the reader to create a new stamper object. You have to create a new instance—which is exactly what the error message tells you.

If you want to fill out a form, you need to have an `AcroFields` object. You can get an instance of this object using the method `getAcroFields()`.

> **FAQ**   *Why do I get a* `DocumentException` *saying "This AcroFields instance is read-only?"* If you look closely at listings 6.18 and 6.19, you'll see that the `getAcro-Fields()` method exists in the `PdfReader` class as well as in the `PdfStamper` class. The `AcroFields` retrieved in listing 6.18 is read-only, and it will throw a `DocumentException` as soon as you try to fill out a field. You need to use the method with `PdfStamper` if you want to update the form.

Filling out the form is easy. If you know the field name, such as "title", you can set its value using only one line:

```
form.setField("title", movie.getMovieTitle());
```

As you can see in listing 6.19 ❶, the filled-out data sheets of movies dating from 2007 are flattened. Figure 6.15 shows such a data sheet. It looks like an ordinary PDF file. The content is stamped on the document; it's no longer an editable form. In figure 6.14, you see a data sheet for a movie made in 2008. It's still a form; you can change the title manually.

There's much more to say about forms, but we can't go into further detail until we've talked about annotations. Also, I haven't said anything about the different types of PDF forms yet: there are forms based on AcroForm technology (like the form you created using Open Office), and there are XFA forms (created with Adobe Designer). This will have to wait until chapter 8, because we have one more group of PDF manipulation classes left to cover.

6.4   *Copying pages with PdfCopy*

In the previous section, each `PdfStamper` object was associated with one and only one `PdfReader` object. As soon as you want to assemble pages from more than one document, you should use another PDF manipulation class: `PdfCopy`.

`PdfCopy` extends `PdfWriter`, and you'll immediately recognize the five steps in the PDF creation process:

> **Listing 6.20   SelectPages.java**

```
public static void main(String[] args)
   throws IOException, DocumentException {
   new MovieTemplates().createPdf(MovieTemplates.RESULT);
   PdfReader reader = new PdfReader(MovieTemplates.RESULT);
   reader.selectPages("4-8");
   ...
   manipulateWithCopy(reader);
}

private static void manipulateWithCopy(PdfReader reader)
   throws IOException, DocumentException {
   int n = reader.getNumberOfPages();
   Document document = new Document();                    ⟵ Step 1
```

```
    PdfCopy copy = new PdfCopy(
      document, new FileOutputStream(RESULT2));          Step 2
    document.open();
    for (int i = 0; i < n;) {                        ←—— Step 3
      copy.addPage(copy.getImportedPage(reader, ++i));    Step 4
    }
    document.close();            ←—— Step 5
  }
```

The main difference between these five steps and the ones from chapter 1 is that you're now using PdfCopy instead of PdfWriter in step 2. You can only add content using addPage(). Listing 6.20 is a variation on listing 6.11, with only one document being involved in this example. Let's extend the example and concatenate two PDFs.

6.4.1 Concatenating and splitting PDF documents

In chapter 2, we created a list with movies containing links to the Internet Movie Database (IMDB). We also created a historical overview of these movies with bookmarks that were generated automatically. Now let's combine those two PDFs into one new document.

Listing 6.21 Concatenate.java

```
String[] files = { MovieLinks1.RESULT, MovieHistory.RESULT };
Document document = new Document();
PdfCopy copy = new PdfCopy(document, new FileOutputStream(RESULT));
document.open();
PdfReader reader;
int n;
for (int i = 0; i < files.length; i++) {
  reader = new PdfReader(files[i]);
  n = reader.getNumberOfPages();
  for (int page = 0; page < n; ) {
    copy.addPage(copy.getImportedPage(reader, ++page));
  }
}
document.close();
```

MovieLinks1.RESULT is a document with 34 pages. MovieHistory.RESULT has 26 pages. The page count of the concatenated file is 60.

> **FAQ** *After merging two PDFs, I'm seeing unnecessary white space. Why are there so many blank areas?* Sometimes people expect that a document with one page concatenated with another document counting one page will result in a document with only one page. They expect that, when the pages of the original document are only half full, the new document will put both halves on one page. That's not how PDF works! In PDF, you work with complete pages; it's not possible to reflow the content on those pages.

There are two different versions of the addPage() method. You can add blank pages if you use a Rectangle and a rotation value as parameters, or you can add a PdfImportedPage obtained from the same PdfCopy instance using getImportedPage().

PRESERVATION OF INTERACTIVE FEATURES

You've used imported pages with PdfWriter in section 6.2 and with PdfStamper in section 6.3. You've scaled these imported pages, rotated them, and so on. All of this isn't possible with the PdfImportedPage objects obtained from PdfCopy. You can only add them to a new document in their original form and size.

This limitation comes with a major advantage: most of the interactive features of the page are preserved. The links that are present in MovieLinks1.RESULT are lost if you import a page using PdfWriter or PdfStamper, but they still work if you import the same page with PdfCopy. Links are a special type of annotation, and we'll discuss the different types of annotations in chapter 7. For now, it's sufficient to know that all annotations are kept with PdfCopy. The bookmarks of MovieHistory.RESULT, on the other hand, are lost.

We'll find a way to work around this in the next chapter.

ADDING CONTENT WITH PDFCOPY

In previous sections, I explained that PdfImportedPage is a read-only subclass of PdfTemplate. You can't add any content to an imported page. This wasn't a big deal when using imported pages with PdfWriter and PdfStamper because we could easily add content over or under the imported page. When using PdfCopy, it would be interesting if we could somehow add extra content too.

It would be interesting if we could add a "page *X* of *Y*" footer that reflects the new page numbers.

Listing 6.22   ConcatenateStamp.java

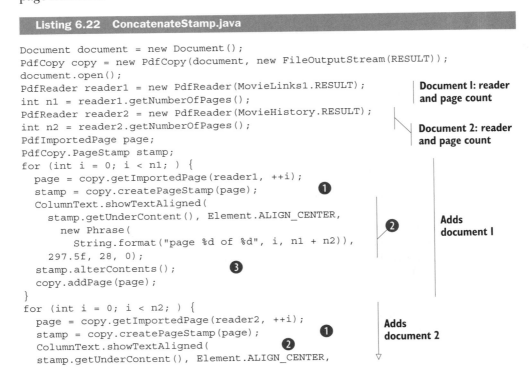

```
Document document = new Document();
PdfCopy copy = new PdfCopy(document, new FileOutputStream(RESULT));
document.open();
PdfReader reader1 = new PdfReader(MovieLinks1.RESULT);         Document 1: reader
int n1 = reader1.getNumberOfPages();                           and page count
PdfReader reader2 = new PdfReader(MovieHistory.RESULT);
int n2 = reader2.getNumberOfPages();                           Document 2: reader
PdfImportedPage page;                                          and page count
PdfCopy.PageStamp stamp;
for (int i = 0; i < n1; ) {
  page = copy.getImportedPage(reader1, ++i);
  stamp = copy.createPageStamp(page);              ❶
  ColumnText.showTextAligned(
    stamp.getUnderContent(), Element.ALIGN_CENTER,              Adds
      new Phrase(                                   ❷          document 1
        String.format("page %d of %d", i, n1 + n2)),
    297.5f, 28, 0);
  stamp.alterContents();             ❸
  copy.addPage(page);
}
for (int i = 0; i < n2; ) {
  page = copy.getImportedPage(reader2, ++i);
  stamp = copy.createPageStamp(page);      ❶       Adds
  ColumnText.showTextAligned(             ❷        document 2
    stamp.getUnderContent(), Element.ALIGN_CENTER,
```

```
    new Phrase(
      String.format("page %d of %d", n1 + i, n1 + n2)),
    297.5f, 28, 0);
  stamp.alterContents();
  copy.addPage(page);                  ❸
}
document.close();
```

❷ Adds
document 2

With `PdfCopy`, we can add content to a `PdfImportedPage` using a `PdfCopy.PageStamp` object. Such an object can be obtained with the `createPageStamp()` method ❶. This object has two methods for getting a direct content layer: `getUnderContent()` and `getOverContent()`. These methods return a `PdfCopy.StampContent` object. `PdfCopy.StampContent` extends `PdfContentByte`, and you can use it just as you'd use any other `PdfContentByte` object. In listing 6.22, you use it to add text at an absolute position ❷. There's one caveat: you mustn't forget to invoke the `alterContents()` method ❸.

SPLITTING A PDF

Using a `PdfReader` instance with `PdfCopy` doesn't *tamper* the reader the way `Pdf-Stamper` does. You can reuse the same reader object for different `PdfCopy` objects. You can, for instance, construct one reader instance that reads the timetable PDF from chapter 3, and create a new `PdfCopy` instance for every page to split the document into individual pages. In PDF terminology, this process is often called *PDF bursting*.

Listing 6.23   Burst.java

```
PdfReader reader = new PdfReader(MovieTemplates.RESULT);
Document document;
PdfCopy copy;
int n = reader.getNumberOfPages();
for (int i = 0; i < n; ) {
  document = new Document();
  copy = new PdfCopy(document,
    new FileOutputStream(String.format(RESULT, ++i)));
  document.open();
  copy.addPage(copy.getImportedPage(reader, i));
  document.close();
}
```

The original file representing the timetable contained 8 pages, and its size was about 15 KB. Bursting this file results in 8 different single-page documents, each with a file size of about 4 KB. 8 times 4 KB is 32 KB, which is more than the original 15 KB, because resources that were shared among pages in the original document are now copied into each separate document. So you might wonder what would happen if you concatenated PDF documents containing duplicate content.

6.4.2   *PdfCopy versus PdfSmartCopy*

In section 6.3.5, you filled out and flattened the film data sheet form to create a separate file for movies made in the year 2007. Wouldn't it be nice to create one single document that contains the data sheets for all the movies in the database?

Here you'll fill the data sheet using `PdfStamper`. The resulting PDF files will be kept in memory just long enough to copy the page into a new document with `PdfCopy`.

Listing 6.24   DataSheets1.java

```
public void createPdf(String filename)
  throws IOException, DocumentException, SQLException {
  Document document = new Document();                        ← Step 1
  PdfCopy copy = new PdfCopy(                             ⎫ Step 2
    document, new FileOutputStream(filename));           ⎭
  document.open();                                          ← Step 3
  addDataSheets(copy);                ← Step 4
  document.close();                   ← Step 5
}
public void addDataSheets(PdfCopy copy)
  throws SQLException, IOException, DocumentException {
  DatabaseConnection connection =
    new HsqldbConnection("filmfestival");
  List<Movie> movies = PojoFactory.getMovies(connection);
  PdfReader reader;
  PdfStamper stamper;
  ByteArrayOutputStream baos;
  for (Movie movie : movies) {
    reader = new PdfReader(DATASHEET);
    baos = new ByteArrayOutputStream();
    stamper = new PdfStamper(reader, baos);       Creates single
    fill(stamper.getAcroFields(), movie);         page in memory
    stamper.setFormFlattening(true);
    stamper.close();

    reader = new PdfReader(baos.toByteArray());   Adds page
    copy.addPage(copy.getImportedPage(reader, 1)); to PdfCopy
  }
  connection.close();
}
```

This example works perfectly, and at first sight you won't find anything wrong with the resulting PDF when you open it in Adobe Reader. Only when you look at the file size will you have doubts. The original datasheet.pdf was less than 60 KB, but the resulting PDF is almost 5 MB.

This document has 120 pages that are almost identical. Only the specific movie information differs from page to page; the form template is repeated over and over again. But `PdfCopy` isn't aware of that: it takes every page you add, including its resources, and copies everything to the writer. The code in listing 6.24 adds the same bits and bytes representing the original form to the same document 120 times. The resulting PDF is full of redundant information.

This can be avoided by using `PdfSmartCopy` instead of `PdfCopy` in step 2.

Listing 6.25   DataSheets2.java

```
public void createPdf(String filename)
  throws IOException, DocumentException, SQLException {
  Document document = new Document();                        ← Step 1
```

```
    PdfSmartCopy copy = new PdfSmartCopy(
      document, new FileOutputStream(filename));                    Step 2
    document.open();                                    ◁─── Step 3
    addDataSheets(copy);                       ◁─── Step 4
    document.close();              ◁─── Step 5
}
```

Now the size of the resulting PDF file is only about 300 KB; that's a much better result.

    PdfSmartCopy extends PdfCopy. It inherits the same functionality, but it checks every page that's added for redundant objects, so it can save plenty of disk space or bandwidth. There's a price to pay for this extra "intelligence." PdfSmartCopy needs more memory and more time to concatenate files than PdfCopy. It will be up to you to decide what's more important: file size and bandwidth, or memory and time. It will also depend on the nature of the documents you want to concatenate. If there is little resemblance between the pages, you might as well use PdfCopy. If different documents all have the same company logo on every page, you might want to consider using PdfSmartCopy to detect that logo.

    In this example, you've concatenated flattened forms. But what happens if you concatenate the original forms? You don't have to try this: it won't work. Although PdfCopy (and PdfSmartCopy) preserve the annotations used to visualize a form, the form functionality will be broken if you try to concatenate two or more documents containing forms using PdfCopy. Your best chance to achieve this is to use PdfCopyFields.

6.4.3 Concatenating forms

Suppose you want to create a film data sheet form with two or more pages. This can easily be done with only four lines of code.

    NOTE   These examples will only work if your forms are created using Acro-Form technology. It's not possible to concatenate XFA forms using iText.

Listing 6.26   ConcatenateForms1.java

```
PdfCopyFields copy = new PdfCopyFields(new FileOutputStream(RESULT));
copy.addDocument(new PdfReader(DATASHEET));
copy.addDocument(new PdfReader(DATASHEET));
copy.close();
```

DATASHEET refers to the file datasheet.pdf. RESULT refers to a new form with two identical pages. This form probably won't work the way you expect it to. You probably want to be able to enter the information about one movie on the first page, and about another movie on the second page. That's impossible with this form. Although the field "title" is physically present in two different locations in the same document, there's only one logical field with the name "title" in the form. This single field can only have one value. If you enter a title on page one, you'll see the same title appear on page two. That may not be your intention; you probably want to create a form with two pages that can be used to enter information about two different movies.

That's only possible if you use forms with different field names, or if you rename the fields.

Listing 6.27   ConcatenateForms2.java

```
public static void main(String[] args)
  throws IOException, DocumentException {
  PdfCopyFields copy = new PdfCopyFields(new FileOutputStream(RESULT));
  copy.addDocument(new PdfReader(renameFieldsIn(DATASHEET, 1)));
  copy.addDocument(new PdfReader(renameFieldsIn(DATASHEET, 2)));
  copy.close();
}
private static byte[] renameFieldsIn(String datasheet, int i)
  throws IOException, DocumentException {
  ByteArrayOutputStream baos = new ByteArrayOutputStream();
  PdfStamper stamper =
    new PdfStamper(new PdfReader(datasheet), baos);          Creates new
  AcroFields form = stamper.getAcroFields();                 version of
  Set<String> keys                                           form
    = new HashSet(form.getFields().keySet());
  for (String key : keys) {                       Renames
    form.renameField(                             fields
      key, String.format("%s_%d", key, i));
  }
  stamper.close();
  return baos.toByteArray();
}
```

This code snippet renames fields such as "title" into "title_1" (on page 1) and "title_2" (on page 2). Now there's no longer a conflict between the field names on the different pages.

> **NOTE**   Don't use `PdfCopyFields` to concatenate PDF documents without form fields. As opposed to concatenating documents using `PdfCopy`, `Pdf-CopyFields` needs to keep all the documents in memory to update the combined form. This can become problematic if you're trying to concatenate large documents.

The `PdfCopyFields` example completes this chapter on the different PDF manipulation classes. It's high time for a summary with an overview that will help you pick the right class for the job.

6.5   *Summary*

In this chapter, you've been introduced to the different PDF manipulation classes available in iText. You've used these classes to solve a series of common problems: *N*-up copying and tiling PDF documents, using a PDF as company stationery, adding headers, footers, watermarks, and "page *X* of *Y*" to existing documents, concatenating and splitting PDFs, and so on.

Every class had its specific specialties and limitations. Table 6.1 gives an overview of the classes that were discussed in this chapter.

Table 6.1 An overview of the PDF manipulation classes

iText class	Usage
PdfReader	Reads PDF files. You pass an instance of this class to one of the other PDF manipulation classes.
PdfImportedPage	A read-only subclass of PdfTemplate. Can be obtained from a PDF manipulation class using the method getImportedPage().
PdfWriter	Generates PDF documents from scratch. Can import pages from other PDF documents. The major downside is that all interactive features of the imported page (annotations, bookmarks, fields, and so forth) are lost in the process.
PdfStamper	Manipulates one (and only one) PDF document. Can be used to add content at absolute positions, to add extra pages, or to fill out fields. All interactive features are preserved, except when you explicitly remove them (for instance, by flattening a form).
PdfCopy	Copies pages from one or more existing PDF documents. Major downsides: PdfCopy doesn't detect redundant content, and it fails when concatenating forms.
PdfSmartCopy	Copies pages from one or more existing PDF documents. PdfSmartCopy is able to detect redundant content, but it needs more memory and CPU than PdfCopy.
PdfCopyFields	Puts the fields of the different forms into one form. Can be used to avoid the problems encountered with form fields when concatenating forms using PdfCopy. Memory use can be an issue.

In the next chapter, we'll focus mainly on PdfStamper. I'll introduce the concept of annotations, and you'll learn that form fields are a special type of annotation. You'll create a form from scratch using iText, and we'll discuss the different types of interactive forms in PDF.

Making documents interactive

7

This chapter covers

- Creating actions and destinations
- Working with outlines and bookmarks
- Adding annotations and JavaScript

In the summary of the previous chapter, table 6.1 outlined the most important iText classes for manipulating documents. You've used these classes to manipulate the content of existing documents to copy pages, add extra content, fill out forms, and so forth. In this chapter, you'll use `PdfStamper` and `PdfCopy` to add interactive features to an existing document.

We'll start by adding actions that will help the end user navigate through the document, similar to what you did with internal and external links in section 2.3.1. Next we'll look at bookmarks, but instead of using `Chapters` and `Sections`, as you did in section 2.3.2, we'll look at how to create a custom outline tree. Finally, we'll add annotations. For example, you'll learn how to put a sticky note on an existing page, and how to show an advertisement when a PDF document is opened.

7.1 Introducing actions

If you're reading this book from beginning to end, actions shouldn't be new to you. You created documents containing actions in chapter 2, but we didn't call them *actions*; instead we talked about *remote* and *local goto links*. In this section, you'll add goto actions using the PdfAction class, and you'll also learn how to introduce new actions, such as actions that trigger JavaScript functions embedded in the document.

But let's start with an example that adds actions to navigate through documents.

7.1.1 Document-navigation actions

Most PDF viewers have buttons that allow the end user of the PDF document to switch to another page. In some cases, these viewer buttons can be removed or the toolbar can be hidden by setting the viewer preferences. Maybe you want to add extra navigational aids to the page itself, to make it easier for the end user to go to the first, previous, next, or last page. For this purpose, ISO-32000-1 defines four named actions that should be supported by every PDF viewer.

NAMED ACTIONS

In figure 7.1, you can find arrows to jump to the first page ($\Leftarrow$), the previous page ($\leftarrow$), the next page ($\rightarrow$), and the last page ($\Rightarrow$).

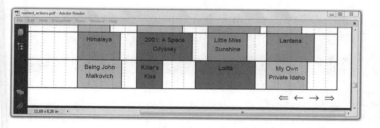

Figure 7.1
Timetable with named actions triggered by clicking the arrows

These arrows correspond to four named actions: /NextPage, /PrevPage, /FirstPage, and /LastPage. You can create these links using the PdfAction class. You can see how to associate an instance of this class with a Chunk using the setAction() method .

Listing 7.1   NamedActions.java

```
Font symbol = new Font(FontFamily.SYMBOL, 20);
PdfPTable table = new PdfPTable(4);
table.getDefaultCell().setBorder(Rectangle.NO_BORDER);
table.getDefaultCell().setHorizontalAlignment(Element.ALIGN_CENTER);
Chunk first = new Chunk(String.valueOf((char)220), symbol);
first.setAction(new PdfAction(PdfAction.FIRSTPAGE));     ⊲┐ Jumps to
table.addCell(new Phrase(first));                          │ first page
Chunk previous = new Chunk(String.valueOf((char)172), symbol);
previous.setAction(new PdfAction(PdfAction.PREVPAGE));   ⊲┐ Jumps to
table.addCell(new Phrase(previous));                       │ previous page
Chunk next = new Chunk(String.valueOf((char)174), symbol);
next.setAction(new PdfAction(PdfAction.NEXTPAGE));       ⊲── Jumps to next page
```

```
table.addCell(new Phrase(next));
Chunk last = new Chunk(String.valueOf((char)222), symbol);
last.setAction(new PdfAction(PdfAction.LASTPAGE));
table.addCell(new Phrase(last));
table.setTotalWidth(120);
```
← **Jumps to last page**

You can add the table from listing 7.1 to the timetable PDF using PdfStamper and the method writeSelectedRows().

> **NOTE**   Most of the functionality discussed in this chapter can also be used when creating documents from scratch.

In the next example, you'll rewrite listing 2.23 using PdfAction instances.

REMOTE AND LOCAL GOTO ACTIONS

The MovieLinks examples in section 2.3.1 resulted in two PDF files. The links and destinations in the first PDF were created using the Anchor class. The document contained external links to the IMDB and local destinations that were referred to by a name or a string. These destinations are called *named destinations*—the country code was the name for the local destination.

The second PDF showed a list of countries with one external link to the IMDB website, an external link to a named destination referring to a country page in the first document, and an internal link to the top of the page. Listing 7.2 duplicates the code from the original MovieLinks2 example but replaces methods such as setRemoteGoto() and setLocalGoto() with setAction().

Listing 7.2   LinkActions.java

```
Chunk imdb = new Chunk(
  "Internet Movie Database", FilmFonts.ITALIC);
imdb.setAction(
  new PdfAction(new URL("http://www.imdb.com/")));
p = new Paragraph("Click on a country, and you'll get a list of movies,"
  + " containing links to the ");
p.add(imdb);
p.add(".");
document.add(p);

p = new Paragraph("This list can be found in a ");
Chunk page1 = new Chunk("separate document");
page1.setAction(new PdfAction("movie_links_1.pdf", 1));
p.add(page1);
p.add(".");
document.add(p);
...
Paragraph country = new Paragraph(rs.getString("country"));
country.add(": ");
Chunk link = new Chunk(
  String.format("%d movies", rs.getInt("c")));
link.setAction(PdfAction.gotoRemotePage(
  "movie_links_1.pdf", rs.getString("country_id"),
  false, true));
country.add(link);
```

❶ Link to external URL

❷ Link to page in external document

❸ Link to named destination in external document

```
document.add(country);
...
p = new Paragraph("Go to ");
top = new Chunk("top");
top.setAction(PdfAction.gotoLocalPage("top", false));
p.add(top);
p.add(".");
document.add(p);
```

4 Link to local named destination

Let's examine all the constructors and methods used to create the `PdfActions` in this example.

JUMP TO AN EXTERNAL URL

The first action added in the listing will create a link to an external URL **1**. This example uses a `URL` object, but passing a `String` with the link address would have worked too. When adding the action to a `Chunk`, a rectangular clickable area is created. If you add a `boolean` as an extra parameter, the X and Y coordinate of the position you've clicked will be added to the URL as a query string. You could define an action like this:

```
new PdfAction("http://www.lowagie.com/", true);
```

Clicking on such a link in the lower-left corner of the clickable area could result in the following hit on the lowagie.com server:

```
http://www.lowagie.com/?5,3
```

Inspecting the query string on the server side will reveal that the user's mouse pointer pointed at the position X = 5, Y = 3 in the clickable rectangle.

JUMP TO A LOCATION IN A DOCUMENT

There are different ways to create a link to an external document. You can use one of the constructors of `PdfAction`, as is done in listing 7.2 **2**:

- `new PdfAction(String filename, String name)`—This will create a link to the document named `filename` and jump to a named destination with the name `name`.

- `new PdfAction(String filename, int page)`—This will create a link to the document named `filename` and jump to a specific page number: `page`.

Executing these actions will replace the document that is currently viewed by the new document. If you want to open the new document in a new viewer window, you can create the action like this:

```
PdfAction action = new PdfAction("other.pdf", 1);
action.put(PdfName.NEWWINDOW, PdfBoolean.PDFTRUE);
```

If you'll look inside iText, you'll see that `PdfAction` is a `PdfDictionary`, which means it's a collection of key-value pairs. The keys are of type `PdfName`, and the value can be (a reference to) any subclass of `PdfObject`; in this case, a `PdfBoolean`. This mechanism will be explained in detail in chapter 13. You can use it to extend iText with functionality that isn't provided out of the box.

NOTE   A new viewer window is not the same as a new browser window. If you tell iText that the action should open a new window, this will only work if you're looking at the document in the standalone Adobe Reader application. It will open a new standalone Adobe Reader window. If you're looking at the document using the Adobe Reader plug-in inside a browser, it will not open a new browser tab or window.

In ❸ in listing 7.2, the static method `gotoRemotePage()` is used to create an instance of class `PdfAction`. This method has four parameters:

- `filename`—Specifies the filename of the external document.
- `dest`—Specifies the named destination inside this document.
- `isName`—Indicates whether the destination is stored as a `PdfName` (when set to `true`) or as a `PdfString` (when set to `false`). These are two different types of PDF objects that can be used to define a named destination. Note that iText creates named destinations as `Strings`.
- `newWindow`—Specifies whether the document will be opened in a new viewer window (if set to `true`) or not.

Actions that jump to a local destination are created using a static `gotoLocalPage()` method. In ❹ this method is used with a `String` for the name; the `boolean` value `false` indicates that the name was stored as a `PdfString`, not as a `PdfName`.

In listing 7.2, you know the names of the named destinations, because you're creating the documents yourself. But suppose somebody gives you an existing document, and you're asked to create a new document that links to the named destinations in this existing document. How can you find out which names to use?

RETRIEVING NAMED DESTINATIONS FROM AN EXISTING DOCUMENT

You can create a `HashMap` and an XML file containing information about the named destinations inside an existing PDF document.

Listing 7.3   LinkActions.java (continued)

```
PdfReader reader = new PdfReader(src);
HashMap<String,String> map =
   SimpleNamedDestination.getNamedDestination(reader, false);
SimpleNamedDestination.exportToXML(map,
   new FileOutputStream(RESULT3), "ISO8859-1", true);
```

With the `boolean` parameter `false`, you indicate that you're interested in the names that are stored as a `PdfString`. If you change this parameter to `true`, you ask iText for the names that are stored as a `PdfName` inside the document.

The keys of such a map are `String` values. In this case, they are the keys of the countries stored in the database: `US`, `AR`, and so on. You can find an example of the values in the `Page` attribute of the XML that is generated:

```
<?xml version="1.0" encoding="ISO8859-1"?>
<Destination>
  <Name Page="1 XYZ 36 802 0">US</Name>
```

```
<Name Page="19 XYZ 36 802 0">AR</Name>
...
</Destination>
```

In this snippet, an XML file is created using the Latin-1 encoding (ISO8859-1), and you ask iText to escape all non-ASCII characters with the `boolean` parameter `true`. The values `1 XYZ 36 802 0` and `19 XYZ 36 802 0` need to be explained in more detail. They refer to explicit destinations.

7.1.2 *Explicit destinations*

If you look at figure 7.1, you'll see that I zoomed in on the arrows at the bottom of the page. If you click on one of the arrows, a named action will be executed. You will jump to another page, and that page will be shown using the same zoom factor.

Suppose you don't want this—suppose you want to instruct the viewer to jump to an exact position on the first, previous, next, or last page using the zoom factor of your choice. In iText, you can achieve this by using the `PdfDestination` class. The constructor of this class always has at least one parameter: `type` defines the destination type.

OVERVIEW OF THE DIFFERENT TYPES

Table 7.1 gives an overview of the available types of explicit destinations.

Table 7.1   **Destination types for creating a `PdfDestination` object**

Type	Extra parameters	Description
FIT	-	The current page is displayed with its contents magnified just enough to fit the document window, both horizontally and vertically.
FITB	-	The current page is displayed magnified just enough to fit the bounding box of the contents (the smallest rectangle enclosing all of its contents).
FITH	float top	The page is displayed so that the page fits within the document window horizontally (the entire width of the page is visible). The extra parameter specifies the vertical coordinate of the top edge of the page.
FITBH	float top	This option is almost identical to FITH, but the width of the bounding box of the page is visible. This isn't necessarily the entire width of the page.
FITV	float left	The page is displayed so that the page fits within the document window vertically (the entire height of the page is visible). The extra parameter specifies the horizontal coordinate of the left edge of the page.
FITBV	float left	This option is almost identical to FITV, but the height of the bounding box of the page is visible. This isn't necessarily the entire height of the page.
XYZ	float left, float top, float zoom	The parameter `left` defines an X coordinate, `top` defines a Y coordinate, and `zoom` defines a zoom factor. If you want to keep the current X coordinate, Y coordinate, or zoom factor, you can pass negative values or 0 for the corresponding parameter.
FITR	float left, float bottom, float right, float top	The parameters define a rectangle. The page is displayed with its contents magnified just enough to fit this rectangle. If the required zoom factors for the horizontal and the vertical magnification are different, the smaller of the two is used.

Table 7.1 can be used to interpret the output generated with the SimpleNamedDestination class. For instance 1 XYZ 36 802 0 means that you want to jump to the coordinate (36, 802) on page 1, keeping the current zoom factor.

The table can also be used to create a new Map of named destinations "manually." PdfWriter has an addNamedDestinations() method that can be used to inject such a map in a document that is built from scratch. This method was originally written to work around a problem with named destinations when using PdfCopy.

NAMED DESTINATIONS AND PDFCOPY

A recurring question on the iText mailing list involves the concatenation of documents that have named destinations. Suppose you want to concatenate the two files created in listing 7.2. In chapter 6, you learned that most of the interactive features are preserved if you use PdfCopy, but there are exceptions. Using PdfCopy with documents that have named destinations is one of these exceptions. All annotations, such as link annotations, are kept with PdfCopy, but they no longer work for links to local named destinations. There is a workaround for this problem.

Listing 7.4   ConcatenateNamedDestinations.java

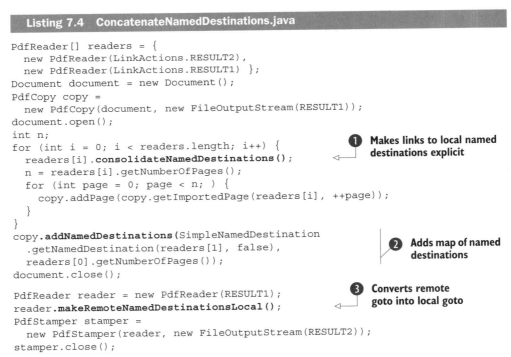

```
PdfReader[] readers = {
  new PdfReader(LinkActions.RESULT2),
  new PdfReader(LinkActions.RESULT1) };
Document document = new Document();
PdfCopy copy =
  new PdfCopy(document, new FileOutputStream(RESULT1));
document.open();
int n;
for (int i = 0; i < readers.length; i++) {          ❶ Makes links to local named
  readers[i].consolidateNamedDestinations();             destinations explicit
  n = readers[i].getNumberOfPages();
  for (int page = 0; page < n; ) {
    copy.addPage(copy.getImportedPage(readers[i], ++page));
  }
}
copy.addNamedDestinations(SimpleNamedDestination
  .getNamedDestination(readers[1], false),           ❷ Adds map of named
  readers[0].getNumberOfPages());                        destinations
document.close();

PdfReader reader = new PdfReader(RESULT1);            ❸ Converts remote
reader.makeRemoteNamedDestinationsLocal();               goto into local goto
PdfStamper stamper =
  new PdfStamper(reader, new FileOutputStream(RESULT2));
stamper.close();
```

If you use listing 6.21 to concatenate the two documents from the previous example (listing 7.2), you'll find out that the link to go to the named destination "top" has the appearance of a link, but if you click it, it won't work. You can work around this problem by using the method consolidateNamedDestinations() ❶. This method translates all the local links referring to a named destination into links that use explicit destinations.

That fixes the internal link problem, but it may not be sufficient. You can link to the file LinkActions.RESULT1 from another file using a named destination, but these destinations are lost in the concatenated file. You can restore these links by injecting them into the PdfCopy object ❷. In listing 7.4, you use SimpleNamedDestination to retrieve a map containing the named destinations you want to preserve. Note that page 1 of the original document is no longer page 1 in the concatenated document. When you use the addNamedDestinations() method, you have to use a page offset based on the number of pages in the documents that were added before the document with the named destinations.

And what about the links to named destinations in external files? These will keep on working, but they'll point to the *original external* document. Maybe you want to concatenate two documents that are linking to each other, and change the *remote* goto actions into *local* goto actions. PdfCopy can't do this. You have to run the file through PdfStamper and use the makeRemoteNamedDestinationsLocal() method ❸. This method will try to convert remote goto links into local goto links. Only the remote links that refer to a name that isn't known as a named destination in the local file are preserved as external links.

With these three mechanisms, you can work around the problems that are caused by the limitations of PdfCopy when dealing with named destinations.

CREATING EXPLICIT DESTINATIONS

Table 7.1 also serves as a reference for creating explicit destinations. The types in the first column are names of public static final int values in the PdfDestination class. You can use these values to construct a PdfDestination object, as follows:

```
PdfDestination dest = new PdfDestination(PdfDestination.XYZ, 36, 802, 0);
```

The static method PdfAction.gotoLocalPage() creates an action that jumps to an explicit destination on a specific page.

Listing 7.5 TimetableDestinations.java

```
public void manipulatePdf(String src, String dest)
  throws IOException, DocumentException {
  PdfReader reader = new PdfReader(src);
  int n = reader.getNumberOfPages();
  PdfStamper stamper
    = new PdfStamper(reader, new FileOutputStream(dest));
  actions = new ArrayList<PdfAction>();
  PdfDestination d;
  for (int i = 0; i < n; ) {
      d = new PdfDestination(PdfDestination.FIT);          // Creates destination
      actions.add(PdfAction.gotoLocalPage(                 // Creates action and
        ++i, d, stamper.getWriter()));                     // adds it to list
  }
  PdfContentByte canvas;
  for (int i = 0; i < n; ) {
    canvas = stamper.getOverContent(++i);
    createNavigationTable(i, n)                            // Creates table containing
      .writeSelectedRows(0, -1, 696, 36, canvas);          // the actions
```

```
    }
    stamper.close();
}
```

This is a rewrite of the first example in this chapter. The output is identical to what is shown in figure 7.1. Instead of using named actions, you create a `List` containing `PdfAction` objects. If you look at the parameters of the `gotoLocalPage()` method, you'll recognize the page number, the destination of choice, and a third parameter that needs further explanation.

PAGE NUMBERS VERSUS PAGE REFERENCES

In listing 7.3, you retrieved information about named destinations using the `Simple-NamedDestination` class. This class uses `reader.getNamedDestination()` to get the named destinations. You could use this method too, but you'd get entries like this:

```
US=[1 0 R, /XYZ, 36, 802, 0]
AR=[210 0 R, /XYZ, 36, 802, 0]
```

The values `1 0 R` and `210 0 R` aren't page numbers but references to page dictionaries. There are no page numbers inside a PDF file. Pages are organized in a *page tree*, and their position in this tree defines the page number. When you create a link to an explicit destination using `gotoLocalPage()`, iText needs to translate the page number (for instance, page 19 to jump to the page with films from Argentina) to a reference (such as `210 0 R`). iText can only do this if you also pass a `PdfWriter` instance. In listing 7.5, you pass the writer associated with a `PdfStamper` object: `stamper.getWriter()`.

You'll create more destinations in section 7.2, when we talk about bookmarks, but first, let's introduce JavaScript into your documents.

7.1.3 *JavaScript in PDF documents*

JavaScript is a scripting language that is primarily used to add client-side functionality to an HTML page and to create dynamic websites. It allows programmatic access to objects within the web browser. JavaScript is also available in PDF viewers such as Adobe Reader.

There's a JavaScript API for PDF documents that extends the core client-side JavaScript specification and gives you access to Acrobat and Adobe Reader objects. Initially JavaScript 1.2 was used; since Acrobat 5.0, the API has been based on JavaScript 1.5. The most recent versions of Acrobat and Adobe Reader (since 8.0) use JavaScript 1.6. If you want to know more about the complete set of objects and functions, you can download the PDFs *Developing Acrobat Applications Using JavaScript* and *JavaScript for Acrobat API Reference* from the adobe.com site (see appendix B for useful links).

We're going to use some of the objects listed in those references to learn how to introduce JavaScript in a PDF document using iText.

DOCUMENT-LEVEL JAVASCRIPT

Here is an example of a simple script that clears the JavaScript console window, makes it visible, and writes information about the viewer and its version number.

Listing 7.6   viewer_version.js

```
console.clear();
console.show();
console.println("Hello");
console.println("You are using: " + app.viewerType);
console.println("The version of " + app.viewerType
  + " is: " + app.viewerVersion);
```

The console is an object that originally wasn't available in Adobe Reader, only in Acrobat. It was introduced in Adobe Reader 7.0 to report errors and show messages. The script in listing 7.6 prints the value of the `viewerType` and `viewerVersion` property of the application (the `app` object) to the console, as shown in figure 7.2.

Figure 7.2 shows that I opened the document in Adobe Reader version 9.2. You can add the script from listing 7.6 to an existing PDF document.

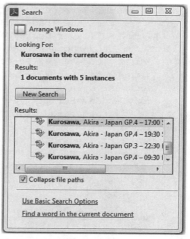

Figure 7.2   JavaScript Console window

Listing 7.7   AddVersionChecker

```
PdfReader reader = new PdfReader(HelloWorld.RESULT);
PdfStamper stamper =
  new PdfStamper(reader, new FileOutputStream(RESULT));
stamper.addJavaScript(Utilities.readFileToString(RESOURCE));
stamper.close();
```

What you're doing in listings 7.6 and 7.7 isn't very elegant. It works, but the `addJava-Script()` method should only be used to add JavaScript functions that can be called from a JavaScript action.

JAVASCRIPT ACTIONS

In chapter 4, you created a day-to-day overview of all the movies that are screened at the festival. The movies are sorted by date and time, but suppose you'd like to offer functionality that allows the end user to search for the occurrence of a specific director in the document. See figure 7.3.

This can be achieved with the `search` object.

Figure 7.3   Search window in Adobe Reader

Listing 7.8   find_director.js

```
function findDirector(name) {
  if (search.available) {
    search.query(name, "ActiveDoc");
  }
  else {
    app.alert("The Search plug-in isn't installed.");
  }
}
```

Note that you first check for the availability of the Search plug-in, because you mustn't assume that the plug-in is installed in every PDF viewer. If the plug-in is missing, you use the app.alert() method to inform the end user that searching for directors won't work. This method is similar to the alert() method in plain JavaScript. The viewer application opens an alert box showing the String that is passed to the method.

FAQ *Why are some of the methods I've found in the API documentation not working?* If you look for the query() method in the API documentation provided by Adobe, you'll see that the method is marked with a red "S". This means that the usage of the method can be restricted because of security reasons. Some methods only work in the full Acrobat application, not in the free Reader. Or, they are only supposed to work when the document is certified (see chapter 12), or reader-enabled (see chapter 8). Please check the *JavaScript for Acrobat API Reference* before reporting problems with JavaScript.

You can call the method shown from an action.

Listing 7.9   FindDirectors

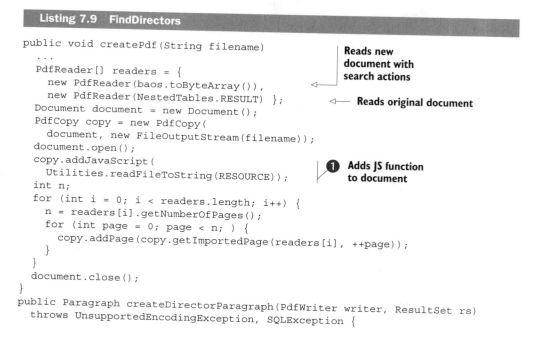

```
public void createPdf(String filename)
  ...
  PdfReader[] readers = {
    new PdfReader(baos.toByteArray()),          ←  Reads new
    new PdfReader(NestedTables.RESULT) };           document with
  Document document = new Document();               search actions
  PdfCopy copy = new PdfCopy(
    document, new FileOutputStream(filename));   ←— Reads original document
  document.open();
  copy.addJavaScript(                          ❶ Adds JS function
    Utilities.readFileToString(RESOURCE));         to document
  int n;
  for (int i = 0; i < readers.length; i++) {
    n = readers[i].getNumberOfPages();
    for (int page = 0; page < n; ) {
      copy.addPage(copy.getImportedPage(readers[i], ++page));
    }
  }
  document.close();
}
public Paragraph createDirectorParagraph(PdfWriter writer, ResultSet rs)
  throws UnsupportedEncodingException, SQLException {
```

```
String n = new String(rs.getBytes("name"), "UTF-8");
Chunk name = new Chunk(n);
name.setAction(PdfAction.javaScript(
    String.format("findDirector('%s');", n), writer));
name.append(", ");
name.append(new String(rs.getBytes("given_name"), "UTF-8"));
return new Paragraph(name);
}
```

❷ Creates action that
uses the function

In this listing, you add the function `findDirector(name)` as document-level JavaScript ❶. You use that function in the first document in actions triggered when the end user clicks on the name of a director ❷.

You'll use more JavaScript later on, when you create bookmarks and we talk about annotations and forms.

7.1.4 More actions

The `PdfAction` object provides more actions—for instance, an action to trigger an action in a Flash application that is embedded in the PDF—but that will be discussed in chapter 16. In this section, we'll look at launch actions. We'll also talk about creating a chain of actions and about triggering actions with events.

LAUNCH ACTIONS

According to ISO-32000-1, you can start an application from a PDF file with a launch action. Here is a harmless example of a clickable `Paragraph` that will open Notepad on a Windows OS showing a simple text file, `test.txt`, that is supposed to be present in the directory `C:\itext-core\book\resources\txt`.

Listing 7.10 LaunchAction

```
Paragraph p = new Paragraph(new Chunk(
    "Click to open test.txt in Notepad.")
    .setAction(new PdfAction("c:/windows/notepad.exe",
    "test.txt", "open", "C:\\itext-core\\book\\resources\\txt")));
```

Recent versions of Adobe Reader show a warning or even disallow this functionality, because executing an external program from a PDF file can be a security hazard. You'll use the example created with listing 7.10 in section 13.3.2, where you'll learn how to remove launch actions from existing PDF files. The example in chapter 13 is used on a mail server—PDFs that are attached to mail messages are checked for launch actions, and if such an action is found, it's replaced with an `app.alert()` JavaScript action using iText.

Suppose that you don't want to start an external program, but you want different actions to be executed one after the other. That sounds like programming, but in PDF it's called *chaining actions together.*

CHAINING ACTIONS

Chaining actions is done with the `next()` method. Let's reuse the timetable, and add the text "print this page" to every page. If an end user clicks these words, you'll cause three actions to be triggered.

Listing 7.11   PrintTimeTable

```
Chunk chunk = new Chunk("print this page");
PdfAction action = PdfAction.javaScript(
  "app.alert('Think before you print!');", stamper.getWriter());
action.next(PdfAction.javaScript(
  "printCurrentPage(this.pageNum);", stamper.getWriter()));
action.next(new PdfAction("http://www.panda.org/savepaper/"));
chunk.setAction(action);
```

❶ **Think!**

❷ **Print!**

⟵ **Read!**

First, you want to show an alert box saying, "Think before you print!" ❶. Then you want the Print dialog box to open with only the current page selected ❷. That can be done using this JavaScript function.

Listing 7.12   print_page.js

```
function printCurrentPage() {
  var pp = this.getPrintParams();
  pp.firstPage = this.pageNum;
  pp.lastPage = pp.firstPage;
  this.print(pp);
}
```

In this context, this refers to the Doc object of the current document. You ask the document for its printer parameters, and you ask it to print itself using a slightly altered print range. The Print dialog box will open with that range already selected. The end user can still decide whether or not to print the document. Once the user closes the dialog box, they'll be invited to visit the "How you can save paper" web page from the World Wide Fund for Nature (WWF).

These three actions happen one after the other because the user clicked a link, but actions can also be started when something happens: they can be triggered by an event.

EVENTS TRIGGERING ACTIONS

In listing 7.7, you used document-level JavaScript that was triggered when the document was opened. But opening a document is an event—it would have been better to trigger the action to open the console from such an event.

If you look at the first day of the Foobar Film Festival on the timetable, you'll see that there's only one movie that isn't reserved for the press: the opening movie. But you know from figure 3.1 that the tickets for this movie are sold out. People consulting the timetable will be disappointed if they're looking to buy tickets. To avoid this, you can use an open action to tell the viewer application to jump to the second page immediately. That way, the end user can still navigate to the first page, but only after having seen the second page.

Furthermore, you'll repeat the "Think before you print" message upon printing, and tell the user to "Think again next time!" afterwards. Upon closing the document, you'll wish the user a good festival.

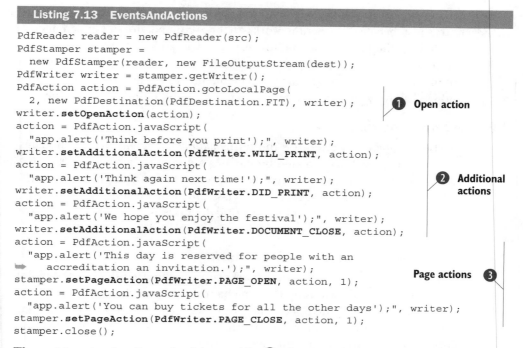

Listing 7.13   EventsAndActions

```
PdfReader reader = new PdfReader(src);
PdfStamper stamper =
  new PdfStamper(reader, new FileOutputStream(dest));
PdfWriter writer = stamper.getWriter();
PdfAction action = PdfAction.gotoLocalPage(
  2, new PdfDestination(PdfDestination.FIT), writer);        ❶ Open action
writer.setOpenAction(action);
action = PdfAction.javaScript(
  "app.alert('Think before you print');", writer);
writer.setAdditionalAction(PdfWriter.WILL_PRINT, action);
action = PdfAction.javaScript(
  "app.alert('Think again next time!');", writer);           ❷ Additional
writer.setAdditionalAction(PdfWriter.DID_PRINT, action);        actions
action = PdfAction.javaScript(
  "app.alert('We hope you enjoy the festival');", writer);
writer.setAdditionalAction(PdfWriter.DOCUMENT_CLOSE, action);
action = PdfAction.javaScript(
  "app.alert('This day is reserved for people with an
     accreditation an invitation.');", writer);
stamper.setPageAction(PdfWriter.PAGE_OPEN, action, 1);       Page actions ❸
action = PdfAction.javaScript(
  "app.alert('You can buy tickets for all the other days');", writer);
stamper.setPageAction(PdfWriter.PAGE_CLOSE, action, 1);
stamper.close();
```

The setOpenAction() method is specific ❶; the corresponding action is triggered when a user opens the document. With the setAdditionalAction() method ❷, you can couple an action to the following events:

- WILL_PRINT—The action is triggered just before printing (part of) the document.
- DID_PRINT—The action is triggered just after printing.
- WILL_SAVE—The action is triggered just before saving the document.
- DID_SAVE—The action is triggered just after saving the document.
- DOCUMENT_CLOSE—The action is triggered just before closing the document.

Note that the WILL_SAVE and DID_SAVE actions aren't triggered if you perform a Save As operation. This implies that these additional actions will only work in the full Acrobat or for Reader-enabled documents.

You can also define page actions ❸. In listing 7.13, you tell the end user that the information on the first page may not be useful; when the user leaves the page, you display the message, "You can buy tickets for all the other days." This is done with the setPageAction() method and one of these values:

- PAGE_OPEN—The action is triggered when you enter a certain page.
- PAGE_CLOSE—The action is triggered when you leave a certain page.

This method exists for both PdfWriter and PdfStamper. The only difference is that with PdfStamper, you have to pass a page number to tell iText which page you want the action added to.

Before we move on to discuss bookmarks, let me repeat what I wrote in the FAQ entry: just because an action works in one context doesn't mean it will work in another. In the chained action, for instance, you added a URL action to open a page on the WWF site. This is an example of an action that will be ignored when triggered automatically. That's good practice. The document should only open a URL when the end user actively clicks a link, or a bookmark, as you'll find out in the next example.

7.2   Adding bookmarks

In PDF language, we often use the terms *outline tree* or *outlines* as synonyms for *bookmarks*. In chapter 2, you created bookmarks automatically by using Chapter and Section objects. The result was nice, but you can do better if you create the outline using PdfOutline objects. The PdfOutline class offers much more functionality, and you can use it to create bookmarks for existing documents.

Let's start using them in a document that's created from scratch.

7.2.1   Creating bookmarks for a new document

Take a look at figure 7.4. The bookmarks consist of movie titles printed in bold; one of the movie titles is shown using Korean characters. If you click one of these titles, you'll jump to the movie in the document. For every movie, there's also a bookmark shown in blue to the corresponding site on IMDB. If you click the Instant Info bookmark, an alert window opens showing the year and run length of the movie.

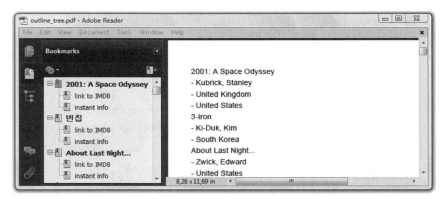

Figure 7.4   Document with bookmarks created using PdfOutline

This is different from what you did before with Chapter and Section objects. These bookmarks aren't referring to a specific destination in the document; they cause the execution of actions.

> **Listing 7.14   CreateOutlineTree**

```
Document document = new Document();
PdfWriter writer =
  PdfWriter.getInstance(document, new FileOutputStream(filename));
```

```
writer.setViewerPreferences(
  PdfWriter.PageModeUseOutlines);
document.open();
PdfOutline root = writer.getRootOutline();
PdfOutline movieBookmark;
PdfOutline link;
String title;
List<Movie> movies = PojoFactory.getMovies(connection);
for (Movie movie : movies) {
  title = movie.getMovieTitle();
  if ("3-Iron".equals(title))
    title = "\ube48\uc9d1";
  movieBookmark = new PdfOutline(root,
    new PdfDestination(PdfDestination.FITH,
      writer.getVerticalPosition(true)),
    true
  );
  movieBookmark.setStyle(Font.BOLD);
  link = new PdfOutline(movieBookmark,
    new PdfAction(
      String.format(RESOURCE, movie.getImdb())),
      "link to IMDB");
  link.setColor(BaseColor.BLUE);
  new PdfOutline(movieBookmark,
    PdfAction.javaScript(String.format(INFO,
      movie.getYear(), movie.getDuration()), writer),
      "instant info");
  document.add(new Paragraph(movie.getMovieTitle()));
  document.add(PojoToElementFactory.getDirectorList(movie));
  document.add(PojoToElementFactory.getCountryList(movie));
}
document.close();
```

Sets viewer preferences for bookmarks

① **Gets root of outline tree**

② **Adds first-level bookmark with internal link**

③ **Adds second-level bookmark with external link**

④ **Adds second-level bookmark with JavaScript action**

The first thing you need is the *root* of the outline tree. You can get this with the get-RootOutline() method **①**. During the creating of the document, you can use this root PdfOutline to create children **②**.

The constructor of the PdfOutline class accepts four parameters:

- *The* parent—Another PdfOutline object of which the newly created bookmark is a kid.
- A destination *or an* action—A PdfDestination if you want to add a local goto link, or a PdfAction object for any other action.
- A title *for the bookmark*—This can be a Paragraph, a String, or even a PdfString.
- A boolean *value* open *(optional)*—Indicates whether the outline has to be open (the default) or closed when the user opens the bookmark panel.

In listing 7.14, you create a PdfDestination to create a traditional bookmark that jumps to the vertical position just before you add a movie title. The zoom factor will be adapted so that the complete horizontal width is visible (look for FITH in table 7.1). Because you are creating the document from scratch, you don't have to pass the page number; iText uses the reference to the current page.

> **NOTE**   When adding basic building blocks to a document, you normally don't have to bother about pagination or the current Y position. But if you want to create a `PdfDestination` object, you need to know the vertical position. You can retrieve this coordinate with the `getVerticalPosition()` method. This method doesn't just "get" the Y value. It can also ensure that you get the position of the next line. That's why you pass the `boolean` value `true` in listing 7.14.

In listing 7.14, you're using actions to create outlines that are added as children of the movie title bookmark. ❸ serves as a link to IMBD using a URL action. ❹ adds a JavaScript action. The script consists of a single line that can be found in the `INFO String`:

```
app.alert('Movie produced in %s; run length: %s');
```

The `String` will be formatted for each movie so that `%s` is replaced with the year and duration found in your database.

> **NOTE**   You can use a `Paragraph` for the bookmark title, but the style of the `Paragraph` object will not be taken into account. You can change the style only with the methods `setStyle()` ❷ and `setColor()` ❸. Observe that Unicode characters are accepted. In listing 7.14, the title of the movie "3-Iron" is replaced with the characters for "Bin-Jip" (which is the original Korean title of this excellent movie).

You've now created a new PDF document with bookmarks, but this part of the book is mainly about manipulating existing documents. Suppose that you receive a document like the one you've just created—how can you retrieve the bookmarks? That's what we're going to look at in the next example.

7.2.2   *Retrieving bookmarks from an existing document*

In section 7.1.1, you used the `SimpleNamedDestination` class to retrieve the named destinations from a document in the form of a `HashMap` or an XML file. Here you use a similar object to extract the bookmarks from an existing PDF: `SimpleBookmark`.

Listing 7.15   CreateOutlineTree

```
PdfReader reader = new PdfReader(src);
List<HashMap<String,Object>> list = SimpleBookmark.getBookmark(reader);
    SimpleBookmark.exportToXML(list,                                       ❶
        new FileOutputStream(dest), "ISO8859-1", true);
```

You first obtain a `List` of `HashMap` objects. Each `HashMap` item contains at least one of the keys listed in table 7.2.

Table 7.2   Possible keys for a bookmark entry

Key	Value	Description
Title	String	The bookmark title that is used in the outline tree.
Color	Three `float` values	Color values for red, green, and blue ranging from 0 to 1, defining the color of the title.

Table 7.2 Possible keys for a bookmark entry *(continued)*

Key	Value	Description
Style	String	Can be empty, `"bold"`, `"italic"`, or `"italic bold"`. Defines the style of the title.
Open	boolean	If `true`, the bookmark is open, showing its kids. If `false`, the end user has to click the + sign in front of the bookmark to see the bookmarks of the sublevel.
Kids	List	A list with the Maps of the sublevel entries of this bookmark.
Action	String	Can be `"GoTo"`, `"GoToR"`, `"URI"`, or `"Launch"`. Due to their possibly complex nature, JavaScript actions aren't shown.
Page	String	A destination on a page; see table 7.1 for the syntax; this entry occurs in combination with GoTo and GoToR actions.
Named / NamedN	String	The name of a named destination; this entry occurs in combination with GoTo and GoToR actions. Named is used when the name is stored as a PdfString; NamedN is used for PdfNames.
File	String	A path to the file to open or execute; this entry occurs in combination with GoToR and Launch actions.
NewWindow	boolean	Indicates whether the file to be opened must be opened in a new window; this entry occurs in combination with the GoToR action.
URI	String	The URL that will be opened if the end user clicks the bookmark. This entry occurs in combination with an URI action.

You can export the bookmarks list to an XML file ❶ (in listing 7.15) using the Latin-1 encoding (see the `"ISO8859-1"` parameter), accepting only ASCII characters (see the true parameter). The resulting XML file looks like this:

```
<?xml version="1.0" encoding="ISO8859-1"?>
<Bookmark>
  <Title Action="GoTo" Page="1 FitH 806"
    Style="bold" >2001: A Space Odyssey
    <Title Action="URI" URI="http://imdb.com/title/tt0062622/"
      Color="0 0 1" >link to IMDB</Title>
    <Title >instant info</Title>
  </Title>
  <Title Action="GoTo" Page="1 FitH 734"
    Style="bold" >&#48712;&#51665;
    <Title Action="URI" URI="http://imdb.com/title/tt0423866/"
      Color="0 0 1" >link to IMDB</Title>
    <Title >instant info</Title>
  </Title>
</Bookmark>
```

You can use table 7.2 to interpret this XML file. The root tag is always named Bookmark. The Title tags are used for its children. There's no Kids tag; the entries of the Kids list are nested Title tags. All other key-value pairs are attributes of the Title tag.

You can also use table 7.2 as a reference to create new bookmarks for an existing document.

7.2.3 *Adding bookmarks to an existing document*

Suppose that you want to add bookmarks to the timetable PDF, as in figure 7.5.

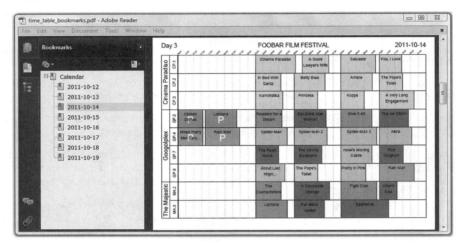

Figure 7.5   Bookmarks added to an existing document

There's a top-level entry in the Bookmarks list for this timetable with the title "Calendar". Nothing happens if you click it; it's just a structural element with eight children: one for each festival day. If you click one of these dates, the corresponding page is opened. You can create this outline tree and add it to an existing document using PdfStamper.

Listing 7.16   BookmarkedTimeTable

```
ArrayList<HashMap<String, Object>> outlines          Creates new
  = new ArrayList<HashMap<String, Object>> ();       bookmarks list
HashMap<String, Object> map = new HashMap<String, Object> ();
outlines.add(map);
map.put("Title", "Calendar");
ArrayList<HashMap<String, Object>> kids              Creates top-
  = new ArrayList<HashMap<String, Object>> ();       level entry
map.put("Kids", kids);
int page = 1;
List<Date> days = PojoFactory.getDays(connection);
for (Date day : days) {
  HashMap<String, Object> kid
    = new HashMap<String, Object> ();
  kids.add(kid);                                      Creates second-
  kid.put("Title", day.toString());                   level entry
  kid.put("Action", "GoTo");
  kid.put("Page", String.format("%d Fit", page++));
}
PdfReader reader = new PdfReader(src);
```

```
PdfStamper stamper =
   new PdfStamper(reader, new FileOutputStream(dest));
stamper.setOutlines(outlines);
stamper.close();
```
⟵ **Adds bookmarks list**

You can use table 7.2 to create Maps with titles, kids, and actions. You can consult table 7.1 to create the destination for the Page value. You can use the setOutlines() method to add the bookmarks to the stamper object. This also works for PdfCopy.

You've concatenated documents with bookmarks in chapter 6, and found that all your bookmarks were lost. We'll see how to fix this in the next example.

7.2.4 Concatenating documents with bookmarks

For this example, you'll take the timetable PDF you created in the previous example, and concatenate it with the MovieHistory document you created in chapter 2. Both documents have bookmarks, and you want these bookmarks to be merged as shown in figure 7.6.

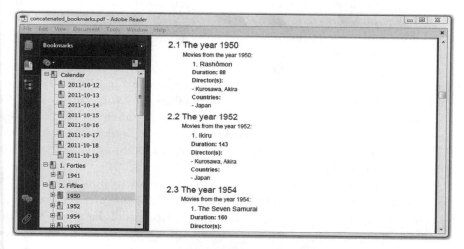

Figure 7.6 Concatenated documents with concatenated bookmarks

In this code sample, we concatenate bookmarks, but in listing 6.21, we concatenated documents.

Listing 7.17 ConcatenateBookmarks

```
Document document = new Document();
PdfCopy copy = new PdfCopy(document, new FileOutputStream(dest));
document.open();
PdfReader reader;
int page_offset = 0;
int n;
ArrayList<HashMap<String, Object>> bookmarks
   = new ArrayList<HashMap<String, Object>>();
List<HashMap<String, Object>> tmp;
```
| **Creates new bookmarks list**

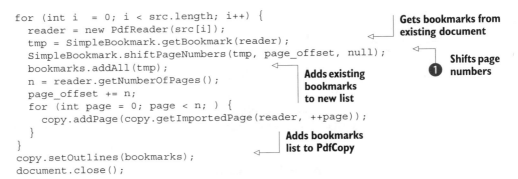

```
for (int i  = 0; i < src.length; i++) {
  reader = new PdfReader(src[i]);
  tmp = SimpleBookmark.getBookmark(reader);
  SimpleBookmark.shiftPageNumbers(tmp, page_offset, null);
  bookmarks.addAll(tmp);
  n = reader.getNumberOfPages();
  page_offset += n;
  for (int page = 0; page < n; ) {
    copy.addPage(copy.getImportedPage(reader, ++page));
  }
}
copy.setOutlines(bookmarks);
document.close();
```

- **Gets bookmarks from existing document**
- **❶ Shifts page numbers**
- **Adds existing bookmarks to new list**
- **Adds bookmarks list to PdfCopy**

Just like in the PdfStamper example, you create an ArrayList for the bookmarks. You could start adding new entries, but for this example you'll get the bookmarks from the existing documents. These bookmarks will work correctly for the first document, but a bookmark that points at the first page in the second document won't. It will point to the first page of the first document in the concatenated PDF. That's why you need to shift the page numbers using the shiftPageNumbers() method ❶. After that's done, you add the bookmarks to the new list. You use setOutlines() to inject the new list of bookmarks into the new document.

One of the parameters in ❶ was null. That's because you want to shift the page numbers of the bookmarks for all the pages. You can also pass an array with an even number of int values that define page ranges for which you want to shift the page numbers with the offset defined by the page_offset parameter. There's also an eliminatePages() method that can be used to remove the bookmarks that point at specific page ranges. That's an interesting method if you want to split existing documents or remove a couple of pages.

Now that you know everything there is to know about bookmarks in PDF, what about creating bookmarks in HTML? With listing 7.3, you retrieved named destinations; with listing 7.15, you retrieved bookmarks. Wouldn't it be nice if you could use that information to create a URL that can be used to open a PDF file in a browser at a specific position? The next section will give you an overview of the open parameters that can be used to achieve this.

7.2.5 *Open parameters*

When starting Adobe Reader from the command line, you can pass an open action (/A) with different parameters. When opening a PDF in a browser using a URL, you can achieve the same result by adding parameters after the # sign.

The following line called from the command line opens the JavaScript API documentation on page 28:

```
AcroRd32.exe /A "page=28=OpenActions" c:/downloads/js_api_reference.pdf
```

The following URL opens the documentation about open actions on page 5 using a magnifying factor that ensures that the complete page fits within the viewer window:

```
http://partners.adobe.com/public/developer/en/acrobat/
➥ PDFOpenParameters.pdf#page=5&view=Fit
```

Table 7.3 lists the parameters that can be passed with the /A option, or that can be added to a URL, involving named and explicit destinations. For more open parameters, consult the *Open Parameters for PDF* document that can be found on the Adobe site (see appendix B for the URL).

Table 7.3 Overview of the open parameters

Parameter and value	Description
nameddest=*name*	Jumps to a named destination with name name in the PDF.
page=*pagenum*	Jumps to the page with page number pagenum. This number indicates the actual page, not the label you may have given the page.
zoom=*scale* zoom=*scale*, *left*, *top*	Sets the zoom and scroll factors. A scale value of 100 gives 100 percent zoom; left and top are set in a coordinate system where the origin is the top left of the visible page, regardless of the document rotation.
view=*fit* view=*fit*, *parameter*	Sets the zoom factor based on the page size. The value for fit can be Fit, FitH, FitV, FitB, FitBH, or FitVH. The parameter has the same meaning as described in table 7.1. This isn't supported with the command-line option.
viewrect=*left*, *top*, *width*, *height*	Opens the file so that the rectangle specified with the parameters is visible. This isn't supported with the command-line option.

You've learned about destinations; you've learned about actions. You've used both with Chunks; you've used both with PdfOutlines. But what really makes a document interactive is annotations.

7.3 *Creating annotations*

According to Merriam-Webster's Online Dictionary, an annotation is a note added by way of comment or explanation. But an annotation in a PDF can be much more. It can be a movie or a sound that will be played in the document. It can be a field with a value that changes depending on other fields. It can be a shape that changes color if you move over it with the mouse.

But let's not get ahead of ourselves; let's start with the simplest type of annotation: a text annotation aka a *sticky note*.

7.3.1 *Text annotations*

Figure 7.7 shows two documents with text annotations. The document in the back has small icons in the form of a note; the document in the front has small text balloons. If you move your mouse over such an icon, a tooltip appears. Double-click the icon, and a sticky note window appears. That's an open text annotation.

The text annotations in the back are created using the Annotation class.

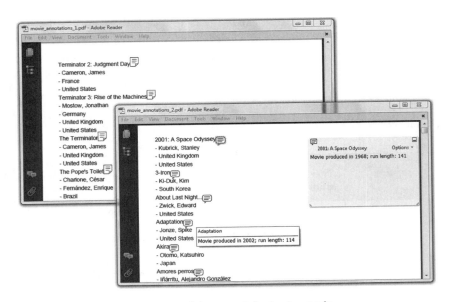

Figure 7.7   Text annotations containing more info about a movie

THE ANNOTATION CLASS

The Annotation class implements the Element interface (see chapter 2), so you can add it to a Document using the add() method. The annotation will be added at the current cursor position in the document.

Listing 7.18   MovieAnnotations1

```
Document document = new Document();
PdfWriter.getInstance(document, new FileOutputStream(filename));
document.open();
for (Movie movie : PojoFactory.getMovies(connection)) {
  document.add(new Phrase(movie.getMovieTitle()));
  document.add(new Annotation(movie.getTitle(),           Adds text
    String.format(INFO,                                   annotation at
      movie.getYear(), movie.getDuration())));            current position
  document.add(PojoToElementFactory.getDirectorList(movie));
  document.add(PojoToElementFactory.getCountryList(movie));
}
document.close(;
```

You create a text annotation using two String values: a title and the contents of the annotation. Note that the functionality of the Annotation class is rather limited. If you want to change the appearance of the annotation, such as to change the color of the open note, you need a more specialized class.

THE PDFANNOTATION CLASS

PdfAnnotation has a series of static methods that create specific types of annotations. The method createText() is used to create a text annotation.

Listing 7.19   MovieAnnotations2

```
Phrase phrase;
Chunk chunk;
for (Movie movie : PojoFactory.getMovies(connection)) {
  phrase = new Phrase(movie.getMovieTitle());
  chunk = new Chunk("\u00a0");
  chunk.setAnnotation(
    PdfAnnotation.createText(writer, null,
    movie.getMovieTitle(), String.format(INFO,
    movie.getYear(), movie.getDuration()),
    false, "Comment"));
  phrase.add(chunk);
  document.add(phrase);
  document.add(PojoToElementFactory.getDirectorList(movie));
  document.add(PojoToElementFactory.getCountryList(movie));
}
```

> **Adds a text annotation to a Chunk**

The createText() method expects six parameters:

- PdfWriter *writer*—An instance of PdfWriter; if you're using PdfStamper, you can use the stamper.getWriter() method to obtain a writer object.
- Rectangle *rect*—The rectangle where you want the annotation to appear. In the example, you don't know in advance where the annotation will be added, so you pass null. The rectangle will be defined as soon as iText renders the Chunk to which the annotation will be added.
- String *title*—A title for the annotations.
- String *contents*—The content of the text annotation.
- boolean *open*—A Boolean value indicating whether the annotation should be open (true) or closed (false).
- String *icon*—The icon that should be used. Possible values are "Comment", "Key", "Note", "Help", "NewParagraph", "Paragraph", and "Insert".

Figure 7.8 illustrates the different types of icons you can use for text annotations. The lower half of this figure shows the comments panel, which gives an overview of all the text annotations present in the PDF document. It was opened by clicking the text balloons at the left in the Adobe Reader window.

The annotations in figure 7.8 were added to the document using a generic tag event (see section 5.2.1). In this case, I used the addAnnotation() method to add the PdfAnnotation object to the PdfWriter. That's the most common way to add annotations.

A GENERIC WAY TO CREATE ANNOTATIONS

In the subsections that follow, you'll discover several types of annotations that are supported in iText. You'll use convenience methods or classes to create link, stamp, line, and other annotations. In chapter 16, we'll discuss different types of rich media annotations.

If this still doesn't meet your requirements, there's a more generic way to create an annotation—*any* type of annotation.

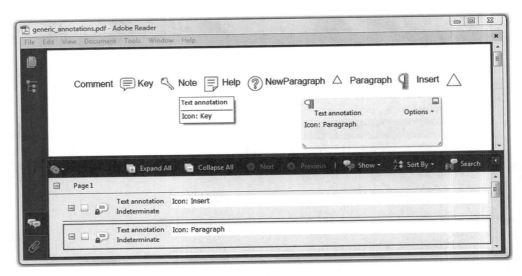

Figure 7.8   Different types of icons for text annotations

Listing 7.20   GenericAnnotations

```
public void onGenericTag(PdfWriter writer, Document document,
  Rectangle rect, String text) {
  PdfAnnotation annotation = new PdfAnnotation(
    writer, new Rectangle(
      rect.getRight() + 10, rect.getBottom(),
      rect.getRight() + 30, rect.getTop()));
  annotation.put(PdfName.SUBTYPE, PdfName.TEXT);
  annotation.setTitle("Text annotation");
  annotation.put(PdfName.OPEN, PdfBoolean.PDFFALSE);
  annotation.put(PdfName.CONTENTS,
    new PdfString(String.format("Icon: %s", text)));
  annotation.put(PdfName.NAME, new PdfName(text));
  writer.addAnnotation(annotation);
}
```

❶ Creates generic annotation

❷ Defines type of annotation

❸ Sets title using convenience class

❹ Sets different properties

Adds annotation to writer

In ❶, you create a generic annotation using a `PdfWriter` instance and a `Rectangle`. In ❷, you tell iText that you want to create a text annotation.

Suppose some new type of annotation is invented; for instance, a "Foobar" annotation. You could create such an annotation like this:

```
annotation.put(PdfName.SUBTYPE, new PdfName("Foobar"));
```

`PdfAnnotation` is a subclass of `PdfDictionary`. Just like `PdfAction`, it's a collection of key-value pairs. The type of the annotation is defined by the /Subtype key. The other entries of the annotation dictionary depend on this value.

> **NOTE**   You can find references to the annotation dictionaries in the /Annots entry of the page dictionary. Visible annotations will always be rendered on top of the other content. They aren't part of the content stream of a page.

A number of keys, such as the title, will be present in many different types of annotations. That's why you'll find methods such as `setTitle()` in the API of the `PdfAnnotation` class ❸. For more exotic annotations, such as the (imaginary) Foobar annotation, you'll have to look at its (future) specification, and add `PdfName` and `PdfObject` pairs using the `put()` method ❹.

> **NOTE** There's a complete range of annotations that are used to visualize text edits: Caret annotations, StrikeThrough annotations, Squiggly annotations, and so on. These annotations are typically added by a human reader using Acrobat. You could add these annotations using iText, but that sort of defeats the purpose of the library: iText is better suited to adding annotations in an automated process. The examples that follow are based on my experience and they're selected to inspire, rather than to give a complete taxonomy.

For more info about annotations, please read section 12.5 of ISO-32000-1. There's a complete overview of all the possible annotations in section 12.5.6 of the ISO specification.

ADDING ANNOTATIONS TO AN EXISTING PDF

Suppose you wanted to provide the timetable online so that people can print it, but you want to add extra information that won't be printed. This is shown in figure 7.9.

To create the timetable in figure 7.9, you'll use `createText()` once more using the Help icon. With the `setColor()` method, you can make sure that the color of the annotation corresponds with the festival category.

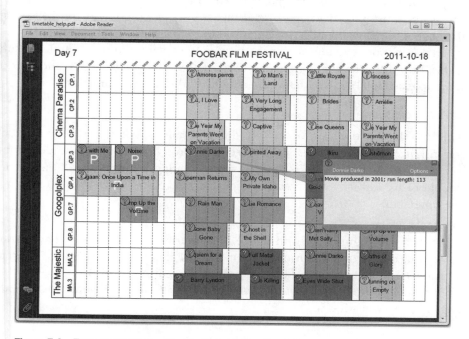

Figure 7.9 Text annotations added to the existing timetable

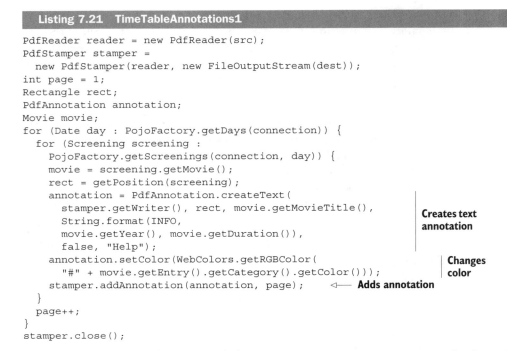

Listing 7.21   TimeTableAnnotations1

```
PdfReader reader = new PdfReader(src);
PdfStamper stamper =
  new PdfStamper(reader, new FileOutputStream(dest));
int page = 1;
Rectangle rect;
PdfAnnotation annotation;
Movie movie;
for (Date day : PojoFactory.getDays(connection)) {
  for (Screening screening :
    PojoFactory.getScreenings(connection, day)) {
    movie = screening.getMovie();
    rect = getPosition(screening);
    annotation = PdfAnnotation.createText(
      stamper.getWriter(), rect, movie.getMovieTitle(),      Creates text
      String.format(INFO,                                    annotation
      movie.getYear(), movie.getDuration()),
      false, "Help");
    annotation.setColor(WebColors.getRGBColor(               Changes
      "#" + movie.getEntry().getCategory().getColor()));     color
    stamper.addAnnotation(annotation, page);      ⊲— Adds annotation
  }
  page++;
}
stamper.close();
```

In the previous example, you used the PdfWriter.addAnnotation() method to add the annotation to the current page. When you add annotations to an existing page, you need to use the PdfStamper.addAnnotation() method, and you have to specify the page number of the page to which you want to add the annotation.

In this section, text annotations were used to explain different annotations mechanisms: how to create them, how to add them to newly created PDFs, and how to add them to existing PDFs. Now let's have a look at other types of annotations.

7.3.2   *Link annotations*

This isn't the first time you've worked with annotations. Whenever you created links—for instance, using the Anchor class (see section 2.3.1) or using the Chunk method setAction() (see section 7.1.1)—you were creating a link annotation. In the next couple of examples, you'll create a clickable image and add clickable rectangles to the timetable.

CLICKABLE IMAGES

If you compare figure 7.10 with figure 3.17, there's one major difference: when you move your mouse over a movie poster on the PDF that's shown in figure 7.10, a tooltip appears, revealing the URL of the corresponding movie on IMDB.

If you click the movie poster, Adobe Reader will ask you if you want to open that page in a browser window.

Figure 7.10 Link annotations have been added to all the images; see, for instance, the link to Donnie Darko at IMDB

Listing 7.22 MoviePosters1

```
Image img;
Annotation annotation;
float x = 11.5f;
float y = 769.7f;
for (Movie movie : PojoFactory.getMovies(connection)) {
  img = Image.getInstance(String.format(RESOURCE, movie.getImdb()));
  img.scaleToFit(1000, 60);
  img.setAbsolutePosition(x + (45 - img.getScaledWidth()) / 2, y);
  annotation = new Annotation(0, 0, 0, 0,
    String.format(IMDB, movie.getImdb()));
  img.setAnnotation(annotation);          ← Makes image clickable    Creates link annotation
  canvas.addImage(img);
  x += 48;
  if (x > 578) {
    x = 11.5f;
    y -= 84.2f;
  }
}
```

You use the simple `Annotation` class to create the link annotation. The first four parameters are meant to pass the coordinates for the clickable area, but listing 7.22 shows how you can make the image clickable using the method `Image.setAnnotation()`, so you don't have to worry about coordinates. iText will set these parameters so they correspond with the image location.

ADDING CLICKABLE AREAS TO AN EXISTING DOCUMENT

You can adapt listing 7.21 so that instead of adding text annotations with extra info about each movie, it adds a link annotation that corresponds with each screening.

Listing 7.23   TimetableAnnotations2

```
int page = 1;
Rectangle rect;
PdfAnnotation annotation;
for (Date day : PojoFactory.getDays(connection)) {
  for (Screening screening :
    PojoFactory.getScreenings(connection, day)) {
    rect = getPosition(screening);
    annotation = PdfAnnotation.createLink(
      stamper.getWriter(), rect,
      PdfAnnotation.HIGHLIGHT_INVERT,
      new PdfAction(String.format(IMDB,
      screening.getMovie().getImdb()))
    );
    stamper.addAnnotation(annotation, page);
  }
  page++;
}
```

Creates link annotation

Adds annotation to existing page

Just as with createText(), you need to pass a PdfWriter and a Rectangle object to the createLink() method. The third parameter should be one of the following values:

- HIGHLIGHT_NONE—No highlighting (the default). The links created with Anchor, Chunk.setAnchor(), or Chunk.setAction() aren't highlighted when you click them.
- HIGHLIGHT_INVERT—Inverts the content of the annotation square when clicked. That's what is used in listing 7.23. If you click a movie block, the colors will be inverted.
- HIGHLIGHT_OUTLINE—Inverts the annotation border when clicked.
- HIGHLIGHT_PUSH—Displays the annotation as if it were being pushed below the surface of the page.

The destination of the link annotation can be a PdfAction, as in listing 7.23, a String for a named destination, or a PdfDestination for an explicit destination.

Now let's continue our overview of "iText's most popular annotations" with file attachments.

7.3.3   *File attachments*

The document shown in figure 7.11 is almost identical to the documents shown in figure 7.7, but the annotation is visualized as a paperclip. This paperclip indicates that an annotation with subtype /FileAttachment was added.

If you click the paperclip icon in the left sidebar of Adobe Reader, you can get an overview of all the files that are attached to the PDF. As you can see, the attachments are a series of JPEG images with names in the form img_*xyz*.jpg, where *xyz* is the primary key of a movie at IMDB. If you click a paperclip next to one of the movie titles, the poster of that movie will be opened using the default image viewer on your computer. Note that, depending on your security preferences, the PDF viewer may ask you if you're sure before opening another application. How was this PDF document created?

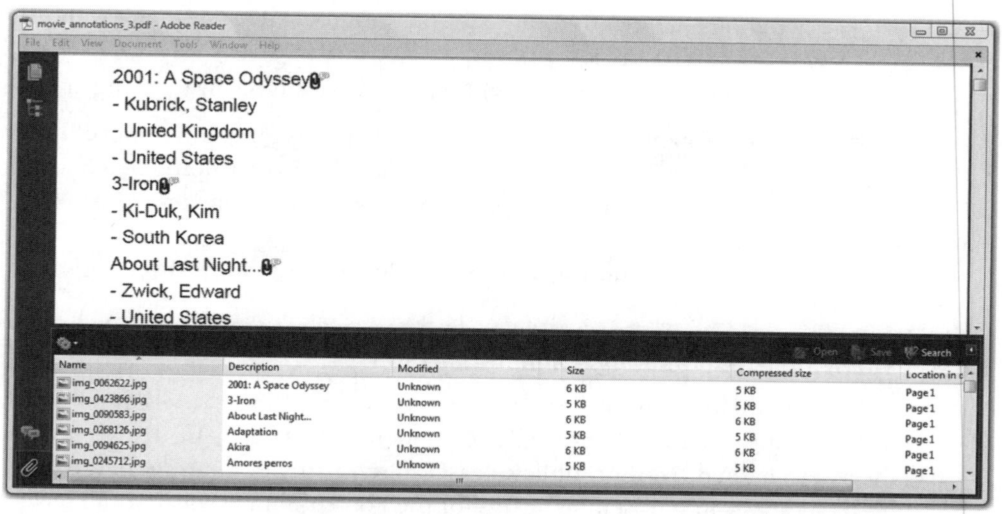

Figure 7.11 Movie list with file attachments

Listing 7.24 MovieAnnotations3

```
Phrase phrase;
Chunk chunk;
PdfAnnotation annotation;
for (Movie movie : PojoFactory.getMovies(connection)) {
  phrase = new Phrase(movie.getMovieTitle());
  chunk = new Chunk("\u00a0\u00a0");
  annotation = PdfAnnotation.createFileAttachment(         Creates file
    writer, null, movie.getMovieTitle(), null,             attachment
    String.format(RESOURCE, movie.getImdb()),              annotation
    String.format("img_%s.jpg", movie.getImdb())));
  annotation.put(PdfName.NAME,                             ➊ Defines name
    new PdfString("Paperclip"));                              for attachment
  chunk.setAnnotation(annotation);          ◁——  Adds annotation
  phrase.add(chunk);                              to existing page
  document.add(phrase);
  document.add(PojoToElementFactory.getDirectorList(movie));
  document.add(PojoToElementFactory.getCountryList(movie));
}
```

There are different ways to embed files. In section 16.2, you'll learn how to create document-level attachments and portable collections. For now, you'll create a file attachment annotation using the createFileAttachment() method and the following parameters:

- PdfWriter *writer*—An instance of PdfWriter.
- Rectangle *rect*—The rectangle where you want the annotation to appear.
- String *contents*—A description for the file attachment.
- byte[] *fileStore*—The bytes of the file you want to attach to the PDF, or null if the file parameter is a valid path to a file.

- String *file*—The path to the file you want to attach. This path will be ignored if fileStore isn't null.
- String *fileDisplay*—The (new) filename that will be given to the attached file.

In ❶, you set the name of the attachment to Paperclip. If you remove this line, every paperclip shown in figure 7.11 will be replaced by a pushpin, which is the default appearance of file attachments. Possible values for the name are "PushPin", "Paperclip", "Graph", and "Tag".

Let's finish this section with an example that combines three different types of annotations.

7.3.4 *Stamp, line, and rectangle annotations*

Rubber stamp annotations are intended to look as if they were stamped on the page with a rubber stamp: "Approved", "Confidential", "Draft". In this section, you'll use the stamp named "NotForPublicRelease" to stamp an annotation on the press visions.

As soon as you start selling tickets for the Foobar Film Festival, you'll have to update your timetable to inform customers which screenings are sold out. In this example, you'll use a line annotation to strike a white line through those screenings and a rectangle annotation with a dashed border to indicate for which screenings there are still tickets available. There are examples of each of these annotation types in figure 7.12.

The screening of the movie *Leaving Las Vegas* on October 18 is sold out. Just as with text annotations, this information is shown when you move your mouse over the

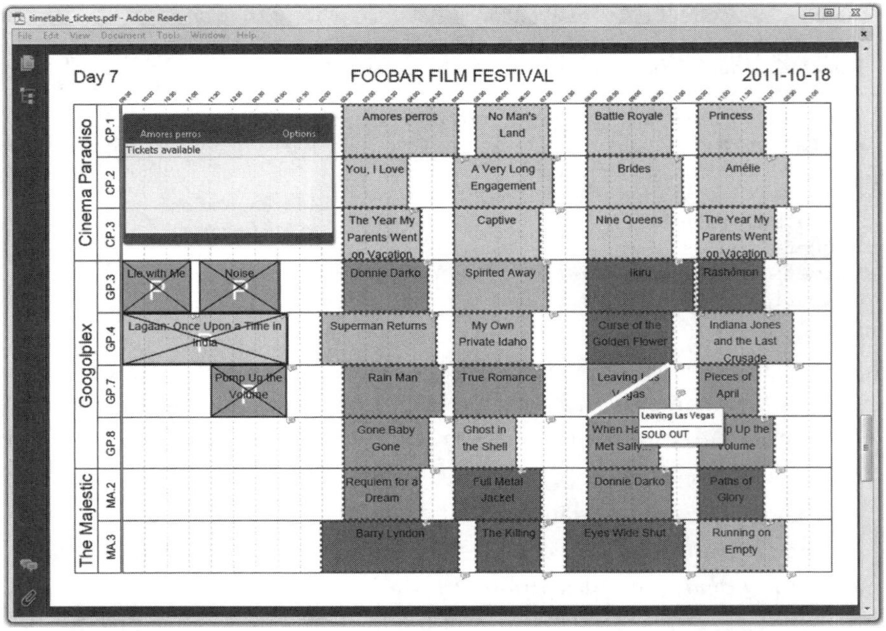

Figure 7.12   Stamp, rectangle, and line annotations added to an existing document

annotation. The annotation for the movie *Amores Perros* is open, because it's been double-clicked. The press screenings have an X stamped over them; they are not open to the public.

Listing 7.25 TimetableAnnotations3

```
int page = 1;
Rectangle rect;
float top;
PdfAnnotation annotation;
Movie movie;
for (Date day : PojoFactory.getDays(connection)) {
  for (Screening screening :
    PojoFactory.getScreenings(connection, day)) {
    rect = getPosition(screening);
    movie = screening.getMovie();
    if (screening.isPress()) {
      annotation = PdfAnnotation.createStamp(
        stamper.getWriter(), rect,
        "Press only", "NotForPublicRelease");
      annotation.setColor(BaseColor.BLACK);
      annotation.setFlags(PdfAnnotation.FLAGS_PRINT);
    }
    else if (isSoldOut(screening)) {
      top =
        reader.getPageSizeWithRotation(page).getTop();
      annotation = PdfAnnotation.createLine(
        stamper.getWriter(), rect, "SOLD OUT",
        top - rect.getTop(), rect.getRight(),
        top - rect.getBottom(), rect.getLeft());
      annotation.setTitle(movie.getMovieTitle());
      annotation.setColor(BaseColor.WHITE);
      annotation.setFlags(PdfAnnotation.FLAGS_PRINT);
      annotation.setBorderStyle(new PdfBorderDictionary(
        5, PdfBorderDictionary.STYLE_SOLID));
    }
    else {
      annotation = PdfAnnotation.createSquareCircle(
        stamper.getWriter(), rect,
        "Tickets available", true);
      annotation.setTitle(movie.getMovieTitle());
      annotation.setColor(BaseColor.BLUE);
      annotation.setFlags(PdfAnnotation.FLAGS_PRINT);
      annotation.setBorder(new PdfBorderArray(
        0, 0, 2, new PdfDashPattern()));
    }
    stamper.addAnnotation(annotation, page);
  }
  page++;
}
```

Adds rubber stamp annotation

1 Sets flag to print annotation

2 Adapts coordinates to rotation

3 Defines border style

Adds line annotation

Sets flag **1** to print annotation

4 Defines border width

Adds rectangle annotation

1 If you print the PDFs created in the previous examples, you won't see any of the annotations you've added showing up on paper. By using `setFlags()` with the `FLAGS_PRINT` flag in this example, you've made the stamp, line, and rectangle visible when printed. Note that this doesn't include the sticky note. For instance, the opened annotation saying that there are tickets available for *Amores Perros* won't be printed; only the dashed lines of the rectangle will be.

2 The width of the media box of a timetable page is smaller than its height, but you define the annotation rectangle as if the page is in landscape orientation, because the rotation of the page is 90 degrees. iText transforms this rectangle internally to make sure it's in the right place. To create a line annotation (or other annotations involving coordinates, such as /Polygon and /PolyLine annotations), however, you need to provide extra coordinates. In this case, you have to perform the transformation yourself if the media box is rotated.

3 You can change the border of the annotation using the setBorderStyle() method. Using the BorderStyleDictionary object, you can create different border styles.

4 You can also change the border using the setBorder() method. This method expects an object of type BorderArray.

> **NOTE** The effect of **3** and **4** depends on the type of annotation, and even on the viewer that is used. You're not creating an appearance using graphics state operators and operands in this example; it's up to the viewer application to decide how to render the annotation.

We could go on with more types of annotations and more properties, but this isn't the place or time to do so. This book doesn't replace the PDF reference or ISO-32000-1, and if we want to create interactive forms in the next chapter, we need to do a little bit of JavaScript programming first.

7.4   *JavaScript programming in PDF*

You've already introduced JavaScript into your PDF files in section 7.1.3. You've added document-level JavaScript, and you've created JavaScript actions triggered from a link annotation or an event. But that isn't the whole story. You didn't know you were using annotations at the time. Now that you do, you can do more cool things. At the end of this section, you'll even create a calculator application in a PDF. Along the way, you'll meet new types of annotations.

7.4.1   *Triggering JavaScript from a button*

The next chapter will be dedicated entirely to interactive forms. Forms consist of fields, and fields are visualized using a special type of annotations: *widget annotations.* In this section, we won't create a fillable form yet, but we'll experiment with the interactive features of widget annotations. In a first example, we'll stamp the timetable PDF once again. We'll add two buttons at the bottom of the page to trigger menu actions.

Listing 7.26 ButtonsActions

```
PdfReader reader = new PdfReader(src);
int n = reader.getNumberOfPages();
PdfStamper stamper = new PdfStamper(reader, new FileOutputStream(dest));
```

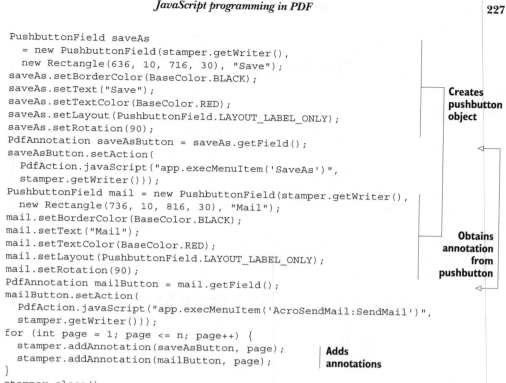

```
PushbuttonField saveAs
  = new PushbuttonField(stamper.getWriter(),
  new Rectangle(636, 10, 716, 30), "Save");
saveAs.setBorderColor(BaseColor.BLACK);
saveAs.setText("Save");
saveAs.setTextColor(BaseColor.RED);
saveAs.setLayout(PushbuttonField.LAYOUT_LABEL_ONLY);
saveAs.setRotation(90);
PdfAnnotation saveAsButton = saveAs.getField();
saveAsButton.setAction(
  PdfAction.javaScript("app.execMenuItem('SaveAs')",
  stamper.getWriter()));
PushbuttonField mail = new PushbuttonField(stamper.getWriter(),
  new Rectangle(736, 10, 816, 30), "Mail");
mail.setBorderColor(BaseColor.BLACK);
mail.setText("Mail");
mail.setTextColor(BaseColor.RED);
mail.setLayout(PushbuttonField.LAYOUT_LABEL_ONLY);
mail.setRotation(90);
PdfAnnotation mailButton = mail.getField();
mailButton.setAction(
  PdfAction.javaScript("app.execMenuItem('AcroSendMail:SendMail')",
  stamper.getWriter()));
for (int page = 1; page <= n; page++) {
  stamper.addAnnotation(saveAsButton, page);
  stamper.addAnnotation(mailButton, page);
}
stamper.close();
```

Creates pushbutton object

Obtains annotation from pushbutton

Adds annotations

You're no longer using a static method of PdfAnnotation to create an instance. Instead, you use a convenience class named PushbuttonField. This class allows you to define the layout of the annotation in a programmer-friendly way. Once you're done, you use getField() to obtain the corresponding PdfAnnotation object, and you can add a JavaScript action.

The JavaScript method execMenuItem() executes a menu item in Adobe Reader. In this case, clicking the buttons will have the same effect as if the user selected File > Save a Copy, and File > Attach to Email.

You've created buttons with a layout that only contained text (LAYOUT_LABEL_ONLY). In the next example, we'll look at how to introduce icons.

7.4.2 *Showing and hiding an annotation*

Do you also hate the aggressive advertisements that prevent you from viewing a web page unless you click a button to make them disappear? If that's the case, I have bad news for you.

I once talked to a manager responsible for a large newspaper group in a very small country (Belgium). I bragged that *The New York Times* had used iText to publish newspaper archives on the internet in the form of PDF documents. The manager said: "Well, that's nice, but we can't do that. We have to make money with our content, and it's almost impossible to add ads to a PDF file. We can only do that in HTML."

I immediately created the PDF shown in figure 7.13 to prove him wrong.

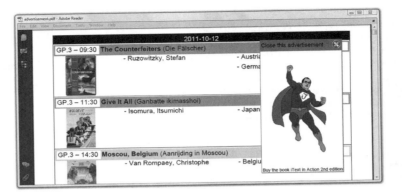

Figure 7.13
An advertisement that can be clicked away, added to an existing document

You'll recognize the original PDF from chapter 4, but I've added a shameless ad to promote this book on top of the existing content. The user can make it disappear by clicking the top bar. The ad consists of two button fields.

Listing 7.27 Advertisement

```
Rectangle rect = new Rectangle(400, 772, 545, 792);
PushbuttonField button = new PushbuttonField(
  stamper.getWriter(), rect, "click");
button.setBackgroundColor(BaseColor.RED);
button.setBorderColor(BaseColor.RED);
button.setFontSize(10);
button.setText("Close this advertisement");
button.setImage(Image.getInstance(IMAGE));
button.setLayout(
  PushbuttonField.LAYOUT_LABEL_LEFT_ICON_RIGHT);
button.setIconHorizontalAdjustment(1);
PdfFormField menubar = button.getField();
String js = "var f1 = getField('click');
    f1.display = display.hidden;
    var f2 = getField('advertisement');
    f2.display = display.hidden;";
menubar.setAction(
  PdfAction.javaScript(js, stamper.getWriter()));
stamper.addAnnotation(menubar, 1);
rect = new Rectangle(400, 550, 545, 772);
button = new PushbuttonField(
  stamper.getWriter(), rect, "advertisement");
button.setBackgroundColor(BaseColor.WHITE);
button.setBorderColor(BaseColor.RED);
button.setText(
  "Buy the book iText in Action 2nd edition");
button.setTemplate(stamper.getImportedPage(ad, 1));
button.setLayout(
  PushbuttonField.LAYOUT_ICON_TOP_LABEL_BOTTOM);
PdfFormField advertisement = button.getField();
advertisement.setAction(
  new PdfAction("http://manning.com/lowagie2/"));
stamper.addAnnotation(advertisement, 1);
```

1 Sets text and image as label and icon

2 Adds JavaScript that hides fields

3 Sets text and XObject as label and icon

Adds link to book site at Manning.com

In this example, you're creating button fields with a label and an icon. You can use an `Image` object for the icon ❶, or a `PdfTemplate` ❸ (in this case, you're using an imported page). I've used this functionality in a real-world project to create online examinations. Every question had a button that allowed the student to get a hint. If that button was clicked, an annotation was made visible and a hidden field was set. The value of this hidden field was posted together with the answers, so that the tutor could see for which questions a hint was used.

Some very simple JavaScript is used to hide (or reveal) the fields (or annotations) ❷. You get a field instance with the `getField()` JavaScript method for interactive fields, or with `getAnnot()` for ordinary annotations. Then you change the properties of these objects as explained in the JavaScript reference. In this example, clicking the upper button (named `click`) hides both buttons. Clicking the lower button (named `advertisement`) opens the web page dedicated to this book at Manning.com.

Pushbuttons aren't always meant to be pushed (or clicked). In the next example, we'll use pushbuttons as "hot areas" that trigger an action when the mouse moves over them.

7.4.3   A popup triggered by a button that doesn't need to be pushed

A popup annotation has no appearance stream or associated actions of its own. It's always associated with a parent annotation. Figure 7.14 shows a text annotation as a popup. If you take a close look at the image, you'll also see a widget annotation on top of the *Donnie Darko* poster. If you move the mouse inside the borders of this widget annotation, the popup with the text annotation will appear; if you move the mouse pointer outside the widget annotation, the popup will disappear.

Figure 7.14   Text annotation in a popup using a button and its events

Here is the mechanism behind this custom-made tooltip.

Listing 7.28   MoviePosters2

```
public void addPopup(PdfStamper stamper, Rectangle rect,
  String title, String contents, String imdb)
  throws IOException, DocumentException {
  PdfAnnotation text = PdfAnnotation.createText(stamper.getWriter(),       ❶
    rect, title, contents, false, "Comment");
  text.setName(String.format("IMDB%s", imdb));
  text.setFlags(
    PdfAnnotation.FLAGS_READONLY | PdfAnnotation.FLAGS_NOVIEW);
  PdfAnnotation popup = PdfAnnotation.createPopup(stamper.getWriter(),     ❷
    new Rectangle(rect.getLeft() + 10, rect.getBottom() + 10,
      rect.getLeft() + 200, rect.getBottom() + 100), null, false);
  popup.put(PdfName.PARENT, text.getIndirectReference());                  ❸
  text.put(PdfName.POPUP, popup.getIndirectReference());
  stamper.addAnnotation(text, 1);                                          ❹
  stamper.addAnnotation(popup, 1);
  PushbuttonField field = new PushbuttonField(stamper.getWriter(),         ❺
    rect, String.format("b%s", imdb));
  PdfAnnotation widget = field.getField();
  PdfAction enter =                                                        ❻
    PdfAction.javaScript(String.format(JS1, imdb), stamper.getWriter());
  widget.setAdditionalActions(PdfName.E, enter);
  PdfAction exit =
    PdfAction.javaScript(String.format(JS2, imdb), stamper.getWriter());
  widget.setAdditionalActions(PdfName.X, exit);
  stamper.addAnnotation(widget, 1);                                        ❼
}
```

❶ You create a text annotation for every movie. Each annotation has a unique name, IMDB*xyz*, where *xyz* is a key in IMDB. You also set the annotation flags so that the text area will be read-only and hidden.

❷ You create a popup annotation using a rectangle that's slightly different from the original one for two reasons: it must be big enough so that it can show the text without scrollbars, and it shouldn't cover the entire movie poster.

❸ You define the text annotation as the parent of the popup annotation. You tell the text annotation that the popup annotation is ... its popup.

❹ You add both annotations to the stamper—or to the writer if you're creating a document from scratch. So far, the text annotation isn't visible.

❺ You create a PushbuttonField and obtain the widget annotation using getField().

❻ You add JavaScript actions to the widget annotation as additional actions.

❼ You add the widget annotation to the stamper.

This listing doesn't define a "push" action for the button, because you're not looking to trigger an action when the user clicks the button. Instead you've defined two additional actions. One action is triggered when the mouse enters the area defined by the button:

```
public static final String JS1 =
  "var t = this.getAnnot(this.pageNum, 'IMDB%1$s'); t.popupOpen = true;
      var w = this.getField('b%1$s'); w.setFocus();";
```

Another action is triggered when the mouse exits the area defined by the button:

```
public static final String JS2 =
  "var t = this.getAnnot(this.pageNum, 'IMDB%s'); t.popupOpen = false;";
```

In these snippets, you set the `popupOpen` property of the text annotation to `true` or `false` depending on the additional action type you want. When the popup is opened, you also set the focus to the corresponding button field.

Enter ("E") and exit ("X") aren't the only additional actions that can be defined for widget annotations.

7.4.4 Additional actions

Table 7.4 lists the annotation events that are available. Most of these additional actions are used to enhance the user experience while filling out a form. In the next chapter, you'll use JavaScript to change the content of a text field to uppercase, to

Table 7.4   Additional actions of an interactive form field

Entry	PdfName	Meaning	The action will be performed when...
PdfName.E	/E	Enter	... the cursor enters the annotation's active area.
PdfName.X	/X	Exit	... the cursor exits the annotation's active area.
PdfName.D	/D	Down	... the mouse button is pressed inside the annotation's active area.
PdfName.U	/U	Up	... the mouse button is released inside the annotation's active area.
PdfName.FO	/Fo	Focus	... the annotation receives the input focus.
PdfName.BL	/Bl	Blurred	... the annotation loses the input focus.
PdfName.K	/K	Keystroke	... the user modifies the content of the field using a keystroke, or by selecting an entry in a list box.
PdfName.F	/F	Formatted	... the content of the field is about to be formatted.
PdfName.V	/V	Validate	... the field value has changed. This action can check the new value for its validity.
PdfName.C	/C	Calculate	... the field needs to be recalculated.
PdfName.PO	/PO	Page open	... the page containing the annotation is opened. The action will be performed after the open action of the document and after the PAGE_OPEN action if such an action is defined (see section 7.1.4).
PdfName.PC	/PC	Page close	... the page containing the annotation is closed. The action will be performed before the PAGE_CLOSE action.
Pdfname.PV	/PV	Page visible	... the page containing the annotation becomes visible in the viewer application's user interface.
PdfName.PI	/PI	Page invisible	... the page containing the annotation is no longer visible in the viewer application's user interface.

validate a date field, and so on. But we'll finish this section as promised: with a PDF calculator application written in JavaScript.

7.4.5 *A PDF calculator*

Figure 7.15 looks like the number pad of a simple calculator. In reality, it's a PDF file with buttons and text fields.

Listing 7.29 contains the method `addTextField()`. It creates a text field that shows the "display" of the calculator (named `result`), and an extra text field (named `move`). The content of this second text field will change when you move over the button fields.

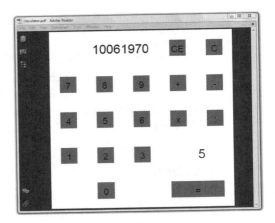

Figure 7.15   A calculator application in a PDF demonstrating the use of annotations and JavaScript

Listing 7.29   Calculator

```
public void addTextField(PdfWriter writer,
  Rectangle rect, String name) {
  PdfFormField field = PdfFormField
    .createTextField(writer, false, false, 0);        Creates single line,
  field.setFieldName(name);                           read-only, right-
  field.setWidget(rect, PdfAnnotation.HIGHLIGHT_NONE); aligned text field
  field.setQuadding(PdfFormField.Q_RIGHT);
  field.setFieldFlags(PdfFormField.FF_READ_ONLY);
  writer.addAnnotation(field);
}
public void addPushButton(PdfWriter writer,
  Rectangle rect, String btn, String script) {
  float w = rect.getWidth();
  float h = rect.getHeight();
  PdfFormField pushbutton                             Creates
    = PdfFormField.createPushButton(writer);          button field
  pushbutton.setFieldName("btn_" + btn);
  pushbutton.setWidget(rect, PdfAnnotation.HIGHLIGHT_PUSH);
  PdfContentByte cb = writer.getDirectContent();
  pushbutton.setAppearance(
    PdfAnnotation.APPEARANCE_NORMAL,
    createAppearance(cb, btn, BaseColor.GRAY, w, h));
  pushbutton.setAppearance(
    PdfAnnotation.APPEARANCE_ROLLOVER,                 Sets different
    createAppearance(cb, btn, BaseColor.RED, w, h));   appearances
  pushbutton.setAppearance(
    PdfAnnotation.APPEARANCE_DOWN,
    createAppearance(cb, btn, BaseColor.BLUE, w, h));
  pushbutton.setAdditionalActions(PdfName.U,           Adds additional
    PdfAction.javaScript(script, writer));             actions
  pushbutton.setAdditionalActions(PdfName.E,
```

```
        PdfAction.javaScript(
          "this.showMove('" + btn + "');", writer));      Adds additional
      pushbutton.setAdditionalActions(PdfName.X,            actions
        PdfAction.javaScript(
          "this.showMove(' ');", writer));
      writer.addAnnotation(pushbutton);
  }
  public PdfAppearance createAppearance(PdfContentByte cb,
    String btn, BaseColor color, float w, float h) {
    PdfAppearance app = cb.createAppearance(w, h);
    app.setColorFill(color);
    app.rectangle(2, 2, w - 4, h - 4);
    app.fill();
    app.beginText();                                        Creates an
    app.setColorFill(BaseColor.BLACK);                      appearance
    app.setFontAndSize(bf, h / 2);
    app.showTextAligned(
      Element.ALIGN_CENTER, btn, w / 2, h / 4, 0);
    app.endText();
    return app;
  }
```

There are 17 buttons on the calculator: 10 digits, 4 operators, 1 equals sign, 1 button to clear the display, and 1 button to clear the display and the memory. Observe that listing 7.29 creates different appearances:

- APPEARANCE_NORMAL—This appearance is used when the annotation is not interacting with the user. It's also used for printing the annotation.
- APPEARANCE_ROLLOVER—This appearance is used when the user moves the cursor into the annotation's active area without pressing the mouse button.
- APPEARANCE_DOWN—This appearance is used when the mouse button is pressed or held down within the annotation's active area.

In the calculator application, the buttons are gray when the document is opened. As soon as you move over a button with the mouse, its color is changed to red. When you click the button, it's blue as long as you keep the mouse button down. This mechanism is often used for link annotations, to show the end user that a specific area can be clicked to go to another page or URL. The different appearances are created the same way you created XObjects in chapter 3.

You've used additional actions to change the value of the text field named move. You can find the implementation of the showMove() function in listing 7.30. Clicking a digit triggers the augment() method. The register() method is called when the end user clicks an operator. The calculateResult() method corresponds to the equals sign. The C and CE buttons trigger reset().

Listing 7.30 calculator.js

```
var previous = 0;
var current = 0;
var operation = '';
```

```
function showCurrent() {
  this.getField('result').value = current;
}
function showMove(s) {
  this.getField('move').value = s;
}
function augment(digit) {
  current = current * 10 + digit;
  showCurrent();
}
function register(op) {
  previous = current;
  current = 0;
  operation = op;
  showCurrent();
}
function calculateResult() {
  if (operation == '+')
    current = previous + current;
  else if (operation == '-')
    current = previous - current;
  else if (operation == '*')
    current = previous * current;
  else if (operation == '/')
    current = previous / current;
  showCurrent();
}
function reset(all) {
  current = 0;
  if(all) previous = 0;
  showCurrent();
}
showCurrent();
```

You compose a number by clicking the digits. This number is stored in the `current` variable until you click an operator. Then it's moved to the `previous` variable; the operator that was clicked is stored in the `operator` variable. A new `current` number is composed. Clicking the equals sign causes the `current` number to be updated with the `previous` number using the `operator`.

This was fun, wasn't it? Let's take a look at what we've done in this chapter.

7.5   *Summary*

In this chapter, we've explored different interactive features that can be added to a document. You already knew that links are actions that jump to a destination, but now you've learned how to create explicit destinations, how to retrieve named destinations from an existing document, and how to preserve links and destinations when concatenating different PDF documents. You found out that there are other types of actions besides link actions; for instance, JavaScript actions. You've used this knowledge to create bookmarks. You also learned how to retrieve and manipulate bookmarks in existing documents. For instance, how to combine the bookmarks of different PDF documents that are concatenated.

Then you discovered that the links you've been creating are a special type of annotation. You used text annotations to get acquainted with the concept, and you've experimented with file attachment, stamp, line, and rectangle annotations. Eventually, you were even able to create an application in a PDF using widget annotations and JavaScript.

In the next chapter, we'll continue working with these widget annotations, and we'll discover how they're related to interactive form fields. Instead of creating a form using Open Office, as you did in the previous chapter, you'll create a form using iText.

Filling out
interactive forms

Adobe products support two ways to create, view, and fill out interactive PDF forms. One is based on *AcroForm technology.* These forms are defined using PDF objects that correspond to subclasses of the `PdfObject` object in iText: `PdfDictionary`, `PdfArray`, and so on. We've already created a form like this with Open Office in chapter 6.

The other type of form uses the XML Forms Architecture (XFA). These are created with the Designer tool that ships with Acrobat. You'll learn how to fill out an XFA form in the second part of this chapter. First, we'll have a closer look at AcroForms.

8.1   *Introducing AcroForms*

You created form fields in the previous chapter. As you saw, you had to use the `getAn-not()` method in JavaScript to get an annotation object from a specific page. But you used `getField()` (without specifying a page) when the annotation corresponded to a form field. The best way to explain the relationship between a widget annotation and a form field is to quote the definition of a form field in ISO-32000-1:

> *Each field in a document's interactive form shall be defined by a field dictionary. For purposes of definition and naming, the fields can be organized hierarchically and can inherit attributes from their ancestors in the field hierarchy. A field's children in the hierarchy may also include widget annotations that define its appearance on the page.*
>
> —ISO-32000-1, section 12.7.1

This definition tells us that fields and widget annotations are two different types of objects. A field is an entry in a form; a widget annotation is its visual representation. However,

> *As a convenience, when a field has only a single associated widget annotation, the contents of the field dictionary and the annotation dictionary may be merged into a single dictionary containing entries that pertain to both a field and an annotation.*
>
> —ISO-32000-1 section 12.5.6.19

That's why the iText `PdfFormField` class extends `PdfAnnotation`, which is in turn a subclass of `PdfDictionary`. We keep the field and widget information in one dictionary. As soon as you add a field dictionary to a PDF, iText creates a form:

> *An interactive form is a collection of fields for gathering information interactively from the user. A PDF document may contain any number of fields appearing on any combination of pages, all of which make up a single, global interactive form spanning the entire document.*
>
> —ISO-32000-1 section 12.7.1

Each PDF document can contain one form, consisting of different types of fields. The type of a field is defined by the `/FT` value in the field dictionary.

AcroForms support four types of fields:

- `/Btn`—Button fields
- `/Tx`—Text fields
- `/Ch`—Choice fields
- `/Sig`—Signature fields

We'll discuss button, text, and choice fields in the next three sections. We'll deal with signature fields in chapter 12.

8.2   Selecting states or trigger actions with button fields

You created buttons in the previous chapter: buttons with and without icons, buttons with and without actions. Now we're going to look at the different types of buttons that are available:

- *Radio button fields*—These contain a set of related buttons that can each be on or off. Typically, at most one radio button in a set may be on at any given time, and selecting any one of the buttons automatically deselects all the others.
- *Check boxes*—These can toggle between two states, on and off.
- *Pushbuttons*—These are purely interactive controls that respond immediately to user input without retaining a permanent value.

Figure 8.1 shows examples of each type of button field.

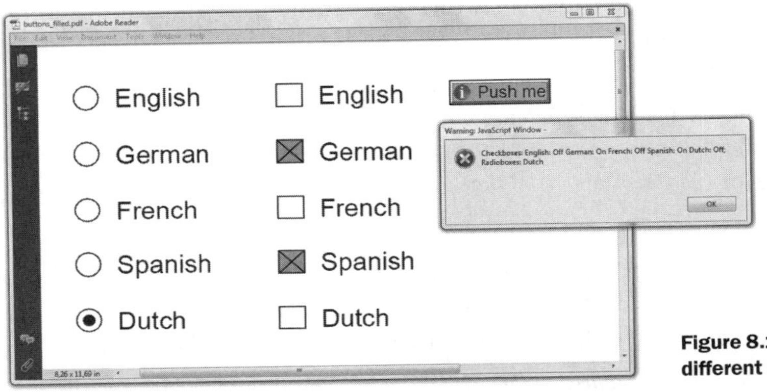

Figure 8.1   A PDF file with different button fields

In listing 7.29, you created a pushbutton field using the `createPushButton()` method. There are more static methods for creating different form fields in the `PdfFormField` class, but they're mainly there for internal use by iText.

In listings 7.26, 7.27, and 7.28, you used the convenience class `PushbuttonField` to create pushbutton fields. You obtained an instance of the `PdfFormField` class using `getField()`. The `PushbuttonField` class extends `BaseField`, and it has two siblings: `RadioCheckField` and `TextField`. These classes help us shape the widget annotations for the field in a programmer-friendly way. In the upcoming examples, you'll learn how to use the appropriate convenience class whenever possible. Creating widget annotations for a radio field, for instance, is best done with the `RadioCheckField` class.

8.2.1   Radio fields and radio buttons

A radio button field is represented by a set of related buttons.

Listing 8.1   Buttons.java

```
PdfContentByte canvas = writer.getDirectContent();
Font font = new Font(FontFamily.HELVETICA, 18);
Rectangle rect;
PdfFormField field;
```

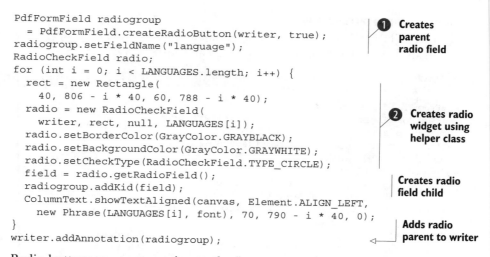

```
PdfFormField radiogroup
  = PdfFormField.createRadioButton(writer, true);
radiogroup.setFieldName("language");
RadioCheckField radio;
for (int i = 0; i < LANGUAGES.length; i++) {
  rect = new Rectangle(
    40, 806 - i * 40, 60, 788 - i * 40);
  radio = new RadioCheckField(
    writer, rect, null, LANGUAGES[i]);
  radio.setBorderColor(GrayColor.GRAYBLACK);
  radio.setBackgroundColor(GrayColor.GRAYWHITE);
  radio.setCheckType(RadioCheckField.TYPE_CIRCLE);
  field = radio.getRadioField();
  radiogroup.addKid(field);
  ColumnText.showTextAligned(canvas, Element.ALIGN_LEFT,
    new Phrase(LANGUAGES[i], font), 70, 790 - i * 40, 0);
}
writer.addAnnotation(radiogroup);
```

1 Creates parent radio field

2 Creates radio widget using helper class

Creates radio field child

Adds radio parent to writer

Radio buttons are an exception to the "use a convenience class" rule: the parent field is created using the static method createRadioButton() **1**. You then use the RadioCheckField class to shape the widgets **2**.

TYPES OF RADIO AND CHECK BOX WIDGET ANNOTATIONS

You can choose one of the types listed in table 8.1 as a parameter for setCheckType() to let iText create appearances for the *on* and *off* states of the button. The second column in the table contains the character code for the ZapfDingbats character that's used to check the radio or check box widget (ZapfDingbats is one of the standard type 1 fonts available in every PDF viewer).

Table 8.1 Different RadioCheckField types

Code	char	Description
TYPE_CHECK	4	A square with a check mark (when selected); the default for check boxes.
TYPE_CIRCLE	1	A circle with a bullet (when selected); the default for radio fields.
TYPE_CROSS	8	A square with an X (when selected).
TYPE_DIAMOND	u	A square with a diamond (when selected).
TYPE_SQUARE	n	A square with a filled square (when selected).
TYPE_STAR	H	A square with a five-pointed star (when selected).

The default for radio field widgets is TYPE_CIRCLE, so the line setting the type in listing 8.1 was redundant. These types also apply to check boxes; the default for check boxes is TYPE_CHECK.

In listing 8.1, we used the LANGUAGES array containing five Strings to add five radio fields on the same page. Adding radio buttons to different pages is more complex.

FIELDS SPANNING DIFFERENT PAGES

To create all the children of the radio field in advance, define the page number where they'll appear ❶ even before the page is created.

Listing 8.2   RadioButtons.java

```
PdfFormField radiogroup
    = PdfFormField.createRadioButton(writer, true);
radiogroup.setFieldName("language");
Rectangle rect = new Rectangle(40, 806, 60, 788);
RadioCheckField radio;
PdfFormField radiofield;
for (int page = 0; page < LANGUAGES.length; ) {
  radio = new RadioCheckField(writer, rect, null, LANGUAGES[page]);
  radio.setBackgroundColor(new GrayColor(0.8f));
  radiofield = radio.getRadioField();
  radiofield.setPlaceInPage(++page);
  radiogroup.addKid(radiofield);
}
writer.addAnnotation(radiogroup);
for (int i = 0; i < LANGUAGES.length; i++) {
  cb.beginText();
  cb.setFontAndSize(bf, 18);
  cb.showTextAligned(Element.ALIGN_LEFT, LANGUAGES[i], 70, 790, 0);
  cb.endText();
  document.newPage();
}
```

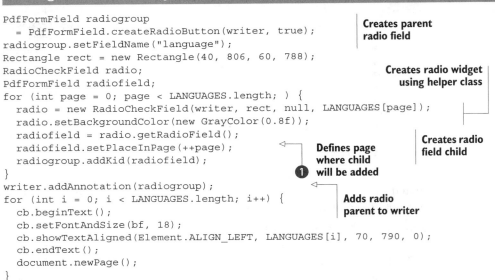

Creates parent radio field

Creates radio widget using helper class

Creates radio field child

Defines page where child ❶ will be added

Adds radio parent to writer

Adding check boxes is much easier, because each check box can only have two values: it's selected or not. There's no need to differentiate between the field and its widgets.

8.2.2   *Check boxes*

In the previous examples, iText has created the appearance of the radio buttons based on one of the types defined in table 8.1. This mechanism also works for check boxes. If you don't like the predefined appearances, you can also create custom appearances. In listing 7.29, you created different PdfAppearance objects for a pushbutton. This is how you create normal appearances for the On and Off states of a check box.

Listing 8.3   Buttons.java

```
PdfAppearance[] onOff = new PdfAppearance[2];
onOff[0] = canvas.createAppearance(20, 20);
onOff[0].rectangle(1, 1, 18, 18);
onOff[0].stroke();
onOff[1] = canvas.createAppearance(20, 20);
onOff[1].setRGBColorFill(255, 128, 128);
onOff[1].rectangle(1, 1, 18, 18);
onOff[1].fillStroke();
onOff[1].moveTo(1, 1);
onOff[1].lineTo(19, 19);
onOff[1].moveTo(1, 19);
onOff[1].lineTo(19, 1);
onOff[1].stroke();
```

Creates array with two appearances

```
RadioCheckField checkbox;
for (int i = 0; i < LANGUAGES.length; i++) {
  rect = new Rectangle(
    180, 806 - i * 40, 200, 788 - i * 40);
  checkbox = new RadioCheckField(
    writer, rect, LANGUAGES[i], "on");
  field = checkbox.getCheckField();
  field.setAppearance(
    PdfAnnotation.APPEARANCE_NORMAL, "Off", onOff[0]);
  field.setAppearance(
    PdfAnnotation.APPEARANCE_NORMAL, "On", onOff[1]);
  writer.addAnnotation(field);
  ColumnText.showTextAligned(canvas, Element.ALIGN_LEFT,
    new Phrase(LANGUAGES[i], font), 210, 790 - i * 40, 0);
}
```

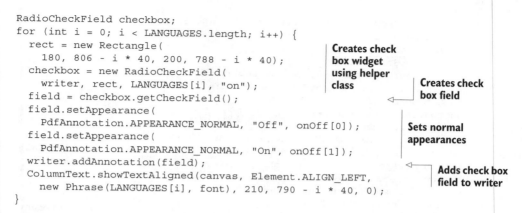

Creates check box widget using helper class

Creates check box field

Sets normal appearances

Adds check box field to writer

Note that "On" and "Off" are also the values that can be used to set the field when you manipulate the form. If you don't know which values are available because you didn't create the fields yourself, you need the getAppearanceStates() method.

Listing 8.4   Buttons.java

```
PdfReader reader = new PdfReader(src);
PdfStamper stamper = new PdfStamper(reader, new FileOutputStream(dest));
AcroFields form = stamper.getAcroFields();
String[] radiostates = form.getAppearanceStates("language");
form.setField("language", radiostates[4]);
for (int i = 0; i > LANGUAGES.length; i++) {
  String[] checkboxstates = form.getAppearanceStates("English");
  form.setField(LANGUAGES[i], checkboxstates[i % 2 == 0 ? 1 : 0]);
}
stamper.close();
```

One of the problems of having plenty of iText examples available online is that many developers copy and paste code snippets without really knowing what they're doing. For instance, they copy this:

```
form.setField("checkbox", "On");
```

This line works for *this* example, but only because On is the name of one of the possible states of the check box we want to check. Other check boxes could have other values, such as Yes, or true, or whatever was defined for the checked state of the field.

Let's finish our overview of button fields with some more information about pushbuttons.

8.2.3   *Pushbuttons*

First you need to create a pushbutton.

Listing 8.5   Buttons.java

```
rect = new Rectangle(300, 806, 360, 788);
PushbuttonField button
  = new PushbuttonField(writer, rect, "Buttons");
```

Creates helper class to create widget

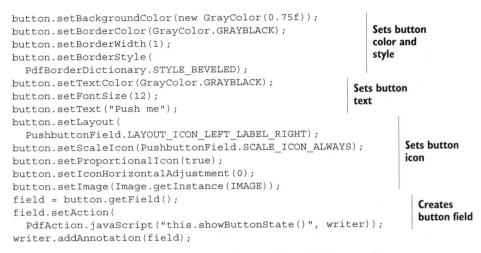

```
button.setBackgroundColor(new GrayColor(0.75f));
button.setBorderColor(GrayColor.GRAYBLACK);
button.setBorderWidth(1);
button.setBorderStyle(
  PdfBorderDictionary.STYLE_BEVELED);
button.setTextColor(GrayColor.GRAYBLACK);
button.setFontSize(12);
button.setText("Push me");
button.setLayout(
  PushbuttonField.LAYOUT_ICON_LEFT_LABEL_RIGHT);
button.setScaleIcon(PushbuttonField.SCALE_ICON_ALWAYS);
button.setProportionalIcon(true);
button.setIconHorizontalAdjustment(0);
button.setImage(Image.getInstance(IMAGE));
field = button.getField();
field.setAction(
  PdfAction.javaScript("this.showButtonState()", writer));
writer.addAnnotation(field);
```

Sets button color and style

Sets button text

Sets button icon

Creates button field

Clicking the pushbutton shown in figure 8.1 will trigger the showButtonState() method. This method (which you should add as document-level JavaScript) opens an alert box showing the state of the radio field and the check boxes.

BORDER STYLES

You've already defined colors with the methods setBackgroundColor() and setBorderColor() in listing 8.2. Now you can use setBorderWidth() and setBorderStyle() to define the width and style of the border of a widget annotation. Possible values for the style are:

- STYLE_SOLID—A solid rectangle surrounding the annotation.
- STYLE_DASHED—A dashed rectangle surrounding the annotation.
- STYLE_BEVELED—A simulated embossed rectangle that appears to be raised above the surface of the page.
- STYLE_INSET—A simulated engraved rectangle that appears to be recessed below the surface of the page.
- STYLE_UNDERLINE—A single line along the bottom of the annotation rectangle.

You've already used methods with the same name in the previous chapter, when you created annotations.

PUSHBUTTON LABELS AND ICONS

The content of the pushbutton consists of an icon and some text, because you changed the layout using the setLayout() method in listing 8.5. Possible values for specifying the layout are:

- LAYOUT_LABEL_ONLY—No icon; caption only (the default).
- LAYOUT_ICON_ONLY—No caption; icon only.
- LAYOUT_ICON_TOP_LABEL_BOTTOM—Caption below the icon.
- LAYOUT_LABEL_TOP_ICON_BOTTOM—Caption above the icon.
- LAYOUT_ICON_LEFT_LABEL_RIGHT—Caption to the right of the icon.

- LAYOUT_LABEL_LEFT_ICON_RIGHT—Caption to the left of the icon.
- LAYOUT_LABEL_OVER_ICON—Caption overlaid directly on the icon.

Note that iText can change this parameter internally. If the icon doesn't fit the button rectangle, iText can decide to switch to LAYOUT_LABEL_ONLY.

You can change the scaling behavior of the icon with setScaleIcon() and one of the following values:

- SCALE_ICON_ALWAYS—Always scale (the default).
- SCALE_ICON_NEVER—Never scale.
- SCALE_ICON_IS_TOO_BIG—Scale only when the icon is bigger than the annotation.
- SCALE_ICON_IS_TOO_SMALL—Scale only when the icon is smaller than the annotation.

The aspect ratio of the icon can be preserved or unlocked when scaling by using the setProportionalIcon() method.

There are also two methods to adjust the position of the icon: setIconHorizontalAdjustment() and setIconVerticalAdjustment(). The parameter is a float value between 0 and 1 indicating the fraction of leftover space to allocate at the left (horizontal adjustment) or at the bottom (vertical adjustment) of the icon. A value of 0 positions the icon at the left or bottom of the annotation rectangle. The default is 0.5, which centers the icon.

The PDF reference told you that pushbuttons don't retain any permanent value. That's true, but you can also use buttons as placeholders for images. In listing 7.27, you used a button to add an advertisement promoting this book to an existing PDF document. But wouldn't people prefer to see the nice woman on the cover instead of me as Superman?

MANIPULATING A PUSHBUTTON

The AcroFields class you use to fill out fields also has a getNewPushbuttonFromField() method. With this method, you can obtain a new PushbuttonField object with the same properties as an existing button in the form. After changing the properties of this object, you can replace the existing button with the new, altered one using replacePushbuttonField().

Listing 8.6 ReplaceIcon.java

```
PdfReader reader = new PdfReader(src);
PdfStamper stamper
  = new PdfStamper(reader, new FileOutputStream(dest));      Replaces
AcroFields form = stamper.getAcroFields();                   pushbutton
PushbuttonField ad
  = form.getNewPushbuttonFromField("advertisement");         Creates new
ad.setLayout(PushbuttonField.LAYOUT_ICON_ONLY);              pushbutton
ad.setProportionalIcon(true);
ad.setImage(Image.getInstance(RESOURCE));                    Changes some
form.replacePushbuttonField("advertisement", ad.getField());  properties
stamper.close();
```

You'll create more buttons in chapter 9, where you'll learn how to submit the content of a form to a server. For now, let's continue our overview of the different types of fields.

8.3   *Filling in data with text fields*

A text field is "a box or space for text fill-in data typically entered from a keyboard. The text may be restricted to a single line or may be permitted to span multiple lines" (ISO-32000-1 12.7.4.3). Figure 8.2 shows examples of such text boxes.

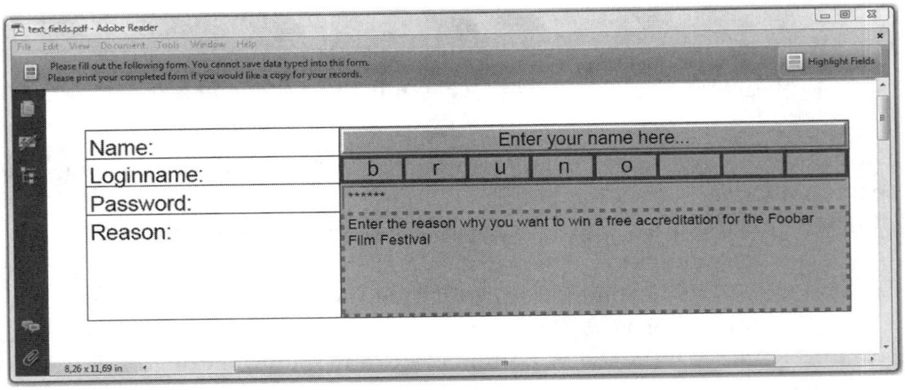

Figure 8.2   A PDF file with different text fields

We'll look at how to use the `TextField` class and the `getTextField()` method to obtain a `PdfFormField` instance.

8.3.1   *Creating text fields*

The text fields in figure 8.2 were created using this code.

Listing 8.7   TextFields.java

```
TextField text
  = new TextField(writer, rectangle, String.format("text_%s", tf));
text.setBackgroundColor(new GrayColor(0.75f));
switch(tf) {
case 1:
  text.setBorderStyle(PdfBorderDictionary.STYLE_BEVELED);     // Creates required
  text.setText("Enter your name here...");                    // text field with
  text.setFontSize(0);                                        // centered text
  text.setAlignment(Element.ALIGN_CENTER);
  text.setOptions(TextField.REQUIRED);
  break;
case 2:
  text.setMaxCharacterLength(8);                              // Creates text field to
  text.setOptions(TextField.COMB);                           // which 8 characters
  text.setBorderStyle(PdfBorderDictionary.STYLE_SOLID);      // can be added
```

```
   text.setBorderColor(BaseColor.BLUE);
   text.setBorderWidth(2);
   break;
case 3:
   text.setBorderStyle(PdfBorderDictionary.STYLE_INSET);
   text.setOptions(TextField.PASSWORD);
   text.setVisibility(TextField.VISIBLE_BUT_DOES_NOT_PRINT);
   break;
case 4:
   text.setBorderStyle(PdfBorderDictionary.STYLE_DASHED);
   text.setBorderColor(BaseColor.RED);
   text.setBorderWidth(2);
   text.setFontSize(8);
   text.setText("Enter the reason why you want to win a free
        accreditation for the Foobar Film Festival");
   text.setOptions(TextField.MULTILINE | TextField.REQUIRED);
   break;
}
try {
   PdfFormField field = text.getTextField();
   if (tf == 3) {
      field.setUserName("Choose a password");
   }
   writer.addAnnotation(field);
}
catch(IOException ioe) {
   throw new ExceptionConverter(ioe);
}
catch(DocumentException de) {
   throw new ExceptionConverter(de);
}
```

Annotations in right margin:
- ↑ **Creates text field to which 8 characters can be added**
- **Creates password field**
- **Creates required, multiline text field** ←

In this listing, you'll recognize several features you used earlier when defining buttons, but it also introduces some new methods.

TEXT PROPERTIES

Previously you used setTextColor(), setFontSize(), and setText() to define captions for pushbuttons. When the text didn't fit a button, it was truncated. The behavior is different for text fields. Three things can happen when an end user enters text that doesn't fit the text field rectangle:

- The full text is present in the field, but it's clipped by the annotation rectangle. The end user has to scroll back and forth to see what has been entered.
- The full text is shown, but the more characters that are added, the smaller the font size gets. This is what happens if you set the font size to 0.
- The end user can't add more than the number of characters that was defined with the setMaxCharacterLength() method.

The alignment of the text is set with the setAlignment() method. You use the same parameters as you've used to define the alignment of paragraphs.

FAQ *Why can't I set the alignment to* ALIGN_JUSTIFIED? If you check the PDF reference, you'll discover that justified text isn't supported in AcroForm text fields. It's impossible to justify the text in a text box, unless you flatten the form, using a technique that will be explained in section 8.5. Note that alignment is referred to as *quadding* in the PDF reference. There's also a setQuadding() method in the PdfFormField class.

Listing 8.7 uses the setVisibility() method to set some flags in the annotation dictionary:

- VISIBLE—The field is visible on screen and can be printed.
- HIDDEN—The field is invisible.
- VISIBLE_BUT_DOES_NOT_PRINT—The field is visible on screen, but is not printed.
- HIDDEN_BUT_PRINTABLE—The field is invisible on screen, but is printed.

When you created annotations, you needed to use setFlags() with the FLAGS_PRINT parameter to make sure the annotation was printed. For widget annotations, iText always uses VISIBLE as default.

FAQ *How can I add a tooltip to a text field?* You need to set the /TU key in the field dictionary with the setUserName() method. This is an alternate name that's used in place of the actual field name wherever the field is identified in the UI. This alternate field name will show up when the user moves the mouse pointer over the field.

You can set flags in the field dictionary with the setOptions() method. You can *or* ('|') the following values:

- READ_ONLY—The end user won't be able to change the value of the field.
- REQUIRED—The end user won't be able to submit the form unless this field is filled in.
- MULTILINE—For text fields: the field can consist of multiple lines.
- DO_NOT_SCROLL—Scrolling will be disabled for the field.
- PASSWORD—The text entered in a text field will be obfuscated.
- FILE_SELECTION—The field will be used to upload a file.
- DO_NOT_SPELL_CHECK—Spell checking (when available) will be disabled.
- EDIT—The values that are presented in a choice field can be edited.
- MULTISELECT—The end user can select more than one value in a choice field.
- COMB—An equal amount of space will be used for every character in the text in a text field.

These are the field flags that can be set when you're using a BaseField class to create the form field. Note that some of the flags only make sense for specific classes.

The COMB flag, for instance, is used in text fields to distribute the characters over a fixed number of small boxes. In figure 8.2, these boxes are drawn by Adobe Reader using the border style and properties of the widget annotation. COMB is often used to enter data that needs to match boxes on preprinted forms; for example, bank forms that can be used to wire money from one account to another.

For every value in the BaseField options list, you'll find a corresponding value in the PdfFormField class. For instance, the value TextField.PASSWORD is equal to Pdf-FormField.FF_PASSWORD. These were the original flags that could be set using the setFieldFlags() method. There were also flags to define the field type. If you wanted to create a pushbutton in earlier iText versions, you had to set the flag FF_PUSHBUTTON, but nowadays this is implicitly done by the BaseField class.

8.3.2 *Filling out text fields*

You've already filled out text fields programmatically in section 6.3.5, but now you'll see not only how to change the value of a field, but also its properties.

Listing 8.8 TextFields.java

```
PdfReader reader = new PdfReader(src);
PdfStamper stamper
  = new PdfStamper(reader, new FileOutputStream(dest));
AcroFields form = stamper.getAcroFields();
System.out.println(form.getField("text_4"));
form.setField("text_1", "Bruno Lowagie");
form.setFieldProperty("text_2", "fflags", 0, null);
form.setFieldProperty("text_2", "bordercolor", BaseColor.RED, null);
form.setField("text_2", "bruno");
form.setFieldProperty("text_3",
                        "clrfflags", TextField.PASSWORD, null);
form.setFieldProperty("text_3",
                    "setflags", PdfAnnotation.FLAGS_PRINT, null);
form.setField("text_3", "12345678", "xxxxxxxx");
form.setFieldProperty("text_4", "textsize", new Float(12), null);
form.regenerateField("text_4");
stamper.close();
```

You can retrieve the value of a field from an existing form with the getField() method. In previous examples, you've used the setField() method to change this value. Up until now, you've only used this method with two parameters: fieldname and value.

For text fields, it can also make sense to use a third parameter: display. This extra String can be used to create the appearance of the text field. If you want to set the value of a field to "1970-06-10" (because that's the way my birthday is stored in your database of dates to remember), but you want that value to be displayed as "10 Jun 1970" in the form, you can use this line:

```
form.setField("birthday", "2007-06-10", "10 Jun 1970");
```

As soon as the user clicks the text field to change it, the actual value of the field will be displayed.

CHANGING THE FLAGS IN THE ANNOTATION OR FLAG DICTIONARY

The annotation and field flag can be changed using the `setFieldProperty()` method. The first parameter refers to the field name, and the second is one of the values in table 8.2.

Table 8.2 Changing the flags in the annotation or flag dictionary

Property	Description
`"flags"`	Replaces all the flags of the widget annotation.
`"setflags"`	Sets one or more flags of the widget annotation.
`"clrflags"`	Removes one or more flags of the widget annotation.
`"fflags"`	Replaces all the flags of the form field.
`"setfflags"`	Sets one or more flags of the form field.
`"clrfflags"`	Removes one or more flags of the form field.

If the second parameter is `"flags"`, `"setflags"`, or `"clrflags"`, the third parameter is one of the flags that can be found in the `PdfAnnotation` class. For instance, adding `FLAGS_PRINT` to the password field will change the visibility of that field from `TextField.VISIBLE_BUT_DOES_NOT_PRINT` to `TextField.VISIBLE`.

If the second parameter is `"fflags"`, `"setfflags"`, or `"clrfflags"`, the third parameter should be one of the `BaseField` options (or a `PdfFormField` constant starting with `FF_`). For instance, removing the `TextField.PASSWORD` flag will change the password field into an ordinary text field.

The fourth parameter wasn't used in listing 8.8; you just passed `null`. If the field was represented by more than one widget (as is the case for radio fields), you could pass an array of `int` values, to sum up the indexes of the widgets for which you want to change the property. Passing `null` means you want to process all the widgets associated with the field.

CHANGING THE PROPERTIES OF WIDGET ANNOTATIONS IN EXISTING FORMS

There's also a `setFieldProperty()` method to change the other properties of a field. Pass the field name as the first parameter. Table 8.3 explains the meanings of the second and third parameters. The fourth parameter has the same meaning as for the `setFieldProperty()` method that was used to change flags.

> **FAQ** *I've changed the properties of a field, yet I don't see any changes. Why not?* iText only creates new appearances for fields when the field value has changed. For example, you change the font size of the field `"text_4"` in listing 8.8, but you don't change its value. If you want to see the font size change, you also have to use the `regenerateField()` method.

Table 8.3 Changing the properties of a field

Property	Value	Description
"textfont"	BaseFont	Changes the font used in the field.
"textcolor"	BaseColor	Changes the text color.
"textsize"	Float	Changes the font size.
"bgcolor"	BaseColor	Changes the background color.
"bordercolor"	BaseColor	Changes the border color.

Up until now, we've avoided one property in the examples: you haven't used set-Font() yet, nor have you changed the "textfont" property.

8.3.3 Text fields and fonts

Figure 8.3 shows three different PDF files with a text field. The text added for the three text fields is identical.

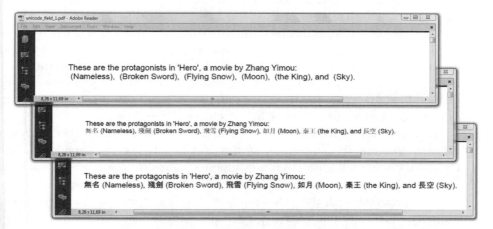

Figure 8.3 Creating text fields containing Unicode characters

As you can see, the Chinese names are missing in the upper example; they're present in the second and third PDFs, but different fonts are used. The code used to create the three different PDFs doesn't differ much.

Listing 8.9 TextFieldFonts.java

```
public void createPdf(
    String filename, boolean appearances, boolean font)
    throws IOException, DocumentException {
  Document document = new Document();
  PdfWriter writer
    = PdfWriter.getInstance(document, new FileOutputStream(filename));
```

```
document.open();
writer.getAcroForm().setNeedAppearances(appearances);
TextField text = new TextField(writer,
  new Rectangle(36, 806, 559, 780), "description");
text.setOptions(TextField.MULTILINE);
if (font) {
  BaseFont unicode = BaseFont.createFont(
    "c:/windows/fonts/arialuni.ttf",
    BaseFont.IDENTITY_H, BaseFont.EMBEDDED);
  text.setExtensionFont(BaseFont.createFont());
  ArrayList<BaseFont> list = new ArrayList<BaseFont>();
  list.add(unicode);
  text.setSubstitutionFonts(list);
}
text.setText(TEXT);
writer.addAnnotation(text.getTextField());
document.close();
}
```

➊ Sets Need-Appearances flag if true

➋ Defines fonts for text field

So far you've been creating forms without ➊ and ➋. This worked because you were only using Western characters. The Chinese characters in the TEXT aren't shown in the appearance of the text field because iText doesn't know where to find a font file containing those characters.

You can work around this by setting the NeedAppearances flag ➊. When set, this flag instructs the PDF viewer to create the appearances for the widget annotations. This way you pass the responsibility for rendering the text correctly to the application that's used to view the PDF. The same mechanism is triggered when the end user clicks the text field to change the text. This won't work on all systems: the PDF viewer needs to have access to a font with the Chinese glyphs.

➋ offers another workaround. With the setExtensionFont() method, you define the main font that should be used for the field. In this case, the default font Helvetica. Helvetica doesn't know how to draw Chinese characters, so you use the setSubstitutionFonts() method to add Arial Unicode. Whenever iText detects a character that can't be rendered with the extension font, it will go through the list of substitution fonts. The first font that has a glyph definition for the needed character will be used (see the third window in figure 8.3). In this case, iText will embed a subset of Arial Unicode in the PDF file.

ADDING UNICODE TO TEXT FIELDS
As soon as you try to fill out the form with other Asian characters than the ones that were in the TEXT string, you'll run into trouble. That's shown in the first and third windows of figure 8.4, which replace the English-Chinese text with a text containing some Korean characters. The upper three windows correspond to the three windows from figure 8.3. As you can see, the workaround ➊ still works (for me, on my OS), but ➋ fails because iText doesn't know where to find a font containing the Korean glyphs.

Again there are two ways to work around this.

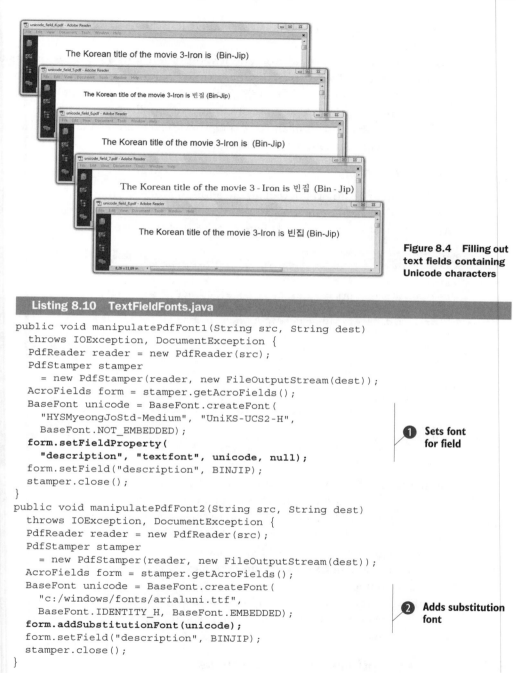

Figure 8.4 Filling out text fields containing Unicode characters

Listing 8.10 TextFieldFonts.java

```java
public void manipulatePdfFont1(String src, String dest)
  throws IOException, DocumentException {
  PdfReader reader = new PdfReader(src);
  PdfStamper stamper
    = new PdfStamper(reader, new FileOutputStream(dest));
  AcroFields form = stamper.getAcroFields();
  BaseFont unicode = BaseFont.createFont(
    "HYSMyeongJoStd-Medium", "UniKS-UCS2-H",
    BaseFont.NOT_EMBEDDED);
  form.setFieldProperty(
    "description", "textfont", unicode, null);
  form.setField("description", BINJIP);
  stamper.close();
}
public void manipulatePdfFont2(String src, String dest)
  throws IOException, DocumentException {
  PdfReader reader = new PdfReader(src);
  PdfStamper stamper
    = new PdfStamper(reader, new FileOutputStream(dest));
  AcroFields form = stamper.getAcroFields();
  BaseFont unicode = BaseFont.createFont(
    "c:/windows/fonts/arialuni.ttf",
    BaseFont.IDENTITY_H, BaseFont.EMBEDDED);
  form.addSubstitutionFont(unicode);
  form.setField("description", BINJIP);
  stamper.close();
}
```

❶ Sets font for field

❷ Adds substitution font

In the first workaround, you change the `"textfont"` property ❶. I'm using a CJK font (see chapter 11) because I want to render Korean characters, and CJK fonts don't need to be embedded. If I had used Arial Unicode, iText would have embedded the complete font file, which would have resulted in a huge file size. It's important to choose your font wisely.

In the second workaround, you add a substitution font ❷. This is similar to the workaround you used when creating the text field, and it has the same disadvantage: as soon as the end user starts typing something else in the text field, you depend entirely on the fonts that are available to the viewer application on the OS.

We'll conclude this section about text fields with an example that uses JavaScript to validate and adapt the content that was entered by an end user.

8.3.4   Validating text fields

Table 7.4 contained an overview of all the additional actions that could be added to an interactive form field. You've used some of these actions to write an application in PDF, but their primary use is to enhance the user experience when filling out a form.

Listing 8.11   TextFieldActions.java

```
TextField date =
  new TextField(writer, new Rectangle(36, 806, 126, 780), "date");
date.setBorderColor(new GrayColor(0.2f));
PdfFormField datefield = date.getTextField();
datefield.setAdditionalActions(                          ❶ Formats date
  PdfName.V, PdfAction.javaScript(                          using pattern
  "AFDate_FormatEx( 'dd-mm-yyyy' );", writer));             "dd-mm-yyyy"
writer.addAnnotation(datefield);
TextField name
  = new TextField(writer, new Rectangle(130, 806, 256, 780), "name");
name.setBorderColor(new GrayColor(0.2f));
namefield.setAdditionalActions(                          ❷ Makes every
  PdfName.K, PdfAction.javaScript(                          character
"event.change = event.change.toUpperCase();", writer));     uppercase
writer.addAnnotation(namefield);
```

The first action ❶ is triggered after the end user has filled in the date field. Adobe Reader comes with canned functions that let you validate and format dates, times, currencies, and so on. The method `AFDate_FormatEx()` is one them. For instance, if you enter `"10 Jun 1970"`, it will be converted to `"10-06-1970"`. If you enter something that can't be recognized as a date, the field is cleared.

The second action ❷ is performed upon every keystroke. You change the key that was pressed to uppercase using the `event` object.

With what you learned in chapter 7, you can create every validation script you need, but now we'll continue with another type of field that can be created using the `TextField` class.

8.4   Selecting options with choice fields

Choice fields are defined in section 12.7.4.4 of ISO-32000-1. A choice field contains several text items, one or more of which shall be selected as the field value. The items may be presented to the user in one of the following two forms:

- A *scrollable list box*—The end user can select one or more values from a fixed list.
- A *combo box*—A drop-down list. The combo box may be accompanied by an editable text box in which the user can type a value other than the predefined choices.

Figure 8.5 demonstrates the different types of choice fields.

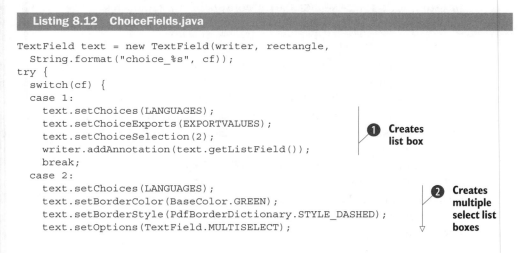

Figure 8.5   A PDF file with different choice fields

The first two are list boxes. As soon as you click the word "French" next to "Language of the movie," a scrollbar appears. The second list box was made big enough that scrollbars aren't needed. The lower two choice fields are combo boxes. If you click the arrow to the right, the full list of choices is shown. Let's find out how these fields were created.

8.4.1   Creating lists and combo boxes

The fields shown in figure 8.5 were created using this code.

Listing 8.12   ChoiceFields.java

```
TextField text = new TextField(writer, rectangle,
  String.format("choice_%s", cf));
try {
  switch(cf) {
  case 1:
    text.setChoices(LANGUAGES);
    text.setChoiceExports(EXPORTVALUES);
    text.setChoiceSelection(2);
    writer.addAnnotation(text.getListField());
    break;
  case 2:
    text.setChoices(LANGUAGES);
    text.setBorderColor(BaseColor.GREEN);
    text.setBorderStyle(PdfBorderDictionary.STYLE_DASHED);
    text.setOptions(TextField.MULTISELECT);
```

1 Creates list box

2 Creates multiple select list boxes

```
            ArrayList<Integer> selections = new ArrayList<Integer>();
            selections.add(0);
            selections.add(2);
            text.setChoiceSelections(selections);
            PdfFormField field = text.getListField();
            writer.addAnnotation(field);
            break;
          case 3:
            text.setBorderColor(BaseColor.RED);
            text.setBackgroundColor(BaseColor.GRAY);
            text.setChoices(LANGUAGES);
            text.setChoiceExports(EXPORTVALUES);
            text.setChoiceSelection(4);
            writer.addAnnotation(text.getComboField());
            break;
          case 4:
            text.setChoices(LANGUAGES);
            text.setOptions(TextField.EDIT);
            writer.addAnnotation(text.getComboField());
            break;
          }
        }
        catch(IOException ioe) {
          throw new ExceptionConverter(ioe);
        }
        catch(DocumentException de) {
          throw new ExceptionConverter(de);
        }
```

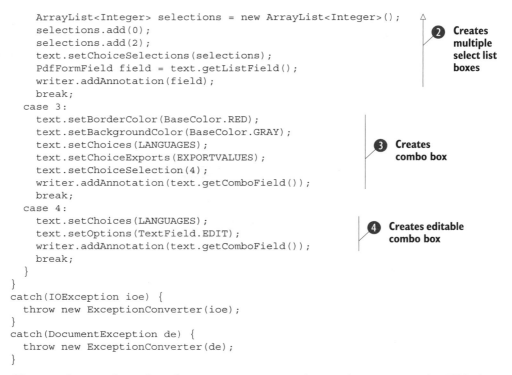

2 Creates multiple select list boxes

3 Creates combo box

4 Creates editable combo box

Observe that you're using the TextField convenience class once again. This is an iText design decision, based on the fact that drawing the appearance of a list or combo box isn't all that different from drawing the appearance of a text box. Instead of using getTextField() to obtain a PdfFormField instance, you now have to use the methods getListField() or getComboField(). You can use the same methods to set properties as you used for the text field widgets.

The values that are shown to the end user are set with the method setChoices(). In listing 8.12, the LANGUAGES array consists of five languages. In **1** and **3**, you use setExportValues(), passing the EXPORTVALUES array. That array looks like this:

```
String[] EXPORTVALUES = { "EN", "DE", "FR", "ES", "NL" };
```

Every export value has to correspond with an option in the choice array. When the form is submitted to a server, the export value will be used. For instance, if the end user selects "English" and submits the form, the corresponding export value "EN" will be submitted. Note that these export values aren't used when you preselect an option—the setChoiceSelection() method expects an int. For multiple select lists, you can also use the setChoiceSelections() method with a list of integers.

You don't define export values in **2** and **4**; in this case, the full language name will be sent to the server. In **4**, you set the EDIT flag, so the end user filling out the form can even add languages that aren't present in the LANGUAGES array.

Now let's find out how to manipulate the values of the choices in an existing PDF document.

8.4.2 Manipulating lists and combo boxes

Let's take the PDF you created in section 8.4.1 and pretend that you forgot which options and export values are available in the choice fields of the form. How could you retrieve those values? And how would you change the selection?

Listing 8.13 ChoiceFields.java (continued)

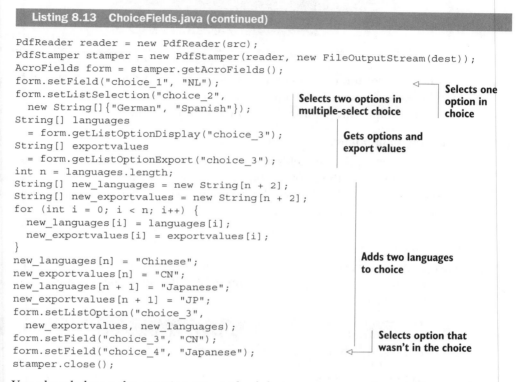

```
PdfReader reader = new PdfReader(src);
PdfStamper stamper = new PdfStamper(reader, new FileOutputStream(dest));
AcroFields form = stamper.getAcroFields();
form.setField("choice_1", "NL");                              Selects one
form.setListSelection("choice_2",                             option in
  new String[]{"German", "Spanish"});    Selects two options in   choice
String[] languages                       multiple-select choice
  = form.getListOptionDisplay("choice_3");
String[] exportvalues                    Gets options and
  = form.getListOptionExport("choice_3");  export values
int n = languages.length;
String[] new_languages = new String[n + 2];
String[] new_exportvalues = new String[n + 2];
for (int i = 0; i < n; i++) {
  new_languages[i] = languages[i];
  new_exportvalues[i] = exportvalues[i];
}
new_languages[n] = "Chinese";            Adds two languages
new_exportvalues[n] = "CN";              to choice
new_languages[n + 1] = "Japanese";
new_exportvalues[n + 1] = "JP";
form.setListOption("choice_3",
  new_exportvalues, new_languages);
form.setField("choice_3", "CN");
form.setField("choice_4", "Japanese");   Selects option that
stamper.close();                         wasn't in the choice
```

You already know the `setField()` method, but now you can also use the `setListSelection()` method to choose more than one value in a multiple-select list box. You can use the methods `getListOptionDisplay()` and `getListOptionExport()` to determine the available options. If you're not happy with the available options, you can use the `setListOption()` method to replace the sets of existing display and export values with new arrays. Or, if the field is an editable combo box, you can set a value that isn't present in the choice field.

Now that you know all the types of fields that can be used in an interactive form, let's have a look at issues you may encounter when filling out form fields.

8.5 Refining the form-filling process

Up until now, you've used field names without any structure. In this section, you'll learn how to create a field hierarchy. We'll also look at ways to speed up the form-filling process and to get more control over the flattening process.

Figure 8.6 shows a form with four fields: a name, a login, a password, and a field for extra info.

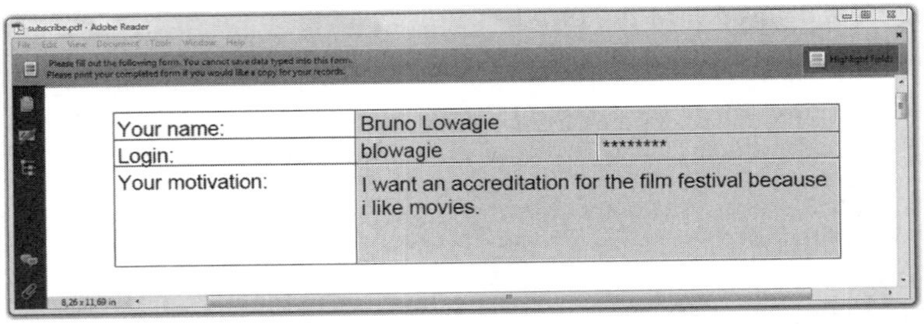

**Figure 8.6
Before: a form
with four fields**

On the outside, there's no significant difference between this form and the forms we've created before, but when you start manipulating this form with iText, you'll notice that something is different on the inside: the fields have dots in their names.

8.5.1   *Choosing field names*

In previous examples, the fields had no (or almost no) hierarchy. The only exception was for radio fields: the parent field had different unnamed children, one for every possible value of the field. A similar hierarchy exists in the form shown in figure 8.6. An empty field was created like this:

```
PdfFormField personal = PdfFormField.createEmpty(writer);
personal.setFieldName("personal");
```

This is a purely structural element. It's not one of the types of fields we've discussed so far in this chapter. It's the parent of a series of child fields that are "adopted" and positioned in a cell event.

Listing 8.14   ChildFieldEvent.java

```
public class ChildFieldEvent implements PdfPCellEvent {
  protected PdfFormField parent;
  protected PdfFormField kid;
  protected float padding;
  public ChildFieldEvent(PdfFormField parent,
    PdfFormField kid, float padding) {
    this.parent = parent;
    this.kid = kid;
    this.padding = padding;
  }
  public void cellLayout(PdfPCell cell,
    Rectangle rect, PdfContentByte[] cb) {
    try {
      parent.addKid(kid);
      kid.setWidget(new Rectangle(
        rect.getLeft(padding), rect.getBottom(padding),
        rect.getRight(padding), rect.getTop(padding)),
        PdfAnnotation.HIGHLIGHT_INVERT);
    } catch (Exception e) {
      throw new ExceptionConverter(e);
    }
  }
}
```

Here, the names of the kids you're adding to the form are "name", "loginname", "password", and "reason". These are the *partial names* of the field. When you fill out the form using iText, you need the *fully qualified name*, which is constructed from the partial field names of the field and all of its ancestors. The names are separated by a period. In the simple form in figure 8.6, the parent element "personal" has four children: "personal.name", "personal.loginname", "personal.password", and "personal.reason".

You can have two different fields with the same partial name, such as "name", provided they have a different parent, such as "sender.name" and "receiver.name". Fully qualified field names are unique in the sense that fields with the same fully qualified name must have the same field type, value, and default value. You can have different representations of fields with the same fully qualified name, provided that they have the same parent, have no children of their own, and differ only in properties that specify their visual appearance.

This is important as soon as you start to fill out the form using iText.

8.5.2 Optimizing the filling process

When you filled out the movie data sheet in chapter 6, iText inspected the same form 120 times—once for every movie in the database. Part of that work was redundant. When filling out the same form multiple times, you can optimize the process significantly by allowing iText to reuse objects that would otherwise have to be created from scratch every time the form is filled out with different data.

FILLING OUT THE SAME FORM MULTIPLE TIMES

In this example, the form in figure 8.6 is filled out three times.

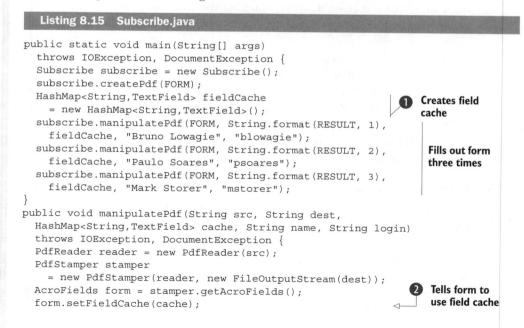

Listing 8.15 Subscribe.java

```
public static void main(String[] args)
  throws IOException, DocumentException {
  Subscribe subscribe = new Subscribe();
  subscribe.createPdf(FORM);
  HashMap<String,TextField> fieldCache                    ❶ Creates field
    = new HashMap<String,TextField>();                       cache
  subscribe.manipulatePdf(FORM, String.format(RESULT, 1),
    fieldCache, "Bruno Lowagie", "blowagie");
  subscribe.manipulatePdf(FORM, String.format(RESULT, 2),   Fills out form
    fieldCache, "Paulo Soares", "psoares");                  three times
  subscribe.manipulatePdf(FORM, String.format(RESULT, 3),
    fieldCache, "Mark Storer", "mstorer");
}
public void manipulatePdf(String src, String dest,
  HashMap<String,TextField> cache, String name, String login)
  throws IOException, DocumentException {
  PdfReader reader = new PdfReader(src);
  PdfStamper stamper
    = new PdfStamper(reader, new FileOutputStream(dest));
  AcroFields form = stamper.getAcroFields();               ❷ Tells form to
  form.setFieldCache(cache);                                  use field cache
```

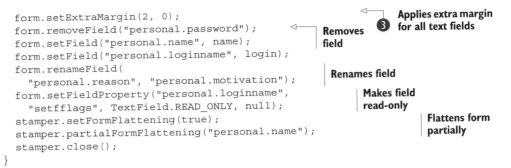

```
form.setExtraMargin(2, 0);
form.removeField("personal.password");
form.setField("personal.name", name);
form.setField("personal.loginname", login);
form.renameField(
  "personal.reason", "personal.motivation");
form.setFieldProperty("personal.loginname",
  "setfflags", TextField.READ_ONLY, null);
stamper.setFormFlattening(true);
stamper.partialFormFlattening("personal.name");
stamper.close();
}
```

Applies extra margin
3 for all text fields

Removes
field

Renames field

Makes field
read-only

Flattens form
partially

Every time you fill out a form, you need to create new `PdfStamper` and `AcroFields` instances. Inside the `AcroFields` object, iText will create a `TextField` object for every text and choice field that's encountered. This is an expensive operation: the original form is read and every property is copied into the new `TextField` object.

You can get a significant speed advantage if you create an empty `HashMap` **1** and use it as a cache for these objects with the `setFieldCache()` method **2**. The first time iText has to fill a form, an entry will be added to the cache for every text or choice field that's filled. This entry will be a key-value pair consisting of the field name and a `TextField` object. The next time the form is filled out, iText will fetch that `TextField` object, which will then be used to create a new appearance based on the new value that was filled in with `setField()`.

In some cases, it may be necessary to adjust the appearance of a text field.

ADJUSTING THE OFFSET OF A TEXT FIELD

Appearances created by iText are an approximation of the way Adobe Reader renders the content of a text field. Depending on the tool used to create the form and the viewer used to open the form, the appearance created by iText won't always correspond to the appearance of the field when you click on it. This can be a serious problem when you want to flatten a form; there could be a consistent discrepancy of the baseline and the X-offset for all of the text fields.

You can work around this problem by using the `setExtraMargin()` method **3**, which corrects the offset in X and Y directions by specifying extra margins to be applied to every text field in the form.

There's more going on in listing 8.15: you're also removing and renaming fields. Moreover the form is flattened, but only partially.

8.5.3   *Partial form flattening*

In section 6.3.5, you created a template using Open Office. The fields were used as placeholders; once they were filled in, you were no longer interested in the form. You didn't have the intention to change the data. With the `setFormFlattening()` method, you threw away the internal form structure. Only the content of the fields was kept; it was added at the absolute positions defined in the template. You won't want this to happen if you're going to use iText to prefill a form, but you may want to make part of the form read-only.

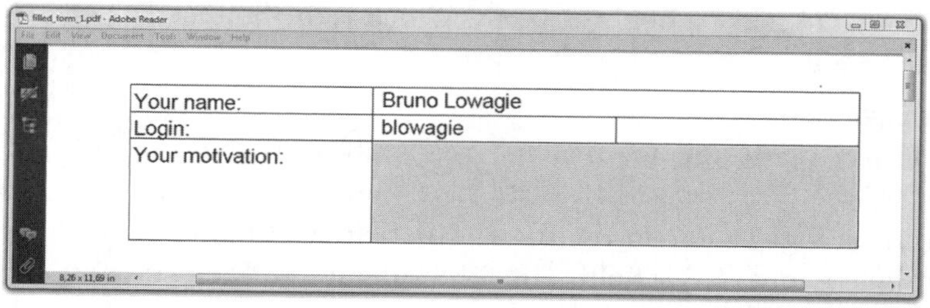

Figure 8.7 After: a form with two fields

Suppose that the form shown in figure 8.6 is one of your standard forms. The first time an end user is confronted with it, he or she has to enter a name, login name, password, and motivation to get an accreditation for the festival. The form is then submitted to the server. The username and password are checked, and if the credentials are correct, you want to allow the end user to change the motivation entry, but not the name and login name. You also don't need the user's password anymore. You want the form to look like figure 8.7.

The form resembles the form shown in figure 8.6, with a few exceptions:

- The password field is removed.
- Internally, one of the field names has been changed.
- The values of the name and loginname fields are still visible, but the end user can no longer change them.

Let's look at the different methods that can be used to achieve this.

REMOVING OR RENAMING FIELDS

There are three different methods that allow you to remove a field:

- removeFieldFromPage(int page)—Removes all field widgets from a page. Fields are removed if they have no other widgets on at least one other page.
- removeField(String name, int page)—Removes the widgets from the field with name name from page page. The field isn't removed entirely if it has widgets on another page.
- removeField(String name)—Removes the entire field and all its widgets.

In this example, it's better to remove the password field instead of flattening it because it doesn't make sense to print a series of stars where the password field used to be. You don't want to remove the field named "personal.reason", you only want to reuse it. In section 6.4.3, you used renameField() before concatenating forms, and you can also use this method to change "reason" into "motivation", but there are some caveats:

- You can only use this method for fields that don't have named children. The following line won't work:

  ```
  form.renameField("personal", "sender");
  ```

- If you rename a field, you can only change the partial name; the first part of the fully qualified name has to be identical. This line won't work either:

  ```
  form.renameField("personal.reason", "motivation");
  ```

There are two ways to make a field read-only. Which is the better way to do it depends on your requirements.

MAKING A FIELD READ-ONLY

In figure 8.7, you made the login name read-only with the `setFieldProperty()` method. You set the flag `TextField.READ_ONLY`, and as a result the end user can no longer change the login name in the form. The field isn't flattened: you can still ask the form for the content of this field. The following line will return `"blowagie"` when used on the form shown in figure 8.7:

```
System.out.println(form.getField("personal.loginname"));
```

Note that it's possible to remove the read-only flag with iText, Acrobat, or another tool. You can even remove it using a JavaScript action executed in the PDF viewer.

If you want the field to be removed, but you want to keep the content, you can use `setFormFlattening()` but restrict the flattening process to a limited number of fields. Only those fields will be flattened for which `partialFormFlattening()` was used. Flattening will remove the field structure, so the following line will return `null` when used on the form shown in figure 8.7:

```
System.out.println(form.getField("personal.name"));
```

Suppose that the way iText flattens PDF forms doesn't meet your needs, in spite of the tips and tricks we've looked at so far. You can work around this by taking control over the flattening process.

8.5.4 *Customized form flattening*

I was once asked to work on a project that involved ads for used cars that had to appear in newspapers and magazines. The design of the advertisement was always the same: it contained the logo and the address of the company that sold used cars, but the main part of the ad consisted of photos, descriptions, and the prices of cars that were on sale that week. That content changed every week, because cars were constantly being bought and sold.

CREATING AN ADVERTISEMENT

I've made a simplified version of that assignment using the movie database for the Foobar Film Festival. See figure 8.8.

Two forms are involved in this example. Take a look at figure 8.9. The form in the back was created using Open Office. The form consists of a nice background and a number of rectangular fields.

The second form is the PDF shown in the foreground of figure 8.9. It's a rectangle with three fields. The upper field is used for an image: a picture of a used car in the real-world example, a movie poster in our example. The middle field is used for text: a description of the car or information about the film. The lower field could be filled with the car price or the production year.

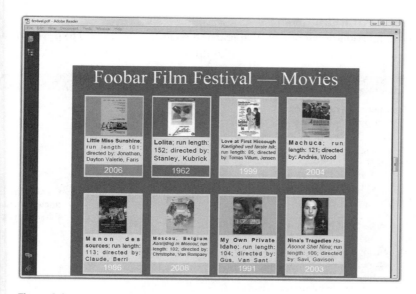

Figure 8.8   Advertisement for the Foobar Film Festival

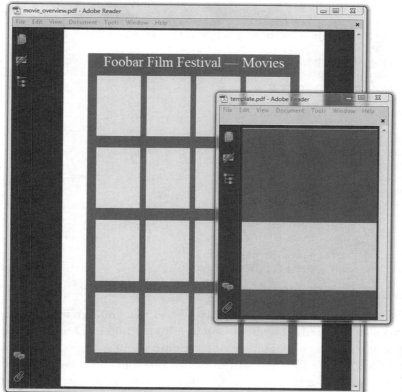

**Figure 8.9
Forms involved in
the Foobar Film
Festival ad**

COMBINING WHAT YOU ALREADY KNOW

If we combine all the knowledge you've learned so far in chapters 6 to 8, we should be able to get close to a solution that looks like the PDF in figure 8.8.

> **Listing 8.16   MovieAds.java**

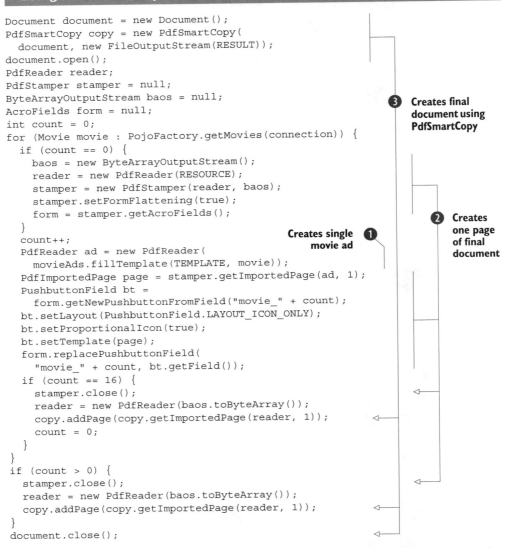

```
Document document = new Document();
PdfSmartCopy copy = new PdfSmartCopy(
  document, new FileOutputStream(RESULT));
document.open();
PdfReader reader;
PdfStamper stamper = null;
ByteArrayOutputStream baos = null;
AcroFields form = null;
int count = 0;
for (Movie movie : PojoFactory.getMovies(connection)) {
  if (count == 0) {
    baos = new ByteArrayOutputStream();
    reader = new PdfReader(RESOURCE);
    stamper = new PdfStamper(reader, baos);
    stamper.setFormFlattening(true);
    form = stamper.getAcroFields();
  }
  count++;
  PdfReader ad = new PdfReader(
    movieAds.fillTemplate(TEMPLATE, movie));
  PdfImportedPage page = stamper.getImportedPage(ad, 1);
  PushbuttonField bt =
    form.getNewPushbuttonFromField("movie_" + count);
  bt.setLayout(PushbuttonField.LAYOUT_ICON_ONLY);
  bt.setProportionalIcon(true);
  bt.setTemplate(page);
  form.replacePushbuttonField(
    "movie_" + count, bt.getField());
  if (count == 16) {
    stamper.close();
    reader = new PdfReader(baos.toByteArray());
    copy.addPage(copy.getImportedPage(reader, 1));
    count = 0;
  }
}
if (count > 0) {
  stamper.close();
  reader = new PdfReader(baos.toByteArray());
  copy.addPage(copy.getImportedPage(reader, 1));
}
document.close();
```

❸ Creates final document using PdfSmartCopy

❷ Creates one page of final document

Creates single movie ad ❶

There's no new functionality in listing 8.16, except that you haven't learned yet what the fillTemplate() method is about. You use this method in ❶ and you can assume that it returns a document containing information about a single movie as a byte[]. You create a PdfReader instance with this small PDF and use it as an icon for one of the 16 buttons on the larger template ❷. Once 16 movies have been added, the large template is full. You add the full page to a new document using PdfSmartCopy ❸, and you continue on the next page.

This may look like a complex example, but this is the code that was written for the used cars advertisement. The fillTemplate() method is the only piece missing from the puzzle.

THE MISSING PIECE OF THE PUZZLE

The field with the information about the used car (in our case, the movie information) is a multiline text field. It's impossible to fill such a field using different font styles (normal, bold, italic), nor can text be left and right justified. You'll also want the font size to adapt to the length of the description. Because of all these specific requirements, it's necessary to bypass the automatic form flattening.

Listing 8.17 MovieAds.java (continued)

```
public byte[] fillTemplate(String filename, Movie movie)
  throws IOException, DocumentException {
  ByteArrayOutputStream baos = new ByteArrayOutputStream();
  PdfReader reader = new PdfReader(TEMPLATE);
  PdfStamper stamper = new PdfStamper(reader, baos);
  AcroFields form = stamper.getAcroFields();
  BaseColor color = WebColors.getRGBColor(
    "#" + movie.getEntry().getCategory().getColor());
  PushbuttonField bt
    = form.getNewPushbuttonFromField(POSTER);
  bt.setLayout(PushbuttonField.LAYOUT_ICON_ONLY);
  bt.setProportionalIcon(true);
  bt.setImage(Image.getInstance(
    String.format(IMAGE, movie.getImdb())));
  bt.setBackgroundColor(color);
  form.replacePushbuttonField(POSTER, bt.getField());
  PdfContentByte canvas = stamper.getOverContent(1);
  float size = 12;
  FieldPosition f
    = form.getFieldPositions(TEXT).get(0);
  while (
    addParagraph(
      createMovieParagraph(movie, size), canvas, f, true)
    && size > 6) {
    size -= 0.2;
  }
  addParagraph(
    createMovieParagraph(movie, size), canvas, f, false);
  form.setField(YEAR, String.valueOf(movie.getYear()));
  form.setFieldProperty(YEAR, "bgcolor", color, null);
  form.setField(YEAR, String.valueOf(movie.getYear()));
  stamper.setFormFlattening(true);
  stamper.close();
  return baos.toByteArray();
}
public boolean addParagraph(
  Paragraph p, PdfContentByte canvas, FieldPosition f, boolean simulate)
  throws DocumentException {
```

❶ Replaces POSTER button

❷ Fills out TEXT field

❸ Fills out YEAR field

```
ColumnText ct = new ColumnText(canvas);
ct.setSimpleColumn(f.position.getLeft(2), f.position.getBottom(2),
   f.position.getRight(2), f.position.getTop());   ct.addElement(p);
return ColumnText.hasMoreText(ct.go(simulate));
}
```

There's nothing new in ❶ and ❸, but let's take a look at ❷. You grab a direct content layer using the method getOverContent(). You try adding a paragraph with the movie information to a rectangle obtained with the getFieldPositions() method. First you try a 12 pt font size, and you add the content using ColumnText in simulation mode. If the paragraph doesn't fit, you try with font size 11.8 pt, and so on. You continue until the complete text fits the rectangle, or until the font has decreased to 6 pt (in which case you truncate the content).

The getFieldPositions() method returns a List of FieldPosition objects. Each contains the page number (f.page), and the Rectangle object defining the coordinates of a widget (f.position).

With this example, we've explored the limits of what is possible with AcroForms. It's time to have a look at the other type of forms supported in PDF: forms based on the XML Forms Architecture.

8.6   *Introducing the XML Forms Architecture (XFA)*

In this section, you'll be introduced to the XML structure that's used to define an XFA form, and we'll try out different alternatives to fill out different types of XFA forms.

If you look at figure 8.10, it's hard to see any difference between it and the forms you've created and used in previous examples. End users won't notice this is a different kind of form.

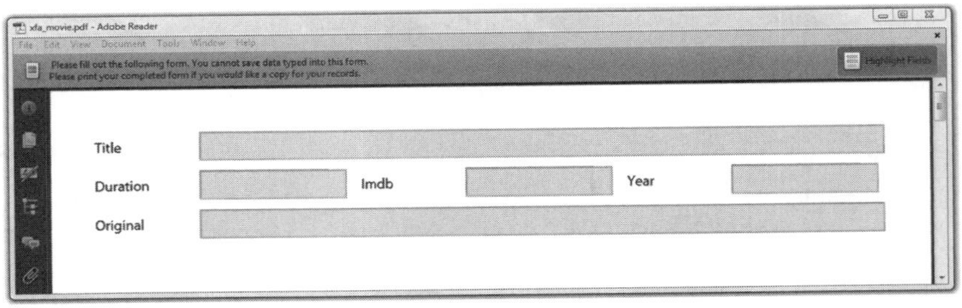

Figure 8.10   A static XFA form

With the next listing, you can inspect the PDF from the inside, and you'll find out it's an XFA form.

Listing 8.18   XfaMovie.java

```
public void readFieldnames(String src, String dest)
  throws IOException {
  PrintStream out = new PrintStream(new FileOutputStream(dest));
  PdfReader reader = new PdfReader(src);
```

```
AcroFields form = reader.getAcroFields();
XfaForm xfa = form.getXfa();                          Checks if form
out.println(                                          is XFA form
  xfa.isXfaPresent() ? "XFA form" : "AcroForm");
Set<String> fields = form.getFields().keySet();       Lists field
for (String key : fields) {                           names
  out.println(key);
}
out.flush();
out.close();
}
```

In this method, you use the method isXfaPresent() to find out if the form is an XFA form or an AcroForm. You also list the names of the fields.

This is the content of the text file with the results:

```
XFA form                              ❶
movies[0].movie[0].imdb[0]
movies[0].movie[0].duration[0]
movies[0].movie[0].title[0]           ❷
movies[0].movie[0].original[0]
movies[0].movie[0].year[0]
```

iText tells us that this is an XFA form ❶, and it returns a list of fields with square brackets in their name ❷. These square brackets are typical for XFA. When listing 8.18 generates a result like this, your PDF contains two different form descriptions: one using XFA technology and one using AcroForm technology. You can conclude that this is a static XFA form.

8.6.1 Static XFA forms

Let's pretend you don't know you're working with a static XFA form, and fill in the form using the AcroFields class and the setField() method. This code will work correctly for most of the forms you'll encounter.

Listing 8.19 XfaMovie.java (continued)

```
public void fillData1(String src, String dest)
  throws IOException, DocumentException {
  PdfReader reader = new PdfReader(src);
  PdfStamper stamper
    = new PdfStamper(reader, new FileOutputStream(dest));
  AcroFields form = stamper.getAcroFields();
  form.setField("movies[0].movie[0].imdb[0]", "1075110");
  form.setField("movies[0].movie[0].duration[0]", "108");
  form.setField("movies[0].movie[0].title[0]", "The Misfortunates");
  form.setField("movies[0].movie[0].original[0]",
    "De helaasheid der dingen");
  form.setField("movies[0].movie[0].year[0]", "2009");
  stamper.close();
}
```

iText will fill out the AcroForm (as it did in all previous examples), and it will make a fair attempt at filling out the XFA form simultaneously. In most cases, this works

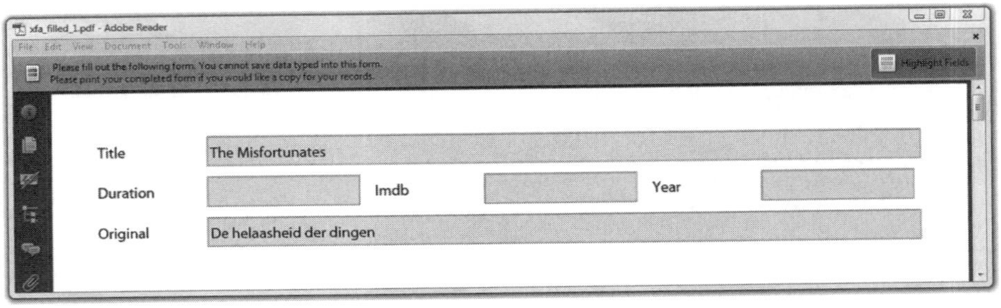

Figure 8.11 Partially filled-in form

transparently: you don't even notice that the two different technologies exist next to each other. However, if you look at figure 8.11, you'll see that this is an example where iText fails. Although you provided values for the year, duration, and the IMDB ID, the corresponding fields remain empty.

I deliberately created the three fields in a way that isn't supported by iText. This way I can explain the mechanism of XFA form filling with iText. There are different workarounds to deal with this problem, but let's inspect the XFA form first.

XFA FORMS: INTERNAL STRUCTURE

When creating an AcroForm using iText, you implicitly create PdfDictionary, PdfArray, and other PdfObject instances. XFA forms are totally different; they aren't defined using PDF objects. XFA forms are described in an XML stream that's embedded in the PDF file.

You can extract this XML into a separate file.

Listing 8.20 XfaMovie.java (continued)

```
public void readXfa(String src, String dest)
  throws IOException, ParserConfigurationException, SAXException,
  TransformerFactoryConfigurationError, TransformerException {
  FileOutputStream os = new FileOutputStream(dest);
  PdfReader reader = new PdfReader(src);                   ⎤ Creates XfaForm
  XfaForm xfa = new XfaForm(reader);                       ⎦ instance
  Document doc = xfa.getDomDocument();        ◁── Gets org.w3c.dom.Document instance
  Transformer tf
    = TransformerFactory.newInstance().newTransformer();      ⎤ Transforms
  tf.setOutputProperty(OutputKeys.ENCODING, "UTF-8");        │ Document
  tf.setOutputProperty(OutputKeys.INDENT, "yes");            │ to XML file
  tf.transform(new DOMSource(doc), new StreamResult(os));    ⎦
  reader.close();
}
```

Note that the Document in this code snippet isn't a com.itextpdf.text.Document object, but an instance of org.w3c.dom.Document. Transforming this Document into an XML file is done using different classes from the javax.xml.transform package.

This is a shortened version of the resulting file.

Listing 8.21   movie_xfa.xml

```xml
<?xml version="1.0" encoding="UTF-8" standalone="no"?>
<xdp:xdp>
  <config>...</config>
  <template>...</template>
  <xfa:datasets>
    <xfa:data>
      <movies>
        <movie duration="" imdb="" year="">
          <title/>
        </movie>
      </movies>
    </xfa:data>
    <dd:dataDescription>
      <movies>
        <movie dd:maxOccur="-1"
          dd:reqAttrs="duration imdb year"
          duration="" imdb="" year="">
          <title/>
          <original dd:minOccur="0" dd:nullType="exclude"/>
        </movie>
      </movies>
    </dd:dataDescription>
  </xfa:datasets>
</xdp:xdp>
```

If you want to understand the full XML file that was extracted, you'll need to consult the XFA specification for more info about the elements that can be found inside an XFA form:

- `config`, `localeSet`, `xmp`, ... —The XFA XML can contain application-defined information and XFA grammar: configuration information, localization info, metadata, information about web connections, and so on. Except for the `config` tag, I've omitted these tags, because they're outside the scope of this book.
- `template`—This is where the appearance and behavior of the form is defined.
- `datasets`—This contains all the sets of data used with the form.
- `data`—Contains the data held by fields in the form.
- `dataDescription`—Defines the schema for the data.

As you can see, XFA separates data from the XFA template, which allows greater flexibility in the structure of the data supported and allows data to be packaged separately from the form.

> **FAQ** *Can I use iText to change the properties and appearance of an XFA form?* Yes and no. In the previous sections of this chapter, you've used iText to manipulate the appearance of AcroForm fields, but none of these examples will change the XML definition inside the XFA stream. Changing an XFA form has to be done using XML tools. First extract the XFA XML from the PDF. Then add, remove, and update the tags and attributes between the `<template>` and `</template>` tags. Once this is done, use iText to replace the existing XFA stream with the updated one.

The template specification is described in about 300 pages in the XFA reference. It would lead us too far off topic to get into the details of manipulating an XFA form, but we'll look at how to replace the full XFA XML in the next example, after changing the data.

THE DATA SPECIFICATION

The `datasets` section of the XFA form consists of a `data` and a `dataDescription` element. You can use any schema you want for the data. This is one of the major advantages of choosing the XFA approach instead of using AcroForms.

The `dataDescription` specification comprises 16 pages in the XFA reference. Here's the introduction:

> *The XFA data description syntax is more concise and readable than XML Schema but does not do as much. XFA data descriptions do not include defaults and do not support validation of text content. They do, however, fully describe the namespaces, element names, attribute names, and the hierarchy which joins them.*

—XML Forms Architecture (XFA) Specification Version 3.1 Part 2 Chapter 21

Let's take a look at the changes made by iText to the `data` element to find out why three fields weren't filled out in figure 8.11. We'll reuse listing 8.20 on the resulting PDF file to have a look at the `data` element that was filled by iText.

Listing 8.22   movie_filled.xml

```
<movies>
  <movie duration="" imdb="" year="">
    <title>The Misfortunates</title>
    <imdb>1075110</imdb>
    <duration>108</duration>
    <original>De helaasheid der dingen</original>
    <year>2009</year>
  </movie>
</movies>
```

The data description in listing 8.21 expects the content of the fields `"imdb"`, `"duration"`, and `"year"` to be added as attributes of the `movie` tag. When you filled the form using listing 8.19, iText used a shortcut: it wrongly assumed that all data should be added between tags, not as attributes. There are three workarounds for this problem:

- *Change the form*—Make sure the form doesn't expect data added as attributes. This may not be an option, because you want the data inside the XFA form to be an identical match with the XML files you're using in your business process.
- *Use XML tools to fill out the data*—This is the most elegant solution. We'll discuss two possible ways to achieve this. In listing 8.23 we'll replace the complete XFA XML; then, in section 8.6.2, we'll let iText replace the data element in a programmer-friendly way.
- *Remove the XFA form, keep the AcroForm*—This is your only option if you want to flatten the form. The resulting form will no longer contain XFA technology—the result will be a pure AcroForm.

The first option should be done with the tool that was used to create the form in the first place. Replacing the XML data can be done the hard way or the easy way; let's look at the hard way first.

REPLACING THE XFA STREAM

Suppose that you've updated the XFA XML manually and saved it in a file named xml. Now you want to take the XFA form src and replace the XFA stream with the new XFA form dest as a result.

Listing 8.23   XfaMovie.java (continued)

```java
public void fillData2(String src, String xml, String dest)
  throws IOException, DocumentException,
  ParserConfigurationException, SAXException {
  PdfReader reader = new PdfReader(src);
  PdfStamper stamper
    = new PdfStamper(reader, new FileOutputStream(dest));
  XfaForm xfa = new XfaForm(reader);
  DocumentBuilderFactory fact = DocumentBuilderFactory.newInstance();
  fact.setNamespaceAware(true);
  DocumentBuilder db = fact.newDocumentBuilder();
  Document doc = db.parse(new FileInputStream(xml));
  xfa.setDomDocument(doc);
  xfa.setChanged(true);
  XfaForm.setXfa(xfa, stamper.getReader(), stamper.getWriter());
  stamper.close();
}
```

Reads XFA XML file into DOM Document

Replaces XFA stream in existing PDF document

For this example, I've changed the XFA XML manually. I've replaced the XML snippet shown in listing 8.22 with this one.

Listing 8.24   xfa.xml

```xml
<movies>
  <movie duration="108" imdb="1075110" year="2009">
    <title>The Misfortunates</title>
    <original>De helaasheid der dingen</original>
  </movie>
</movies>
```

The result is shown in figure 8.12. All the fields are now filled in correctly.

Figure 8.12   Correctly filled-out XFA form

The code in listing 8.23 is rather complex. We'll find a better way to replace only the data XML in section 8.6.2. You can use this method, however, if you want to change other parts of the XFA form. For instance, if you want to change the appearance of the form.

Note that iText doesn't parse what's inside the template tag. One of the consequences is that you have to use an XML tool to apply changes to the form. Another consequence is that iText can't flatten a pure XFA form; iText can't translate the XFA syntax to draw a form field, captions, and lines into PDF syntax. A form can only be flattened with iText if it's also defined using AcroForm technology.

CHANGING AN XFA FORM INTO AN ACROFORM

If a form is defined twice, once using XFA technology once as an AcroForm, you can choose to remove the XFA technology with the removeXfa() method.

Listing 8.25   XfaMovie.java (continued)

```
public void fillData3(String src, String dest)
  throws IOException, DocumentException {
  PdfReader reader = new PdfReader(src);
  PdfStamper stamper
    = new PdfStamper(reader, new FileOutputStream(dest));
  AcroFields form = stamper.getAcroFields();
  form.removeXfa();                                              Removes XFA
  form.setField("movies[0].movie[0].imdb[0]", "1075110");       technology
  ...
  stamper.close();
}
```

If you run listing 8.18 on the resulting form, you get the following output:

```
AcroForm
movies[0].movie[0].title[0]
movies[0].movie[0].duration[0]
movies[0].movie[0].imdb[0]
movies[0].movie[0].year[0]
movies[0].movie[0].original[0]
```

After this operation, you can use all the iText functionality discussed in sections 8.2 to 8.5. That's an advantage. The disadvantage is that you lose all the benefits you can have from XFA. This only works for static XFA forms with an AcroForm counterpart; it won't work for dynamic XFA forms.

8.6.2   *Dynamic XFA forms*

One of the major advantages of XFA is you can define forms that can grow dynamically. In traditional PDF files, the layout of the content is fixed: the coordinate of every dot, every line, every glyph on the page is known in advance. PDF was created because there was a need for a document format that was predictable. When you create a document containing three pages, you don't want it to be rendered as a document with two or four pages when opened on another OS or using a different viewer application. XFA makes an exception to this rule. A dynamic XFA form can grow dynamically depending on the data that's entered.

XML DATA

Suppose that your movie data is stored as an XML file using this XML schema.

Listing 8.26   movies.xsd

```xml
<?xml version="1.0" encoding="UTF-8"?>
<xs:schema xmlns:xs="http://www.w3.org/2001/XMLSchema"
 elementFormDefault="qualified">
 <xs:element name="movies">
  <xs:complexType><xs:sequence>
    <xs:element maxOccurs="unbounded" ref="movie"/>
   </xs:sequence></xs:complexType>
 </xs:element>
 <xs:element name="movie">
  <xs:complexType>
   <xs:sequence>
    <xs:element ref="title"/>
    <xs:element minOccurs="0" ref="original"/>
    <xs:element ref="directors"/>
    <xs:element ref="countries"/>
   </xs:sequence>
   <xs:attribute name="duration" use="required" type="xs:string"/>
   <xs:attribute name="imdb" use="required" type="xs:string"/>
   <xs:attribute name="year" use="required" type="xs:string"/>
  </xs:complexType>
 </xs:element>
 <xs:element name="title" type="xs:string"/>
 <xs:element name="original" type="xs:string"/>
 <xs:element name="directors">
  <xs:complexType><xs:sequence>
    <xs:element maxOccurs="unbounded" ref="director"/>
   </xs:sequence></xs:complexType>
 </xs:element>
 <xs:element name="director" type="xs:string"/>
 <xs:element name="countries">
  <xs:complexType><xs:sequence>
    <xs:element maxOccurs="unbounded" ref="country"/>
   </xs:sequence></xs:complexType>
 </xs:element>
 <xs:element name="country" type="xs:string"/>
</xs:schema>
```

Here is a shortened example of an XML file that follows this schema. The full version contains 120 movies.

Listing 8.27   movies.xml

```xml
<?xml version="1.0" encoding="UTF-8" ?>
<movies>
  <movie duration="141" imdb="0062622" year="1968">
    <title>2001: A Space Odyssey</title>
    <directors><director>Kubrick, Stanley</director></directors>
    <countries>
      <country>United Kingdom</country>
```

```
      <country>United States</country>
    </countries>
  </movie>
  ...
</movie>
```

If you want to create a form that can be filled with all the information in this XML file, regardless of the number of movies, the number of directors per movie, and the number of countries per movie, you need to use Adobe LiveCycle Designer.

CREATING A DYNAMIC XFA FORM

Adobe LiveCycle Designer can be started as a separate product, but as it's shipped with Acrobat, you can also start it from the Acrobat menu: Forms > Start Form Wizard.

You want to create a form from scratch, so select No Existing Form (Create an Adobe Form from Scratch or from a Template). A dialog box opens, assisting you in creating the form by offering the following options:

- *Getting Started*—Choose the Use a Blank Form option.
- *Document Setup*—Choose the defaults and click Next.

This is shown in figure 8.13. Observe the difference between Acrobat in the background and Adobe LiveCycle Designer in the foreground.

You could start adding text boxes manually, but that's a lot of work. It's easier to create a new data connection: File > New Data Connection. A dialog box opens, and

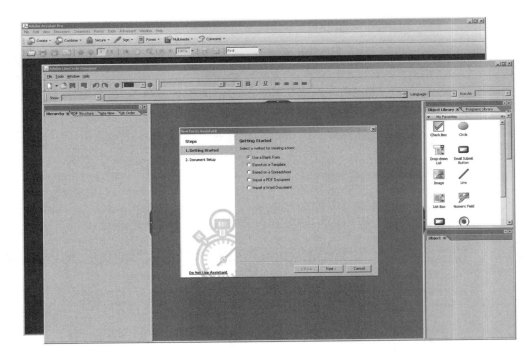

Figure 8.13   Creating a new form with Adobe LiveCycle Designer

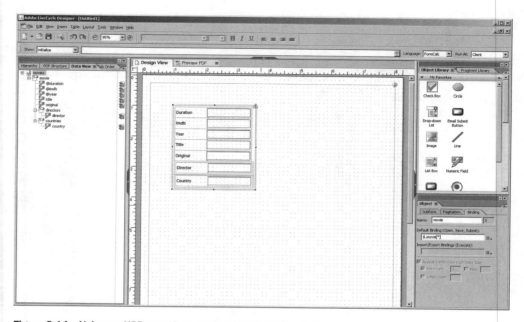

Figure 8.14   Using an XSD as a data connection to create the form

you can import the XSD from listing 8.26: XML Schema > movies.xsd > Finish. You can see the result in the Data View panel to the left in figure 8.14.

The next step is easy. You can drag the movies tree from the Data View panel to your form. Designer will automatically create a form with all the text fields you need. The form consists of fields that are organized in *subforms*.

The yellow triangle in the upper-right corner of the rectangle enclosing the fields indicates that there's an inconsistency between the top-level subform and the underlying subforms. You can solve this problem by selecting the outer rectangle corresponding with the top-level subform. Right-click and choose Palettes > Object. An extra panel will open. Checking the Allow Page Breaks within Content check box will remove the warning.

Let's reorganize the fields. In the Object panel at the bottom right, change the Content setting of the top-level subform from Positioned to Flowed. Then select the subform named `movie` and set that Content value to Positioned. You can now move around the fields. If you lose the overview, select the Hierarchy panel that's shown on the left in figure 8.15.

If you want the form to start a new page if a movie doesn't fit on the current page, you have to uncheck the Allow Page Breaks within Content check box in the Object panel. Now save this form as a dynamic form, and you'll get a PDF as shown in figure 8.16.

Running listing 8.18 with this form as resource will give you the following result:

```
XFA form
```

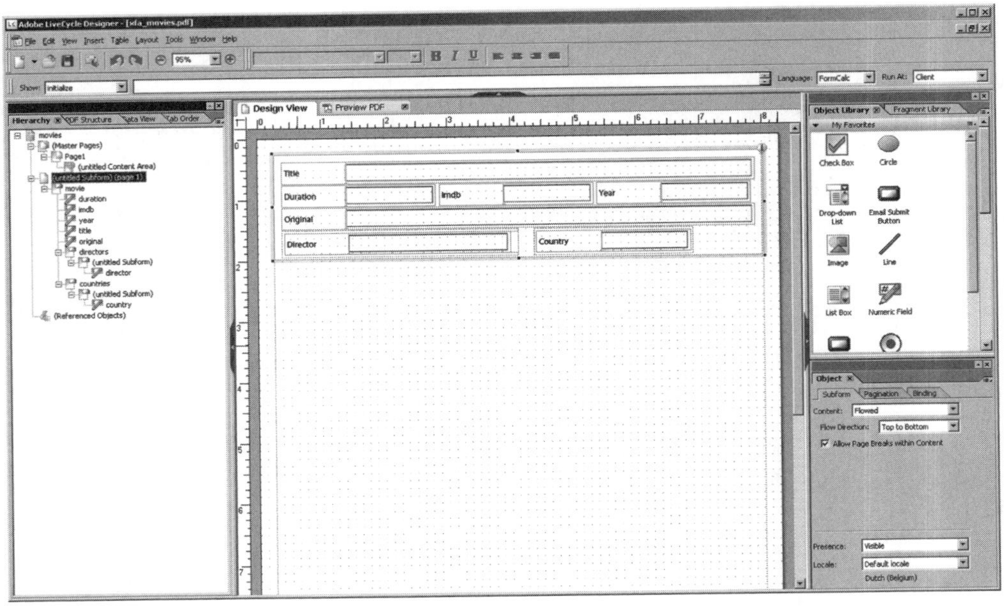

Figure 8.15   Reorganizing the fields in the form

The form you've just created is a pure XFA form. There are no AcroForm fields inside the PDF.

FILLING A DYNAMIC XFA FORM

The PDF shown in figure 8.16 is a dynamic form, so when you fill it with an XML file containing 120 movies, you'd expect it to look like figure 8.17.

The original form only had one page, but the resulting PDF counts 23 pages! Because the form is dynamic, the movie subform is repeated 120 times. Observe that the same goes for the lists with the directors and countries. If there are two directors, the director field is duplicated; if there are two countries, the country field is duplicated.

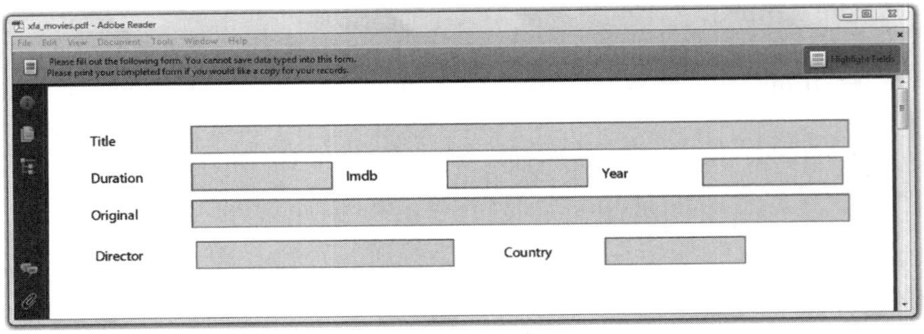

Figure 8.16   Empty dynamic XFA form

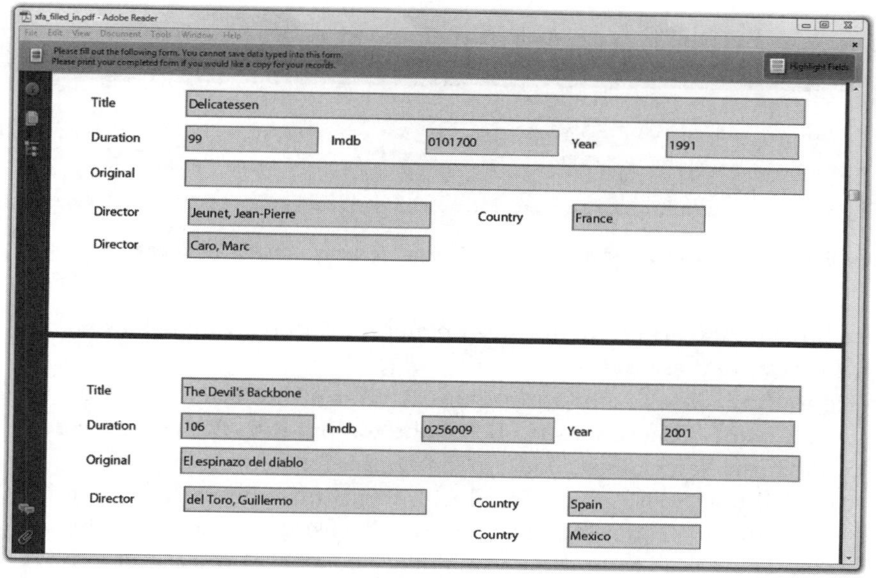

Figure 8.17 Dynamic XFA form filled with movie XML

You can use iText to fill such a dynamic PDF form.

Listing 8.28 XfaMovies.java

```
public void manipulatePdf(String src, String xml, String dest)
  throws IOException, DocumentException {
  PdfReader reader = new PdfReader(src);
  PdfStamper stamper =
    new PdfStamper(reader, new FileOutputStream(dest));
  AcroFields form = stamper.getAcroFields();
  XfaForm xfa = form.getXfa();
  xfa.fillXfaForm(new FileInputStream(XMLDATA));   ◁── Injects XML data
  stamper.close();                                      into dynamic form
}
```

In this example, XMLDATA is the path to the XML file from listing 2.27. As you can see, XFA technology is very powerful. This is a simple example, containing only text fields, but this code also works with barcode fields, check boxes, and so on. A good graphical designer skilled at creating forms with Adobe LiveCycle Designer can create very complex dynamic forms. All you need to do to fill them out is inject an XML stream using the fillXfaForm() method. There's one major caveat: if your form is Reader-enabled, filling it out will break the Reader-enabling.

8.7 *Preserving the usage rights of Reader-enabled forms*

With what you've learned so far, you can use iText to fill out PDF forms created with Open Office, Adobe Acrobat, LiveCycle Designer, or other tools. When creating a form using Adobe products, the form's designer can enable usage rights that unlock

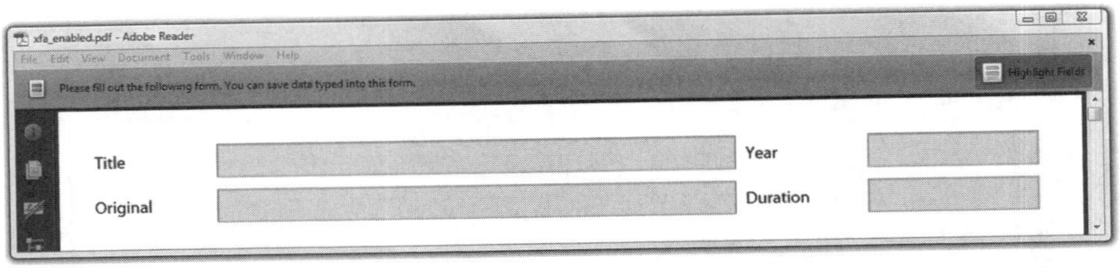

Figure 8.18   A Reader-enabled form can be filled out and saved in Adobe Reader

extra functionality when the form is opened in Adobe Reader. This section explains how to preserve these rights.

Figure 8.18 shows a PDF form that's significantly different from the forms we've dealt with before. There's a strip below the toolbar with the text: "Please fill out the following form. You can save data typed into this form."

Up until now, we've only worked with forms that showed the following message: "Please fill out the following form. You can't save data typed into this form. Please print your completed form if you would like a copy for your records."

> **FAQ**   *Can I fill out any PDF form and save it locally using Adobe Reader?* No, you
> can only save forms filled out manually with Adobe Reader if they have been
> "Reader-enabled."

If you provide a PDF form in a web application, people can fill out the form in their browser and submit the data to your server. We're going to look at how to do this in the next chapter. If you want to allow people to save the data locally before submitting the form, you need to enable your form using the LiveCycle Reader Extensions or the full Acrobat.

8.7.1   *Reader-enabling a form using Adobe Acrobat*

Choose Advanced > Extend Features in Adobe Acrobat. A dialog box titled Enable Usage Rights in Adobe Reader will open, explaining which features will become available in the free Adobe Reader: saving a form locally, but also commenting, signing, and so on.

> **FAQ**   *Can I create a Reader-enabled form using iText?* The technology that's used
> to enable a form is based on public-key cryptography, where the viewer of the
> document (in this case Adobe Reader) has the public key and the authoring
> software for the document has the private key. Because iText (or any other
> non-Adobe software) has no access to Adobe's private key, you can only
> enable documents using Adobe products.

Once you've made the form Reader-enabled, you can prefill it using iText; but you have to be aware that users risk being confronted with the alert box shown in figure 8.19.

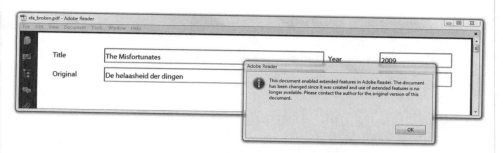

Figure 8.19   Filling out a form programmatically can break Reader-enabling

The full text of the warning tells you exactly what happened:

This document enabled extended features in Adobe Reader. The document has been changed since it was created and use of extended features is no longer available. Please contact the author for the original version of this document.

When making a document Reader-enabled using Acrobat, a hash of the content was signed with Adobe's private key. Adobe Reader decrypts this embedded hash and compares it with the current content. If the content hasn't changed, there's a match, and the additional usage rights are active. When filling out a form, iText changes the document structure, and therefore breaks Reader-enabling.

8.7.2   *Filling out Reader-enabled forms using iText*

If you don't want to confront your end users with this warning, you can remove the usage rights. You'll end up with a "normal" form, without the extra features. Or, you can use PdfStamper in append mode. The result of these two workarounds is shown in figure 8.20. The code for both workarounds is in listing 8.29.

The form in the background can no longer be saved locally. The extended features of the form in the foreground remain intact.

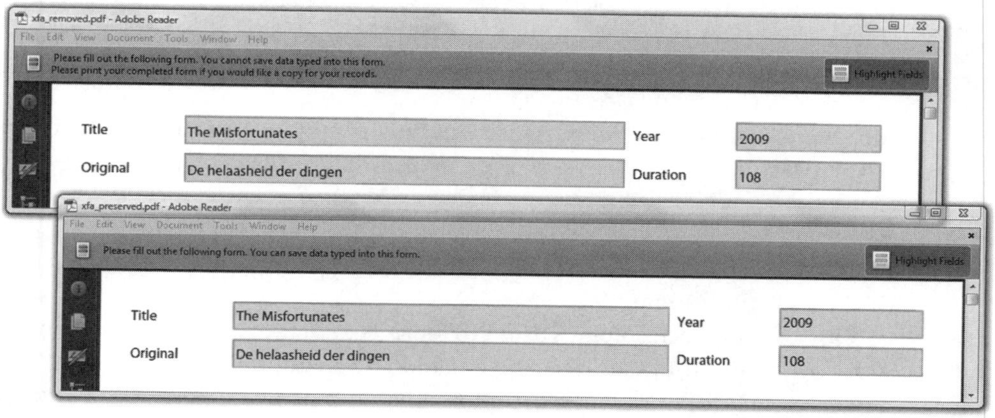

Figure 8.20   Two workarounds to fill out a Reader Enabled form

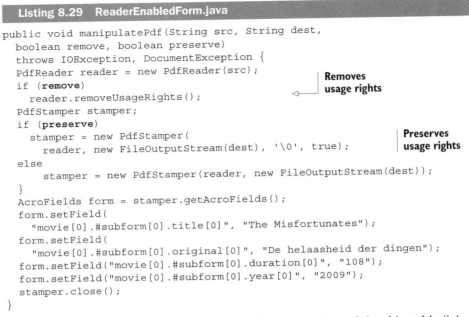

Listing 8.29   ReaderEnabledForm.java

```
public void manipulatePdf(String src, String dest,
  boolean remove, boolean preserve)
  throws IOException, DocumentException {
  PdfReader reader = new PdfReader(src);                    Removes
  if (remove)                                               usage rights
    reader.removeUsageRights();
  PdfStamper stamper;
  if (preserve)                                             Preserves
    stamper = new PdfStamper(                               usage rights
      reader, new FileOutputStream(dest), '\0', true);
  else
    stamper = new PdfStamper(reader, new FileOutputStream(dest));
  }
  AcroFields form = stamper.getAcroFields();
  form.setField(
    "movie[0].#subform[0].title[0]", "The Misfortunates");
  form.setField(
    "movie[0].#subform[0].original[0]", "De helaasheid der dingen");
  form.setField("movie[0].#subform[0].duration[0]", "108");
  form.setField("movie[0].#subform[0].year[0]", "2009");
  stamper.close();
}
```

The meaning of the parameters remove and preserve is explained in table 8.4.

Table 8.4   Filling out a Reader-enabled form

remove	preserve	Result
false	false	You fill out the form as before. This breaks Reader-enabling and causes a scary warning.
true	false	You fill out the form as before, with removal of the usage rights. With Reader-enabling gone, there's also no more scary warning.
false	true	You fill out the form, but not as before. By using a different constructor for PdfStamper, you'll create the new PDF in append mode. This means that iText will keep the original PDF intact and append all the changes instead of reorganizing the internal structure.

Although a static XFA form is used in this example, this also works for plain old AcroForms.

8.8   Summary

In this chapter, we've explored the two types of interactive forms that are supported in the PDF specification.

One of these technologies uses PDF objects to define a form; these forms are called AcroForms, and they can easily be created and manipulated using iText. You learned how to create different types of button, text, and choice fields. At the same time, you found out how to change the properties of these fields in an existing PDF document.

We focused on filling out forms. Form fields can be organized hierarchically, which changes how forms are filled out. You learned to optimize the process using a field cache. We also looked at flattening a form partially and taking over the flattening process altogether.

Then we looked at the other type of form. XFA forms are based on the XML Forms Architecture, and they come in two flavors: static XFA forms and dynamic XFA forms. Most of the static XFA forms can be filled with iText in the same way as AcroForms, using the same code. But when we inspected what an XFA form looks like on the inside, you discovered that there were exceptions. You created a dynamic XFA form using Adobe LiveCycle Designer, and you used iText to inject an XML data file into that form.

Finally, you learned more about Reader-enabled forms. Filling such a form with iText can break the extra features that are added to the form, but you learned how to avoid this.

This chapter concludes the second part of this book about manipulating existing PDF files. You had an overview of the different manipulation classes in chapter 6; you added links, bookmarks, and annotations to existing documents in chapter 7; and you've learned almost everything about filling out interactive forms in this chapter.

In the next chapter, you'll discover how to integrate the standalone examples we've looked at so far in a Java servlet; for instance, how to integrate a PDF form in a web application.

Part 3

Essential iText skills

Parts 1 and 2 showed you how to build a standalone application that is able to create or manipulate a PDF document in black and white, using standard fonts, and so on. The four chapters in part 3 will show you how to integrate such an application into a web application, how to create images and colors, how to choose and use different fonts, and how to protect your document.

Integrating iText in your web applications

9

This chapter covers

- Making interactive forms "web ready"
- Converting HTML and XML to PDF
- Using iText in servlets

Every month, I visit Google Analytics to look at the statistics for my different sites; I click Export > PDF and save a printable report for my archives. When I want to travel by train or by plane, I can download a ticket or a boarding pass from a website. When you download an eBook from Manning, your email address is automatically stamped on every page. Most of these reports, vouchers, stamped books, and so on, are "powered by iText." iText was one of the first libraries that combined ease of use with speed, and that's why it's omnipresent in applications generating PDFs for the web.

Let's take a look at how these applications work and see how easy it is to integrate iText in a Java servlet.

9.1   *Creating a PDF from a servlet*

Up until now, you've only worked with standalone examples. You compiled them using the `javac` command and executed them with `java`, resulting in one or more PDF documents.

For this chapter, you need to install an application server. If you've written and deployed Java servlets before, you shouldn't have any problem setting up the examples. If you don't have any experience with J2EE applications, please consult a book about writing web applications in Java, as this is outside the scope of this book.

I use Tomcat in combination with Eclipse. This allows me to choose Run As > Run on Server instead of Run As > Java Application. Eclipse will start up an instance of Tomcat, and a browser window opens inside my IDE. If I'm pleased with the result, I deploy the application on my web server. See figure 9.1. The window at the lower right in the foreground is Eclipse; the windows in the background are browser windows: Firefox, Google Chrome, Microsoft Internet Explorer (MSIE).

To get to this result, you need to integrate the five steps in the PDF creation process in a servlet.

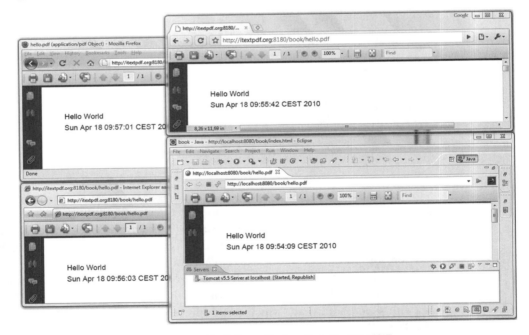

Figure 9.1   Hello World servlet opened in Eclipse, Firefox, Chrome, and MSIE

9.1.1   *The five steps of PDF creation in a web application*

When we discussed step 2 in the PDF creation process, writing a simple Hello World example to a `FileOutputStream`, you learned that we could have used any other `OutputStream`. For instance, a `ServletOutputStream` obtained from the `HttpServletResponse` with the `getOutputStream()` method.

Listing 9.1   Hello.java

```java
public class Hello extends HttpServlet {
  protected void doGet(
    HttpServletRequest request, HttpServletResponse response)
    throws ServletException, IOException {
    response.setContentType("application/pdf");        ◀── Sets Content-
    try {                                                  Type to PDF
      Document document = new Document();                        ❶
      PdfWriter.getInstance(document, response.getOutputStream());  ❷
      document.open();                                          ❸
      document.add(new Paragraph("Hello World"));
      document.add(new Paragraph(new Date().toString()));    ❹
      document.close();                                      ❺
    } catch (DocumentException de) {
      throw new IOException(de.getMessage());
    }
  }
}
```

The difference between this and the standalone "Hello World" example from chapter 1 is that here you subclass HttpServlet and override the doGet() or doPost() method, or both. You copy and paste the five steps into this method:

- ❶ Create the Document.
- ❷ Create an instance of PdfWriter and use response.getOutputStream() for the second parameter.
- ❸ Open the Document.
- ❹ Add content.
- ❺ Close the Document.

This is probably the simplest iText servlet you can write.

If you want to deploy it in a web application, you have to adapt the web.xml configuration file of your application. Note that most IDEs have a wizard that updates this XML file for you. I made my web.xml file using a wizard in Eclipse.

Listing 9.2   web.xml

```xml
<?xml version="1.0" encoding="UTF-8"?>
<web-app id="WebApp_ID" version="2.4" ...>
  <display-name>book</display-name>
  <servlet>
    <description></description>
    <display-name>Hello</display-name>
    <servlet-name>Hello</servlet-name>
    <servlet-class>part3.chapter09.Hello</servlet-class>
  </servlet>
  <servlet-mapping>
    <servlet-name>Hello</servlet-name>
    <url-pattern>/hello.pdf</url-pattern>
  </servlet-mapping>
</web-app>
```

You'll put all the examples from this chapter in a web application named book. As you move on, you'll have to add more servlet and servlet-mapping tags to this file.

You'll use /hello.pdf as the URL pattern for your first servlet. The URL to run the servlet on the localhost will look like this: http://localhost:8080/book/hello.pdf. You can also see the servlet in action on http://itextpdf.org:8180/book/hello.pdf; that's where I deployed the WAR file of the application. You can use the ANT files that come with the examples to create your own WAR file if you want to test this functionality on your own server.

The screenshots in figure 9.1 prove that this servlet works for recent versions of the most common browsers and PDF viewers, but you may experience problems that are not iText-related with specific browser and viewer combinations. How can you determine whether a problem is caused by the browser, by the server, or by (the wrong use of) iText?

9.1.2   Troubleshooting web applications

Let's start with rules of thumb that can save you from a lot of frustration when trying to get your PDF servlet online. These rules may seem trivial, but they're very important.

- *Always begin writing code that runs as a standalone example*. If the example doesn't work in its standalone version, it won't work in a web application either, but at least you can rule out all problems related to the server or the browser.
- *Start with simple code samples based on the examples in this book*. Gradually add complexity until something goes wrong. Look at the stack trace in the server logs. Most of the time, the error messages will tell you exactly what to do. If not, post the stack-trace to the iText mailing list, and don't forget to mention what application server you're using, as well as the Java version and the iText release number.
- *Always test your application on different machines, using different browsers, even if there isn't any problem*. Some web applications won't show any problems when tested on one type of browser, but will fail when using another browser.
- *Create a file on the server's filesystem if no file appears in the browser*. An easy way to find out if a problem is caused by iText or by the browser is to replace the ServletOutputStream in step ❷ with a FileOutputStream (for debugging reasons only). If the file is generated correctly on your server, you can rule out iText as the cause of the problem.

By following this last rule, you should be able to determine whether the problem is a client-side or a server-side problem.

SERVER-SIDE PROBLEMS

Throughout the years, I've compiled a list of things that can go wrong on the server side, based on what other users have posted on the mailing list.

- *Bad Exception handling*　The first thing you shouldn't like about listing 9.1 is the way the `DocumentException` is handled. If something goes wrong in the try block, an `IOException` is thrown, resulting in an internal server error. If you're using Tomcat, an HTML page with the header "HTTP Status 500" is sent to the browser, showing (part of) the stack trace of the exception. That's not something you want to show to the visitors of your site. You're probably used to providing error pages that are less technical than the one generated by Tomcat, but remember that you're creating PDFs. If you send HTML to a PDF viewer, it will throw an error saying "the file doesn't begin with %PDF."

- *Mixing HTML and PDF syntax*　Be careful not to mix HTML error messages in a stream of PDF bytes. If a PDF viewer is already opened as a browser plug-in, it will tell you that the PDF is corrupt because it can't interpret the HTML code. The best way to debug problems like this is by saving the stream that is sent to the browser as a file. First try opening it in Adobe Reader. If it doesn't open correctly, have a look at it in a text editor that preserves binary characters. Don't forget to scroll down beyond the `%EOF` end of file marker (if possible). I've seen web applications that were adding a stream of plain HTML to the PDF file. Newer versions of the Adobe Reader plug-in may ignore the HTML, but older versions will complain that the file is corrupt.

- *The blank-page problem*　If you don't find HTML syntax, but you see an unusual amount of question marks inside blocks marked with `stream` and `endstream`, the problem is server-related. The question marks should be binary characters. You'll probably be able to open the PDF in the browser plug-in because the page structure of the PDF is OK, but you'll only see blank pages because the content of the pages is corrupted. This can happen when your server flattens all bytes with a value higher than 127. Consult your web (or application) server manual to find out how to make sure binary data is sent correctly to the browser.

- *Problems with JARs*　For instance, a `ClassNotFoundException` is thrown. Check whether you have added all the JARs you need to the classpath of your web application. If an iText class is missing, make sure you don't have more than one version of the iText.jar in the classpath; for instance, one version in the lib directory of your web application, and a different version in the lib directory of the application server. Different versions can lead to conflicts. Finally, check whether the application is compiled with the correct compiler. iText is compiled with Java 5, you can't run it on a server that is running in an older Java Runtime Environment (JRE).

- *A resource can't be found*　Many server-related problems are caused by an image, a font, or another resource that can't be found. A file that was available for the standalone example might not be available for the web application. Normally, the exception will give you an indication where to look. Maybe the working directory of the servlet is different from what you expected. The problem can also be caused by permission issues, or simply by the fact that a resource isn't present on the server. If the cause isn't obvious, try reproducing the problem in a servlet that doesn't involve iText. For instance, read the bytes of the resource file, and write them to the `ServletInputStream`. If this fails, your problem isn't iText-related.

If the file generated on the server side is OK, or if none of the situations mentioned so far matches your problem, chances are that your problem is browser-related.

THE BROWSER DOESN'T RECOGNIZE THE FILE AS A PDF

When an end user installs Adobe Reader, the browsers on the user's OS should be detected and configured automatically. When a browser is installed, it should detect Adobe Reader if it's present. If there's no PDF viewer on the end user's system, or if the PDF viewer isn't configured correctly, the user will see content that looks like gibberish starting with %PDF-1.4 %âãïÓ.

If this "gibberish problem" only occurs for a handful of end users, not for *all* your users, you'll have to ask these people to install or reinstall their PDF viewer. If all users experience the same problem, the problem is caused on the server side. The viewer receives the PDF syntax, but shows it as if it were plain text. Maybe you didn't set the content type correctly, in which case you need to add this line to your servlet:

```
response.setContentType("application/pdf");
```

Old versions of MSIE ignore the content type; they only look at the file extension. PDFs ending with .pdf are rendered fine, but if you use a different URL pattern, the browser plug-in isn't opened. The most elegant way to solve this problem is by using a URL pattern as shown in listing 9.2. If this is not an option, you could add a parameter ending in .pdf. For instance,

```
http://myserver.com/servlet/MyServlet?dummy=dummy.pdf;
```

Use this solution as a last recourse. A better solution is to set the content disposition in the response header:

```
response.setHeader("Content-Disposition", " inline; filename=\"my.pdf\"");
```

Note that not every version of every browser deals with this header correctly.

THE PDF IS CORRUPT FOR ONLY A COUPLE OF BROWSERS

When no content length is specified in the header of your dynamically generated file, the browser reads blocks of bytes sent by the web server. Most browsers detect when the stream is finished and use the correct size of the dynamically generated file. Some browsers are known to have problems truncating the stream to the right size—the real size of the PDF is smaller than the size assumed by the browser. The surplus of bytes can contain gibberish, and this can cause the viewer plug-in to show an error message saying the file is corrupt.

If you can't ask the end user to upgrade to a more recent browser and reader combination, there's only one solution. You have to specify the content length of the PDF file in the response header. Setting this header has to be done *before* any content is sent. Unfortunately, you only know the length of the file *after* you've created it. This means you can't send the PDF to the `ServletOutputStream` obtained with `response.getOutputStream()` right away. Instead, you must create the PDF on your filesystem or in memory first (the next listing), so you can retrieve the length, add it to the response header, and send the PDF. This is also true for some other binary file formats.

Listing 9.3 PdfServlet.java

```
protected void service(
  HttpServletRequest request, HttpServletResponse response)
  throws ServletException, IOException {
  try {
    String text = request.getParameter("text");
    if (text == null || text.trim().length() == 0) {
      text = "You didn't enter any text.";
    }
    Document document = new Document();
    ByteArrayOutputStream baos
      = new ByteArrayOutputStream();
    PdfWriter.getInstance(document, baos);
    document.open();
    document.add(new Paragraph(String.format(          Creates PDF
      "You have submitted the following text            in memory
          using the %s method:",
      request.getMethod())));
    document.add(new Paragraph(text));
    document.close();
    response.setHeader("Expires", "0");
    response.setHeader("Cache-Control",
      "must-revalidate, post-check=0, pre-check=0");    ❶ Adds extra
    response.setHeader("Pragma", "public");               response headers
    response.setContentType("application/pdf");        ◀── Sets content type
    response.setContentLength(baos.size());                           Sets
    OutputStream os = response.getOutputStream();                     content
    baos.writeTo(os);                                  Writes PDF to  length
    os.flush();                                        OutputStream ❷
    os.close();
  }
  catch(DocumentException e) {
    throw new IOException(e.getMessage());
  }
}
```

Mailing list subscribers have shared their experience with the community and told us that it's also safe to set extra response header values ❶. These headers make sure that the end user always gets the most recent version of the PDF, and not a PDF that is loaded from the cache on the client side. This is important if the content of the PDF changes frequently, which would happen if it reports about real-time data.

❷ solves the problem caused by old browser and PDF viewer configurations. Note that there are several serious downsides to this solution. When you need to generate large files, you risk an OutOfMemoryException on the server side, and a timeout on the client side. You can work around the server-side problem by writing the PDF to a temporary file on the server and asking the end user to fetch the file when it's finished. Don't forget to delete the file once it's served to the browser.

The second problem, avoiding a browser timeout, can be solved by moving the five steps of the PDF creation process to a separate thread. You can add your `Runnable` implementation as an attribute to the `HttpSession` object. As long as the PDF document isn't ready, send an HTML page to the browser that is refreshed on a regular basis, such as every three seconds. Check the thread with every hit; serve the PDF as soon as the document is closed. Not only does this solution solve the technical timeout problem, it also works on a psychological level. People tend to be impatient. They don't like to wait for that internet page to come, not knowing if the connection got lost, whether or not they should hit the reload button, or if the server went down... Give them feedback—if possible, a progress bar showing the percentage of data that has been processed—and time seems to go a lot faster!

Usually, I implement the `doPost()` method to accept parameters and to set up the thread; then I cause a redirect to trigger the `doGet()` method that serves the HTML and eventually the finished PDF.

GET VERSUS POST

A trivial problem, but one that is easily overlooked, is what happens when people bookmark pages that are the result of a `POST` action. When they want to return to that page using the bookmark, they initiate a `GET` request, getting a result that differs from what they expect. You can do the experiment with the example from listing 9.3.

Figure 9.2 shows the URL http://itextpdf.org:8180/book/ opened in a Firefox window. This page contains two simple forms: one that uses the `GET` method, the other

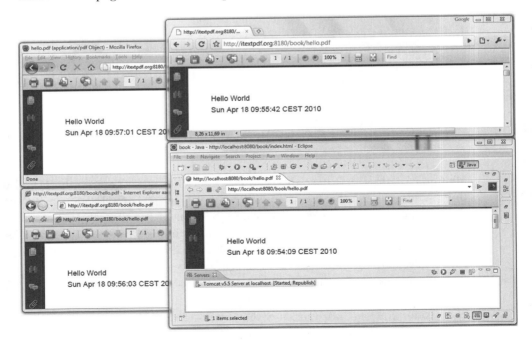

Figure 9.2 PDFs created with GET and POST actions

using the POST method. Recall that neither doGet() nor doPost() were implemented in listing 9.3. Instead you overrode the service() method that works in both cases.

We'll conclude the list of client-side issues with the "multiple-hit" problem.

PROBLEMS CAUSED BY MULTIPLE HITS

In web analytics, a hit is when an end user requests a page from your web server and this page is sent to the user's browser directly. For example, when you enter the URI http://itextpdf.org:8180/book/hello.pdf in the location bar, one PDF file opens in your browser window using a PDF viewer plug-in. If I look in my server logs, I should see one line corresponding with this hit. This is true for most browsers, but some browsers hit the server several times for every dynamically generated binary file. You can't predict how many hits a single request will generate; it could be two or three hits, or occasionally just one.

If you want to avoid this multiple-hit problem, you can try setting the cache parameters like this:

```
response.setHeader("Cache-control",
    "must-revalidate, post-check=0, pre-check=0");
```

Another way to solve the multiple-hit problem is to embed the PDF in an HTML page using the embed tag.

Listing 9.4   embedded.html

```
<html>
<body leftMargin="0" topMargin="0" scroll="No">
  <embed src="/book/hello.pdf" width="100%" height="100%"
    type="application/pdf" fullscreen="yes" />
</body>
</html>
```

If you skip to section 9.3, you'll also find an example of how to embed a PDF in an HTML page using the object tag.

Using the tips and tricks summed up in this section, you should be able to tackle all the problems that can occur when writing a servlet that produces a PDF document. Writing a JSP page generating a PDF is another story.

9.1.3   *Generating a PDF from a JSP page*

It's a bad idea to use JSP to generate binary content. That's considered improper use of the technology. JSP wasn't created to produce images, PDF files, or any other binary file type.

But that doesn't mean it's impossible. Go to http://itextpdf.org:8180/book/helloworld.jsp and you'll see a JSP page in action.

Listing 9.5   helloworld.jsp

```
<%@
page import="java.io.*, com.itextpdf.text.*, com.itextpdf.text.pdf.*"
%><%
```

```
response.setContentType( "application/pdf" );
Document document = new Document();
ByteArrayOutputStream buffer = new ByteArrayOutputStream();
PdfWriter.getInstance( document, buffer );
document.open();
document.add(new Paragraph("Hello World"));
document.close();
DataOutput output = new DataOutputStream( response.getOutputStream() );
byte[] bytes = buffer.toByteArray();
response.setContentLength(bytes.length);
for( int i = 0; i < bytes.length; i++ ) { output.writeByte( bytes[i] ); }
%>
```

Please take my advice and don't use this example. I'm only including it because the question, "How can I produce a PDF from a JSP page?" turns up on the mailing list on a regular basis. Let me explain why that is a bad idea, using this (working!) example.

Several things can go wrong if you ignore my advice and deploy the code from listing 9.5 on your server. If you write the bytes of the ByteArrayOutputStream to a file on the server, the PDF will be OK, but this doesn't mean that the PDF will be OK when you send the same bytes to the browser. These are some potential problems:

- *The blank page problem for JSP pages*   It's possible that the PDF opens when served on the client, showing nothing but blank pages. Some servers assume that JSP output isn't binary, and every byte higher than 127 will show up as a question mark.

- *Whitespace corrupting the binary data*   JSP pages are compiled to a servlet internally. If you think writing a PDF servlet is more difficult than writing a PDF JSP page, think again. If you copy listing 9.5 and start working from there, you'll probably add indentation, newlines, spaces, and carriage returns, inside as well as outside the <% and %> marks to make the JSP file more readable. Although this is good practice when you write JSP that produces HTML, it can be deadly if you want to generate binary content. If you look at the code of the servlet that is automatically generated based on the JSP file, you'll see that the whitespace characters outside these marks are written to the OutputStream. This has the same effect as when you would open a JPG in a text editor and insert whitespace characters in arbitrary places.

- *OutputStream opened twice*   Your JSP code may go wrong even before you get the chance to corrupt your PDF file. If you've added whitespace before invoking response.getOutputStream(), an exception will be thrown, saying "getOutputStream() has already been called for this response." Calling this method was done implicitly the moment the first unwanted whitespace characters appeared, and it's forbidden to call that method a second time.

If you take all these warnings into consideration, you might be able to write a PDF-producing JSP page, but sooner or later you'll run into troubles. Maybe a colleague will open that JSP in an IDE that automatically formats the code to make it more readable. While debugging problems like this, you'll probably end up inspecting the servlet that is generated, and eventually, you may want to replace the JSP page with a servlet. That's why it's better to stay away from JSP in the first place if you want to produce a PDF document. Write a servlet, and you'll save time not only for yourself, but also for your employer. Maybe you can use this argument if using JSP is a requirement in your project.

Enough about JSP already. Let's continue with servlets that involve PDF forms.

9.2   *Making a form "web ready"*

Now that you know how to integrate iText in a web application, you can combine this knowledge with what you learned about interactive PDF forms in the previous chapter. In this section, you'll add buttons to submit the data entered in a PDF form to the server; then you'll interpret this data and create a new PDF (pre)filled with the submitted data. Note that most of the functionality discussed in this section is AcroForm-specific; it won't work for XFA forms.

9.2.1   *Adding a submit button to an existing form*

Figure 9.3 shows a form you created in section 8.5 (see figure 8.6) opened with the Adobe Reader plug-in in Google Chrome. I've manually filled out the form with my name, login, and the most obvious reason why I want to visit the Foobar Film Festival. I've also added buttons to the form that will allow you to submit this data to a server.

There are four ways to submit this data:

- *As an HTML form*—The server will receive a query string
- *As FDF*—This is the Forms Data Format
- *As XFDF*—This is the XML version of the Forms Data Format
- *As PDF*—The full PDF, including the data that was entered, is sent to the server

Sending the form as a full PDF is only possible if the end user is filling out the form in the full Acrobat, so there's no button for that option in figure 9.3. In this example, we're only looking at the first three options. The fourth button in the form, Reset, can be used to reset the data that was entered manually.

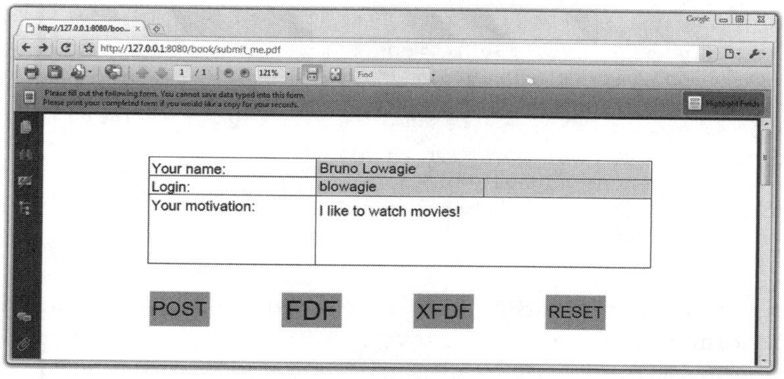

Figure 9.3 Adding submit buttons to an existing form

Listing 9.6   SubmitForm.java

```
PdfReader reader = new PdfReader(src);
PdfStamper stamper = new PdfStamper(reader,
  new FileOutputStream(dest));
PushbuttonField button1 = new PushbuttonField(
  stamper.getWriter(),
  new Rectangle(90, 660, 140, 690), "post");
button1.setText("POST");
button1.setBackgroundColor(new GrayColor(0.7f));
button1.setVisibility(
  PushbuttonField.VISIBLE_BUT_DOES_NOT_PRINT);
PdfFormField submit1 = button1.getField();
submit1.setAction(PdfAction.createSubmitForm(
  "/book/request", null, PdfAction.SUBMIT_HTML_FORMAT
  | PdfAction.SUBMIT_COORDINATES));
stamper.addAnnotation(submit1, 1);
PushbuttonField button2 = new PushbuttonField(
  stamper.getWriter(),
  new Rectangle(200, 660, 250, 690), "FDF");
button2.setBackgroundColor(new GrayColor(0.7f));
button2.setText("FDF");
button2.setVisibility(
  PushbuttonField.VISIBLE_BUT_DOES_NOT_PRINT);
PdfFormField submit2 = button2.getField();
submit2.setAction(PdfAction.createSubmitForm(
  "/book/request", null,
  PdfAction.SUBMIT_EXCL_F_KEY));
stamper.addAnnotation(submit2, 1);
PushbuttonField button3 = new PushbuttonField(
  stamper.getWriter(),
  new Rectangle(310, 660, 360, 690), "XFDF");
button3.setBackgroundColor(new GrayColor(0.7f));
button3.setText("XFDF");
button3.setVisibility(
  PushbuttonField.VISIBLE_BUT_DOES_NOT_PRINT);
PdfFormField submit3 = button3.getField();
submit3.setAction(PdfAction.createSubmitForm(
  "/book/request", null, PdfAction.SUBMIT_XFDF));
stamper.addAnnotation(submit3, 1);
PushbuttonField button4 = new PushbuttonField(
  stamper.getWriter(),
  new Rectangle(420, 660, 470, 690), "reset");
button4.setBackgroundColor(new GrayColor(0.7f));
button4.setText("RESET");
button4.setVisibility(
  PushbuttonField.VISIBLE_BUT_DOES_NOT_PRINT);
PdfFormField reset = button4.getField();
reset.setAction(PdfAction.createResetForm(null, 0));
stamper.addAnnotation(reset, 1);
stamper.close();
```

Button to
POST as HTML

Button to
POST as FDF

Button to
POST as XFDF

Button to reset
the form

NOTE   There's one button missing in figure 9.3 and listing 9.6: a button that submits the form using the option PdfAction.SUBMIT_PDF. This was a deliberate choice, because this button won't work if the end user only has Adobe Reader, not the full Acrobat.

You'll recognize the methods to create and shape the `PushbuttonField` and to obtain the corresponding `PdfFormField`. The key methods in this code snippet are two static methods from the `PdfAction` class we haven't discussed before.

- `createSubmitForm()`—Expects three parameters. The first parameter is a `String` representing a URL. In listing 9.6, you specify the path `/book/request`. This is a path to a servlet in the `book` application. We'll have a look at this servlet in listing 9.7. The second parameter is an array of `Object` values. You can pass an array of `String` values with field names, or an array of `PdfAnnotation` values representing fields. This can be used to limit the data that is sent to the server. The third parameter defines the submit method and extra options.

- `createResetForm()`—Expects two parameters. The first parameter has the same meaning as the second parameter of the `createSubmitForm()` method. The second parameter is a flag, specifying whether the fields in the array should be included (`0`) or excluded (`1`). The use of `null` and `0` in listing 9.6 will reset all the fields.

Before discussing the different submit methods and options, we'll take a look at what happens on the server side if you use the `/request` URL pattern. This pattern corresponds with this `ShowData` servlet.

Listing 9.7 ShowData.java

```java
public class ShowData extends HttpServlet {
  protected void doGet(
    HttpServletRequest request, HttpServletResponse response)
    throws ServletException, IOException {
    response.setContentType("text/plain");
    PrintWriter out = response.getWriter();
    Enumeration<String> parameters
      = request.getParameterNames();
    String parameter;
    while (parameters.hasMoreElements()) {          // Shows parameters/
      parameter = parameters.nextElement();         // values sent with GET
      out.println(String.format("%s: %s",
        parameter, request.getParameter(parameter)));
    }
  }
  protected void doPost(
    HttpServletRequest request, HttpServletResponse response)
    throws ServletException, IOException {
    response.setContentType("text/plain");
    OutputStream os = response.getOutputStream();
    InputStream is = request.getInputStream();
    byte[] b = new byte[256];
    int read;                                       // Shows request sent
    while ((read = is.read(b)) != -1) {             // to server with POST
      os.write(b, 0, read);
    }
  }
}
```

296 CHAPTER 9 *Integrating iText in your web applications*

This is an interesting servlet for debugging web applications. If you send a GET request to it, you'll get an overview of the query string parameters and values that are received on the server side. If you use the POST method, the servlet returns the byte stream that was received by the request. We can use this servlet to inspect the data that is sent to the server from the PDF form.

SUBMITTING A PDF FORM AS HTML POST

If you create a submit button with the flag PdfAction.SUBMIT_HTML_FORMAT, the form will be submitted as if the PDF document were an HTML form. It will use the POST method. Figure 9.4 shows what the ShowData servlet received.

You'll recognize the fields personal.loginname, personal.name, personal.password, and personal.reason, as well as two unexpected fields: post.x and post.y. You created a submit button with the name post, measuring 50 pt x 30 pt. You also added the PdfAction.SUBMIT_COORDINATES option. As a result, the server receives the X and Y coordinates of the position you've clicked inside the 50 pt x 30 pt rectangle. Using this option turns your button into a clickable map.

> **NOTE** The PDF specification also provides the option to submit the data using the GET method (adding the option PdfAction.SUBMIT_HTML_GET), but I don't advise you to do so (just like with using JSP, use this at your own risk).

The default submit option for AcroForms is *submit as FDF.*

SUBMITTING A PDF FORM AS FDF

When you click the second button shown in figure 9.3, the request servlet will return a file in the FDF. See figure 9.5.

FDF is based on PDF; it uses the same syntax and the same file structure. This format is used to export form data to standalone files that can be stored, transmitted electronically, and imported back into the corresponding PDF interactive form. In the next section, you'll take an FDF file similar to the one shown in figure 9.5 and you'll use iText to import the data embedded in the FDF file into a form. FDF is an interesting and compact format if you want to take the data that was posted by end users and save it on the filesystem on server side.

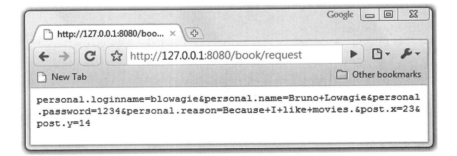

Figure 9.4 InputStream **of the** HttpServletRequest **(POST)**

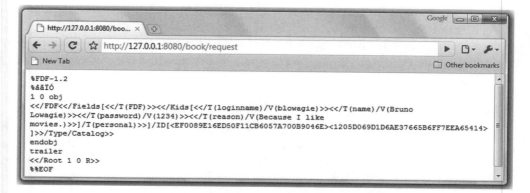

Figure 9.5 `InputStream` of the `HttpServletRequest` (FDF)

You don't need to set any flags to create a submit button that posts an FDF file; just use 0 if you don't need any options. In listing 9.6, you set the option `PdfAction.SUBMIT_EXCL_F_KEY`. If you omit this option, the URL of the original form (for instance, http://127.0.0.1:8080/book/submit_me.pdf) will be added to the FDF document. There are some other options, but most of them only work if the end user has the full Acrobat; they don't work with Adobe Reader.

There's also a limited XML implementation of the FDF: XFDF.

SUBMITTING A PDF FORM AS XFDF

If you look at figure 9.6, you'll see that the XFDF result is more human readable than what was returned in figure 9.5.

```
<?xml version="1.0" encoding="UTF-8"?>
<xfdf xmlns="http://ns.adobe.com/xfdf/" xml:space="preserve"
><f href="http://127.0.0.1:8080/book/submit_me.pdf"
/><fields
><field name="XFDF"
/><field name="personal"
/><field name="loginname"
><value
>blowagie</value
></field
><field name="name"
><value
>Bruno Lowagie</value
></field
><field name="password"
/><field name="reason"
><value
>I like to watch movies!</value
></field
></field
></fields
><ids original="EF0089E16ED50F11CB6057A700B9046E" modified="1205D069D1D6AE37665B6FF7EEA65414"
/></xfdf
>
```

Figure 9.6 `InputStream` of the `HttpServletRequest` (XFDF)

The value of the `personal.name` field can be found in the `value` tag that is nested inside the `field` tags with names `personal` and `name`.

This concludes the overview of the submit methods. In the upcoming examples, you'll use these methods to submit data to a servlet that fills out a form on the server side.

9.2.2   Filling out a form on the server side

Typically, you won't use iText to create interactive forms, but Acrobat, Open Office, or another authoring tool. You'll use iText to automatically fill out forms that were designed manually. In section 9.1.1, we've integrated the five steps of PDF creation in a servlet; now we'll do the same with a PDF manipulation example.

> **Listing 9.8   FormServlet.java**

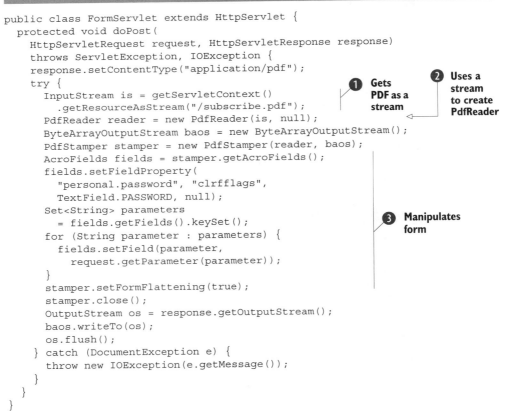

```
public class FormServlet extends HttpServlet {
  protected void doPost(
    HttpServletRequest request, HttpServletResponse response)
    throws ServletException, IOException {
    response.setContentType("application/pdf");
    try {
      InputStream is = getServletContext()
        .getResourceAsStream("/subscribe.pdf");
      PdfReader reader = new PdfReader(is, null);
      ByteArrayOutputStream baos = new ByteArrayOutputStream();
      PdfStamper stamper = new PdfStamper(reader, baos);
      AcroFields fields = stamper.getAcroFields();
      fields.setFieldProperty(
        "personal.password", "clrfflags",
        TextField.PASSWORD, null);
      Set<String> parameters
        = fields.getFields().keySet();
      for (String parameter : parameters) {
        fields.setField(parameter,
          request.getParameter(parameter));
      }
      stamper.setFormFlattening(true);
      stamper.close();
      OutputStream os = response.getOutputStream();
      baos.writeTo(os);
      os.flush();
    } catch (DocumentException e) {
      throw new IOException(e.getMessage());
    }
  }
}
```

Annotations in the figure: **1** Gets PDF as a stream   **2** Uses a stream to create PdfReader   **3** Manipulates form

This example accepts parameters that correspond with the fields in the subscribe.pdf form you created in section 8.5. This form is in the root of the book web application. **1** creates an `InputStream` to read the original form from the WAR file, or from the book subdirectory of the `webapps` folder of your Tomcat installation. You can use this `Input-Stream` to construct a `PdfReader` instance **2**. The second parameter in this constructor is reserved for the password of the PDF. Since you're not using a password-protected file, you can pass null. From here on, you can use all the functionality that was discussed in the previous chapter. In ❸, you use the input sent to the request to fill out the form. You also clear the password flag from the password field and flatten the form.

In your application, you could get info from the database, and use that data to prefill the form. That's just a matter of combining what you learned in chapter 8 with the tips and tricks from section 9.1.2. We'll continue with examples that use FDF and XFDF as formats to store and transmit data from the client to the server, and vice versa.

9.2.3 FDF and XFDF in web applications

Suppose you're working for the Foobar Film Festival, and you need to create a form that allows people to subscribe, but you also need to ask them to post a photograph of the applicant. Figure 9.7 shows the original subscribe.pdf form with an extra field that allows the end user to upload a file. In the example, I added a picture of myself from the c:\TEMP\pdf\ directory. You can see the uploaded picture in the resulting PDF at the bottom of figure 9.7.

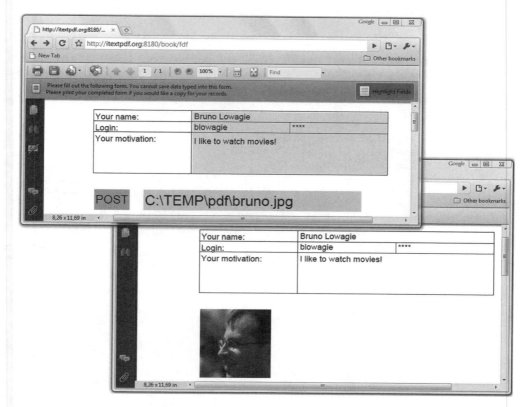

Figure 9.7 Uploading a file using FDF

If you submit this form as HTML, the server will receive a multipart/form-data request. Processing such a request increases the complexity of your servlet. It may be a better idea to post the data as FDF—the uploaded file will be embedded inside the FDF document as an attachment.

TRANSMITTING DATA AS FDF

There are benefits to this approach.

Listing 9.9   FDFServlet.java

```java
public class FDFServlet extends HttpServlet {
  protected void doGet(
    HttpServletRequest request, HttpServletResponse response)
    throws ServletException, IOException {
    response.setContentType("application/pdf");
    try {
      InputStream is
        = getServletContext().getResourceAsStream("/subscribe.pdf");
      PdfReader reader = new PdfReader(is, null);
      ByteArrayOutputStream baos = new ByteArrayOutputStream();
      PdfStamper stamper = new PdfStamper(reader, baos);
      PushbuttonField button = new PushbuttonField(
        stamper.getWriter(),
        new Rectangle(90, 660, 140, 690), "submit");
      button.setText("POST");
      button.setBackgroundColor(new GrayColor(0.7f));
      button.setVisibility(
        PushbuttonField.VISIBLE_BUT_DOES_NOT_PRINT);
      PdfFormField submit = button.getField();
      submit.setAction(PdfAction.createSubmitForm(
        "/book/fdf", null, 0));
      stamper.addAnnotation(submit, 1);
      TextField file = new TextField(
        stamper.getWriter(),
        new Rectangle(160, 660, 470, 690), "image");
      file.setOptions(TextField.FILE_SELECTION);
      file.setBackgroundColor(new GrayColor(0.9f));
      PdfFormField upload = file.getTextField();
      upload.setAdditionalActions(PdfName.U,
        PdfAction.javaScript(
          "this.getField('image').browseForFileToSubmit();"
          + "this.getField('submit').setFocus();",
          stamper.getWriter()));
      stamper.addAnnotation(upload, 1);
      stamper.close();
      OutputStream os = response.getOutputStream();
      baos.writeTo(os);
      os.flush();
    } catch (DocumentException e) {
      throw new IOException(e.getMessage());
    }
  }

  protected void doPost(
```

Annotations in right margin:
- **Defines FDF submit button** (next to the `PushbuttonField button` ... `stamper.addAnnotation(submit, 1);` block)
- **Defines file-selection text field** (next to the `TextField file` ... block)
- **Sets action to select file** (next to the `upload.setAdditionalActions` block)

```
HttpServletRequest request, HttpServletResponse response)
throws ServletException, IOException {
response.setContentType("application/pdf");
response.setHeader("Content-Disposition",
  "inline; filename=\"your.pdf\"");
try {
  FdfReader fdf
    = new FdfReader(request.getInputStream());
  InputStream is
    = getServletContext().getResourceAsStream("/subscribe.pdf");
  PdfReader reader = new PdfReader(is, null);
  ByteArrayOutputStream baos = new ByteArrayOutputStream();
  PdfStamper stamper = new PdfStamper(reader, baos);
  AcroFields fields = stamper.getAcroFields();
  fields.setFields(fdf);
  stamper.setFormFlattening(true);
  try {
    Image img = Image.getInstance(
      fdf.getAttachedFile("image"));
    img.scaleToFit(100, 100);
    img.setAbsolutePosition(90, 590);
    stamper.getOverContent(1).addImage(img);
  }
  catch(IOException ioe) {
    ColumnText.showTextAligned(stamper.getOverContent(1),
      Element.ALIGN_LEFT, new Phrase("No image posted!"), 90, 660, 0);
  }
  stamper.close();
  OutputStream os = response.getOutputStream();
  baos.writeTo(os);
  os.flush();
} catch (DocumentException e) {
  throw new IOException(e.getMessage());
}
}
}
}
```

- **Specifies filename of resulting PDF**
- **① Reads FDF from request**
- **② Uses shortcut to set fields**
- **③ Gets uploaded file from FDF**

In the doGet() part of listing 9.9, you add a submit button and a text field that will act as an <input type="File"> field in an HTML form. You also add an additional action that opens a "browse for file" dialog box. That way, the end user doesn't have to enter the file path manually.

The doPost() method is more interesting. In listing 9.7, you sent the FDF bytes back to the browser; now you use them to create an instance of FdfReader ①. You could use FdfReader to retrieve the data with the getFieldValue() method. For instance,

```
fields.setField("personal.name", fdf.getField("personal.name"));
```

But it's easier to set the fields all at once with the setFields() method ②. This method loops over all the fields in the FDF document and sets the value of the corresponding fields in the AcroForm. ③ demonstrates how easy it is to extract the uploaded file from the FDF stream. You use it to create an Image that will be added to the form.

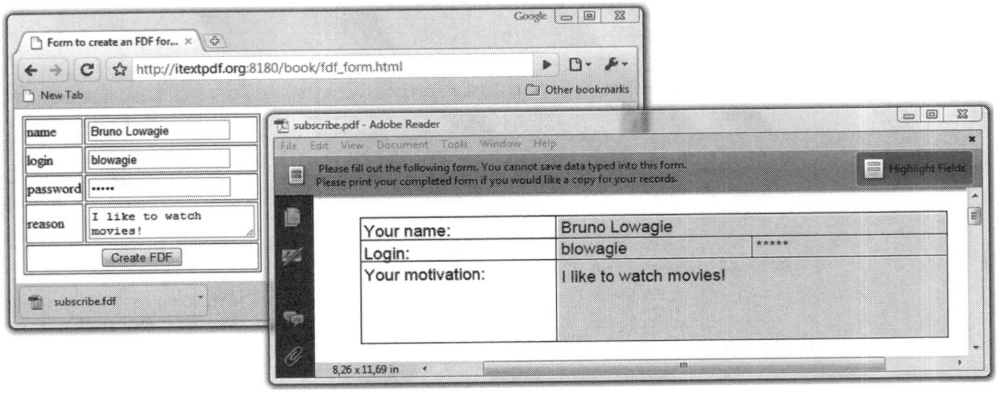

Figure 9.8   Creating FDF based on data sent from an HTML form

This is a useful FDF example if you want to transmit data from the browser to the server. You can also benefit from FDF if you want to store data on a filesystem.

STORING DATA AS FDF

Suppose you're organizing a conference. People who want to register need to enter data into an HTML form on your site. As soon as they've paid the conference fee, you have to print a configuration letter that will be sent by snail mail. You can put all the registrations in a database, but depending on your requirements, storing the data on the filesystem as a series of FDF documents (one per subscriber) may be a valid alternative. The window on the left in figure 9.8 shows a simple HTML form where I've added information about myself. Let's submit that form. Instead of storing the data on the server side, we'll use a servlet that sends the FDF back to the client. See the download bar on the bottom of the Google Chrome window with the button labeled "subscribe.fdf". If you open that file, it will try to find the form that corresponds with the data, open that form, and fill it out with the data from the FDF. This is shown in the left window of figure 9.8.

Listing 9.10   CreateFDF.java

```
public class CreateFDF extends HttpServlet {
  protected void service(
    HttpServletRequest request, HttpServletResponse response)
    throws ServletException, IOException {
    response.setContentType(                              ❶ Sets content
      "application/vnd.adobe.fdf");                           type
    response.setHeader("Content-Disposition",            ❷ Forces download
      "attachment; filename=\"subscribe.fdf\"");             dialog
    FdfWriter fdf = new FdfWriter();
    fdf.setFieldAsString(                                  Creates FDF
      "personal.name", request.getParameter("name"));      document
    fdf.setFieldAsString("personal.loginname",
      request.getParameter("loginname"));
```

```
      fdf.setFieldAsString("personal.password",
        request.getParameter("password"));
      fdf.setFieldAsString("personal.reason",
        request.getParameter("reason"));
      fdf.setFile("subscribe.pdf");
      fdf.writeTo(response.getOutputStream());
    }
  }
```

→ Creates FDF document

Up until now, you've used the application/pdf content type. For FDF files, you need to use application/vnd.adobe.fdf ❶. You want the end user to download the file, so you're also setting the Content-Disposition header. As opposed to the previous example, you use the word attachment (instead of inline) to force the browser to download the file locally (instead of showing it in the browser window) ❷. You create the FDF document with the FdfWriter class. The contents of the file will be kept in memory until you write the file to an OutputStream.

You can set fields in different ways. Listing 9.10 uses setFieldAsString(), but it's also possible to use setFieldAsName(). The former method stores the field value as a PdfString object; the latter stores it as a PdfName. There are also different set-Fields() methods to which you can pass an AcroFields object, a PdfReader, or an FdfReader instance.

An FDF file can contain a reference to a PDF document containing a form that accepts the FDF data. If you save the file subscribe.fdf in the same directory as sub-scribe.pdf, clicking the FDF file will open the PDF file as shown in the left window of figure 9.8. Note that you can also use a URL to open the form online, but this can cause security issues, depending on the version of the PDF viewer.

iText doesn't offer a class to create XFDF files, but it's easy to write your own server-side script to transform the key-value pairs from an HTML submit into an XFDF file.

TRANSMITTING DATA AS XFDF

If you create a button to submit data using the XFDF format, you can read the incoming stream with the XfdfReader class.

Listing 9.11   XFDFServlet.java

```
protected void doPost(
  HttpServletRequest request, HttpServletResponse response)
  throws ServletException, IOException {
  response.setContentType("application/pdf");
  try {
    XfdfReader xfdf = new XfdfReader(request.getInputStream());
    InputStream is
      = getServletContext().getResourceAsStream("/subscribe.pdf");
    PdfReader reader = new PdfReader(is, null);
    ByteArrayOutputStream baos = new ByteArrayOutputStream();
    PdfStamper stamper = new PdfStamper(reader, baos);
    AcroFields fields = stamper.getAcroFields();
    fields.setFields(xfdf);
    stamper.close();
```

```
        OutputStream os = response.getOutputStream();
        baos.writeTo(os);
        os.flush();
    } catch (DocumentException e) {
        throw new IOException(e.getMessage());
    }
}
```

Note that XFDF is more limited than FDF. For example, you can't upload files with XFDF. Another limitation of both FDF and XFDF is that they are based on AcroForm technology; these examples won't work for XFA forms.

We have one web example left involving forms.

9.3   *JavaScript communication between HTML and PDF*

In this section, we'll write an example that demonstrates how to establish communication between JavaScript in an HTML page and JavaScript inside a PDF document.

Imagine the following situation: you have a catalog with thousands of items stored in a database. People can purchase these items online using a PDF form. How will you create that form? Surely you don't want to embed your complete article database in a choice field inside your PDF. It would be much easier to provide browse or search functionality in an HTML page, then find a way to pass this data from the HTML pages to the PDF form.

Figure 9.9 shows an HTML page with a form and an embedded PDF document. The HTML form has two fields and a button. If you fill out a name and login and click the button, the values entered in the fields are passed as a message to the PDF document. The PDF document accepts these values and fills out the corresponding fields in the AcroForm.

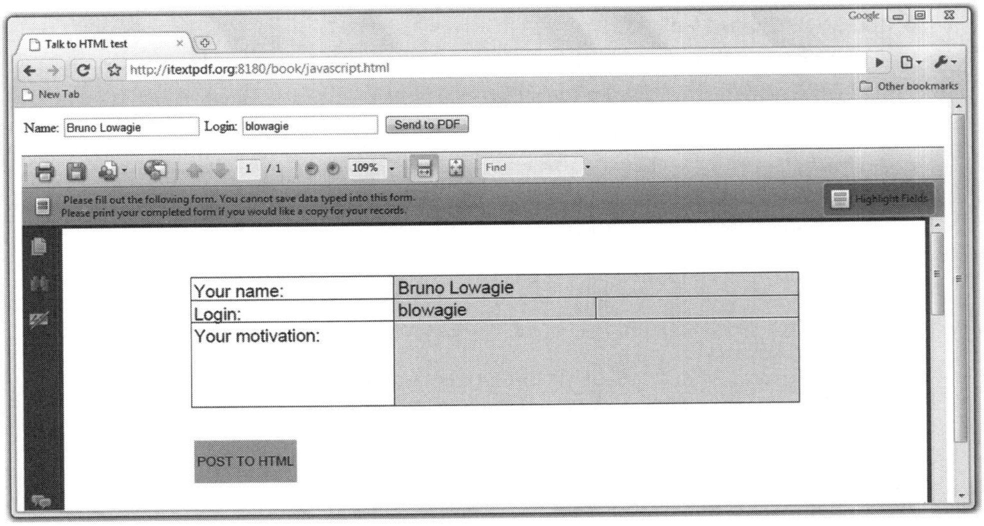

Figure 9.9   JavaScript communication between HTML and PDF

Passing the values in the opposite direction is also possible. If you change the name and login in the PDF form, and click the Post To HTML button, the entries are passed from the PDF form to the HTML form.

EMBEDDING A PDF DOCUMENT AS AN HTML OBJECT

Let's start by looking at the HTML side of this functionality. This example shows the JavaScript needed to accept the data from the PDF, and how to embed the PDF inside the HTML page.

Listing 9.12   javascript.html

```html
<html>
<head>
  <script language="javascript">
    function createMessageHandler() {
      var PDFObject = document.getElementById("myPdf");
      PDFObject.messageHandler = {
        onMessage: function(msg) {
          document.personal.name.value = msg[0];
          document.personal.loginname.value = msg[1];
        },
        onError: function(error, msg) {
          alert(error.message);
        }
      }
    }
    function sendToPdf() {
      var PDFObject = document.getElementById("myPdf");
      if(PDFObject!= null){
        PDFObject.postMessage(
          [document.personal.name.value,
           document.personal.loginname.value]);
      }
    }
  </script>
</head>
<body onLoad="createMessageHandler();">
  <form name="personal">
    <table>
      <tr>
        <td>Name:</td>
        <td><input type="Text" name="name"></td>
        <td>Login:</td>
        <td><input type="Text" name="loginname"></td>
        <td><input type="Button" value="Send to PDF"
          onClick="return sendToPdf();"></td>
      </tr>
    </table>
  </form>
  <object id="myPdf" type="application/pdf"
    data="javascript.pdf"
      height="100%" width="100%"></object>
</body>
</html>
```

1 JavaScript to get data from PDF

2 JavaScript to send data to PDF

HTML form

Embedding PDF as object

In listing 9.4, you used the embed tag to embed a PDF document inside an HTML file. In listing 9.12, the PDF is treated as an object. If you give it an id, such as myPdf, you can create a variable using document.getElementById("myPdf"). You use this variable in ❶ to accept data from the PDF, and in ❷ to send data to the PDF.

HTML TO PDF COMMUNICATION

The JavaScript sendToPdf() method is triggered when the end user clicks the button in the HTML form. It passes a message to the PDF object. This message is an array of String values. It will only be accepted if the PDF is *disclosed* and if there's a message handler in place. The JavaScript code shown next was added as an *Open action* to the javascript.pdf document.

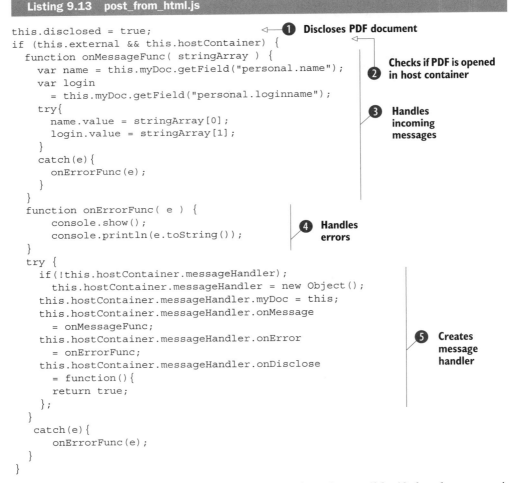

Listing 9.13   post_from_html.js

```
this.disclosed = true;                              ◁──❶ Discloses PDF document
if (this.external && this.hostContainer) {
  function onMessageFunc( stringArray ) {                  Checks if PDF is opened
    var name = this.myDoc.getField("personal.name");    ❷ in host container
    var login
      = this.myDoc.getField("personal.loginname");
    try{                                                  ❸ Handles
      name.value = stringArray[0];                           incoming
      login.value = stringArray[1];                          messages
    }
    catch(e){
      onErrorFunc(e);
    }
  }
  function onErrorFunc( e ) {
      console.show();                                   ❹ Handles
      console.println(e.toString());                       errors
  }
  try {
    if(!this.hostContainer.messageHandler)
      this.hostContainer.messageHandler = new Object();
    this.hostContainer.messageHandler.myDoc = this;
    this.hostContainer.messageHandler.onMessage
      = onMessageFunc;                                  ❺ Creates
    this.hostContainer.messageHandler.onError              message
      = onErrorFunc;                                       handler
    this.hostContainer.messageHandler.onDisclose
      = function(){
      return true;
    };
  }
   catch(e){
      onErrorFunc(e);
   }
}
```

JavaScript communication between documents is only possible if the document is disclosed ❶. You also need to check if the document is opened in an external window.

If so, you need access to the host container ②. In this case, the host container is the web browser.

> **NOTE** The hostContainer property doesn't work on Mac OS X. Because of that limitation, this example may not work for you or for a segment of your customers.

⑤ creates a message handler for the host container. It also defines a function to handle messages ③ and errors ④. The postMessage() method in the HTML passes a message to the onMessage method of the messageHandler. In this implementation, the first entry in the message array is used to fill in the personal.name field, the second entry to fill in the personal.loginname field.

Now let's take a look at the communication in the opposite direction.

PDF TO HTML COMMUNICATION

When an end user clicks the Post to HTML button in the PDF document, this JavaScript snippet is executed.

Listing 9.14   post_to_html.js

```
if(this.hostContainer) {
  var names = new Array();
  names[0] = this.getField("personal.name").value.toString();
  names[1] = this.getField("personal.loginname").value.toString();
  try{
    this.hostContainer.postMessage(names);
  }
  catch(e){
    app.alert(e.message);
  }
}
```

In the example, you check whether the PDF is opened in a host container. If it is, you put the values you want to transmit to the HTML JavaScript in an array and use the post-Message() method of the host container. This message will only be accepted if there's a message handler in place for the PDF object. This message handler is created in the createMessageHandler() (① in listing 9.12) that was triggered when the HTML page was loaded; see the onLoad attribute of the body tag. This method is similar to what you did in listing 9.13. The onMessage:function accepts an array of String values. In this implementation, these values are used to fill out fields in the HTML form.

This example was a little bit out of scope for a book about iText. You'll find more information about HTML to PDF communication (and vice versa) in the *JavaScript for Acrobat API Reference*. We'll continue looking at web-related functionality with examples that convert HTML snippets and XML files into a sequence of iText building blocks.

9.4   *Creating basic building blocks from HTML and XML*

You created many different basic building blocks through code in chapters 2 and 4. You've written createObject() methods and a PojoToElementFactory class for your convenience. In this section, you'll learn how to take a shortcut, and to let iText create these objects for you.

In section 9.4.1, we'll take HTML as the source to create objects, in section 9.4.2, we'll use XML.

9.4.1   *Parsing HTML*

One of the frequently asked questions on the iText mailing list is, "Does iText provide HTML2PDF functionality?" The official answer is *no*. Usually you'll get advice to use another product; for instance, xhtmlrenderer, aka Flying Saucer—a project that is built on top of iText. You can find the URL of that project in appendix B.

In some cases, you don't need a full-blown HTML renderer. Many web applications come with a small HTML editor that allows users to post messages with limited markup. For example, perhaps only <b> and <i> tags are allowed. Often these HTML snippets are stored in a database or somewhere on the filesystem. The initial question for HTML to PDF functionality could be rephrased as: "Can we insert those HTML snippets into a PDF file using iText?" The answer is *yes*; you can do this with iText if you use HTMLWorker.

HTML SNIPPETS

You can use the method parseToList() to parse a snippet of HTML into a List of iText Elements.

Listing 9.15   HtmlMovies1.java

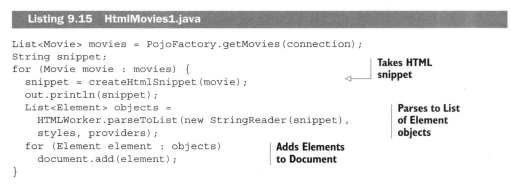

```
List<Movie> movies = PojoFactory.getMovies(connection);
String snippet;
for (Movie movie : movies) {                          Takes HTML
  snippet = createHtmlSnippet(movie);        ◁────┘   snippet
  out.println(snippet);
  List<Element> objects =                              Parses to List
    HTMLWorker.parseToList(new StringReader(snippet),  of Element
    styles, providers);                                objects
  for (Element element : objects)       Adds Elements
    document.add(element);              to Document
}
```

The method createHtmlSnippet() returns a very simple HTML snippet containing information about a movie. If you want to know what it looks like, you can open the file movies_1.html that is generated simultaneously with the PDF file (the out object is an instance of a PrintStream). It has entries like this:

```
<span class="title">Little Miss Sunshine</span><br />
<ul>
  <li class="country">United States</li>
</ul>
Year: <i>2006 minutes</i><br />
Duration: <i>101 minutes</i><br />
<ul>
  <li><span class="director">Dayton, Jonathan</span></li>
  <li><span class="director">Faris, Valerie</span></li>
</ul>
```

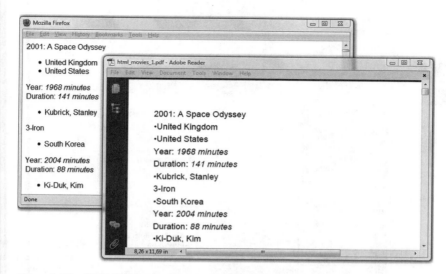

Figure 9.10   HTML snippets converted to PDF without using styles

`HTMLWorker` will parse this snippet to a `java.util.List` of `Paragraph` and `com.itext-pdf.text.List` objects. Figure 9.10 compares the HTML file opened in Firefox with the corresponding PDF opened in Adobe Reader.

Note that the content is rendered differently. That's to be expected: HTML wasn't designed to define the exact layout of a document. You can tune the way an object is created by using the `StyleSheet` object and by creating a `HashMap` with providers.

DEFINING STYLES

The `styles` and `providers` parameters were `null` in the previous example. You'll reuse listing 9.15 in the next example, but this time you'll create instances for these parameters.

Listing 9.16   HtmlMovies2.java

```
HtmlMovies2 movies = new HtmlMovies2();
StyleSheet styles = new StyleSheet();
styles.loadTagStyle("ul", "indent", "10");
styles.loadTagStyle("li", "leading", "14");
styles.loadStyle("country", "i", "");
styles.loadStyle("country", "color", "#008080");
styles.loadStyle("director", "b", "");
styles.loadStyle("director", "color", "midnightblue");
movies.setStyles(styles);
HashMap map = new HashMap();
map.put("font_factory", new MyFontFactory());
map.put("img_provider", new MyImageFactory());
movies.setProviders(map);
```

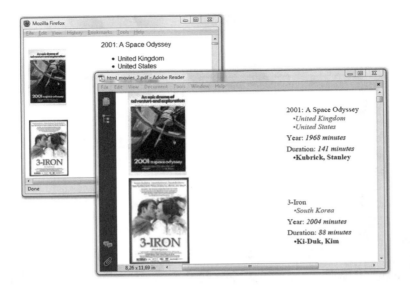

Figure 9.11 HTML snippets converted to PDF using styles

With the `loadTagStyle()` method, you can adapt the style of specific tags. In listing 9.16, you change the indentation of unordered lists and reduce the leading of the list items. The method `loadStyle()` is used to change the style of the tags with a class attribute. The style for `country` elements is changed to italic; the style is changed to bold for the `director` class. The color is changed too. The result is shown in figure 9.11.

Observe that, although you didn't specify a font face or size in the `StyleSheet`, another font was used. You could change the font using `loadTagStyle()` or `loadStyle()`. For instance,

```
styles.loadTagStyle("li", "face", "courier");
styles.loadStyle("country", "size", "10pt");
```

For this example, you can use a custom `FontProvider` instead.

IMPLEMENTING THE FONTPROVIDER INTERFACE

The next listing is a simple example of how you can implement the two methods of the `FontProvider` interface. The `getFont()` method returns a Times-Roman font, no matter what font is defined in the HTML snippet or the `StyleSheet`.

Listing 9.17 HtmlMovies2.java

```java
public static class MyFontFactory implements FontProvider {
  public Font getFont(String fontname,
    String encoding, boolean embedded, float size,
    int style, BaseColor color) {
    return new Font(FontFamily.TIMES_ROMAN, size, style, color);
  }
  public boolean isRegistered(String fontname) {
    return false;
  }
}
```

Another implementation of the `FontProvider` interface can be found in iText's source code. If you don't define a `font_factory`, `HTMLWorker` will use the class `Font-FactoryImp`, which is much more elaborate than this simple `MyFontFactory` example. This class will be discussed in more detail in chapter 11.

Figure 9.11 also shows that the HTML snippet used in this second HTML example is a tad more complex than the snippet used in the first one. It now involves a `<table>` tag that will result in a `PdfPTable` object and an `<img>` tag that should result in an `Image` object.

IMPLEMENTING THE IMAGEPROVIDER INTERFACE

The `<img>` tag, more specifically its `src` attribute, can cause a problem when you're using relative paths for the images. You're creating an HTML file with the HTML snippets in the ./results/part3/chapter09/ directory, but you're referring to images that are in the ./resources/posters/ folder. This is an example of such an `<img>` tag:

```
<img src="../../../resources/posters/0062622.jpg" />
```

If you use `HTMLWorker` without an `ImageProvider`, iText won't be able to find this image because it will be looking for it in the directory ../../../resources/posters/ instead of in the ./resources/posters/ folder. You can resolve this by defining an img_provider in listing 9.16. Here is the implementation.

Listing 9.18   HtmlMovies2.java

```java
public static class MyImageFactory implements ImageProvider {
  public Image getImage(String src, HashMap h,
    ChainedProperties cprops, DocListener doc) {
    try {
      return Image.getInstance(String.format("resources/posters/%s",
        src.substring(src.lastIndexOf("/") + 1)));
    } catch (DocumentException e) {
      e.printStackTrace();
    } catch (IOException e) {
      e.printStackTrace();
    }
    return null;
  }
}
```

We're working with HTML snippets in these examples. We haven't defined at which point a snippet becomes a complete HTML page. If you inspect the source code of the `HtmlMovies2` example, you'll see that there's also a `createPdf()` method that parses the complete HTML file. It's certainly possible to use iText to parse larger HTML files, but remember that iText wasn't designed for this kind of work. It's not a full-blown HTML parser; there are better tools available if converting HTML to PDF is your main purpose.

The same goes for parsing XML. When talking about XML and PDF, people often refer to Formatting Objects (FO), and Formatting Objects Parsers (FOP), such as Apache FOP. But that doesn't mean you can't use iText to convert XML to PDF, as you'll see in the next section.

9.4.2 *Parsing XML*

In chapter 8, you injected an XML file containing information about movies into an XFA form. Here you're going to use the same XML file to create a PDF document from scratch. The XML file is shown on the right in figure 9.12. The result is shown in the Adobe Reader window to the left.

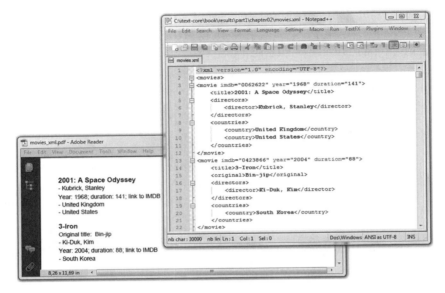

Figure 9.12   An XML file converted to PDF

The schema used for the movie information is custom made; iText doesn't know what the tags `movie`, `title`, `directors`, and so on, mean. You'll have to tell iText how to interpret these tags by writing your own XML handler.

WRITING AN XML HANDLER

You need to extend `org.xml.sax.helpers.DefaultHandler` and implement at least three methods:

- *The* `characters()` *method*—To put all the characters that are encountered between the tags of the XML file into a `Chunk` object.
- *The* `startElement()` *method*—To create specific `TextElementArray` objects that correspond with each tag that is encountered. You can also inspect the attributes to define the properties of the basic building blocks. Once a `Text-ElementArray` is created, you can push it to a `Stack`, where it will wait for further processing.
- *The* `endElement()` *method*—To update or flush the `Stack`.

A possible implementation for the XML file shown in figure 9.12 can be found in the next example.

Listing 9.19 XmlHandler.java

```java
protected Document document;
protected Stack<TextElementArray> stack =
  new Stack<TextElementArray>();
protected Chunk currentChunk = null;

protected String year = null;
protected String duration = null;
protected String imdb = null;

public XmlHandler(Document document) {
  this.document = document;
}

public void characters(char[] ch, int start, int length)
  throws SAXException {
  String content = new String(ch, start, length);
  if (content.trim().length() == 0)
    return;
  if (currentChunk == null) {
    currentChunk = new Chunk(content.trim());
  }
  else {
    currentChunk.append(" ");
    currentChunk.append(content.trim());
  }
}

public void startElement(String uri, String localName,
  String qName, Attributes attributes) throws SAXException {
  try {
    if ("directors".equals(qName)
      || "countries".equals(qName)) {
      stack.push(new List(List.UNORDERED));
    }
    else if ("director".equals(qName)
      || "country".equals(qName)) {
      stack.push(new ListItem());
    }
    else if ("movie".equals(qName)) {
      flushStack();
      Paragraph p = new Paragraph();
      p.setFont(new Font(
        FontFamily.HELVETICA, 14, Font.BOLD));
      stack.push(p);
      year = attributes.getValue("year");
      duration = attributes.getValue("duration");
      imdb = attributes.getValue("imdb");
    }
    else if ("original".equals(qName)) {
      stack.push(new Paragraph("Original title: "));
    }
  } catch (Exception e) {
    e.printStackTrace();
  }
}
```

Adds characters to current Chunk

Adds List to Stack for directors and countries

Adds ListItems for director or country

Adds Paragraph to Stack for movie title

Keeps track of attributes

Pushes Paragraph with some text to Stack

```
public void endElement(String uri, String localName,
  String qName) throws SAXException {
  try {
    updateStack();
    if ("directors".equals(qName)) {
      flushStack();
      Paragraph p = new Paragraph(String.format(
        "Year: %s; duration: %s; ", year, duration));
      Anchor link = new Anchor("link to IMDB");
      link.setReference(String.format(
        "http://www.imdb.com/title/tt%s/", imdb));
      p.add(link);
      stack.push(p);
    }
    else if ("countries".equals(qName)
      || "title".equals(qName)) {
      flushStack();
    }
    else if ("original".equals(qName)
      || "movie".equals(qName)) {
      currentChunk = Chunk.NEWLINE;
      updateStack();
    }
    else if ("director".equals(qName)
      || "country".equals(qName)) {
      ListItem listItem = (ListItem) stack.pop();
      List list = (List) stack.pop();
      list.add(listItem);
      stack.push(list);
    }
  } catch (Exception e) {
    e.printStackTrace();
  }
}
```

Adds extra info after directors List

Flushes Stack after countries and title

Adds Chunk.NEWLINE after original and movie

Adds ListItems to List

The helper method updateStack() adds the current Chunk to the top TextElementArray on the Stack. If the Stack is empty, a Paragraph is created and added to the Stack. The helper method flushStack() will try to compose elements on the Stack; for instance, adding Phrase objects to a Paragraph. It will try to add TextElementArrays to the Document as soon as possible.

PARSING THE XML FILE USING THE HANDLER

Once you've written your XmlHandler implementation, creating the PDF is a matter of a handful of lines. All it takes is a servlet that reads the XML from the server and serves a PDF to the browser.

Listing 9.20   MovieServlet.java

```
public class MovieServlet extends HttpServlet {
  protected void doGet(
    HttpServletRequest request, HttpServletResponse response)
    throws ServletException, IOException {
    try {
```

```
            Document document = new Document();
            PdfWriter.getInstance(document, response.getOutputStream());
            document.open();
            InputStream is
              = getServletContext().getResourceAsStream("/movies.xml");
            SAXParser parser = SAXParserFactory.newInstance().newSAXParser();
            parser.parse(new InputSource(is), new XmlHandler(document));
            document.close();
        } catch (DocumentException e) {
          throw new IOException(e.getMessage());
        } catch (ParserConfigurationException e) {
          throw new IOException(e.getMessage());
        } catch (SAXException e) {
          throw new IOException(e.getMessage());
        }
    }
}
```

This may not be the easiest way to create a PDF document, but as soon as you've gained experience implementing the different DefaultHandler methods, you can create very powerful XML converters. I've frequently used this functionality in projects where the XML schema is unlikely to change, but the XML content changes frequently; for instance, in projects where the content of a letter is described in XML. The structure of the letter—defined in the XML schema—is always the same, but because of changing rules and laws, some of the clauses have to be adapted on a regular basis. For this situation, I wrote the XmlHandler once upon a time, very long ago, but I'm asked to change the content of the XML file on a regular basis.

Up until now, HTML and XML to PDF conversion hasn't been part of the core business of iText because there are plenty of other tools that have made it their specialty. But as we're moving more and more toward XFA, you'll probably see more activity on the iText XML front in the years to come. For now, let's summarize what we've done in this chapter.

9.5   *Summary*

Generating PDFs for the web isn't all that different from generating PDFs in a standalone application. That's what could be concluded after the first example in this chapter, where you integrated the five steps of the PDF creation process in a servlet. Nevertheless, there are different pitfalls that have been reported on the mailing list over the years. You can benefit from the experience of other developers by following some simple rules of thumb. When in need, you'll be able to fall back on the section about troubleshooting web applications. Generating PDFs using JSP isn't impossible, but it's not done.

In the previous chapter, you created interactive PDF forms. In this chapter, you learned how to make these forms "web ready" by adding buttons that allow end users to submit data to a server in different formats. You filled a form on the server-side using data that was submitted as an HTML POST, but you also explored the possibilities of the FDF. You used FDF as a means to transmit data, including file uploads. You also found out that you can use FDF and XFDF to store data on the filesystem. You used a PDF form to demonstrate how to establish the communication between a PDF document and its host container, the web browser, and you sent messages back and forth between an HTML page and a PDF document.

Finally, you learned how to use HTMLWorker to convert HTML snippets to basic building blocks, and eventually to PDF. You also converted XML to PDF using a custom-made XmlHandler.

In the next chapter, we'll look at another aspect that we discussed in previous parts but that needs to be discussed in more detail: images and colors.

Brightening your document with color and images

This chapter covers

- Using color in PDF documents
- Introducing transparency
- Using images in PDF documents

You've already used color and images in previous chapters. You set the background and changed the font color of a Chunk using the BaseColor class in chapter 2. You used setColorFill() and setColorStroke() methods when you painted movie blocks on a calendar sheet in chapter 3. But that doesn't mean we've talked about everything. One could write an entire book about color.

The same goes for images. We looked at the Image class in chapter 2, but there are many other classes involved when creating an Image object: Jpeg, GifImage, TiffImage, and so on. It would lead us too far astray to go into too much detail about color and images, but this chapter will help you if you need more color or image functionality than we covered in part 1.

10.1   *Working with the iText color classes*

Colors are defined using values, and these values are interpreted according to a color space. Color spaces are expressed as PDF dictionaries, and there are eleven different color spaces available in PDF. You can find a reference to these dictionaries in the resources entry of a PDF stream. This is explained in great detail in the PDF reference; but don't worry, iText provides color classes that hide the complex theory.

The most common group of color spaces is the device color space family.

10.1.1   *Device colors*

Device colors enable a conforming writer to control color precisely for a particular device. The family consists of three color spaces:

- *DeviceRGB*—The iText BaseColor class defines an RGB color. This is an additive color: red, green, and blue light is used to produce the other colors. If you add red light (#FF00000) to green light (#00FF000), for example, you get yellow light (#FFFF00). This is how a TV screen works: the colors are composed of red, green, and blue dots. RGB is typically used for graphics that need to be rendered on a screen.
- *DeviceCMYK*—The opposite of RGB is a subtractive color model. If you look at an object using white light, you see a color because the object reflects and absorbs some of the wavelengths that make up the white light. A yellow object absorbs blue and reflects red and green. White (#FFFFFF) minus blue (#0000FF) equals yellow (#FFFF00). The subtractive color model is used when printing a document. You don't use red, green, and blue, but cyan, magenta, yellow, and black. The CMY in CMYK correspond with the colors in the cartridge of an ink-jet printer. The K (key) stands for black. Such a color can be created using one of BaseColor's subclasses: CMYKColor.
- *DeviceGray*—The default color space when drawing lines or shapes in PDF is gray. It is expressed as the intensity of achromatic light, represented by a single number in the range 0 to 1, where 0 corresponds to black, 1 to white, and intermediate values to different gray levels. The corresponding class in iText is GrayColor, another subclass of BaseColor.

The BaseColor, CMYKColor, and GrayColor classes have different constructors. The color values can be expressed as int values from 0 to 255, or as float values from 0.0 to 1.0. The BaseColor and GrayColor classes also have a series of predefined colors.

Listing 10.1   DeviceColor.java

```
public void colorRectangle(PdfContentByte canvas,
  BaseColor color, float x, float y,
  float width, float height) {
  canvas.saveState();
  canvas.setColorFill(color);
  canvas.rectangle(x, y, width, height);
  canvas.fillStroke();
```

Method that draws colored rectangle

```
    canvas.restoreState();                          Method that draws
  }                                                 colored rectangle
  public void createPdf(String filename)
    throws IOException, DocumentException {
    Document document = new Document();
    PdfWriter writer = PdfWriter.getInstance(
      document, new FileOutputStream(filename));
    document.open();
    PdfContentByte canvas = writer.getDirectContent();
    colorRectangle(canvas,
      new BaseColor(0x00, 0x00, 0xFF), 90, 770, 36, 36);     RGB colors
    colorRectangle(canvas,
      new BaseColor(1f, 1f, 0f), 360, 770, 36, 36);
    colorRectangle(canvas,
      BaseColor.LIGHT_GRAY, 470, 770, 36, 36);
    colorRectangle(canvas,
      new CMYKColor(0x00, 0x00, 0xFF, 0x00),                 CMYK colors
      90, 716, 36, 36);
    colorRectangle(canvas,
      new CMYKColor(0f, 1f, 0f, 0.5f), 252, 716, 36, 36);
    colorRectangle(canvas,
      new GrayColor(0x20), 36, 662, 36, 36);
    colorRectangle(canvas,
      new GrayColor(0x40), 90, 662, 36, 36);                 Gray colors
    colorRectangle(canvas,
      new GrayColor(0.75f), 306, 662, 36, 36);
    colorRectangle(canvas,
      GrayColor.GRAYBLACK, 416, 662, 36, 36);
    canvas.setRGBColorFill(0x00, 0x80, 0x80);
    canvas.rectangle(36, 608, 36, 36);
    canvas.fillStroke();
    canvas.setRGBColorFillF(0.5f, 0.25f, 0.60f);
    canvas.rectangle(90, 608, 36, 36);
    canvas.fillStroke();
    canvas.setGrayFill(0.5f);                                Alternative
    canvas.rectangle(144, 608, 36, 36);                      methods that
    canvas.fillStroke();                                     define colors
    canvas.setCMYKColorFill(0xFF, 0xFF, 0x00, 0x80);
    canvas.rectangle(198, 608, 36, 36);
    canvas.fillStroke();
    canvas.setCMYKColorFillF(0f, 1f, 1f, 0.5f);
    canvas.rectangle(252, 608, 36, 36);
    canvas.fillStroke();
    document.close();
  }
```

Observe that you don't need a BaseColor class when writing to the direct content. You can instead use a number of variations on the setColorFill() method.

NOTE By convention, integers for colors are written in their hexadecimal form in iText. This isn't an obligation, but it improves the readability of the code if you're familiar with the way colors are expressed in HTML. The expression new BaseColor(0, 128, 128) is the equivalent of new BaseColor(0x00, 0x80, 0x80), but in the latter, you'll recognize the HTML notation #008080, aka teal.

In part 4, we'll talk about different flavors of PDF. One of the first ISO specifications for PDF was PDF/X. The X stands for *exchange*. It was proposed by the prepress sector to make PDF documents more predictable when printing. Among other restrictions, it's forbidden to use RGB in a PDF/X document, because the results of the transformation of the red, green, and blue values to cyan, magenta, yellow, and black ink might not be consistent for all printers.

There are also printing devices that work with special colors that can't be achieved with CMYK. For instance, metallic colors, fluorescent colors, and special textures. If that's the case, you probably need spot colors.

10.1.2   Spot colors

A spot color is any color generated by an ink (pure or mixed) that is printed in a single run. Section 8.6.6.4 of ISO-32000-1, titled "Separation Color Spaces," contains the following note:

> *When printing a page, most devices produce a single composite page on which all process colorants (and spot colorants, if any) are combined. However, some devices, such as image setters, produce a separate, monochromatic rendition of the page, called a separation, for each colorant. When the separations are later combined—on a printing press, for example—and the proper inks or other colorants are applied to them, the result is a full-color page.*
>
> *The term separation is often misused as a synonym for an individual device colorant. In the context of this discussion, a printing system that produces separations generates a separate piece of physical medium (generally film) for each colorant. It is these pieces of physical medium that are correctly referred to as separations. A particular colorant properly constitutes a separation only if the device is generating physical separations, one of which corresponds to the given colorant. The Separation color space is so named for historical reasons, but it has evolved to the broader purpose of controlling the application of individual colorants in general, regardless of whether they are actually realized as physical separations.*
>
> —ISO-32000-1, section 8.6.6.4

Every colorant in the Separation color space has a name. Every color value consists of a single tint component in the range 0.0 to 1.0. A tint value of 0.0 denotes the lightest color that can be achieved with the given colorant, and 1.0 is the darkest. Listing 10.2 shows how the PdfSpotColor class is used to define the colorant; the actual color is created with the SpotColor class.

Listing 10.2   SeparationColor.java

```
PdfSpotColor psc_g = new PdfSpotColor(
    "iTextSpotColorGray", new GrayColor(0.9f));
PdfSpotColor psc_rgb = new PdfSpotColor(
    "iTextSpotColorRGB",
    new BaseColor(0x64, 0x95, 0xed));
PdfSpotColor psc_cmyk = new PdfSpotColor(
```

Defines
colorants

```
      "iTextSpotColorCMYK",
      new CMYKColor(0.3f, .9f, .3f, .1f));       Defines colorants
colorRectangle(canvas,
      new SpotColor(psc_g, 0.5f), 36, 770, 36, 36);
colorRectangle(canvas,
      new SpotColor(psc_rgb, 0.1f), 90, 770, 36, 36);
colorRectangle(canvas,
      new SpotColor(psc_rgb, 0.2f), 144, 770, 36, 36);      Defines spot
colorRectangle(canvas,                                      colors
      new SpotColor(psc_rgb, 0.3f), 198, 770, 36, 36);
...
colorRectangle(canvas,
      new SpotColor(psc_cmyk, 0.25f), 470, 770, 36, 36);
canvas.setColorFill(psc_g, 0.5f);
canvas.rectangle(36, 716, 36, 36);
canvas.fillStroke();
canvas.setColorFill(psc_rgb, 0.5f);          Defines spot colors
canvas.rectangle(144, 716, 36, 36);          with alternative
canvas.fillStroke();                         methods
canvas.setColorFill(psc_cmyk, 0.5f);
canvas.rectangle(252, 716, 36, 36);
canvas.fillStroke();
```

Observe that I've used dummy names—iTextSpotColorRGB and iTextSpotColor-CMYK—referring to the way the spot color was created.

> **NOTE** The dominant spot-color printing system in the United States is Pantone. Pantone Inc. is a New Jersey company, and the company's list of color names and values is its intellectual property. Free use of the list isn't allowed, but if you buy a house style, and the colors include Pantones, you can replace the dummy names with the names of your Pantone colors as well as the corresponding color values.

The next type of color isn't really a color in the strict sense of the word. It's listed with the special color spaces in ISO-32000-1.

10.1.3 Painting patterns

When stroking or filling a path, you've always used a single color in this book, but it's also possible to apply paint that consists of repeating graphical figures or a smoothly varying color gradient. In this case, we're talking about pattern colors that use either a *tiled pattern* (a repeating figure) or a *shading pattern* (a smooth gradient).

TILING PATTERNS

To create a tiled pattern color, you must construct a *pattern cell.* This cell is a subclass of PdfTemplate named PdfPatternPainter. You can obtain such a cell from the PdfContentByte object with the method createPattern(). This cell will be repeated at fixed horizontal and vertical intervals when you fill a path. See figure 10.1.

There are two kinds of tiling patterns: *colored tiling patterns* and *uncolored tiling patterns.* A colored tiling pattern is self-contained. In the course of painting the pattern cell, the pattern's content stream explicitly sets the color of each graphical element it

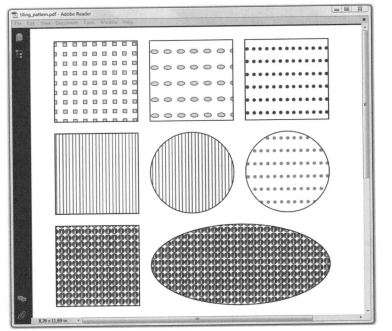

**Figure 10.1
Tiling patterns**

paints. An uncolored tiling pattern has no inherent color. You can define a default color, but normally you specify the actual color whenever the pattern is used. The content stream defines a stencil through which the color is poured.

Listing 10.3   TilingPatternColor.java

```
PdfContentByte canvas = writer.getDirectContent();
PdfPatternPainter square = canvas.createPattern(15, 15);
square.setColorFill(new BaseColor(0xFF, 0xFF, 0x00));
square.setColorStroke(new BaseColor(0xFF, 0x00, 0x00));
square.rectangle(5, 5, 5, 5);
square.fillStroke();
PdfPatternPainter ellipse
  = canvas.createPattern(15, 10, 20, 25);
ellipse.setColorFill(new BaseColor(0xFF, 0xFF, 0x00));
ellipse.setColorStroke(new BaseColor(0xFF, 0x00, 0x00));
ellipse.ellipse(2f, 2f, 13f, 8f);
ellipse.fillStroke();
PdfPatternPainter circle = canvas.createPattern(
  15, 15, 10, 20, BaseColor.BLUE);
circle.circle(7.5f, 7.5f, 2.5f);
circle.fill();
PdfPatternPainter line
  = canvas.createPattern(5, 10, null);
line.setLineWidth(1);
line.moveTo(3, -1);
line.lineTo(3, 11);
line.stroke();
```

Creates colored
pattern cell
with squares

Creates colored
pattern cell
with ellipses

Creates uncolored
pattern cell with
circles

Creates uncolored
pattern cell with
lines

```
Image img = Image.getInstance(RESOURCE);
img.scaleAbsolute(20, 20);
img.setAbsolutePosition(0, 0);
PdfPatternPainter img_pattern
  = canvas.createPattern(20, 20, 20, 20);
img_pattern.addImage(img);
img_pattern.setPatternMatrix(
  -0.5f, 0f, 0f, 0.5f, 0f, 0f);
colorRectangle(canvas,
  new PatternColor(square), 36, 696, 126, 126);
colorRectangle(canvas,
  new PatternColor(ellipse), 180, 696, 126, 126);
colorRectangle(canvas,
  new PatternColor(circle), 324, 696, 126, 126);
colorRectangle(canvas,
  new PatternColor(line), 36, 552, 126, 126);
colorRectangle(canvas,
  new PatternColor(img_pattern), 36, 408, 126, 126);
canvas.setPatternFill(line, BaseColor.RED);
canvas.ellipse(180, 552, 306, 678);
canvas.fillStroke();
canvas.setPatternFill(circle, BaseColor.GREEN);
canvas.ellipse(324, 552, 450, 678);
canvas.fillStroke();
canvas.setPatternFill(img_pattern);
canvas.ellipse(180, 408, 450, 534);
canvas.fillStroke();
```

Creates pattern cell with image

Creates and uses color with pattern cell

Uses pattern colors with alternative methods

Observe that there are different versions of the createPattern() method. The simplest version accepts two float values: one for the width and one for the height of the pattern cell. Additionally, you can also specify an X and Y step. This is the desired horizontal and vertical spacing between pattern cells. These are the methods used to create a colored pattern.

When you add a default color (or null), you create an uncolored pattern. This default color is used when you create a PatternColor object, but typically you'll want to use an uncolored pattern with the setPatternFill() method, passing the PdfPatternPainter object and a different color. Uncolored patterns are monochrome, whereas a colored pattern can consist of different colors. It can even contain images, as demonstrated with img_pattern. In listing 10.3, you use the method setPatternMatrix() to scale and mirror the cell; this method corresponds to the setMatrix() method in PdfTemplate and PdfContentByte.

The other pattern type is more complex. Let's look at simple examples to get an idea.

SHADING PATTERNS

Shading patterns provide a smooth transition between colors across an area to be painted. ISO-32000-1 lists seven types of shading; iText provides convenience methods for two: *axial shading* and *radial shading*. These two shadings are demonstrated in figure 10.2.

The background color of the first page of figure 10.2 (the left half) changes from orange in the lower-left corner to blue in the upper-right corner. This is an axial

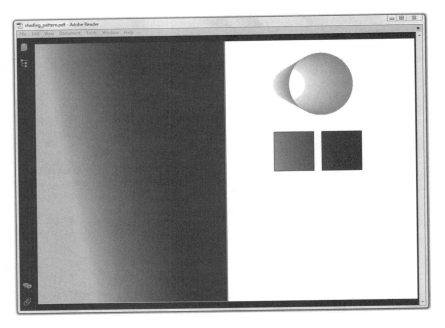

Figure 10.2   Shading patterns

shading. The circular shape on the second page (the right half) is the result of a radial shading:

- *Axial shadings (Type 2 in ISO-32000-1)*—These define a color blend that varies along a linear axis between two endpoints and extends indefinitely perpendicular to that axis. In the iText object PdfShading, a static simpleAxial() method allows you to pass the start and end coordinates of the axis, as well as a start and end color.
- *Radial shadings (type 3 in ISO 32000-1)*—These define a color blend that varies between two circles; see the shape in the right side of figure 10.2. This shape was created with the static simpleRadial() method. With this method, you define two circles, using the coordinates of the center point and a radius. You also pass a start and end color.

The methods simpleAxial() and simpleRadial() also accept two boolean values that indicate whether or not you want the shading to be extended at the start and end. These values were true for the axial shading on the left side of figure 10.2 and false for the radial shading on the right side.

Listing 10.4   ShadingPatternColor.java

```
PdfContentByte canvas = writer.getDirectContent();
PdfShading axial = PdfShading.simpleAxial(writer,
  36, 716, 396, 788, BaseColor.ORANGE, BaseColor.BLUE);
canvas.paintShading(axial);
```

```
document.newPage();
PdfShading radial = PdfShading.simpleRadial(writer,
  200, 700, 50, 300, 700, 100,
  new BaseColor(0xFF, 0xF7, 0x94),
  new BaseColor(0xF7, 0x8A, 0x6B),
  false, false);
canvas.paintShading(radial);
PdfShadingPattern shading
  = new PdfShadingPattern(axial);
colorRectangle(canvas,
  new ShadingColor(shading), 150, 420, 126, 126);
canvas.setShadingFill(shading);
canvas.rectangle(300, 420, 126, 126);
canvas.fillStroke();
```

The first part of this code snippet shows how to create and paint the shading with the method `paintShading()`. In the second part, you use the shading to create a `Pdf-ShadingPattern` and a `ShadingColor`.

NOTE Shadings are created using specific types of functions. So far we've seen an example involving type 2 and type 3 functions. ISO-32000-1 includes five more types. If you want to use the other types, you need to combine one or more of the static `type()` methods of the `PdfShading` class. Please consult ISO-32000-1, section 8.7.4, for more info, and inspect the implementation of the `simpleAxial()` and `simpleRadial()` methods in the iText source code for inspiration.

We've looked at drawing different graphical objects in different colors. If these objects overlap, as shown in figures 3.1 and 3.2, the color at each point on the page will, by default, be the color of the topmost object. But you can change this. You can introduce transparency so that the color is composed using a combination of the color of the topmost object with the colors of the objects below, aka the backdrop.

10.1.4 *Transparency*

Transparency is very complex matter, but let me try to select the most important rules from chapter 11 of ISO-32000-1:

A given object shall be composited with a backdrop. Ordinarily, the backdrop consists of the stack of all objects that have been specified previously. The result of compositing shall then be treated as the backdrop for the next object. However, within certain kinds of transparency groups, a different backdrop may be chosen.

During the compositing of an object with its backdrop, the color at each point shall be computed using a specified blend mode, which is a function of both the object's color and the backdrop color ...

Two scalar quantities called shape and opacity mediate compositing of an object with its backdrop ... Both shape and opacity vary from 0.0 (no contribution) to 1.0 (maximum contribution) ... Shape and opacity are conceptually very similar. In fact, they can usually be combined into a single value, called alpha, which controls both the color compositing computation and the fading between an object and its backdrop. However, there are a few situations in which they shall be treated separately; see knockout groups.

—ISO-32000-1 11.2

You've already used transparency to draw the layers in figures 3.2 and 6.2. These figures were created with the source code shown in listing 10.5 taken from an example in chapter 6. This code snippet draws the transparent white rectangle that was used as the background for every page. When you overlap the `PdfImportedPage` objects, you can see what is beneath each page.

Listing 10.5   Layers.java (from chapter 6)

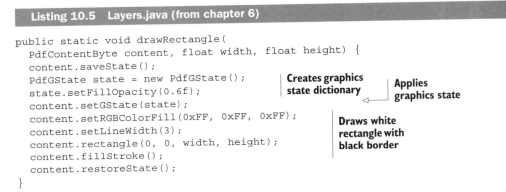

```
public static void drawRectangle(
    PdfContentByte content, float width, float height) {
    content.saveState();
    PdfGState state = new PdfGState();          Creates graphics     Applies
    state.setFillOpacity(0.6f);                 state dictionary     graphics state
    content.setGState(state);
    content.setRGBColorFill(0xFF, 0xFF, 0xFF);  Draws white
    content.setLineWidth(3);                    rectangle with
    content.rectangle(0, 0, width, height);     black border
    content.fillStroke();
    content.restoreState();
}
```

When transparency is involved, you need to create a `PdfGState` object and apply it with the method `setGState()`. The rectangle that is drawn in listing 10.5 has an opaque black border, but the `setFillOpacity()` method is used to change the opacity of the white "paint" to 0.6.

Let's look at examples to learn more about transparency groups, isolation, and knockout.

TRANSPARENCY GROUPS

Figure 10.3 shows four identical paths. The background is a square that is half gray, half white. Inside the square, three circles are painted. The first one is red, the second is yellow, and the third is blue. Each version of these paths is filled using a different transparency model.

In the two upper figures, the circles are painted as independent objects (no grouping). There's no transparency involved in the upper-left figure; the circles in the upper-right figure are drawn with an opacity of 0.5 causing them to composite with each other and with the gray and white backdrop.

In the two lower figures, the circles are combined as a transparency group. At the left, the individual circles have an opacity of 1 within the group, but the group as a whole is painted in the Normal blend mode with an opacity of 0.5. The objects overwrite each other within the group, but the resulting group composites transparently with the backdrop. At the right, the circles have an opacity of 0.5 within the group,

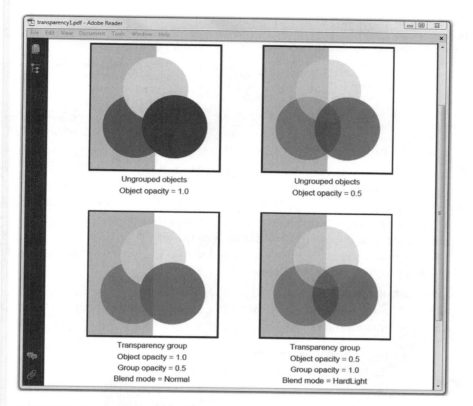

Figure 10.3 Transparency groups

and the group as a whole is painted against the backdrop with an opacity of 1.0, but in a different blend mode.

The `pictureCircles()` method draws the figures shown in figure 10.3. You'll use this method in different graphics states.

Listing 10.6   Transparency1.java

```
pictureCircles(gap, 500, cb);
cb.saveState();
PdfGState gs1 = new PdfGState();
gs1.setFillOpacity(0.5f);                                          Changes
cb.setGState(gs1);                                                 opacity to 0.5
pictureCircles(200 + 2 * gap, 500, cb);
cb.restoreState();
cb.saveState();
PdfTemplate tp = cb.createTemplate(200, 200);                      Creates
PdfTransparencyGroup group = new PdfTransparencyGroup();           transparency
tp.setGroup(group);                                                group for XObject
pictureCircles(0, 0, tp);
cb.setGState(gs1);                                                 Draws template
cb.addTemplate(tp, gap, 500 - 200 - gap);                          using opacity 0.5
```

```
cb.restoreState();
cb.saveState();
tp = cb.createTemplate(200, 200);
tp.setGroup(group);
PdfGState gs2 = new PdfGState();
gs2.setFillOpacity(0.5f);
gs2.setBlendMode(PdfGState.BM_HARDLIGHT);
tp.setGState(gs2);
pictureCircles(0, 0, tp);
cb.addTemplate(tp, 200 + 2 * gap, 500 - 200 - gap);
cb.restoreState();
```

Defines group with opacity 0.5 and hard light blend mode

Draws template using opacity I

To group objects, you create a `PdfTemplate` object. When you define a `PdfTranspar-encyGroup` for this XObject, the objects drawn to it—in this case, circles—belong to the same transparency group. Observe the difference between the lower-left figure where you set the opacity for the complete group and the lower-right figure where you set the opacity and blend mode within the group.

The `PdfTransparencyGroup` class has two methods: `setIsolated()` and `setKnock-out()`. Let's find out what these concepts are about.

ISOLATION AND KNOCKOUT

Figure 10.4 shows four squares filled with a shading pattern. Four circles are added inside these squares as a group.

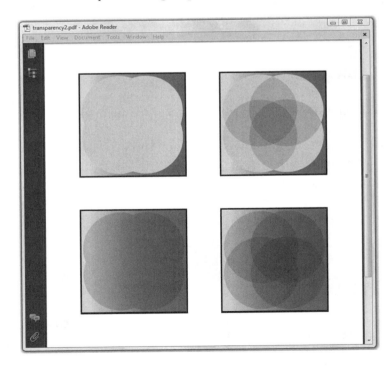

Figure 10.4
Isolation and knockout

The code that draws the four figures is identical. All the circles have the same CMYK color: C, M, and Y are set to 0 and K to 0.15. Their opacity is 1.0 and the blend mode is Multiply; the only difference is the *isolation* and *knockout* modes.

- *Isolation*—For the two upper squares, the group is isolated: it doesn't interact with the backdrop. For the two lower squares, the group is nonisolated: the group composites with the backdrop.
- *Knockout*—For the squares at the left, knockout is set to `true`: the circles don't composite with each other. For the two on the right, it's set to `false`: they composite with each other.

Listing 10.7 shows how the upper-right figure was drawn. The other figures are created by changing the `boolean` values for the methods `setIsolated()` and `setKnockout()`.

Listing 10.7 Transparency2.java

```
tp = cb.createTemplate(200, 200);
pictureCircles(0, 0, tp);
group = new PdfTransparencyGroup();
group.setIsolated(true);
group.setKnockout(true);
tp.setGroup(group);
cb.addTemplate(tp, gap, 500);
```

Note that figure 10.3 was inspired by figure L.16 in ISO-32000-1. Figure 10.4 is very similar to figure L.17. You may also want to take a look at the overview of the different blend modes in figures L.18 (RGB) and L.19 (CMYK). The blend modes are listed in section 11.3.5 of ISO-32000-1. They are all supported in iText (see the constant values starting with `BM_` in the `PdfGState` class), but it would lead us too far off topic to discuss them in detail.

It would be interesting to apply transparency to images, but before you can do so, you need to know which types of images are supported in iText.

10.2 Overview of supported image types

When we needed images in the previous chapters, we used `Image.getInstance()`, passing the path to an image without considering which type of image we were using. Figure 10.5 shows a document with 12 images.

The first nine images were created with the `getInstance()` method; the last three are special cases. Let's start with the standard types.

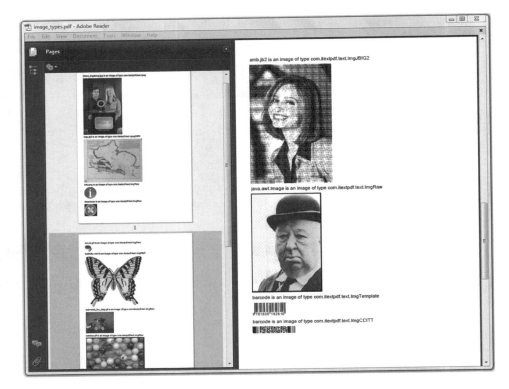

Figure 10.5   Different image types

10.2.1   *JPEG, JPEG2000, GIF, PNG, BMP, WMF, TIFF, and JBIG2*

Table 10.1 lists the types of images supported by the Image class and indicates which format is best to use in which context. For example, JPEG is a better format for photographs than GIF. GIF is better for charts than JPG.

Table 10.1   Standard image types supported by com.itextpdf.text.Image

Type	Extension	Description
JPEG JPG	.jpg	JPEG (Joint Photographic Experts Group) is commonly used to refer to a lossy compression technique, reducing the size of a graphic file by as much as 96 percent. Usually this is the best file format for photographs on the web.
JPEG 2000	.jp2 .j2k	The successor to JPEG, providing better efficiency in compression. JPEG 2000 has multiple versions for use, including a lossless version and a tiling version that allows for zooming in to detailed areas of the image file.
GIF	.gif	GIF (Graphics Interchange Format) is a format that is suitable for images containing large areas of the same color. GIF files of simple images are often smaller than the same files would be if stored in JPEG format, but GIF doesn't store photographic images as well as JPEG. A GIF file can contain multiple frames, in which case it's referred to as an animated GIF.

Table 10.1   Standard image types supported by `com.itextpdf.text.Image` *(continued)*

Type	Extension	Description
PNG	.png	The PNG (Portable Network Graphics) format was designed as the successor to GIF. It features compression, transparency, and progressive loading, like GIF.
BMP	.bmp .dib	BMP (Windows bitmap) is a common form of bitmap file in Microsoft Windows. Most BMP files have a relatively large file size due to the lack of any compression.
WMF	.wmf	WMF (Windows Metafile) is a vector graphics format for Windows-compatible computers, used mostly for word processing clip art.
TIFF	.tiff .tif	TIFF (Tagged Image File Format) is commonly used for digital scanned images. It was originally a binary image format with only two possible values for each pixel. Nowadays, it's a popular format for high color-depth images, along with JPEG and PNG. A TIFF image can consist of multiple pages.
JBIG2	.jb2	JBIG2 (Joint Bi-level Image Experts Group) is an image compression standard for bilevel images. Bi-level images are digital images in which each pixel is represented by only one bit. For instance, a pixel can be either black or white. JBIG2 is intended for images sent using a fax. A JBIG2 image can consist of multiple pages.

`Image` is an abstract class, which means you can't construct an instance directly. The `getInstance()` method returns an instance of a specific image implementation. iText has a separate image class for each type that is supported. These classes process the image data, and possibly change the bits and bytes into a format that is supported in PDF. For instance, JPEG images are copied *as is* into an image XObject, but a BMP will be decoded into raw image bytes that are compressed using the zlib/deflate compression method. A WMF file will be translated into PDF syntax; if you look inside the PDF, you'll see that the WMF image is changed into a form XObject.

Table 10.2 gives an overview of the most important image classes and how they relate to each other. The second column indicates whether the class is a subclass of `com.itextpdf.text.Image`.

Table 10.2   Image classes in iText

Classname	Subclass	Produces
Jpeg	Yes	The image is copied byte by byte into the PDF. Inspecting the PDF, you'll find out that the DCTDecode filter can be used to decompress the data. DCT stands for Discrete Cosine Transform.
Jpeg2000	Yes	The filter used for these images is JPXDecode. This means that the image was encoded using the wavelet-based JPEG 2000 standard.
ImgRaw	Yes	Raw images can either be compressed using zlib/flate compression or using the CCITT facsimile standard. See sections 10.2.2 and 10.2.3 for more details.
GifImage	No	Although PDF supports images with LZW compression, iText decodes the GIF image into a raw image. If you create an `Image` with a path to a GIF file, you'll get an instance of the `ImgRaw` class.

Table 10.2   Image classes in iText *(continued)*

Classname	Subclass	Produces
PngImage	No	Just like GIF images, iText decodes PNG images into raw images. If the color space of the image is DeviceGray and if it only has 1 bit per component, CCITT is used as compression. In all other cases, the image data is zlib/flate compressed.
BmpImage	No	Just like GIF images, iText decodes BMP images into raw images. Likewise, the filter in the image dictionary is FlateDecode.
ImgTemplate	Yes	This is an image that consists of PDF syntax. If you look inside the PDF, you won't find an image XObject, but a form XObject. In iText lingo, it's a PdfTemplate wrapped in an Image object for reasons of convenience when scaling, rotating, and adding the image to the document.
ImgWMF	Yes	If you create an Image using a WMF file, you'll get an instance of ImgWMF, but internally the image will be translated into a PdfTemplate. Inside the PDF, you'll find a form XObject instead of an image XObject.
ImgCCITT	Yes	The filter for these images is CCITTFaxDecode. The data was encoded using the CCITT facsimile standard. It's typically a monochrome image with 1 bit per pixel. See section 10.2.3.
TiffImage	No	The TiffImage class will inspect the TIFF file and, depending on its parameters, it can return an ImgCCITT, an ImgRaw, or even a Jpeg instance.
ImgJBIG2	Yes	An ImgJBIG2 object is an Image instance produced by the JBIG2Image.

In table 10.2, you'll find some image types that don't map directly to an image type in table 10.1. For instance, what do we mean when we talk about a raw image?

10.2.2   *Creating a raw image*

An image consists of a series of pixels, and each pixel has a color. The color value of the sequence of pixels can be stored in a byte array, and the byte array can be compressed, for instance using zlib/flate compression. Figure 10.6 shows images that were created byte by byte.

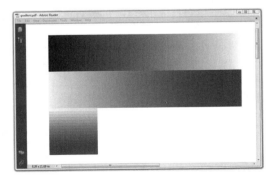

Figure 10.6   Images built using raw image data

This source code was used to create the images in figure 10.6.

Listing 10.8   RawImage.java

```
byte gradient[] = new byte[256];
for (int i = 0; i < 256; i++)
  gradient[i] = (byte) i;
Image img1 = Image.getInstance(256, 1, 1, 8, gradient);        ❶ Creates
img1.scaleAbsolute(256, 50);                                      DeviceGray, 8
document.add(img1);                                               bpc image
byte cgradient[] = new byte[256 * 3];
for (int i = 0; i < 256; i++) {
  cgradient[i * 3] = (byte) (255 - i);
  cgradient[i * 3 + 1] = (byte) (255 - i);
  cgradient[i * 3 + 2] = (byte) i;
}                                                               ❷ Creates RGB,
Image img2 = Image.getInstance(256, 1, 3, 8, cgradient);           8 bpc image
img2.scaleAbsolute(256, 50);
document.add(img2);
Image img3 = Image.getInstance(16, 16, 3, 8, cgradient);        Creates RGB,
img3.scaleAbsolute(64, 64);                                     ❸ 8 bpc image
document.add(img3);
```

You're creating three images in listing 10.8. The first one has 256 pixels x 1 pixel. The color space is DeviceGray (1 component), and you're using 8 bits per component (bpc) ❶. When you create the image data, you let the color value vary from 0 to 255. This results in the gradient from black to white in figure 10.6 (note that the height of the image is scaled).

For the second and third images, you use three components with 8 bits per component. This means that you'll need 256 bytes x 3 bytes to describe an image that consists of 256 pixels. You use the image data to create an image of 256 pixels x 1 pixel ❷, and to create an image of 16 pixels x 16 pixels ❸. Note that this image uses the DeviceRGB color space; if you create an image with four components, you're working in the DeviceCMYK color space. The getInstance() method used in listing 10.8 also accepts an extra parameter to define a transparency range. We'll discuss transparency for images in more detail in section 10.3.1.

What you're doing manually in this example is done automatically with GIF, PNG, BMP, and some TIFF images internally. These bytes are added to a zipped stream using the zlib/flate algorithm, except for some TIFF and PNG images that are CCITT-encoded.

10.2.3 *CCITT compressed images*

CCITT stands for Comité Consultatif International Téléphonique et Télégraphique, a standards organization that is now part of the International Telecommunication Union (ITU). This organization is responsible for defining many of the standards for data communications. PDF supports Group 3 and Group 4 compression, which are facsimile (fax) standards.

With iText, you can insert CCITT-encoded images using the following method:

```
Image.getInstance(int width, int height, boolean reverseBits,
    int typeCCITT, int parameters, byte[] data)
```

The `reverseBits` parameter indicates whether the bits need to be swapped (bit 7 swapped with bit 0, and so on). The type can be `Element.CCITTG31D`, `Element.CCITTG32D`, or `Element.CCITT4`. The `parameters` value is a combination of the following flags:

- `Element.CCITT_BLACKIS1`—A flag indicating whether 1 bits are interpreted as black pixels and 0 bits as white pixels.
- `Element.CCITT_ENCODEDBYTEALIGN`—A flag indicating whether the filter expects extra 0 bits before each encoded line so that the line begins on a byte boundary.
- `Element.CCITT_ENDOFLINE`—A flag indicating whether end-of-line bit patterns are required to be present in the encoding.
- `Element.CCITT_ENDOFBLOCK`—A flag indicating whether the filter expects the encoded data to be terminated by an end-of-block pattern.

The CCITT protocols described in this section are used to send a document as an image from one fax to another. You could use iText to import a stream received from your fax into a PDF file. iText also uses CCITT internally to create images that need to be read by a machine, such as two-dimensional barcodes.

10.2.4 *Creating barcodes*

You may not look at barcodes as images, but in iText it's common to add a barcode to a document as an instance of the `Image` object. The same goes for matrix codes, which are often referred to as two-dimensional barcodes. Listing 10.9 shows how these barcodes were created.

Figure 10.5 has a barcode in the EAN-13 format containing the ISBN number of this book. The second barcode is a matrix code in the PDF417 format containing the text "iText in Action, a book by Bruno Lowagie." Internally, the first barcode is added to the document as an instance of `ImgTemplate`; the second one is an `ImgCCITT` object.

Listing 10.9   ImageTypes.java

```
BarcodeEAN codeEAN = new BarcodeEAN();
codeEAN.setCodeType(Barcode.EAN13);
codeEAN.setCode("9781935182610");
img = codeEAN.createImageWithBarcode(
  writer.getDirectContent(), null, null);
document.add(img);
BarcodePDF417 pdf417 = new BarcodePDF417();
String text = "iText in Action, a book by Bruno Lowagie.";
pdf417.setText(text);
img = pdf417.getImage();
document.add(img);
```

The classes to create regular (one-dimensional) barcodes extend the abstract class `Barcode`.

NORMAL BARCODES

Table 10.3 shows an overview of these subclasses, along with the types of barcodes they can produce.

Table 10.3   Barcode classes and barcode types

iText class	Barcode type	Description
BarcodeEAN	EAN-13, UPC-A, EAN-8, UPC-E	EAN stands for European Article Number code; UPC for Universal Product Code. Each type represents a number with a different number of digits.
BarcodeEANSUPP	Supplemental 2, Supplemental 5	EAN-13, UPC-A, EAN-8, and UPC-E allow for a supplemental two- or five-digit number to be appended to the main barcode. For instance, if you add a supplemental five-digit barcode to an EAN-13 barcode representing an International Standard Book Number (ISBN), you get a *Bookland* code.
Barcode128	Plain code 128, raw code 128, UCC/EAN-128	Code 128 provides much more detail than the single-product EAN barcodes. It's used to describe properties such as the number of products included, weight, dates, and so on.
BarcodeInter25	Interleaved 2 of 5	A numerical barcode that encodes pairs of digits: the first digit is encoded in the bars; the second digit is encoded in the spaces interleaved with them. Two out of every five bars or spaces are wide (hence 2 of 5).
BarcodePostnet	POSTNET, PLANET	The United States Postal Service (USPS) uses a combination of the Postal Numeric Encoding Technique (POSTNET) sorting code and the Postal Alphanumeric Encoding Technique (PLANET) code to direct and identify mail. Currently, three forms of POSTNET codes are in use: a 5-digit ZIP code, a 9-digit ZIP+4, and an 11-digit delivery point code. The PLANET code is an 11-digit code assigned by USPS.
Barcode39	Barcode 3 of 9, 3 of 9 extended	The 3 of 9 code can encode numbers, uppercase letters (A–Z), and symbols (- . ' '$ / + % *).
BarcodeCodabar	Codabar	Codabar is used to store numerical data only, but the letters A, B, C, and D are used as start and stop characters.

The value that has to be shown by the barcode is set with the method setCode(), except for BarcodeEANSUPP. The example shows how to create a Bookland barcode composed of two BarcodeEAN instances: one with type EAN13 and one with type SUPP5.

Listing 10.10   Barcodes.java

```
document.add(new Paragraph("Bookland"));
document.add(new Paragraph("ISBN 0-321-30474-8"));
codeEAN.setCodeType(Barcode.EAN13);
codeEAN.setCode("9781935182610");
BarcodeEAN codeSUPP = new BarcodeEAN();
codeSUPP.setCodeType(Barcode.SUPP5);
codeSUPP.setCode("55999");
```

```
codeSUPP.setBaseline(-2);
BarcodeEANSUPP eanSupp = new BarcodeEANSUPP(codeEAN, codeSUPP);
document.add(eanSupp.createImageWithBarcode(cb, null, BaseColor.BLUE));
```

The barcodes example contains code samples for every type of barcode. The barcodes are added to the document as an `Image` that is created with the `createImageWithBarcode()` method. As an alternative, you can write the barcode directly to a `PdfContentByte` object with `placeBarcode()`, or create a `PdfTemplate` with `createTemplateWithBarcode()`. These methods take three parameters:

- `PdfContentByte cb`—The direct content of the `PdfWriter` to which the barcode has to be added
- `BaseColor barColor`—The color of the bars
- `BaseColor textColor`—The color of the text

You can also create a `java.awt.Image` of the barcode using the `createAwtImage()` method. This method expects two colors of type `java.awt.Color` (as opposed to `com.itextpdf.text.BaseColor`). The first one represents the color of the bars; the second one defines the background color. No text is added to these barcodes.

The subclasses of the `Barcode` class have a lot of properties in common that can be set with methods in the abstract superclass. Table 10.4 presents an overview showing the default value for each property.

Table 10.4   Default properties of the different barcode classes

Code:	EAN	EANSUPP	128	Inter25	39	Codabar	Postnet
type	EAN13	-	CODE128	-	-	CODABAR	POSTNET
x	0.8f						0.02f * 72f
n	-	8	-	2			72f / 22f
font	BaseFont.createFont(BaseFont.HELVETICA, BaseFont.WINANSI, BaseFont.NOT_EMBEDDED);						-
size	8						0.05f * 72f
baseline	size						-
bar height	size * 3						0.125f * 72f
text align	-	-	Element.ALIGN.CENTER				-
guardbars	true	-	-	-	-	-	-
generate checksum	User	User	-	false	false	false	-
text checksum	-	-	-	false	false	false	-
start/stop text	-	-	-	-	true	false	-

Note that some barcode classes require a value for the type variable. For example, BarcodeEAN can produce barcodes of type EAN13, EAN8, UPCA, UPCE, SUPP2, and SUPP5, whereas BarcodeInter25 can produce only one type of barcode.

The property x—adjustable with the setX() method—holds the minimum width of a bar. Except for the POSTNET code, this value is set to 0.8 by default. You can set the amount of ink spreading with setInkSpreading(). This value is subtracted from the width of each bar. The actual value depends on the ink and the printing medium; it's 0 by default. The property n holds the multiplier for wide bars for some types, the distance between two barcodes in EANSUPP, and the distance between the bars in the USPS barcodes.

The font property defines the font of the text (if any). If you want to produce a barcode without text, you have to set the barcode font to null with setFont(). You can change the size of the font with setSize(). With setBaseline() you can change the distance between text and barcode; negative values put the text above the bar. Changing the bar height can be done with setBarHeight(). For USPS codes, you can also change the height of the short bar with setSize(). USPS codes don't have text.

Finally, there are methods to generate a checksum and to make the calculated value visible in the human-readable text (or not). You can also set the start/stop sequence visible for those barcodes that use these sequences.

MATRIX CODES

iText supports three types of matrix codes. Table 10.5 lists the classes that are available for each type.

Table 10.5 Overview of the matrix code classes

iText class	Matrix code	Description
BarcodePDF417	PDF417	In this context, PDF stands for *Portable Data File*. It's a stacked linear barcode that can store up to 2,170 characters, and the symbology is capable of encoding the entire ASCII set.
BarcodeDatamatrix	Data Matrix	This code consists of black and white pixels arranged in a square or rectangular pattern. A Data Matrix symbol can store up to 2,335 alphanumeric characters.
BarcodeQRCode	QRCode	This is a matrix code created for Quick Response. These codes can be read by mobile phones with their camera in the context of mobile tagging.

The different matrix codes don't have a common superclass in iText. Each type has its own typical set of properties. PDF417 codes can be segmented, and you can set the aspect ratio. For Data Matrix, you can set the width, height, and encoding options. The same goes for QRCode, where you define a width and a height, along with hints that are listed in the API documentation. But let's return to real images.

There's one type of image used in figure 10.5 we haven't discussed yet. The picture of Alfred Hitchcock was added using a java.awt.Image.

10.2.5 *Working with java.awt.Image*

You have to pay attention not to confuse the iText object com.itextpdf.text.Image with the standard Java image class java.awt.Image. If you're using both classes in the same source file, you must use the full class name for at least one of them to avoid ambiguity and compile errors.

This shows how Hitchcock was added to the document shown in figure 10.5.

Listing 10.11   ImageTypes.java

```
java.awt.Image awtImage
  = Toolkit.getDefaultToolkit().createImage(RESOURCE);
img = com.itextpdf.text.Image.getInstance(awtImage, null);
document.add(img);
```

The second parameter in the getInstance() method is null in this example. In section 10.3.1, you'll learn that you can pass a java.awt.Color object. This color will replace the transparent color when the com.itextpdf.text.Image is added to the document. One of the possible reasons why you'd prefer using java.awt.Image is to reduce the quality of an image so that the resulting file size is significantly lower.

10.2.6 *Compressing images*

The different compression algorithms are listed in table 10.2, but it's important to realize that iText doesn't reduce the quality of an image. If you create an Image with a high-quality image, the image will be added to the PDF at the same quality. If you change the width and the height of the image, the resolution will change, but the number of pixels will remain the same.

CHANGING THE COMPRESSION LEVEL

You can try to reduce the size of an image that is flate-compressed by changing the compression level.

Listing 10.12   CompressImage.java

```
Image img = Image.getInstance(RESOURCE);
img.setCompressionLevel(9);
document.add(img);
```

Compression levels vary from 1 for best speed to 9 for best compression. If you set the compression to 0, the stream won't be compressed. iText uses default compression: -1. In some cases, a compression level of 9 will result in a smaller stream, but that's no guarantee.

Usually, you won't save a lot of space by changing the compression level. The RESOURCE in the example is a BMP image with a size of 492 KB. Before changing the compression, the resulting PDF file is 13 KB; with compression level 9, it's reduced to 11 KB. (With compression 0, it would have been 370 KB.) Lossless compression won't result in dramatic file size reduction. However, if lossy compression is acceptable, you could use java.awt.Image to reduce the quality.

USING JAVA.AWT.IMAGE FOR JPEG COMPRESSION

Figure 10.7 shows the same picture three times. The original `hitchcock.png` image is 16 KB. Due to the way the `Image` object is constructed, it's compressed using JPEG compression. The image in the first PDF in figure 10.7 is shown with a quality of 100 percent; the size of the file is 35 KB. The quality is reduced to 20 percent in the second PDF, resulting in a file size of 6 KB. At 10 percent quality, the size is 5 KB.

This is how you convert the image from PNG to JPEG.

Listing 10.13   CompressAwt.java

```
java.awt.Image awtImage
  = Toolkit.getDefaultToolkit().createImage(RESOURCE);
Image img = Image.getInstance(writer, awtImage, quality);
img.setAbsolutePosition(15, 15);
document.add(img);
```

For the `quality` parameter, you can pass a `float` varying from 0.0 to 1.0. Note that if you added the PNG as is, without `using.java.awt.Image`, the file size of the resulting PDF would have been 17 KB, which is almost half of the file size with the JPEG at 100 percent. If you really want to compress an image, you'll have to fine-tune your application to make sure you don't end up with unexpected results.

> **NOTE** As an alternative to using this limited functionality to compress images, you may want to use the Java Advanced Imaging (JAI) library or `java.awt.Image` to preprocess images. You can use standard Java transformations to reduce the size of the image, or even to change the appearance of the image before adding it to a document using iText. Although this is outside the scope of a book about iText, you'll use this technique in chapter 16 to reduce the resolution of an image in an existing document.

Table 10.1 showed that TIFF, JBIG2, and GIF files can contain more than one image. But when you added these files to obtain figure 10.5, only one image was added. Let's find out how to retrieve the other images in the file (if there are any).

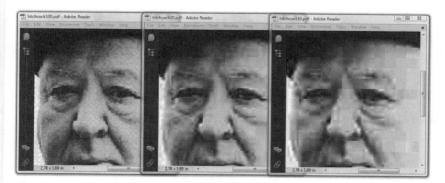

Figure 10.7   Compressed image with quality loss

10.2.7 *Images consisting of multiple pages or frames*

TIFF and JBIG2 were originally created for scanners and fax machines, and when you scan or fax a document, it can contain multiple pages. The next listing shows how you can use the `TiffImage` and `JBIG2Image` objects to get the number of pages in the image file ❶, and how to get an `Image` instance ❷ that can be added to a `Document`.

Listing 10.14   PagedImages.java

```java
public void addTif(Document document, String path)
  throws DocumentException, IOException {
  RandomAccessFileOrArray ra = new RandomAccessFileOrArray(RESOURCE1);
  int n = TiffImage.getNumberOfPages(ra);                                    ❶
  Image img;
  for (int i = 1; i <= n; i++) {
    img = TiffImage.getTiffImage(ra, i);              ❷
    img.scaleToFit(523, 350);
    document.add(img);
  }
}
public void addJBIG2(Document document, String path)
  throws IOException, DocumentException {
  RandomAccessFileOrArray ra = new RandomAccessFileOrArray(RESOURCE2);
  int n = JBIG2Image.getNumberOfPages(ra);                                   ❶
  Image img;
  for (int i = 1; i <= n; i++) {
    img = JBIG2Image.getJbig2Image(ra, i);                                   ❷
    img.scaleToFit(523, 350);
    document.add(img);
  }
}
```

The GIF format, on the other hand, can be used to create small animations. An animated GIF contains different images that are referred to as frames. That's why the terminology for extracting the different frames from an animated GIF is slightly different from what you saw in listing 10.14. Instead of getting the number of pages, you get the frame count.

Listing 10.15   PagedImages.java (continued)

```java
public void addGif(Document document, String path)
  throws IOException, DocumentException {
  GifImage img = new GifImage(RESOURCE3);
  int n = img.getFrameCount();
  for (int i = 1; i <= n; i++) {
    document.add(img.getImage(i));
  }
}
```

Figure 10.8 shows a series of photographs that animate the pangram, "Quick brown fox jumps over the lazy dog." (A *pangram* is a phrase that contains all the letters of the alphabet.)

Note that animated GIF images aren't supported in PDFs. You can only add static GIF images. If you want to add an animation, you need to create a movie file, and add that movie as an annotation, but that will have to wait until you've reached chapter 16.

We've discussed all the different types of images that are supported in iText; now let's combine this knowledge about images with what you've learned about transparency.

10.3 Making images transparent

All the image types listed in table 10.1 are raster images, except for WMF, which is a vector graphics image, aka line work. A raster graphics image is a data structure representing a rectangular grid of pixels. Suppose you want to add a raster image to a document shaped as a circle instead of a rectangle. There are different solutions for achieving this. Let's have a look at them one by one.

10.3.1 Images and transparency

Some image types, such as GIF and PNG, support transparency; others, such as JPEG, don't. Figure 10.9 shows a JPEG image in the background. Three other images were added on top of it.

Figure 10.8   Different frames taken from an animated GIF

The circle with the letter "i" is a PNG that is partly transparent. When you add this file to a document, the transparency of the original image is preserved. The other two images are GIFs that aren't transparent. If you open them in another application, you'll see that they are completely opaque.

Figure 10.9   Making images transparent

COLOR KEY MASKING

You can make part of those images transparent using color key masking.

Listing 10.16   TransparentImage.java

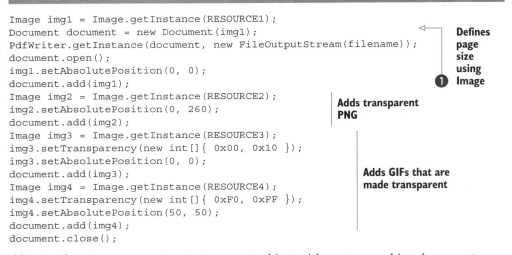

```
Image img1 = Image.getInstance(RESOURCE1);
Document document = new Document(img1);
PdfWriter.getInstance(document, new FileOutputStream(filename));
document.open();
img1.setAbsolutePosition(0, 0);
document.add(img1);
Image img2 = Image.getInstance(RESOURCE2);
img2.setAbsolutePosition(0, 260);
document.add(img2);
Image img3 = Image.getInstance(RESOURCE3);
img3.setTransparency(new int[]{ 0x00, 0x10 });
img3.setAbsolutePosition(0, 0);
document.add(img3);
Image img4 = Image.getInstance(RESOURCE4);
img4.setTransparency(new int[]{ 0xF0, 0xFF });
img4.setAbsolutePosition(50, 50);
document.add(img4);
document.close();
```

Defines page size using Image ❶

Adds transparent PNG

Adds GIFs that are made transparent

Observe that you can construct a `Document` object with an `Image` object because `Image` extends the `Rectangle` class ❶. You don't need to do anything special for the PNG that is already transparent, but you need to use the `setTransparency()` method for the two GIF images. This method expects an array specifying a range of colors to be masked out. The array needs to contain 2 x *n* values, with *n* being the number of components in the image's color space. For an RGB image, you need six values: a range for red, green, and blue. The GIFs in listing 10.16 use the *Indexed* color space. In this case, the PDF contains a color map with 256 RGB values. Every pixel of the image can be expressed as 1 byte, corresponding to a color in the color map.

> **NOTE**   We started this chapter saying that there are 11 color spaces in PDF, but we only discussed 5 of them in section 10.1: DeviceGray, DeviceRGB, DeviceCMYK, Pattern, and Separation. The other six color spaces, including Indexed and ICCBased, are supported in iText when they are needed to embed images in a PDF document. You won't be confronted with them directly; that's why they aren't discussed in detail in this book.

For `RESOURCE3`, you make the colors with index values of 0 to 16 transparent; the colors blue and orange of the iText logo are made transparent. For `RESOURCE4`, you make the white pixels transparent.

TRANSPARENCY AND JAVA.AWT.IMAGE

To create figure 10.10, you'll use a GIF file that was already transparent. If you add it the way you did in listing 10.16, the foreground will be red, the background will be transparent.

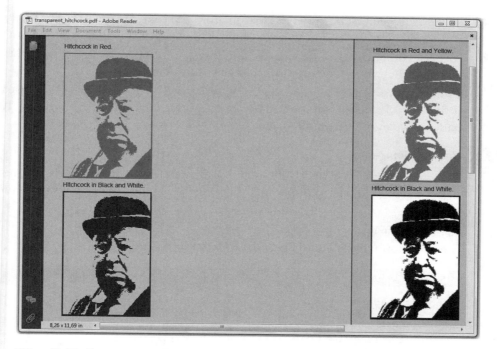

Figure 10.10 **Transparency with** `java.awt.Image`

For this example, you'll use a `java.awt.Image` object and create four different instances of `com.itextpdf.Image` with it.

Listing 10.17 TransparentAwt.java

```
java.awt.Image awtImage                                    Creates a
  = Toolkit.getDefaultToolkit().createImage(RESOURCE);     java.awt.Image
Image img1 = Image.getInstance(awtImage, null);            ①
document.add(img1);
Image img2 = Image.getInstance(awtImage, null, true);      ②
document.add(img2);
Image img3 = Image.getInstance(awtImage,
  new Color(0xFF, 0xFF, 0x00));                            ③
document.add(img3);
Image img4 = Image.getInstance(awtImage,
  new Color(0xFF, 0xFF, 0x00), true);                      ④
document.add(img4);
```

❶ If you add the image exactly the way you did in listing 10.11, the foreground of the image is red, and the background is transparent.

❷ With an extra `boolean` parameter, you can tell iText to change the image into a black and white image (with 1 bit per component). In the second image, all the red is changed into black, and the transparency is preserved.

③ You keep the colors, but you tell iText that the transparent pixels should be replaced with a `java.awt.Color`; in this case, yellow. The image is no longer transparent.

④ This is a combination of **②** and **③**. The transparent pixels are replaced by another color, but then the image is changed to black and white.

If you look inside the PDF generated with listing 10.17, you'll see that the transparency of the GIF is achieved using color key masking. The PNG image from listing 10.16 is made transparent using a soft mask.

10.3.2 *Masking images*

The image used in figure 10.11 is the same JPEG used in figure 10.9. The JPEG format doesn't support transparency, but you can apply either an *explicit mask* or a *soft mask*.

EXPLICIT MASKING

The PDF shown to the left in figure 10.11 uses a *stencil mask*.

Listing 10.18 ImageMask.java

```
byte circledata[] = {
  (byte) 0x3c, (byte) 0x7e, (byte) 0xff, (byte) 0xff,          Specifies
  (byte) 0xff, (byte) 0xff, (byte) 0x7e, (byte) 0x3c };        image data
Image mask = Image.getInstance(8, 8, 1, 1, circledata);        Creates
mask.makeMask();                                               mask
mask.setInverted(true);
```

Figure 10.11   Hard and soft image masks

You create an image with 8 pixels x 8 pixels, using one component and 1 bit per component, which makes 64 bits in total. You can store these bits in an array containing 8 bytes. Internally, iText will create a CCITT image.

When you make it a mask with the method `makeMask()`, you tell iText that this image is a stencil mask. This means that the bit value doesn't define a color (black or white), but rather whether the pixel is opaque or transparent. Normally, the value 1 will be opaque, and 0 transparent, but you change this with the method `setInverted()`. You can now apply the mask to the JPEG image:

```
Image img = Image.getInstance(RESOURCE);
img.setImageMask(mask);
```

The mask parameter can also be a soft mask. That's the case in the image shown to the right in figure 10.11.

SOFT MASKING

The code in the next listing should look very familiar. The first part is identical to what you did in listing 10.8 when you created a gradient in the DeviceGray color space.

> **Listing 10.19   ImageMask.java**

```
byte gradient[] = new byte[256];
for (int i = 0; i < 256; i++)
  gradient[i] = (byte) i;
mask = Image.getInstance(256, 1, 1, 8, gradient);
mask.makeMask();
```

The only difference here is that you now use the `makeMask()` method so that you can use the resulting `Image` as a parameter for the `setImageMask()` on another `Image`.

If using masks is too complex for what you need, you can also use simple PDF syntax to clip an image.

10.3.3 *Clipping images*

The first image in figure 10.5 is a picture of my wife and me, taken at the Flanders International Film Festival in Ghent. In the foreground you see a phenakistoscope. That's an early animation device, invented in 1832 by Joseph Plateau, (also) a citizen of Ghent. Nowadays, it's the Belgian version of the Oscar statue. Unfortunately, I didn't win one of these Belgian Oscars (yet); the picture was an initiative of one of the sponsors of the film festival.

Suppose I want to use only the upper half of this photograph in a PDF document because the lower half shows the name of the sponsor. This is done in figure 10.12. Using a mask isn't the best way to achieve this. Instead, we'll clip the image.

TEMPLATE CLIP

If you want to cut a rectangle out of the original image, as is done in the PDF to the left in figure 10.12, you could create a `PdfTemplate` object that is smaller than the original picture, and add the `Image` object to it.

Figure 10.12   Clipping images

Listing 10.20   TemplateClip.java

```
Image img = Image.getInstance(RESOURCE);
float w = img.getScaledWidth();
float h = img.getScaledHeight();
PdfTemplate t = writer.getDirectContent().createTemplate(850, 600);
t.addImage(img, w, 0, 0, h, 0, -600);
Image clipped = Image.getInstance(t);
clipped.scalePercent(50);
document.add(clipped);
```

What happens with the image in the template is true for all the objects you add to the direct content. Everything that is added outside the boundaries of a PdfTemplate or a page will be present in the PDF, but you won't see it in a PDF viewer. It's important to understand that iText may change the way the image is compressed, but it doesn't remove pixels. In this case, the complete picture—including the name of the festival sponsor in the lower half of the image—will be in the PDF file, but it won't be visible when looking at the PDF document.

If you aren't satisfied with a rectangle, you can define a clipping path.

CLIPPING PATH

You defined different paths in chapter 3, when you wrote lines and shapes to the direct content. With the combination of the clip() and newPath() methods, you can use such a path as a clipping path. You can reuse listing 10.20 to create the PDF shown to the right in figure 10.12. You only have to add a couple of lines.

Listing 10.21   ClippingPath.java

```
PdfTemplate t = writer.getDirectContent().createTemplate(850, 600);
t.ellipse(0, 0, 850, 600);
t.clip();
t.newPath();
t.addImage(img, w, 0, 0, h, 0, -600);
```

Any graphical shape can be used as a clipping path, including text.

**Figure 10.13
Clipped image with a
transparent overlay**

Let's finish this chapter with one more example that demonstrates another, less obvious, way to hide part of an image.

USING A SOFT MASK FOR DIRECT CONTENT

The PDF in figure 10.13 looks similar to the one in figure 10.12, but it also has a soft mask applied. The main difference between this and what you did for figure 10.11 is that you don't use the soft mask for the Image object, but for the GState of the direct content.

The code to achieve this is rather complex, as you can see.

Listing 10.22   TransparentOverlay.java

```java
PdfTemplate t2 = writer.getDirectContent()
  .createTemplate(850, 600);
PdfTransparencyGroup transGroup
  = new PdfTransparencyGroup();
transGroup.put( PdfName.CS, PdfName.DEVICEGRAY);
transGroup.setIsolated(true);
transGroup.setKnockout(false);
t2.setGroup(transGroup);
int gradationStep = 30;
float[] gradationRatioList = new float[gradationStep];
for(int i = 0; i < gradationStep; i++) {
  gradationRatioList[i] = 1 - (float)Math.sin(
    Math.toRadians(90.0f / gradationStep * (i + 1)));
}
for(int i = 1; i < gradationStep + 1; i++) {
  t2.setLineWidth(5 * (gradationStep + 1 - i));
  t2.setGrayStroke(
    gradationRatioList[gradationStep - i]);
  t2.ellipse(0, 0, 850, 600);
  t2.stroke();
}
```

*Creates XObject/
transparency group*

*Adds ellipses in
shades of gray*

```
PdfDictionary maskDict = new PdfDictionary();
maskDict.put(PdfName.TYPE, PdfName.MASK );              Creates
maskDict.put(PdfName.S, new PdfName("Luminosity"));     Image mask
maskDict.put(                                           dictionary
  new PdfName("G"), t2.getIndirectReference());
PdfGState gState = new PdfGState();            Sets graphics
gState.put(PdfName.SMASK, maskDict);           state
canvas.setGState(gState);
canvas.addTemplate(t2, 0, 0);      ⊲── Adds XObject
```

This is an example that should be studied with this book in one hand and ISO-32000-1 in the other. This isn't "the definitive chapter" about colors, images, and transparency, but we've looked at a selection of the most important functionality from the perspective of the iText developer.

10.4   *Summary*

We started this chapter with an introduction to color spaces. We discussed three device color spaces (RGB, CMYK, and Gray), as well as two special device color spaces (Separation and Pattern). These are the color spaces for which iText has specific color classes that can be used as font, fill, or stroke color. You also learned about making colors transparent. You can change the opacity and the blend mode of objects added to the direct content using the GState object, and you can group objects in a transparency group for which you can define isolation and knockout.

After this overview of colors and transparency, we took a look at the different image types that are supported by iText. We mapped these image types to the different image classes in iText. You created an image byte by byte, color by color to find out what images are about. You learned that iText changes the way some image types are compressed, but it doesn't reduce the quality, unless you use java.awt.Image.

Finally, you made images transparent using masking (color key masking, explicit masking, and soft masking) and you learned to clip images. Although you may have the impression that we've covered a lot of functionality, we've only been scratching the surface. ISO-32000-1 contains much more information about color spaces, blending modes, image types, and so on.

We can't go into more detail. We have to move on to chapter 11 and take a closer look at fonts, font programs, and glyphs.

Choosing the right font

11

This chapter covers

- Font files, types, and classes
- Writing systems and advanced typography
- Automatic font creation and selection

We discussed two font classes in chapter 2: `Font` and `BaseFont`. You used the `Font` class in section 2.2.1 for the 14 *standard Type 1 fonts*. These fonts are supposed to be "known" by every PDF viewer and are therefore never embedded by iText. In section 2.2.2, you used the `Font` class in combination with `BaseFont` to embed fonts. You created a `BaseFont` object by telling iText where to find a font program; for instance, a .ttf file. In chapter 3, you needed the `BaseFont` class to set the font when writing text to the direct content. You've also learned how to measure `Strings` in a certain font, how to change the render mode, and so on.

You know how to use fonts in your applications, but how do you choose them? Which font files can be used with iText? How about special writing systems? In some languages, you have to write from right to left, and from top to bottom. Furthermore, there are some convenience classes that make it easier to select a font. You'll find the answers to all these questions in this chapter.

11.1 Getting fonts from a file

Figure 11.1 shows a PDF containing a sentence written nine times using different fonts.

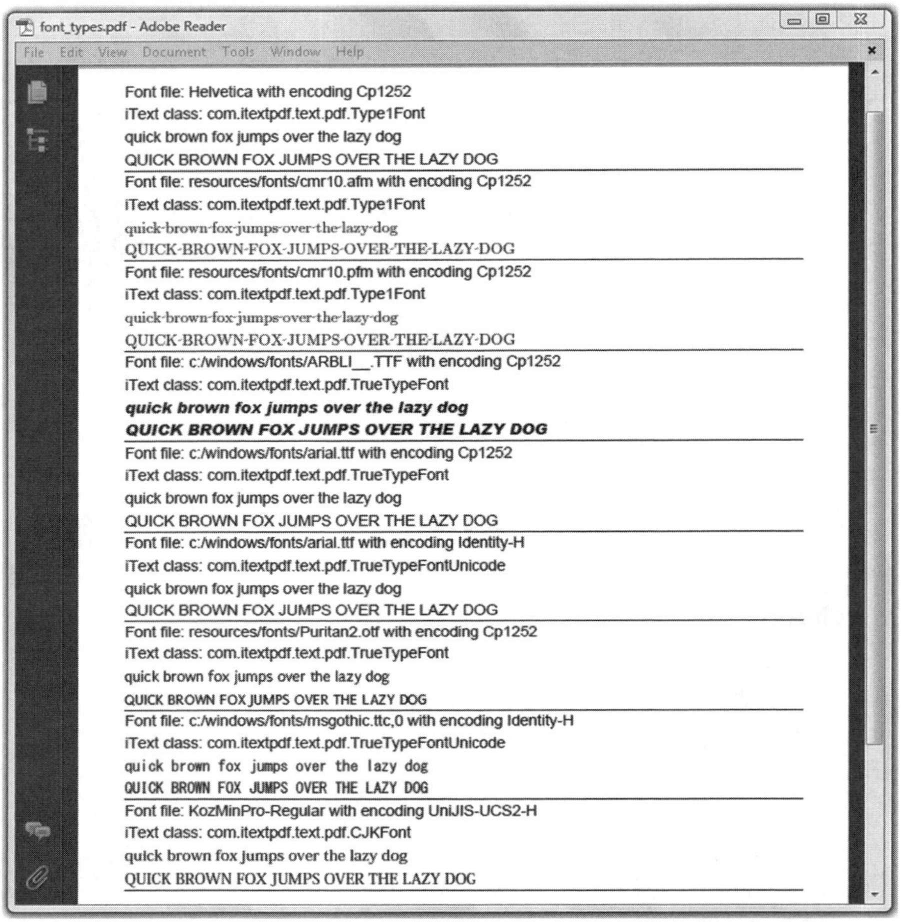

Figure 11.1 One sentence written in different fonts

The document also shows which font program and encoding was used, and which iText class was responsible for interpreting the font. In the next subsections, we'll approach this example from different angles. First, let's take a look at the font files that can be used.

11.1.1 *Font files and their extensions*

Table 11.1 lists the extensions of the files that contain the font metrics or the font program, or both. Type 1 was originally a proprietary specification owned by Adobe, but after Apple introduced TrueType as a competitor, the specification was published, and third-party font manufacturers were allowed to create Type 1 fonts, provided they adhered to the specification. In 1991, Microsoft started using TrueType as its standard font.

Table 11.1   Font files and their extension

Font type	Extension	Description
Type 1 font files	.afm, .pfm, .pfb	A Type 1 font is composed of two files: one containing the metrics (.afm or .pfm), and one containing the mathematical descriptions for each character (.pfb).
TrueType font files	.ttf	A font based on a specification developed by Apple to compete with Adobe's Type 1 fonts.
OpenType font files	.otf, .ttf, .ttc	A cross-platform font file format based on Unicode. OpenType font files containing Type 1 outlines have an .otf extension. Filenames of OpenType fonts containing TrueType data have a .ttf or .ttc extension. The .ttc extension is used for TrueType collections.

For a long time, TrueType was the most common font on both Mac OS and MS Windows systems, but both companies, Apple as well as Microsoft, added their own proprietary extensions, and soon they had their own versions and interpretations of (what once was) the standard. When looking for a commercial font, you had to be careful to buy a font that could be used on your system. A TrueType font for Windows didn't necessarily work on a Mac. To resolve the platform dependency of TrueType fonts, Microsoft started developing a new font format. Microsoft was joined by Adobe, and support for Adobe's Type 1 fonts was added. In 1996, a new font format was born: OpenType fonts. The glyphs in an OpenType font can be defined using either True-Type or Type 1 technology.

This demonstrates how the PDF shown in figure 11.1 was created.

Listing 11.1   FontTypes.java

```
public static String[][] FONTS = {
  {BaseFont.HELVETICA, BaseFont.WINANSI},
  {"resources/fonts/cmr10.afm", BaseFont.WINANSI},       Type I
  {"resources/fonts/cmr10.pfm", BaseFont.WINANSI},                    OpenType
  {"c:/windows/fonts/ARBLI__.TTF", BaseFont.WINANSI},  <--- TrueType   with
  {"c:/windows/fonts/arial.ttf", BaseFont.WINANSI},                    TrueType
  {"c:/windows/fonts/arial.ttf", BaseFont.IDENTITY_H},                 outlines
  {"resources/fonts/Puritan2.otf", BaseFont.WINANSI},  <--
  {"c:/windows/fonts/msgothic.ttc",0",              TrueType   OpenType
    BaseFont.IDENTITY_H},                            collection  with Type I
  {"KozMinPro-Regular", "UniJIS-UCS2-H"}                         outlines
};
public void createPdf(String filename)
  throws IOException, DocumentException {
  Document document = new Document();
  PdfWriter.getInstance(document, new FileOutputStream(filename));
  document.open();
  BaseFont bf;
  Font font;
  for (int i = 0; i < FONTS.length; i++) {
    bf = BaseFont.createFont(
      FONTS[i][0], FONTS[i][1], BaseFont.EMBEDDED);
    document.add(new Paragraph(String.format(
```

```
      "Font file: %s with encoding %s", FONTS[i][0], FONTS[i][1])));
    document.add(new Paragraph(String.format(
      "iText class: %s", bf.getClass().getName())));
    font = new Font(bf, 12);
    document.add(new Paragraph(TEXT, font));
    document.add(new LineSeparator(0.5f, 100, null, 0, -5));
  }
  document.close();
}
```

There are many things going on in this code snippet, but for now we'll focus on the files that were used to create the BaseFont object.

11.1.2 *Type 1 fonts*

If you open the iText JAR, you'll find a com/itextpdf/text/pdf/fonts folder containing 14 .afm files. These are the Adobe Font Metrics (AFM) files for the 14 standard Type 1 fonts: 4 Helvetica fonts (normal, bold, oblique, and bold-oblique), 4 Times-Roman fonts (normal, bold, italic, and bold-italic), 4 Courier fonts (normal, bold, oblique, and bold-oblique), Symbol, and Zapf Dingbats.

ADOBE FONT METRICS (AFM) FILES

The AFM files are used when you create a Font like this:

```
Font f = new Font(FontFamily.COURIER, 10, Font.BOLD);
```

Or when you create a BaseFont like this:

```
BaseFont bf = BaseFont.createFont(
  BaseFont.TIMES_ITALIC, BaseFont.WINANSI, BaseFont.EMBEDDED);
```

The former will fetch the Courier-Bold.afm file from the iText JAR; the latter will get the Times-Italic.afm file. The AFM files only contain metrics for each glyph: the bounding box, the character advance, and so on.

> **FAQ** *Why do I get an* IOException *when I use the default or a standard font?* If you get an exception with a message saying something like "Helvetica not found as resource." this means that the AFM file containing the font metrics of the font Helvetica can't be loaded as a resource. This will happen if you build the JAR from source code but forget to include the AFM file. Add them to the iText JAR, or check if you have access to the com/itextpdf/text/pdf/fonts/ *.afm files for the standard Type 1 fonts.

Note that the BaseFont.EMBEDDED parameter will be ignored for the standard Type 1 fonts. That's because iText doesn't ship with the PostScript Font Binary (PFB) files of these fonts.

POSTSCRIPT FONT BINARY FILES

The actual outlines of each glyph aren't stored in the metrics file, but in a separate PFB file. In listing 11.1, the cmr10.afm AFM file is used. This is the metrics file for Computer Modern Regular, a font designed by Donald Knuth. When you tell iText to embed this font, it will check whether the cmr10.pfb file is present in the same directory as the AFM file. If that file is missing, you'll get an exception saying "resources/fonts/cmr10.pfb not found as file or resource." Computer Modern Regular is used twice in our example: once with an AFM file and once with a PFM file.

PRINTER FONT METRICS (PFM) FILES

Printer Font Metrics (PFM) files are the Microsoft version of AFM, and iText is able to convert PFM into AFM. The same PFB file is used for both types of metrics files. Type 1 fonts aren't subset by iText; when you choose to embed a Type 1 font, the outlines of all glyphs in the font are embedded, including those that aren't used in the document.

Now let's take a look at the difference between TrueType fonts and OpenType fonts.

11.1.3 *TrueType and OpenType fonts*

Files with the .ttf extension can be either a TrueType font, or an OpenType font with TrueType outlines. Figure 11.2 shows a fragment of the fonts folder on Windows. The snippet contains icons for two .ttc and four .ttf files.

Thanks to the icon that's used, you can distinguish the TrueType fonts—the ones with the TT icon—from the OpenType fonts with TrueType outlines—the ones with the O icon. This difference doesn't matter much if you're using iText; you only have to be careful if you're using a TrueType collection—with the TC icon.

TRUETYPE COLLECTIONS

A TrueType collection is, as the name indicates, a collection of TrueType fonts bundled in one .ttc file. Figure 11.3 shows the fonts available in the file msgothic.ttc.

In the next example, you'll use the `enumerateTTCNames()` method to find the names of the fonts inside the collection.

Figure 11.2 TrueType fonts, TrueType collections, OpenType fonts with TrueType outlines

Figure 11.3 TrueType collection example

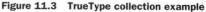

Listing 11.2　TTCExample.java

```
String[] names = BaseFont.enumerateTTCNames(FONT);
for (int i = 0; i < names.length; i++) {
  bf = BaseFont.createFont(String.format("%s,%s", FONT, i),
    BaseFont.IDENTITY_H, BaseFont.EMBEDDED);
  font = new Font(bf, 12);
  document.add(new Paragraph("font " + i + ": " + names[i], font));
  document.add(new Paragraph("Rash\u00f4mon", font));
  document.add(new Paragraph("Directed by Akira Kurosawa", font));
  document.add(new Paragraph("\u7f85\u751f\u9580", font));
  document.add(Chunk.NEWLINE);
}
```

The FONT parameter contains the path to msgothic.ttc. Observe that you have to add the index of the font to the font file when you want to create a BaseFont object. For instance, if you want to use the font MS-PGothic, you need to add the index 1:

```
BaseFont bf = BaseFont.createFont("c:/windows/fonts/msgotic.ttc,1",
  BaseFont.IDENTITY_H, BaseFont.EMBEDDED);
```

When you ask iText to embed a TrueType or an OpenType font with TrueType outlines, iText will not embed the complete font, as is the case with Type 1 fonts or OpenType fonts with Type 1 outlines. Instead, it will only embed a subset of the font, containing only those glyphs that were used in the document. iText will ignore the embedded parameter and always embed a subset of the font if you use the encoding IDENTITY_H or IDENTITY_V.

If you want to understand what this encoding means, you have to look at the different ways a font can be stored inside a PDF.

11.2　*Examining font types from a PDF perspective*

In this section, we'll examine font types from a PDF perspective, and we'll find out the difference between simple and composite fonts.

Table 11.1 looked at the way fonts can be organized in different files; table 11.2 lists the font subtypes that can be present in a PDF document. This table corresponds to Table 110 in ISO-32000-1, omitting the subtype MMType1. Multiple Master fonts have been discontinued. They can be present in a PDF document, but there's no support for Multiple Master fonts in iText's BaseFont class.

Table 11.2　Subtype values for fonts (ISO-32000-1 Table 110)

Subtype	Description
/Type1	A font that defines glyph shapes using Type 1 font technology
/Type3	A font that defines glyphs with streams of PDF graphics operators
/TrueType	A font based on the TrueType font format
/Type0	A composite font—a font composed of glyphs from a descendant CIDFont

Table 11.2   Subtype values for fonts (ISO-32000-1 Table 110) *(continued)*

Subtype	Description
/CIDFontType0	A CIDFont whose glyph descriptions are based on the Compact Font Format (CFF)
/CIDFontType2	A CIDFont whose glyph descriptions are based on TrueType font technology

The first three subtypes are used in the context of simple fonts; Type 0 are fonts called composite fonts. Let's start with simple fonts.

11.2.1   Simple fonts

Glyphs in a simple font are selected using a single byte. Each glyph corresponds to a character that has a value from 0 to 255. The mapping between the characters and the glyphs is called the *character encoding*. A Type 1 font can have a special built-in encoding, as is the case for Symbol and Zapf Dingbats. With other fonts, multiple encodings may be available. For instance, the glyph known as *dagger* (†) corresponds with (char) 134 in the encoding known as WinAnsi, aka Western European Latin (code page 1252), a superset of Latin 1 (ISO-8859-1). The same dagger glyph corresponds to different character values in the Adobe Standard encoding (178), Mac Roman encoding (160), and PDF Doc Encoding (129). Figure 11.4 shows the available code pages for three of the fonts used in figure 11.1.

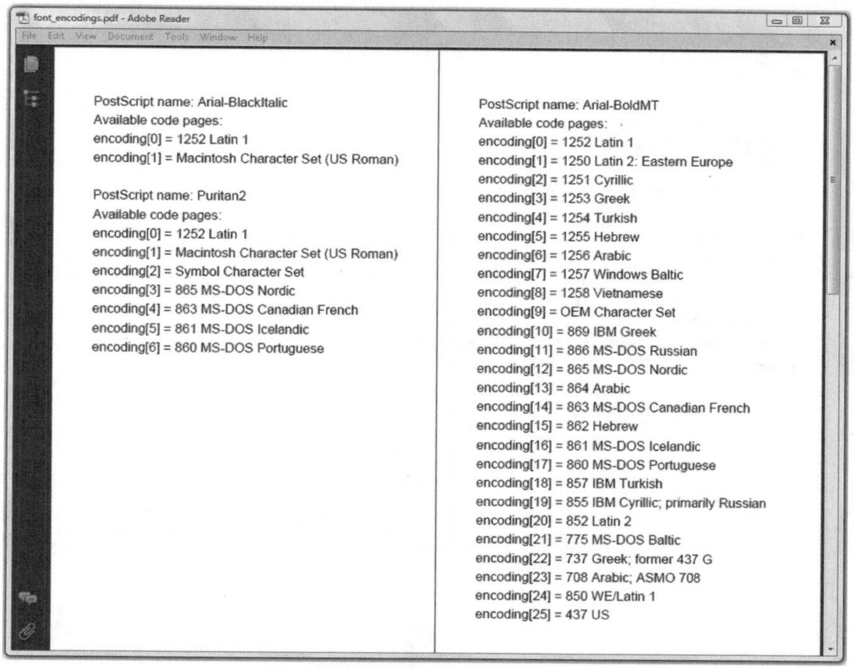

Figure 11.4   Encodings available in different font files

These encoding names were obtained using the `getCodePagesSupported()` method. *Code page* is the traditional IBM term for character encoding.

Listing 11.3   EncodingNames.java

```
String[] encoding = bf.getCodePagesSupported();
for (int i = 0; i < encoding.length; i++) {
  document.add(new Paragraph("encoding[" + i + "] = " + encoding[i]));
}
```

If you use a simple font, it's up to you to decide which encoding to use. Some Western languages (for instance, French) have letters that get a *cedilla* (˛) or a *circumflex* (ˆ). Those letters are in code page 1252 (Latin 1). If you need a *hacek* or a *caron* (ˇ), you should use code page 1250 (Latin 2). Figure 11.5 shows examples using different encodings available in Arial-BoldMT, including examples in Cyrillic (code page 1251) and Greek (code page 1253).

Listing 11.4, which produced what you see in figure 11.5, shows that four different `BaseFont` objects were created using the same font, but with different encodings. If you look at the document properties (see the window on the right in figure 11.5), you'll find four embedded subsets of Arial-BoldMT: one using Ansi encoding (`Cp1252`) and three using a custom encoding.

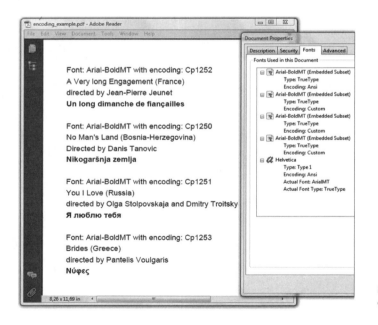

Figure 11.5   Using different encodings of the same font

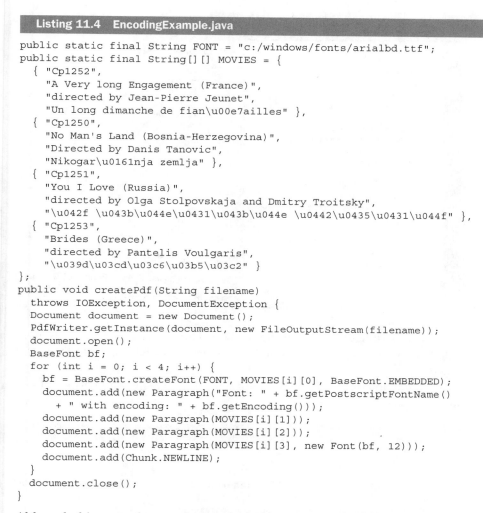

Listing 11.4 EncodingExample.java

```java
public static final String FONT = "c:/windows/fonts/arialbd.ttf";
public static final String[][] MOVIES = {
  { "Cp1252",
    "A Very long Engagement (France)",
    "directed by Jean-Pierre Jeunet",
    "Un long dimanche de fian\u00e7ailles" },
  { "Cp1250",
    "No Man's Land (Bosnia-Herzegovina)",
    "Directed by Danis Tanovic",
    "Nikogar\u0161nja zemlja" },
  { "Cp1251",
    "You I Love (Russia)",
    "directed by Olga Stolpovskaja and Dmitry Troitsky",
    "\u042f \u043b\u044e\u0431\u043b\u044e \u0442\u0435\u0431\u044f" },
  { "Cp1253",
    "Brides (Greece)",
    "directed by Pantelis Voulgaris",
    "\u039d\u03cd\u03c6\u03b5\u03c2" }
};
public void createPdf(String filename)
  throws IOException, DocumentException {
  Document document = new Document();
  PdfWriter.getInstance(document, new FileOutputStream(filename));
  document.open();
  BaseFont bf;
  for (int i = 0; i < 4; i++) {
    bf = BaseFont.createFont(FONT, MOVIES[i][0], BaseFont.EMBEDDED);
    document.add(new Paragraph("Font: " + bf.getPostscriptFontName()
      + " with encoding: " + bf.getEncoding()));
    document.add(new Paragraph(MOVIES[i][1]));
    document.add(new Paragraph(MOVIES[i][2]));
    document.add(new Paragraph(MOVIES[i][3], new Font(bf, 12)));
    document.add(Chunk.NEWLINE);
  }
  document.close();
}
```

Although this example uses characters that are expressed using more than one byte in the source code, the characters will be stored as single bytes inside the PDF file because you're using Arial-BoldMT as a simple font. This is OK if you have a document that consists of only one language, but if you have a document where you constantly need to switch between languages, it would probably be easier if you didn't have to worry about switching the encoding. You can achieve this by using Arial-BoldMT as a *composite font*.

11.2.2 *Composite fonts*

A composite font obtains its glyphs from a font-like object called a CIDFont. A composite font is represented by a font dictionary with subtype /Type0. The Type 0 font is known as the *root font*, and its associated CIDFont is called its *descendant*.

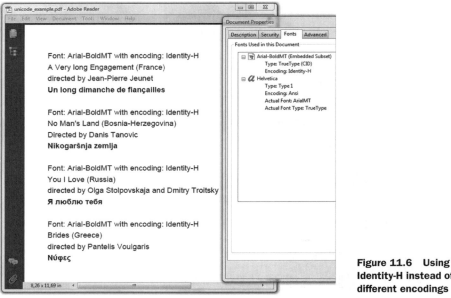

Figure 11.6   Using Identity-H instead of different encodings

Please compare figure 11.6 with figure 11.5. The content of the page is identical, but now Arial-BoldMT only appears once in the list of fonts, as a CIDFont with Identity-H encoding.

The code to create this PDF is almost identical to the code in listing 11.4; you need only to replace the encoding.

Listing 11.5   UnicodeExample.java

```
BaseFont bf;
for (int i = 0; i < 4; i++) {
  bf = BaseFont.createFont(FONT, BaseFont.IDENTITY_H, BaseFont.EMBEDDED);
  document.add(new Paragraph("Font: " + bf.getPostscriptFontName()
    + " with encoding: " + bf.getEncoding()));
  document.add(new Paragraph(MOVIES[i][1]));
  document.add(new Paragraph(MOVIES[i][2]));
  document.add(new Paragraph(MOVIES[i][3], new Font(bf, 12)));
  document.add(Chunk.NEWLINE);
}
```

CIDFonts are collections of glyphs that can't be used directly. They can only be used as a component of a Type 0 font.

CHARACTER COLLECTION

CID stands for *character identifier*. A character identifier is used as the index of the *character collection* to access the glyphs in the font. For simple fonts, you had an index ranging from 0 to 255; in contrast, a CID can be a number from 0 to 65,535. This is a great advantage when dealing with languages that have huge character sets, such as Chinese, Japanese, and Korean.

CMAP

Note that 65,535 is less than the number of code points available in Unicode (1,114,112). The association between the Unicode code points and their CIDs in the font is specified in a *CMap*, which is like a very large code page.

In listing 11.5, you have used the CMap named Identity-H. This is a generic identity mapping for 2-byte CIDs in a horizontal writing system. The same mapping also exists for vertical writing systems: Identity-V. You'll use Identity-V when we discuss vertical writing systems. You'll use other CMaps in an example that uses a CJKFont.

CIDFONT TYPES

As you can see in table 11.2, there are two types of CIDFonts:

- *Type 0 CIDFonts*—These contain glyphs based on the Compact Font Format (CFF; this is a Type 2 font in PostScript terms). If you want to embed such a font, you'll need to buy an .otf file that supports this format. You won't find many free fonts that support this format.
- *Type 2 CIDFonts*—These contain glyphs based on the TrueType format. You can embed such a font if you have a file containing an OpenType font with True-Type outlines (.ttf) or a TrueType collection (.ttc).

Note that the way fonts are named can be very confusing: Type 0 in the context of CID-Fonts has a different meaning than for Type 0 fonts; Type 2 in PostScript has a different meaning than for CIDFonts. Moreover, when you look at the Fonts tab in the Document properties, you'll see that a font with subtype CIDFontType0 is listed as a Type 1 (CID) font.

Font technology isn't simple, but it's described in great detail in ISO-32000-1 and in additional technical notes published by Adobe. Right now, we're more interested in the way iText deals with these different types of fonts.

11.3 Using fonts in iText

In the previous sections, we had a short overview of the different font files that can be used to create a BaseFont object, as well as the different font types one can find inside a PDF file. You saw some examples using different files resulting in different font types, but we've overlooked some types: we haven't discussed Type 3 fonts yet, and we should also take a look at CMaps other than Identity-H. Before we can do this, we must have a look at the different iText classes that deal with fonts.

11.3.1 Overview of the Font classes

In the first column of table 11.3, you can find the most important font classes in iText. You already know Font and BaseFont, but more classes are used under the hood, most of which are subclasses of BaseFont (see the subclass column).

Table 11.3 covers all the file types listed in table 11.1, as well as all the font subtypes listed in table 11.2. You don't need to address classes such as Type1Font and True-TypeFont directly; just as you used the Image class to select the correct image type in the previous chapter, you can let the BaseFont class decide which font class applies.

Table 11.3   iText Font classes

iText class	Subclass	Description
Font	NA	This is the most simple Font class. There are different constructors to create one of the standard Type 1 font types (not embedded). You can also create a Font instance using a BaseFont object and a font size as a parameter.
BaseFont	NA	This is the abstract superclass; the createFont() method returns an instance of one of its subclasses, depending on the font file used.
Type1Font	Yes	You'll get a Type1Font instance if you create a standard Type 1 font, or if you pass an .afm or .pfm file. Standard Type 1 fonts are never embedded; for other Type 1 fonts, it depends on the value of the embedded parameter and the presence of a .pfb file.
Type3Font	Yes	Type 3 fonts are special: they don't come in files. You need to create them using PDF syntax. Type 3 fonts are always embedded.
TrueTypeFont	Yes	In spite of its name, this class isn't only used for TrueType fonts (.ttf), but also for OpenType fonts with TrueType (.ttf) or Type 1 (.otf) outlines. This class will create a TrueType or a Type 1 font subtype in a PDF document.
TrueTypeFontUnicode	Yes	Files with extension .ttf or .otf can also result in this subclass of TrueTypeFont if you use them as composite fonts. So will files with extension .ttc. Inside the PDF, you'll find the subtype /Type0 along with /CIDFontType2 (.ttf and .ttc files) or /CIDFontType0 (.otf files). Contrary to its superclass, TrueTypeFontUnicode ignores the embedded parameter. iText will always embed a subset of the font.
CFFFont	No	OpenType fonts with extension .otf use the Compact Font Format (CFF). Although creating a font using an .otf file results in an instance of TrueTypeFont, it's the CFFFont class that does the work.
CJKFont	Yes	This is a special class for Chinese, Japanese, and Korean fonts for which the metrics files are shipped in a separate JAR. Using a CJK font results in a Type 0 font; the font is never embedded.

Table 11.3 is nevertheless useful for finding out about important implementation differences. For instance, the TrueTypeFontUnicode class always embeds a subset of the font. This reduces the file size.

FONTS AND FILE SIZE

In this example, you use the font arial.ttf to write a document with the text "quick brown fox jumps over the lazy dog" using different settings for the font.

Listing 11.6   FontFileAndSizes.java

```
public static final String FONT = "c:/windows/fonts/arial.ttf";
public static String TEXT
  = "quick brown fox jumps over the lazy dog";
public static String OOOO
  = "ooooo ooooo ooo ooooo oooo ooo oooo ooo";
public static void main(String[] args)
  throws IOException, DocumentException {
  FontFileAndSizes ffs = new FontFileAndSizes();
  BaseFont bf;
  bf = BaseFont.createFont(
    FONT, BaseFont.WINANSI, BaseFont.NOT_EMBEDDED);
  ffs.createPdf(RESULT[0], bf, TEXT);
  bf = BaseFont.createFont(
    FONT, BaseFont.WINANSI, BaseFont.EMBEDDED);
  ffs.createPdf(RESULT[1], bf, TEXT);
  ffs.createPdf(RESULT[2], bf, OOOO);
  bf = BaseFont.createFont(
    FONT, BaseFont.WINANSI, BaseFont.EMBEDDED);
  bf.setCompressionLevel(9);
  ffs.createPdf(RESULT[3], bf, TEXT);
  bf = BaseFont.createFont(
    FONT, BaseFont.WINANSI, BaseFont.EMBEDDED);
  bf.setSubset(false);
  ffs.createPdf(RESULT[4], bf, TEXT);
}
```

❶ ❷ ❸ ❹

If you compare the file sizes of the different files that are created, you'll see that the smallest file is the one for which you didn't embed the font: 2 KB ❶.

In ❷, you embed a subset of the glyphs. You create a PDF containing 27 different glyphs (the 26 letters of the alphabet and the space character) with a file size of 24 KB. If you reduce the number of glyphs to two, the size is only 16 KB. The file size varies depending on the number of different glyphs used.

Setting the compression level as is done in ❸ doesn't save space; the resulting file is also 24 KB.

FAQ   *Can I prevent iText from creating a subset of the font?* Yes, you can. If your requirements demand full embedding of the font, you can use the setSubset(false) method to change the default behavior ❹. This comes at a cost: the resulting file is 414 KB.

Two classes in table 11.3 demand an extra example: Type3Font and CJKFont. See figure 11.7.

11.3.2   *Type 3 fonts*

In a Type 3 font, the glyphs are described using PDF graphics operators. You used these operators in chapter 3 when you wrote to the direct content. You can use this knowledge to create a user-defined font. Figure 11.7 shows custom characters created for the Greek capitals Delta and Sigma. They even use colors. This is how it was created.

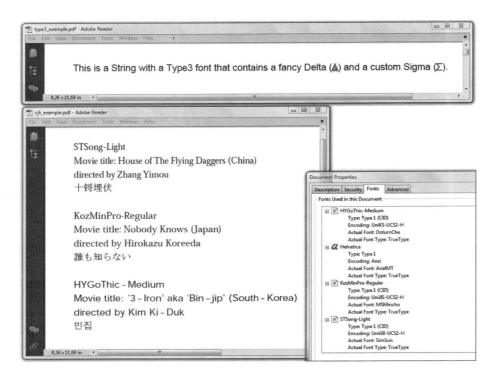

Figure 11.7   Type 3 and CJK font example

Listing 11.7   Type3Example.java

```
Type3Font t3 = new Type3Font(writer, true);      ⟵ Creates BaseFont
PdfContentByte d
  = t3.defineGlyph('D', 600, 0, 0, 600, 700);
d.setColorStroke(new BaseColor(0xFF, 0x00, 0x00));     Creates Delta
d.setColorFill(new GrayColor(0.7f));                   (corresponds to "D")
d.setLineWidth(100);
d.moveTo(5, 5);
d.lineTo(300, 695);
d.lineTo(595, 5);
d.closePathFillStroke();
PdfContentByte s
  = t3.defineGlyph('S', 600, 0, 0, 600, 700);
s.setColorStroke(new BaseColor(0x00, 0x80, 0x80));
s.setLineWidth(100);
s.moveTo(595,5);                                       Creates Sigma
s.lineTo(5, 5);                                        (corresponds to "S")
s.lineTo(300, 350);
s.lineTo(5, 695);
s.lineTo(595, 695);
s.stroke();
Font f = new Font(t3, 12);
```

```
Paragraph p = new Paragraph();
p.add(
  "This is a String with a Type3 font that contains a fancy Delta (");
p.add(new Chunk("D", f));                    ⊲── Uses Delta
p.add(") and a custom Sigma (");
p.add(new Chunk("S", f));                     ⊲── Uses Sigma
p.add(").");
document.add(p);
```

There's no `createFont()` method for Type 3 fonts; instead you need to use the `Type3Font` constructor. The first parameter is the `PdfWriter` to which the glyph descriptions will be written; the second parameter is a `boolean` indicating whether or not you want to use color. If you change this parameter to `false`, the glyphs in figure 11.7 will change into black and white. You define two characters using the `defineGlyph()` method. The first parameter of this method is the character that corresponds to the custom glyph. The other parameters contain the metrics for the glyph: the char advance and the coordinates of the bounding box of the glyph (lower-left X, lower-left Y, upper-right X, and upper-right Y).

The other PDF shown in figure 11.7 contains Chinese, Japanese, and Korean glyphs. This was achieved using the `CJKFont` class.

11.3.3 CJK fonts

If you look at the iText source code repository, you'll see that the directory com/itext-pdf/text/pdf/fonts doesn't only contain fourteen AFM files, but also a series of *.properties and *.cmap files. These files aren't shipped with the iText JAR, but you can download them separately. Look for iTextAsian.jar and add this JAR to your class-path if you want to use CJK fonts. The properties and CMap files in this JAR do not contain the glyph descriptions, which means that iText won't embed these fonts.

> **NOTE** If you open a file using these CJK fonts in Adobe Reader, and if the fonts aren't available, a dialog box will open. You'll be asked if you want to update the Reader. If you agree, the necessary font packs will be downloaded and installed. You'll find the font files in the folder where Adobe Reader was installed; for example, C:/Program Files/Adobe/Reader 9.0/Resource/CID-Font/. These fonts are only licensed for use in combination with Adobe Reader; you're not allowed to use them in any other application (unless you've bought a license from Adobe).

The files from iTextAsian.jar correspond with the values in the second and third column of table 11.4. You can use this table to create a `CJKFont` object. If you want to use a `CJKFont` in a different style, you can add one of the following modifiers to the font name: `Bold`, `Italic`, or `BoldItalic`. For instance, replace `"STSong-Light"` in listing 11.8 with `"STSong-Light,Italic"`, and the title of the movie by Zhang Yimou will be printed in italics.

Table 11.4   CJK fonts in iTextAsian.jar

Language	Font	CMap name
Chinese (simplified)	STSong-Light STSongStd-Light	UniGB-UCS2-H UniGB-UCS2-V
Chinese (traditional)	MHei-Medium MSung-Light MSungStd-Light	UniCNS-UCS2-H UniCNS-USC2-V
Japanese	HeiseiMin-W3 HeiseiKakuGo-W5 KozMinPro-Regular	UniJIS-UCS2-H UniJIS-UCS2-V UniJIS-UCS2-HW-H UniJIS-UCS2-HW-V
Korean	HYGoThic-Medium HYSMyeongJo-Medium HYSMyeongJoStd	UniKS-UCS2-H UniKS-UCS2-V

Listing 11.8   CJKExample.java

```java
public static final String[][] MOVIES = {
  { "STSong-Light", "UniGB-UCS2-H",
    "Movie title: House of The Flying Daggers (China)",
    "directed by Zhang Yimou", "\u5341\u950a\u57cb\u4f0f" },
  { "KozMinPro-Regular", "UniJIS-UCS2-H",
    "Movie title: Nobody Knows (Japan)", "directed by Hirokazu Koreeda",
    "\u8ab0\u3082\u77e5\u3089\u306a\u3044" },
  { "HYGoThic-Medium", "UniKS-UCS2-H",
    "Movie title: '3-Iron' aka 'Bin-jip' (South-Korea)",
    "directed by Kim Ki-Duk", "\ube48\uc9d1" }
};
public void createPdf(String filename) throws IOException, DocumentException
    {
  Document document = new Document();
  PdfWriter.getInstance(document, new FileOutputStream(filename));
  document.open();
  BaseFont bf;
  Font font;
  for (int i = 0; i < 3; i++) {
    bf = BaseFont.createFont(
      MOVIES[i][0], MOVIES[i][1], BaseFont.NOT_EMBEDDED);
    font = new Font(bf, 12);
    document.add(new Paragraph(bf.getPostscriptFontName(), font));
    for (int j = 2; j < 5; j++)
      document.add(new Paragraph(MOVIES[i][j], font));
      document.add(Chunk.NEWLINE);
  }
  document.close();
}
```

Observe that the CMaps come in pairs: one for horizontal writing systems (-H) and one for vertical writing systems (-V).

THE VERTICAL WRITING SYSTEM

In figure 11.7, some Asian movie titles were written from left to right, but some Eastern languages were originally written from top to bottom, in columns from right to left. See, for instance, figure 11.8.

My knowledge of Japanese is limited to "konishiwa" and "arigato," so I've used the title of a movie by Akira Kurosawa and the English translation of a quote from this movie for this example. The PDF shown to the left in figure 11.8 is created using this code.

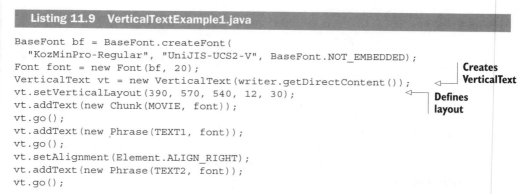

Figure 11.8 The vertical writing system

Listing 11.9   VerticalTextExample1.java

```java
BaseFont bf = BaseFont.createFont(
  "KozMinPro-Regular", "UniJIS-UCS2-V", BaseFont.NOT_EMBEDDED);
Font font = new Font(bf, 20);
VerticalText vt = new VerticalText(writer.getDirectContent());
vt.setVerticalLayout(390, 570, 540, 12, 30);
vt.addText(new Chunk(MOVIE, font));
vt.go();
vt.addText(new Phrase(TEXT1, font));
vt.go();
vt.setAlignment(Element.ALIGN_RIGHT);
vt.addText(new Phrase(TEXT2, font));
vt.go();
```

Creates VerticalText ← (annotation pointing to `VerticalText vt = new VerticalText(...)`)

Defines layout ← (annotation pointing to `vt.setVerticalLayout(...)`)

You use the `VerticalText` object to achieve this. It's very similar to the `ColumnText` object, but instead of defining a simple column, you define a layout. The first two parameters define the coordinates where the column has to start, in this case (390, 570). The second parameter defines the height of each column: 540. Then follows the maximum number of lines that may be written (12) and the leading. Observe that the leading is no longer the vertical distance between two horizontal baselines, but the horizontal distance between two vertical lines. Likewise, you also have to turn your head 90 degrees to the right if you want to set the alignment: `ALIGN_RIGHT` aligns the column to the bottom.

The PDF on the right in figure 11.8 is created in a slightly different way.

Listing 11.10   VerticalTextExample2.java

```java
public void createPdf(String filename)
  throws IOException, DocumentException {
...
  BaseFont bf = BaseFont.createFont(
```

```
    "KozMinPro-Regular", "Identity-V", BaseFont.NOT_EMBEDDED);
  Font font = new Font(bf, 20);
  VerticalText vt = new VerticalText(writer.getDirectContent());
  vt.setVerticalLayout(390, 570, 540, 12, 30);
  font = new Font(bf, 20);
  vt.addText(new Phrase(convertCIDs(TEXT1), font));
  vt.go();
  vt.setAlignment(Element.ALIGN_RIGHT);
  vt.addText(new Phrase(convertCIDs(TEXT2), font));
  vt.go();
  ...
}
public String convertCIDs(String text) {
  char cid[] = text.toCharArray();
  for (int k = 0; k < cid.length; ++k) {
  char c = cid[k];
  if (c == '\n')
    cid[k] = '\uff00';
  else
    cid[k] = (char) (c - ' ' + 8720);
  }
  return new String(cid);
}
```

You still use `KozMinPro-Regular`, but now you use `Identity-V`. This font contains Western characters that are rotated 90 degrees clockwise, as shown in figure 11.8. You use the custom-made formula in the `convertCIDs()` method to translate the normal characters into rotated characters. This example demonstrates more or less what needs to be done when you're confronted with `Strings` in different encodings.

USING OTHER CMAPS

The *UCS2* in the CMap names listed in table 11.4 stands for Universal Character Set. There's also a JAR named iTextAsianCmaps.jar with the contents of the com/itextpdf/text/pdf/cmaps/ directory. These CMaps can be used in combination with the `PdfEncodings` class to convert a `String` in a specific encoding to a `String` with 2-byte CIDs.

For example, if you have a `char[]` encoded in the GB 18030-2000 character set, you need to load the CMap GBK2K-H and convert it to a sequence of Identity-H CIDs like this:

```
PdfEncodings.loadCmap("GBK2K-H", PdfEncodings.CRLF_CID_NEWLINE);
byte text[] = my_GB_encoded_text;
String cid = PdfEncodings.convertCmap("GBK2K-H", text);
BaseFont bf = BaseFont.createFont(
  "STSong-Light", BaseFont.IDENTITY_H, BaseFont.NOT_EMBEDDED);
Paragraph p = new Paragraph(cid, new Font(bf, 14));
document.add(p);
```

We've discussed Asian languages written vertically. Now let's find out how to write Semitic languages such as Hebrew and Arabic; these are written from right to left.

11.3.4 *Writing from right to left*

Figure 11.9 shows an XML file with the text "Say Peace in all languages" in English, Arabic, and Hebrew. The XML is encoded using UTF-8, and in the top left of the figure it's

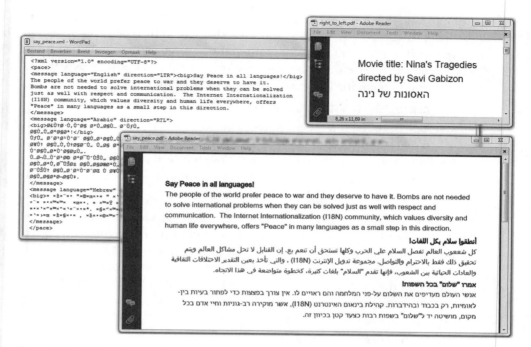

Figure 11.9 Writing from right to left

opened in WordPad, which assumes it's plain text, hence the strange characters. You'll use this XML file to create the PDF document shown in the foreground. But you'll start by creating the PDF showing the movie title *Nina's Tragedies* in Hebrew.

Writing from right to left is only supported when using `ColumnText` or `PdfPCell` objects.

RUN DIRECTION IN COLUMNTEXT OBJECTS

If you don't know Hebrew, you'll probably try to read the glyphs of the Hebrew movie title from left to right. You see four glyphs, a space, two glyphs, a space, and the rest of the title. Let's compare this with the original `String` here.

Listing 11.11   RightToLeftExample.java

```java
BaseFont bf = BaseFont.createFont(
  "c:/windows/fonts/arial.ttf", BaseFont.IDENTITY_H, true);
Font font = new Font(bf, 14);
document.add(new Paragraph("Movie title: Nina's Tragedies"));
document.add(new Paragraph("directed by Savi Gabizon"));
ColumnText column = new ColumnText(writer.getDirectContent());
column.setSimpleColumn(36, 770, 569, 36);
column.setRunDirection(PdfWriter.RUN_DIRECTION_RTL);          ← Sets run direction
column.addElement(new Paragraph(
  "\u05d4\u05d0\u05e1\u05d5\u05e0\u05d5\u05ea "
  + "\u05e9\u05dc \u05e0\u05d9\u05e0\u05d4", font));           Adds paragraph to column
column.go();
```

The String that is passed to the ColumnText object includes seven 2-byte characters, a space, two characters, a space, and four characters. In reality, the first glyph on the title line in figure 11.9 is \u05d4, followed by \u05e0, and so on: iText has added the characters in reverse order because you changed the run direction with the setRun-Direction() method. This method accepts one of the following options:

- RUN_DIRECTION_DEFAULT—Uses the default direction
- RUN_DIRECTION_LTR—Uses bidirectional reordering with a left-to-right preferential run direction
- RUN_DIRECTION_NO_BIDI—Doesn't use bidirectional reordering
- RUN_DIRECTION_RTL—Uses bidirectional reordering with a right-to-left preferential run direction

The best way to understand what bidirectional means is to look at the message of peace in figure 11.9. In this text, the term I18N (Internationalization) is used. If you choose RTL as the run direction, you don't want this term to be reordered as N81I; you want to preserve the order of the Latin text. Choosing the option RUN_DIRECTION_RTL means that the characters are reordered from right to left by preference, but if Latin text is encountered, the left-to-right order is preserved. The PDF containing the message of peace was created using a PdfPTable.

RUN DIRECTION IN PDFPCELL OBJECTS
You can use the technique explained in chapter 9 to convert the XML file into a PDF document. This is what to do when an opening or a closing tag is encountered.

Listing 11.12   SayPeace.java

```java
public void startElement(
  String uri, String localName, String qName, Attributes attributes)
  throws SAXException {
  if ("message".equals(qName)) {
    buf = new StringBuffer();
    cell = new PdfPCell();
    cell.setBorder(PdfPCell.NO_BORDER);
    if ("RTL".equals(attributes.getValue("direction"))) {
      cell.setRunDirection(PdfWriter.RUN_DIRECTION_RTL);
    }
  }
  else if ("pace".equals(qName)) {
    table = new PdfPTable(1);
    table.setWidthPercentage(100);
  }
}
public void endElement(String uri, String localName, String qName)
  throws SAXException {
  ...
  if ("message".equals(qName)) {
    Paragraph p = new Paragraph(strip(buf), f);
    p.setAlignment(Element.ALIGN_LEFT);
    cell.addElement(p);
```

```
    table.addCell(cell);;
    buf = new StringBuffer();
  }
  else if ("pace".equals(qName)) {
    try {
      document.add(table);
    } catch (DocumentException e) {
      throw new ExceptionConverter(e);
    }
  }
}
```

The Arabic text produced by this example looks all right, but it's important to understand that iText has done a lot of work behind the scenes. Not every character in the XML file was rendered as a separate glyph. Some characters or glyphs were combined and replaced.

To understand what happens, we need to talk about diacritics and ligatures.

11.3.5 Advanced typography

If you want to see a Thai cowboy movie about a poor hero who falls in love with a girl from the upper classes, you should buy a ticket for *Tears of the Black Tiger* at the Foobar Film Festival. Figure 11.10 shows the poster featuring the protagonists.

As you can see in the figure, the Thai title is also printed:

```
public static final String MOVIE =
  "\u0e1f\u0e49\u0e32\u0e17\u0e30\u0e25\u0e32\u0e22\u0e42\u0e08\u0e23";
```

This `String` is written twice, using two different fonts: Angsana New and Arial Unicode MS.

```
public static final String[] FONTS = {
  "c:/windows/fonts/angsa.ttf",
  "c:/windows/fonts/arialuni.ttf"
};
```

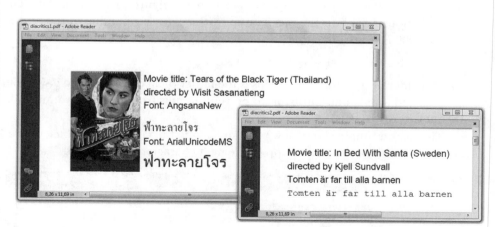

Figure 11.10 Using diacritics, ancillary glyphs added to a letter

This shows how the title was added to the `Document`.

```java
for (int i = 0; i < 2; i++) {
  bf = BaseFont.createFont(
    FONTS[i], BaseFont.IDENTITY_H, BaseFont.EMBEDDED);
  document.add(new Paragraph("Font: " + bf.getPostscriptFontName()));
  font = new Font(bf, 20);
  document.add(new Paragraph(MOVIE, font));
}
```

If you look at the poster, you'll see that there's a special curl above the first character. This curl is a diacritical mark.

DIACRITICAL MARKS

You've used diacritical marks before. In figure 11.5, you'll find a cedilla, a hacek, and so on, but there's a difference between listing 11.4 and listing 11.13. When you printed c cedilla (ç), you only used one Unicode character (\u00e7). In listing 11.13, the diacritical mark is a separate character: \u0e49 has to be combined with \u0e1f.

That's unusual for Western languages. Suppose that you want to type the French word être (to be) on a French keyboard (AZERTY instead of QWERTY); you'd need to hit five different keys: ^etre. If you save a text file with this `String`, only four bytes would be used, because there's a character value for the *e* with a circumflex.

In other languages that use diacritics more frequently, it's common to store both characters separately. For instance: ^etre or e^tre instead of être. That's what happened in the Thai example. The fonts Angsana New and Arial Unicode MS used a negative character advance for this glyph to create the illusion that the two characters are actually one.

CHANGING THE CHARACTER ADVANCE

The character advance is stored in the font's metrics, but you can change this value in the iText `BaseFont` object. The second example in figure 11.10 is somewhat artificial, but it demonstrates how the mechanism works. The original title of the best Swedish film of 1999 is written like this:

```java
public static final String MOVIE = "Tomten ¨ar far till alla barnen";
```

The title literally means "Santa Claus is the father of all children," but it was translated into "In bed with Santa," probably to prevent parents from bringing young children to the movie.

The next example shows how you can change the character advance of the ¨ character so that it's positioned on top of the next character that is added.

```java
BaseFont bf = BaseFont.createFont(
  FONTS[0], BaseFont.CP1252, BaseFont.EMBEDDED);
Font font = new Font(bf, 12);
```

Title in Arial

```
bf.setCharAdvance('"', -100);
document.add(new Paragraph(MOVIE, font));
bf = BaseFont.createFont(
  FONTS[1], BaseFont.CP1252, BaseFont.EMBEDDED);
bf.setCharAdvance('"', 0);
font = new Font(bf, 12);
document.add(new Paragraph(MOVIE, font));
```

Title in Arial

Title in Courier

The width of the umlaut (or dieresis) glyph is 333 units in Arial (glyph space). To get the umlaut or dieresis above the letter that follows the diacritical mark, you change the advance to a negative value.

The value used here is ideal for the letter *a*, but there's no guarantee that it will fit perfectly above the other vowels, because they may have a different width and character advance. Arial is a *proportional font,* meaning that different glyphs have different widths. This problem doesn't occur when you use a *fixed-width* or *monospaced font* such as Courier. Every character in Courier has the same width (600 units in glyph space). To make the diacritical mark fit above the next character, it's sufficient to set its advance to 0.

CHANGING THE CHARACTER WIDTH

In listing 11.15, a proportional font is changed into a fixed width font. You use the method getWidths() to get an array containing the widths of every character in the font (measured in glyph space). You then change the width to 600 units for every glyph with a width greater than 0.

Listing 11.15   Monospace.java

```
BaseFont bf3 = BaseFont.createFont(
  "c:/windows/fonts/arialbd.ttf", BaseFont.CP1252, BaseFont.EMBEDDED);
Font font3 = new Font(bf3, 12);
int widths[] = bf3.getWidths();
for (int k = 0; k < widths.length; ++k) {
  if (widths[k] != 0)
    widths[k] = 600;
}
bf3.setForceWidthsOutput(true);
```

You force iText to use the changed widths with the method setForceWidthsOutput(). This feature is very useful if you want to print a Chinese text where every ideogram needs to have the same width, but it's not very elegant when you use it for Western fonts. If you want to use it to attribute more space to every character to get t h i s e f f e c t, you should use the setCharacterSpacing() method.

Listing 11.16   ExtraCharSpace.java

```
Chunk chunk = new Chunk(MOVIE, font1);
chunk.setCharacterSpacing(10);
document.add(new Paragraph(chunk));
```

Ligatures are another example involving advanced typography.

LIGATURES

A ligature occurs when a combination of two or more characters is considered to be one and only one glyph. A letter with a diacritic isn't usually called a ligature, but the same principle applies. One of the ligatures we all know—though we may have forgotten it's a ligature—is the & character. The ampersand sign was originally a ligature for the Latin word *et* (meaning *and*). Figure 11.11 shows a movie title with ligatures in Danish and Arabic.

As is the case with diacritics, you usually don't have to worry about ligatures in languages using Latin text. Usually, you'll use only one character for the ligature:

```
document.add(
  new Paragraph("K\u00e6rlighed ved f\u00f8rste hik", font));
```

If you want to use more than one character, you'll need to write code that makes the ligature for you. Suppose you want to add a `String` like this:

```
document.add(
  new Paragraph(ligaturize("Kaerlighed ved f/orste hik"), font));
```

You need to write your own `ligaturize()` method as is done next.

Listing 11.17   Ligatures1.java

```java
public String ligaturize(String s) {
  int pos;
  while ((pos = s.indexOf("ae")) > -1) {
    s = s.substring(0, pos) + '\u00e6' + s.substring(pos + 2);
  }
  while ((pos = s.indexOf("/o")) > -1) {
    s = s.substring(0, pos) + '\u00f8' + s.substring(pos + 2);
  }
  return s;
}
```

The combination "ae" is changed into "æ", the combination "/o" into "ø". Similar code, but much more complex than this small snippet, is present in iText to make Arabic ligatures.

Figure 11.11   Using ligatures, joining different glyphs into one

WRITING ARABIC

In figure 11.11, the Arabic translation of the movie title *Lawrence of Arabia* has been added three times. The first version of the title is wrong because the glyphs are added from left to right, whereas Arabic is written from right to left (see section 11.3.4). In the second version, the glyphs are written in reverse order, but a space was added between all characters. No ligatures are made, so the title isn't rendered correctly. Compare this line with the next one. The omission of the extra spaces is the only difference, but if you look closely, you can see that some character combinations were replaced by another glyph. That was done by the iText class `ArabicLigaturizer`.

If you study listing 11.18, you can see that you don't have to do anything special to start up the `ArabicLigaturizer`. If the run direction is RTL and if iText detects Unicode characters in the Arabic character set, this is done automatically.

Listing 11.18   Ligatures2.java

```
public static final String MOVIE =
  "\u0644\u0648\u0631\u0627\u0646\u0633 "
  + "\u0627\u0644\u0639\u0631\u0628";
public static final String MOVIE_WITH_SPACES =
  "\u0644 \u0648 \u0631 \u0627 \u0646 \u0633  "
  + " \u0627 \u0644 \u0639 \u0631 \u0628";
...
document.add(new Paragraph("Wrong: " + MOVIE, font));
ColumnText column = new ColumnText(writer.getDirectContent());
column.setSimpleColumn(36, 730, 569, 36);
column.setRunDirection(PdfWriter.RUN_DIRECTION_RTL);
column.addElement(new Paragraph("Wrong: " + MOVIE_WITH_SPACES, font));
column.addElement(new Paragraph(MOVIE, font));
column.go();
```

Note that the `setRunDirection()` method only exists for the classes `PdfPCell` and `ColumnText`. Both classes also have a `setArabicOption()` method to tell iText how to deal with vowels in Arabic. These are the possible values for the parameter:

- `ColumnText.AR_NOVOWEL`—Eliminates Arabic vowels
- `ColumnText.AR_COMPOSEDTASHKEEL`—Composes the Tashkeel on the ligatures
- `ColumnText.AR_LIG`—Does extra double ligatures

None of these options has any effect on this example, but it can be useful information if you need advanced Arabic support.

This is highly specialized functionality; it's time to return to everyday use of iText and look at some classes that make working with fonts easier.

11.4   *Automating font creation and selection*

In this section, you'll add two classes that make it easier for you to select a font: the `FontFactory` and the `FontSelector` classes.

When you created `Font` objects in part 1, you mostly used one of the standard Type 1 fonts. In this chapter, you've always created `Font` objects in two steps. For example,

```
BaseFont bf = BaseFont.createFont(
  "c:/windows/fonts/arial.ttf", BaseFont.CP1252, BaseFont.EMBEDDED);
Font font = new Font(bf, 12);
```

One of the major disadvantages of this approach is that you need to pass a path to a font program. I'm working on Windows XP and Vista, and I know that the font arial.tff is present in the directory c:/windows/fonts/. But this code won't work if you try to run it on a Mac or a Linux machine. You may need to look for the font in the directory /Library/Fonts/ or /usr/share/X11/fonts/.

It would be nice if there were a more generic way to select fonts to make your code platform-independent. The FontFactory class can help you.

11.4.1   *Getting a Font from the FontFactory*

The FontFactory class has a series of static getFont() methods that allow you to get a Font object without explicitly creating a BaseFont instance:

```
Font font = FontFactory.createFont(
  "c:/windows/fonts/arial.ttf", BaseFont.CP1252, BaseFont.EMBEDDED, 12);
```

This doesn't solve the platform (in)dependence problem yet. But you should be able do something like this:

```
Font font = FontFactory.getFont("Times-Roman");
document.add(new Paragraph("Times-Roman", font));
Font fontbold = FontFactory.getFont("Times-Roman", 12, Font.BOLD);
document.add(new Paragraph("Times-Roman, Bold", fontbold));
```

This code snippet will work because Times-Roman is one of the font families that is supported by default by the font factory; so are all the standard Type 1 fonts. It won't work with other fonts, unless they are registered.

REGISTERING A FONT

You can register an individual font like this:

```
FontFactory.register("c:/windows/fonts/garabd.ttf", "my_bold_font");
Font myBoldFont = FontFactory.getFont("my_bold_font");
```

This code registers the font Garamond Bold and gives it the alias my_bold_font. From now on, you can use this custom name to get the font from the factory.

The alias parameter is optional. You can also use one of the names that is stored in the font to retrieve a Font object. This bit of code shows how to read not only the PostScript name, but also the full font names in different languages.

Listing 11.19   FontFactory.java

```
BaseFont bf = myBoldFont.getBaseFont();
document.add(new Paragraph(bf.getPostscriptFontName(), myBoldFont));
String[][] name = bf.getFullFontName();
for (int i = 0; i < name.length; i++) {
  document.add(new Paragraph(name[i][3] + " (" + name[i][0]
    + "; " + name[i][1] + "; " + name[i][2] + ")"));
```

```
}
Font myBoldFont2 = FontFactory.getFont("Garamond vet");
document.add(new Paragraph("Garamond Vet", myBoldFont2));
```

The output contains the following entries:

```
Garamond Bold (3; 1; 1033)
Garamond Gras (3; 1; 1036)
Garamond Vet (3; 1; 1043)
```

If i is an index of the two-dimensional name array, you're interested in name[i][3], because that's the String you can use to get the font from the FontFactory. In listing 11.19, the Dutch name of the font "Garamond Vet" is used. "Garamond Bold", "Garamond Gras", or any other of the names in the name array would also work.

> **NOTE** The other values in the array only make sense for fonts that contain a *cmap* (not to be confused with the CMap mapping Unicode characters to CIDs from section 11.2.2). A cmap is an internal structure that maps character codes directly to glyph descriptions. A cmap table may contain one or more subtables that represent multiple encodings intended for use on different platforms. Each subtable is identified by two numbers that represent a combination of a platform ID (name[i][0]) and a platform-specific encoding ID (name[i][1]). There's also a language id (name[i][2]). You can find a full overview of all these codes in naming table pages published on the developer pages at adobe.com and microsoft.com (see appendix B.3.2 for the full URLs). If you look up the IDs from the output of listing 11.19, you'll see that 3 is the platform ID for Microsoft encoding and that the encoding ID 1 means Unicode BMP only. The language IDs are expressed in hexadecimal, but if you convert them to decimal, you'll find out that 1033 stands for English, 1036 for French, and 1043 for Dutch.

You probably won't use the register() method directly; instead you could register a complete directory.

REGISTERING A FONT DIRECTORY

The examples in this book come with a resources directory; in this directory, there's a fonts folder. You can register all the fonts in this folder at once like this:

```
FontFactory.registerDirectory("resources/fonts");
```

This method will call the register() method for every font file in the directory. You can list all the available names like this:

```
for (String f : FontFactory.getRegisteredFonts()) {
  document.add(new Paragraph(
    f, FontFactory.getFont(f, "", BaseFont.EMBEDDED)));
}
```

One of the fonts in the list that is produced has a very cryptic name: cmr10. You used this font in section 11.1.2, and you know that the real font name is Computer Modern Regular. If you want to use the full name as an alias, you can change the PostScript name of the BaseFont like this:

```
Font cmr10 = FontFactory.getFont("cmr10");
cmr10.getBaseFont().setPostscriptFontName("Computer Modern Regular");
Font computerModern = FontFactory.getFont(
  "Computer Modern Regular", "", BaseFont.EMBEDDED);
document.add(new Paragraph("Computer Modern", computerModern));
```

This is an interesting way to get fonts that are shipped with an application, but what you really want is to register all the system fonts, be it on Windows, Mac, or Linux.

REGISTERING SYSTEM FONTS

The `registerDirectories()` method will attempt to register all the system fonts at once:

```
FontFactory.registerDirectories();
```

This method calls the method `registerDirectory()` using the following paths as a parameter:

- c:/windows/fonts—A possible font directory on Windows
- c:/winnt/fonts—A possible font directory on Windows
- d:/windows/fonts—A possible font directory on Windows
- d:/winnt/fonts—A possible font directory on Windows
- /Library/Fonts—A possible font directory on OS X
- /System/Library/Fonts—A possible font directory on OS X
- /usr/share/X11/fonts—A possible font directory on UNIX/Linux
- /usr/X/lib/X11/fonts—A possible font directory on UNIX/Linux
- /usr/openwin/lib/X11/fonts—A possible font directory on UNIX/Linux
- /usr/share/fonts—A possible font directory on UNIX/Linux
- /usr/X11R6/lib/X11/fonts—A possible font directory on UNIX/Linux

The `registerDirectory()` method for the Linux directories is used with an extra `boolean` that tells iText also to scan the subdirectories.

> **NOTE**   `registerDirectories()` is an "expensive" method if you have a lot of fonts on your system. Don't use it in a servlet because it takes time to scan the font directories; it's better to use it when the JVM starts up, so that you can use the font factory throughout your web application.

If you list the available font names now, you'll see that the list is much longer. You can also list the font families.

FONT FAMILIES

The first font you registered was Garamond Bold. This font belongs to a family of three different fonts: Garamond (gara.ttf), Garamond-Italic (garait.ttf), and Garamond-Bold (garabd.ttf). You can list the names of all the families just like you listed the names of all the individual fonts.

```
for (String f : FontFactory.getRegisteredFamilies()) {
  document.add(new Paragraph(f));
}
```

Font family names are very useful when you want to switch between styles. Instead of using the full font name as the first parameter—for instance, Garamond-Italic—you could use the family name with an extra parameter for the style:

```
Font garamondItalic = FontFactory.getFont(
  "Garamond", BaseFont.WINANSI, BaseFont.EMBEDDED, 12, Font.ITALIC);
document.add(new Paragraph("Garamond-Italic", garamondItalic));
```

Normally, the font factory would look for a font named "Garamond" and find the font gara.ttf. But if you pass an extra parameter saying you want an italic font, iText will search for an italic font in the Garamond family. You've registered all the system fonts, so if garait.ttf is present on your system, the font factory will return Garamond-Italic.

> **NOTE** If you look inside iText, you'll see that `FontFactory` delegates most of the work to the `FontFactoryImp` class. This class implements the `FontProvider` interface, which is the interface you implemented when you converted HTML to PDF in chapter 9. The mechanism to switch between styles within the same font family is used frequently by `HTMLWorker` when the font family is defined with the font tag and the style with em, i, strong, or b tags.

We've solved several problems with the `FontFactory` class: you can make the creation of fonts platform-independent, and you can easily switch between styles using only the family name of the font. In the next section, we'll solve another problem.

If you have a text that contains characters from many different languages, you have to switch between fonts, because there's not a single font that contains every possible glyph for every possible language. Up until now, you've manually selected different fonts for different languages. In the next section, you'll let iText select the appropriate fonts.

11.4.2 *Automatic font selection*

Imagine that you need to write text in Times-Roman, but the text contains a number of Chinese glyphs. The document in the background of figure 11.12 shows such an example. It lists the names of the protagonists in the movie *Hero* by Zhang Yimou.

It would be possible to construct this sentence using different Chunks or Phrases, with the English text in Times-Roman and the Chinese names in a traditional Chinese

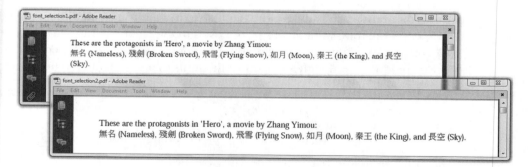

Figure 11.12   Automatic font selection

font. But there's an easier way; you can use the `FontSelector` class to do this work for you.

Listing 11.20   FontSelectionExample.java

```
public static final String TEXT
    = "These are the protagonists in 'Hero', a movie by Zhang Yimou:\n"
    + "\u7121\u540d (Nameless), \u6b98\u528d (Broken Sword), "
    + "\u98db\u96ea (Flying Snow), \u5982\u6708 (Moon), "
    + "\u79e6\u738b (the King), and \u9577\u7a7a (Sky).";
...
FontSelector selector = new FontSelector();
selector.addFont(
    FontFactory.getFont(FontFactory.TIMES_ROMAN, 12));                ❶    Creates
selector.addFont(FontFactory.getFont("MSung-Light",                        selector and
    "UniCNS-UCS2-H", BaseFont.NOT_EMBEDDED));                        ❷    adds fonts
Phrase ph = selector.process(TEXT);                             ⟵— Processes String
document.add(new Paragraph(ph));
```

What happens in here? You have a `String` containing characters referring to glyphs from the Latin alphabet as well as to Chinese glyphs. You pass this `String` to a `FontSe-lector` object for processing, and the `FontSelector` will look at the `String`, character by character. If the corresponding glyph is available in the first font that was added (in this case, Times-Roman), the character is added to a `Chunk` with the Times-Roman font. If the character isn't available, the selector looks it up in the next font that was added (in this case, MSung-Light). The selector goes on until the glyph is found, or until there are no fonts left.

> **NOTE**   The order in which the fonts are added to the selector is important. If you switch ❶ and ❷ in listing 11.20, you get the PDF shown in the foreground of figure 11.12. All glyphs are printed in MSung-Light, because that font also has descriptions for Western characters.

Figure 11.13 shows an XML file with the word *Peace* in different languages. This XML was converted to PDF using iText. In this example, you see different mechanisms at work: font selection, but also bidirectional writing and ligatures.

If you try this example (named `Peace`) on your own system, you'll see that some translations for the word Peace are missing or wrong. If you see a question mark, it's because the translation is unknown. You'll also find a question mark in the XML file. (If you know the translation, feel free to post it to the iText mailing list.)

If you see an empty space where a translation was expected, it's because the font selector couldn't find the glyph in any of the fonts that were added to the selector.

> **FAQ**   *I've tried all the examples in the book, but as soon as I change the text into a* `String` *in language X, the text disappears. Why?* That's because the glyphs that are needed can't be found in the font. You are either using the wrong encoding, or the glyphs just aren't there. Try using another encoding or another font.

Some of the translations are rendered incorrectly because iText doesn't have support for ligatures for Hindic languages. Just as we have the `ArabicLigaturizer`, we need a

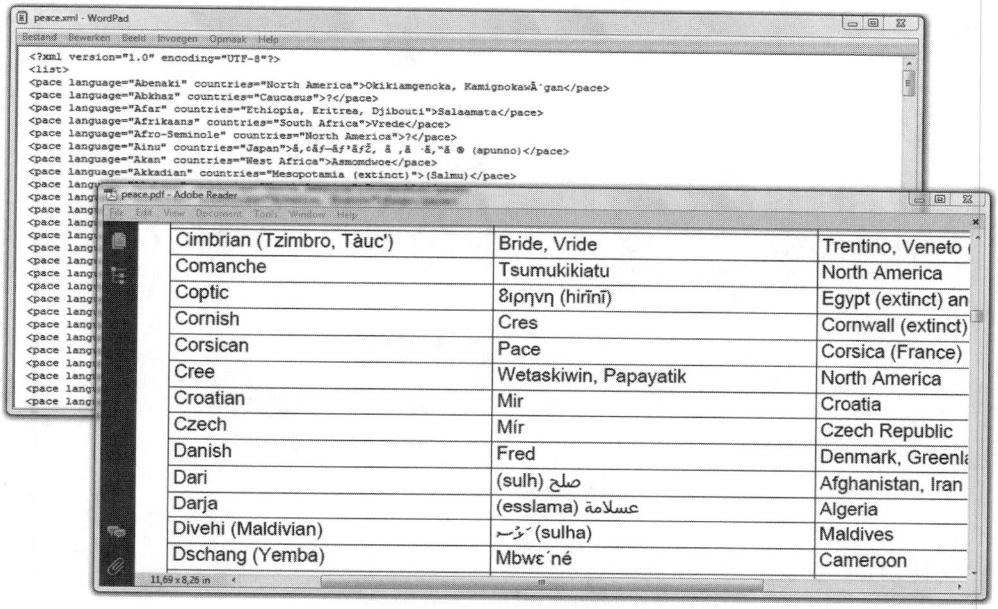

Figure 11.13   Using iText for different languages

HindicLigaturizer, but so far we haven't found anyone who could write such a class for iText. Maybe that's something for the third edition of *iText in Action*.

Let's take a look at what we've covered in this chapter.

11.5   Summary

First we approached fonts from three different angles:

- *Table 11.1*—Lists the different types of font files that can be used to create a BaseFont object
- *Table 11.2*—Lists the different font types that can be stored in a PDF file, divided into two groups: simple fonts and composite fonts
- *Table 11.3*—Lists the different font classes that are available in iText

After looking at examples for every type that was discussed, we studied different writing systems: vertical text, written in columns from right to left, and horizontal text written from right to left. We also looked at some advanced typography issues, such as using diacritical marks and making ligatures.

Finally, you learned ways to make the font creation and selection easier. With the FontFactory class, you learned how to make your applications platform independent; with the FontSelector class you delegated the font selection process to iText.

We'll conclude this part about essential iText skills with a chapter about protecting your documents by using encryption and digital signatures.

Protecting your PDF

This chapter covers

- Providing metadata
- Compressing and decompressing PDFs
- Encrypting documents
- Adding digital signatures

You have created many different documents containing data, such as movies, directors, and movie screenings taken from a database, but you haven't added any information about the owner of this data. You could make sure that people find out who created the document by adding metadata.

You've also peeked inside some of the PDF files you created, and you've seen that the content of a document is compressed by default. You could use iText to decompress content streams to read the PDF syntax that makes up a page or a form XObject.

For confidential documents, you'll want to protect the document. To achieve this, we're going to discuss how to encrypt content streams. You can do this using a password, or you can encrypt a PDF using a public key. Only the person who owns the corresponding private key will be able to open the document.

Digital signatures work the other way around: you sign a document using your private key, and whoever reads your document can use your public key (or the root certificate of a certificate authority) to make sure the document wasn't forged by somebody else.

But let's begin with the beginning, and start by adding metadata.

12.1   Adding metadata

There are two ways to store metadata inside a PDF document. The original way was to store a limited number of keys and values in a special dictionary; a newer way is to embed the data as an XML stream inside the PDF. Let's discuss both to find out the difference.

12.1.1   The info dictionary

In figure 12.1, the document properties from the Hello World example you made in chapter 1 are compared to a new Hello World example with metadata added.

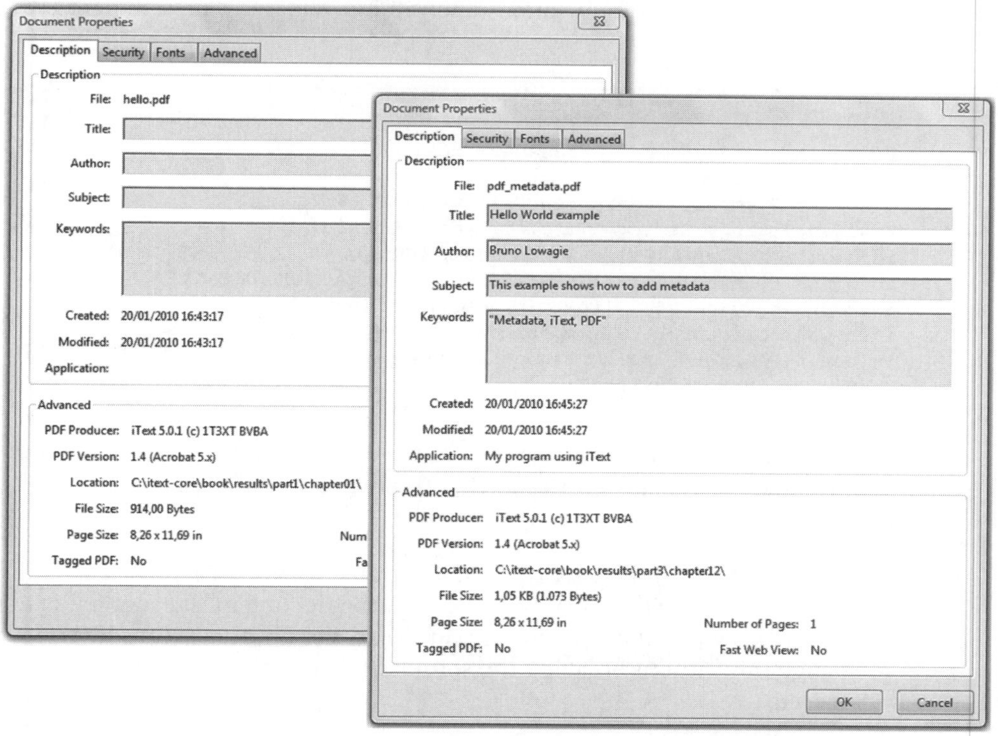

Figure 12.1   Metadata in PDF files

The metadata shown in the window to the right was added using this code:

Listing 12.1   MetadataPdf.java

```
document.addTitle("Hello World example");
document.addAuthor("Bruno Lowagie");
document.addSubject("This example shows how to add metadata");
document.addKeywords("Metadata, iText, PDF");
document.addCreator("My program using iText");
```

This code snippet adds the title of the document, its author, the subject, some key-words, and the application that was used to create the PDF as metadata. If you look inside the PDF, you see that this information is stored in a dictionary, named the *info dictionary*, along with the creation date, modification date, and PDF producer. This is the limited set of metadata key-value pairs that is supported in PDF.

Three metadata entries are filled in automatically by iText (and you can't change them). If you create a PDF from scratch, iText will use the time on the clock of your local computer as the creation and modification date. If you manipulate a PDF with PdfStamper, only the modification date will be changed. The same goes for the producer name.

Listing 12.2   MetadataPdf.java

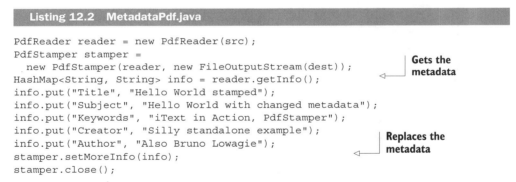

```
PdfReader reader = new PdfReader(src);
PdfStamper stamper =
  new PdfStamper(reader, new FileOutputStream(dest));    ⟵  Gets the
HashMap<String, String> info = reader.getInfo();              metadata
info.put("Title", "Hello World stamped");
info.put("Subject", "Hello World with changed metadata");
info.put("Keywords", "iText in Action, PdfStamper");
info.put("Creator", "Silly standalone example");
info.put("Author", "Also Bruno Lowagie");            ⟵  Replaces the
stamper.setMoreInfo(info);                                 metadata
stamper.close();
```

With the getInfo() method, you can retrieve the keys and values as Strings. You can add, remove, or replace entries in the HashMap, and put the altered metadata in the PDF using setMoreInfo().

> **FAQ**   *Can I change the producer info?* The value for the PDF producer tells you which version of iText was used to create the document. It's also a way to tell the end users of the document that iText was used to create it. You can't change this without breaking the software license that allows you to use iText for free.

A dictionary is a PDF object, and the values that are stored in this dictionary are also PDF objects. PDF viewers such as Adobe Reader don't have any problem interpreting these objects, but applications that aren't PDF-aware can't find or read this meta-information. The *Extensible Metadata Platform* (XMP) was introduced to solve this problem.

12.1.2 *The Extensible Metadata Platform (XMP)*

The Extensible Metadata Platform provides a standard format for the creation, processing, and interchange of metadata. An XMP stream can be embedded in a number of popular file formats (TIFF, JPEG, PNG, GIF, PDF, HTML, and so on) without breaking their readability by non-XMP-aware applications.

The XMP specification defines a model that can be used with any defined set of metadata items. It also defines particular schemas; for instance, the Dublin Core schema provides a set of commonly used properties such as the title of the document, a description, and so on. For PDF files, there's a PDF schema with information about the keywords, the PDF version, and the PDF producer. This way, an application that can't interpret PDF syntax can still extract the metadata from the file by detecting and parsing the XML that is embedded inside the PDF. What follows is an example of such an XMP metadata stream.

Listing 12.3   xmp.xml

```xml
<?xpacket begin="?" id="W5M0MpCehiHzreSzNTczkc9d"?>
<x:xmpmeta xmlns:x="adobe:ns:meta/">
  <rdf:RDF xmlns:rdf="http://www.w3.org/1999/02/22-rdf-syntax-ns#">
    <rdf:Description
        rdf:about="" xmlns:dc="http://purl.org/dc/elements/1.1/">
        <dc:format>application/pdf</dc:format>
        <dc:description><rdf:Alt>
          <rdf:li>This example shows how to add metadata</rdf:li>
        </rdf:Alt></dc:description>
        <dc:subject><rdf:Bag>
          <rdf:li>This example shows how to add metadata</rdf:li>
        </rdf:Bag></dc:subject>
        <dc:title><rdf:Alt>
          <rdf:li>Hello World example</rdf:li>
        </rdf:Alt></dc:title>
        <dc:creator><rdf:Seq>
          <rdf:li>Bruno Lowagie</rdf:li>
        </rdf:Seq></dc:creator>
    </rdf:Description>
    <rdf:Description rdf:about="" xmlns:pdf="http://ns.adobe.com/pdf/1.3/">
        <pdf:Producer>iText 5.0.1 (c) 1T3XT BVBA</pdf:Producer>
        <pdf:keywords>Metadata, iText, PDF</pdf:keywords>
    </rdf:Description>
    <rdf:Description rdf:about="" xmlns:xmp="http://ns.adobe.com/xap/1.0/">
        <xmp:CreateDate>2010-01-22T16:31:00+01:00</xmp:CreateDate>
        <xmp:ModifyDate>2010-01-22T16:31:01+01:00</xmp:ModifyDate>
        <xmp:CreatorTool>My program using iText</xmp:CreatorTool>
    </rdf:Description>
  </rdf:RDF>
</x:xmpmeta>
<?xpacket end="w"?>
```

This stream was created with iText using the `XmpWriter` class. The following bit of code shows how to add an XMP stream as metadata.

Listing 12.4   MetadataXmp.java

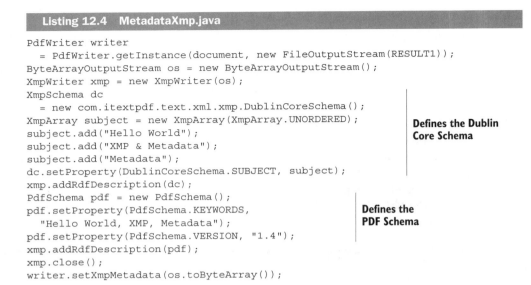

```
PdfWriter writer
  = PdfWriter.getInstance(document, new FileOutputStream(RESULT1));
ByteArrayOutputStream os = new ByteArrayOutputStream();
XmpWriter xmp = new XmpWriter(os);
XmpSchema dc
  = new com.itextpdf.text.xml.xmp.DublinCoreSchema();
XmpArray subject = new XmpArray(XmpArray.UNORDERED);
subject.add("Hello World");
subject.add("XMP & Metadata");
subject.add("Metadata");
dc.setProperty(DublinCoreSchema.SUBJECT, subject);
xmp.addRdfDescription(dc);
PdfSchema pdf = new PdfSchema();
pdf.setProperty(PdfSchema.KEYWORDS,
  "Hello World, XMP, Metadata");
pdf.setProperty(PdfSchema.VERSION, "1.4");
xmp.addRdfDescription(pdf);
xmp.close();
writer.setXmpMetadata(os.toByteArray());
```

Defines the Dublin Core Schema

Defines the PDF Schema

You use the `byte[]` created with `XmpWriter` with the `setXmpMetadata()` method to add the stream to the `PdfWriter`. This XMP stream covers the complete document. It's also possible to define an XML stream for individual pages. In that case you need to use the `setPageXmpMetadata()` method.

You can delegate the creation of the XMP stream to iText. Just create the metadata as done in listing 12.1, and add the following line:

```
writer.createXmpMetadata();
```

Suppose you have a PDF file that only contains metadata in an info dictionary. In that case, you can use the following to add an XMP stream.

Listing 12.5   MetadataXmp.java

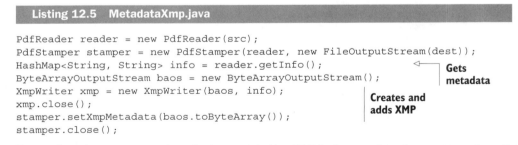

```
PdfReader reader = new PdfReader(src);
PdfStamper stamper = new PdfStamper(reader, new FileOutputStream(dest));
HashMap<String, String> info = reader.getInfo();
ByteArrayOutputStream baos = new ByteArrayOutputStream();
XmpWriter xmp = new XmpWriter(baos, info);
xmp.close();
stamper.setXmpMetadata(baos.toByteArray());
stamper.close();
```

Gets metadata

Creates and adds XMP

Extracting the XMP metadata from an existing PDF is done using the `getMetadata()` method on a `PdfReader` instance.

Tools or applications that aren't PDF-aware will search through the file for an `xpacket` with the `id` shown in listing 12.3, so it's important that the stream containing the XMP metadata is never compressed.

12.2 PDF and compression

iText will never compress an XMP metadata stream; all other content streams are compressed by default. You've already used the setCompressionLevel() method for the Image and BaseFont classes; you can also use it for PdfWriter to set the compression level for the other stream objects that are written to the OutputStream.

12.2.1 Compression levels

The next example uses different techniques to change the compression settings of a newly created PDF document.

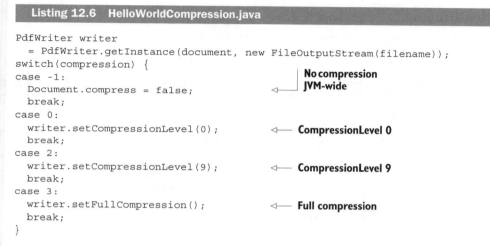

Listing 12.6   HelloWorldCompression.java

```
PdfWriter writer
  = PdfWriter.getInstance(document, new FileOutputStream(filename));
switch(compression) {
case -1:                                           No compression
  Document.compress = false;          ◁───┐        JVM-wide
  break;
case 0:
  writer.setCompressionLevel(0);      ◁───          CompressionLevel 0
  break;
case 2:
  writer.setCompressionLevel(9);      ◁───          CompressionLevel 9
  break;
case 3:
  writer.setFullCompression();        ◁───          Full compression
  break;
}
```

The Document class has a static member variable, compress, that can be set to false if you want to avoid having iText compress the content streams of pages and form XObjects. Use this for debugging purposes only! It changes the behavior of iText for the whole JVM, and that's not a good idea because it will also affect PDF documents created in other processes using the same JVM.

One option in listing 12.6 uses the method setFullCompression(). In the resulting PDF file, content streams will be compressed, but so will some other objects, such as the cross-reference table. This is only possible since PDF version 1.5. This is an example where iText will change the version number in the PDF header automatically from PDF-1.4 to PDF-1.5.

Table 12.1 compares the file sizes of the PDFs produced with listing 12.6.

Table 12.1   PDF and compression

Option	File size	Percentage
Without any compression (Document.compress = false)	43,237 bytes	99.23%
Compression level 0	43,567 bytes	100.00%

Table 12.1   PDF and compression *(continued)*

Option	File size	Percentage
Default compression	12,066 bytes	27.70%
Compression level 9	11,943 bytes	27.41%
Full compression	9,836 bytes	22.58%

As you can see, compressing as many objects as possible is the most effective option in this example, but be aware that the compression percentage largely depends on the type of content in the document.

12.2.2   Compressing and decompressing existing files

Next you'll see how to compress the content streams of the pages in an existing file.

Listing 12.7   HelloWorldCompression.java

```
PdfReader reader = new PdfReader(src);
PdfStamper stamper = new PdfStamper(
  reader, new FileOutputStream(dest), PdfWriter.VERSION_1_5);
stamper.getWriter().setCompressionLevel(9);
int total = reader.getNumberOfPages() + 1;
for (int i = 1; i < total; i++) {
  reader.setPageContent(i, reader.getPageContent(i));
}
stamper.setFullCompression();
stamper.close();
```

You want the `PdfStamper` class to create a file with header PDF-1.5, because you're using the `setFullCompression()` method after the header has been written to the `OutputStream`. That's why you add the PDF version number to the parameter list of the `PdfStamper` constructor.

Decompressing can be done exactly the same way by setting the compression level to zero, or by using the following code.

Listing 12.8   HelloWorldCompression.java

```
PdfReader reader = new PdfReader(src);
PdfStamper stamper = new PdfStamper(reader, new FileOutputStream(dest));
Document.compress = false;
int total = reader.getNumberOfPages() + 1;
for (int i = 1; i < total; i++) {
  reader.setPageContent(i, reader.getPageContent(i));
}
stamper.close();
Document.compress = true;
```

The result is a document whose PDF syntax can be seen in the content streams of each page when opened in a text editor. This can be handy when you need to debug a PDF document. We'll take a closer look inside the content stream of a PDF in part 4.

NOTE PdfStamper keeps existing stream objects intact when it manipulates a document, which means the compression level won't be changed. As a work-around, you can use the getPageContent() method to get the content stream of a page, and the setPageContent() method to put it back. When you do so, iText thinks the stream has changed, and it will use the compression level that was defined for PdfStamper's writer object.

Suppose your PDF contains confidential information that should only be seen by a limited number of people. Or you want to enforce access permissions to the people who download the PDF; for instance, they can view it, but they are not allowed to print it. In that case, you'll want these content streams to be encrypted.

12.3 *Encrypting a PDF document*

The PDF standard security handler allows access permissions and up to two passwords to be specified for a document: a *user password* (sometimes referred to as the *open password*) and an *owner password* (sometimes referred to as the *permissions password*).

In this section, we'll start with encrypting and decrypting PDFs using passwords, and we'll move on to public-key encryption, which is a much more robust way to protect your documents.

WARNING The examples in the remainder of the chapter involve encryption or digital signing. If you want them to work, you'll need extra encryption JARs in your classpath. For iText 5.0.x, the Bouncy Castle JARs are required (see section B.3.1). Later versions of iText can use different libraries. Check itextpdf.com for the most current information.

12.3.1 *Creating a password-encrypted PDF*

Listing 12.9 shows how to create a PDF document that is protected with two passwords. The maximum password length is 32 characters. You can enter longer passwords, but only the first 32 characters will be taken into account. One or both of the passwords can be null.

Listing 12.9   EncryptionPdf.java

```
public static byte[] USER = "Hello".getBytes();
public static byte[] OWNER = "World".getBytes();
public void createPdf(String filename)
   throws IOException, DocumentException {
  Document document = new Document();
  PdfWriter writer
    = PdfWriter.getInstance(document, new FileOutputStream(filename));
  writer.setEncryption(USER, OWNER,
    PdfWriter.ALLOW_PRINTING, PdfWriter.STANDARD_ENCRYPTION_128);
  writer.createXmpMetadata();
  document.open();
  document.add(new Paragraph("Hello World"));
  document.close();
}
```

A user who wants to open the resulting PDF file has to enter the password—"Hello" in this example—and will be able to perform only the actions that were specified in the permissions parameter. In this case, the user will be allowed to print the document but won't be able to copy and paste content.

The document will also open if the user enters the password "World". Using this owner password on Adobe Acrobat (not Reader), allows the user to change the permissions to whatever they want. If you don't specify a user password, all users will be able to open the document without being prompted for a password, but the permissions and restrictions (if any) will remain in place.

Note that iText will create a random password if the owner password isn't specified. In that case, you'll never know which password to use if you ever want to change the access permissions.

ACCESS PERMISSIONS

Table 12.2 shows an overview of the permissions that are available. If you pass 0 as a parameter for the permissions in the setEncryption() method, the end user can only view the document. By composing the values of table 12.2 in an or (|) sequence (such as PdfWriter.ALLOW_PRINTING | PdfWriter.ALLOW_COPY), you can grant the end user permissions (for instance to print the document and to extract text).

Half of these permissions can only be revoked when 128-bit encryption is used for one of the available encryption algorithms.

Table 12.2   Overview of the permissions parameters

Static final in `PdfWriter`	Description
ALLOW_PRINTING	The user is permitted to print the document.
ALLOW_DEGRADED_PRINTING	The user is permitted to print the document, but not with the quality offered by ALLOW_PRINTING (for 128-bit encryption only).
ALLOW_MODIFY_CONTENTS	The user is permitted to modify the contents—for example, to change the content of a page, or insert or remove a page.
ALLOW_ASSEMBLY	The user is permitted to insert, remove, and rotate pages and add bookmarks. The content of a page can't be changed unless the permission ALLOW_MODIFY_CONTENTS is granted too (for 128-bit encryption only).
ALLOW_COPY	The user is permitted to copy or otherwise extract text and graphics from the document, including using assistive technologies such as screen readers or other accessibility devices.
ALLOW_SCREENREADERS	The user is permitted to extract text and graphics for use by accessibility devices (for 128-bit encryption only).
ALLOW_MODIFY_ANNOTATIONS	The user is permitted to add or modify text annotations and interactive form fields.
ALLOW_FILL_IN	The user is permitted to fill form fields (for 128-bit encryption only).

ENCRYPTION ALGORITHMS

The standard encryption used in PDF documents is a proprietary algorithm known as RC4. RC4 was initially a trade secret, but in September 1994 a description of it was posted anonymously on the Cypherpunks mailing list. This algorithm is often referred to as ARC4 or ARCFOUR (the Alleged RC4). iText uses this unofficial implementation.

Beginning with PDF 1.6, you can also use the Advanced Encryption Standard (AES). iText supports the algorithms listed in table 12.3.

Static final in `PdfWriter`	Description
STANDARD_ENCRYPTION_40	40-bit ARC4 encryption
STANDARD_ENCRYPTION_128	128-bit ARC4 encryption
ENCRYPTION_AES_128	128-bit AES encryption

Table 12.3 Overview of the encryption algorithms

There's one major problem with listing 12.9. You're adding XMP metadata, but this metadata won't be readable by a non-PDF-aware application, because the XMP stream will be encrypted too. To avoid this, you need to add DO_NOT_ENCRYPT_METADATA to the encryption parameter; for instance, use ENCRYPTION_AES_128 | DO_NOT_ENCRYPT_METADATA as the encryptionType parameter.

> **FAQ**   *How do I revoke the permission to save a PDF file?* It isn't possible to restrict someone from saving or copying a PDF file. You can't disable the Save (or Save As) option in Adobe Reader. And even if you could, people would always be able to retrieve and copy the file with another tool. If you really need this kind of protection, you must look for a Digital Rights Management (DRM) solution. DRM tools give you fine-grained control over documents.

If you want to use an encrypted PDF document with PdfReader, for instance, to fill out fields, add annotations, or even decrypt it, you always need the owner password, regardless of the permissions that were set.

DECRYPTING AND ENCRYPTING AN EXISTING PDF DOCUMENT

Decrypting or encrypting an existing document is easily done with PdfStamper.

Listing 12.10   EncryptionPdf.java

```
public void decryptPdf(String src, String dest)
  throws IOException, DocumentException {
  PdfReader reader = new PdfReader(src, OWNER);
  PdfStamper stamper
    = new PdfStamper(reader, new FileOutputStream(dest));
  stamper.close();
}
public void encryptPdf(String src, String dest)
  throws IOException, DocumentException {
  PdfReader reader = new PdfReader(src);
  PdfStamper stamper
```

```
      = new PdfStamper(reader, new FileOutputStream(dest));
   stamper.setEncryption(USER, OWNER, PdfWriter.ALLOW_PRINTING,
      PdfWriter.ENCRYPTION_AES_128 | PdfWriter.DO_NOT_ENCRYPT_METADATA);
   stamper.close();
}
```

You can also combine both methods from listing 12.10 to change the permissions of an already encrypted PDF document. PdfReader has a getPermissions() method that returns an integer value that can interpreted as a bit-set containing the values listed in table 12.2.

> **FAQ**   *I have an encrypted PDF document with permissions that allow me to fill in a form, but iText throws a BadPasswordException. Why?* The decryption process in iText isn't fine-grained. As soon as you start manipulating a document, iText will decrypt it, and this always requires the owner password. Note that if you've created the PDF using iText, passing null as the password, you won't be able to change the document because you don't know the randomly created password.

Encrypting a PDF document using passwords isn't a waterproof solution. Password protection has to be seen as a psychological and legal barrier. If the document is encrypted, the author intends to protect the document against abuse. If you remove that protection without permission (that is, without the passwords), you're deliberately doing something you're not supposed to do. Extra restrictions were added to iText to prevent the use of the API for password removal.

If you need better protection for your documents, you can use public-key encryption.

12.3.2   *Public-key encryption*

With symmetric key algorithms, a single secret key has to be shared between the creator and the consumer of a document. The same key is used to encrypt and decrypt the content.

Public-key cryptography uses asymmetric key algorithms, where the key used to encrypt a message is not the same as the key used to decrypt it. Each user has a pair of cryptographic keys: one that is kept secret—the *private key*—and one that is publicly distributed—the *public key*. In the next example, you'll use a public key to encrypt a PDF document. This way, only the person who owns the corresponding private key will be able to open the document in Adobe Reader.

But before you can do this, you need to find out how to create a public-private key pair.

CREATING A PUBLIC-PRIVATE KEY PAIR WITH KEYTOOL

You're developing in Java, so you can use the keytool application that comes with the JDK. Let's use the -genkey option to create a key store for somebody called Bruno Specimen:

```
$ keytool -genkey -alias foobar -keyalg RSA -keystore .keystore
Enter keystore password:  f00b4r
What is your first and last name?
```

```
     [Unknown]:  Bruno Specimen
What is the name of your organizational unit?
     [Unknown]:  ICT
What is the name of your organization?
     [Unknown]:  Foobar Film Festival
What is the name of your City or Locality?
     [Unknown]:  Foobar
What is the name of your State or Province?
     [Unknown]:
What is the two-letter country code for this unit?
     [Unknown]:  BE
Is CN=Bruno Specimen, OU=ICT, O=Foobar Film Festival, L=Foobar,
 ST=Unknown, C=BE correct?
     [no]:  yes

Enter key password for <foobar>
          (RETURN if same as keystore password):  f1lmf3st
```

This file, .keystore, is protected with the password f00b4r; the private key stored in this file is protected with the password f1lmf3st. Do not share this key store or these passwords with anyone, but extract a public certificate with the -export option:

```
$ keytool -export -alias foobar -file foobar.cer -keystore .keystore
Enter keystore password:  f00b4r
Certificate stored in file <foobar.cer>
```

You can now share the file foobar.cer, which contains your public key, with the world. People can use this file to encrypt a PDF document that can be read by nobody else but you, the owner of the corresponding private key.

CREATING A PUBLIC-KEY ENCRYPTED PDF

In the next listing, you'll encrypt a document using two public keys. The first one is the public key you've created for testing purposes (Bruno Specimen); the second one is my own public key (Bruno Lowagie).

Listing 12.11   EncryptWithCertificate.java

```java
public Certificate getPublicCertificate(String path)
  throws IOException, CertificateException {
  FileInputStream is = new FileInputStream(path);
  CertificateFactory cf
    = CertificateFactory.getInstance("X.509");        Creates Certificate
  X509Certificate cert                                object
    = (X509Certificate) cf.generateCertificate(is);
  return cert;
}
public void createPdf(String filename)
  throws IOException, DocumentException, GeneralSecurityException {
  Document document = new Document();
  PdfWriter writer
    = PdfWriter.getInstance(document, new FileOutputStream(RESULT1));
  Certificate cert1
    = getPublicCertificate("resources/encryption/foobar.cer");
  Certificate cert2
```

```
        = getPublicCertificate(properties.getProperty("PUBLIC"));
  writer.setEncryption(
    new Certificate[]{cert1, cert2},
    new int[]{
      PdfWriter.ALLOW_PRINTING, PdfWriter.ALLOW_COPY},
    PdfWriter.ENCRYPTION_AES_128);
  document.open();
  document.add(new Paragraph("Hello World!"));
  document.close();
}
```

Sets encryption using certificates

Note the different permissions defined for the different certificates. Bruno Specimen will only be able to print the document; I won't be able to print it. I'll only be able to extract text, for instance with copy/paste, provided that my private key is registered on my operating system.

Listing 12.11 will only work if the unlimited strength jurisdiction policy files are installed in your runtime environment.

> **FAQ** *When I try to encrypt a document using public-key encryption, an* Invalid-KeyException *is thrown, saying the key size is invalid. Why?* Due to import control restrictions by the governments of a few countries, the encryption libraries shipped by default with the JDK restrict the length, and as a result the strength, of encryption keys. If you want these examples to work, you need to replace the default JARs with the *Java Cryptography Extension (JCE) Unlimited Strength Jurisdiction Policy Files.* These JARs are available for download from http://java.sun.com/ in eligible countries.

The document was encrypted for Bruno Specimen and for myself. If somebody else tries to open the document, they will get an Acrobat Security error, saying that "A digital ID was used to encrypt this document but no digital ID is present to decrypt it. Make sure your digital ID is properly installed or contact the document author." See figure 12.2.

Suppose that the document was created for you. In that case, you should use the keytool utility to export the private key from your key store to a .p12 file. To install

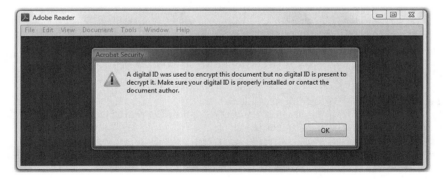

Figure 12.2 A protected public-key encrypted PDF document

your private key on the Windows OS, you need to double-click this file (for instance, private.p12) and follow the instructions.

> **NOTE** The path to my personal key store and certificate, along with the corresponding passwords that are used in the examples, are stored in a properties file on my OS. For obvious reasons, this file is not distributed with the examples.

When you open the document that was created using listing 12.11 and your public key, the PDF will be shown, as in figure 12.3. When you open the Document Properties window, you can check the permissions and the security method that was used.

While this is a safer way to protect your document than using user and owner passwords, it's hard to enforce the permissions. Private key holders can always use a PDF library to decrypt the content that was encrypted with their own public key.

DECRYPTING AND ENCRYPTING EXISTING PDFS

In the previous section, you used PdfStamper to decrypt existing password-protected PDF files using the owner password; or to encrypt an unprotected PDF file by adding a user and an owner password. In this listing, you'll do the same with public-key encryption.

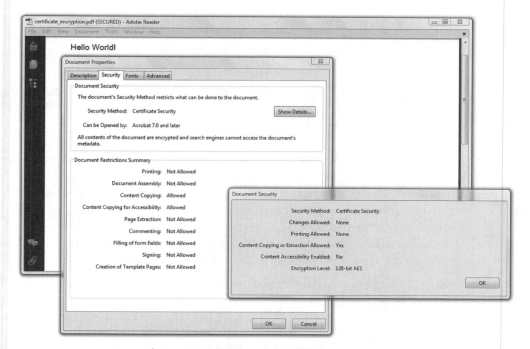

Figure 12.3   An opened public-key-encrypted PDF document

Listing 12.12   EncryptWithCertificate.java

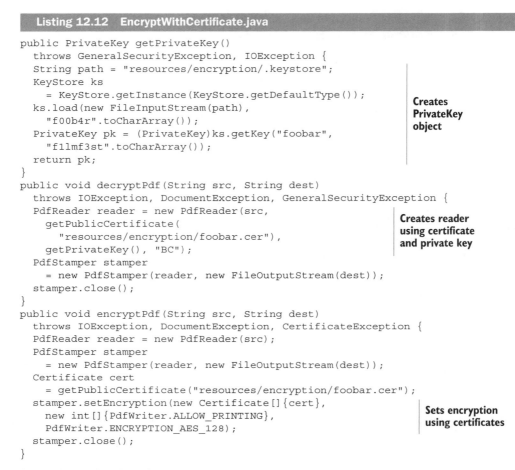

```
public PrivateKey getPrivateKey()
  throws GeneralSecurityException, IOException {
  String path = "resources/encryption/.keystore";
  KeyStore ks
    = KeyStore.getInstance(KeyStore.getDefaultType());
  ks.load(new FileInputStream(path),
    "f00b4r".toCharArray());
  PrivateKey pk = (PrivateKey)ks.getKey("foobar",
    "f1lmf3st".toCharArray());
  return pk;
}
```

> Creates
> PrivateKey
> object

```
public void decryptPdf(String src, String dest)
  throws IOException, DocumentException, GeneralSecurityException {
  PdfReader reader = new PdfReader(src,
    getPublicCertificate(
      "resources/encryption/foobar.cer"),
    getPrivateKey(), "BC");
  PdfStamper stamper
    = new PdfStamper(reader, new FileOutputStream(dest));
  stamper.close();
}
```

> Creates reader
> using certificate
> and private key

```
public void encryptPdf(String src, String dest)
  throws IOException, DocumentException, CertificateException {
  PdfReader reader = new PdfReader(src);
  PdfStamper stamper
    = new PdfStamper(reader, new FileOutputStream(dest));
  Certificate cert
    = getPublicCertificate("resources/encryption/foobar.cer");
  stamper.setEncryption(new Certificate[]{cert},
    new int[]{PdfWriter.ALLOW_PRINTING},
    PdfWriter.ENCRYPTION_AES_128);
  stamper.close();
}
```

> Sets encryption
> using certificates

Apart from the fact that the access permissions got lost in the decryption process, there's another problem that is inherent to the way Bruno Specimen's key was created. What if Bruno Specimen actually exists? You could distribute the public key you created for him, and you could pretend to be him. He wouldn't like that.

Anybody can generate a private key and a self-signed certificate. To solve this problem, Bruno Specimen can call in a third party that is beyond suspicion: a *certificate authority* (CA). He could create a *certificate signing request* (CSR) like this:

```
$ keytool -certreq -keystore .keystore -alias foobar -file foobar.csr
Enter keystore password:  f00b4r
Enter key password for f1lmf3st
```

A file, foobar.csr, is generated. Bruno Specimen can send this file to a CA, and this third party will check if Bruno Specimen is really who he says he is. If his identity can be verified, he'll receive a *Privacy Enhanced Mail* (PEM) file, which will contain his public certificate signed by the CA using the CA's private key. This certificate can be decrypted with the CA's public key, which comes in the form of a *Distinguished Encoding Rules* (DER) file.

Many applications ship with a number of root certificates from CAs. This is necessary to check the validity of digital signatures.

12.4 Digital signatures, OCSP, and timestamping

Digital signatures in PDF also involve asymmetric cryptography. Suppose that you receive an official PDF document from Bruno Specimen. How do you make sure that this document was originally created by Bruno and not by somebody else? Also, how do you make sure that nobody changed the document after Bruno created it and before you received it?

This is only possible if the document was digitally signed by Bruno. The signing application will make a digest of the document's content, and encrypt it using Bruno's private key. This encrypted digest will be stored in a signature field. When you open the signed PDF, the viewer application will decrypt the encrypted digest using the author's public key, and compare it with a newly created digest of the content. If there's a match, the document wasn't tampered with; if there's a difference, somebody else has tried to forge the author's signature, or the document was changed after it was signed.

Let's start by creating a document that has a signature field.

12.4.1 Creating an unsigned signature field

When you created AcroForms in chapter 8, we discussed button (/Btn), text (/Tx), and choice (/Ch) fields, but we skipped signature fields (/Sig). Figure 12.4 shows two PDF files. The one to the left has a signature field without a digital signature. This file was signed using my own private key. The resulting PDF is shown on the right.

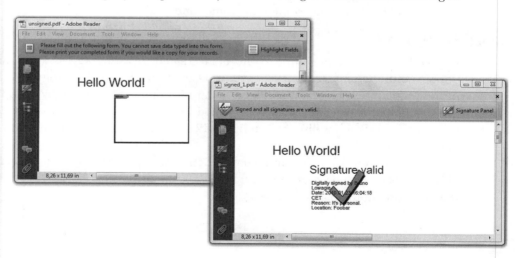

Figure 12.4 PDFs with signature fields

This code shows how to add a signature field without a signature.

Listing 12.13   SignatureField.java

```
public void createPdf(String filename)
  throws IOException, DocumentException {
  Document document = new Document();
  PdfWriter writer
    = PdfWriter.getInstance(document, new FileOutputStream(filename));
  document.open();
  document.add(new Paragraph("Hello World!"));
  PdfFormField field
    = PdfFormField.createSignature(writer);
  field.setWidget(new Rectangle(72, 732, 144, 780),      Creates field
    PdfAnnotation.HIGHLIGHT_INVERT);                      (widget, name, ...)
  field.setFieldName("mySig");
  field.setFlags(PdfAnnotation.FLAGS_PRINT);
  field.setPage();
  field.setMKBorderColor(BaseColor.BLACK);
  field.setMKBackgroundColor(BaseColor.WHITE);
  PdfAppearance tp
    = PdfAppearance.createAppearance(writer, 72, 48);    Creates
  tp.rectangle(0.5f, 0.5f, 71.5f, 47.5f);                appearance
  tp.stroke();
  field.setAppearance(
    PdfAnnotation.APPEARANCE_NORMAL, tp);
  writer.addAnnotation(field);              ←— Adds field
  document.close();
}
```

Normally, you won't have to use the code in listing 12.13. The signature field will either be present because it was added by another application (such as Adobe Acrobat); or you'll be presented with a document that has no signature field. In that case, you can add the field and sign it at the same time.

12.4.2 *Signing a PDF*

Listing 12.14 adds a signature to the field created in listing 12.13. There are two options: with the parameter `certified`, you can choose whether or not to use a certification signature. In figure 12.5 there's a bar with the text "Certified by Bruno Lowagie <bruno@lowagie.com>, certificate issued by CA Cert Signing Authority." This is different from what was displayed in figure 12.4, where it only said "Signed and all signatures are valid."

There's also a `graphic` parameter to define whether or not to use a graphical object instead of a text message. In figure 12.5, the 1T3XT logo was used to visualize the signature on the page.

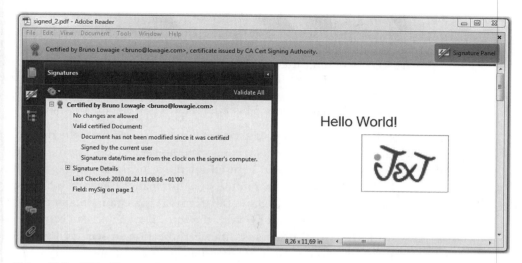

Figure 12.5 PDF with a certifying signature

Listing 12.14 SignatureField.java

```java
KeyStore ks = KeyStore.getInstance("pkcs12", "BC");
ks.load(new FileInputStream(path), keystore_password.toCharArray());
String alias = (String)ks.aliases().nextElement();
PrivateKey pk = (PrivateKey)ks.getKey(alias, key_password.toCharArray());
Certificate[] chain = ks.getCertificateChain(alias);
PdfReader reader = new PdfReader(ORIGINAL);
PdfStamper stamper = PdfStamper.createSignature(
  reader, new FileOutputStream(dest), '\0');                            ❶
PdfSignatureAppearance appearance
  = stamper.getSignatureAppearance();                                   ❷
appearance.setVisibleSignature("mySig");
appearance.setReason("It's personal.");                                ❸
appearance.setLocation("Foobar");
appearance.setCrypto(
  pk, chain, null, PdfSignatureAppearance.WINCER_SIGNED);               ❹
if (certified)
  appearance.setCertificationLevel(
    PdfSignatureAppearance.CERTIFIED_NO_CHANGES_ALLOWED);               ❺
if (graphic) {
  appearance.setAcro6Layers(true);
  appearance.setSignatureGraphic(Image.getInstance(RESOURCE));
  appearance.setRenderingMode(                                          ❻
    PdfSignatureAppearance.RenderingMode.GRAPHIC);
}
stamper.close();
```

This listing no longer uses the constructor to create an instance of PdfStamper, but the method createSignature() ❶. You create a PdfSignatureAppearance and define it as a visible signature ❷. In this example, the signature field uses the name "mySig".

FAQ   *How can I sign a document if it doesn't have a signature field?* If there's no signature field present, you can make a small change to the code from listing 12.14 to add a signature that will show up in the signature panel (see the left side of figure 12.5). If you omit the setVisibleSignature() method, the signature won't show up on any page. This is called an *invisible signature*. Or you can use the setVisibleSignature() method with a Rectangle object, a page number, and a field name as parameters. This will create a new signature field.

The name of the person who signs the document is retrieved from the private key. You can add a reason for signing and a location with the setReason() and setLocation() methods ❸. This information can be used for the appearance in the signature field (see figure 12.4) and it's also shown in the signature panel (see figure 12.5).

You pass the PrivateKey object and the Certificate chain obtained from the key store to the setCrypto() method ❹. With the third parameter, you can pass *certificate revocation lists* (CRLs). We'll discuss certificate revocation in section 12.4.6. With the final parameter, you choose a security handler. The corresponding cryptographic filters that are supported in iText are listed in table 12.4.

Table 12.4   Security handlers

iText constant	Filter name	Description
SELF_SIGNED	Adobe.PPKLite	This uses a self-signed security handler.
VERISIGN_SIGNED	VeriSign.PPKVS	To sign documents with the VeriSign CA, you need a key that is certified with VeriSign. You can acquire a 60-day trial key or buy a permanent key at verisign.com.
WINCER_SIGNED	Adobe.PPKMS	The Microsoft Windows Certificate Security works with any trusted certificate. For instance, I'm using a public-private key pair obtained from CACert (http://cacert.org).

The signature shown in figure 12.4 is an *ordinary signature*, aka an *approval* or a *recipient signature*. A document can be signed for approval by one or more recipients.

The signature shown in figure 12.5 is a *certification signature*, aka an *author signature*. There can only be one certification signature in a document. In iText, you create a certification signature by using the setCertificationLevel() method ❺ with one of the following values:

- CERTIFIED_NO_CHANGES_ALLOWED—No changes are allowed.
- CERTIFIED_FORM_FILLING—The document is certified, but other people can still fill out form fields without invalidating the signature.
- CERTIFIED_FORM_FILLING_AND_ANNOTATIONS—The document is certified, but other people can still fill out form fields and add annotations without invalidating the signature.

If you use NOT_CERTIFIED as parameter, an approval signature will be added.

Just like other form fields, a signature field has an appearance. Only the normal appearance is supported; the rollover and down attributes aren't used. There are two approaches to generating those appearances. In ❻, you use the `setAcro6Layers()` method and pass the 1T3XT logo as signature graphic with the `setSignature-Graphic()` method, because listing 12.14 uses the `GRAPHIC` option for the rendering mode. The following options are available for the `setRenderingMode()` method:

- `DESCRIPTION`—The rendering mode is just the description.
- `NAME_AND_DESCRIPTION`—The rendering mode is the name of the signer and the description.
- `GRAPHIC_AND_DESCRIPTION`—The rendering mode is an image and the description.
- `GRAPHIC`—The rendering mode is just an image.

The `setAcro6Layers()` method refers to Acrobat 6. In earlier versions of Acrobat, the signature appearance consisted of five different layers that are drawn on top of each other:

- *n0*—Background layer.
- *n1*—Validity layer, used for the unknown and valid state; contains, for instance, a yellow question mark.
- *n2*—Signature appearance, containing information about the signature. This can be text or an XObject that represents the handwritten signature.
- *n3*—Validity layer, containing a graphic that represents the validity of the signature when the signature is invalid.
- *n4*—Text layer, for a text presentation of the state of the signature.

If you omit `setAcro6Layers()`, iText will create a default appearance for these layers, or you can use the method `getLayer()` with a number ranging from 0 to 4 to get a `PdfTemplate` that allows you to create a custom appearance. You can also use the methods `setLayer2Text()` and `setLayer4Text()` to add a custom text for the signature appearance and the text layer. Note that the use of layers n1, n3, and n4 is no longer recommended since Acrobat 6.

In the next example, you'll add more than one signature.

12.4.3 *Adding multiple signatures*

Figure 12.6 shows another Hello World document, but now it has been signed twice. Once by myself with a signature that could be validated, and once by Bruno Specimen, who isn't trusted because "None of the parent certificates are trusted identities." This is normal: the certificate was self-signed; there was no CA such as VeriSign involved.

If you know and trust Bruno Specimen, you can add his public certificate to the list of trusted identities in Adobe Reader. You can import the file foobar.cer through Document > Manage Trusted Identities and edit the trust as a "trusted root." If you do, the second signature can also be verified (figure 12.7).

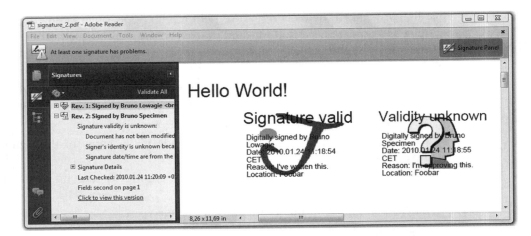

Figure 12.6 Document with two signatures, one of which has "validity unknown"

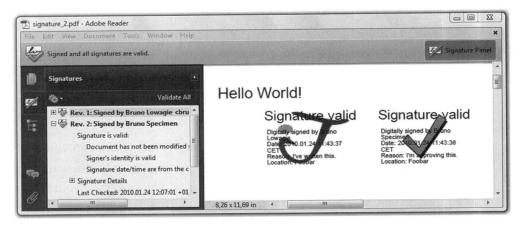

Figure 12.7 Document with two valid signatures

The original Hello World example of the document shown in figures 12.6 and 12.7 didn't have a signature field. Here is how the first signature was added.

Listing 12.15 Signatures.java

```java
PdfReader reader = new PdfReader(src);
FileOutputStream os = new FileOutputStream(dest);
PdfStamper stamper
  = PdfStamper.createSignature(reader, os, '\0');
PdfSignatureAppearance appearance
  = stamper.getSignatureAppearance();
appearance.setCrypto(key, chain, null,
PdfSignatureAppearance.WINCER_SIGNED);
appearance.setImage(Image.getInstance(RESOURCE));
appearance.setReason("I've written this.");
```

```
appearance.setLocation("Foobar");
appearance.setVisibleSignature(
  new Rectangle(72, 732, 144, 780), 1, "first");
stamper.close();
```

You don't have to create a `PdfFormField` explicitly as in listing 12.13. The field is created by iText using the parameters of the `setVisibleSignature()` method. Note that this time you add an `Image` that will be added in the background of layer 2. Compare listing 12.15 with this one to find out how to add a second approval signature.

Listing 12.16   Signatures.java

```
PdfReader reader = new PdfReader(src);
FileOutputStream os = new FileOutputStream(dest);
PdfStamper stamper
  = PdfStamper.createSignature(reader, os, '\0', null, true);
PdfSignatureAppearance appearance
  = stamper.getSignatureAppearance();
appearance.setCrypto(key, chain, null,
PdfSignatureAppearance.WINCER_SIGNED);
appearance.setReason("I'm approving this.");
appearance.setLocation("Foobar");
appearance.setVisibleSignature(
  new Rectangle(160, 732, 232, 780), 1, "second");
stamper.close();
```

You have to add two extra parameters to the `createSignature()` method if you want to add a second signature. One parameter can be used to store the resulting PDF as a temporary file. If you pass a `File` object that's a directory, a temporary file will be created there; if it's a file, it will be used directly. The file will be deleted on exit unless the `os` output stream is `null`. In that case, the document can be retrieved directly from the temporary file. This is a way to keep the memory use low. In this example, you're signing a simple Hello World file. You don't need a temporary file; the signing will be done in memory.

The fifth parameter of `createSignature()` indicates whether or not the file has to be manipulated in *append mode*. Working in append mode means that the original file will be kept intact; the new content will be appended after the `%EOF` marker.

> **NOTE**   You can also use append mode if you want the file to keep the complete history of the changes made to the document. We'll look at the implications of using append mode outside the context of digital signatures in chapter 13.

Using append mode is *mandatory* if you want to add content to a document that has been signed. If you set the `append` value to `false`, the original signature will be invalidated, as shown in figure 12.8.

When a document is signed multiple times, you get a PDF file with multiple revisions (see the signature panel in figures 12.6 and 12.7). For one revision, the signature name is "first"; for the other it's "second". In figure 12.6, you can see a link

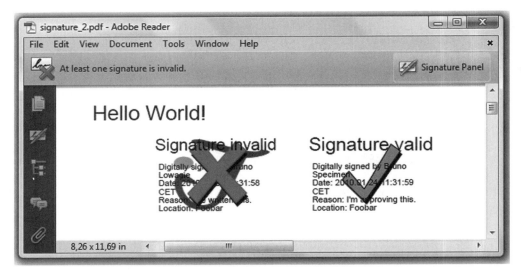

Figure 12.8   Document with one valid and one invalid signature

in the signature panel saying "Click to view this version." This allows you to manually retrieve the original files for each signature. This listing shows how to extract such a revision programmatically.

Listing 12.17   Signatures.java

```java
public void extractFirstRevision() throws IOException {
  PdfReader reader = new PdfReader(SIGNED2);
  AcroFields af = reader.getAcroFields();
  FileOutputStream os = new FileOutputStream(REVISION);
  byte bb[] = new byte[8192];
  InputStream ip = af.extractRevision("first");
  int n = 0;
  while ((n = ip.read(bb)) > 0)
    os.write(bb, 0, n);
  os.close();
  ip.close();
}
```

With this code snippet, you can extract the first revision, the one that only has the signature field named "first".

   We've now checked for the validity of a signature using Adobe Reader, but you can also automate the process.

12.4.4   *Verifying the signatures in a document*

The root certificates of CAs that are trusted by the distributor of the Java Runtime you use are stored in a file named cacerts. You can find this key store in the lib directory of the JAVA_HOME directory. Depending on the use case, different collections of CA certificates may be required, which may not include those already in that file.

If a root certificate isn't present, you can import it with the keytool utility. This key store can be loaded into a KeyStore object like this:

```
KeyStore ks = PdfPKCS7.loadCacertsKeyStore();
```

The next bit of code uses the getSignatureNames() method to get all the names of the signature fields in the document. Then you can use the root certificates in a Key-Store to verify each signature.

Listing 12.18 Signatures.java

```
PdfReader reader = new PdfReader(SIGNED2);
AcroFields af = reader.getAcroFields();
ArrayList<String> names = af.getSignatureNames();
for (String name : names) {
  out.println("Signature name: " + name);
  out.println("Signature covers whole document: "
    + af.signatureCoversWholeDocument(name));
  out.println("Document revision: "
    + af.getRevision(name) + " of " + af.getTotalRevisions());
  PdfPKCS7 pk = af.verifySignature(name);
  Calendar cal = pk.getSignDate();
  Certificate[] pkc = pk.getCertificates();
  out.println("Subject: "
    + PdfPKCS7.getSubjectFields(pk.getSigningCertificate()));
  out.println("Revision modified: " + !pk.verify());
  Object fails[] = PdfPKCS7.verifyCertificates(pkc, ks, null, cal);
  if (fails == null)
    out.println("Certificates verified against the KeyStore");
  else
    out.println("Certificate failed: " + fails[1]);
}
```

You can check whether the signature covers the whole document by using the signatureCoversWholeDocument() method. This is true for the second signature, but the first signature only covers revision 1 of 2, and that's not the complete document.

You can get the revision number for the signature with the getRevision() method, and the total number of revisions with getTotalRevisions(). The verification of the signature is done with the PdfPKCS7 object. This object can give you the public certificate of the signer and its parent certificates, as well as the signing date. You can use the verify() method to find out if the document was tampered with, and the verifyCertificates() method to check the certificates in the PDF against the certificates in the cacerts key store. In this example, you didn't pass any CRLs, so the third parameter of the method is null.

12.4.5 *Creating the digest and signing externally*

In the previous examples, we've let iText make the digest, and we've let iText decide how to sign it using the PrivateKey object. But it isn't always possible to create a PrivateKey object. If the private key is put on a token or a smart card, you can't retrieve it programmatically. In this case, making and signing the digest has to be done on external hardware, such as a smart-card reader.

FAQ   *How do I get a private key that is on my smart card?* There would be a serious security problem if you could extract a private key from a smart card. Your private key is secret, and the smart card should be designed to keep this secret safe. You don't want an external application to use your private key. Instead, you send a hash to the card, and the card returns a signature or a PKCS#7 message. PKCS refers to a group of Public Key Cryptography Standards, and PKCS#7 defines the Cryptographic Message Syntax Standard.

Signing a PDF document using a smart-card reader involves middleware, and the code will depend on the type of smart-card reader you're using. To get an idea of what needs to be done, we'll look at some examples where the digest is made or signed externally.

The first part of this listing looks similar to what you've done before.

Listing 12.19   Signatures.java

```
PdfStamper stamper = PdfStamper.createSignature(reader, os, '\0');
PdfSignatureAppearance appearance = stamper.getSignatureAppearance();
appearance.setCrypto(
  null, chain, null, PdfSignatureAppearance.SELF_SIGNED);          ❶
appearance.setReason("External hash example");
appearance.setLocation("Foobar");
appearance.setVisibleSignature(
  new Rectangle(72, 732, 144, 780), 1, "sig");
appearance.setExternalDigest(new byte[128], null, "RSA");          ❷
appearance.preClose();                                             ❸
Signature signature = Signature.getInstance("SHA1withRSA");        ❹
signature.initSign(key);
byte buf[] = new byte[8192];
int n;
InputStream inp = appearance.getRangeStream();
while ((n = inp.read(buf)) > 0) {                                  ❺
  signature.update(buf, 0, n);
}
PdfPKCS7 sig = appearance.getSigStandard().getSigner();
sig.setExternalDigest(signature.sign(), null, "RSA");              ❻
PdfDictionary dic = new PdfDictionary();
dic.put(PdfName.CONTENTS,
  new PdfString(sig.getEncodedPKCS1()).setHexWriting(true));
appearance.close(dic);
```

Let's pretend you don't have access to the private key, so you pass null to the set-Crypto() method ❶. You use the setExternalDigest() method to reserve space in the signature dictionary for keys whose content isn't known yet ❷. You don't close the Pdf-Stamper, but you preClose() the signature appearance ❸. Then you create a Signature object using the private key ❹; this is something that could happen outside of your program. You pass the document bytes obtained with getRangeStream() to the Signature ❺, and you create the /Contents (the signed digest) of the signature field ❻. When you close the appearance, the signature will be added.

The following listing shows a variation where you create a digest using the Secure Hash Algorithm 1 (SHA-1), and if sign is true, you sign it with the RSA algorithm.

Listing 12.20   Signatures.java

```
appearance.setCrypto(
  key, chain, null, PdfSignatureAppearance.WINCER_SIGNED);
appearance.setExternalDigest(null, new byte[20], null);
appearance.preClose();
MessageDigest messageDigest = MessageDigest.getInstance("SHA1");
byte buf[] = new byte[8192];
int n;
InputStream inp = appearance.getRangeStream();
while ((n = inp.read(buf)) > 0) {
  messageDigest.update(buf, 0, n);
}
byte hash[] = messageDigest.digest();
PdfSigGenericPKCS sg = appearance.getSigStandard();
PdfLiteral slit = (PdfLiteral)sg.get(PdfName.CONTENTS);
byte[] outc = new byte[(slit.getPosLength() - 2) / 2];
PdfPKCS7 sig = sg.getSigner();
if (sign) {
  Signature signature = Signature.getInstance("SHA1withRSA");
  signature.initSign(key);
  signature.update(hash);
  sig.setExternalDigest(signature.sign(), hash, "RSA");
}
else
  sig.setExternalDigest(null, hash, null);
PdfDictionary dic = new PdfDictionary();
byte[] ssig = sig.getEncodedPKCS7();
System.arraycopy(ssig, 0, outc, 0, ssig.length);
dic.put(PdfName.CONTENTS, new PdfString(outc).setHexWriting(true));
appearance.close(dic);
```

If you look at the resources that come with this book, you'll also find an example that explains how to sign a PDF document using an external library.

NOTE   Signing can become even more generic. There may be situations in which you don't know the certificate chain before the signature is generated. Or you may have to split the signing process into parts, in which case you can't keep the PdfStamper open all the time. It would lead us too far afield to discuss all the possible workarounds for each of these situations. More examples, including examples involving smart-card readers, can be found on SourceForge and on the official iText site (see section B.1, for the URLs).

Now let's discuss some technologies that provide extra security features.

12.4.6   CRLs, OCSP, and timestamping

Suppose you receive a contract from person *X* who works at company *Y*. The contract is signed with a valid digital signature, corresponding to the e-mail address *X@Y.com.* You can safely assume that the document is genuine, unless ... person *X* was fired, but he still owns a copy of the private key of company *Y.* Such a contract probably wouldn't be legal. Surely there must be a way for company *Y* to revoke the certificate for employee *X* so that he no longer can act on behalf of his former company.

CERTIFICATE REVOCATION LIST

Every certificate authority keeps lists of certificates that are no longer valid, whether because the owner thinks the private key was compromised, or the token containing the private key was lost or stolen, or the original owner of the key is no longer entitled to use it. Such a list is called a *certificate revocation list* (CRL), and they are made public at one or more URLs provided by the CA who signed the certificate.

You can create a CRL object like this:

```
InputStream is = new URL(url_of_crl).openStream();
CertificateFactory cf = CertificateFactory.getInstance("X.509");
CRL crl = (CRL)cf.generateCRL(is);
```

An array of CRL objects can be passed as a parameter to the setCrypto() method. However, CRLs are generally large, and this technique is considered to be "old technology."

It might be a better idea to use the *Online Certificate Status Protocol* (OCSP).

ONLINE CERTIFICATE STATUS PROTOCOL

OCSP is an internet protocol for obtaining the revocation status of a certificate online. You can post a request to check the status of a certificate over HTTP, and the CA's OCSP server will send you a response. You no longer need to parse and embed long CRLs. An OCSP response is small and constant in size, and can easily be included in the PKCS#7 object.

> **NOTE**   Revocation information in a PDF document is a signed attribute, which means that the signing software must capture the revocation information before signing. A similar requirement in this use case applies to the chain of certificates. The signing software must capture and validate the certificate's chain before signing. CRLs will lead to bigger PDF documents, and using OCSP will not take as much space. But the OCSP connection to check the status can take time, whereas CRLs can easily be cached on the filesystem. It's always a tradeoff.

Now let's look at another problem that might arise. Suppose somebody sends you a signed contract. He has used a private key that is still valid, and you're sure that the document you've received is genuine. However, at some point the author of the document regrets what he's written. By resetting the clock on his computer, he could create a new document with a new digital signature that is as valid as the first one. This way, you could end up with two documents signed with the same private key at almost the same time, but with slightly different content. How can anybody know which document is more genuine?

TIMESTAMPING

This problem can be solved by involving a third party: a *timestamping authority* (TSA). The TSA will take the hash of the document and concatenate a timestamp to it. This is

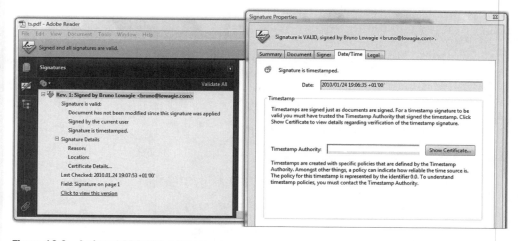

Figure 12.9   A signed PDF with a timestamp

done on a timestamp server that is contacted during the signing process. The time-stamp server will return a hash that is signed using the private key of the TSA.

Figure 12.9 shows a PDF with a timestamped signature. In previous examples and screen shots, the signature panel informed you that the "Signature date/time are from the clock on the signer's computer." Now it says: "Signature is timestamped." You can also check the certificate of the TSA in the signature properties. That solves the potential problem of antedated documents.

The next listing can be used to add a timestamp (if `withTS` is `true`) and to check the revocation status of the certificate with OCSP (if `withOCSP` is `true`).

Listing 12.21   Signatures.java

```java
PdfReader reader = new PdfReader(src);
FileOutputStream fout = new FileOutputStream(dest);
PdfStamper stp = PdfStamper.createSignature(reader, fout, '\0');
PdfSignatureAppearance sap = stp.getSignatureAppearance();
sap.setVisibleSignature(
  new Rectangle(72, 732, 144, 780), 1, "Signature");
sap.setCrypto(null, chain, null, PdfSignatureAppearance.SELF_SIGNED);
PdfSignature dic = new PdfSignature(
  PdfName.ADOBE_PPKLITE,
  new PdfName("adbe.pkcs7.detached"));          Creates
dic.setReason(sap.getReason());                 signature
dic.setLocation(sap.getLocation());             dictionary
dic.setContact(sap.getContact());
dic.setDate(new PdfDate(sap.getSignDate()));
sap.setCryptoDictionary(dic);
int contentEstimated = 15000;
HashMap<PdfName,Integer> exc                    Reserves space
  = new HashMap<PdfName,Integer>();             for signature
exc.put(PdfName.CONTENTS,                        content
  new Integer(contentEstimated * 2 + 2));
```

```
sap.preClose(exc);
InputStream data = sap.getRangeStream();
MessageDigest messageDigest
  = MessageDigest.getInstance("SHA1");
byte buf[] = new byte[8192];
int n;
while ((n = data.read(buf)) > 0) {
  messageDigest.update(buf, 0, n);
}
byte hash[] = messageDigest.digest();
Calendar cal = Calendar.getInstance();
TSAClient tsc = null;
if (withTS) {
  String tsa_url = properties.getProperty("TSA");
  String tsa_login
    = properties.getProperty("TSA_LOGIN");
  String tsa_passw
    = properties.getProperty("TSA_PASSWORD");
  tsc = new TSAClientBouncyCastle(
    tsa_url, tsa_login, tsa_passw);
}
byte[] ocsp = null;
if (withOCSP) {
  String url
    = PdfPKCS7.getOCSPURL((X509Certificate)chain[0]);
  CertificateFactory cf
    = CertificateFactory.getInstance("X509");
  FileInputStream is = new FileInputStream(
    properties.getProperty("ROOTCERT"));
  X509Certificate root
    = (X509Certificate) cf.generateCertificate(is);
  ocsp = new OcspClientBouncyCastle(
    (X509Certificate)chain[0], root, url).getEncoded();
}
PdfPKCS7 sgn = new PdfPKCS7(
  pk, chain, null, "SHA1", null, false);
byte sh[] = sgn.getAuthenticatedAttributeBytes(
  hash, cal, ocsp);
sgn.update(sh, 0, sh.length);
byte[] encodedSig
  = sgn.getEncodedPKCS7(hash, cal, tsc, ocsp);
if (contentEstimated + 2 < encodedSig.length)
  throw new DocumentException("Not enough space");
byte[] paddedSig = new byte[contentEstimated];
System.arraycopy(
  encodedSig, 0, paddedSig, 0, encodedSig.length);
PdfDictionary dic2 = new PdfDictionary();
dic2.put(PdfName.CONTENTS,
  new PdfString(paddedSig).setHexWriting(true));
sap.close(dic2);
```

Creates hash
of content

Creates
Timestamp
client

Creates
OCSP client

Creates
signed hash

Adds signature
content

In this example, you use the PdfSignature dictionary to create a *detached* PKCS#7 signature, as opposed to PKCS#7 signatures where the data is encapsulated in the digest. Before you preclose the appearance, you also need to estimate the length of the signature's content.

Note that you need an account with a TSA (with a `TSA_LOGIN` and `TSA_PASSWORD`) to create a TSA client object. An account with a trustworthy TSA isn't free, but you can probably find some free timestamp server for testing purposes.

The URL of the OCSP server that is needed to create an OCSP client object is available in the public certificate. That is, if the CA that signed the certificate supports OCSP. You retrieve it with the `getOCSPURL()` method.

If you set `withTS` and `withOCSP` to `false` in listing 12.21, you'll get an example that shows how to create a detached signature with *authenticated attributes*. By combining the code snippets in this chapter, we could make many more examples, experimenting with almost every option that is described in ISO-32000-1.

We'll finish this chapter by introducing a set of restrictions and extensions to the PDF standard developed by the European Telecommunications Standards Institute (ETSI) regarding PDF Advanced Electronic Signatures (PAdES) profiles.

12.4.7 *PDF Advanced Electronic Signatures (PAdES) profiles*

ETSI is a European standardization organization in the telecommunications industry. This institute issues technical specifications such as TS 101 733 (first published in 2000), "Cryptographic Message Syntax (CMS) Advanced Electronic Signatures (CAdES)," and TS 101 903 (first published in 2002), "XML Advanced Electronic Signatures (XAdES)." More recently, in 2009, ETSI brought the same capabilities pioneered in CAdES and XAdES to PDF, resulting in a five-part specification describing PDF Advanced Electronic Signatures profiles:

- *Part 1*—This is an overview of support for signatures in PDF documents, and it lists the features of the PDF profiles in the other documents.
- *Part 2*—PAdES Basic is based on ISO-32000-1. If you want to know more about digital signatures in PDF, you should read this specification before starting to dig into the PDF reference. Everything mentioned in PAdES part 2 is supported in iText.
- *Part 3*—PAdES Enhanced describes profiles that are based on CAdES: PAdES Basic Electronic Signature (BES) and Explicit Policy Electronic Signature (EPES). If you want to implement PAdES part 3 using iText, you need to switch to creating a detached CMS signature and use `ETSI.CAdES.detached` as the `/SubFilter`.
- *Part 4*—PAdES Long-Term Validation (LTV) is about protecting data beyond the expiry of the user signing certificate. This mechanism requires a Document Security Store (DSS), and this mechanism isn't available in ISO-32000-1. PAdES part 4 isn't supported in iText yet.
- *Part 5*—PAdES for XML content describes profiles for XAdES signatures. For instance, after filling an XFA form, which is XML content embedded in a PDF file, a user may sign selected parts of the form. This isn't supported in iText yet.

At the time this book was written, neither Adobe Acrobat nor iText supported parts 3, 4, or 5. PAdES will solve one major issue that hasn't been discussed in this chapter: certificates have an expiration date. A document that is signed and verified today may be difficult to verify in seven years when the certificate has expired, or when it has been revoked (the validation data may not be available in the future).

The idea is to add new validation data and a new document timestamp to a Document Security Store in the PDF before the last document timestamp expires. This can be repeated multiple times, always before the expiration of the last document timestamp. This way, PAdES LTV makes it possible to extend the lifetime of protection for the document.

Note that the DSS isn't part of ISO-32000-1 and it's not available in iText yet; it will be introduced in ISO-32000-2. We'll find out more about ISO-32000-2 in the next part of this book, but first let's summarize what we've learned in this chapter.

12.5   *Summary*

With this chapter, we close part 3 of this book. You've discovered that you can add different types of metadata to the documents created in parts 1 and 2. We discussed the compression of content streams, and we'll use the decompression methods in the next part to inspect the PDF syntax that's used to describe the content of a page.

In the sections about encryption and digital signatures, we talked about the protection of PDF documents. You used public-key cryptography to encrypt and decrypt a PDF document, and to digitally sign a PDF document. You've worked with key stores and certificates, signing documents in different ways. You've also learned about certificate and timestamp authorities, about certificate revocation lists, and the Online Certificate Status Protocol.

This chapter completes the overview of essential iText skills you may need when creating or manipulating PDF documents. In the next part, we'll dive into the PDF specification, and look at PDF at a much lower level. While doing this, you'll learn about different types of PDFs such as PDF/X and PDF/A. We'll work with PDF-specific functionality, such as optional content and marked content, and we'll inspect different types of streams.

Part 4

Under the hood

P art 4 provides an overview of the history of PDF, and it shows you the inner workings of a PDF document. It explains the different parts of a PDF file: the header, the body, the cross-reference table, and the trailer. The body of a PDF file consists of a series of objects, and you'll learn about the different types of objects in the Carousel Object System.

The three final chapters focus on stream objects. First you'll learn more about the content stream of a page. You'll learn about graphics state and text state, and about marked content. In the final chapter, you'll learn how to deal with streams that contain images, fonts, file attachments, and rich media.

PDFs inside-out

One of the initial strengths that made iText a success was that a developer was—and still is—able to create documents in the PDF format without having to know anything about the PDF specification. In the first versions of iText, you only had to know how a Chunk related to a Phrase, a Phrase to a Paragraph, and so on. The functionality was simple, but rather limited. Features that are specific to PDF, such as forms, optional content, and file attachments, weren't supported yet. The more functionality was added, the more there was a need for developers to understand what PDF is about. That's why we're going to take a look inside.

But before you open up a PDF file, let's look at why PDF was invented and how the format evolved from a de facto to an ISO standard.

13.1   PDF, why and how?

We can't talk about the history of PDF without talking about the history of the inventors of PDF, Adobe Systems Incorporated. Adobe was founded in 1982 by John Warnock and Chuck Geschke. Its first products were digital fonts, but nowadays Adobe offers a wide range of products and technologies. In this section, we'll look at the ancestors of PDF, and you'll learn about the different types of PDF that were created for different purposes.

13.1.1   The ancestors of PDF

In 1985, Adobe introduced the PostScript (PS) Page Description Language (PDL). PS is an interpretive programming language. Its primary goal is to describe the appearance of text, graphical shapes, and sampled images. It also provides a framework for controlling printing devices; for example, it can specify the number of copies to be printed, activate duplicate printing, and so forth.

Also in 1985, Adobe developed an application for the Apple Macintosh called Adobe Illustrator, a vector-based drawing program with its own format, AI, which was derived from PS. Illustrator was ported to Windows in 1989, so it covered an important market in the graphical industry.

Producing high-quality visual materials was the privilege of specialists for a long time, but with the advent of PostScript and Illustrator, anyone with a computer could accomplish high-end document publishing. By introducing these two technologies, Adobe started the desktop publishing revolution. But the founders of Adobe felt there was something missing.

In 1991, John Warnock wrote the "Camelot paper," in which he said:

> *The specific problem is that most programs print to a wide range of printers, but there is no universal way to communicate and view this printed information electronically ... What industries badly need is a universal way to communicate documents across a wide variety of machine configurations, operating systems, and communication networks.*

> —*The Camelot Project*, John Warnock

As a result of this writing, a new development project was started, and the engineers at Adobe enhanced the PostScript and Illustrator technologies to create a suite of applications with which to create and visualize documents of this format. *Carousel* was the original code name for what later became Acrobat. The new document format was originally called Interchange PostScript (IPS) but was soon known as the Portable Document Format (PDF).

13.1.2   The history of PDF

In February 1993, Jim King, Adobe's principal scientist, talked about "liberating" the information locked up on computer systems. In many cases, you had to use the computer application that was used to collect and assemble a document in order to read it on screen or to print it.

This is analogous to requiring the reader of a newspaper to own a photo-typesetting machine. Or the reader of a book to own a printing press. Acrobat frees the computer industry from this ridiculous model, establishing a standard for electronic final-form documents and providing simple viewing and printing tools that are widely and generally usable. Acrobat is an information liberation system!

—Jim King, principal scientist, Adobe

PDF is called the *Portable* Document Format because a PDF document can be viewed and printed on any platform: Windows, Mac, Linux, and so on. In theory, a PDF document looks the same on any of these platforms (although we've looked at some exceptions, such as in chapters 2 and 11 when we talked about embedding fonts). In analogy with Java's Write Once, Run Anywhere, you could say PDF is Write Once, Read Anywhere—but in a more reliable way than the catchy Java advertising phrase promises.

In June 1993, Adobe announced its new product, Acrobat. The first documentation on PDF was called the *Portable Document Format Reference Manual* and published by Addison-Wesley. Five more editions would follow, although not all of them were printed on paper—the sixth edition for PDF version 1.7 was only available as a PDF document. Figure 13.1 shows the cover of the first PDF reference, as well as an advertisement for the Acrobat Starter Kit, and the diskettes on which Acrobat was distributed.

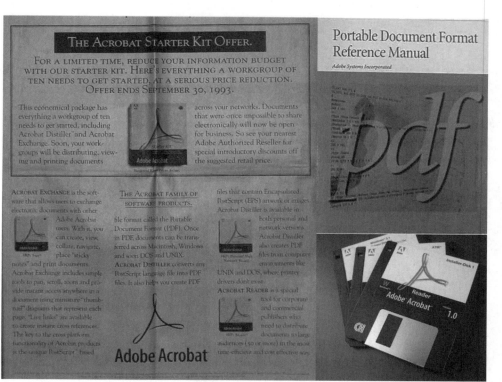

Figure 13.1 PDF reference cover, Acrobat Starter Kit advertisement, and Acrobat diskettes

In September 1993, Acrobat Exchange was the software that allowed users to exchange electronic documents with other Adobe Acrobat users. They could create, view, collate, navigate, place sticky notes, and print documents for $195. Acrobat Distiller converted (and still converts) PS to PDF. Distiller was priced at $695; Network Distiller at $2495. Finally, there was Acrobat Reader, described as "a special tool for corporate and commercial publishers who need to distribute documents to large audiences (50 or more) in the most time-efficient and cost effective way." In those days, Reader wasn't distributed for free; it was sold at $2500 for 50 copies. By version 2.0, released in 1994, the Reader was made available for free and Distiller was included with Acrobat Pro.

THE RELATIONSHIP BETWEEN PDF AND PS

Although PS and PDF are related, they're different formats. PDF leverages the ability of the PS language to render complex text and graphics, and brings this feature to the screen as well as to the printer. With PDF, reduced flexibility was traded for improved efficiency and predictability. Unlike PS, PDF can contain a lot of document structure, links, and other related information, but PDF can't tell the printer to use a certain input tray, change the resolution, or use any other hardware-specific features.

PDF isn't a programming language like PS. A PDF file consists of a number of objects. In his presentations about the PDF format, Jim King often refers to PDF as "object-oriented PostScript" because this object structuring is something that doesn't exist in PS. We'll have a closer look at the different objects in the *Carousel Object System* (COS) in section 13.2.

One of the key advantages PDF has over PS is page independence. With PS, something in the description of page 1 can affect page 1000, so to view page 1000, you have to interpret all the pages before it. PDF and PS share the same underlying Adobe imaging model, but in PDF, each page is self-contained and can be drawn individually. Each page has access to the text, font specifications, margins, layout, graphical elements, and background and text colors. We'll have a closer look at the syntax for drawing content in chapter 14, and at the way font specifications and graphical elements are embedded in the document in chapter 16.

But let's continue with the historical overview of PDF and Acrobat.

PDF VERSION HISTORY

In some of the examples you've made so far, you've changed the PDF version of a document because you were using technology that was introduced in a later version than the default. Table 13.1 shows a nonexhaustive list of new features that were added in each version.

The final part of this table needs more explaining. Up until PDF 1.7, Adobe owned the copyright of the PDF specification. To promote the use of the format for information exchange among diverse products and applications—including, but not necessarily limited to, Acrobat products—Adobe gave anyone copyright permission to do the following:

- Prepare files whose content conforms to the specification
- Write drivers and applications that produce output represented in PDF
- Write software that accepts input in PDF and displays, prints, or otherwise interprets the contents
- Copy Adobe's copyrighted list of data structures and operators, as well as the example code and PostScript language function definitions to the extent necessary to use PDF for the purposes above

Table 13.1 New features in different PDF versions

PDF version	Year	Version	New features
PDF-1.0	1993	Acrobat 1	■ Render complex text and graphics to the screen as well as to the printer
PDF-1.1	1994	Acrobat 2	■ Password-protected PDFs ■ External links ■ Device-independent color
PDF-1.2	1996	Acrobat 3	■ Flate compression ■ Interactive fill-in forms ■ Chinese, Japanese, Korean (CJK) support
PDF-1.3	1999	Acrobat 4	■ File attachments ■ Digital signatures ■ Logical page numbering
PDF-1.4	2001	Acrobat 5	■ 128-bit encryption ■ Transparency ■ Tagged PDF
PDF-1.5	2003	Acrobat 6	■ Additional compression and encryption options ■ Optional content groups ■ Enhanced support for embedding and playback of multimedia
PDF-1.6	2004	Acrobat 7	■ Customizable user unit value ■ Support for Advanced Encryption Standard (AES) ■ Page-scaling option for printing
PDF-1.7	2006	Acrobat 8	■ Portable collections ■ More printer controls ■ Major improvements to 3D
PDF-1.7 Extension Level 3	2008	Acrobat 9.0	■ PDF 1.7 specification used as the basis for ISO-32000-1; the version number remains 1.7, but companies can add their own extensions, such as Adobe's level 3 extensions, including support for rich media, geospatial data, and so on
PDF-1.7 Extension Level 5	2009	Acrobat 9.1	■ Adobe's level 5 extensions, including enhancements for transparency, portable collections, and rich text strings
PDF-2.0	2011	Acrobat 10?	■ ISO-32000-2, scheduled for release in the summer of 2011; the version number of PDFs will be augmented to 2.0

These were the conditions of such copyright permissions:

- Authors of software that accepts input in the form of PDF must make reasonable efforts to ensure that the software they create respects the access permissions and permissions controls.
- Anyone who uses the copyrighted list of data structures and operators, as stated above, must include an appropriate copyright notice.

These permissions granted by Adobe made it possible for me to start writing iText. Looking at the success of iText, I must have found a hole in the market. Whereas Acrobat was an information liberation system for data locked away on your computer, iText enabled you to liberate the data on your server. At the time iText was developed, the End User License Agreement of Acrobat (EULA) prevented the use of the product to produce PDF documents for multiple users on a server. The EULA of Acrobat still prevents this use, but Adobe now offers LiveCycle Enterprise Suite as a very powerful server solution.

13.1.3   *PDF as an ISO standard*

In spite of the far-reaching freedom provided by Adobe, there were always people who didn't consider the format open enough. They pestered Adobe because the company kept the privilege of owning and controlling the language specification, whereas the trend of the new millennium was to make everything as open as possible. At some point, Adobe must have decided the time was ripe to make this decision:

> *SAN JOSE, Calif.—Jan. 29, 2007—Adobe Systems Incorporated (Nasdaq:ADBE) today announced that it intends to release the full Portable Document Format (PDF) 1.7 specification to AIIM, the Enterprise Content Management Association, for the purpose of publication by the International Organization for Standardization (ISO).*

—Adobe Press Release

Jim King explains why this decision was made:

> *It was not a simple or easy decision for Adobe to make, but it has come up nearly every year since we first announced PDF and each time we've decided not to do it. I view it as a balance scale for weighing things. We put positive things on the right side and negative things on the left. Negative and positive for all of Adobe, our customers, our competitors, etc. It always has come out not to do it. Things do change and this year it came out (to my surprise) that the scale tipped the other way for the first time. There were just too many good reasons to do it and not many not so good. We believe that it will benefit everyone. I have been asked if this was in response to the pressure from government for open specifications or because of something Microsoft has done or might do, or because we think the language is becoming mature. Well my answer is yes, of course, but not because of any single one of those kinds of things. Just the accumulated long list of benefits and the scale tipped.*

—The Future of PDF and Flash, Jim King

The standard was published by the ISO on July 1, 2008. To us, iText users and developers working with PDF, the corporate politics didn't really matter; my personal reason why I liked Adobe bringing the specification to ISO was nicely phrased by Jim King:

> *From what I have been able to figure out there are over a billion PDF files being stored on computers in this world—could be a lot bigger number. What we want to do is to help ISO get an accurate specification under their control that documents the rules all those PDF files obey. We think they all, well nearly all, obey Adobe's current PDF 1.7 specification so a clean clear ISO version of that is what we're after. Please note that this is not tied in any significant way to Adobe products like Acrobat. It is your billion PDF files we're interested in documenting, not Acrobat. Once the ISO standard has been established, Adobe will be just one other (key we hope) company working together with other companies to make any changes to ISO PDF that are needed.*

> *—The Future of PDF and Flash,* Jim King

From now on, any company can write their own extensions to the Portable Document Format and submit them to ISO as proposed changes to the PDF specification. ISO may or may not accept these extensions; for instance, Adobe submitted a series of proposals for inclusion in ISO-32000-2. This new ISO will be published in 2011 and will result in PDF version 2.0. (There will be no PDF version 1.8.)

Extensions to the PDF specification aren't identified by PDF version identifiers. They use the extension mechanism defined in ISO-32000-1. The new convention lets companies and other entities identify their own extensions relative to a base version of PDF. Additionally, the convention identifies extension levels relative to that base version. Table 13.1 listed extension levels 3 and 5. These are two extensions published by Adobe for Acrobat 9.0 and 9.1.

The intent of the extensions convention is twofold:

- To enable developers of PDF-producing applications to identify the use of company-specific extensions they have added to a PDF document and to associate those extensions with their own publicly available specifications.
- To enable developers of PDF-consuming applications to determine which extensions are present in a PDF document and to associate those extensions with the specifications that describe them.

To avoid collisions over company names and company-specific extension names, ISO provides the prefix name registry. The prefix registry designates a 4-character, case-sensitive prefix that identifies a company or other entity. This prefix is used for company-specific version identifiers. For example, ADBE is the prefix registered by Adobe; ITXT is the prefix used for iText. For more info about the use of these prefixes, read appendix E of ISO-32000-1.

ISO-32000 wasn't the first ISO standard for PDF, nor will it be the last.

13.1.4 *PDF/X, PDF/A, PDF/E, PDF/UA, and other types of PDF*

There are many different ways to create a valid PDF file. This freedom is an advantage, but it can be a disadvantage too. Not all valid PDF files are usable in every context. To tackle this problem, different ISO standards were created, the first one dating from 2001: PDF/X.

X FOR EXCHANGE

The prepress sector uses PDF for a very specific purpose: to create digital documents that are meant to be produced on a printing press. Quality press output requires depositing precise amounts of different colors of ink at resolutions as high as 5000 dots per inch. Such high resolution also calls for images to have been sampled at a high rate. Not just any old PDF file can be used to produce high-quality press output under these conditions.

Confronted with a number of issues relating to parts of the PDF reference, a consortium of prepress companies got together and released specifications for PDF/X. This is a set of ISO standards (ISO 15930-1 to ISO 15930-8) describing well-defined subsets of the PDF specification that promise predictable and consistent output for press printing. Because these standards are subsets of PDF, files meeting these standards also meet the standard as normal PDF files. Each of these PDF/X standards has its own specific requirements and constraints, but in general you can say that functionality that will probably break PDF/X conformance includes encryption, the use of fonts that aren't embedded, RGB colors, layers, image masks, transparency, and some blend modes.

The two most useful PDF/X standards are supported by iText: PDF/X-1a:2001 and PDF/X-3:2002. The main goal of PDF/X-1a is to support *blind exchange* of PDF documents. Blind exchange means you can deliver PDF documents to a print service provider with hardly any technical discussion. PDF/X-3 is a superset of PDF/X-1a. The primary difference is that a PDF/X-3 file can also contain color-managed data. This listing shows how to set the PDF/X conformance. You can replace the parameter `PdfWriter.PDFX1A2001` with `PdfWriter.PDFX32002` to change the conformance to PDF/X-3.

Listing 13.1 PdfXPdfA.java

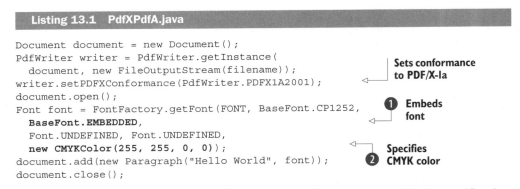

```
Document document = new Document();
PdfWriter writer = PdfWriter.getInstance(
  document, new FileOutputStream(filename));          Sets conformance
writer.setPDFXConformance(PdfWriter.PDFX1A2001);      to PDF/X-la
document.open();
Font font = FontFactory.getFont(FONT, BaseFont.CP1252,  ❶ Embeds
  BaseFont.EMBEDDED,                                       font
  Font.UNDEFINED, Font.UNDEFINED,
  new CMYKColor(255, 255, 0, 0));                       Specifies
document.add(new Paragraph("Hello World", font));      ❷ CMYK color
document.close();
```

As soon as you introduce functionality that isn't allowed in the PDF/X specification you've chosen, iText will throw an exception explaining what went wrong. For instance, try making these changes:

- Replace `BaseFont.EMBEDDED` ❶ with `BaseFont.NOT_EMBEDDED`. Try executing the example, and it will throw an exception saying, "All the fonts must be embedded. This one isn't: ArialMT."
- Replace the `CMYKColor` ❷ used for the font color by an instance of the `BaseColor` class. iText will throw the following error: "Colorspace RGB is not allowed."

The exceptions help you discover what is missing.

iText has similar functionality for PDF/A, although iText won't always throw an exception if you forget some of the requirements. You need a PDF validator after creating a PDF/A file with iText to see if you've met all the conditions and restrictions.

A FOR ARCHIVING

The PDF/A specification is also known as ISO 19005-1:2005: *Document Management—Electronic Document File Format for Long-Term Preservation—Part 1: Use of PDF 1.4 (PDF/A-1)*. The standard was approved in September 2005. The initiative for PDF/A was started by the Association for Information and Image Management (AIIM) and the Association for Suppliers of Printing, Publishing, and Converting Technology (NPES).

There are many electronic formats and technologies to choose from for archiving electronic data. The proprietary nature of many of these formats is one of the biggest disadvantages. There's no guarantee that a Word document created with the latest Microsoft Word version will open up in the newest version ten years from now. And even if you're able to open it, you can't expect it to look like it looked in the version of Word that was used to create it.

As opposed to most word-processing formats, PDF represents not only the data contained in the document, but also the exact form the document takes. The file can be viewed without the originating application. Adobe also made sure that all the revisions of the PDF specification are backward compatible, so no matter the version number, the PDF will always look the same even on newer PDF viewers. Even before PDF was published as an ISO standard, the PDF version of the specification was available for free. Anyone, at any time, using any hardware or software, can create programs to access PDF documents. This makes PDF (ISO-32000) an interesting candidate as a format for archiving.

PDF/A goes a step further. It's a subset of PDF-1.4, and like PDF/X, PDF/A imposes requirements and constraints.

PDF/A LEVEL B

In order to meet level-B conformance, all fonts must be embedded, encryption isn't allowed, audio and video content are forbidden, JavaScript and executable file launches are not permitted, and so forth. Each PDF/A document must contain metadata in the form of an XMP stream.

Here is how to create a level-B PDF/A document using iText.

Listing 13.2   PdfXPdfA.java

```
Document document = new Document();
PdfWriter writer = PdfWriter.getInstance(document,
  new FileOutputStream(filename));
```

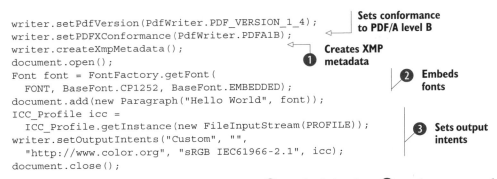

```
writer.setPdfVersion(PdfWriter.PDF_VERSION_1_4);
writer.setPDFXConformance(PdfWriter.PDFA1B);
writer.createXmpMetadata();
document.open();
Font font = FontFactory.getFont(
  FONT, BaseFont.CP1252, BaseFont.EMBEDDED);
document.add(new Paragraph("Hello World", font));
ICC_Profile icc =
  ICC_Profile.getInstance(new FileInputStream(PROFILE));
writer.setOutputIntents("Custom", "",
  "http://www.color.org", "sRGB IEC61966-2.1", icc);
document.close();
```

Sets conformance to PDF/A level B

❶ Creates XMP metadata

❷ Embeds fonts

❸ Sets output intents

In this example, you create XMP metadata ❶, embed the font ❷, and create a color profile. The constant PROFILE refers to a color profile saved on disk. This profile is used to set the output intents ❸. When color values are specified in a PDF file using the device color spaces, those values are to directly control the quantity of colorant (ink) used on a particular device or device class. The output intent supplies the color characteristics of that device so that the actual colors to be produced can be know in a device-independent way.

PDF/A LEVEL A

Level-A conformance includes all the requirements and constraints of level-B, but also requires that the PDF be tagged. Tagged PDF is a stylized use of PDF; it defines a set of standard structure types and attributes that allow page content to be extracted and reused for other purposes. Page content is represented so that the characters, words, and text order can be determined reliably. We'll learn about some more advantages of tagged PDFs when we discuss PDF/UA, and we'll create tagged PDFs in chapter 15.

Another important step in the history of PDF ISO specifications is PDF/E.

E FOR ENGINEERING

PDF/E, or ISO 24517-1:2008, was ratified by ISO as an open standard in June 2007. Based on PDF 1.6, it's meant to be used in engineering workflows. It was designed to be an open and neutral exchange format for engineering and technical documentation. PDF/E provides secure distribution of intellectual property and reliable exchange and change management. It also reduces costs associated with paper (including the cost to store and archive paper). It covers three primary areas:

- Compact, accurate printing of engineering drawings.
- Support for exchanging and managing annotation and comment data.
- Incorporation of complex data into PDF (3D, object-level data, and so on)

There's no direct support for PDF/E in iText yet. But there's already some functionality added that will be mandatory for PDF/UA.

UA FOR UNIVERSAL ACCESSIBILITY

To make the document accessible for the visually impaired, a PDF file should contain a logical reading order, images should be given alternate descriptions, and so on. All of these requirements will be bundled in the soon to be published ISO/AWI 14289.

The mission of PDF/UA is to develop technical and other standards for the authoring, remediation, and validation of PDF content to ensure accessibility for people who use assistive technology, such as screen readers.

> *This is not meant to be a techniques (how to) specification, but rather a set of guidelines for creating accessible PDF. The components and their structure are highly dependent upon which objects (graphics, text, multimedia, form fields) are to be present in the PDF file. The specification will describe such components and the conditions governing their inclusion in a PDF file in order to be considered accessible for a particular document type.*

> —AIIM, PDF/UA, Universal Accessibility Committee Scope

The mechanism of tagged PDF offers a number of techniques for different aspects of PDF accessibility. We'll take a look at some of these techniques in section 15.2.2. For instance, you can add extra tags that make it easier to understand a text that's read out loud by the speech software that's integrated into Adobe Reader.

> **FAQ** *Can I use iText to convert a plain PDF document to PDF/X, PDF/A, … ?* This is not possible out of the box for several reasons: external resources are needed (for instance, fonts need to be embedded), iText doesn't have the "intelligence" to add tags (for PDF/A level A, you need to add structure information that isn't there), iText doesn't convert RGB colors into CMYK, and so on. There are commercial tools that can help you to turn a plain PDF into a PDF/X, PDF/A, … document, but these tools usually need human input to make decisions.

We've talked about different ISO specifications for PDF, but there are plenty of other flavors of PDF files.

OTHER TYPES OF PDF

This is a nonexhaustive list of PDF and PDF-related types of documents you can encounter:

- *Tagged PDF*—As explained when we talked about PDF/A and PDF/UA, you can add extra structure to a PDF file that allows a PDF consumer to "understand" the content.
- *Linearized PDF*—A *linearized* PDF file is organized in a special way to enable efficient incremental access, thus enhancing the viewing performance. Its primary goal is to display the first page as quickly as possible without the need to read all of the rest of the file or to read the cross-reference table that normally is at the end of the file. This enhances the experience when viewing a PDF file over a streaming communications channel such as the internet. Linearized PDF is sometimes referred to as PDF for "fast web view." When data for a page is delivered over a slow channel, you'd like to have the page content displayed incrementally as it arrives. With the essential cross-reference table at the end of the file, this is not possible unless the file is linearized.

  Linearization can only be done after the PDF file is complete and after all resources are known. iText can read linearized PDFs, but it can't create a linearized PDF, nor can you linearize an existing PDF using iText.

- *PDF/H*—PDF for the healthcare providers and consumers. PDF/H is described in a "Best Practices Guide." It aims to provide a more secure electronic container for storing and transferring healthcare information, including documents, XML data, DICOM images and data, clinical notes, lab reports, electronic forms, scanned images, photographs, digital X-rays, and ECGs.
- *XML Data Package (XDP)*—When we discussed dynamic XFA forms, we had a PDF that was used as the container and an XML stream embedded in the PDF representing the content of the PDF. In an XDP file, it's the other way around. An XDP file is an XML file that packages a PDF file (base64 encoded), along with XML form and template data. PDF and XDP are interchangeable representations of the same underlying electronic form. PDF offers advantages for large documents, when file size is important, or when forms contain images. XDP is interesting when forms have to fit in an XML workflow and data needs to be manipulated by software that isn't PDF-aware. XDP files aren't supported in iText.

There are other types of PDF in the works, such as PDF/VT (for the variable and transactional printing industry). Some specifications have emerged, and then disappeared, never to be heard about again; for example, Adobe Mars was another XML alternative for PDF by Adobe.

But that's outside the scope of this book. Let's return to the PDF and find out why Jim King sometimes calls it object-oriented PostScript.

13.2 *Understanding the Carousel Object System*

Although Carousel was only a code name for what later became Acrobat, the name is still used to refer to the way a PDF file is composed. In part 1 of this book, you worked with the high-level API of iText, creating a document using objects that implement the `Element` interface. On the lowest level, iText works with objects that are derived from the abstract class `PdfObject`. This was one of the first iText classes that was written, immediately followed by the basic PDF objects in the *Carousel Object System.*

13.2.1 *Basic PDF objects*

There are eight basic types of objects in PDF. They're explained in sections 7.3.2 to 7.3.9 in ISO-32000-1. Table 13.2 lists these types as well as their corresponding objects in iText.

Table 13.2   Overview of the basic PDF objects

PDF object	iText object	Description
Boolean	PdfBoolean	This type is similar to the Boolean type in programming languages and can be `true` or `false`.
Numeric object	PdfNumber	There are two types of numeric objects: integer and real. You've used them frequently to define coordinates, font sizes, and so on.

Table 13.2 Overview of the basic PDF objects *(continued)*

PDF object	iText object	Description
String	`PdfString`	String objects can be written in two ways: ■ As a sequence of literal characters enclosed in parentheses: ( ) ■ As hexadecimal data enclosed in angle brackets: < > Beginning with PDF 1.7, the type string is further qualified in the documentation as text string, PDFDocEncoded string, ASCII string, and byte string depending upon how the string is used in each particular context.
Name	`PdfName`	A name object is an atomic symbol uniquely defined by a sequence of characters. You've been using names as keys for dictionaries, to define a destination on a page, and so on. You can easily recognize them in a PDF file because they're all introduced with a forward slash: /.
Array	`PdfArray`	An array is a one-dimensional collection of objects, arranged sequentially between square brackets. You've used arrays to define the size of a page; for instance, [0 0 595 842].
Dictionary	`PdfDictionary`	A dictionary is an associative table containing pairs of objects known as dictionary entries. The key is always a name; the value can be (a reference to) any other object. The collection of pairs is enclosed by double angle brackets: << and >>.
Stream	`PdfStream`	Like a string object, a stream is a sequence of bytes. The main difference is that a PDF consumer reads a string entirely, whereas a stream is best read incrementally. Strings are generally used for small pieces of data; streams are used for large amounts of data. Each stream consists of a dictionary followed by zero or more bytes bracketed between the keywords `stream` (followed by newline) and `endstream`.
Null object	`PdfNull`	This type is similar to the `null` object in programming languages. Setting the value of a dictionary to `null` is equivalent to omitting the entry.

You've used subclasses of these objects frequently in previous chapters:

■ `PdfAction`, `PdfFormField`, and `PdfOutline` are only a few of the many subclasses of the `PdfDictionary` class.

■ `PdfRectangle` is a special type of `PdfArray` because it's a sequence of four values: [llx, lly, urx, ury].

■ `PdfDate` extends `PdfString` because a date is a special type of string.

These objects are called *direct* when they're used as shown in the following code snippet:

```
<<
  /CreationDate(D:20100219095234+01'00')
  /Producer(iText 5.0.2 \(c\) 1T3XT BVBA)
  /ModDate(D:20100219095234+01'00')
>>
```

This is a dictionary with three entries. The key of each entry is a name; in this case the value of each entry is a string.

An object can also be labeled as an *indirect* object:

```
5 0 obj
<<
  /Type/Catalog
  /Pages 3 0 R
>>
endobj
```

Using the keywords `obj` and `endobj`, the object is given a unique object identifier by which other objects can refer to it. The value of the `/Pages` entry is such a reference: `3 0 R` is an indirect reference to the indirect object with number 3.

> **NOTE**   A stream object may never be used as a direct object. For example, if an entry in a dictionary is a stream, the value always has to be an indirect reference to an indirect object containing a stream. The stream dictionary always has to be a direct object. This dictionary contains information about the stream, such as its length in bytes and the filter that was used to compress the stream.

When you look inside a PDF file, you'll find out that a large part of the PDF consists of a series of indirect objects.

13.2.2   *The PDF file structure*

Figure 13.2 shows two PDF files opened in Notepad++. Extra lines were added to identify the different parts.

In general, a PDF has four parts:

- *The header*—Discussed in section 1.3.3. It specifies the PDF version (which can be overruled in the Catalog dictionary) and contains a comment section that ensures that the file's content is treated as binary content.
- *The body*—Contains a sequence of indirect objects that make up the document: pages, outlines, annotations, and so on.
- *The cross-reference table*—Contains information that allows random access to the indirect objects in the body.
- *The trailer*—Gives the location of the cross-reference table and of certain special objects in the body of the file.

You can see these four parts in the PDF in the background of figure 13.2. The PDF in the foreground is slightly different. That PDF is *fully compressed* (see section 12.2.1). The trailer is shorter. The cross-reference table isn't missing, but it's compressed in the object with number 8. Object 5 is a so-called object stream, in which a sequence of indirect objects may be stored as an alternative to their being stored at the outermost file level. The purpose of such an object stream is to allow objects other than streams to be stored more compactly by using the facilities provided by stream compression filters.

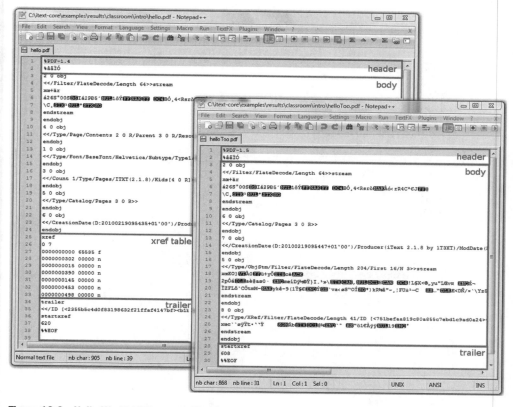

Figure 13.2 Hello World PDFs opened in Notepad++

It's also possible to create a PDF in append mode. In this case, the four parts of the original file are kept intact, and an extra body, cross-reference table, and trailer are added. There are different reasons why you might choose to work in append mode:

- To avoid signatures being invalidated when adding multiple signatures (see section 12.4.3)
- To preserve the usage rights when filling out Reader-enabled forms (see section 8.7)
- To make it possible to restore previous revisions of a document (see listings 13.4 and 13.5)

There will also be more than one body, xref, and trailer when you open a linearized PDF in a text editor. Linearized PDF files have the first page's cross-reference table at the beginning of the file. This way, a PDF viewer has all the necessary information to show the first page, even before the content of the second page is downloaded. Page two can be shown before page three is downloaded, and so on. Linearized PDFs are the exception to the rule. In all other cases, a PDF viewer has to start reading a PDF file at the end.

EXAMINING THE CONTENT OF A PDF FILE

Let's look at a simple PDF file that isn't fully compressed and that isn't linearized.

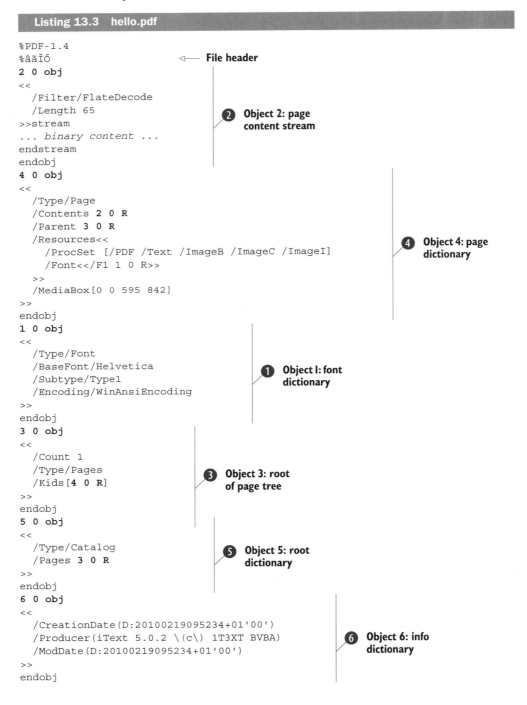

Listing 13.3   hello.pdf

```
%PDF-1.4
%âãÏÓ                          ◁── File header
2 0 obj
<<
  /Filter/FlateDecode
  /Length 65                   ❷ Object 2: page
>>stream                           content stream
... binary content ...
endstream
endobj
4 0 obj
<<
  /Type/Page
  /Contents 2 0 R
  /Parent 3 0 R
  /Resources<<
    /ProcSet [/PDF /Text /ImageB /ImageC /ImageI]   ❹ Object 4: page
    /Font<</F1 1 0 R>>                                  dictionary
  >>
  /MediaBox[0 0 595 842]
>>
endobj
1 0 obj
<<
  /Type/Font
  /BaseFont/Helvetica
  /Subtype/Type1               ❶ Object I: font
  /Encoding/WinAnsiEncoding        dictionary
>>
endobj
3 0 obj
<<
  /Count 1
  /Type/Pages                  ❸ Object 3: root
  /Kids[4 0 R]                     of page tree
>>
endobj
5 0 obj
<<
  /Type/Catalog                ❺ Object 5: root
  /Pages 3 0 R                     dictionary
>>
endobj
6 0 obj
<<
  /CreationDate(D:20100219095234+01'00')
  /Producer(iText 5.0.2 \(c\) 1T3XT BVBA)   ❻ Object 6: info
  /ModDate(D:20100219095234+01'00')             dictionary
>>
endobj
```

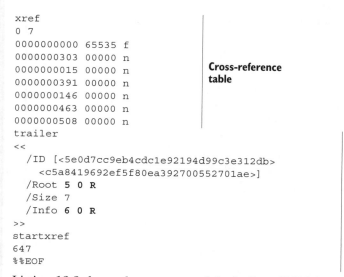

```
xref
0 7
0000000000 65535 f
0000000303 00000 n
0000000015 00000 n
0000000391 00000 n
0000000146 00000 n
0000000463 00000 n
0000000508 00000 n
trailer
<<
  /ID [<5e0d7cc9eb4cdc1e92194d99c3e312db>
    <c5a8419692ef5f80ea392700552701ae>]
  /Root 5 0 R
  /Size 7
  /Info 6 0 R
>>
startxref
647
%%EOF
```

Cross-reference table

Trailer

Listing 13.3 shows the contents of the hello.pdf file. You created this file in listing 1.1 of chapter 1. Note that the file has been slightly reorganized to improve its readability.

You need to start reading this file at the end. The last line of each PDF file should contain the end-of-file marker, %EOF. The two preceding lines contain the keyword startxref and the byte offset of the cross-reference table. That's the position of the word xref counted from the start of the file.

THE TRAILER

The trailer begins with the keyword trailer, followed by the *trailer dictionary*. In listing 13.3, the first entry of this dictionary is a *file identifier*. The /Size entry shows the total number of entries in the file's cross-reference table. There are two references to special dictionaries: the /Info key to the *info dictionary* and the /Root key to the *catalog dictionary*. The info dictionary contains the metadata discussed in section 12.1.1; we'll take a closer look at the catalog in section 13.3.

> **NOTE** For fully compressed PDF files, startxref is followed by the byte offset of the cross-reference stream. In the compressed file shown in figure 13.2, the entries of the trailer dictionary were moved to the /XRef dictionary in the cross-reference stream.

Other possible entries in the trailer dictionary are the /Encrypt key, which is required if the document is encrypted, and the /Prev key, which is present only if the file has more than one cross-reference section.

This listing creates a PDF file with two cross-reference tables, reusing the hello.pdf file created in listing 1.1.

Listing 13.4   AppendMode.java

```java
PdfReader reader = new PdfReader(src);
PdfStamper stamper =
  new PdfStamper(reader, new FileOutputStream(dest), '\0', true);
```

```
PdfContentByte cb = stamper.getUnderContent(1);
cb.beginText();
cb.setFontAndSize(BaseFont.createFont(), 12);
cb.showTextAligned(Element.ALIGN_LEFT, "Hello People!", 36, 770, 0);
cb.endText();
stamper.close();
```

At first sight, this looks like a typical PdfStamper example from part 2 of this book. The only difference is that you use extra parameters to create the stamper object. The binary null ('/0') ensures that the PDF version of the original PDF file won't be changed. The boolean value indicates whether the original file should be appended (true) or not (false). This example tells iText to preserve the original file; the extra content is added after the end-of-file marker of the original file.

When you open the resulting file in a text editor, you'll see the exact same content as shown in listing 13.3, followed by the content of this listing.

Listing 13.5   appended.pdf

```
... Unaltered content of listing 13.3 ...
7 0 obj
<<
  /Type/Font
  /BaseFont/Helvetica              ❼  Object 7: font
  /Subtype/Type1                       dictionary
  /Encoding/WinAnsiEncoding
>>
endobj
8 0 obj
<<
  /Filter/FlateDecode
  /Length 63                       ❽  Object 8: part of page
>>stream                              content stream
... binary content ...
endstream
endobj
4 0 obj
<<
  /Type/Page
  /Contents[8 0 R 2 0 R]
  /Parent 3 0 R
  /Resources<<
    /ProcSet [/PDF /Text /ImageB /ImageC /ImageI]   ❹  Object 4: page
    /Font<</F1 1 0 R/Xi0 7 0 R>>                         dictionary
  >>
  /MediaBox[0 0 595 842]
>>
endobj
3 0 obj
<<
  /Count 1
  /Type/Pages                      ❸  Object 3: root
  /Kids[4 0 R]                         of page tree
>>
endobj
```

```
6 0 obj
<<
  /CreationDate(D:20100220120417+01'00')
  /Producer(iText 5.0.2 \(c\) 1T3XT BVBA)
  /ModDate(D:20100220120417+01'00')
>>
endobj
xref
0 1
0000000000 65535 f
3 2
0000001324 00000 n
0000001150 00000 n
6 3
0000001396 00000 n
0000000933 00000 n
0000001021 00000 n
trailer
<<
  /Prev 647
  /ID [<a98da95e3ed2cce8ce81c963fab0f64f>
    <eabe5f84e63aa0be734786337345d78b>]
  /Root 5 0 R
  /Size 9
  /Info 6 0 R
>>
startxref
1535
%%EOF
```

6 Object 6: info dictionary

Cross-reference table

Trailer

You'll recognize the indirect objects in the body. They can occur in any order; for instance, **2**, **4**, **1**, **3**, **5**, **6** in listing 13.3, and **7**, **8**, **4**, **3**, **6** in listing 13.5. An application reading the PDF (for instance, using the PdfReader class), can find the different objects thanks to the cross-reference table.

THE CROSS-REFERENCE TABLE

The cross-reference table stores the information required to locate every indirect object in the body.

For reasons of performance, a PDF consumer doesn't read the entire file. Imagine a document with 10,000 pages. If you only need to see the last page, a PDF viewer doesn't have to know what's inside the 9999 previous pages. It can use the cross reference to find the resources for the requested page in no time.

The cross-reference table contains two types of lines:

- *Lines with two numbers*—For example, 6 3 in listing 13.5 means the next line is about object 6 in a series of three consecutive objects: 6, 7, and 8.
- *Lines with exactly 20 bytes*—A 10-digit number represents the byte offset; a 5-digit number indicates the generation of the object. If these numbers are followed by the keyword n, the object is in use. Otherwise, the keyword f is present, meaning the object is free. These three parts are separated by a space character and end with a 2-byte end-of-line sequence.

The first entry in the xref table is always free and has a generation number of 65,535. Except for this 0 object, all objects in the cross-reference table have a generation number 0. In theory, the generation number of objects 3, 4, and 6 in listing 13.5 should have been 1; these objects replace the objects with the same number in listing 13.3. In practice, the use of generation numbers has been abandoned. It was one of the items that was eligible for removal when writing ISO-32000-1, but eventually the concept remained part of the specification, although not many products implement it.

Now pretend that you're a PDF viewer; how do you read a PDF file?

13.2.3 *Climbing up the object tree*

You need to start at the end to find the offset of the cross-reference tree. The first object you need is the *root object*, aka the *catalog*. The *trailer dictionary* tells you that you need object 5:

```
5 0 obj
<<
  /Type/Catalog
  /Pages 3 0 R
>>
endobj
```

The catalog contains a reference to a *pages dictionary*. This is the root of the page tree; see the following indirect object:

```
3 0 obj
<<
  /Count 1
  /Type/Pages
  /Kids[4 0 R]
>>
endobj
```

Such a dictionary can refer to branches—other /Pages dictionaries—and leaves—/Page dictionaries. This is a simple example containing only one page (/Count 1).

The /Kids array only has one value, a reference to object 4:

```
4 0 obj
<<
  /Type/Page
  /Contents[8 0 R 2 0 R]
  /Parent 3 0 R
  /Resources<<
    /ProcSet [/PDF /Text /ImageB /ImageC /ImageI]
    /Font<</F1 1 0 R/Xi0 7 0 R>>
  <<
  /MediaBox[0 0 595 842]
>>
endobj
```

This page has references to the original content, the stream in indirect object ❷ in listing 13.3, and the new content added with listing 13.4, object ❽. Each page also has a back-reference to its parent, in this case object ❸ in listing 13.3. The /Resources dictionary tells you which resources are needed to render the page. In this case, you'll find references to font objects, but in more complex examples you'll find references to form and image XObjects. If a page has annotations, there will also be an /Annots entry in the page dictionary. The size of the page is defined by the /MediaBox rectangle (there's no /CropBox in this example).

A PDF viewer has no problem finding, using, and reusing the different objects that compose a page. Although you've pretended to be a PDF viewer, you're not. In the past, I've "climbed the object tree" of many PDF files looking for bugs in the PDF, scrolling up and down in a text editor. This may be easy for a simple file, as shown in listings 13.3 and 13.5, but it's far from easy in larger files, especially if they contain more than one trailer or if objects are compressed in a stream. That's why I wrote a tool named RUPS. *Rups* is a Dutch word meaning *caterpillar*. It's also an acronym for *Reading and Updating PDF Syntax*. It's not possible to update the syntax of a PDF document yet, but you can already use RUPS to browse through the internal structure like a caterpillar.

Figure 13.3 shows the ebook version of the first edition of *iText in Action* opened in RUPS.

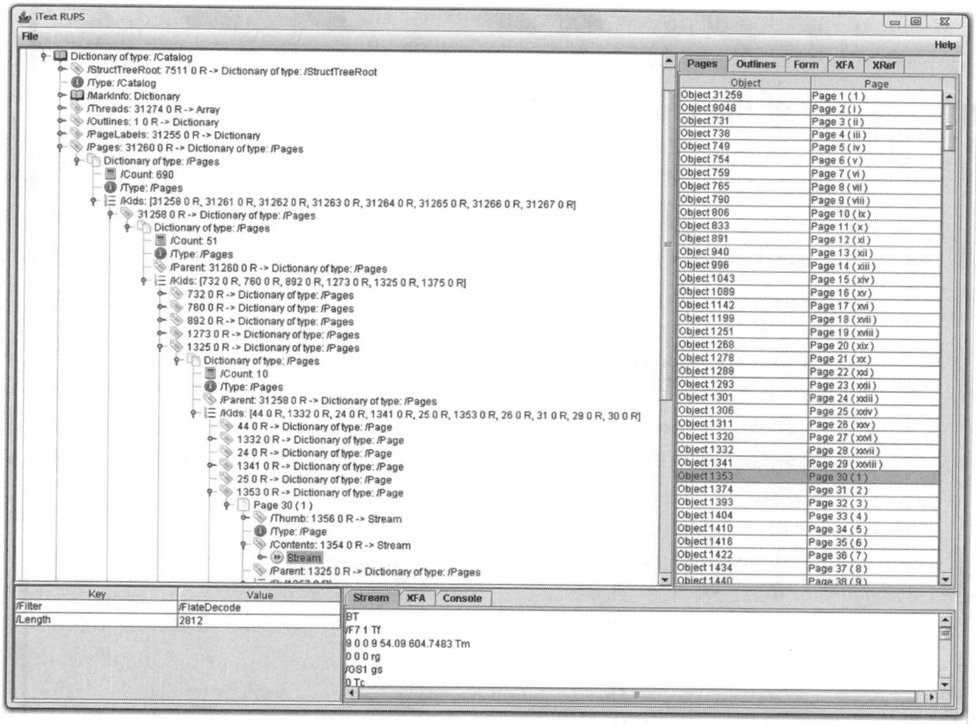

Figure 13.3   The *iText in Action*, first edition ebook opened in RUPS

In the left panel, you can see the objects that make up the PDF file in a tree. In this figure, I started with the catalog dictionary, opened the /Pages entry (object 31260), went into the /Kids array, and selected indirect object 1325 which is in turn a /Pages dictionary. I went into that /Kids array and selected object 1253. This is page 30 of the PDF, labeled page 1 (the first 29 pages are numbered *i, ii, iii, iv,* and so on). To see what's inside that page, I opened the /Contents entry of the page dictionary. I clicked the word Stream, which allows me to consult the stream dictionary in the bottom-left panel. The actual stream is shown in the bottom-right panel.

That's one way to find page 30. A simpler way is to select page 30 in the Pages panel on the right. The tree will open automatically, showing the /Page dictionary of the selected page. The right pane also contains panels that allow you to jump to the objects that form the outline tree, an AcroForm, or an XFA form, and there's also a complete overview of the cross-reference table.

This tool is under development; the GUI may change, and more functionality may be added in the near future, but I'm already using it extensively when people post questions about "PDFs that don't work." If you know the PDF specification, you can use RUPS to find out what's wrong with a broken PDF.

In the next section, we'll dig into ISO-32000-1 to find out more about the entries in the catalog dictionary that deal with viewer preferences, pages, destinations, and AcroForms.

13.3 *Exploring the root of a PDF file*

Table 28 in ISO-32000-1 lists the possible entries in the catalog dictionary. Some of these entries should already look familiar because we've discussed them before:

- Version *and* Extensions—As explained in section 1.3.3, the PDF version can be found in the header of a PDF file, but this version number can be overruled if the /Version key is present in the catalog. As shown in table 13.1, you can also specify which extensions from which company are used. The version is set using the method PdfWriter.setPdfVersion(); the extension can be defined using the PdfDeveloperExtension class, and it can be added to the PDF with Pdf-Writer.addDeveloperExtension().

- OpenAction *and* AA—In section 7.1.4, you added actions triggered by events to a PDF: an open action and additional actions. If the document has an open action, you'll find an array specifying a destination or an action dictionary in the /Open-Action entry. The /AA entry can contain a dictionary with keys referring to events such as PdfWriter.WILL_PRINT or PdfWriter.DOCUMENT_CLOSE. If you look at the source code of PdfWriter, you'll see that these constants are PdfName objects.

- Metadata—This refers to an XMP stream containing metadata about the complete document; see section 12.1.2. Note that a stream always has to be added as an indirect object, and that an XMP stream can never be compressed or encrypted.

- OutputIntents—Listing 13.2 defines an output intent. The catalog contains an array of dictionaries that specify the color characteristics of output devices on which the document might be rendered.

We won't go into further detail as far as these entries are concerned, but we'll select some other entries for a closer look.

13.3.1 Page layout, page mode, and viewer preferences

If you open a document in Adobe Reader, and no viewer preferences are specified inside the document, the Reader shows the document using default settings for the zoom factor, the visibility of toolbars, and so on. The panes or panels to the left, showing bookmarks, for example, are closed by default. You can change this default behavior by setting three entries in the catalog dictionary: /PageLayout, /PageMode, and /ViewerPreferences. You can do this using the setViewerPreferences() and addViewerPreference() convenience methods, which are present in PdfWriter as well as in PdfStamper. The setViewerPreferences() method expects an int value that's a combination of the values for the page layout (table 13.3) and the page mode (table 13.4).

PAGE LAYOUT

With the values in table 13.3, you can specify the page layout to be used when a document is opened.

Table 13.3   Page layout values

Value	Description
PageLayoutSinglePage	Displays one page at a time (this is the default).
PageLayoutOneColumn	Displays the pages in one column.
PageLayoutTwoColumnLeft	Displays the pages in two columns, with odd-numbered pages on the left.
PageLayoutTwoColumnRight	Displays the pages in two columns, with odd-numbered pages on the right.
PageLayoutTwoPageLeft	Displays the pages two at a time, with odd-numbered pages on the left.
PageLayoutTwoPageRight	Displays the pages two at a time, with odd-numbered pages on the right.

Figure 13.4 shows documents that are opened using (from left to right) PageLayout-TwoColumnLeft, PageLayoutTwoColumnRight, and PageLayoutOneColumn. You can change the page layout by choosing View > Page Display. Note that features described in the PDF reference are often referred to by another name in end-user products. In Acrobat terminology, you have the choice of displaying Single Page, Single Page Continuous, Two-Up, and Two-Up Continuous.

The version number is set to PDF 1.5 in listing 13.6, because that's when the values /TwoPageLeft and /TwoPageRight were introduced.

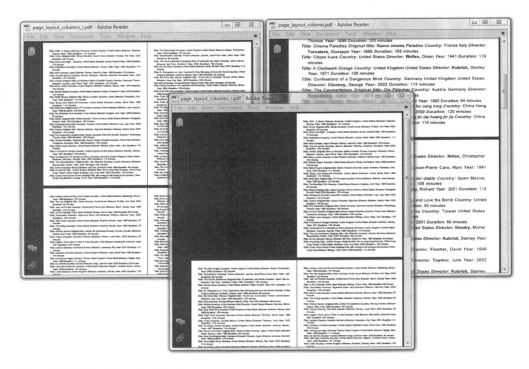

Figure 13.4   Page layout with columns

Listing 13.6   PageLayoutExample.java

```
PdfWriter writer
  = PdfWriter.getInstance(document, new FileOutputStream(filename));
writer.setPdfVersion(PdfWriter.VERSION_1_5);
writer.setViewerPreferences(viewerpreference);
```

With page layout preferences, you define how the pages are organized in the document window. With page mode preferences, you can define how the document opens in Adobe Reader.

PAGE MODE

Table 13.4 lists page mode preferences. This gives you an idea of the different panels available in Adobe Reader.

Table 13.4   Page mode values

Value	Description
PageModeUseNone	None of the tabs on the left are selected (this is the default).
PageModeUseOutlines	The document outline is visible (bookmarks).
PageModeUseThumbs	Images corresponding with the page are visible.

Table 13.4 Page mode values *(continued)*

Value	Description
PageModeFullScreen	Full-screen mode; no menu bar, window controls, or any other windows are visible.
PageModeUseOC	The optional content group panel is visible (since PDF 1.5).
PageModeUseAttachments	The attachments panel is visible (since PDF 1.6).

Typically, these page modes are set to stress the fact that the document has book-marks, optional content, and so on. We'll discuss optional content in chapter 15 and attachments in chapter 16.

With page layout and page mode, you're supposed to choose one option from each list. It doesn't make sense to choose two different page layout or page mode values, but you can always combine a page mode with a page layout option. For instance,

```
PdfWriter.PageLayoutTwoColumnRight | PdfWriter.PageModeUseThumbs
```

If you choose a full-screen mode, you can add another option related to the panel to the left. This preference specifies how to display the document on exiting full-screen mode; see table 13.5.

Table 13.5 Page mode values on exiting full-screen mode

Value	Description
NonFullScreenPageModeUseNone	None of the tabs at the left are visible.
NonFullScreenPageModeUseOutlines	The document outline is visible.
NonFullScreenPageModeUseThumbs	Thumbnail images corresponding with the pages are visible.
NonFullScreenPageModeUseOC	The optional content group panel is visible.

These options only make sense if the page mode is full screen. For instance,

```
PdfWriter.PageModeFullScreen | PdfWriter.NonFullScreenPageModeUseOutlines
```

Note that you can exit full-screen mode using the Escape key.

The value that's set when you choose one of these NonFullScreenPageMode options can be found as an entry in the /ViewerPreferences dictionary.

VIEWER PREFERENCES

In the View menu of Adobe Reader, you can select toolbar items that must be shown or hidden. You can control the initial state of some of these items by setting the viewer preferences listed in table 13.6.

Table 13.6   Values for the viewer preferences

Value	Description
HideToolbar	Hides the toolbar when the document is opened.
HideMenubar	Hides the menu bar when the document is opened.
HideWindowUI	Hides UI elements in the document's window (such as scrollbars and navigation controls), leaving only the document's contents displayed.
FitWindow	Resizes the document's window to fit the size of the first displayed page.
CenterWindow	Puts the document's window in the center of the screen.
DisplayDocTitle	Displays the title that was added in the metadata in the top bar (otherwise the filename is displayed).

With the following preference values, you can determine the predominant order of the pages.

- DirectionL2R—Left to right (the default).
- DirectionR2L—Right to left, including vertical writing systems such as Chinese, Japanese, and Korean.

This preference also has an effect on the way pages are shown when displayed side by side.

> **FAQ** *How can I show the title of the PDF in my browser window? How can I hide the location bar of my browser?* We're talking about viewer preferences, not about browser preferences. The Reader plug-in isn't able to control the settings of the browser, unless you embed the PDF as an object in an HTML page and use JavaScript as described in section 9.3.

These viewer preferences can also be set using the setViewerPreferences() method. For example,

```
writer.setViewerPreferences(PdfWriter.FitWindow | PdfWriter.HideToolbar);
```

You can also add the entries of the viewer preferences dictionary using the addViewerPreference() method, like this:

```
writer.addViewerPreference(PdfName.FITWINDOW, PdfBoolean.TRUE);
writer.addViewerPreference(PdfName.HIDETOOLBAR, PdfBoolean.TRUE);
```

This method can also be used with the keys shown in table 13.7 and one of the page boundaries discussed in section 5.3 as the value: PdfName.MEDIABOX, PdfName.CROPBOX, PdfName.BLEEDBOX, PdfName.TRIMBOX, or PdfName.ARTBOX.

Table 13.7   More viewer preferences

Key	Description
PdfName.VIEWAREA	Defines the area of the pages that will be displayed when viewing the document on the screen.
PdfName.VIEWCLIP	Clips the contents of the pages when viewing the document on the screen.
PdfName.PRINTAREA	Defines the area of the pages that will be rendered when printing the document.
PdfName.PRINTCLIP	Clips the contents of the pages when printing the document.

The viewer preferences also include a number of printing preferences.

PRINTING PREFERENCES

When an end user chooses to print a document, a Print dialog box is displayed, in which the page range, the number of copies, and so on, can be set. You can help the end user by predefining values for some of the keys listed in table 13.8.

Table 13.8   Keys and values of printing preferences

Key	Possible values
PdfName.PRINTSCALING	Valid values are PdfName.NONE, which indicates no page scaling, and PdfName.APPDEFAULT, which indicates the conforming Reader's default print scaling.
PdfName.DUPLEX	The value can be PdfName.SIMPLEX (print single-sided), PdfName.DUPLEXFLIPSHORTEDGE (duplex printing, flip on the short edge of the sheet), PdfName.DUPLEXFLIPLONG-EDGE (duplex printing, flip on the long edge of the sheet).
PdfName.PICKTRAYBYPDFSIZE	Expects a PdfBoolean. If set to PDFTRUE, the check box in the Print dialog box associated with input paper tray will be checked.
PdfName.PRINTPAGERANGE	Expects a PdfArray containing an even number of integers to be interpreted in pairs, with each pair specifying the first and last pages in a subrange of pages to be printed. The first page of the PDF file is denoted by 1.
PdfName.NUMCOPIES	Expects a PdfNumber. Supported values are the integers 2 through 5. Values outside this range are ignored.

Figure 13.5 shows a Print dialog box with some values that were set using viewer preferences.

Listing 13.7 shows how it was done.

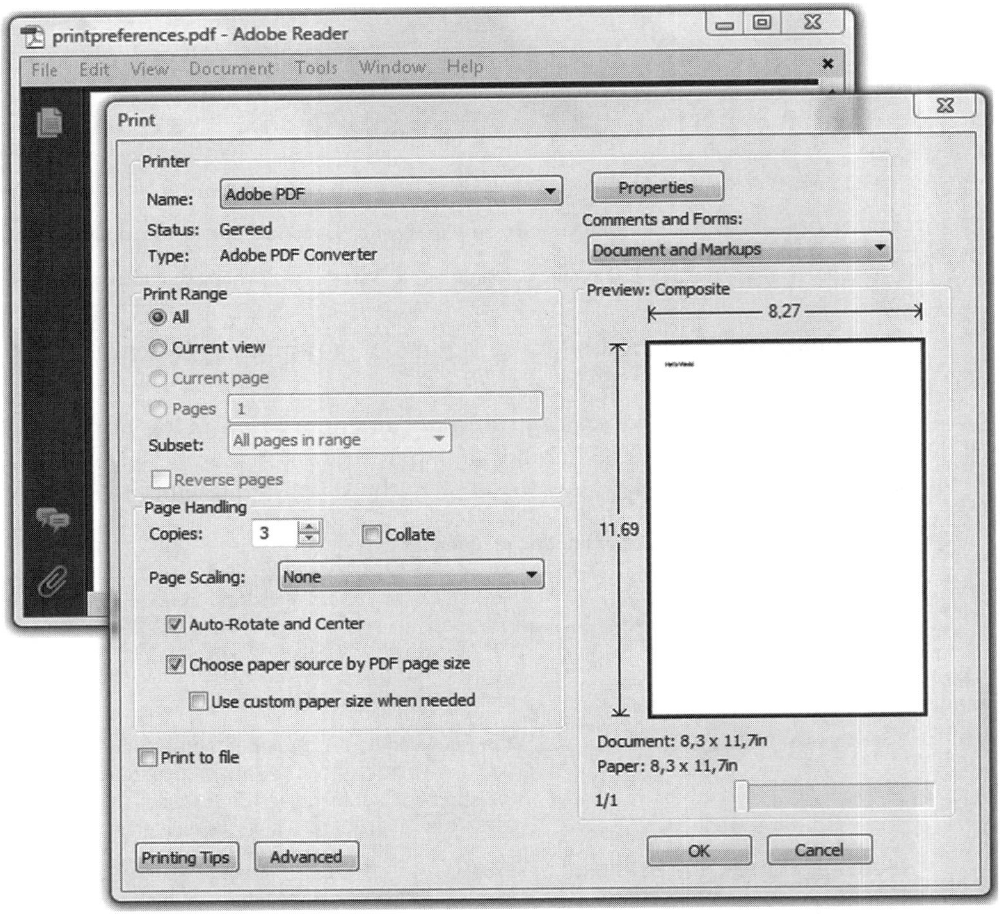

Figure 13.5   Print dialog box with default values set using viewer preferences

Listing 13.7   PrintPreferencesExample.java

```
PdfWriter writer
  = PdfWriter.getInstance(document, new FileOutputStream(filename));
writer.setPdfVersion(PdfWriter.VERSION_1_5);
writer.addViewerPreference(PdfName.PRINTSCALING, PdfName.NONE);
writer.addViewerPreference(PdfName.NUMCOPIES, new PdfNumber(3));
writer.addViewerPreference(PdfName.PICKTRAYBYPDFSIZE, PdfBoolean.PDFTRUE);
```

Not every viewer supports all these viewer preferences. ISO-32000-1 warns that most viewers disregard /ViewArea, /ViewClip, /PrintArea, /PrintClip, and that /Pick-TrayByPDFSize only works on operating systems that have the ability to pick the input tray by size. You also can't force an end user to use these preferences: they can always change the page layout, the page mode, the properties of the viewer, and the printer settings.

FAQ *Why are the measurements not correct when I print a PDF?* A lot of printers have margin limitations; they can't print anything close to the borders of the page. The amount of space that's left blank varies from printer to printer. If you look at figure 13.5, you'll see that there's a property named *Page Scaling*. Possible values for this property are None, Fit to Printable Area, Shrink to Printable Area, Multiple Pages per Sheet, and Booklet Printing. You need to set the page scaling to none if you don't want the measurements to be scaled down.

This concludes our overview of the viewer preferences that can be set for a PDF document. Let's continue with the catalog entries concerning pages.

13.3.2 *Pages and page labels*

The value of the /Pages entry in the catalog dictionary refers to the root of the page tree. ISO-32000-1 explains how pages are organized inside a PDF document:

> *The pages of a document are accessed through a structure known as the page tree, which defines the ordering of pages in the document. Using the tree structure, [PDF] readers using only limited memory, can quickly open a document containing thousands of pages. The tree contains nodes of two types—intermediate nodes, called page tree nodes, and leaf nodes, called page objects—whose form is described in the subsequent subclauses ... The simplest structure can consist of a single page tree node that references all of the document's page objects directly. However, to optimize application performance, a [PDF] writer can construct trees of a particular form, known as balanced trees.*
>
> —ISO-32000-1 section 7.7.3.1

In section 5.2.4, you learned that iText automatically creates a balanced tree, unless you use the setLinearPageMode() method. Linear page mode was necessary if you wanted to be able to reorganize the order of the pages.

MANIPULATING PAGE DICTIONARIES

If you want to inspect the resources of a specific page, you don't have to walk through the page tree; iText can do this for you if you use the method getPageN(). The next listing shows how you can get the page dictionary to change the page boundaries.

Listing 13.8 CropPages.java

```java
public void manipulatePdf(String src, String dest)
  throws IOException, DocumentException {
  PdfReader reader = new PdfReader(src);
  int n = reader.getNumberOfPages();
  PdfDictionary pageDict;
  PdfRectangle rect = new PdfRectangle(55, 76, 560, 816);     Loops over
  for (int i = 1; i <= n; i++) {                              all pages
    pageDict = reader.getPageN(i);
    pageDict.put(PdfName.CROPBOX, rect);         ⟵ Adds entry
  }
  PdfStamper stamper
    = new PdfStamper(reader, new FileOutputStream(dest));     Creates
  stamper.close();                                            altered PDF
}
```

Listing 13.8 demonstrates a technique that's very powerful. In previous examples, you've created `PdfReader` instances to retrieve properties from PDF files. Now you also change some of the objects in the PDF. In this case, you add an extra entry to the page dictionary of every page. Once you've applied all the changes, you create a new, altered PDF document using `PdfStamper`. This is different from what you did in part 2; you're manipulating a PDF file at the lowest level.

The next listing is similar to listing 13.8. Instead of adding an entry, you change the `/Rotate` entry, adding 90 degrees to the original value.

Listing 13.9   RotatePages.java

```
public void manipulatePdf(String src, String dest)
  throws IOException, DocumentException {
  PdfReader reader = new PdfReader(MovieTemplates.RESULT);
  int n = reader.getNumberOfPages();
  int rot;
  PdfDictionary pageDict;
  for (int i = 1; i <= n; i++) {
    rot = reader.getPageRotation(i);
    pageDict = reader.getPageN(i);
    pageDict.put(PdfName.ROTATE, new PdfNumber(rot + 90));
  }
  PdfStamper stamper
    = new PdfStamper(reader, new FileOutputStream(RESULT));
  stamper.close();
}
```

Table 30 in ISO-32000-1 lists all the possible entries in the page dictionary. For instance, you can find an array referring to all the annotations that are present on the page (`/Annots`).

REMOVING LAUNCH ACTIONS

I was once asked to write code that removed every launch action. Launch actions are triggered from an annotation on a page, but instead of looping over all the pages, I wrote a loop over all the objects in the PDF file, looking for action dictionaries. Whenever a launch action was encountered, I replaced it with a JavaScript action.

Listing 13.10   RemoveLaunchActions.java

```
PdfReader reader = new PdfReader(src);
PdfObject object;
PdfDictionary action;
for (int i = 1; i < reader.getXrefSize(); i++) {          ① Gets
  object = reader.getPdfObject(i);                            object
  if (object instanceof PdfDictionary) {
    action = ((PdfDictionary)object).getAsDict(PdfName.A);
    if (action == null) continue;
    if (PdfName.LAUNCH.equals(action.getAsName(PdfName.S))) {
      action.remove(PdfName.F);
      action.remove(PdfName.WIN);
      action.put(PdfName.S, PdfName.JAVASCRIPT);
      action.put(PdfName.JS, new PdfString(
        "app.alert('Launch Application Action removed by iText');\r"));
    }
```

```
    }
}
PdfStamper stamper = new PdfStamper(reader, new FileOutputStream(dest));
stamper.close();
```

Observe that you can ask the `reader` object for an indirect object with the `getPdfOb-ject()` method, passing the number of the object as a parameter ❶. This code is used on a mail server that needs to remove possible security hazards from attachments.

There are no references to page numbers in the page dictionary. Every page is self-contained and doesn't care about the other pages in the page tree. The page number is determined by the order of the page dictionaries in the page tree. When walking through the page tree, the first page dictionary that's encountered is the dictionary of page 1, the second of page 2, and so on. If you want to create page numbers for "human consumption"—for instance, i, ii, iii for pages 1 to 3, followed by 1, 2, 3 for pages 4 to 6—you can define page labels.

ADDING PAGE LABELS

With the `/PageLabels` entry in the catalog, you can define the page labeling for the document. You can define *page label dictionaries* for the page indices of your choice. Each page index will denote the first page in a labeling range to which the specified page label dictionary applies.

Figure 13.6 shows a PDF opened on page 3 of 10, but the page label says it's page 1, because the first two pages in the page tree are labeled A and B. Starting with page 6 (labeled page 4), the page numbers get a prefix.

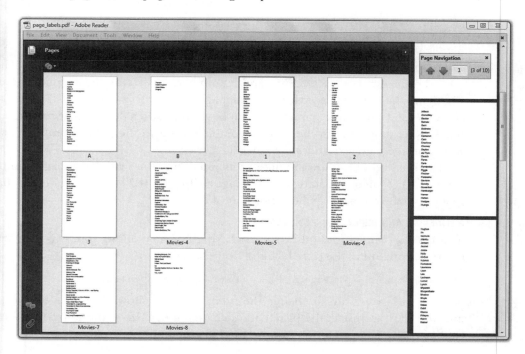

Figure 13.6   Page numbers versus page labels

This listing shows how shows how the PDF in figure 13.6 was created.

Listing 13.11   PageLabelExample.java

```
PdfPageLabels labels = new PdfPageLabels();
labels.addPageLabel(1, PdfPageLabels.UPPERCASE_LETTERS);
labels.addPageLabel(3, PdfPageLabels.DECIMAL_ARABIC_NUMERALS);
labels.addPageLabel(6,
  PdfPageLabels.DECIMAL_ARABIC_NUMERALS, "Movies-", 4);
writer.setPageLabels(labels);
```

This example uses two of the six possible numbering types for the page labels. The numbering types are listed in table 13.9.

Table 13.9   Page label numbering types

Type	Description
DECIMAL_ARABIC_NUMERALS	Decimal Arabic numerals
UPPERCASE_ROMAN_NUMERALS	Uppercase Roman numerals
LOWERCASE_ROMAN_NUMERALS	Lowercase Roman numerals
UPPERCASE_LETTERS	Uppercase letters: A to Z for the first 26 pages, AA to ZZ for the next 26, and so on
LOWERCASE_LETTERS	Lowercase letters: a to z for the first 26 pages, aa to zz for the next 26 and so on
EMPTY	No page numbers

There are different addPageLabel() methods in the PdfPageLabels class. They all take a page number as the first and a numbering style as the second parameter. Changing the numbering style resets the page number to 1.

A method with three parameters can be used to add a String that serves as a prefix. This method can also be used in combination with the EMPTY numbering style if you want to create text-only page labels.

The method with four parameters lets you define the first logical page number. In listing 13.11, when you start labeling pages with "Movies-", you can define that the first page labeled that way should be page 4.

RETRIEVING AND REPLACING PAGE LABELS

The PdfPageLabels class also has a static method that allows you to get an array of Strings, containing the page labels of every page:

```
String[] labels = PdfPageLabels.getPageLabels(new PdfReader(src));
```

Now suppose you want to change the prefix Movies- shown in figure 13.6 to Film-, and you want to restart the page count, changing Movies-4 into Film-1. You can do this using the same technique you've used to crop and rotate pages.

Listing 13.12   PageLabelExample.java

```
PdfReader reader = new PdfReader(src);
PdfDictionary root = reader.getCatalog();
PdfDictionary labels = root.getAsDict(PdfName.PAGELABELS);
PdfArray nums = labels.getAsArray(PdfName.NUMS);
int n;
PdfDictionary pagelabel;
for (int i = 0; i < nums.size(); i++) {          ◁── Loops over page
  n = nums.getAsNumber(i).intValue();                 label definitions
  i++;
  if (n == 5) {
    pagelabel = nums.getAsDict(i);
    pagelabel.remove(PdfName.ST);               ◁── Removes start value
    pagelabel.put(PdfName.P, new PdfString("Film-"));   for page number
  }                                              ◁── Replaces
}                                                    prefix
PdfStamper stamper = new PdfStamper(reader, new FileOutputStream(dest));
stamper.close();
```

Here you don't have a method, such as `getPageN()`, that takes you straight to the dictionary you need. Instead, you climb up the object tree, jumping from object to object starting from the root.

RETRIEVING OBJECTS FROM AN ARRAY OR DICTIONARY

`PdfDictionary` has a `get()` method that returns the `PdfObject` that corresponds with a specific `PdfName`. This can be a `PdfIndirectReference`, in which case you have to look up the corresponding indirect object; or it can be a direct object in the form of a `PdfObject` that needs to be cast to the proper type. If you know in advance which type of object you'll get, you can use one of the convenience methods listed in table 13.10 (as was done in listing 13.12).

Method	Return value
getAsBoolean()	A PdfBoolean or null
getAsNumber()	A PdfNumber or null
getAsString()	A PdfString or null
getAsName()	A PdfName or null
getAsArray()	A PdfArray or null
getAsDict()	A PdfDictionary or null
getAsStream()	A PdfStream or null

Table 13.10 Convenience methods for getting specific objects

These methods exist for the classes `PdfArray`, `PdfDictionary`, and `PdfStream`. If you don't know which object to expect, you can use the `getDirectObject()` method . If the value in the array is referenced, the reference will be resolved. If you want to get the `PdfIndirectReference` object instead of the actual object, you need the `getAsIndirectObject()` method .

You need the PDF reference to understand what happens in listing 13.12—as will always be the case when you manipulate a PDF at the lowest level. Section 12.4.2 of ISO-32000-1 tells us that the value of the `/PageLabels` entry is a *number tree*: an array (`/Nums`) with ordered pairs of numbers and values. Each number corresponds with the index of a page for which a style was defined in listing 13.11. It's important to note that page 1 has index 0; if you want to change the page label with prefix `Movie-` (starting on page 6), you have to look for the page label value corresponding with index 5. This value is a dictionary whose entries are explained in table 159 of ISO-32000-1. The key `/St` is used for the numeric portion for the first page label in the range. If you remove this entry, the default value will be used: 1. The `/P` key is used for the label prefix. You can replace it with `Film-`.

The functionality offered by iText is comprehensive, but once in a while you're confronted with a requirement for which there is no high-level method. The examples in this chapter are inspired by some of the more exceptional requests that have been posted to the mailing list. In cases like this, you need to manipulate the PDF at the lowest level.

Let's continue with another not so trivial assignment and explore another feature: how to add an extra object to an existing PDF file.

13.3.3   *Outlines, destinations, and names*

In section 7.1.1, you learned how to retrieve the named destinations from a document. In section 7.2, you did the same with bookmarks. In the next listing you read the `/Outlines` entry directly from the catalog dictionary. You can use the information retrieved from the bookmarks to create named destinations.

Listing 13.13   Bookmarks2NamedDestinations.java

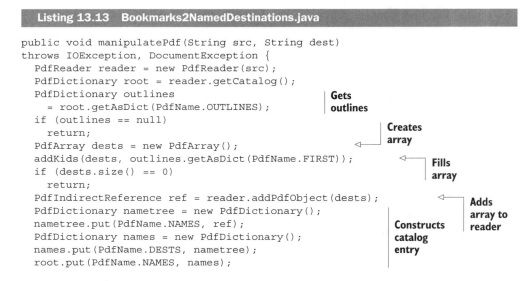

```
public void manipulatePdf(String src, String dest)
throws IOException, DocumentException {
  PdfReader reader = new PdfReader(src);
  PdfDictionary root = reader.getCatalog();
  PdfDictionary outlines
    = root.getAsDict(PdfName.OUTLINES);            Gets
  if (outlines == null)                            outlines
    return;
  PdfArray dests = new PdfArray();                 Creates
  addKids(dests, outlines.getAsDict(PdfName.FIRST));  array
  if (dests.size() == 0)                           Fills
    return;                                        array
  PdfIndirectReference ref = reader.addPdfObject(dests);  Adds
  PdfDictionary nametree = new PdfDictionary();    array to
  nametree.put(PdfName.NAMES, ref);                reader
  PdfDictionary names = new PdfDictionary();       Constructs
  names.put(PdfName.DESTS, nametree);              catalog
  root.put(PdfName.NAMES, names);                  entry
```

```
    PdfStamper stamper
      = new PdfStamper(reader, new FileOutputStream(dest));
    stamper.close();
  }
  public void addKids(PdfArray dests, PdfDictionary outline) {
    while (outline != null) {
      dests.add(outline.getAsString(PdfName.TITLE));
      dests.add(outline.getAsArray(PdfName.DEST));
      addKids(dests, outline.getAsDict(PdfName.FIRST));
      outline = outline.getAsDict(PdfName.NEXT);
    }
  }
}
```

> **Adds entry to name tree**

You've already worked with a number tree for page labels; now you'll work with a *name tree*: an array with ordered pairs of strings and values. In the addKids() method, you use the title of the outlines as the key and the destination of the outline, an array, as the value. You add the name tree to the document with the method addPdfObject(). An indirect object will be created, and you'll receive a PdfIndirectReference object that refers to this new object. You replace the /Names entry in the catalog with a new one that has a /Dests item. This /Dests item has a /Names entry referring to the newly created indirect object.

> **WARNING** If the catalog already has a /Names entry, the put() method will replace it, and you may break existing functionality. The examples in this chapter explain a mechanism; you shouldn't copy and paste the code snippets and use them as definitive solutions.

Changing outlines into named destinations is one of the more exotic requirements I've encountered. A more common situation where you may need low-level access to a PDF involves forms.

13.3.4 *AcroForms revisited*

The catalog has two entries concerning forms: /AcroForm and /NeedsRendering. The value of /NeedsRendering is a flag (a boolean). If true, documents containing XFA forms will be regenerated when the document is first opened. You could check whether there's an XFA form inside a PDF by looking for an XFA entry in the Acro-Form dictionary, but you've used easier methods in section 8.6 to get the same result. In this section, we'll have a closer look at some problems related to AcroForms that can be solved using low-level functionality.

FIXING A BROKEN FORM

There's a plethora of tools that are able to create PDF documents, but the quality of the PDF that's produced isn't always as good. We regularly get questions on the mailing list about forms created by a free UNIX tool. These forms can be filled out using Acrobat, but not with iText. After inspecting such a form, we discovered that the widget dictionaries of the form fields were present in the /Annots array of the page dictionary, but were missing from the /Fields array of the AcroForm. As a result, the widgets were rendered correctly on the page, but when seen from the perspective of the AcroFields object, the form was empty. Such forms are broken, and iText can't fill them until they're fixed. Let's look at how to fix them.

The next bit of code makes the assumption that every annotation in each page is a widget annotation corresponding to one field. It loops over every page and puts the references to each annotation into the fields array.

Listing 13.14   FixBrokenForm.java

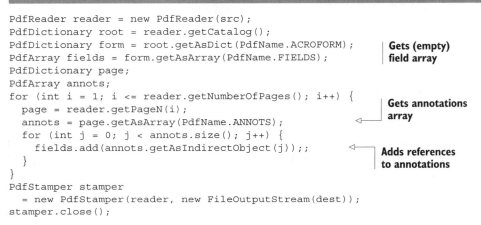

```
PdfReader reader = new PdfReader(src);
PdfDictionary root = reader.getCatalog();
PdfDictionary form = root.getAsDict(PdfName.ACROFORM);      Gets (empty)
PdfArray fields = form.getAsArray(PdfName.FIELDS);          field array
PdfDictionary page;
PdfArray annots;
for (int i = 1; i <= reader.getNumberOfPages(); i++) {      Gets annotations
  page = reader.getPageN(i);                                array
  annots = page.getAsArray(PdfName.ANNOTS);
  for (int j = 0; j < annots.size(); j++) {
    fields.add(annots.getAsIndirectObject(j));;;            Adds references
  }                                                         to annotations
}
PdfStamper stamper
  = new PdfStamper(reader, new FileOutputStream(dest));
stamper.close();
```

The annots object is an array, and this listing assumes that all the elements in this array are indirect references (instead of direct objects). You get these references with the getAsIndirectObject() method.

Although this code sample isn't perfect, it has already helped many developers.

INSPECTING FIELDS AT A LOW LEVEL

In chapter 8, you used the AcroFields class to manipulate form fields in a PDF document. This class offers the most common functionality you'll need, but sometimes you'll need more. For instance, how could you find out whether a text field is a password field, or a multiline field?

In the next listing, you'll get the fields as instances of the inner class Acro-Fields.Item. From this inner class, you'll retrieve a dictionary that merges the field and the widget dictionary. You'll inspect the field flags, /FF, to see if the PASSWORD or the MULTILINE bits are set.

Listing 13.15   InspectForm.java

```
PdfReader reader = new PdfReader(src);
AcroFields form = reader.getAcroFields();
Map<String,AcroFields.Item> fields = form.getFields();
AcroFields.Item item;
PdfDictionary dict;
int flags;
for (Map.Entry<String,AcroFields.Item> entry : fields.entrySet()) {
  out.write(entry.getKey());
  item = entry.getValue();
```

```
dict = item.getMerged(0);
flags = dict.getAsNumber(PdfName.FF).intValue();
if ((flags & BaseField.PASSWORD) > 0)
  out.write("-> password");
if ((flags & BaseField.MULTILINE) > 0)
  out.write("-> multiline");
out.write('\n');
}
```

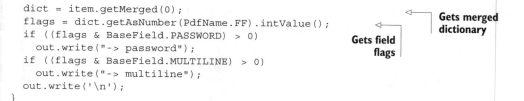

Gets merged dictionary

Gets field flags

If you use this code to inspect the form used in section 8.5.2, the following output is returned:

```
personal.loginname
personal.name
personal.reason -> multiline
personal.password -> password
```

You may wonder why the getMerged() method needs a parameter. In chapter 8, you learned that a field can be represented by different widget annotations. You can ask an Item object how many widgets are associated with the field by using the size() method. In the form you've inspected here, there was only one widget per field, and it had the index 0. You can get more info about a widget with index idx using the methods from table 13.11.

Table 13.11 AcroFields.Item **methods**

Method	Description
getValue(idx)	Returns a dictionary where the /V entry is present. This entry holds the field value whose format varies depending on the field type.
getWidget(idx)	Returns one of the widget dictionaries of the field.
getWidgetRef(idx)	Returns the PdfIndirectReference for the widget.
getMerged(idx)	Retrieves the merged dictionary for the given instance. This PdfDictionary contains all the keys present in the parent fields, though they may have been overwritten (or modified) by children.
getPage(idx)	Retrieves the page number on which the widget with index idx is placed.
getTabOrder(idx)	Returns the tab index of the given field widget.

You can use these methods to inspect the widget annotations of a field, and even to manipulate a field at the lowest level.

ADDING JAVASCRIPT TO A FIELD

Imagine an IRS form asking a citizen if they are married. This could be done using a radio field named Married with possible values Yes and No. There could also be a Partner text box to which a name could be added. This text field should only be filled in if the value for Married is Yes.

Listing 13.16 shows how to add the setReadOnly() JavaScript method to the radio field button. The method is triggered when one of the buttons gets the focus. This

method is written so that the content of the Partner field is blanked out and made
read-only if Married is set to No. When changed back to Yes, the read-only status is set
to `false`.

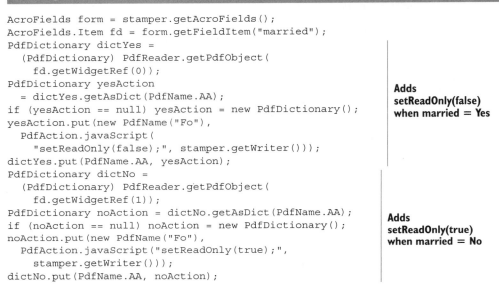

```
AcroFields form = stamper.getAcroFields();
AcroFields.Item fd = form.getFieldItem("married");
PdfDictionary dictYes =
  (PdfDictionary) PdfReader.getPdfObject(
    fd.getWidgetRef(0));
PdfDictionary yesAction                              Adds
  = dictYes.getAsDict(PdfName.AA);                   setReadOnly(false)
if (yesAction == null) yesAction = new PdfDictionary();  when married = Yes
yesAction.put(new PdfName("Fo"),
  PdfAction.javaScript(
    "setReadOnly(false);", stamper.getWriter()));
dictYes.put(PdfName.AA, yesAction);
PdfDictionary dictNo =
  (PdfDictionary) PdfReader.getPdfObject(
    fd.getWidgetRef(1));
PdfDictionary noAction = dictNo.getAsDict(PdfName.AA);   Adds
if (noAction == null) noAction = new PdfDictionary();    setReadOnly(true)
noAction.put(new PdfName("Fo"),                          when married = No
  PdfAction.javaScript("setReadOnly(true);",
    stamper.getWriter()));
dictNo.put(PdfName.AA, noAction);
```

There's more than one way to achieve this. This example uses the `PdfReader.getPdf-`
`Object()` method with a `PdfIndirectReference` to the widget as a parameter. You
fetch the additional actions dictionary from the widget dictionary; if such a dictionary
isn't present, you create a new one. The JavaScript stream is added to `stamper.get-`
`Writer()` implicitly.

REPLACING THE URL OF A SUBMIT BUTTON
You could have used a shortcut to get the widget dictionary in listing 13.16. You'll use
this shortcut in the next example to replace the submit URL of the Post button of an
AcroForm.

```
PdfReader reader = new PdfReader(src);
AcroFields form = reader.getAcroFields();
AcroFields.Item item = form.getFieldItem("post");
PdfDictionary field = item.getMerged(0);
PdfDictionary action = field.getAsDict(PdfName.A);
PdfDictionary f = action.getAsDict(PdfName.F);
f.put(PdfName.F, new PdfString("http://itextpdf.com:8080/book/request"));
PdfStamper stamper = new PdfStamper(reader, new FileOutputStream(dest));
stamper.close();
```

Almost every example in this chapter is what we call a *hack*. Each example solves a specific problem, but it probably won't work for every PDF. Manipulating PDFs at the lowest level gives you a lot of power, but you can seriously damage a PDF file if you add, change, or remove objects directly. You should always remember the words of Spider-Man's Uncle Ben: "With great power comes great responsibility." It's your responsibility to check ISO-32000-1 to see if your changes result in a valid PDF file.

You should also consult the ISO specification if you want to know more about the following entries of the root dictionary: /Threads, /URI, /Lang, /SpiderInfo, /PieceInfo, /Legal, /Requirements, and /Perms. But please read on if you want to know more about /OCProperties, /StructTreeRoot, /MarkInfo, or /Collection, because these will be discussed in the upcoming chapters.

13.4 Summary

We started this chapter with a short historical overview: why did the world need PDF, and how did PDF evolve from a de facto standard owned by a company to an ISO standard? We looked at different flavors of PDF, such as PDF/A and PDF/X. The history lesson was necessary to understand how and why the Carousel Object System was invented.

You opened up one of the PDF documents you created in chapter 1 and learned about the different objects that make a PDF file. You attempted to read this file the same way a PDF viewer would read it, interpreting the different parts in the file structure. You jumped from indirect object to indirect object in the body, following the path defined by indirect references. As you saw, you can do this for a small PDF file, but you need a tool such as iText RUPS as soon as you want to inspect the objects of a larger PDF document.

The examples in this book solved specific problems by manipulating PDF documents at the lowest level. These examples were taken from the collection of code snippets that accumulated in the "sandbox" directory on my computer. Most of these snippets were written in answer to a question on the mailing list, but I selected them in such a way that they explained the mechanisms that can be used to select, change, add, or remove objects when manipulating an existing PDF document.

One type of object was deliberately overlooked: PdfStream. When we studied the structure of the Hello World document, we didn't look at the part marked as binary content, and we didn't look at streams representing fonts and images. That's what the next chapters are about.

The imaging model 14

This chapter covers
- The PDF imaging model
- All methods in `PdfContentByte`
- Using `Graphics2D` to create PDF content

We studied the Carousel Object System in the previous chapter. We used iText to find, remove, change, and replace objects in a PDF file. In this chapter, we'll look at one specific type of object: the stream containing the syntax that makes up a page.

First we'll look at the PDF imaging model and learn how to draw graphics and text using PDF syntax. Then we'll look at the Java class `java.awt.Graphics2D` as an alternative solution for achieving the same results. In both cases, we'll add content at absolute positions as we did in chapter 3. Chapter 3 explained the mechanisms available in iText, but this chapter dives straight into the PDF syntax.

This chapter includes different tables listing all the possible graphics and text operators and operands. This chapter will serve as a reference that can be used to look up the meaning of the syntax in a PDF file, and to find the iText methods that correspond with this syntax.

14.1 Examining the content stream

Let's start by looking at the content streams of some PDF samples you've created in previous parts of the book. A first step is to get the content of a page.

> **Listing 14.1   GetContentStream.java**

```
public void readContent(String src, String result) throws IOException {
    PdfReader reader = new PdfReader(src);
    FileOutputStream out = new FileOutputStream(result);
    out.write(reader.getPageContent(1));
    out.flush();
    out.close();
}
```

If you try this example on your Hello World example from chapter 1, you'll get this stream:

```
q
BT
36 806 Td
0 -18 Td
/F1 12 Tf
(Hello World!)Tj
0 0 Td
ET
Q
```

This stream contains mainly text operators, and using the tables in section 14.4, you'll be able to interpret every character in this stream. If you execute the code in listing 14.1 on the first superhero example in chapter 5, you'll get the following stream:

```
q
BT
-1156 1649 Td
ET
Q
q 1 0 0 1 -1192 -1685 cm /Xf1 Do Q
-595 0 m
595 0 l
0 -842 m
0 842 l
S
```

This stream contains mainly graphics operators, but the syntax that draws Superman is missing. We'll look into where to find it, and we'll discuss these operators, in sections 14.2 and 14.3.

PDF SYNTAX NOTATION

PDF (and PS) use a notation known as postfix, aka reverse Polish notation. In reverse Polish notation, the operators follow their operands. Table 14.1 shows the different notations that can be used to note down the addition of the integers 10 and 6.

Table 14.1   Mathematical notations

Notation	Example	Description
Prefix	+ 10 6	Polish notation
Infix	10 + 6	The common arithmetic and logical formula notation
Postfix	10 6 +	Reverse Polish notation

Interpreters of the postfix notation are often stack-based. Operands are pushed onto a stack, and when an operation is performed, its operands are popped from a stack and its result pushed back on. This has the advantage of being easy to implement and very fast.

When you look at the content stream snippets extracted from a PDF file using listing 14.1, you'll see operations such as -595 0 m, where -595 and 0 are the operands (in this case, representing a translation), and where m is the operator (which will cause the cursor to move 595 points to the left and 0 points up).

In iText, this syntax is generated by the PdfContentByte class. This class was introduced in section 3.1, where you used it to draw paths and text at absolute positions—to create a movie calendar, for instance. One of the member variables of this object is a ByteBuffer, storing the PDF syntax until it can be put into a stream object. This stream can be added to a PDF file as the content of a page, as a form XObject, or as the appearance of an annotation.

This chapter contains a series of tables listing graphics and text operators in PDF, along with the corresponding methods in the PdfContentByte class.

14.2   *Path construction and painting operators*

The first series of operators we'll look at can be used to construct paths that will be used to stroke lines and to fill shapes.

14.2.1   *Constructing paths*

Figure 14.1 shows a series of paths that are constructed using PdfContentByte methods.

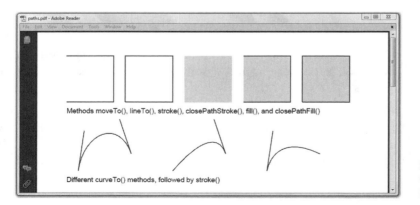

**Figure 14.1
Constructing and
painting paths**

These methods and the corresponding PDF operators are listed in table 14.2.

Table 14.2 PDF path construction operators and operands

PDF	iText method	Parameters	Description
m	moveTo	(x, y)	Moves the current point to coordinates (x,y), omitting any connecting line segment. This begins a new (sub) path.
l	lineTo	(x, y)	Moves the current point to coordinates (x,y), appending a line segment from the previous to the new current point.
c	curveTo	(x1, y1, x2, y2, x3, y3)	Moves the current point to coordinates (x3,y3), appending a cubic Bézier curve from the previous to the new current point, using (x1,y1) and (x2,y2) as Bézier control points.
v	curveTo	(x2, y2, x3, y3)	Moves the current point to coordinates (x3, y3), appending a cubic Bézier curve from the previous to the new current point, using the previous current point and (x2,y2) as Bézier control points.
y	curveFromTo	(x1, y1, x3, y3)	Moves the current point to coordinates (x3, y3), appending a cubic Bézier curve from the previous to the new current point, using (x1,y1) and (x3,y3) as Bézier control points.
h	closePath	()	Closes the current subpath by appending a straight line segment from the current point to the starting point of the subpath.
re	rectangle	(x, y, width, height)	Appends a rectangle to the current path as a complete sub-path. (x,y) is the lower-left corner; width and height define the dimensions of the rectangle.

You can move the cursor to specific coordinates using moveTo(). Straight lines are constructed with the lineTo() method. The first series of paths shown in figure 14.1 are drawn using one moveTo() and three lineTo() operations. The first path is an open shape because I didn't "close the path" as was done for the second path.

Curves are constructed using the curveTo() or curveFromTo() methods. The curve segments added to the path are *Bézier curves.*

BÉZIER CURVES

Bézier curves are parametric curves developed in 1959 by Paul de Casteljau (using *de Casteljau's algorithm*). They were widely publicized in 1962 by Paul Bézier, who used them to design automobile bodies. Nowadays they're important in computer graphics.

Cubic Bézier curves are defined by four points: the two *endpoints*—the current point and point (x3,y3)—and two *control points*—(x1,y1) and (x2,y2). The curve starts at the first endpoint going onward to the first control point, and it arrives at the second endpoint coming from the second control point. In general, the curve doesn't pass through the control points. They're there only to provide directional information. The distance between an endpoint and its corresponding control point determines how long the curve moves toward the control point before turning toward the other endpoint.

The Bézier curves shown in figure 14.1 demonstrate the different curve methods from table 14.2. The extra straight lines connect the endpoints with the corresponding control points. In the second example, the endpoint to the left coincides with the first control point (the PDF operator v is used instead of c). In the third example, the endpoint to the right coincides with the second control point (the PDF operator y was used).

14.2.2   *Painting and clipping paths*

The methods listed in table 14.2 can be used to construct a path, using different straight and curved segments, but these methods won't *draw* any line or shape on the page.

> **FAQ**   *I've used methods such as* moveTo(), lineTo(), *and* curveTo() *to draw a shape, but this shape doesn't show up on my page.* This is normal; you have been constructing a path using different subpaths, but this path wasn't drawn because you forgot to stroke or fill the line or shape. Not all shapes are meant to be drawn—a shape can also be used to clip content.

Table 14.3 lists the different path-painting and -clipping operators. Note that they don't have any operands.

Table 14.3   PDF path-painting and -clipping operators

PDF	iText method	Description
S	stroke()	Strokes the path (lines only; the shape isn't filled).
s	closePathStroke()	Closes and strokes the path. This is the same as doing closePath() followed by stroke().
f	fill()	Fills the path using the nonzero winding number rule. Open subpaths are closed implicitly.
F	-	Deprecated! Equivalent to f, and included for compatibility. ISO-32000-1 says that PDF writer applications should use f instead.
f*	eoFill()	Fills the path using the even-odd rule.
B	fillStroke()	Fills the path using the nonzero winding number rule, and then strokes the path. This is equivalent to fill() followed by stroke().
B*	eoFillStroke()	Fills the path using the even-odd rule, and then strokes the path. This is equivalent to eoFill() followed by stroke().
b	closePathFillStroke()	Closes, fills, and strokes the path, as is done with closePath() followed by fillStroke().
b*	closePathEoFillStroke()	Closes, fills, and strokes the path, as is done with closePath() followed by eoFillStroke().
n	newPath()	Ends the path object without filling or stroking it. Used primarily after defining a clipping path.

Table 14.3   PDF path-painting and -clipping operators *(continued)*

PDF	iText method	Description
W	clip()	Modifies the current clipping path by intersecting it with the current path, using the nonzero winding rule.
W*	eoClip()	Modifies the current clipping path by intersecting it with the current path, using the even-odd rule.

When you construct a path using the methods from table 14.2, you can stroke those paths. *Stroking* a path means you're going to draw the line segments of the subpaths. The color used by default is black, but you can change this color with one of the set-ColorStroke() methods in table 14.8.

Filling a path means you're going to paint the entire region enclosed by the path. By default, shapes are filled using the *nonzero winding number rule*.

NONZERO WINDING NUMBER RULE VERSUS EVEN-ODD RULE

When I close my eyes, I can still see how our professor of analytic geometry filled two of his nine blackboards explaining how to determine whether or not a given point is inside a path.

With the nonzero winding number rule, you need to draw a line from that point in any direction, and examine every intersection of the path with this line. Start with a count of zero; add one each time a subpath crosses the line from left to right; subtract one each time a subpath crosses from right to left. Do this until there are no more path segments to cross. If the result is zero, the point is outside the path; otherwise, it's inside.

An alternative to the nonzero winding number rule is the *even-odd rule*. Again, you need to draw a line from the point that's being examined to infinity. Now count the number of path segments that are crossed, regardless of the direction. If this number is odd, the point is inside; if even, the point is outside.

If you don't like to read definitions, have a look at the stars and circles in figure 14.2.

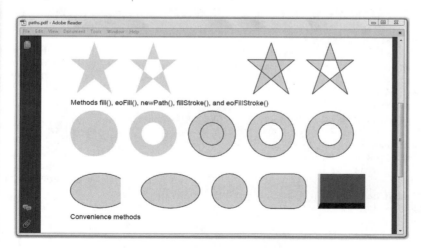

**Figure 14.2
Constructing and
painting shapes**

The paths of the star and circle shapes are constructed using listing 14.2. Observe that the star is composed of five straight lines, four of which are created using the lineTo() method and one implicitly using closePath().

Listing 14.2   PathConstructionAndPainting.java

```java
public static void createStar(PdfContentByte canvas, float x, float y) {
  canvas.moveTo(x + 10, y);
  canvas.lineTo(x + 80, y + 60);
  canvas.lineTo(x, y + 60);
  canvas.lineTo(x + 70, y);
  canvas.lineTo(x + 40, y + 90);
  canvas.closePath();
}
public static void createCircle(PdfContentByte canvas, float x, float y,
  float r, boolean clockwise) {
  float b = 0.5523f;
  if (clockwise) {
    canvas.moveTo(x + r, y);
    canvas.curveTo(x + r, y - r * b, x + r * b, y - r, x, y - r);
    canvas.curveTo(x - r * b, y - r, x - r, y - r * b, x - r, y);
    canvas.curveTo(x - r, y + r * b, x - r * b, y + r, x, y + r);
    canvas.curveTo(x + r * b, y + r, x + r, y + r * b, x + r, y);
  } else {
    canvas.moveTo(x + r, y);
    canvas.curveTo(x + r, y + r * b, x + r * b, y + r, x, y + r);
    canvas.curveTo(x - r * b, y + r, x - r, y + r * b, x - r, y);
    canvas.curveTo(x - r, y - r * b, x - r * b, y - r, x, y - r);
    canvas.curveTo(x + r * b, y - r, x + r, y - r * b, x + r, y);
  }
}
```

The circle is constructed using four Bézier curves. With the method createCircle(), you can construct the path clockwise and counterclockwise.

Now look at the next listing to see how the shapes in figure 14.2 were added.

Listing 14.3   PathConstructionAndPainting.java (continued)

```java
createStar(canvas, x, y);
createCircle(canvas, x + radius, y - 70, radius, true);          ❶ Fills using
createCircle(canvas, x + radius, y - 70, radius / 2, true);         nonzero winding
canvas.fill();                                                      number rule
x += 2 * radius + gutter;
createStar(canvas, x, y);
createCircle(canvas, x + radius, y - 70, radius, true);
createCircle(canvas, x + radius, y - 70, radius / 2, true);      ❷ Fills using
canvas.eoFill();                                                    even-odd rule
x += 2 * radius + gutter;
createStar(canvas, x, y);                                         ❸ Discards
canvas.newPath();                                                   previous path
createCircle(canvas, x + radius, y - 70, radius, true);
createCircle(canvas, x + radius, y - 70, radius / 2, true);
x += 2 * radius + gutter;
createStar(canvas, x, y);
createCircle(canvas, x + radius, y - 70, radius, true);
```

```
createCircle(canvas, x + radius, y - 70, radius / 2, false);
canvas.fillStroke();
x += 2 * radius + gutter;
createStar(canvas, x, y);
createCircle(canvas, x + radius, y - 70, radius, true);
createCircle(canvas, x + radius, y - 70, radius / 2, true);
canvas.eoFillStroke();
```

◄─── Fills and strokes using nonzero winding number rule **4**

◄─**5** Fills using even-odd rule

The paths for the stars and circles are filled in different ways. The first pair is filled using the nonzero winding number rule **1**. The inner circle overlaps the outer circle, but it has the same color; you can't distinguish the inner circle from the outer one.

In the second pair, the star and the circle are filled using the even-odd rule **2**. The middle part of the star isn't filled, nor is the inner circle.

The star seems to be missing in the third example. This time the newPath() method is used **3**, and it has discarded the subpaths that were on the stack. Only the circles are drawn. They're filled and stroked using the nonzero winding number rule **4**.

Note the difference between the third and the fourth concentric circles. In the third column, the subpaths of the circles are constructed clockwise—the curves are drawn in that direction. In the fourth column, the path of the outer circle is constructed clockwise, and the path of the inner circle is constructed counterclockwise.

By definition, the direction of the paths doesn't matter when filling the circles using the even-odd rule, as is the case in the fifth pair of circles **5**.

Computing the values to draw Bézier curves representing a simple circle or an ellipse isn't easy. That's why iText provides convenience methods.

14.2.3 Convenience methods to draw shapes

Table 14.4 lists the convenience methods that were used to draw the final row of shapes shown in figure 14.2. These shapes can't be drawn using a single operator in PDF. The path is constructed using different subpaths as was done for the circle in listing 14.2.

Table 14.4 iText convenience methods for graphics

iText method	Parameters	Description
arc	(x1, y1, x2, y2, startAng, extent)	Constructs the path of a partial ellipse inscribed within the rectangle [x1 y1 x2 y2], starting at startAng degrees and covering extent degrees. Angles start with 0 to the right and increase counterclockwise.
ellipse	(x1, y1, x2, y2)	Constructs the path of an ellipse using the arc method, starting at 0 degrees and covering 360 degrees.
circle	(x, y, r)	Constructs the path of a circle with center (x,y) and radius r using one moveTo() and four curveTo() instructions.
roundRectangle	(x, y, w, h, r)	Constructs the path of a rounded rectangle.
rectangle	(rect)	Draws a Rectangle object. Constructs the path, fills it with the background color of rect (if any) and strokes the borders.

The first four methods in this table construct the path, but don't draw it; this is similar to what the `rectangle()` method in table 14.2 does. If you want to see the shapes, you need to `stroke()` or `fill()` the paths, or both. The `rectangle()` method in table 14.4 calls these methods implicitly, because there are different colors and line widths involved.

To draw lines and shapes using different stroke and fill properties, you'll need to change the graphics state.

14.3   *Overview of the graphics state methods*

The mechanism of the graphics state stack was explained in section 3.1.2, but we didn't get a complete overview of all the methods that were available. Table 14.5 lists a series of graphics state operators.

Let's work through some examples involving lines and their characteristics, and take a closer look at the different parameters that can be used for the methods that change the graphics state for stroking lines.

Table 14.5   Graphics state operators

PDF	iText method	Parameters	Description
w	setLineWidth	(width)	Sets the line width. The parameter represents the thickness of the line in user units (default = 1).
J	setLineCap	(style)	Defines the line cap style.
j	setLineJoin	(style)	Defines the line join style.
M	setMiterLimit	(miterLimit)	Defines a limit for joining lines. When it's exceeded, the join is converted from a miter to a bevel.
d	setLineDash	(phase) (unitsOn, phase) (unitsOn, unitsOff, phase) (array, phase)	Sets the line dash type. The default line dash is a solid line, but by using the different iText methods that change the dash pattern, you can create all sorts of dashed lines.
i	setFlatness	(flatness)	Sets the maximum permitted distance, in device pixels, between the mathematically correct path and an approximation constructed from straight line segments. This is a value between 0 and 100. Smaller values yield greater precision at the cost of more computation.
q	saveState	()	Saves the current graphics state on the graphics state stack.
Q	restoreState	()	Restores the graphics state by removing the most recently saved state from the stack, making it the current stack.
gs	setGState	(gstate)	Sets a group of parameters in the graphics state using a graphics state parameter dictionary.

Table 14.5   Graphics state operators *(continued)*

PDF	iText method	Parameters	Description
/RI	PdfGState .setRenderingIntent	(name)	Sets the color rendering intent in the graphics state. Possible values are /AbsoluteColorimetric, /RelativeColorimetric, /Saturation, and /Perceptual.
cm	concatCTM	(a, b, c, d, e, f)	Modifies the current transformation matrix (CTM) by concatenating the matrix defined by the parameters a, b, c, d, e, and f.

14.3.1 Line characteristics

Figure 14.3 shows some of the characteristics that can be defined for lines.

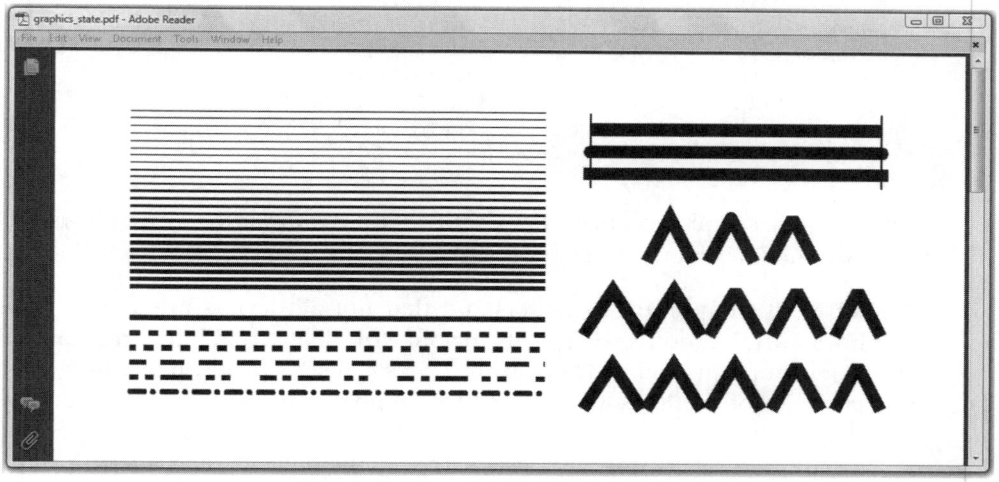

Figure 14.3   Examples of different line characteristics

This listing demonstrates how all but the dashed lines in figure 14.3 were drawn.

Listing 14.4   GraphicsStateOperators.java

```
canvas.saveState();
for (int i = 25; i > 0; i--) {
  canvas.setLineWidth((float) i / 10);        ◁── Changes line width
  canvas.moveTo(50, 806 - (5 * i));
  canvas.lineTo(320, 806 - (5 * i));
  canvas.stroke();
}
canvas.restoreState();
canvas.moveTo(350, 800); canvas.lineTo(350, 750);
canvas.moveTo(540, 800); canvas.lineTo(540, 750);
canvas.stroke();
```

```
canvas.saveState();
canvas.setLineWidth(8);
canvas.setLineCap(PdfContentByte.LINE_CAP_BUTT);
canvas.moveTo(350, 790); canvas.lineTo(540, 790);
canvas.stroke();
canvas.setLineCap(PdfContentByte.LINE_CAP_ROUND);
canvas.moveTo(350, 775); canvas.lineTo(540, 775);
canvas.stroke();
canvas.setLineCap(
  PdfContentByte.LINE_CAP_PROJECTING_SQUARE);
canvas.moveTo(350, 760); canvas.lineTo(540, 760);
canvas.stroke();
canvas.restoreState();
canvas.saveState();
canvas.setLineWidth(8);
canvas.setLineJoin(PdfContentByte.LINE_JOIN_MITER);
canvas.moveTo(387, 700); canvas.lineTo(402, 730);
canvas.lineTo(417, 700); canvas.stroke();
canvas.setLineJoin(PdfContentByte.LINE_JOIN_ROUND);
canvas.moveTo(427, 700); canvas.lineTo(442, 730);
canvas.lineTo(457, 700); canvas.stroke();
canvas.setLineJoin(PdfContentByte.LINE_JOIN_BEVEL);
canvas.moveTo(467, 700); canvas.lineTo(482, 730);
canvas.lineTo(497, 700); canvas.stroke();
canvas.restoreState();
```

Changes
line cap

Changes
line join

In this code sample, you first draw a series of lines with widths varying from 0.1 pt to 2.5 pt. See the lines on the top-left of figure 14.3.

NOTE   It's important to understand that not all devices are able to render lines with the widths you specify in your PDF. The actual line width can differ from the requested width by as much as 2 device pixels, depending on the positions of the lines with respect to the pixel grid. When drawing lines and shapes, the *flatness tolerance* (i in table 14.5) controls the maximum permitted distance in device pixels between the mathematically correct path and an approximation constructed from straight line segments.

The three thick lines at the top right in figure 14.3 are drawn from x = 350 to x = 540, but they appear to have different lengths. That's because they're drawn using different line cap styles. The line cap styles are listed in table 14.6.

Table 14.6   Line cap styles

Style	Description
LINE_CAP_BUTT	The stroke is squared off at the endpoint of the path. This is the default.
LINE_CAP_ROUND	A semicircular arc with diameter equal to the line width is drawn around the endpoint.
LINE_CAP_PROJECTING_SQUARE	The stroke continues beyond the endpoint of the path for a distance equal to half the line width.

The three hook shapes under these thick lines demonstrate the different line join styles shown in table 14.7.

Table 14.7 Line join styles

Style	Description
LINE_JOIN_MITER	The outer edges of the strokes for two segments are extended until they meet at an angle. This is the default.
LINE_JOIN_ROUND	An arc of a circle with diameter equal to the line width is drawn around the point where the two line segments meet.
LINE_JOIN_BEVEL	The two segments are finished with butt caps.

When you define miter joins, and two line segments meet at a sharp angle, it's possible for the miter to extend far beyond the thickness of the line stroke. If φ is the angle between both line segments, the miter limit equals the line width divided by $\sin(\varphi/2)$.

You can define a maximum value for the ratio of the miter length to the line width. This maximum is called the *miter limit*. When this limit is exceeded, the join is converted from a miter to a bevel. Figure 14.3 shows two rows of hooks that were drawn using the same PdfTemplate object hooks. The angle of the hooks decreases from left to right. In spite of the fact that the PDF syntax to draw the hooks is identical, the appearance of the third hook is different when comparing both lines because of the different miter limit:

```
canvas.saveState();
canvas.setMiterLimit(2);
canvas.addTemplate(hooks, 300, 600);
canvas.restoreState();
canvas.saveState();
canvas.setMiterLimit(2.1f);
canvas.addTemplate(hooks, 300, 550);
canvas.restoreState();
```

Figure 14.3 also demonstrates how you can create dashed lines. The next listing shows how these lines were created.

Listing 14.5 GraphicsStateOperators.java

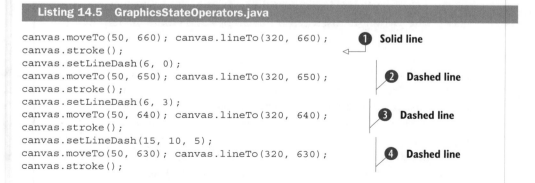

```
canvas.moveTo(50, 660); canvas.lineTo(320, 660);     ❶  Solid line
canvas.stroke();
canvas.setLineDash(6, 0);
canvas.moveTo(50, 650); canvas.lineTo(320, 650);     ❷  Dashed line
canvas.stroke();
canvas.setLineDash(6, 3);
canvas.moveTo(50, 640); canvas.lineTo(320, 640);     ❸  Dashed line
canvas.stroke();
canvas.setLineDash(15, 10, 5);
canvas.moveTo(50, 630); canvas.lineTo(320, 630);     ❹  Dashed line
canvas.stroke();
```

```
float[] dash1 = { 10, 5, 5, 5, 20 };
canvas.setLineDash(dash1, 5);
canvas.moveTo(50, 620); canvas.lineTo(320, 620);
canvas.stroke();
float[] dash2 = { 9, 6, 0, 6 };
canvas.setLineCap(PdfContentByte.LINE_CAP_ROUND);
canvas.setLineDash(dash2, 0);
canvas.moveTo(50, 610); canvas.lineTo(320, 610);
canvas.stroke();
```

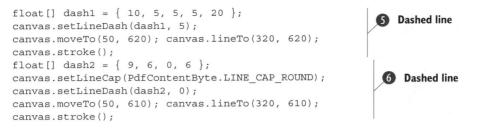

5 Dashed line

6 Dashed line

The first line is drawn using the default line style, which is solid **1**. For the second line, the line dash is set to a pattern of 6 units with phase 0 **2**. This means that the line starts with a dash of 6 units long, then there's a gap of 6 units, and then there's a dash of 6 units, and so on. The same goes for the third line, but it uses a different phase **3**. In line **4**, you have a dash of 15 units and a gap of 10 units. The phase is 5, so the first dash is only 10 units long (15 – 5). Line **5** uses a more complex pattern. You start with a dash of 5 (10 – 5), then there's a gap of 5, followed by a dash of 5, a gap of 5, and a dash of 20. The next sequence is as follows: a gap of 10, a dash of 5, a gap of 5, a dash of 5, a gap of 20, and so on. Situation **6** is also special: a dash of 9, a gap of 6, a dash of 0, and a gap of 6. The dash of 0 may seem odd, but as you're using round caps, a dot is drawn instead of a 0-length dash.

Most of these characteristics can also be set outside the content stream, in a reusable graphics state parameter dictionary.

GRAPHICS STATE PARAMETER DICTIONARY

The graphics state stack is initialized at the beginning of each page using the default value for every graphics state parameter. You can change the state with the operators described in this chapter, and then save and restore the state with saveState() and restoreState(). If you want to reuse a set of parameters, you can store them in an external dictionary with /Type /ExtGState, and refer to that dictionary with the setG-State() method.

In such a dictionary, the key /LW is used for the line width parameter, /LC for the line cap, /LJ for the line join, /ML for the miter limit, /D for the dash pattern, and so on. For the complete list, see table 58 in ISO-32000-1.

One of the operators in that table also appears in our table 14.5; with /RI, you can set the color rendering intent by using a method in the PdfGState class. You used this class earlier, when we discussed transparency and colors in chapter 10.

14.3.2   *Colors*

You can change the color of the current graphics state using the methods setColor-Stroke() and setColorFill(). These methods accept an instance of the BaseColor class. This class has many different subclasses, and the type of the subclass will determine which operator is used. Table 14.8 lists the different operators and operands that are at play.

Before we move on to the text operators, we need to discuss one more mechanism in more detail: the coordinate system that's used in PDF.

Table 14.8   Color and shading methods

PDF	iText method	Parameters	Description
g	setGrayFill	(gray)	Changes the current gray tint for filling paths to a float value from 0 (black) to 1 (white),
G	setGrayStroke	(gray)	Changes the current gray tint for stroking paths to a float value from 0 (black) to 1 (white).
rg	setRGBColorFill	(red, green, blue)	Sets the color space to DeviceRGB and changes the current color for filling paths. The color values are integers from 0 to 255.
RG	setRGBColorStroke	(gray)	Sets the color space to DeviceRGB and changes the current color for stroking paths. The color values are integers from 0 to 255.
rg	setRGBColorFillF	(red, green, blue)	Sets the color space to DeviceRGB and changes the current color for filling paths. The color values are floats from 0 to 1.
RG	setRGBColorStrokeF	(gray)	Sets the color space to DeviceRGB and changes the current color for stroking paths. The color values are floats from 0 to 1.
k	setCMYKColorFill	(cyan, magenta, yellow, black)	Sets the color space to DeviceCMYK and changes the current color for filling paths. The color values are integers from 0 to 255.
K	setCMYKColorStroke	(cyan, magenta, yellow, black)	Sets the color space to DeviceCMYK and changes the current color for stroking paths. The color values are integers from 0 to 255.
k	setCMYKColorFillF	(cyan, magenta, yellow, black)	Sets the color space to DeviceCMYK and changes the current color for filling paths. The color values are floats from 0 to 1.
K	setCMYKColorStrokeF	(cyan, magenta, yellow, black)	Sets the color space to DeviceCMYK and changes the current color for stroking paths. The color values are floats from 0 to 1.
CS		name	Sets the color space for nonstroking operations. This is done implicitly when necessary by iText.
cs		name	Sets the color space for nonstroking operations. This is done implicitly when necessary by iText.
SC		c1 c2 c3 . . .	Sets the color to use for stroking operations in a device, CIE-based (other than ICCBased), or Indexed color space. Not used in iText.
sc		c1 c2 c3 . . .	Same as SC for nonstroking operations. Not used in iText.

Table 14.8   Color and shading methods *(continued)*

PDF	iText method	Parameters	Description
SCN		c1 c2 c3 ... name	Same as SC but also supports Pattern, Separation, DeviceN, and ICCBased color spaces. It's used in the methods `setColorStroke(PdfSpotColor sp, float tint)`, `setPatternStroke(PdfPatternPainter p)`, `setPatternStroke(PdfPatternPainter p, BaseColor color)`, `setPatternStroke(PdfPatternPainter p, BaseColor color, float tint)`, and `setShadingStroke(PdfShadingPattern shading)`.
scn		c1 c2 c3 ... name	Same as SC but also supports Pattern, Separation, DeviceN, and ICCBased color spaces. It's used in the methods `setColorFill(PdfSpotColor sp, float tint)`, `setPatternFill(PdfPatternPainter p)`, `setPatternFill(PdfPatternPainter p, BaseColor color)`, `setPatternFill(PdfPatternPainter p, BaseColor color, float tint)`, and `setShadingFill(PdfShadingPattern shading)`.
sh	paintShading	(shading)	Paints the shape and color shading described by a shading dictionary. In iText the shading dictionary can be a `PdfShading` or `PdfShadingPattern` object.

14.3.3   *Changing the coordinate system*

In chapter 3, you learned that the origin of the coordinate system can usually be found in the lower-left corner of the page. For an A4 page in portrait orientation, the upper-right corner has the coordinates (595,842). We amended this in chapter 5,

where you created a superhero PDF with page size A0 with the origin of the coordinate system centered in the middle of the page.

Figure 14.4 is similar. The origin of the coordinate system is marked by two lines, where $Y = 0$ (the X axis) and $X = 0$ (the Y axis).

To this page, the same logo was added six times using the method addTemplate (template, 0, 0). However, the template is added at a different places and the shape changes. It looks translated, scaled, skewed, and rotated because the current transformation matrix is changed. This shows how it is done.

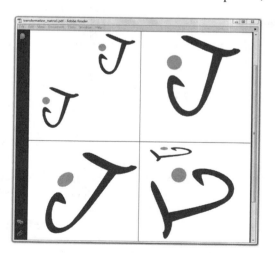

Figure 14.4   The current transformation matrix

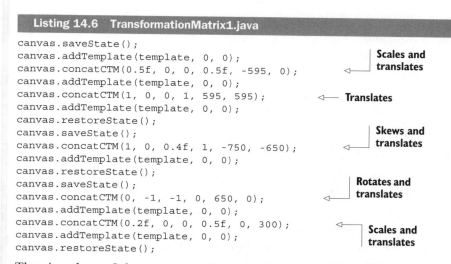

Listing 14.6 TransformationMatrix1.java

```
canvas.saveState();
canvas.addTemplate(template, 0, 0);
canvas.concatCTM(0.5f, 0, 0, 0.5f, -595, 0);        Scales and
canvas.addTemplate(template, 0, 0);                 translates
canvas.concatCTM(1, 0, 0, 1, 595, 595);          Translates
canvas.addTemplate(template, 0, 0);
canvas.restoreState();
canvas.saveState();                                 Skews and
canvas.concatCTM(1, 0, 0.4f, 1, -750, -650);        translates
canvas.addTemplate(template, 0, 0);
canvas.restoreState();
canvas.saveState();                                 Rotates and
canvas.concatCTM(0, -1, -1, 0, 650, 0);             translates
canvas.addTemplate(template, 0, 0);
canvas.concatCTM(0.2f, 0, 0, 0.5f, 0, 300);         Scales and
canvas.addTemplate(template, 0, 0);                 translates
canvas.restoreState();
```

The six values of the `concatCTM()` method are elements of a matrix that has three rows and three columns:

$$\begin{bmatrix} a & b & 0 \\ c & f & 0 \\ e & f & 1 \end{bmatrix}$$

You can use this matrix to express a transformation in a two-dimensional system:

$$[\; x'\; y'\; 1\;] = [\; x\; y\; 1\;] \times \begin{bmatrix} a & b & 0 \\ c & d & 0 \\ e & f & 1 \end{bmatrix}$$

Carrying out this multiplication results in this:

```
x' = a * x + c * y + e
y' = b * x + d * y + f
```

The third column in the matrix is fixed: you're working in two dimensions, so you don't need to calculate a new z coordinate.

There's one big difference here from what you were taught at school; in most math books you can read about transforming objects (points, lines, shapes), rather than coordinate systems. This demands a slightly different point of view.

To understand the mathematics of coordinate transformations in PDF, it's vital to remember what is written in ISO-32000-1 (section 8.3.4):

All objects painted before a transformation is applied shall be unaffected by the transformation. Objects painted after the transformation is applied, shall be interpreted in the transformed coordinate system.

Transformation matrices specify the transformation from the new (transformed) coordinate system to the original (untransformed) coordinate system. All coordinates used after the transformation shall be expressed in the transformed coordinate system.

Translating the coordinate system in direction (dX, dY) is done like this:

```
x' = 1 * x + 0 * y + dX
y' = 0 * x + 1 * y + dY
```

These formulas scale the coordinate system with factors sX in the *X* direction and sY in the *Y* direction:

```
x' = sX * x + 0 * y + 0
y' = 0 * x + sY * y + 0
```

To rotate the coordinate system with an angle φ, you need to use the following equations:

```
x' = cos(φ) * x - sin(φ) * y + 0
y' = sin(φ) * x + cos(φ) * y + 0
```

Skewing the coordinates is done like this:

```
x' = 1 * x + tan(β) * y + 0
y' = tan(α) * x + 1 * y + 0
```

where α is the new angle of the *X* axis and β is the new angle of the *Y* axis.

You can use these formulas to compute the values for a, b, c, d, e, and f. For example, if you want to combine a translation (dX, dY), a scaling (sX, sY), and a rotation φ, you'd use these values:

```
a = sX * cos(φ);
b = sY * sin(φ);
c = sX * -sin(φ);
d = sY * cos(φ);
e = dX;
f = dY;
```

If you combine different concatCTM() operations, you can compute the resulting transformation by multiplying the matrices with each other.

> **NOTE**   The order is important when performing transformations one after the other. This can be demonstrated by switching the lines with concatCTM() methods in the sequence between saveState() and restoreState() in listing 14.6.

Suppose you want the same result as shown in figure 14.4 but without using concatCTM() directly. In that case, you'll need a version of the addTemplate() method that takes a, b, c, d, e, and f parameters.

ADDING TEMPLATES AND IMAGES

Listing 14.7 is exactly equivalent to listing 14.6. First you add the template without any transformation ❶ in listing 14.7. Then you add two templates, ❷ and ❸, which are scaled and translated: ❹ skews and translates the template, and ❺ rotates and translates the template. Finally, the template is rotated, scaled, and translated ❻.

Listing 14.7   TransformationMatrix2.java

```
canvas.addTemplate(template, 0, 0);                              ❶
canvas.addTemplate(template, 0.5f, 0, 0, 0.5f, -595, 0);         ❷
canvas.addTemplate(template, 0.5f, 0, 0, 0.5f, -297.5f, 297.5f); ❸
canvas.addTemplate(template, 1, 0, 0.4f, 1, -750, -650);         ❹
canvas.addTemplate(template, 0, -1, -1, 0, 650, 0);              ❺
canvas.addTemplate(template, 0, -0.2f, -0.5f, 0, 350, 0);        ❻
```

The transformation matrix elements in ❸ are the result of the following multiplication:

$$\begin{bmatrix} 1 & 0 & 0 \\ 0 & 1 & 0 \\ 595 & 595 & 1 \end{bmatrix} \times \begin{bmatrix} 0.5 & 0 & 0 \\ 0 & 0.5 & 0 \\ -595 & 0 & 1 \end{bmatrix} = \begin{bmatrix} 0.5 & 0 & 0 \\ 0 & 0.5 & 0 \\ -297.5 & -297.5 & 1 \end{bmatrix}$$

The parameters in ❻ were computed like this:

$$\begin{bmatrix} 0.2 & 0 & 0 \\ 0 & 0.5 & 0 \\ 0 & 300 & 1 \end{bmatrix} \times \begin{bmatrix} 0 & -1 & 0 \\ -1 & 0 & 0 \\ 650 & 0 & 1 \end{bmatrix} = \begin{bmatrix} 0 & 0.2 & 0 \\ -0.5 & 0 & 0 \\ 350 & 0 & 1 \end{bmatrix}$$

Observe that you get a different result if you switch the order of the multiplication:

$$\begin{bmatrix} 0 & -1 & 0 \\ -1 & 0 & 0 \\ 650 & 0 & 1 \end{bmatrix} \times \begin{bmatrix} 0.2 & 0 & 0 \\ 0 & 0.5 & 0 \\ 0 & 300 & 1 \end{bmatrix} = \begin{bmatrix} 0 & -0.5 & 0 \\ -0.2 & 0 & 0 \\ 130 & 0 & 1 \end{bmatrix}$$

This proves that the order of the `concatCTM()` methods in listing 14.6 matters.

Table 14.9 lists the methods that can be used to add templates and images using iText.

Table 14.9 `PdfTemplate` and `Image` methods in `PdfContentByte`

PDF	iText method	Parameters	Description
Do	addTemplate	(template, e, f) (template, a, b, c, d, e, f)	The operator Do, preceded by a name of a form XObject, such as /Xf1, paints the XObject. iText will take care of handling the template object, as well as saving the state, performing a transformation of the CTM that's used for adding the XObject, and restoring the state.
Do	addImage	(image) (image, false) (image, a, b, c, d, e, f) (image, a, b, c, d, e, f, false)	The operator Do, preceded by a name of an image XObject, such as /img0, paints the image. iText will take care of storing the image stream correctly, as well as saving the state, performing a transformation of the CTM that's used for adding the image, and restoring the state.
BI EI	addImage	(image, true) (image, a, b, c, d, e, f, true)	As discussed in section 3.4.1, images can also be added inline. In that case, there's no Do operator, but the image properties and bytes are added inside a BI and EI sequence.

If you're not familiar with PDF matrix calculations, you can also use an alternative way to perform transformations.

14.3.4 *Affine transformations using Java*

Most Java programmers are more familiar with the java.awt package than with the PDF reference. In section 14.5, we'll look at how to draw graphics and text using standard Java methods available in the class PdfGraphics2D. Right now, we'll use the class java.awt.geom.AffineTransform as an alternative way to define a transformation.

According to the Java API documentation, the AffineTransform class represents "a 2D affine transform that performs a linear mapping from 2D coordinates to other 2D coordinates. Affine transformations can be constructed using sequences of translations, scales, flips, rotations, and shears."

The next bit of code is yet another rewrite of listings 14.6 and 14.7.

Listing 14.8   TextStateOperators.java

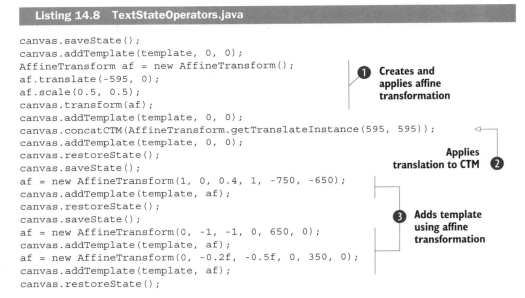

```java
canvas.saveState();
canvas.addTemplate(template, 0, 0);
AffineTransform af = new AffineTransform();
af.translate(-595, 0);
af.scale(0.5, 0.5);
canvas.transform(af);
canvas.addTemplate(template, 0, 0);
canvas.concatCTM(AffineTransform.getTranslateInstance(595, 595));
canvas.addTemplate(template, 0, 0);
canvas.restoreState();
canvas.saveState();
af = new AffineTransform(1, 0, 0.4, 1, -750, -650);
canvas.addTemplate(template, af);
canvas.restoreState();
canvas.saveState();
af = new AffineTransform(0, -1, -1, 0, 650, 0);
canvas.addTemplate(template, af);
af = new AffineTransform(0, -0.2f, -0.5f, 0, 350, 0);
canvas.addTemplate(template, af);
canvas.restoreState();
```

① Creates and applies affine transformation

② Applies translation to CTM

③ Adds template using affine transformation

Listing 14.8 demonstrates different ways to compose and use the affine transformation:

① Create an AffineTransform class. In this listing, you add a translation and a scaling operation and use the transform() method as an alternative for concatCTM().

② Create an instance of AffineTransform using one of its many static methods. In the listing, this method is used with the already discussed concatCTM() method.

③ Create AffineTransform objects using the same parameters as in listing 14.7, and use these transformations as parameters for the addTemplate() method.

Table 14.10 lists the PdfContentByte methods that accept an AffineTransform object. For more info about the AffineTransform class, please consult the Java documentation; for instance, see the tutorials on Oracle's Sun Developer Network site (see appendix B).

One method in table 14.10 demands further explanation: setTextMatrix(). This method results in a text-positioning operation.

Table 14.10 `AffineTransform` **methods**

iText method	Parameters	Description
addTemplate	`(PdfTemplate template, AffineTransform transform)`	Equivalent to the `addTemplate()` methods in table 14.7.
addImage	`(Image image, AffineTransform transform)`	Equivalent to the `addImage()` methods in table 14.7.
concatCTM	`(AffineTransform transform)`	Modifies the current transformation matrix (CTM).
transform	`(AffineTransform af)`	Alternative for `concatCTM()`.
setTextMatrix	`(AffineTransform transform)`	Sets the text matrix and the text-line matrix; see table 14.11.

14.4 Overview of the text and text state methods

A PDF text object consists of operators that may set the text state, move the text position, and show text. A text object is defined using the text object operators shown in table 14.11.

Table 14.11 Text object operators

PDF	iText method	Description
BT	`beginText()`	Begins a text object. Initializes the text, text line, and identity matrix. Don't nest text objects; a second BT is forbidden before an ET.
ET	`endText()`	Ends a text object, discards the text matrix.

If you set the fill color in the graphics state outside a BT/ET sequence, this color will be used as the color of the glyphs inside the text object, but PDF also has some text-specific state operators.

14.4.1 Text state operators

The text state is a subset of the graphics state. The available text state operators are listed in table 14.12.

Table 14.12 Text state operators

PDF	iText method	Parameters	Description
Tf	`setFontAndSize`	`(font, size)`	Sets the text font (a `BaseFont` object) and size. If you try showing text without having set a `font` and a `size`, an exception will be thrown.
Tc	`setCharacterSpacing`	`(charSpace)`	Sets the character spacing (initially 0).

Table 14.12   Text state operators *(continued)*

PDF	iText method	Parameters	Description
Tw	setWordSpacing	(wordSpace)	Sets the word spacing (initially 0).
Tz	setHorizontalScaling	(scale)	Sets the horizontal scaling (initially 100).
TL	setLeading	(leading)	Sets the leading (initially 0)
Ts	setTextRise	(rise)	Sets the text rise (initially 0).
Tr	setTextRenderingMode	(render)	Specifies a rendering mode (a combination of stroking and filling). By default, glyphs are filled.
/TK	PdfGState.setTextKnockout	(true | false)	Determines whether text elements are considered elementary objects for purposes of color compositing in the transparent imaging model.

These aren't the only text-specific operators. There are also operators to position and show text.

14.4.2 *Text-positioning and text-showing operators*

A glyph is a graphical shape and is subject to all graphical manipulations, such as coordinate transformations defined by the CTM, but there are also three matrices for text that are valid inside a text object:

- *The text matrix*—This is updated by the text-positioning and text-showing operators listed in table 14.13.
- *The text-line matrix*—This captures the value of the text matrix at the beginning of a line of text.
- *The text-rendering matrix*—This is an intermediate result that combines the effects of text state parameters, the text matrix, and the CTM.

Note that the value of these matrix parameters isn't persisted from one text object to another. Table 4.13 lists the operators that allow you to choose a position and put the text on the page based on that position.

Table 14.13   Text-positioning and -showing operators

PDF	iText method	Parameters	Description
Td	moveText	(tx, ty)	Moves to the start of the next line, offset from the start of the current line by (tx, ty).
TD	moveTextWithLeading	(tx, ty)	Same as moveText() but sets the leading to -ty.
Tm	setTextMatrix	(e, f) (a, b, c, d, e, f)	Sets the text matrix and the text-line matrix. The parameters a, b, c, d, e, and f are the elements of a matrix that will replace the current text matrix.

Table 14.13   Text-positioning and -showing operators *(continued)*

PDF	iText method	Parameters	Description
T*	newLineText	()	Moves to the start of the next line (depending on the leading).
Tj	showText	(string)	Shows a text string.
'	newlineShowText	(string)	Moves to the next line, and shows a text string.
"	newlineShowText	(aw, ac, string)	Moves to the next line, and shows a text string using aw as word spacing and ac as character spacing.
TJ	showText	(array)	Shows one or more text strings, allowing individual glyph positioning.

In figure 14.5, you can see some of these text state operators in action.

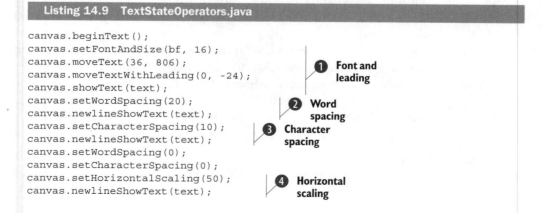

**Figure 14.5
Demonstrating
the different text
state operators**

This listing shows how the seven lines at the left of figure 14.5 were drawn.

Listing 14.9   TextStateOperators.java

```
canvas.beginText();
canvas.setFontAndSize(bf, 16);
canvas.moveText(36, 806);                    ❶ Font and
canvas.moveTextWithLeading(0, -24);             leading
canvas.showText(text);
canvas.setWordSpacing(20);                   ❷ Word
canvas.newlineShowText(text);                   spacing
canvas.setCharacterSpacing(10);              ❸ Character
canvas.newlineShowText(text);                   spacing
canvas.setWordSpacing(0);
canvas.setCharacterSpacing(0);
canvas.setHorizontalScaling(50);             ❹ Horizontal
canvas.newlineShowText(text);                   scaling
```

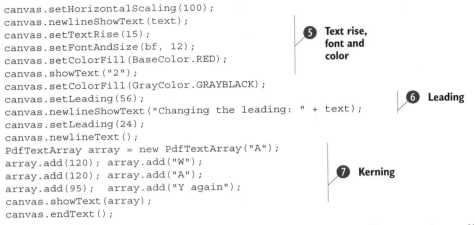

```
canvas.setHorizontalScaling(100);
canvas.newlineShowText(text);
canvas.setTextRise(15);                           ❺ Text rise,
canvas.setFontAndSize(bf, 12);                       font and
canvas.setColorFill(BaseColor.RED);                  color
canvas.showText("2");
canvas.setColorFill(GrayColor.GRAYBLACK);
canvas.setLeading(56);                            ❻ Leading
canvas.newlineShowText("Changing the leading: " + text);
canvas.setLeading(24);
canvas.newlineText();
PdfTextArray array = new PdfTextArray("A");
array.add(120); array.add("W");
array.add(120); array.add("A");                   ❼ Kerning
array.add(95);  array.add("Y again");
canvas.showText(array);
canvas.endText();
```

❶ For the first line, you start a new line at position (36, 806). Then you immediately move 24 pt down. This sets the leading to -24 because you use moveTextWithLeading() instead of moveText(). You draw the text with showText().

❷ There's more space between the words "AWAY" and "again". That's because the word spacing is changed to 20 pt.

❸ The word spacing is still 20 pt, but now there's also a character spacing of 10 pt. In sections 2.2.4, 3.3.1, and 4.2.1, you used the setSpaceCharRatio() method to fine-tune the spacing of a justified line of text. Internally iText uses the word and character spacing to achieve this.

❹ Word and character spacing are changed back to their defaults (0 pt), and you scale the glyphs horizontally to 50 percent.

❺ You add a red exponent "2". The color is changed using a graphics state operator, and the glyph is raised 15 pt using setTextRise().

❻ In ❶ you implicitly set the leading to 24; now you change the leading to 56 pt with the setLeading() method. Note that the text rise is still active, so the text is only moved down 41 pt.

❼ In previous lines, the characters of the word "AWAY" were added using the character advance as described in the font program. Here you move the glyphs closer together. You use the method showText() with a PdfTextArray as a parameter; this array contains a sequence of strings and numbers. With the numbers, you specify extra positioning information in glyph space (in thousandths of a unit). The amount is subtracted from the current horizontal or vertical coordinate, depending on the writing mode. You don't have to construct this array yourself. If your font has *kerning* information, you can use the method getKernArray(text, font), and use the return value as a parameter.

The lines to the right in figure 14.5 demonstrate the different rendering modes.

RENDERING MODES

At first sight, there seem to be seven "AWAY again" lines at the right. But in reality, there are eight. The first four are added using this code snippet:

```
canvas.setColorFill(BaseColor.BLUE);
canvas.beginText();
canvas.setTextMatrix(360, 770);
canvas.setTextRenderingMode(PdfContentByte.TEXT_RENDER_MODE_FILL);
canvas.setFontAndSize(bf, 24);
canvas.showText(text);
canvas.endText();
```

This snippet is repeated four times using different coordinates and different rendering modes. See table 14.14.

Table 14.14 Rendering mode modes

Rendering mode	Description
TEXT_RENDER_MODE_FILL	This is the default: glyphs are shapes that are filled.
TEXT_RENDER_MODE_STROKE	With this mode, the paths of the glyphs are stroked, not filled.
TEXT_RENDER_MODE_FILL_STROKE	Glyphs are filled and stroked.
TEXT_RENDER_MODE_INVISIBLE	Glyphs are neither filled nor stroked: this is why the fourth line is invisible.

The code for the final four lines looks like this:

```
PdfTemplate template = canvas.createTemplate(200, 36);
template.setLineWidth(2);
for (int i = 0; i < 6; i++) {
  template.moveTo(0, i * 6);
  template.lineTo(200, i * 6);
}
template.stroke();
canvas.saveState();
canvas.beginText();
canvas.setTextMatrix(360, 610);
canvas.setTextRenderingMode(
  PdfContentByte.TEXT_RENDER_MODE_FILL_CLIP);
canvas.setFontAndSize(bf, 24);
canvas.showText(text);
canvas.endText();
canvas.addTemplate(template, 360, 610);
canvas.restoreState();
```

Creates template with series of lines

Adds text (clip render mode)

Adds template (clipped)

These are the render modes that were used for the last four lines in figure 14.5:

- TEXT_RENDER_MODE_FILL_CLIP
- TEXT_RENDER_MODE_STROKE_CLIP
- TEXT_RENDER_MODE_FILL_STROKE_CLIP
- TEXT_RENDER_MODE_CLIP

They have the same meaning as the four render modes shown in table 14.14, except that by adding _CLIP, the text will function as a clipping area for the content that's added afterwards.

This chapter serves as a reference to the graphics and text operators in the PDF imaging model. The methods in tables 14.12 and 14.13 could be useful one day, but in general, you'll probably use convenience classes (such as `ColumnText`) or methods.

14.4.3 *Convenience methods for text*

Table 14.15 lists the extra methods available in `PdfContentByte` that can be used to draw text or to compute the text width, taking into account the text state.

Table 14.15   iText convenience methods for text

iText method	Parameters	Description
showTextKerned	(text)	This is the equivalent of `showText(getKernArray(text, bf))`.
getEffectiveStringWidth	(text, kerned)	Computes the width of the given string taking into account the current values of character spacing, word spacing, and horizontal scaling. Takes the kerning into account if kerned is `true`.
showTextAligned	(alignment, text, x, y, rot) (alignment, text, x, y, rot, k)	Shows the text at position `(x,y)` with rotation `rot`, aligned left, right, or centered depending on the value of `alignment`. The text will be kerned if k is `true`.
showTextAlignedKerned	(alignment, text, x, y, rot)	Same as `showTextAligned(alignment, text, x, y, rot, true)`.

Figure 14.6 demonstrates how these methods can be used.

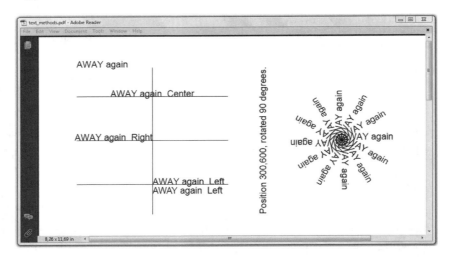

Figure 14.6   Demonstrating the convenience methods for text

The code that produced the PDF in figure 14.6 is shown here.

Listing 14.10   TextMethods.java

```
String text = "AWAY again ";
BaseFont bf = BaseFont.createFont();
cb.beginText();
cb.setFontAndSize(bf, 12);
cb.setTextMatrix(50, 800);
cb.showText(text);
cb.showTextAligned(PdfContentByte.ALIGN_CENTER,
  text + " Center", 150, 760, 0);                    Centered text
cb.showTextAligned(PdfContentByte.ALIGN_RIGHT,
  text + " Right", 150, 700, 0);                      Right-aligned text
cb.showTextAligned(PdfContentByte.ALIGN_LEFT,
  text + " Left", 150, 640, 0);                       Left-aligned text
cb.showTextAlignedKerned(PdfContentByte.ALIGN_LEFT,
  text + " Left", 150, 628, 0);                       Left-aligned and kerned text
cb.setTextMatrix(0, 1, -1, 0, 300, 600);
cb.showText("Position 300,600, rotated 90 degrees.");
for (int i = 0; i < 360; i += 30) {
  cb.showTextAligned(PdfContentByte.ALIGN_LEFT, text, 400, 700, i);
}
cb.endText();
```

Apart from these convenience methods for text, `PdfContentByte` has additional methods that can be useful in special situations:

- `setLiteral()`—Allows you to add literal PDF syntax to the `ByteBuffer`. Use this method only if you know exactly what the syntax does and if you're aware of all the possible side effects.
- `add(PdfContentByte other)`—Appends the content of another `PdfContent-Byte` object to the current one (provided that both were created for the same `PdfWriter`).
- `reset()`—Empties the `ByteBuffer`.

If you have experience with imaging models in other programming or markup languages, such as in Flex, SVG, XAML, and so on, many of the concepts explained in this chapter will have sounded familiar. Principles such as the nonzero winding number rule and the even-odd rule exist for almost every language where you can describe and fill shapes. Almost every programming language that allows you to create a GUI has methods to draw text.

Let's conclude this chapter by taking a look at how it's done in Java, and how iText allows you to create PDFs using those methods.

14.5   *Using java.awt.Graphics2D*

In *Star Trek*, Dr. Leonard "Bones" McCoy is often heard to say things like "Dammit, man! I'm a doctor, not a physicist!" After reading the previous sections, you may have a similar reaction: "I'm a Java developer, not a PDF specialist. I want to use iText so that I can avoid learning PDF syntax!" If that's the case, I have good news for you.

In this section, you'll learn how to draw paths, shapes, and text using Java's Graphics2D API. Although this seems easy to achieve, you'll also learn how to avoid common pitfalls.

14.5.1 *Drawing content to PdfGraphics2D*

Swing is an API for providing a GUI for Java programs. It consists of different GUI components and a series of graphical classes, including an abstract class named Graphics2D. PdfContentByte has a series of createGraphics() methods that allow you to create a special implementation of this class called PdfGraphics2D. This subclass overrides all the Graphics2D methods, translating them into the PdfContentByte calls described in the previous sections.

DRAWING SHAPES TO SWING OBJECTS

The Java API says that java.awt.Graphics is "the abstract base class for all graphics contexts that allow an application to draw onto components that are realized on various devices, as well as onto off-screen images." The abstract class java.awt.Graphics2D extends this Graphics class "to provide more sophisticated control over geometry, coordinate transformations, color management, and text layout. This is the fundamental class for rendering 2-dimensional shapes, text and images on the Java platform."

If you go to Oracle's Sun Developer Network (SDN), you'll find a tutorial "Constructing Complex Shapes from Geometry Primitives." There's an example named Pear.java in this tutorial for drawing a shape as shown in figure 14.7.

The window on the right in figure 14.7 is a JFrame containing a JPanel. The JPanel was constructed and painted using the next bit of code. This code snippet is almost identical to the sample that can be found on SDN.

Figure 14.7
Graphics2D for
Swing and PDF; the
Pear example from
the Java tutorial

Listing 14.11   PearExample.java

```java
public class PearExample extends JPanel {
  Ellipse2D.Double circle, oval, leaf, stem;
  Area circ, ov, leaf1, leaf2, st1, st2;
  public PearExample() {
    circle = new Ellipse2D.Double();
    oval = new Ellipse2D.Double();
    leaf = new Ellipse2D.Double();
    stem = new Ellipse2D.Double();
    circ = new Area(circle);
    ov = new Area(oval);
    leaf1 = new Area(leaf);
    leaf2 = new Area(leaf);
    st1 = new Area(stem);
    st2 = new Area(stem);
  }
  public void paint(Graphics g) {
    Graphics2D g2 = (Graphics2D)g;
    double ew = 75; double eh = 75;
    g2.setColor(Color.GREEN);
    leaf.setFrame(ew - 16, eh - 29, 15.0, 15.0);
    leaf1 = new Area(leaf);
    leaf.setFrame(ew - 14, eh - 47, 30.0, 30.0);
    leaf2 = new Area(leaf);
    leaf1.intersect(leaf2);
    g2.fill(leaf1);
    leaf.setFrame(ew + 1, eh - 29, 15.0, 15.0);
    leaf1 = new Area(leaf);
    leaf2.intersect(leaf1);
    g2.fill(leaf2);
    g2.setColor(Color.BLACK);
    stem.setFrame(ew, eh - 42, 40.0, 40.0);
    st1 = new Area(stem);
    stem.setFrame(ew + 3, eh - 47, 50.0, 50.0);
    st2 = new Area(stem);
    st1.subtract(st2);
    g2.fill(st1);
    g2.setColor(Color.YELLOW);
    circle.setFrame(ew - 25, eh, 50.0, 50.0);
    oval.setFrame(ew - 19, eh - 20, 40.0, 70.0);
    circ = new Area(circle);
    ov = new Area(oval);
    circ.add(ov);
    g2.fill(circ);
  }
}
```

Initializes different shapes

Draws green leaves

Draws black stem

Draws yellow pear body

This is a book about PDF, not a book about Java, so we won't go into detail discussing the different geometry primitives and how to use them. That is all explained on SDN. Instead, we'll try to draw this complex shape to PDF as shown in the window to the right in figure 14.7.

DRAWING SHAPES TO PDFGRAPHICS2D

In listing 14.12 you'll reuse the code from listing 14.11. You'll construct a JPanel, more specifically a PearExample object, create a PdfGraphics2D instance, and draw the

JPanel to `PdfGraphics2D` using the `paint()` method. Don't forget to use the `dispose()` method ❶, or you'll end up with unpredictable errors in the resulting PDF file.

Listing 14.12   PearToPdf.java

```
Document document = new Document(new Rectangle(150, 150));
PdfWriter writer
  = PdfWriter.getInstance(document, new FileOutputStream(filename));
document.open();
PdfContentByte canvas = writer.getDirectContent();
PearExample pear = new PearExample();
Graphics2D g2 = canvas.createGraphics(150, 150);
pear.paint(g2);
g2.dispose();
document.close();
```

❶ Warning: don't forget dispose ()

Observe that there's not a single line referring to iText in the `PearExample` constructor, nor in its `paint()` method. This is a very powerful feature. If you have an existing application that draws shapes to a `Graphics2D` object, you can use this code snippet to add these shapes to a PDF file.

Figure 14.8 shows how you can integrate charts generated with the JFreeChart library into a PDF file through the `PdfGraphics2D` mechanism.

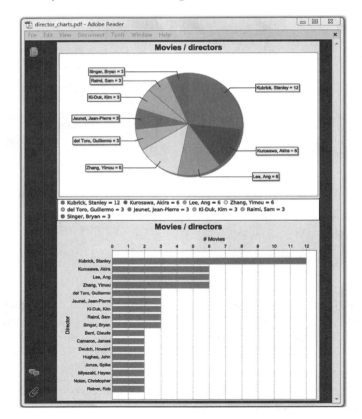

Figure 14.8   Combining JFreeChart and iText

The pie chart in figure 14.8 was created using the next code snippet. It charts the result of a database query selecting nine directors and the number of movies by these directors in the movie database.

Listing 14.13   DirectorCharts.java

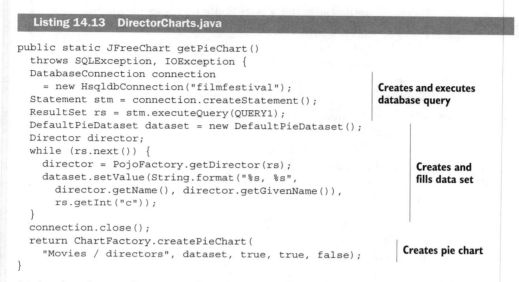

```
public static JFreeChart getPieChart()
  throws SQLException, IOException {
  DatabaseConnection connection
    = new HsqldbConnection("filmfestival");
  Statement stm = connection.createStatement();
  ResultSet rs = stm.executeQuery(QUERY1);
  DefaultPieDataset dataset = new DefaultPieDataset();
  Director director;
  while (rs.next()) {
    director = PojoFactory.getDirector(rs);
    dataset.setValue(String.format("%s, %s",
      director.getName(), director.getGivenName()),
      rs.getInt("c"));
  }
  connection.close();
  return ChartFactory.createPieChart(
    "Movies / directors", dataset, true, true, false);
}
```

Creates and executes database query

Creates and fills data set

Creates pie chart

Again, there's no reference to iText in this method. The iText magic happens here:

Listing 14.14   DirectorCharts.java (continued)

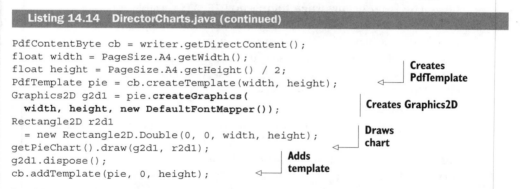

```
PdfContentByte cb = writer.getDirectContent();
float width = PageSize.A4.getWidth();
float height = PageSize.A4.getHeight() / 2;
PdfTemplate pie = cb.createTemplate(width, height);
Graphics2D g2d1 = pie.createGraphics(
  width, height, new DefaultFontMapper());
Rectangle2D r2d1
  = new Rectangle2D.Double(0, 0, width, height);
getPieChart().draw(g2d1, r2d1);
g2d1.dispose();
cb.addTemplate(pie, 0, height);
```

Creates PdfTemplate

Creates Graphics2D

Draws chart

Adds template

In this code snippet, you obtain a PdfGraphics2D object from a PdfTemplate. This makes it easier to position the chart on the page.

TROUBLESHOOTING PDFGRAPHICS2D APPLICATIONS

So far, the Graphics2D examples have been simple compared to the previous examples in this chapter. It would be surprising if there weren't any caveats.

Numerous developers have posted problems to the mailing list that can be avoided by following these guidelines:

- Don't forget to call the dispose() method once you've finished drawing to the PdfGraphics2D object (❶ in listing 14.12). Seriously, this is an FNA: a Frequently Needed Answer.

- The coordinate system in Java's `Graphics2D` is different from the default coordinate system in PDF's graphics state. The origin of user space in Java `Graphics` is the upper-left corner of the component's drawing area. The *X* coordinate increases to the right; the *Y* coordinate increases downward.
- Java works in standard Red-Green-Blue (sRGB) as the default color space internally, but colors need to be translated. Be aware that anything with four color values is assumed to be ARGB, even when it's probably CMYK. (ARGB includes the RGB components plus an alpha transparency factor that specifies what happens when one color is drawn over another.)
- Watch out when using fonts. There's a big difference between the `java.awt.Font` and `com.itextpdf.text.Font` font classes. We'll discuss this in section 14.5.2.
- It's possible that you'll need to install a virtual X11 server to make the examples involving Java's Abstract Window Toolkit (AWT), such as the `Graphics2D` examples, work on Linux servers.

Let's have a closer look at the last point in the list. If you use `java.awt` classes in applications on Linux servers, you can get exceptions like, "Can't connect to X11 window server using xyz as the value of the DISPLAY variable" or "No X11 DISPLAY variable was set, but this program performed an operation which requires it." The former error message occurs when a `DISPLAY` variable was set, but there was no X display server running. The latter occurs when there's no `DISPLAY` variable set at all.

The Sun AWT classes on UNIX and Linux have a dependency on the X Window System. You must have X installed in the machine; otherwise none of the packages from `java.awt` will be installed. If you use these classes, they'll attempt to load X client libraries and try to talk to an X display server. This makes sense if your client has a GUI. Unfortunately, it's required even if your application uses AWT but, like iText, doesn't have a GUI.

In some cases, you can work around this issue by running the AWT in headless mode. This can be achieved by starting the Java Virtual Machine (JVM) with the parameter `java.awt.headless=true`. In other cases, you'll have to install a virtual X server. Xvfb, for instance, emulates an X server without outputting it to the monitor.

Suppose you're working on Fedora Linux—you could install Xvfb using this line:

```
yum install xorg-x11-server-Xvfb
```

Once Xvfb is started, you can execute it like this:

```
Xvfb :100 -ac
```

Before starting your application, export the `DISPLAY` variable like this:

```
export DISPLAY=:100.0
```

You'll have to do something similar for other Linux distributions; Please consult your Linux manual for the correct commands to install a virtual X server.

In the next section, we'll look at how to render text using `Graphics2D`.

14.5.2 *Drawing text to PdfGraphics2D*

Drawing text to a `Graphics2D` object is straightforward:

```
g2d.setFont(new java.awt.Font("SansSerif", Font.PLAIN, 12));
g2d.drawString("Hello World", 36, 54);
```

Drawing the same text to a `PdfGraphics2D` object isn't as trivial as the previous examples suggest. In the code snippet, you tell Java to use a `java.awt.Font` named "Sans-Serif", but how does iText know where to find such a font?

USING A FONTMAPPER

One way to deal with the difference between the way fonts are handled in AWT and in PDF is to create the `PdfGraphics2D` object and pass in an instance of the `FontMapper` interface:

```
FontMapper mapper = new DefaultFontMapper();
Graphics2D g2d = cb.createGraphics(width, height, mapper);
```

The font mapper interface has two methods. One returns an iText `BaseFont` when you pass a Java AWT `Font`, and the other returns a Java AWT `Font` when you pass an iText `BaseFont`:

```
public BaseFont awtToPdf(java.awt.Font font);
public java.awt.Font pdfToAwt(BaseFont font, int size);
```

Every class implementing this interface needs to establish a mapping between the two font objects.

There's a default font mapper class called `DefaultFontMapper`. This class maps the following AWT font names to the standard Type 1 fonts:

- *DialogInput, Monospaced, and Courier*—Mapped to a font from the Courier family.
- *Serif and TimesRoman*—Mapped to a font from the Times-Roman family.
- *Dialog and SansSerif*—Mapped to a font from the Helvetica family (this is also the default if the font name isn't recognized).

You can get the names of the font families that are available in AWT like this:

```
GraphicsEnvironment ge = GraphicsEnvironment.getLocalGraphicsEnvironment();
String[] fontFamily = ge.getAvailableFontFamilyNames();
```

On Windows, you'll get names such as these:

```
Arial
Arial Black
Arial Narrow
Arial Unicode MS
```

These names won't be recognized by the `DefaultFontMapper` unless you help the mapper by inserting a directory. In the next listing, you add all the fonts that are present in the directory c:/windows/fonts and list the fonts that were registered.

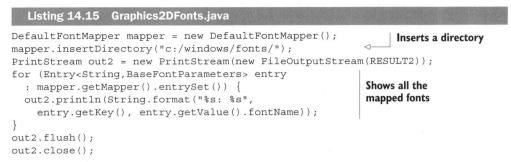

```
DefaultFontMapper mapper = new DefaultFontMapper();                    ⟵┤ Inserts a directory
mapper.insertDirectory("c:/windows/fonts/");
PrintStream out2 = new PrintStream(new FileOutputStream(RESULT2));
for (Entry<String,BaseFontParameters> entry
  : mapper.getMapper().entrySet()) {                                      Shows all the
  out2.println(String.format("%s: %s",                                    mapped fonts
    entry.getKey(), entry.getValue().fontName));
}
out2.flush();
out2.close();
```

The insertDirectory() method will examine all the font files in that directory, get the name of each font, and add it to a map. You can get the entries in this map with the getMapper() method.

   If you search the results of listing 14.15 for the Arial family, you'll see that DefaultMapper has found four matches in the fonts directory on Windows:

```
Arial: c:\windows\fonts\arial.ttf
Arial Bold: c:\windows\fonts\arialbd.ttf
Arial Italic: c:\windows\fonts\ariali.ttf
Arial Bold Italic: c:\windows\fonts\arialbi.ttf
```

In addition to getMapper(), there's a getAliases() method that returns all the names that can be used to create the Java AWT Font object. This includes the name of the font in different languages, provided that the translations are present in the font file. You can also add your own aliases with the putAlias() method. All of these aliases can be used when creating a java.awt.Font object.

   We've solved one major problem with DefaultFontMapper: how to map the name of a font in Java with the path to a font for iText. But what about the encoding?

CHOOSING A DIFFERENT ENCODING

Figure 14.9 shows a JPanel containing English and Japanese text.

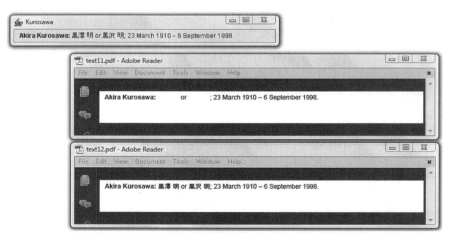

Figure 14.9   Demonstration and solution of the encoding problem

The text was added to the JPanel in the paint() method of the next listing. It specifies a SansSerif font and MS PGothic.

Listing 14.16 TextExample1.java

```
public class TextExample1 extends JPanel {
  private static AttributedString akira;
  public TextExample1() {
    akira = new AttributedString(
      "Akira Kurosawa: \u9ed2\u6fa4 \u660e or \u9ed2\u6ca2 \u660e; "
      + "23 March 1910 - 6 September 1998.");
    akira.addAttribute(TextAttribute.FONT,
      new Font("SansSerif", Font.PLAIN, 12));
    akira.addAttribute(TextAttribute.FONT,
      new Font("SansSerif", Font.BOLD, 12), 0, 15);
    akira.addAttribute(TextAttribute.FONT,
      new Font("MS PGothic", Font.PLAIN, 12), 16, 20);
    akira.addAttribute(TextAttribute.FONT,
      new Font("MS PGothic", Font.PLAIN, 12), 24, 28);
  }
  public void paint(Graphics g) {
    Graphics2D g2d = (Graphics2D) g;
    g2d.drawString(akira.getIterator(), 10, 16);
  }
}
```

In this listing, you try to draw the content of the JPanel to PDF.

Listing 14.17 Text1ToPdf1.java

```
DefaultFontMapper mapper = new DefaultFontMapper();
mapper.insertDirectory("c:/windows/fonts/");
Graphics2D g2 = canvas.createGraphics(600, 60, mapper);
TextExample1 text = new TextExample1();
text.paint(g2);
g2.dispose();
```

If you search the map generated by the example listing, you'll discover that the mapper is able to find the correct font:

```
MS PGothic: c:\windows\fonts\msgothic.ttc,1
```

But the Japanese text isn't rendered because the DefaultFontMapper assumes that each font uses the encoding Cp1252 (WinAnsi). This won't work for Japanese.

You can fix this by adding a custom BaseFontParameters object to the mapper as was done here.

Listing 14.18 Text1ToPdf2.java

```
DefaultFontMapper mapper = new DefaultFontMapper();
BaseFontParameters parameters = new BaseFontParameters(
  "c:/windows/fonts/msgothic.ttc,1");          Creates font
                                                mapping
parameters.encoding = BaseFont.IDENTITY_H;                Adds it to
mapper.putName("MS PGothic", parameters );                mapper
Graphics2D g2 = canvas.createGraphics(600, 60, mapper);
```

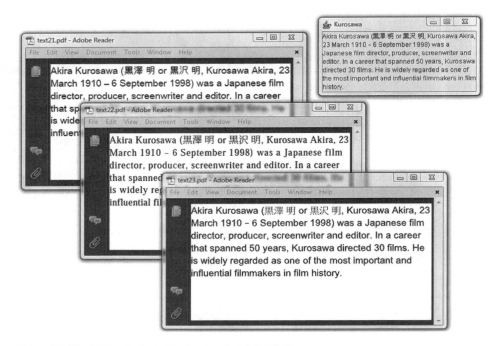

Figure 14.10   Different strategies for drawing Asian fonts

An alternative to this approach would be to subclass the `DefaultFontMapper` so that it uses a different encoding, or even a different font.

CUSTOM IMPLEMENTATIONS OF THE FONTMAPPER

You can render the text shown in figure 14.10 to PDF using three different strategies: by creating a custom `FontMapper` forcing the `PdfGraphics2D` object to use MS Arial Unicode with encoding Identity-H, by using `AsianFontMapper`, or by adding the glyphs as shapes instead of characters stored in a font.

Experienced Java programmers won't like the `paint()` method in the next listing, but we'll look at rewriting the code in listing 14.21.

Listing 14.19   TextExample2.java

```java
private LineBreakMeasurer lineMeasurer;
public static final String AKIRA =
  "Akira Kurosawa (\u9ed2\u6fa4 \u660e or \u9ed2\u6ca2 \u660e, " +
  "Kurosawa Akira, 23 March 1910 - 6 September 1998) was a " +
  "Japanese film director, producer, screenwriter and editor. " +
  "In a career that spanned 50 years, Kurosawa directed 30 films. " +
  "He is widely regarded as one of the most important and " +
  "influential filmmakers in film history.";
public TextExample2() {
  akira = new AttributedString(AKIRA);
  akira.addAttribute(
```

```
      TextAttribute.FONT, new Font("Arial Unicode MS", Font.PLAIN, 12));
}
public void paint(Graphics g) {
  Graphics2D g2d = (Graphics2D) g;
  g2d.setFont(new Font("Arial Unicode MS", Font.PLAIN, 12));
  if (lineMeasurer == null) {
    AttributedCharacterIterator paragraph = akira.getIterator();
    paragraphStart = paragraph.getBeginIndex();
    paragraphEnd = paragraph.getEndIndex();
    FontRenderContext frc = g2d.getFontRenderContext();
    lineMeasurer = new LineBreakMeasurer(paragraph, frc);
  }
  float breakWidth = (float)getSize().width;
  float drawPosY = 0;
  lineMeasurer.setPosition(paragraphStart);
  int start = 0;
  int end = 0;
  while (lineMeasurer.getPosition() < paragraphEnd) {
    TextLayout layout = lineMeasurer.nextLayout(breakWidth);
    drawPosY += layout.getAscent();
    end = start + layout.getCharacterCount();
    g2d.drawString(AKIRA.substring(start, end), 0, drawPosY);
    start = end;
    drawPosY += layout.getDescent() + layout.getLeading();
  }
}
```

The drawString() method is similar to iText's showTextAligned() method. It doesn't wrap the text when the end of the line is reached. Figure 14.10 shows a longer text containing English and Japanese spanning multiple lines.

Here, you're dividing the long AKIRA text into smaller String objects using the LineBreakMeasurer object with an AttributedString. The substrings are added using the drawString() method.

CREATING A CUSTOM FONTMAPPER
The first of the three proposed strategies for rendering the text shown in figure 14.10 to PDF is to create a custom FontMapper class.

Listing 14.20   Text2ToPdf1.java

```
FontMapper arialuni = new FontMapper() {
  public BaseFont awtToPdf(Font font) {
    try {
      return BaseFont.createFont(
        "c:/windows/fonts/arialuni.ttf",
        BaseFont.IDENTITY_H, BaseFont.EMBEDDED);
    } catch (DocumentException e) {
      e.printStackTrace();
    } catch (IOException e) {
      e.printStackTrace();
    }
    return null;
  }
```

```
  public Font pdfToAwt(BaseFont font, int size) {
    return null;
  }
};
Graphics2D g2 = canvas.createGraphics(300, 150, arialuni);
```

This is a quick and dirty solution that forces `PdfGraphics2D` to use `arialuni.ttf` no matter which font was selected on the Java side.

USING ASIANFONTMAPPER

A similar solution is to use the `AsianFontMapper` class, as is done in the `Text2ToPdf2` class, which demonstrates the second strategy for rendering the text:

```
Graphics2D g2 = canvas.createGraphics(300, 150,
  new AsianFontMapper(AsianFontMapper.JapaneseFont_Min,
    AsianFontMapper.JapaneseEncoding_H));
```

The `AsianFontMapper` class contains static `String` values corresponding with the CJK fonts discussed in section 11.3.3. One of the most difficult problems when using this approach lies with the font metrics. As far as the Java part is concerned, the font Arial Unicode is used. This choice is respected in the `Text2ToPdf1` example in listing 14.20, but you use a different font in the `Text2ToPdf2` example. This different font may have different metrics. If that's the case, the size of each line will be different from what was expected. The text may even exceed the designated area.

Let's consider a third strategy. You can drop the idea of using a `FontMapper` and let the Java code draw the shapes of the glyphs.

DRAWING GLYPH SHAPES INSTEAD OF USING A PDF FONT

If you create a `PdfGraphics2D` object using the `createGraphicsShapes()` method instead of `createGraphics()`, you don't need to map any fonts. This is what happens in the example named `Text2ToPdf3`:

```
Graphics2D g2 = canvas.createGraphicsShapes(300, 150);
```

Internally, iText will use the Java object `java.awt.font.TextLayout` to draw the glyphs to the `Graphics2D` object. This object will address the font program directly and copy the path of each glyph to the page.

There's a significant difference between this approach and using a `FontMapper`. If you open the Fonts tab in File > Properties, you won't find any font. This has the following consequences:

- The file size will generally be larger because the glyph descriptions will be repeated in the content stream instead of being stored in a font stream from which they can be reused.
- Selecting text will be impossible because there is no text. Each glyph is a path that has been filled.
- Glyph resolution for glyphs that are stored in a font will render much better than glyphs drawn as shapes, such as when printed on low-resolution printers.

These are all disadvantages. An advantage could be that you will prevent end users from copying and pasting, or that you can obfuscate email addresses in your document so that they can't be "harvested" by engines spidering your PDF. Finally, there's the advantage that Java supports Hindic languages, whereas iText can't make the ligatures when writing Hindi.

    This phenomenon is also a side effect of using the `LineBreakMeasurer` correctly. The following example is a rewrite of listing 14.19.

Listing 14.21   TextExample3.java

```
private LineBreakMeasurer lineMeasurer;
private static AttributedString akira;
public TextExample3() {
  akira = new AttributedString(
    "Akira Kurosawa (\u9ed2\u6fa4 \u660e or \u9ed2\u6ca2 \u660e, " +
    "Kurosawa Akira, 23 March 1910 - 6 September 1998) was a " +
    "Japanese film director, producer, screenwriter and editor. " +
    "In a career that spanned 50 years, Kurosawa directed 30 films. " +
    "He is widely regarded as one of the most important and " +
    "influential filmmakers in film history.");
    akira.addAttribute(
      TextAttribute.FONT, new Font("SansSerif", Font.PLAIN, 12));
    akira.addAttribute(
      TextAttribute.FONT, new Font("SansSerif", Font.BOLD, 12), 0, 14);
    akira.addAttribute(
      TextAttribute.FONT, new Font("MS PGothic", Font.PLAIN, 12), 16, 20);
    akira.addAttribute(
      TextAttribute.FONT, new Font("MS PGothic", Font.PLAIN, 12), 24, 28);
}
public void paint(Graphics g) {
  Graphics2D g2d = (Graphics2D) g;
  if (lineMeasurer == null) {
    AttributedCharacterIterator paragraph = akira.getIterator();
    paragraphStart = paragraph.getBeginIndex();
    paragraphEnd = paragraph.getEndIndex();
    FontRenderContext frc = g2d.getFontRenderContext();
    lineMeasurer = new LineBreakMeasurer(paragraph, frc);
  }
  float breakWidth = (float)getSize().width;
  float drawPosY = 0;
  lineMeasurer.setPosition(paragraphStart);
  while (lineMeasurer.getPosition() < paragraphEnd) {
    TextLayout layout = lineMeasurer.nextLayout(breakWidth);
    drawPosY += layout.getAscent();
    layout.draw(g2d, 0, drawPosY);
    drawPosY += layout.getDescent() + layout.getLeading();
  }
}
```

You `draw()` the substring available in the `TextLayout` object instead of taking substrings of the long text and using `drawString()`. Using `TextLayout.draw()` has the same effect as using `createGraphicsShapes()` instead of `createGraphics()`. The same disadvantages apply: problems with file sizes, selecting text, and resolution.

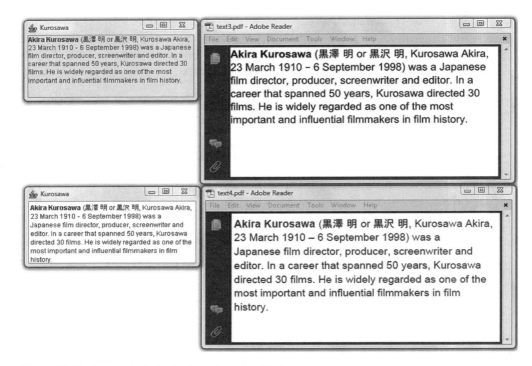

Figure 14.11   Different strategies for using mixed fonts

Suppose that you want to mix different fonts and styles in one `String`, force line breaks, and avoid the disadvantages of using `draw()`. To do this, you'll need another solution.

The upper-right PDF in figure 14.11 is drawn using listing 14.21. There are no fonts in the PDF; the glyph descriptions are added as PDF syntax in the content stream.

The lower-right PDF uses a different mechanism. It's the result of printing a `JTextPane` to a `PdfGraphics2D` object.

PRINTING SWING COMPONENTS TO PDF

The Java class `java.awt.Component` has a method named `print()` that takes a `Graphics` object as a parameter. You can use this method to print any component to a `PdfGraphics2D` object: `JTables`, `JTrees`, and so on.

The next listing creates a `JTextPane` and adds the different components of a text to a `StyledDocument`. The `JTextPane` will make sure the content is distributed over different lines, and render it correctly using the right fonts. The `JTextPane` is shown in the bottom-left window in figure 14.11.

Listing 14.22   TextExample4.java

```
public class TextExample4 {
  public static final String[] AKIRA = {
    "Akira Kurosawa", " (", "\u9ed2\u6fa4 \u660e",     ◁──  Contains text
    " or ",                                                  snippets
```

```
      "\u9ed2\u6ca2 \u660e",
      ", Kurosawa Akira, 23 March 1910" +
      " - 6 September 1998) was a Japanese film director,"
      + " producer, screenwriter and editor. In a career "
      + "that spanned 50 years, Kurosawa directed 30 "
      + "films. He is widely regarded as one of the most "
      + "important and influential filmmakers in film "
      + "history." };
   public static final String[] STYLES =  {
      "bold", "regular", "japanese", "regular",
      "japanese", "regular" };
   public static void initStyles(StyledDocument doc) {
      Style def = StyleContext.getDefaultStyleContext()
        .getStyle(StyleContext.DEFAULT_STYLE);
      StyleConstants.setFontFamily(def, "SansSerif");
      Style regular = doc.addStyle("regular", def);
      Style bold = doc.addStyle("bold", regular);
      StyleConstants.setBold(bold, true);
      Style japanese = doc.addStyle("japanese", def);
      StyleConstants.setFontFamily(
        japanese, "MS PGothic");
   }
   public static JTextPane createTextPane()
     throws BadLocationException {
     JTextPane textPane = new JTextPane();
     StyledDocument doc = textPane.getStyledDocument();
     initStyles(doc);
     for (int i=0; i < AKIRA.length; i++) {
       doc.insertString(doc.getLength(), AKIRA[i],
       doc.getStyle(STYLES[i]));
     }
     return textPane;
   }
}
```

- Contains text snippets
- Lists corresponding styles
- Initializes styles
- Creates JTextPane
- Adds snippets of text

The JTextPane class extends the Component class, and you'll use its print() method in the next listing.

Listing 14.23   Text4ToPdf.java

```
DefaultFontMapper mapper = new DefaultFontMapper();
BaseFontParameters parameters = new BaseFontParameters(
"c:/windows/fonts/msgothic.ttc,1");
parameters.encoding = BaseFont.IDENTITY_H;
mapper.putName("MS PGothic", parameters );
Graphics2D g2 = canvas.createGraphics(300, 150, mapper);
JTextPane text = TextExample4.createTextPane();
text.setSize(new Dimension(300, 150));
text.print(g2);
g2.dispose();
```

- Creates font mapper
- Creates Graphics2D
- Creates JTextPane
- Prints JTextPane to PDF

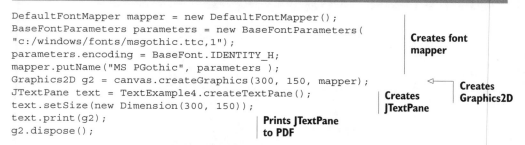

This technique is frequently used in Swing applications. For instance, if you have an application with a JTable that's shown on the screen, you can print that JTable to PDF using its print() method instead of using PdfPTable.

NOTE   The two methods for creating a `PdfGraphics2D` object, `createGraph-ics()` and `createGraphics2D()`, also exist with two extra parameters: `con-vertImagesToJPEG` and `quality`. Use these parameters to tell iText that it should convert all the images that are added to JPEGs. This can be an interesting way to reduce the size of the resulting PDF document. The `quality` parameter has the same meaning as the parameter with the same name in section 10.2.6.

In the next chapter, you'll use the `PdfGraphics2D` class to convert files in the Scalable Vector Graphics (SVG) format to PDF. Right now, it's time to summarize what this chapter was about.

14.6   *Summary*

We started this chapter by peeking into the content stream of a page, and we were confronted with PDF syntax for stroking and filling paths and shapes. To understand this syntax, we first looked at path construction and painting operators, and then we moved on to the operators that change the graphics state. The coordinate system received our special attention. Along the way, you learned about some convenience methods provided by iText.

We did the same for text and text state, looking at reference tables listing all the methods that are available in the `PdfContentByte` object. Then we repeated more or less what we did before, drawing paths and shapes and drawing text, but we didn't use any of the methods discussed previously. Instead, we used the standard Java methods that are available in the abstract class `PdfGraphics2D`.

In the next chapter, we'll continue examining the content of a PDF page, but we'll focus on optional content and PDF tags. We'll also try to parse a content stream to extract text from a page.

Page content and structure

This chapter covers

- Making content optional
- Working with marked content
- Parsing PDF files

The previous chapter was devoted entirely to page content; you learned how to add content the PDF way and the Java way. We'll continue discussing content in this chapter. We'll add operators and operands to make part of the content optional. We'll use marked content to add custom parameters to graphical objects, to make the content accessible for the visually impaired, and to store the structure of the document. Finally, we'll make a fair attempt at parsing a PDF document and extracting content from a page.

15.1 Making content visible or invisible

All the content you've added to a page so far was either visible or it was invisible, whether because it was clipped or because the rendering mode was set to invisible. Beginning with PDF 1.5, you can also add *optional* content: content that can be selectively viewed or hidden by document authors or consumers.

15.1.1 Optional content groups

Graphics and text that can be made visible or invisible dynamically are grouped in an *optional content group* (OCG). Content that belongs to a certain group is visible when the group is *on*, and invisible when the group is *off*. Figure 15.1 demonstrates this functionality.

Figure 15.1
Making content visible and invisible

The text, "Do you see me?" is added as normal content. The text, "Peek-a-Boo!!!" is added as optional content that's visible in the upper window, but not in the lower window. In both windows, the Layers panel is opened. "Do you see me?" is the caption of a *layer* (which is another name for an OCG). By clicking the group's check box in the Layers panel, end users can make the content visible or invisible.

The next listing shows how the "Do you see me?" layer was created using iText's `PdfLayer` object, and how the "Peek-a-Boo!!!" text was made optional using the `PdfContentByte` methods `beginLayer()` and `endLayer()`.

Listing 15.1 PeekABoo.java

```
Document document = new Document();
PdfWriter writer
  = PdfWriter.getInstance(document, new FileOutputStream(filename));
writer.setViewerPreferences(PdfWriter.PageModeUseOC);
writer.setPdfVersion(PdfWriter.VERSION_1_5);
document.open();
PdfLayer layer = new PdfLayer("Do you see me?", writer);      ⟵ Creates layer
layer.setOn(on);
BaseFont bf = BaseFont.createFont();
PdfContentByte cb = writer.getDirectContent();
cb.beginText();
cb.setFontAndSize(bf, 18);
cb.showTextAligned(Element.ALIGN_LEFT,
  "Do you see me?", 50, 790, 0);
```
⟵ Adds normal content

```
cb.beginLayer(layer);
cb.showTextAligned(Element.ALIGN_LEFT,          Adds optional
  "Peek-a-Boo!!!", 50, 766, 0);                 content
cb.endLayer();
cb.endText();
document.close();
```

Note that in this listing the viewer preferences are set so that the optional content panel is shown when the document is opened. The state of the layers can be specified with the setOn() method, which expects a Boolean value. If true, the layer will be visible (this is the default). If false, the layer will be hidden.

If you peek into the content stream of the resulting page, you'll see this construct:

```
/OC /Pr1 BDC
1 0 0 1 50 766 Tm
(Peek-a-Boo!!!)Tj
EMC
```

The optional content is put between the *marked-content operators* BDC and EMC. This marked content is recognized as optional because of the /OC tag. The operand /Pr1 was created by iText.

You'll find a reference to the OCG in the resources dictionary of the page:

```
/Properties<</Pr1 1 0 R>>
```

The indirect object 1 looks like this:

```
1 0 obj
<</Type/OCG/Name(Do you see me?)>>
endobj
```

The OCGs and their properties are listed in the catalog (see section 13.3):

```
<<
  /Type/Catalog
  /Pages 4 0 R
  /OCProperties<<
    /D<<
      /Order[1 0 R]
      /ListMode/VisiblePages
    >>
    /OCGs[1 0 R]
  >>
  /PageMode/UseOC
>>
```

The optional content of a group can reside anywhere in the document. It doesn't have to be consecutive in drawing order or belong to the same content stream (or page).

The previous example was simple, with one layer and one sequence of optional content. Let's see how to work with different layers that are organized in structures.

15.1.2 *Adding structure to layers*

Figure 15.2 shows different features of the PdfLayer object.

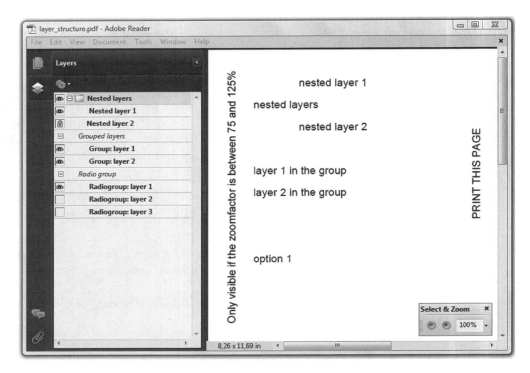

Figure 15.2   Different groups of optional content

We'll start with the structure that is visible in the Layers tab. It shows a tree with branches: Nested Layers, Grouped Layers, and Radio Group.

NESTED LAYERS

The nested layers in figure 15.2 are visible by default; if you click the eye icon next to Nested Layer 1, the words "nested layer 1" disappear from the page on the right. You can't change the visibility of "nested layer 2" separately because it has been locked, but if you click the eye icon next to the Nested Layers parent layer, everything that is added to the parent layer is made invisible, as well as everything that is added to its children. This is how it's done.

Listing 15.2   OptionalContentExample.java

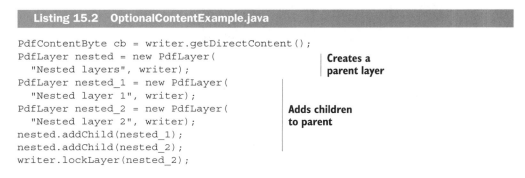

```
PdfContentByte cb = writer.getDirectContent();
PdfLayer nested = new PdfLayer(                    Creates a
  "Nested layers", writer);                        parent layer
PdfLayer nested_1 = new PdfLayer(
  "Nested layer 1", writer);
PdfLayer nested_2 = new PdfLayer(                  Adds children
  "Nested layer 2", writer);                       to parent
nested.addChild(nested_1);
nested.addChild(nested_2);
writer.lockLayer(nested_2);
```

```
cb.beginLayer(nested);
ColumnText.showTextAligned(cb, Element.ALIGN_LEFT,
  new Phrase("nested layers"), 50, 775, 0);       Adds content
cb.endLayer();                                     parent
cb.beginLayer(nested_1);
ColumnText.showTextAligned(cb, Element.ALIGN_LEFT,
  new Phrase("nested layer 1"), 100, 800, 0);
cb.endLayer();                                     Adds content
cb.beginLayer(nested_2);                           children
ColumnText.showTextAligned(cb, Element.ALIGN_LEFT,
  new Phrase("nested layer 2"), 100, 750, 0);
cb.endLayer();
```

The nested structure is defined by using the addChild() method. It's not necessary to nest the beginLayer() and endLayer() sequences, but it isn't forbidden either. Layers can be locked with the lockLayer() method. The visibility of a locked layer can't be changed using the eye icon in the Layers panel.

Grouped layers are similar to nested layers.

GROUPED LAYERS

If you look at the Layers panel, you'll see that the Grouped Layers layer can't be clicked. This layer was constructed with the createTitle() method.

Listing 15.3   OptionalContentExample.java

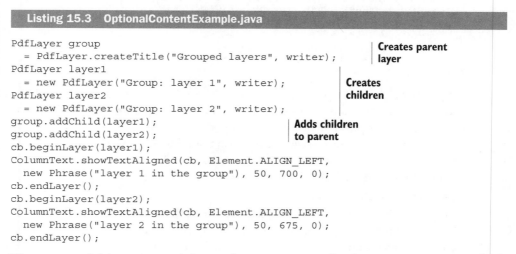

```
PdfLayer group                                     Creates parent
  = PdfLayer.createTitle("Grouped layers", writer);  layer
PdfLayer layer1
  = new PdfLayer("Group: layer 1", writer);        Creates
PdfLayer layer2                                    children
  = new PdfLayer("Group: layer 2", writer);
group.addChild(layer1);                    Adds children
group.addChild(layer2);                    to parent
cb.beginLayer(layer1);
ColumnText.showTextAligned(cb, Element.ALIGN_LEFT,
  new Phrase("layer 1 in the group"), 50, 700, 0);
cb.endLayer();
cb.beginLayer(layer2);
ColumnText.showTextAligned(cb, Element.ALIGN_LEFT,
  new Phrase("layer 2 in the group"), 50, 675, 0);
cb.endLayer();
```

The parent of this group can't be used as a parameter for the beginLayer() method. The PdfLayer object returned by createTitle() is a structural element and doesn't represent an OCG.

RADIO GROUP

This listing uses the same method to create a parent object for a radio group.

Listing 15.4   OptionalContentExample.java

```
PdfLayer radiogroup                                Creates
  = PdfLayer.createTitle("Radio group", writer);   parent layer
```

```
PdfLayer radio1
  = new PdfLayer("Radiogroup: layer 1", writer);
radio1.setOn(true);
PdfLayer radio2                                          Creates
  = new PdfLayer("Radiogroup: layer 2", writer);        children
radio2.setOn(false);
PdfLayer radio3
  = new PdfLayer("Radiogroup: layer 3", writer);
radio3.setOn(false);
radiogroup.addChild(radio1);                   Adds children
radiogroup.addChild(radio2);                   to parent
radiogroup.addChild(radio3);
ArrayList<PdfLayer> options                    Groups
  = new ArrayList<PdfLayer>();                 children in
options.add(radio1);                           ArrayList
options.add(radio2);                                      Defines list as
options.add(radio3);                                      radio group
writer.addOCGRadioGroup(options);
cb.beginLayer(radio1);
ColumnText.showTextAligned(cb, Element.ALIGN_LEFT,
  new Phrase("option 1"), 50, 600, 0);
cb.endLayer();
cb.beginLayer(radio2);
ColumnText.showTextAligned(cb, Element.ALIGN_LEFT,
  new Phrase("option 2"), 50, 575, 0);
cb.endLayer();
cb.beginLayer(radio3);
ColumnText.showTextAligned(cb, Element.ALIGN_LEFT,
  new Phrase("option 3"), 50, 550, 0);
cb.endLayer();
```

If you open the PDF shown in figure 15.2 in Adobe Reader, clicking another option in the radio group makes "option 1" invisible. Depending on the layer you chose, "option 2" or "option 3" becomes visible.

The PDF shown in the screenshot also contains two sequences of optional content for which there's no entry in the Layers panel. These layers are visible or invisible depending on the usage of the PDF file.

VISIBILITY DEPENDING ON USAGE

In listing 15.5, two PdfLayer objects are created, and setOnPanel(false) is used for both. An extra method determines the visibility: The method setPrint() was used to create a layer that will only be visible on screen; the content won't be printed on paper. The method setZoom() ensures that the layer is only visible if the zoom factor is between 75% and 125% (in the screenshot, the zoom factor is 100%).

Listing 15.5 OptionalContentExample.java

```
PdfLayer not_printed = new PdfLayer("not printed", writer);
not_printed.setOnPanel(false);
not_printed.setPrint("Print", false);
cb.beginLayer(not_printed);
ColumnText.showTextAligned(cb, Element.ALIGN_CENTER,
  new Phrase("PRINT THIS PAGE"), 300, 700, 90);
cb.endLayer();
PdfLayer zoom = new PdfLayer("Zoom 0.75-1.25", writer);
```

```
zoom.setOnPanel(false);
zoom.setZoom(0.75f, 1.25f);
cb.beginLayer(zoom);
ColumnText.showTextAligned(cb, Element.ALIGN_LEFT,
  new Phrase("Only visible if the zoomfactor is between 75 and 125%"),
  30, 530, 90);
cb.endLayer();
```

Table 15.1 lists the different methods that can be used to add entries to the *usage dictionary* of an OCG. This dictionary describes the nature of the content controlled by the OCG.

Table 15.1 `PdfLayer` methods for changing the usage dictionary

Method	Parameters	Description
setCreatorInfo	(creator, subtype)	Stores application-specific data associated with this OCG. The creator parameter is a String specifying the group; subtype defines the type of content, such as "Artwork" or "Technical".
setLanguage	(lang, preferred)	Specifies the language of the content controlled by this OCG. The lang parameter is a String defining the locale, such as "en-US". If you've specified a language, the layer that matches the system language is visible (ON), unless preferred is set to true.
setExport	(export)	Indicates the recommended state for content in this group when the document is saved by an application to a format that doesn't support optional content. If export is true, the layer is visible (ON).
setZoom	(min, max)	Specifies a range of magnifications at which the content is best viewed. The parameters min and max are the minimum and maximum recommended zoom factors. Using a negative value for min sets the default to 0; for max a negative value corresponds with the largest possible magnification supported by the viewer.
setPrint	(subtype, printstate)	Specifies the state if the content in this group is to be printed. Possible values for subtype are "Print", "Trapped", "PrinterMarks", and "Watermark"; printstate is a boolean.
setView	(view)	Indicates that the group should be set to that state when the document is opened in a viewer application. If view is true, the layer is visible (ON).
setUser	(type, names)	Specifies one or more users for whom this OCG is primarily intended. Possible values for type are "Ind" (individual), "Ttl" (title), or "Org" (organization). The names parameter can be one or more String objects.
setPageElement	(pe)	Indicates that the OCG contains a pagination artifact. Possible values include "HF" (header or footer), "FG" (foreground image or graphic), "BG" (background image or graphic), or "L" (logo).

The decision as to whether or not an object should be visible can depend on the state of a series of other layers that are grouped in an optional content membership.

15.1.3 *Optional content membership*

In the previous examples, you've added content to a single OCG. This content is visible if the status of the group is *on* and invisible when it's *off*. Consider more complex visibility possibilities, with content not belonging directly to a specific layer, but where the visibility depends on the states of different layers.

DEFINING A VISIBILITY POLICY

Suppose you have three layers, one with the word "dog", one with the word "tiger", and one with the word "lion". Next, define a membership with the word "cat" that is visible only if *either* of the words "tiger" or "lion" are visible, and a membership with the words "no cat" if *none* of these words are visible.

This can be achieved with this code.

Listing 15.6   LayerMembershipExample1.java

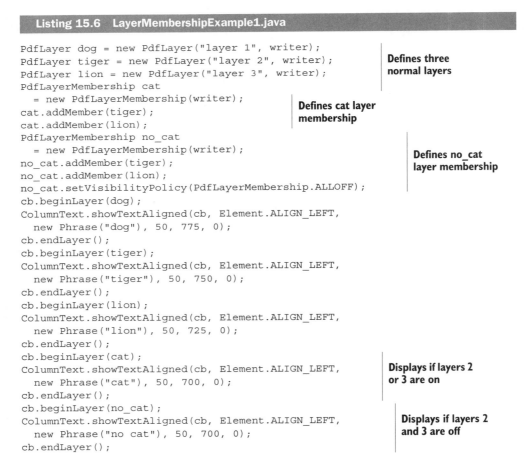

```
PdfLayer dog = new PdfLayer("layer 1", writer);      Defines three
PdfLayer tiger = new PdfLayer("layer 2", writer);    normal layers
PdfLayer lion = new PdfLayer("layer 3", writer);
PdfLayerMembership cat
  = new PdfLayerMembership(writer);                  Defines cat layer
cat.addMember(tiger);                                membership
cat.addMember(lion);
PdfLayerMembership no_cat
  = new PdfLayerMembership(writer);                  Defines no_cat
no_cat.addMember(tiger);                             layer membership
no_cat.addMember(lion);
no_cat.setVisibilityPolicy(PdfLayerMembership.ALLOFF);
cb.beginLayer(dog);
ColumnText.showTextAligned(cb, Element.ALIGN_LEFT,
  new Phrase("dog"), 50, 775, 0);
cb.endLayer();
cb.beginLayer(tiger);
ColumnText.showTextAligned(cb, Element.ALIGN_LEFT,
  new Phrase("tiger"), 50, 750, 0);
cb.endLayer();
cb.beginLayer(lion);
ColumnText.showTextAligned(cb, Element.ALIGN_LEFT,
  new Phrase("lion"), 50, 725, 0);
cb.endLayer();
cb.beginLayer(cat);                                  Displays if layers 2
ColumnText.showTextAligned(cb, Element.ALIGN_LEFT,   or 3 are on
  new Phrase("cat"), 50, 700, 0);
cb.endLayer();
cb.beginLayer(no_cat);                               Displays if layers 2
ColumnText.showTextAligned(cb, Element.ALIGN_LEFT,   and 3 are off
  new Phrase("no cat"), 50, 700, 0);
cb.endLayer();
```

In this listing, you first create three normal `PdfLayer` objects. Then you create two `PdfLayerMembership` objects, `cat` and `no_cat`.

This example uses two out of four possible *visibility policies*:

- `ALLON`—Visible if all the entries are on.
- `ANYON`—Visible if any of the entries are on.
- `ANYOFF`—Visible if any of the entries are off.
- `ALLOFF`—Visible if all of the entries are off.

You didn't explicitly define a visibility policy for the `cat` membership. It was set to `ANYON`, which is the default value.

DEFINING A VISIBILITY EXPRESSION

Since PDF 1.6, visibility policies are still accepted, but preference is given to a *visibility expression*. This allows you to specify an arbitrary Boolean expression for computing the visibility from the states of OCGs. The layer memberships in the next listing are equivalent to those in listing 15.6. The end user will not notice any difference.

Listing 15.7   LayerMembershipExample2.java

```
PdfLayerMembership cat = new PdfLayerMembership(writer);
PdfVisibilityExpression ve1
  = new PdfVisibilityExpression(PdfVisibilityExpression.OR);
ve1.add(tiger);
ve1.add(lion);
cat.setVisibilityExpression(ve1);
PdfLayerMembership no_cat = new PdfLayerMembership(writer);
PdfVisibilityExpression ve2
  = new PdfVisibilityExpression(PdfVisibilityExpression.NOT);
ve2.add(ve1);
no_cat.setVisibilityExpression(ve2);
```

Using a `PdfVisibilityExpression` offers a more general way to define a layer membership. Possible values for the parameter when constructing a `PdfVisibilityExpression` are `AND`, `OR`, and `NOT`. You can add `PdfLayer` objects to a visibility expression, and you can nest `PdfVisibilityExpression` objects. If the value is `NOT`, you may only add one element. If it's `AND` or `OR`, you can add more elements.

Another way to switch content on or off is by using actions.

15.1.4 *Changing the state of a layer with an action*

You used the `PdfAction` class in chapter 7 to jump to another location in a PDF file, to execute JavaScript, and so on. In this section, you'll create actions to change the visibility of an OCG.

Figure 15.3 shows three questions about movies. The answers are also added to the document, but each answer is added to a separate OCG. They aren't visible by default, so that you can test your own knowledge about movies and directors.

In this example, the layers are added to the Layers panel, so that you can switch the answers on or off, but the more questions and answers there are in your questionnaire,

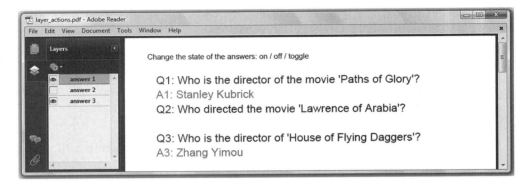

Figure 15.3 Changing visibility using actions

the less user-friendly this panel will be. It would be better to add clickable areas to the document that allow you to make one or more answers visible. This is illustrated in the next example.

Listing 15.8 OptionalContentActionExample.java

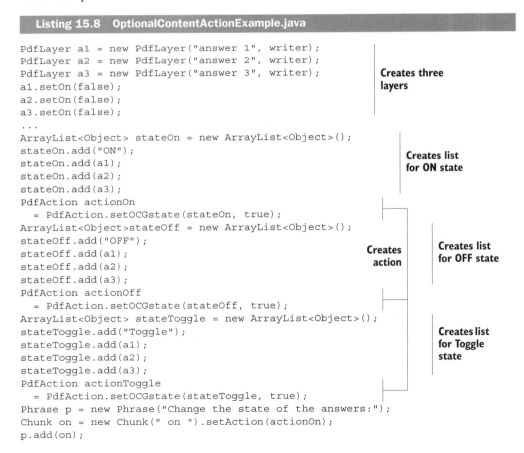

```java
PdfLayer a1 = new PdfLayer("answer 1", writer);
PdfLayer a2 = new PdfLayer("answer 2", writer);
PdfLayer a3 = new PdfLayer("answer 3", writer);
a1.setOn(false);
a2.setOn(false);
a3.setOn(false);
...
ArrayList<Object> stateOn = new ArrayList<Object>();
stateOn.add("ON");
stateOn.add(a1);
stateOn.add(a2);
stateOn.add(a3);
PdfAction actionOn
  = PdfAction.setOCGstate(stateOn, true);
ArrayList<Object>stateOff = new ArrayList<Object>();
stateOff.add("OFF");
stateOff.add(a1);
stateOff.add(a2);
stateOff.add(a3);
PdfAction actionOff
  = PdfAction.setOCGstate(stateOff, true);
ArrayList<Object> stateToggle = new ArrayList<Object>();
stateToggle.add("Toggle");
stateToggle.add(a1);
stateToggle.add(a2);
stateToggle.add(a3);
PdfAction actionToggle
  = PdfAction.setOCGstate(stateToggle, true);
Phrase p = new Phrase("Change the state of the answers:");
Chunk on = new Chunk(" on ").setAction(actionOn);
p.add(on);
```

Creates three layers

Creates list for ON state

Creates action

Creates list for OFF state

Creates list for Toggle state

```
Chunk off = new Chunk("/ off ").setAction(actionOff);
p.add(off);
Chunk toggle = new Chunk("/ toggle").setAction(actionToggle);
p.add(toggle);
document.add(p);
```

The setOCGState() static method returns a PdfAction object ❶. The first parameter is an ArrayList, and the first element in this list defines the action: the layers that are added can be turned on ("ON"), turned off ("OFF"), or toggled ("Toggle"). The second parameter makes sense only if you've defined radio groups. If it's false, the fact that a layer belongs to a radio group is ignored. If it's true, turning on a layer that belongs to a radio group turns off the other layers in the radio group.

Up until now, you've marked content as optional in the content stream, using Pdf-ContentByte methods. You can also mark specific objects as optional.

15.1.5 *Optional content in XObjects and annotations*

Three types of iText objects are often drawn in an OCG: Images, PdfTemplates, and PdfAnnotations. For convenience, these objects have a setLayer() method that can be used to define the OCG to which the object belongs.

Figure 15.4 shows a map of Foobar. People from all over the world will be coming to the Foobar Film Festival, and to make sure these people find their way to the movie theater, you'll create a map of the city. You'll add the street names in three languages—English, French, and Dutch—and put these street names in different layers, organized as a radio group, so that only one layer is visible at a time. You'll also add more layers showing information about restaurants, movie theaters, and so on. End users can switch these layers on and off depending on what they're looking for in the city of Foobar.

This PDF is created from an SVG file, foobarcity.svg containing the map (lines and shapes), and three SVG files, foobarstreets.svg, foobarrues.svg, and foobarstraten.svg, containing the street names in English, French, and Dutch (text only). iText can't

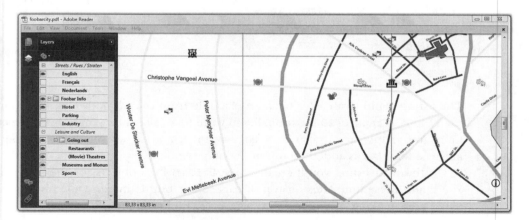

Figure 15.4   The interactive map of Foobar

interpret these files. You could try to write your own SVG handler (as was done in the first edition of this book), but it's easier to use a library that already exists, such as Apache Batik. This listing creates the map without the optional content layers.

Listing 15.9   SvgToPdf.java

```java
protected SAXSVGDocumentFactory factory;
protected BridgeContext ctx;
protected GVTBuilder builder;
public SvgToPdf() {
  String parser
    = XMLResourceDescriptor.getXMLParserClassName();
  factory = new SAXSVGDocumentFactory(parser);
  UserAgent userAgent = new UserAgentAdapter();
  DocumentLoader loader = new DocumentLoader(userAgent);
  ctx = new BridgeContext(userAgent, loader);
  ctx.setDynamicState(BridgeContext.DYNAMIC);
  builder = new GVTBuilder();
}
public void drawSvg(PdfTemplate map, String resource)
  throws IOException {
  Graphics2D g2d = map.createGraphics(6000, 6000);
  SVGDocument city = factory.createSVGDocument(
    new File(resource).toURL().toString());
  GraphicsNode mapGraphics = builder.build(ctx, city);
  mapGraphics.paint(g2d);
  g2d.dispose();
}
public void createPdf(String filename)
  throws IOException, DocumentException {
  Document document = new Document(new Rectangle(6000, 6000));
  PdfWriter writer
    = PdfWriter.getInstance(document, new FileOutputStream(RESULT));
  document.open();
  PdfContentByte cb = writer.getDirectContent();
  PdfTemplate map = cb.createTemplate(6000, 6000);
  drawSvg(map, CITY);
  cb.addTemplate(map, 0, 0);
  PdfTemplate streets = cb.createTemplate(6000, 6000);
  drawSvg(streets, STREETS);
  cb.addTemplate(streets, 0, 0);
  document.close();
}
```

Annotations:
- **Performs Batik-specific initializations** (applies to the `SvgToPdf()` constructor block)
- **Draws SVG to PdfTemplate** (applies to the `drawSvg` method block)
- **Creates and adds city template**
- **Creates and adds streets template**

The listing could easily have been an example from the previous chapter, where you used the PdfGraphics2D functionality to write to a java.awt.Graphics2D object. The lines and shapes are drawn to a PdfTemplate, and so are the street names. The streets template is added on top of the map template.

In the next listing you'll create three PdfTemplate objects for the street names. You'll add these templates on top of each other but define an OCG for each of the templates, making sure that only one layer is visible at a time.

Listing 15.10 SvgLayers.java

```java
PdfLayer streetlayer = PdfLayer.createTitle(
  "Streets / Rues / Straten", writer);
PdfLayer streetlayer_en
  = new PdfLayer("English", writer);
streetlayer_en.setOn(true);
streetlayer_en.setLanguage("en", true);
PdfLayer streetlayer_fr
  = new PdfLayer("Fran\u00e7ais", writer);
streetlayer_fr.setOn(false);
streetlayer_fr.setLanguage("fr", false);
PdfLayer streetlayer_nl
  = new PdfLayer("Nederlands", writer);
streetlayer_nl.setOn(false);
streetlayer_nl.setLanguage("nl", false);
streetlayer.addChild(streetlayer_en);
streetlayer.addChild(streetlayer_fr);
streetlayer.addChild(streetlayer_nl);
ArrayList<PdfLayer> radio = new ArrayList<PdfLayer>();
radio.add(streetlayer_en);
radio.add(streetlayer_fr);
radio.add(streetlayer_nl);
writer.addOCGRadioGroup(radio);
PdfContentByte cb = writer.getDirectContent();
PdfTemplate map = cb.createTemplate(6000, 6000);
drawSvg(map, CITY);
cb.addTemplate(map, 0, 0);
PdfTemplate streets = cb.createTemplate(6000, 6000);
drawSvg(streets, STREETS);
streets.setLayer(streetlayer_en);
cb.addTemplate(streets, 0, 0);
PdfTemplate rues = cb.createTemplate(6000, 6000);
drawSvg(rues, RUES);
rues.setLayer(streetlayer_fr);
cb.addTemplate(rues, 0, 0);
PdfTemplate straten = cb.createTemplate(6000, 6000);
drawSvg(straten, STRATEN);
straten.setLayer(streetlayer_nl);
cb.addTemplate(straten, 0, 0);
cb.saveState();
```

Creates street layers

Adds layers to radio group

Sets layers for PdfTemplate

The setLayer() method is often used for watermark images, such as for a layer that is only visible when a document is printed, or for specific form fields (widget annotations) that need to be made visible or invisible depending on the values of other fields.

This listing uses a method from table 15.1 to set the language of the street layers. For a watermark image, you'll use the setPageElement() method with the parameter "BG". The interactive map of Foobar is meant as an inspiring example, showing that you can create really interesting interactive PDF files using the OCG functionality.

Optional content uses the marked-content operators BDC and EMC. In the next section, you'll learn about more features involving marked content.

15.2   *Working with marked content*

Marked-content operators are used to identify a portion of a PDF content stream as an element of interest to a particular application or PDF plug-in extension. In this section, we'll take a closer look at three situations in which marked content is important: adding custom data to objects, making a PDF accessible, and storing the structure of a document along with its content.

15.2.1   *Object data*

In the map of Foobar, you have icons of movie theaters, but you may want to add extra information, such as the theater name, address, and so on. Figure 15.5 shows different movie posters with the names of the directors added.

The properties of each poster in figure 15.5 are shown in the Model Tree panel. This panel is opened if you activate the object data tool by selecting Tools > Analysis > Object Data Tool in the menu. You can check whether this tool is activated by looking at the Analysis toolbar; if it is, there will be an icon with a page, an information symbol, and a crosshair. If this option is selected, you can click a poster of a movie.

When a poster is clicked, the Model Tree panel will open. In this case, there are seven sets of object data, named director1 to director7, one for each director who has a poster in the PDF. In figure 15.5, one of the six posters of movies by Akira Kurosawa has been clicked on, so director2 is selected. You can see more information about this entry in the lower panel:

- Name: Kurosawa
- Given name: Akira
- Posters: 6

All the objects for which these properties are valid—six posters—are highlighted in the page with a red border around the poster.

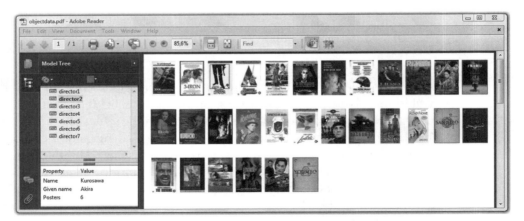

Figure 15.5   Using marked content for object data

The next bit of code creates the structure tree that makes this possible.

Listing 15.11 ObjectData.java

```
writer.setTagged();                                     ❶
writer.setUserProperties(true);                         ❷
...
PdfStructureTreeRoot tree                               Gets root of
  = writer.getStructureTreeRoot();                      structure tree
PdfStructureElement top = new PdfStructureElement(
  tree, new PdfName("Directors"));                      Creates top
Map<Integer,PdfStructureElement> directors             element
  = new HashMap<Integer,PdfStructureElement>();
Statement stm = connection.createStatement();
ResultSet rs = stm.executeQuery(SELECTDIRECTORS);
int id;
Director director;
PdfStructureElement e;
while (rs.next()) {
  id = rs.getInt("id");
  director = PojoFactory.getDirector(rs);
  e = new PdfStructureElement(                           Creates
    top, new PdfName("director" + id));                  branch
  PdfDictionary userproperties = new PdfDictionary();
  userproperties.put(
    PdfName.O, PdfName.USERPROPERTIES);
  PdfArray properties = new PdfArray();
  PdfDictionary property1 = new PdfDictionary();
  property1.put(PdfName.N, new PdfString("Name"));
  property1.put(
    PdfName.V, new PdfString(director.getName()));
  properties.add(property1);
  PdfDictionary property2 = new PdfDictionary();
  property2.put(
    PdfName.N, new PdfString("Given name"));             Creates user
  property2.put(                                         properties
    PdfName.V, new PdfString(director.getGivenName()));
  properties.add(property2);
  PdfDictionary property3 = new PdfDictionary();
  property3.put(PdfName.N, new PdfString("Posters"));
  property3.put(
    PdfName.V, new PdfNumber(rs.getInt("c")));
  properties.add(property3);                             Adds
  userproperties.put(PdfName.P, properties);             properties
  e.put(PdfName.A, userproperties);           ◀───       to branch
  directors.put(id, e);
}
```

If you tell the `PdfWriter` to create a tagged PDF ❶, the `getStructureTreeRoot()` method will create a `/StructTreeRoot` entry for the root dictionary of the document. The children of the top element contain attributes (`/A`) that are owned (`/O`) by user properties (`/UserProperties`). These properties are defined as an array of dictionaries with a name (`/N`) and a value (`/V`). Don't forget to tell the writer that the structure contains elements that have user properties ❷; otherwise the object data tool won't be able to identify objects.

If you have a map containing Movie objects and director IDs, you can create the PDF shown in figure 15.5 using the next listing.

Listing 15.12   ObjectData.java (continued)

```
for (Map.Entry<Movie,Integer> entry : map.entrySet()) {
  img = Image.getInstance(
    String.format(RESOURCE, entry.getKey().getImdb()));
  img.scaleToFit(1000, 60);
  img.setAbsolutePosition(x + (45 - img.getScaledWidth()) / 2, y);
  canvas.beginMarkedContentSequence(          Writes BDC and
    directors.get(entry.getValue()));         its operands
  canvas.addImage(img);
  canvas.endMarkedContentSequence();      ◁──  Writes
  x += 48;                                     EDC
  if (x > 578) {
    x = 11.5f;
    y -= 84.2f;
  }
}
```

User properties are one type of attribute that can be added to a marked content sequence. You'll find more in ISO-32000-1. In the next section, we'll work with the optional entries that can be added for accessibility support.

15.2.2 *Section 508 and accessibility*

In the U.S., federal agencies are required to make their electronic and information technology accessible to people with disabilities. This is enforced by law: section 508, an amendment to the Rehabilitation Act of 1973.

Section 508 is about electronic information in general, so it also applies to PDF. We've briefly discussed PDF/UA (aka ISO/AWI 14289) in chapter 13. This standard is currently under development. It will be to PDF what the World Wide Web Consortium (W3C)'s Web Content Accessibility Guidelines (WCAG) are to web pages. The Web Accessibility Initiative (WAI) is an effort to improve the accessibility of the web for people with disabilities by defining principles, guidelines, success criteria, benefits, and examples that explain the requirements for making web-based information and applications accessible.

> **FAQ** *Does iText support the creation of PDF documents that are compliant with section 508?* You can use iText to create a document that passes all the criteria that are listed in section 508. It's technically impossible, however, to provide a setPDFUAConformance() method that checks whether the PDF you're creating is accessible. This is true for *any* PDF creator, not just for iText. Even a "pass" from Acrobat's Accessibility Checker doesn't verify compliance with section 508. Many of the accessibility requirements, such as alternate text, tooltips, and color use, will always require human validation.

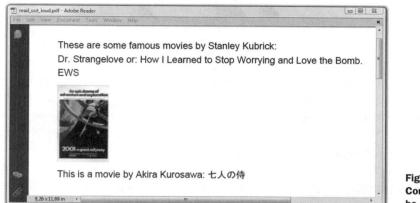

**Figure 15.6
Content that can
be read out loud**

PDF includes several facilities in support of accessibility. Documents can be made available for the visually impaired by using screen readers. In Adobe Reader, you can select View > Read out Loud, but you need marked content to enable proper vocalization. Consider the document shown in figure 15.6.

A screen reader doesn't know that "Dr." should be read as "Doctor," nor that EWS is the abbreviation of the movie title *Eyes Wide Shut*. Viewers will render the poster of *2001: A Space Odyssey*, but you should provide alternate text so that the screen reader knows this too. Also, you want Adobe Reader to say "Seven Samurai" instead of the Japanese title.

To achieve this, you'll use a marked-content operator with /Span as the first operand, and a dictionary with the extra information as the second operand. You could add these elements as PdfStructureElement objects that are part of the structure tree, as was done in listing 15.11, but in this case you'll add the marked content tag and dictionary directly to the content stream.

EXPANSION OF ABBREVIATIONS AND ACRONYMS

This demonstrates how to use the /E entry to expand abbreviations.

Listing 15.13   ReadOutLoud.java

```
cb.beginText();
cb.moveText(36, 788);
cb.setFontAndSize(bf, 12);
cb.setLeading(18);
cb.showText("These are some famous movies by Stanley Kubrick: ");
dict = new PdfDictionary();
dict.put(PdfName.E, new PdfString("Doctor"));
cb.beginMarkedContentSequence(new PdfName("Span"), dict, true);
cb.newlineShowText("Dr.");
cb.endMarkedContentSequence();
cb.showText(" Strangelove or: How I Learned to Stop Worrying and Love
➥ the Bomb.");
dict = new PdfDictionary();
```

```
dict.put(PdfName.E, new PdfString("Eyes Wide Shut."));
cb.beginMarkedContentSequence(new PdfName("Span"), dict, true);
cb.newlineShowText("EWS");
cb.endMarkedContentSequence();
cb.endText();
```

Instead of passing a `PdfStructureElement`, you now pass three parameters to the `beginMarkedContentSequence()` method: the name of the tag (`/Span`), the dictionary with the entries, and a parameter that specifies whether the dictionary has to be added inline (inside the content stream) or as a reference to an indirect object.

ALTERNATE DESCRIPTIONS AND LANGUAGE

If you know HTML, you know that the `img` tag has an attribute named `alt`. This attribute can be used to specify alternate text for the image, which can be used if the image is missing on the server, or if your browser doesn't download images to save bandwidth, or to conform with accessibility standards. The first two reasons don't apply for PDF, but to make your document compliant with PDF/UA and section 508, you have to use marked content with an `/Alt` entry to define alternate text for images, formulas, or other items that are part of the content and that do not translate naturally into text. This is done here.

Listing 15.14   ReadOutLoud.java

```
dict = new PdfDictionary();
dict.put(PdfName.LANG, new PdfString("en-us"));
dict.put(new PdfName("Alt"), new PdfString("2001: A Space Odyssey."));
cb.beginMarkedContentSequence(new PdfName("Span"), dict, true);
Image img = Image.getInstance(RESOURCE);
img.scaleToFit(1000, 100);
img.setAbsolutePosition(36, 640);
cb.addImage(img);
cb.endMarkedContentSequence();
```

Note that the listing also uses the `/Lang` entry to indicate that it's using the English title.

REPLACEMENT TEXT

Just as alternate descriptions can be provided for images, replacement text can be specified for content that translates into text but that is represented in a nonstandard way: glyphs for ligatures or custom characters, inline graphics corresponding to dropped capitals or to letters in an illuminated manuscript, and so on. The next listing shows the title of the movie *Seven Samurai* in Japanese, but it uses the English title as `/ActualText`.

Listing 15.15   ReadOutLoud.java

```
cb.beginText();
cb.moveText(36, 620);
cb.setFontAndSize(bf, 12);
cb.showText("This is a movie by Akira Kurosawa: ");
```

```
dict = new PdfDictionary();
dict.put(PdfName.ACTUALTEXT, new PdfString("Seven Samurai."));
cb.beginMarkedContentSequence(new PdfName("Span"), dict, true);
cb.setFontAndSize(bf2, 12);
cb.showText("\u4e03\u4eba\u306e\u4f8d");
cb.endMarkedContentSequence();
cb.endText();
```

If you try this example, open the document in Adobe Reader and listen to the result. "Dr." will be vocalized as "Doctor," "EWS" as "Eyes Wide Shut," you'll hear text for the image, and "Seven Samurai" for the Japanese title.

15.2.3 *Adding structure*

We talked about marked content in chapter 13 when we discussed standards such as PDF/UA and PDF/A. In the previous section, you saw why marked content is important for PDF/UA. In this section, we'll discuss the extra requirement for PDF/A level A conformance: the PDF needs to be tagged. Tagged PDF is a stylized use of PDF.

In part 1 of this book, you added all kinds of objects to the Document: paragraphs, lists, tables, and so on. Once PdfWriter translated these objects to PDF syntax, all structure was lost; if you have a PDF file, it's not possible to extract a Paragraph, List, or PdfPTable object. The content inside a PDF consists of a series of operators such as showText(), and there's no way to know if a snippet of PDF syntax is part of a paragraph, a list, or a table.

When you create a tagged PDF file that conforms with PDF/A level A, you use marked content to store information about the document structure along with the content. The standard structure types that can be used for this purpose are defined in ISO-32000-1. They are divided into these four categories:

- Grouping elements—These group other elements into sequences and hierarchies, but they have no direct effect on layout. For example, /Document, /Part, /Sect, /Div, /TOC, and so on.
- Block-level structure elements (BLSEs)—These describe the overall layout of content on the page: paragraph-like elements (/P, /H, /H1-/H6), list elements (/L, /LI, /Lbl, /LBody), and the table element (/Table).
- Inline-level structure elements (ILSEs)—These describe the layout of content within a BLSE: /Span, /Quote, /Note, /Reference, and so on.
- Illustration elements—These compact sequences of content that are considered to be unitary objects with respect to page layout: /Figure, /Formula, and /Form.

The content of such a structure is enclosed in a marked-content sequence, such as the /Span element used in the previous example. For a full list of all the available elements, see ISO-32000-1 section 14.8.4.

CREATING A TAGGED PDF

Suppose that you have an XML file containing the first paragraphs of the book *Moby Dick*. This XML file uses the custom tags chapter, title, and para. You want to convert this XML file into a tagged PDF file and use the structure elements, but keep the original tags.

The following listing demonstrates the first step in doing this. It creates the root of a structure tree and maps the custom tags to structure elements listed in ISO-32000-1. That way, you can use your custom tags in the rest of the document.

Listing 15.16   StructuredContent.java

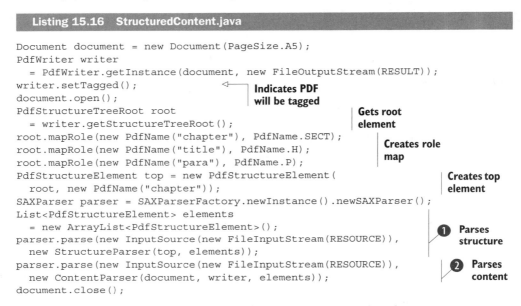

```
Document document = new Document(PageSize.A5);
PdfWriter writer
  = PdfWriter.getInstance(document, new FileOutputStream(RESULT));
writer.setTagged();                          ◁──┐ Indicates PDF
document.open();                                 │ will be tagged
PdfStructureTreeRoot root                                    Gets root
  = writer.getStructureTreeRoot();                           element
root.mapRole(new PdfName("chapter"), PdfName.SECT);
root.mapRole(new PdfName("title"), PdfName.H);               Creates role
root.mapRole(new PdfName("para"), PdfName.P);                map
PdfStructureElement top = new PdfStructureElement(           Creates top
  root, new PdfName("chapter"));                             element
SAXParser parser = SAXParserFactory.newInstance().newSAXParser();
List<PdfStructureElement> elements
  = new ArrayList<PdfStructureElement>();                    ❶ Parses
parser.parse(new InputSource(new FileInputStream(RESOURCE)),    structure
  new StructureParser(top, elements));
parser.parse(new InputSource(new FileInputStream(RESOURCE)),  ❷ Parses
  new ContentParser(document, writer, elements));                content
document.close();
```

In listing 15.16, you create a top element for the structure using the custom tag chapter. A PDF reader will look up what this tag means in the /RoleMap and find out it's a /Sect element. The XML file containing the first paragraphs of *Moby Dick* is parsed twice: once to examine the structure ❶ and once to read the content ❷.

This listing reads the structure elements into a List.

Listing 15.17   StructureParser.java

```
public class StructureParser extends DefaultHandler {
  protected PdfStructureElement top;
  protected List elements;
  public StructureParser(
    PdfStructureElement top, List<PdfStructureElement> elements) {
    this.top = top;
    this.elements = elements;
  }
  public void startElement(
    String uri, String localName, String qName, Attributes attributes)
    throws SAXException {
    if ("chapter".equals(qName)) return;
    elements.add(new PdfStructureElement(top, new PdfName(qName)));
  }
}
```

The structure elements obtained in listing 15.17 are used in the `ContentParser`, whose two most important methods are shown here.

Listing 15.18   ContentParser.java

```java
public void startElement(
  String uri, String localName, String qName, Attributes attributes)
  throws SAXException {
  if ("chapter".equals(qName)) return;
  current = elements.get(0);
  elements.remove(0);
  canvas.beginMarkedContentSequence(current);
}
public void endElement(String uri, String localName, String qName)
  throws SAXException {
  if ("chapter".equals(qName)) return;
  try {
    String s = buf.toString().trim();
    buf = new StringBuffer();
    if (s.length() > 0) {
      Paragraph p = new Paragraph(s, font);
      p.setAlignment(Element.ALIGN_JUSTIFIED);
      column.addElement(p);
      int status = column.go();
      while (ColumnText.hasMoreText(status)) {
        canvas.endMarkedContentSequence();
        document.newPage();
        canvas.beginMarkedContentSequence(current);
        column.setSimpleColumn(36, 36, 384, 569);
        status = column.go();
      }
    }
  } catch (DocumentException e) {
    e.printStackTrace();
  }
  canvas.endMarkedContentSequence();
}
```

Creating tagged PDFs with iText is possible, but it demands a lot of discipline. It's certainly an area where there's still a lot of work for the iText developers to do. The same goes for parsing tagged PDF files.

PARSING A TAGGED PDF

The code in this listing parses the Moby Dick PDF into an XML file.

Listing 15.19   ParseTaggedPdf.java

```java
public static void main(String[] args)
  throws IOException, DocumentException,
  SAXException, ParserConfigurationException {
  StructuredContent.main(args);
  TaggedPdfReaderTool reader = new TaggedPdfReaderTool();
  reader.convertToXml(new PdfReader(StructuredContent.RESULT),
    new FileOutputStream(RESULT));
}
```

The `TaggedPdfReaderTool` class fetches the `/StructTreeRoot` object from the catalog. Then it recursively inspects all the children of the tree:

```
PdfDictionary catalog = reader.getCatalog();
PdfDictionary struct = catalog.getAsDict(PdfName.STRUCTTREEROOT);
inspectChild(struct.getDirectObject(PdfName.K));
```

The `convertToXml()` method writes an XML file to the `OutputStream` that is the equivalent of the XML file originally used to create the PDF. Because the structure is stored in the PDF document, you can convert an XML file to PDF and back. The tagged PDF reader tool won't work for PDF documents that don't have any structure (which is the case for most PDF files), but it will work for most tagged PDF files.

> **NOTE**   This functionality is very new (it was originally written as an example for this book) and there's plenty of room for improvement.

The tool is built on top of the PDF parsing classes that were recently added to iText. Parsing traditional PDFs is extremely difficult, but we'll make a fair attempt in the next section.

15.3   *Parsing PDFs*

The first edition of *iText in Action* had a section named "Why iText doesn't do text extraction." It was preceded by an example that demonstrated how to retrieve the content stream of a page using the `getPageContent()` method, just like you did in section 14.1. The simple Hello World example from chapter 1 resulted in the following stream:

```
q
BT
36 806 Td
0 -18 Td
/F1 12 Tf
(Hello World!)Tj
0 0 Td
ET
Q
```

The PDF string (`Hello World!`) followed by the text operator `Tj` is visible in clear text. Surely it must be possible to write some code to extract that string? When the first edition was written, the only way to achieve this was by using the `PRTokeniser` class (mind the British *s* in the name, instead of the American *z*).

In this section, we'll learn how iText has evolved, and find out how to parse the content of PDF content streams to retrieve text and images.

15.3.1   *Examining the content stream with PRTokeniser*

With `PRTokeniser`, you can split a PDF content stream into its most elementary parts. Each part has a specific type. The possible types, shown in table 15.2, are enumerated in the enum named `TokenType`.

Table 15.2 Overview of the token types

TokenType	Symbol	Description
NUMBER		The current token is a number.
STRING	( )	The current token is a string.
NAME	/	The current token is a name.
COMMENT	%	The current token is a comment.
START_ARRAY	[	The current token starts an array.
END_ARRAY	]	The current token ends an array.
START_DIC	<<	The current token starts a dictionary.
END_DIC	>>	The current token ends a dictionary.
REF	R	The current token ends a reference.
OTHER		The current token is probably an operator.
ENDOFFILE		There are no more tokens.

This listing shows the simplest PDF parser one could write. It gets the page content of page 1, passes the content to a PRTokeniser object, and writes all the tokens with TokenType.STRING to a PrintWriter.

Listing 15.20 ParsingHelloWorld.java

```java
public void parsePdf(String src, String dest) throws IOException {
  PdfReader reader = new PdfReader(src);
  byte[] streamBytes = reader.getPageContent(1);
  PRTokeniser tokenizer = new PRTokeniser(streamBytes);
  PrintWriter out = new PrintWriter(new FileOutputStream(dest));
  while (tokenizer.nextToken()) {
    if (tokenizer.getTokenType() == PRTokeniser.TokenType.STRING) {
      out.println(tokenizer.getStringValue());
    }
  }
  out.flush();
  out.close();
}
```

If you try this example with your first Hello World example, you'll have a very good result:

```
Hello World!
```

But as soon as you have more complex PDF files, this simple parser won't work. Listing 15.21 creates a PDF file with the text "Hello World", but those words are added in different parts: first "ld", then "Wor", then "llo", and finally "He". Because of the choice of coordinates, the text reads "Hello World" when opened in a PDF viewer. It also adds the text "Hello People" as a form XObject.

Listing 15.21   ParsingHelloWorld.java

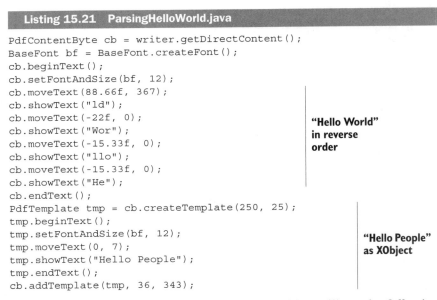

```
PdfContentByte cb = writer.getDirectContent();
BaseFont bf = BaseFont.createFont();
cb.beginText();
cb.setFontAndSize(bf, 12);
cb.moveText(88.66f, 367);
cb.showText("ld");
cb.moveText(-22f, 0);
cb.showText("Wor");
cb.moveText(-15.33f, 0);
cb.showText("llo");
cb.moveText(-15.33f, 0);
cb.showText("He");
cb.endText();
PdfTemplate tmp = cb.createTemplate(250, 25);
tmp.beginText();
tmp.setFontAndSize(bf, 12);
tmp.moveText(0, 7);
tmp.showText("Hello People");
tmp.endText();
cb.addTemplate(tmp, 36, 343);
```

"Hello World" in reverse order

"Hello People" as XObject

When you use the simple parser from listing 15.20, you'll get the following output:

```
ld
Wor
llo
He
```

PRTokeniser offers the strings in the order they appear in the content stream, not in the order they are shown on the screen. Moreover, the text "Hello People" is missing because it's not part of the content stream. It's inside an external object that is referred to from the page dictionary.

Even if all the characters are in the right order, there may be kerning information between substrings, adjusting the space between letters so they look better (for instance between the two letter *l*s of the word "Hello"). However, the spacing can also be used instead of a whitespace character. That's one aspect that should be considered and that makes it difficult to extract text from a content stream.

Another aspect is the encoding. It's possible for a PDF to have a font containing characters that appear in a content stream as a, b, c, and so on, but for which the shapes drawn in the PDF file show a completely different glyph, such as α, β, γ, and so on. An application can create a different encoding for each specific PDF document—for example, in an attempt to obfuscate. More likely, the PDF-generating software does this deliberately, such as when a font with many characters is used but all the text can be shown using only 256 different glyphs. In this case, the software picks character names at random according to the glyphs that are used. Another possibility is that the content stream consists of raw glyph indexes; you then have to write code that goes through the character mappings and finds the right letters.

You'll also encounter PDF files that were created from scanned images. The content stream of each of the pages in such a document contains a reference to an image XObject. There will be no PDF strings in the stream. In the previous chapter, you created PDF documents with the glyphs drawn by the Java `TextLayout` object, and you wouldn't find any strings in this case either. Optical character recognition (OCR) will be your only recourse if you want to extract text from such a PDF document.

The section about text extraction in the first edition was followed by a section entitled "Why you shouldn't use PDF as a format for editing." Again, an example and a list of reasons was given for why it's extremely difficult and not very wise to edit a content stream. But that was then, and this is now. It's still true that you shouldn't edit a PDF, but with regards to text extraction, we've welcomed a new iText developer, Kevin Day, who has contributed a package (`com.itextpdf.text.pdf.parser`) containing classes that are able to parse and interpret PDF content.

> **WARNING** The API of this package is subject to change, because other developers—including myself—are still experimenting with it, adding new features, and fixing bugs.

Given the different obstacles I've outlined, not every PDF document that can be found in the wild can be parsed effectively, but the functionality does make a good effort at trying to find words and sentences, even if they're drawn on a page in random order, as was the case with our second "Hello World" example.

15.3.2 *Processing content streams with PdfContentStreamProcessor*

If you look at the `com.itextpdf.text.pdf.parser` package, you'll find utility classes such as `ContentByteUtils` with static methods to extract byte arrays from a PDF file, and tools such as `PdfContentReaderTool` with methods to create a `String` representation of objects and to output lists of objects and contents. For instance,

```
PdfContentReaderTool.listContentStream(new File(pdf), out);
```

This code snippet will write all the information that is needed to extract the content of a page, including the extracted text.

The next listing gives an idea of what to expect. Note that the content streams are replaced by ellipses (. . .).

Listing 15.22   calendar_info.txt generated with InspectPageContent.java

```
=============Page 1====================
- - - - - Dictionary - - - - - -
(/Type=/Page, /Contents=Stream, /Parent=Dictionary of type: /Pages,
/Resources=Dictionary, /MediaBox=[0, 0, 595, 842], /Rotate=90)
   Subdictionary /Parent = (/Count=8, /Type=/Pages, /ITXT=5.0.2_SNAPSHOT,
   /Kids=[6 0 R, 8 0 R, 10 0 R, 12 0 R, 14 0 R, 16 0 R, 18 0 R, 20 0 R])
   Subdictionary /Resources = (/ProcSet=[/PDF, /Text, /ImageB, /ImageC,
```

```
  /ImageI], /XObject=Dictionary, /Font=Dictionary)
    Subdictionary /XObject = (/Xf2=Stream of type: /XObject,
    /Xf1=Stream of type: /XObject)
    Subdictionary /Font = (/F1=Dictionary of type: /Font)
      Subdictionary /F1 = (/Type=/Font, /BaseFont=/Helvetica,
      /Subtype=/Type1, /Encoding=/WinAnsiEncoding)
- - - - - XObject Summary - - - - - -
------ /Xf2 - subtype = /Form = 671 bytes ------
...
------ /Xf2 - subtype = /FormEnd of Content------
------ /Xf1 - subtype = /Form = 162 bytes ------
...
------ /Xf1 - subtype = /FormEnd of Content------
- - - - - Content Stream - - - - - -
...
- - - - - Text Extraction - - - - - -
Day 1 FOOBAR FILM FESTIVAL 2011-10-12
...
```

This is the first step toward text extraction: collecting all the resources. Now you need to process the information. Listing 15.23 shows a new version of parsePdf() from listing 15.20. The PRTokeniser class is still used, but its complexity is hidden by the Pdf-ContentStreamProcessor class.

Listing 15.23   ParsingHelloWorld.java

```
public void extractText(String src, String dest) throws IOException {
  PrintWriter out = new PrintWriter(new FileOutputStream(dest));
  PdfReader reader = new PdfReader(src);
  RenderListener listener
    = new MyTextRenderListener(out);                    Creates processor
  PdfContentStreamProcessor processor                   with listener
    = new PdfContentStreamProcessor(listener);
  PdfDictionary pageDic = reader.getPageN(1);
  PdfDictionary resourcesDic                            Gets resources
    = pageDic.getAsDict(PdfName.RESOURCES);             for page
  processor.processContent(ContentByteUtils
    .getContentBytesForPage(reader, 1), resourcesDic);  Processes content
  out.flush();                                          and resources
  out.close();}
```

The output of this listing depends on the listener. This is an instance of the Render-Listener interface to which the processor passes information about the text and images in the page. The following listing is an experimental implementation that will help you understand the mechanism.

Listing 15.24   MyTextRenderListener.java

```
public class MyTextRenderListener implements RenderListener {
  protected PrintWriter out;
  public MyTextRenderListener(PrintWriter out) {
```

```
    this.out = out;
  }
  public void beginTextBlock() {
    out.print("<");                          BT is
  }                                          encountered
  public void endTextBlock() {
    out.println(">");                        ET is
  }                                          encountered
  public void renderImage(ImageRenderInfo renderInfo) {
  }
  public void renderText(TextRenderInfo renderInfo) {
    out.print("<");
    out.print(renderInfo.getText());         Info about text
    out.print(">");                          content
  }
}
```

You're not concerned with images yet. Angle brackets are placed at the start and end of text blocks, and every text segment is enclosed in angle brackets. If you use this method on the PDF created with listing 15.21, you'll get the following results:

```
<>
<<ld><Wor><llo><He>>
<<Hello People>>
```

The words "Hello World" are still mangled, but the text "Hello People" is picked up correctly.

In listing 15.24, you use the class `TextRenderInfo` to get a chunk of text with the `getText()` method, but the render info class also provides methods to get `LineSegment` objects containing information about the location of the text on the page, to get the font that was used, and so on. With this information, you could write a `RenderListener` implementation that returns a result that is much better than the output provided by `MyTextRenderListener`.

Fortunately, this has already been done for you in the form of text-extraction strategies. The `TextExtractionStrategy` interface extends `RenderListener`, adding a `getResultantText()` method. The different implementations of this interface, in combination with the `PdfReaderContentParser` or `PdfTextExtractor`, dramatically reduce the number of code lines needed to extract text.

15.3.3 Extracting text with PdfReaderContentParser and PdfTextExtractor

Figure 15.7 shows two pages—the preface from the first edition of *iText in Action*. The PDF was extracted from the eBook version of the book. It's a traditional PDF without structure.

Let's try to convert the content from these two pages to a plain text file.

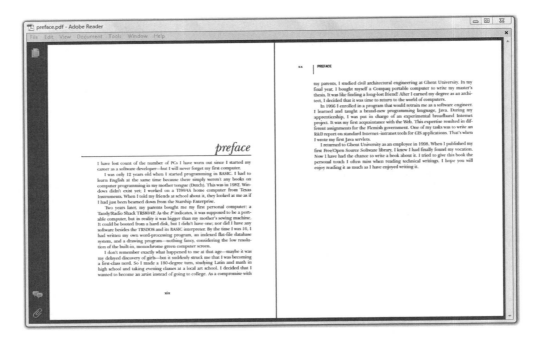

Figure 15.7   Preface from the first edition

SIMPLE TEXT EXTRACTION

The next example shows how to use `SimpleTextExtractionStrategy` in combination with `PdfReaderContentParser` to create a plain text file with the content of the preface.

Listing 15.25   ExtractPageContent.java

```
PdfReader reader = new PdfReader(pdf);
PdfReaderContentParser parser = new PdfReaderContentParser(reader);
PrintWriter out = new PrintWriter(new FileOutputStream(txt));
TextExtractionStrategy strategy;
for (int i = 1; i <= reader.getNumberOfPages(); i++) {
  strategy = parser.processContent(i, new SimpleTextExtractionStrategy());
  out.println(strategy.getResultantText());
}
out.flush();
out.close();
```

The `PdfReaderContentParser` uses the `PdfContentStreamProcessor` internally. The `processContent()` method performs the same actions you did in listing 15.23, saving you a handful of lines of code.

The `SimpleTextExtractionStrategy` class is a special implementation of the `RenderListener`. It stores all the `TextRenderInfo` snippets in the order they occur in the stream, but it's intelligent enough to detect which snippets should be combined into one word, and which snippets should be separated with a space character.

This `TextExtractionStrategy` object, containing all the text of a specific page, is returned by the `processContent()` method. When you get the resulting text of the first page of the Preface, it starts like this:

```
xix
preface
I have lost count of the number of PCs I have worn out since I started my
career as a software developer—but I will never forget my first computer.
 I was only 12 years old when I started programming in BASIC. I had to
learn English at the same time because there simply weren't any books on
computer programming in my mother tongue (Dutch). This was in 1982. Win-
dows didn't exist yet; I worked on a TI99/4A home computer from Texas
Instruments. When I told my friends at school about it, they looked at
me as if I had just been beamed down from the Starship Enterprise.
```

The first text element in the content stream is "xix", the Roman page number that appears at the bottom of the page. The fact that the rest of the text reads correctly is a coincidence. It's not necessary for an application to put all the paragraphs in the correct order.

LOCATION-BASED TEXT EXTRACTION

Let's change one line in listing 15.25:

Listing 15.26   ExtractPageContentSorted1.java

```
PdfReader reader = new PdfReader(pdf);
PdfReaderContentParser parser = new PdfReaderContentParser(reader);
PrintWriter out = new PrintWriter(new FileOutputStream(txt));
TextExtractionStrategy strategy;
for (int i = 1; i <= reader.getNumberOfPages(); i++) {
  strategy
    = parser.processContent(i, new LocationTextExtractionStrategy());
  out.println(strategy.getResultantText());
}
out.flush();
out.close();
```

The `LocationTextExtractionStrategy` class will accept all the `TextRenderInfo` objects from the processor, just like the simple text-extraction strategy, but it will sort all the snippets of text based on their position on the page, before creating the resultant text.

The next example makes this code even more compact by using the `PdfTextExtractor` class.

Listing 15.27   ExtractPageContentSorted2.java

```
PdfReader reader = new PdfReader(pdf);
PrintWriter out = new PrintWriter(new FileOutputStream(txt));
for (int i = 1; i <= reader.getNumberOfPages(); i++) {
  out.println(PdfTextExtractor.getTextFromPage(reader, i));
}
out.flush();
out.close();
```

Listings 15.26 and 15.27 have the same output. If you look at the resulting text file, you'll see that it starts with the word "preface", and that the page number has moved to the middle:

```
... As a compromise with
xix
xx PREFACE
my parents, I studied civil architectural engineering at Ghent University.
```

The strings "xix" and "xx" are page numbers; "PREFACE" is a running header. In tagged documents, these elements would have been referred to as *artifacts*. Screen readers would have ignored these snippets of text because they are not part of the actual content. When parsing our preface, it would be nice to add a filter that removes the page numbers and headers from the resulting text.

USING RENDER FILTERS

The special `FilteredTextRenderListener` text-extraction strategy combines a normal `TextExtractionStrategy` implementation with one or more render filters. The next listing uses a subclass of the abstract `RenderFilter` class, named `RegionText-RenderFilter`.

Listing 15.28 ExtractPageContentArea.java

```
PdfReader reader = new PdfReader(pdf);
PrintWriter out = new PrintWriter(new FileOutputStream(txt));
Rectangle rect = new Rectangle(70, 80, 420, 500);         Creates region
RenderFilter filter = new RegionTextRenderFilter(rect);   filter
TextExtractionStrategy strategy;
for (int i = 1; i <= reader.getNumberOfPages(); i++) {
  strategy = new FilteredTextRenderListener(              Creates filtered text-
    new LocationTextExtractionStrategy(), filter);       extraction strategy
  out.println(PdfTextExtractor
    .getTextFromPage(reader, i, strategy));               Extracts text
}
out.flush();out.close();
```

In this listing, you create a `Rectangle` whose dimensions are chosen in such a way that the page numbers and the running headers are outside the rectangle. You then use this rectangle to create a `RegionTextRenderFilter`. This filter will examine all the text and images that are processed and ignore everything that falls outside the chosen area.

> **NOTE** The `rect` object is currently not an instance of `com.itextpdf.text.Rectangle`; it's a `java.awt.Rectangle` (internally, a `java.awt.geom.Rectangle2D` object is used). This may change in the future; the API of the PDF parsing functionality hasn't been finalized yet.

The filter is combined with a text-extraction strategy in a `FilteredTextRenderListener` object, and from there on the code is similar to the code in listing 15.27, with the exception that you now pass a custom strategy as a parameter for the `getTextFromPage()` method. The result is the preface text without page numbers and running headers.

15.3.4 *Finding text margins*

The goal of parsing the content of a page isn't always to retrieve text. A frequently asked question involves finding the position where the last line of text ends on a page, so that extra text can be added. This can be done using a special `RenderLis-tener` implementation.

Figure 15.8 shows the same pages as figure 15.7, but with bounding rectangles for the text added.

The positions needed to draw these rectangles were retrieved using a `TextMarginFinder`:

Listing 15.29 ShowTextMargins.java

```
PdfReader reader = new PdfReader(src);
PdfReaderContentParser parser = new PdfReaderContentParser(reader);
PdfStamper stamper = new PdfStamper(reader, new FileOutputStream(RESULT));
TextMarginFinder finder;
for (int i = 1; i <= reader.getNumberOfPages(); i++) {
  finder = parser.processContent(i, new TextMarginFinder());
  PdfContentByte cb = stamper.getOverContent(i);
  cb.rectangle(finder.getLlx(), finder.getLly(),
    finder.getWidth(), finder.getHeight());
  cb.stroke();
}
stamper.close();
```

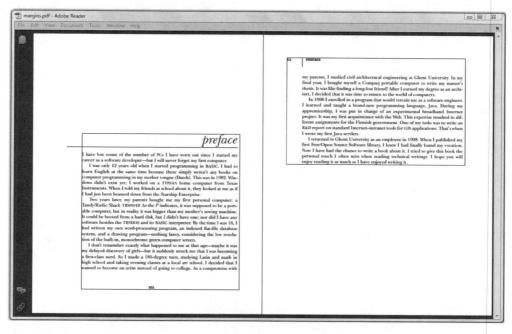

Figure 15.8 Finding the location of text in existing PDFs

Note that only text is taken into account. Graphics, such as the line that is drawn under the title "preface," are ignored by the parser in its current version. The content stream processor only returns objects of type `TextRenderInfo` and `ImageRenderInfo`.

15.3.5 *Extracting images*

Just like `TextRenderInfo` gives you information about a snippet of text, `ImageRender-Info` will give you info about an image: the position of the image and an instance of the `PdfImageObject` class that encapsulates the image XObject dictionary and the raw image bytes. The next listing processes all the pages of a PDF document and uses a custom `ImageRenderListener` to extract the images to a file.

Listing 15.30   ExtractImages.java

```
PdfReader reader = new PdfReader(filename);
PdfReaderContentParser parser = new PdfReaderContentParser(reader);
MyImageRenderListener listener = new MyImageRenderListener(RESULT);
for (int i = 1; i <= reader.getNumberOfPages(); i++) {
  parser.processContent(i, listener);
}
```

The following example shows a special implementation of the `RenderListener` to extract images. The methods you implemented in the custom text render listener in listing 15.24 are left empty. In this case, you're not interested in the text; only the `renderImage()` method is implemented.

Listing 15.31   MyImageRenderListener.java

```
public class MyImageRenderListener implements RenderListener {
  protected String path = "";
  public MyImageRenderListener(String path) {
    this.path = path;
  }
  public void beginTextBlock() { }
  public void endTextBlock() { }
  public void renderImage(ImageRenderInfo renderInfo) {
    try {
      String filename;
      FileOutputStream os;
      PdfImageObject image = renderInfo.getImage();
      PdfName filter = (PdfName)image.get(PdfName.FILTER);
      if (PdfName.DCTDECODE.equals(filter)) {
        filename = String.format(path,
          renderInfo.getRef().getNumber(), "jpg");       
        os = new FileOutputStream(filename);            
        os.write(image.getStreamBytes());               
        os.flush();                                      
        os.close();                                      
      }
      else if (PdfName.JPXDECODE.equals(filter)) {       
        filename = String.format(path,
          renderInfo.getRef().getNumber(), "jp2");        
        os = new FileOutputStream(filename);              
        os.write(image.getStreamBytes());
```

Deals with
JPEG images

Deals with
JPEG2000 images

```
      os.flush();                    ▲  Deals with
      os.close();                    |  JPEG2000 images
    }
    else {
      BufferedImage awtimage =
        renderInfo.getImage().getBufferedImage();
        if (awtimage != null) {              Handles other
        filename = String.format(path,       image types
          renderInfo.getRef().getNumber(), "png");
        ImageIO.write(awtimage, "png",
          new FileOutputStream(filename));
      }
    }
  } catch (IOException e) {
    e.printStackTrace();
  }
}
public void renderText(TextRenderInfo renderInfo) { }
}
```

In listing 15.31, the filename that is chosen for each image has a reference to the indirect object number of the image stream. The bytes of image streams with the filter /DCTDE-CODE or /JPXDECODE will be written to a file as is, resulting in valid JPEG and JPEG2000 files. For the other types of images, you also need to inspect the stream dictionary for values such as the number of bits per component, the color space, the width and the height, and so on. The getBufferedImage() method will attempt to do this in your place, and return an instance of java.awt.image.BufferedImage. But when you try this example on your own system, you'll notice that not all images are extracted.

Please don't report this as a bug. Not all the different types of images are supported yet. This is only a preview of new functionality that has been added to iText recently. Just like with parsing text, a best effort is done; when more types of images are supported will depend on code contributors and paying iText users.

15.4 Summary

This chapter was like a sequel to chapter 14. We continued talking about the content stream of a page, but in the first two sections we added structures that made part of the content optional or that added extra information to the content, like extra properties that belong to objects on the screen, information that improves the accessibility of the document, and structures that allow you to discover elements from the original source, such as paragraphs, lists, and tables.

To demonstrate the power of these structure elements, you've seen how to convert an existing PDF document to XML. This only works for PDF documents that are tagged. Other PDF documents can't be converted to XML, but you can parse them and write the output to a plain text file. We've discussed the different strategies that are at play and looked at how you can extract text from a PDF, find margins, and even extract images.

In the next chapter, we'll start by looking at image and other streams. We won't return to content streams, but we'll look at fonts streams and embedded files, and we'll even look at how to integrate a Flash application into a PDF document.

PDF streams

16

We've arrived at the final chapter of part 4. In this part, we're turning PDF files inside out. In chapter 13, we explored the file structure and discussed the different objects. We focused on the content stream of pages in chapters 14 and 15.

In this chapter, we'll continue working with streams: we'll look at image and font streams, and you'll find out how to add streams containing other files as attachments, and how to organize these files in a portable collection. We'll finish this chapter with some really cool examples of adding multimedia annotations to a document and integrating a Flash application into a PDF document.

16.1 Finding and replacing image and font streams

When you create an image using the Image class, or a font using the Font or Base-Font class, you don't have to worry about the way these objects are stored in the finished document. For example, when you use a standard Type 1 font, iText will add a font dictionary to the PDF file. When you use a font that is embedded, the font dictionary will also refer to a stream with a full or partial font program that is copied into the PDF file.

In this section, we'll look at advanced techniques that address the lowest level of PDF creation and manipulation with iText. The examples that follow were inspired by questions that were posted to the mailing list (see appendix B for more info about the list).

16.1.1 Adding a special ID to an Image

In the previous chapter, you learned how to extract *all* the images from a page, but what if you want to pick *one specific* image programmatically?

An image is a stored in a stream object. Each stream consists of a dictionary followed by zero or more bytes bracketed between the keywords `stream` and `endstream` (see table 13.2). The entries of the stream dictionary are filled in by iText. In the case of images, you'll have at least entries for the width and the height of the image, and a value defining the compression filter, but there's no reference to the original filename. The original bits and bytes of the image may have been changed completely.

One of the mailing-list subscribers wanted to solve the problem of retrieving specific images by adding an extra entry to the image stream dictionary. Listing 16.1 was written in answer to his question.

Listing 16.1 SpecialId.java

```
Image img = Image.getInstance(RESOURCE);
img.scaleAbsolute(400, 300);                                        ❶
img.setAbsolutePosition(0, 0);
PdfImage stream = new PdfImage(img, "", null);                      ❷
stream.put(new PdfName("ITXT_SpecialId"), new PdfName("123456789")); ❸
PdfIndirectObject ref = writer.addToBody(stream);                   ❹
img.setDirectReference(ref.getIndirectReference());                 ❺
document.add(img);                                                  ❻
```

❶ You create an instance of the high-level `Image` object, and set some properties, as described in chapter 2.

❷ You use this `Image` object to create a low-level `PdfImage` object. This object extends the `PdfStream` class. With the second parameter, you can pass a name for the image; the third parameter can be used for the reference to a mask image.

❸ `PdfStream` extends `PdfDictionary`. Just like with plain dictionaries, you can add key-value pairs. In this case, you choose a name for the key using the prefix reserved for iText (ITXT): `ITXT_SpecialId`. The value of the entry is also a name of your choice, in this case `/123456789`.

❹ You add the stream object to the body of the file that is written by the `PdfWriter` object. The `addToBody()` method returns a `PdfIndirectObject`. Because it's the first element that's added to the writer in this example, the reference of this object will be `1 0 R`.

❺ You tell the `Image` object that it has already been added to the writer with the method `setDirectReference()`.

❻ Finally, you add the image to the document. The image bytes have already been written to the `OutputStream` in ❹. Line ❻ writes the `Do` operator and its operands to the content stream of the page, and adds the correct reference to the image bytes ❺ to the page dictionary.

This example unveils the mechanism that's used by iText internally to add streams.

You'll use the PDF file that was created by listing 16.1 in the next example. You'll search for an image with the special ID `/123456789`, and you'll replace it with another image that has a lower resolution.

16.1.2 *Resizing an image in an existing document*

Here's another question that is often posted to the mailing list: "How do I reduce the size of an existing PDF containing lots of images?" There are many different answers to this question, depending on the nature of the PDF file. Maybe the same image is added multiple times, in which case passing the PDF through `PdfSmartCopy` could result in a serious file size reduction. Maybe the PDF wasn't compressed, or maybe there are plenty of unused objects. You could try to see if the `PdfReader`'s `removeUnusedObjects()` method has any effect.

It's more likely that the PDF contains high-resolution images, in which case the original question should be rephrased as, "How do I reduce the resolution of the images inside my PDF?" To achieve this, you should extract the image from the PDF, downsample it, then put it back into the PDF, replacing the high-resolution image.

The next example uses brute force instead of the `PdfReaderContentParser` to find images. With the `getXrefSize()` method, you get the highest object number in the PDF document, and you loop over every object, searching for a stream that has the special ID you're looking for.

Listing 16.2 ResizeImage.java

```java
PdfName key = new PdfName("ITXT_SpecialId");
PdfName value = new PdfName("123456789");
PdfReader reader = new PdfReader(SpecialId.RESULT);
int n = reader.getXrefSize();
PdfObject object;
PRStream stream;
for (int i = 0; i < n; i++) {
  object = reader.getPdfObject(i);
  if (object == null || !object.isStream())          // Finds image stream
    continue;
  stream = (PRStream)object;
  if (value.equals(stream.get(key))) {
    PdfImageObject image = new PdfImageObject(stream);  // Gets BufferedImage
    BufferedImage bi = image.getBufferedImage();
    if (bi == null) continue;
    int width = (int)(bi.getWidth() * FACTOR);          // Creates new BufferedImage
    int height = (int)(bi.getHeight() * FACTOR);
```

```
      BufferedImage img = new BufferedImage(
        width, height, BufferedImage.TYPE_INT_RGB);      Creates new
      AffineTransform at = AffineTransform                BufferedImage
        .getScaleInstance(FACTOR, FACTOR);
      Graphics2D g = img.createGraphics();
      g.drawRenderedImage(bi, at);
      ByteArrayOutputStream imgBytes
        = new ByteArrayOutputStream();                    Writes JPG
      ImageIO.write(img, "JPG", imgBytes);                bytes
      stream.clear();
      stream.setData(imgBytes.toByteArray(),
        false, PRStream.NO_COMPRESSION);
      stream.put(PdfName.TYPE, PdfName.XOBJECT);
      stream.put(PdfName.SUBTYPE, PdfName.IMAGE);          Replaces content of
      stream.put(key, value);                             image stream and
      stream.put(PdfName.FILTER, PdfName.DCTDECODE);       stream dictionary
      stream.put(PdfName.WIDTH, new PdfNumber(width));
      stream.put(PdfName.HEIGHT, new PdfNumber(height));
      stream.put(PdfName.BITSPERCOMPONENT,
        new PdfNumber(8));
      stream.put(PdfName.COLORSPACE, PdfName.DEVICERGB);
    }
  }
PdfStamper stamper = new PdfStamper(reader, new FileOutputStream(RESULT));
stamper.close();
```

Once you've found the stream you need, you create a PdfImageObject that will create a java.awt.image.BufferedImage named bi; you'll create a second BufferedImage named img that is a factor smaller. In this example, the value of FACTOR is 0.5. You draw the image bi to the Graphics2D object of the image image using an affine transformation that scales the image down with a factor of FACTOR.

You write the image as a JPEG to a ByteArrayOutputStream, and use the bytes from this OutputStream as the new data for the stream object you've retrieved from PdfReader. You reset all the entries in the image dictionary and add all the keys that are necessary for a PDF viewer to interpret the image bytes correctly. After changing the PRStream object in the reader, you use PdfStamper to write the altered file to a FileOutputStream. Again, you get a look at the way iText works internally. When you add a JPEG to a document the normal way, iText selects all the entries for the image dictionary for you.

Working at the lowest level is fun and gives you a lot of power, but you really have to know what you're doing, or you can seriously damage a PDF file. Because of the high complexity, some requirements are close to impossible. For instance, it's very hard to replace a font. Let's start by finding a way to list the fonts that are used in a PDF document.

16.1.3 *Listing the fonts used*

In listing 11.1, you created a PDF document demonstrating different font types. You can now use listing 16.3 to inspect this document and create a set containing all the fonts that were used. This time you won't look at every object in the PDF, as done in the previous listing—even those that weren't relevant. This time you'll process the resources of every page in the document.

Listing 16.3   ListUsedFonts.java

```java
public Set listFonts(String src) throws IOException {
  Set<String> set = new TreeSet<String>();                     // Creates Set
  PdfReader reader = new PdfReader(src);                        // for fonts
  PdfDictionary resources;
  for (int k = 1;
    k <= reader.getNumberOfPages(); ++k) {                      // Processes
    resources = reader.getPageN(k)                              // resources of
      .getAsDict(PdfName.RESOURCES);                            // every page
    processResource(set, resources);
  }
  return set;
}
public static void processResource(
  Set<String> set, PdfDictionary resource) {
  if (resource == null)
    return;
  PdfDictionary xobjects
    = resource.getAsDict(PdfName.XOBJECT);
  if (xobjects != null) {                                       // Uses recursion
    for (PdfName key : xobjects.getKeys()) {                    // to get fonts in
      processResource(set, xobjects.getAsDict(key));            // form XObjects
    }
  }
  PdfDictionary fonts                                           // Gets font
    = resource.getAsDict(PdfName.FONT);                         // dictionary
  if (fonts == null)
    return;
  PdfDictionary font;
  for (PdfName key : fonts.getKeys()) {
    font = fonts.getAsDict(key);
    String name                                                 // Gets font
      = font.getAsName(PdfName.BASEFONT).toString();            // name
    if (name.length() > 8 && name.charAt(7) == '+') {
      name = String.format("%s subset (%s)",                    // Checks for prefix
       name.substring(8), name.substring(1, 7));                // subsetted fonts
    }
    else {
      name = name.substring(1);
      PdfDictionary desc
        = font.getAsDict(PdfName.FONTDESCRIPTOR);
      if (desc == null)
        name += " nofontdescriptor";
      else if (desc.get(PdfName.FONTFILE) != null)
        name += " (Type 1) embedded";
      else if (desc.get(PdfName.FONTFILE2) != null)            // ❶ Gets type
        name += " (TrueType) embedded";                        //   of fully
      else if (desc.get(PdfName.FONTFILE3) != null)            //   embedded
        name +=                                                //   fonts
          " (" + font.getAsName(PdfName.SUBTYPE)
            .toString().substring(1) + ") embedded";
    }
```

```
        set.add(name);
    }
}
```

In this listing, you check for a series of keys in the font descriptor dictionary to determine the font type ❶. Table 16.1 explains which key corresponds with which font type.

Table 16.1   Stream references in the font descriptor

Key	Description
FONTFILE	The value for this key (if present) is a stream containing a Type 1 font program.
FONTFILE2	The value for this key (if present) is a stream containing a TrueType font program.
FONTFILE3	The value for this key (if present) is a stream containing a font program whose format is specified by the /Subtype entry in the stream dictionary. It can be /Type1C, /CIDFontType0C, or /OpenType.

If you try this example on the file created in chapter 11, you'll get the following result:

```
Arial-BlackItalic subset (IAEZOI)
ArialMT subset (WTBBZY)
ArialMT subset (XKYIQK)
CMR10 (Type 1) embedded
Helvetica nofontdescriptor
KozMinPro-Regular-UniJIS-UCS2-H nofontdescriptor
MS-Gothic subset (ZGXOUP)
Puritan2 (Type1) embedded
```

The standard Helvetica Type 1 font isn't embedded, and there's no font descriptor. The same goes for the KozMinPro-Regular CJK font. Embedded Type 1 fonts are always *fully* embedded by iText. TrueType and OpenType fonts are *subsetted* unless you changed the default behavior with the setSubset() method. This was explained in chapter 11.

   Observe that there are two entries of ArialMT. This is caused by the use of two variations of the Arial font: one using WinAnsi encoding and one using Identity-H. You can't store both types of the font in the same font dictionary and stream; two different font objects with different names will be created. In this case, the font names are WTB-BZY+ArialMT and XKYIQK+ArialMT. The six-letter code is chosen at random and will change every time you execute the example.

> **FAQ**   *Can I combine different subsetted fonts into one font?* The easy answer is "no." The not-so-easy answer is that merging subsets is really hard. It may require the page content of all the pages to be rewritten.

In the next example, you'll replace a font that isn't embedded with a fully embedded font. This will give you an idea of the difficulties you can expect if you ever try to combine different subsetted fonts into one.

16.1.4 Replacing a font

Figure 16.1 shows two PDF files that were created in the very same way, except for one difference: in the upper PDF, the font (Walt Disney Script v4.1) wasn't embedded. It's

Figure 16.1   Non-embedded versus embedded fonts

a font I downloaded from a site with plenty of free fonts. The font isn't installed on my OS, so Adobe Reader doesn't find it, and the words "iText in Action" are shown in Adobe Sans MM, which is quite different from the font shown in the PDF that has the font embedded.

Suppose you have the upper PDF as well as the font file for the Walt Disney Script font. You could use this listing to embed that font after the fact.

Listing 16.4   EmbedFontPostFacto.java

```
RandomAccessFile raf = new RandomAccessFile(FONT, "r");
byte fontfile[] = new byte[(int)raf.length()];
raf.readFully(fontfile);
raf.close();
PdfStream stream = new PdfStream(fontfile);
stream.flateCompress();
stream.put(PdfName.LENGTH1,
  new PdfNumber(fontfile.length));
PdfReader reader = new PdfReader(RESULT1);
int n = reader.getXrefSize();
PdfObject object;
PdfDictionary font;
PdfStamper stamper
  = new PdfStamper(reader, new FileOutputStream(RESULT2));
PdfName fontname = new PdfName(FONTNAME);
for (int i = 0; i < n; i++) {
  object = reader.getPdfObject(i);
  if (object == null || !object.isDictionary())
    continue;
  font = (PdfDictionary)object;
  if (PdfName.FONTDESCRIPTOR.equals(
    font.get(PdfName.TYPE)) && fontname.equals(
    font.get(PdfName.FONTNAME))) {
```

Reads font file into byte array

Creates PDF stream

Finds unembedded font

```
    PdfIndirectObject objref                          Adds stream
        = stamper.getWriter().addToBody(stream);      to writer
    font.put(PdfName.FONTFILE2,                    Adds
        objref.getIndirectReference());            reference to stream
  }
}
stamper.close();
```

In this listing, you're adding the complete font file. You add the reference to the stream using the FONTFILE2 key because you know in advance that the font has True-Type outlines. That's not the only assumption you make. You also assume that the metrics of the font that is used in the PDF correspond to the metrics of the new font you're embedding.

When we talked about parsing PDFs, I explained that we could only make a fair attempt, but that the functionality could fail for PDFs using exotic encodings. Several warnings that were mentioned in section 15.3.1 also apply here. In real-world examples, replacing one font with another can be very difficult.

Now that you know what a PDF looks like on the inside, these examples complement your knowledge about images (discussed in chapter 10) and fonts (chapter 11). In the sections that follow, we'll take a close look at annotations (chapter 7) that are associated with a PDF stream.

16.2 Embedding files into a PDF

You've already created a document with file attachment annotations in section 7.3.3. You can embed different files of any type—images, Word documents, XML files, other PDF files—into a PDF document as an annotation, but there's also an alternative way to do this.

In this section, we'll briefly return to file attachment annotations, and you'll learn about document-level attachments and create actions to open these annotations. We'll also discuss the concept of portable collections.

16.2.1 File attachment annotations

Figure 16.2 shows a list of Kubrick movies available in video stores. There's a pushpin next to every movie title, and if you click the pushpin, the movie poster is shown. All the file attachments are also listed in the file attachments panel at the bottom.

The next listing demonstrates how you can extract the attached files by looping over all the pages of the document, inspecting the /Annots array.

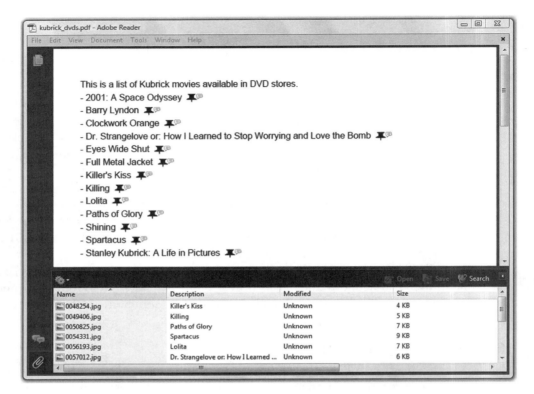

Figure 16.2   File attachment annotations

Listing 16.5   KubrickDvds.java

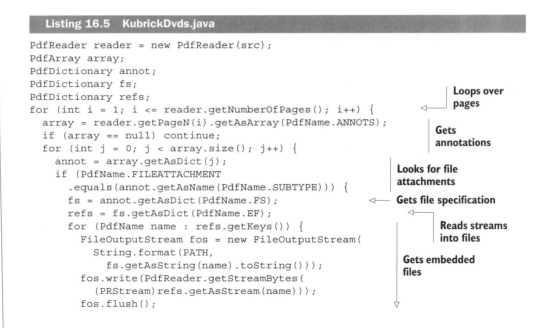

```
PdfReader reader = new PdfReader(src);
PdfArray array;
PdfDictionary annot;
PdfDictionary fs;
PdfDictionary refs;
for (int i = 1; i <= reader.getNumberOfPages(); i++) {        ◁── Loops over pages
  array = reader.getPageN(i).getAsArray(PdfName.ANNOTS);       ── Gets annotations
  if (array == null) continue;
  for (int j = 0; j < array.size(); j++) {
    annot = array.getAsDict(j);
    if (PdfName.FILEATTACHMENT                                 ── Looks for file attachments
      .equals(annot.getAsName(PdfName.SUBTYPE))) {
      fs = annot.getAsDict(PdfName.FS);                        ◁── Gets file specification
      refs = fs.getAsDict(PdfName.EF);
      for (PdfName name : refs.getKeys()) {                    ── Reads streams into files
        FileOutputStream fos = new FileOutputStream(
          String.format(PATH,
            fs.getAsString(name).toString()));
        fos.write(PdfReader.getStreamBytes(                    ── Gets embedded files
          (PRStream)refs.getAsStream(name)));
        fos.flush();
```

```
        fos.close();
      }                          ⇧ Gets embedded
    }                              files
  }
}
```

If you don't want to add an attachment using a visible annotation, you can attach files at the document level.

16.2.2 *Document-level attachments*

In the next listing, you'll create a page listing the movies that are discussed in the documentary, *Stanley Kubrick: A Life in Pictures*. When you add the movies to a List, you create an XML file. You then add this XML file to the document as an attachment with the addFileAttachment() method.

Listing 16.6   KubrickDocumentary.java

```
ByteArrayOutputStream txt = new ByteArrayOutputStream();
PrintStream out = new PrintStream(txt);
out.println("<movies>");
List list = new List(List.UNORDERED, 20);
ListItem item;
for (Movie movie : movies) {
  out.println("<movie>");
  out.println(String.format("<title>%s</title>",
    SimpleXMLParser.escapeXML(movie.getMovieTitle(), true)));
  out.println(String.format("<year>%s</year>",
    movie.getYear()));
  out.println(String.format("<duration>%s</duration>",
    movie.getDuration()));
  out.println("</movie>");
  item = new ListItem(movie.getMovieTitle());
  list.add(item);
}
document.add(list);
out.print("</movies>");
out.flush();
out.close();
PdfFileSpecification fs                                    Adds document-
  = PdfFileSpecification.fileEmbedded(writer,              level attachment
    null, "kubrick.xml", txt.toByteArray());
writer.addFileAttachment(fs);
```

Suppose you've created a report based on different spreadsheets; you could add the original spreadsheets to your document as attachments. This is also an ideal way to combine any presentation for human consumption with the data for automated consumption.

The following listing shows how you can extract the XML from the PDF document you created in the previous one.

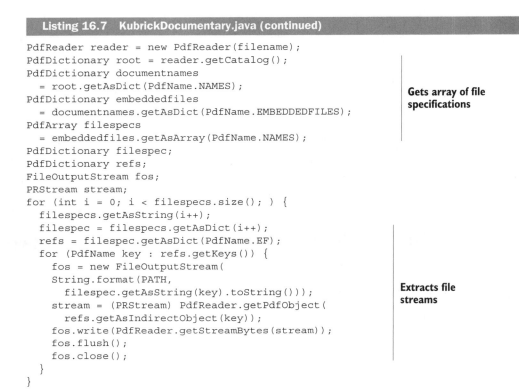

Listing 16.7   KubrickDocumentary.java (continued)

```java
PdfReader reader = new PdfReader(filename);
PdfDictionary root = reader.getCatalog();
PdfDictionary documentnames
  = root.getAsDict(PdfName.NAMES);                          // Gets array of file
PdfDictionary embeddedfiles                                 // specifications
  = documentnames.getAsDict(PdfName.EMBEDDEDFILES);
PdfArray filespecs
  = embeddedfiles.getAsArray(PdfName.NAMES);
PdfDictionary filespec;
PdfDictionary refs;
FileOutputStream fos;
PRStream stream;
for (int i = 0; i < filespecs.size(); ) {
  filespecs.getAsString(i++);
  filespec = filespecs.getAsDict(i++);
  refs = filespec.getAsDict(PdfName.EF);
  for (PdfName key : refs.getKeys()) {
    fos = new FileOutputStream(
    String.format(PATH,
      filespec.getAsString(key).toString()));              // Extracts file
    stream = (PRStream) PdfReader.getPdfObject(             // streams
      refs.getAsIndirectObject(key));
    fos.write(PdfReader.getStreamBytes(stream));
    fos.flush();
    fos.close();
  }
}
```

The references to the file specifications of document-level attachments can be found through the /EmbeddedFiles entry in the catalog's name tree. These reference are in turn part of a name tree. In section 13.3.3, you learned that a name tree is an array with ordered pairs of strings and values. In this case, you ignore the names—you only want the values, which are the file specifications of the embedded files.

16.2.3   *Go to embedded file action*

Embedded files—be they added as annotations, or at the document level—are listed in the attachments panel where the end user can select and open them. If you want to provide a better way for end users to find an attachment, you can create *goto actions* to switch to an embedded file, or to the parent of an embedded file.

The document in figure 16.3 shows a PDF listing the DVDs that are packaged in the Kubrick box: eight Kubrick movies and a documentary. The PDF has nine attachments in the PDF format, one per movie. When you click "see info," one of these attached files will open. There's a "Go to original document" link in each of these files to return you to the original document. This is done with a /GoToE action specifying a destination in an embedded or embedding file (an attachment or a parent of an attachment).

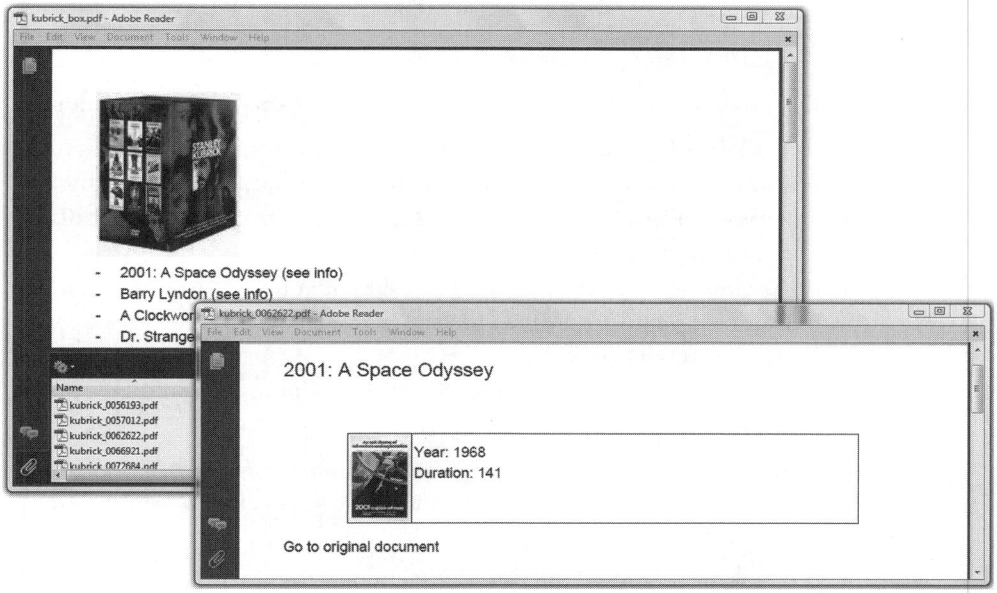

Figure 16.3 Go to embedded files

This example shows how such a /GoToE action in the parent document is created.

Listing 16.8 KubrickBox.java

```
PdfDestination dest
  = new PdfDestination(PdfDestination.FIT);
dest.addFirst(new PdfNumber(1));
...
fs = PdfFileSpecification.fileEmbedded(writer, null,
  String.format("kubrick_%s.pdf", movie.getImdb()),
  createMoviePage(movie));
fs.addDescription(movie.getTitle(), false);
writer.addFileAttachment(fs);
item = new ListItem(movie.getMovieTitle());
target = new PdfTargetDictionary(true);
target.setEmbeddedFileName(movie.getTitle());
action = PdfAction.gotoEmbedded(
  null, target, dest, true);
chunk = new Chunk(" (see info)");
chunk.setAction(action);
item.add(chunk);
list.add(item);
```

Annotations:
- Creates destination
- Creates document-level attachment
- Creates target
- Creates Chunk with action

You do something similar in the PDF files that are attached to the parent document:

```
PdfDestination dest = new PdfDestination(PdfDestination.FIT);
dest.addFirst(new PdfNumber(1));
PdfTargetDictionary target = new PdfTargetDictionary(false);
Chunk chunk = new Chunk("Go to original document");
```

```
PdfAction action = PdfAction.gotoEmbedded(null, target, dest, false);
chunk.setAction(action);
document.add(chunk);
```

How does this work? The gotoEmbedded() method expects four parameters:

- *A filename*—The name of the PDF file that has attachments. This parameter can be null if you want to go to an attachment in the current document.
- *A target*—An instance of the class PdfTargetDictionary. We'll discuss this dictionary in a moment.
- *A destination*—A PdfString or a PdfName if you want to jump to a named destination (see section 7.1.1); a PdfDestination if you want to go to an explicit destination (see section 7.1.2).
- *A Boolean value*—If true, the destination document should be opened in a new window.

When you create a PdfTargetDictionary, you specify whether you are targeting a child document (true) or a parent document (false). If you want to jump to a child document, you have two options:

- If you want to go to a file that is attached at the document-level, which could be the case if you are targeting a child document, you need to specify the name of this file with the setEmbeddedFileName() method.
- If you're targeting a file that was added as a file attachment annotation, you need to use setFileAttachmentPage() or setFileAttachmentPagename() to specify to which page the attachment belongs. The former method expects a page number; the latter expects a named destination. A page can contain more than one file attachment, so you also have to pass the index (0-based) of the attachment with setFileAttachmentIndex(), or its name with setFileAttachmentName()—the name is the value corresponding with the /NM key in the annotation dictionary.

It's also possible to nest target dictionaries. For instance, you might want to go to a child document of a child document, to the parent of a parent document, or to a sibling. This is done with the setAdditionalPath() method. We'll use this method in a more complex example involving portable collections.

16.2.4 *PDF packages, portable collections, or portfolios*

Suppose that you want to bundle a set of documents that belong together into one PDF, and organize them in a way that the attachment panel can't accommodate. Suppose you want to add your own keys, and to allow the end user to sort the entries in the collection of documents based on those custom keys.

This functionality was introduced in PDF 1.7, and it's known under different names. People working with it on the lowest level will talk about *portable collections*, because that's the name that is used in the PDF reference and in ISO-32000-1. People who work on a higher level using Adobe Acrobat or Adobe Reader will say that a PDF

Figure 16.4 A portable collection containing PDF files

document as shown in figure 16.4 is a *portfolio*. And if you ever hear people talk about *PDF packages*, that's the original name of this functionality.

Figure 16.4 shows a collection of PDF files with information about the movies of Stanley Kubrick. The end user gets an overview with the year the movie was made, the movie title, the run length, and the file size. The user can also sort the entries based on these fields. Clicking one of the lines in the overview opens the file.

The fields in this UI are defined in a *collection schema dictionary*. This dictionary consists of a variable number of individual *collection field dictionaries*. The next listing shows how to create these dictionaries.

Listing 16.9 KubrickMovies.java

```java
private static PdfCollectionSchema getCollectionSchema() {
  PdfCollectionSchema schema = new PdfCollectionSchema();
  PdfCollectionField size
    = new PdfCollectionField("File size", PdfCollectionField.SIZE);
  size.setOrder(4);
  schema.addField("SIZE", size);
  PdfCollectionField filename
    = new PdfCollectionField("File name", PdfCollectionField.FILENAME);
  filename.setVisible(false);
  schema.addField("FILE", filename);
```

```
PdfCollectionField title
  = new PdfCollectionField("Movie title", PdfCollectionField.TEXT);
title.setOrder(1);
schema.addField("TITLE", title);
PdfCollectionField duration
  = new PdfCollectionField("Duration", PdfCollectionField.NUMBER);
duration.setOrder(2);
schema.addField("DURATION", duration);
PdfCollectionField year
  = new PdfCollectionField("Year", PdfCollectionField.NUMBER);
year.setOrder(0);
schema.addField("YEAR", year);
return schema;
}
```

In listing 16.9, you create five PdfCollectionField objects. The constructor of this class accepts a name that will be used as the caption of a column in the detail view of the collection. It also expects a field type, which must be one of values listed in table 16.2.

Table 16.2 Collection field types

Parameter	Name	Description
TEXT	/S	The field value will contain text; iText will use the object PdfString internally.
DATE	/D	The field value will contain a date; iText will use the object PdfDate internally.
NUMBER	/N	The field value will contain a number; iText will use the object PdfNumber internally.
FILENAME	/F	The value will be obtained from the /UF entry in the file specification.
DESC	/Desc	The value will be obtained from the /Desc entry in the file specification.
MODDATE	/ModDate	The value will be obtained from the /ModDate entry in the file specification.
CREATIONDATE	/CreationDate	The value will be obtained from the /CreationDate entry in the file specification.
SIZE	/Size	The size of the embedded file as identified by the /Size entry in the /Params dictionary of the stream dictionary of the embedded file.

You can set the order of the fields in the UI with the setOrder() method. Observe that in listing 16.9 you set one field invisible with setVisible(false). As a result, there's no column with that filename in figure 16.4. The default is true; all other fields are visible. Finally, you can make the field editable with the setEditable() method. By default, fields are not editable.

NOTE If the collection schema is absent, the Reader will choose useful defaults taken from the file specification dictionary, such as the filename and the file size.

The collection schema is used in the *collection dictionary* of the PDF document. You construct a `PdfCollection` dictionary with one of the following preferences as a parameter:

- `DETAIL`—The collection view is presented in detail mode, with all information in the schema dictionary presented in a multicolumn format. This mode provides the most information to the user. See figure 16.4.
- `TILE`—The collection view is presented in tile mode, with each file in the collection denoted by a small icon and a subset of information from the schema dictionary. This mode provides top-level information about the file attachments to the user. See figure 16.5.
- `HIDDEN`—The collection view is initially hidden, without preventing the user from obtaining a file list via explicit actions.
- `CUSTOM`—The collection view is presented by a custom navigator. This option isn't described in ISO-32000-1, but in Adobe's extensions to ISO-32000-1 (level 3).

The end user can always switch from the initial view to another view.

The files presented in the UI can be sorted in different ways, and you can define the sort order using a `PdfCollectionSort` object. You construct this object by passing the name of a field that has to be used to sort the items as a parameter. With the `setSortOrder()` method, you can sort the items in ascending (`true`) or descending (`false`) order. If you want to involve multiple fields, you have to pass an array of field names as a parameter of the `PdfCollectionSort` constructor as well as a corresponding array of Boolean values for the sort order.

Each collection has a cover page. In listing 16.10, the cover page has the text, "This document contains a collection of PDFs, one per Stanley Kubrick movie." But when you open the document, you'll see a different page because you've used the `setInitialDocument()` method to choose one of the embedded files as the initial page.

Once you've completed setting all the parameters of the `PdfCollection` dictionary, you can use `setCollection()` as is done here.

Listing 16.10   KubrickMovies.java (continued)

```
public byte[] createPdf()
  throws DocumentException, IOException, SQLException {
  Document document = new Document();
  ByteArrayOutputStream baos = new ByteArrayOutputStream();
  PdfWriter writer = PdfWriter.getInstance(document, baos);
  document.open();
  document.add(new Paragraph(
    "This document contains a collection of PDFs, one per
        Stanley Kubrick movie."));
  PdfCollection collection
    = new PdfCollection(PdfCollection.DETAILS);
```

Defines
collection

```
collection.setInitialDocument("Eyes Wide Shut");
PdfCollectionSchema schema = getCollectionSchema();
collection.setSchema(schema);
PdfCollectionSort sort
  = new PdfCollectionSort("YEAR");
sort.setSortOrder(false);
collection.setSort(sort);
writer.setCollection(collection);
PdfFileSpecification fs;
PdfCollectionItem item;
DatabaseConnection connection = new HsqldbConnection("filmfestival");
java.util.List movies = PojoFactory.getMovies(connection, 1);
connection.close();
for (Movie movie : movies) {
  fs =
    PdfFileSpecification.fileEmbedded(writer, null,
    String.format("kubrick_%s.pdf", movie.getImdb()),
    createMoviePage(movie));
  fs.addDescription(movie.getTitle(), false);
  item = new PdfCollectionItem(schema);
  item.addItem("TITLE", movie.getMovieTitle(false));
  if (movie.getMovieTitle(true) != null) {
    item.setPrefix("TITLE",
      movie.getMovieTitle(true));
  }
  item.addItem("DURATION", movie.getDuration());
  item.addItem("YEAR", movie.getYear());
  fs.addCollectionItem(item);
  writer.addFileAttachment(fs);
}
document.close();
return baos.toByteArray();
}
```

Defines collection

Defines file specification

Defines collection item for file

Adds file as document-level attachment

As soon as there are fields of type TEXT, DATE, or NUMBER in the collection schema, you need to create a PdfCollectionItem for each file specification. This class comes with a plethora of addItem() methods that allow you to set the values of the different fields present in the collection schema.

> **NOTE** If you sorted the collection shown in figure 16.4 alphabetically in ascending order based on the titles, you'd want the movie *A Clockwork Orange* to follow *Barry Lyndon,* and not the other way around. To achieve this, you need to pass the string "Clockwork Orange" with the addItem() method and the article "A" with the setPrefix() method. The title would be shown as *A Clockwork Orange,* but the sorting order wouldn't be affected by the article "A".

You've created your first portable collection. If you open it in Adobe Reader, there will be an extra entry named Portfolio in the View menu. You can use it to switch to another UI, such as from a detailed view to a tiled view, or to return to the cover page.

Figure 16.5 shows a second portable collection opened in tiled view. As you can see, some of the PDFs created in this section have been bundled along with a JPEG and a plain text file. The image was created using the following listing.

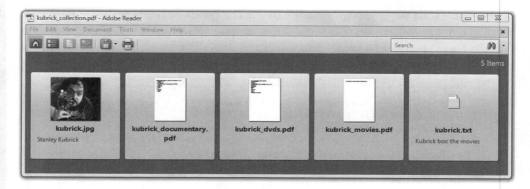

Figure 16.5 **A portable collection containing different file types**

Listing 16.11   KubrickCollection.java

```
PdfCollectionItem collectionitem = new PdfCollectionItem(schema);
PdfFileSpecification fs;
fs = PdfFileSpecification
  .fileEmbedded(writer, IMG_KUBRICK, "kubrick.jpg", null);
fs.addDescription("Stanley Kubrick", false);
collectionitem.addItem(TYPE_FIELD, "JPEG");
fs.addCollectionItem(collectionitem);
writer.addFileAttachment(fs);
```

If the file type is supported by the viewer, the end user will be able to view the file directly. This is the case for the JPEG and the plain text file in figure 16.5. You can choose to open these files in an external application too. That's also an option for file types that can't be opened in the viewer, unless special permissions are set to avoid security hazards.

This second portfolio example, named KubrickCollection, was written to demonstrate nested /GoToE actions. The file kubrick_movies.pdf shown in figure 16.5 is the collection you created with the KubrickMovies example. The following listing adds links from the cover page of the collection to the files embedded in a file that is part of the collection.

Listing 16.12   KubrickCollection.java (continued)

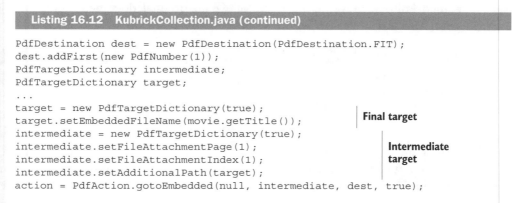

```
PdfDestination dest = new PdfDestination(PdfDestination.FIT);
dest.addFirst(new PdfNumber(1));
PdfTargetDictionary intermediate;
PdfTargetDictionary target;
...
target = new PdfTargetDictionary(true);                          Final target
target.setEmbeddedFileName(movie.getTitle());
intermediate = new PdfTargetDictionary(true);
intermediate.setFileAttachmentPage(1);                           Intermediate
intermediate.setFileAttachmentIndex(1);                          target
intermediate.setAdditionalPath(target);
action = PdfAction.gotoEmbedded(null, intermediate, dest, true);
```

The final target is a movie page that is the child of an intermediate target, namely the first attachment on page 2, which is the page with index 1. The next bit of code shows how this attachment was added.

Listing 16.13   KubrickCollection.java (continued)

```
PdfPCell cell = new PdfPCell(new Phrase("All movies by Kubrick"));
cell.setBorder(PdfPCell.NO_BORDER);
fs = PdfFileSpecification.fileEmbedded(writer, null,
  KubrickMovies.FILENAME, new KubrickMovies().createPdf());
collectionitem.addItem(TYPE_FIELD, "PDF");
fs.addCollectionItem(collectionitem);
target = new PdfTargetDictionary(true);
target.setFileAttachmentPagename("movies");
target.setFileAttachmentName("The movies of Stanley Kubrick");
cell.setCellEvent(new PdfActionEvent(writer,
  PdfAction.gotoEmbedded(null, target, dest, true)));
cell.setCellEvent(new FileAttachmentEvent(writer, fs,
  "The movies of Stanley Kubrick"));
cell.setCellEvent(new LocalDestinationEvent(writer, "movies"));
table.addCell(cell);
writer.addFileAttachment(fs);
```

In this code snippet, we have another example of a /GoToE action, demonstrating the use of the setFileAttachmentPagename() and setFileAttachmentName() methods as alternatives for setFileAttachmentPage() and setFileAttachmentIndex(). But the main reason to look at this snippet is the final line: writer.addFileAttachment(fs);.

The kubrick_movies.pdf file is added as an attachment annotation. Internally, this annotation will appear in the /Annots array of the page dictionary. These file attachment annotations do not appear in the list of embedded files and are therefore not a part of the portable collection, unless you also add them as document-level attachments.

Don't worry, the bits and bytes of the file will only be present once inside the PDF file. The file specification will be referenced from two places: from a file attachment annotation on the page level, and from the /EmbeddedFiles name tree at the document level.

If you've experimented with the examples while reading this book, you've probably noticed that the files with the movie information that were embedded in the PDF named kubrick_movies.pdf contain a "Go to original document" link that doesn't work. This link is created with this listing:

Listing 16.14   KubrickMovies.java (continued)

```
PdfTargetDictionary target = new PdfTargetDictionary(false);
target.setAdditionalPath(new PdfTargetDictionary(false));
Chunk chunk = new Chunk("Go to original document");
PdfAction action
  = PdfAction.gotoEmbedded(null, target, new PdfString("movies"), false);
```

This creates a link to the parent of a parent. It's normal that this link doesn't work in the context of the standalone kubrick_movies.pdf file, because there's no grandparent. This link will only work when the file with the movie information is opened in the context of the kubrick_collection.pdf file in which the kubrick_movies.pdf file is embedded. While it's fun to make constructions like this, you shouldn't confuse the end user by making the family structure of embedded files and embedded goto actions too complex.

Let's move on and look at special types of annotations that allow you to add movies, sound, and other multimedia formats as part of a document.

16.3 Integrating rich media

ISO-32000-1 has a complete chapter about multimedia, explaining how to embed movies and sound and even 3D images into pages, but the supplement to ISO-32000-1 (extension level 3), also adds the concept of rich media. If you look for the term "Rich Media" on Wikipedia, you'll be forwarded to a page about "Interactive media":

> *Interactive media normally refers to products and services on digital computer-based systems which respond to the user's actions by presenting content such as text, graphics, animation, video, audio.*

> —"Interactive media," Wikipedia

Let's start with the more traditional multimedia, such as movies, then have a look at a 3D example, and finish this chapter with a rich media annotation that embeds a Flash application into a PDF document.

16.3.1 Movie annotations

In chapter 10, you created a document containing the different frames of an animated GIF showing a fox jumping over a dog. You learned that animated GIFs aren't supported in PDF, but if you want to add a movie with a fox jumping over a dog, you can create an annotation using the media types shown in table 16.3.

Table 16.3   Multimedia files supported in PDF

Extension	MIME-type	Description
.aiff	audio/aiff	Audio Interchange File Format
.au	audio/basic	NeXT/Sun Audio Format
.avi	video/avi	AVI (Audio/Video Interleaved)
.mid	audio/midi	MIDI (Musical Instrument Digital Interface)
.mov	video/quicktime	QuickTime
.mp3	audio/x-mp3	MPEG Audio Layer-3
.mp4	audio/mp4	MPEG-4 Audio
.mp4	video/mp4	MPEG-4 Video
.mpeg	video/mpeg	MPEG-2 Video
.smil	application/smil	Synchronized Multimedia Integration Language
.swf	application/x-shockwave-flash	Macromedia Flash

Depending on the viewer, other types of multimedia may be supported too, but these are the ones listed in appendix H of the PDF specification.

Adding a movie with iText is done with a screen annotation. You can use the `createScreen()` method to add an annotation that refers to an external file, or you can embed the file as is done next.

Listing 16.15   MovieAnnotation.java

```
PdfFileSpecification fs = PdfFileSpecification
  .fileEmbedded(writer, RESOURCE, "foxdog.mpg", null);
writer.addAnnotation(PdfAnnotation.createScreen(writer,
  new Rectangle(200f, 700f, 400f, 800f), "Fox and Dog", fs,
  "video/mpeg", true));
```

The constant value `RESOURCE` contains the path to the file that needs to be embedded; foxdog.mpg is the name that will be used inside the PDF.

NOTE   The viewer will warn you about possible security hazards before you can play a movie or any other multimedia file, because one never knows if the file contains a Trojan horse. (I'm not referring to a wooden construction concealing Brad Pitt.)

You can also add sound with a sound annotation, but currently there are no convenience methods in iText to do this. If you need to embed an .au file, you'll have to create `PdfDictionary` objects describing a sound object, a sound annotation, and possibly a sound action. The same goes for 3D annotations.

In the next section, we'll learn how to create specific objects that are described in ISO-32000-1, but for which there are no convenience classes or methods.

16.3.2 *3D annotations*

The 3D Industry Forum is a special consortium that brought together a diverse group of companies and organizations, including Adobe Systems, HP, and Intel. They've developed a format named the *Universal 3D* (U3D) file format, a compressed file format for 3D computer graphics. The format was standardized by Ecma International in 2005.

This format is natively supported by the PDF format. 3D objects in U3D format can be inserted into PDF documents and interactively visualized by Adobe Reader 7.0 and higher. This is done with a 3D annotation that provides a virtual camera through which the artwork is viewed. Figure 16.6 shows a 3D image of a teapot. You can change the view of the object in the PDF by using the mouse and the 3D controls in the bar on top of the annotation.

To produce a PDF like the one shown in figure 16.6, you need to use basic `PdfObject` classes to create a 3D stream object ❶ in listing 16.16, a 3D view dictionary ❷, and a 3D annotation ❸.

Figure 16.6 Document with a 3D annotation

Listing 16.16 Pdf3D.java

```
Rectangle rect = new Rectangle(100, 400, 500, 800);
PdfStream stream3D
  = new PdfStream(new FileInputStream(RESOURCE), writer);
stream3D.put(PdfName.TYPE, new PdfName("3D"));
stream3D.put(PdfName.SUBTYPE, new PdfName("U3D"));
stream3D.flateCompress();
PdfIndirectObject streamObject = writer.addToBody(stream3D);
stream3D.writeLength();
PdfDictionary dict3D = new PdfDictionary();
dict3D.put(PdfName.TYPE, new PdfName("3DView"));
dict3D.put(new PdfName("XN"), new PdfString("Default"));
dict3D.put(new PdfName("IN"), new PdfString("Unnamed"));
dict3D.put(new PdfName("MS"), PdfName.M);
dict3D.put(new PdfName("C2W"), new PdfArray(
  new float[] { 1, 0, 0, 0, 0, -1, 0, 1, 0, 3, -235, 28 } ));
dict3D.put(PdfName.CO, new PdfNumber(235));
PdfIndirectObject dictObject = writer.addToBody(dict3D);
PdfAnnotation annot = new PdfAnnotation(writer, rect);
annot.put(PdfName.CONTENTS, new PdfString("3D Model"));
annot.put(PdfName.SUBTYPE, new PdfName("3D"));
annot.put(PdfName.TYPE, PdfName.ANNOT);
annot.put(new PdfName("3DD"), streamObject.getIndirectReference());
annot.put(new PdfName("3DV"), dictObject.getIndirectReference());
PdfAppearance ap = writer.getDirectContent()
```

1 Creates 3D stream object

2 Creates 3D view dictionary

3 Creates 3D annotation

```
.createAppearance(rect.getWidth(), rect.getHeight());
annot.setAppearance(PdfAnnotation.APPEARANCE_NORMAL, ap);
annot.setPage();
writer.addAnnotation(annot);
```

 ❸ Creates 3D annotation

In ❶, you create a PdfStream using a FileInputStream that allows iText to read a U3D file. You add the keys /Type and /Subtype to the stream dictionary to indicate that you're creating a /3D stream of type /U3D—you do this because it's described that way in ISO-32000-1. You then compress the stream and add the compressed stream to the body of the PDF file with the addToBody() method.

> **NOTE** If you create a PdfStream by passing an array of bytes, the stream object can immediately determine the length of the stream. This length will change when you invoke flatecompress(). In this example, you're creating the stream using a FileInputStream, and iText doesn't know the length of the stream until after the stream has been written to the body, so iText will create an indirect reference for the value of the /Length key. It's up to us to write the object with the actual value to the body once the length is known. This is done with the writeLength() method.

When you add the stream to the body, you obtain the indirect reference streamObject.

You also need a 3D view dictionary ❷. In this dictionary, you can specify parameters for the virtual camera associated with a 3D annotation: the orientation and position of the camera, details regarding the projection of camera coordinates, and so on.

In listing 16.16, you define an external (/XN) and an internal (/IN) name. The matrix system (/MS) indicates that you'll specify a matrix (/M) using a *Camera to World* entry (/C2W). This is a 12-element 3D transformation matrix that specifies a position and orientation of the camera in world coordinates. The /CO value is a non-negative number indicating a distance in the camera coordinate system along the Z axis to the center of orbit for this view. For the complete description of these values, and of the other options that are available, please read section 13.6 of ISO-32000-1.

You add the 3D view dictionary to the body with the addToBody() method, just as you did with the 3D stream. You obtain the indirect reference dictObject. Finally, you create a 3D annotation ❸ as you did before in listing 7.20. You can consult ISO-32000-1 to find out which keys are required in the annotation dictionary, and you add the annotation to the PDF document using the addAnnotation() method.

3D is hot, and it will probably become even hotter, because Adobe's supplement to ISO-32000-1 and Acrobat 9 came with plenty of new features for 3D. If you need 3D functionality, please check itextpdf.com to find out if 3D classes have been added to iText before you add 3D streams the hard way—as described in listing 16.16.

We'll conclude this chapter with an example of brand new functionality described in the supplement to ISO-32000-1 by Adobe (extension level 3).

16.3.3 *Embedding Flash into a PDF*

You can embed a Flash application (a .swf file) into a PDF document using a movie annotation as described in section 16.3.1. This works well for a Flash *movie*, but if you

Figure 16.7 Integrating a Flash application in a PDF document

want to embed a Flash *application*, you'll discover that the interactive features are rather limited. If you want to take advantage of all the functionality of a Flash application, you'll need to embed the .swf file as a rich media annotation. This was the case for the PDF shown in figure 16.7.

The combo box with dates, the button for selecting a day, and the table listing screenings on a particular day are all part of a Flash application written in Flex.

WRITING A FLEX APPLICATION

This listing shows the source code of the Flex application.

Listing 16.17 FestivalCalendar1.mxml

```
<?xml version="1.0" encoding="utf-8"?>
<mx:Application xmlns:mx="http://www.adobe.com/2006/mxml"
  layout="absolute"
  applicationComplete="stage.scaleMode = StageScaleMode.EXACT_FIT;      ❶
  initList(Application.application.parameters.day);">                    ❷
  <mx:Script>
    <![CDATA[
      private function initList(day:Object):void {
        days.selectedItem = day;
        getDateInfo(days.selectedItem);
      }
      private function getDateInfo(day:Object):void {
        screeningsService.url=
          'http://flex.itextpdf.org/fff/day_'
          + day + '.xml';
        screeningsService.send();
        screeningsDataGrid.invalidateList();
      }
```

Initializes
date

Gets data for
specific day

```
        ]]>
      </mx:Script>
      <mx:HTTPService
        id="screeningsService" resultFormat="e4x" />
      <mx:Grid id="formgrid">
        <mx:GridRow id="row1">
          <mx:GridItem>
            <mx:ComboBox id="days" dataProvider="{[
              '2011-10-12', '2011-10-13', '2011-10-14',
              '2011-10-15', '2011-10-16', '2011-10-17',
              '2011-10-18', '2011-10-19' ]}" />
          </mx:GridItem>
          <mx:GridItem>
            <mx:Button id="date" label="Select day"
              click="getDateInfo(days.selectedItem);" />
          </mx:GridItem>
        </mx:GridRow>
        <mx:GridRow id="row2">
          <mx:GridItem colSpan="2">
            <mx:DataGrid id="screeningsDataGrid"
              dataProvider=
                "{screeningsService.lastResult.screening}">
              <mx:columns>
                <mx:DataGridColumn
                  headerText="Time" dataField="time"/>
                <mx:DataGridColumn headerText="Location"
                  dataField="location"/>
                <mx:DataGridColumn headerText="Duration"
                  dataField="duration"/>
                <mx:DataGridColumn
                  headerText="Title" dataField="title"/>
                <mx:DataGridColumn
                  headerText="Year" dataField="year"/>
              </mx:columns>
            </mx:DataGrid>
          </mx:GridItem>
        </mx:GridRow>
      </mx:Grid>
    </mx:Application>
```

Fetches XML file

Displays combo box with dates

Displays button to trigger getDateInfo method

Displays grid containing screening info

This listing is easy to understand even if you've never written a Flex application. There are two methods written in ActionScript inside the Script tag. The object defined with the HTTPService tag will be responsible for making a connection to a site and retrieving data about screenings in the form of an XML file (resultFormat="e4x").

The layout of the UI is defined using a Grid containing two GridRows. The first row has two GridItems: a ComboBox with days ranging from 2011-10-12 to 2011-10-19, and a Button with the label "Select day". The item in the second row has colspan 2, and contains a DataGrid with five DataGridColumns: Time, Location, Duration, Title, and Year. The data provider for this data grid is the last result of the HTTPService with id screeningsService.

This .mxml file was compiled into an .swf file using Flex Builder. This .swf file can be embedded into an HTML file, but you're going to integrate it into a PDF document.

FETCHING XML DATA FROM A SERVER

This example shows the XML file that is fetched by this service for October 12.

Listing 16.18   http://flex.itextpdf.org/fff/day_2011-10-12.xml

```xml
<day date="2011-10-12">
<screening>
  <location>GP.3</location>
  <time>09:30:00</time>
  <duration>98</duration>
  <title>The Counterfeiters</title>
  <year>2007</year>
</screening>
<screening>
  <location>GP.3</location>
  <time>11:30:00</time>
  <duration>120</duration>
  <title>Give It All</title>
  <year>1998</year>
</screening>
...
</day>
```

You've indicated that you're looking for `screening` nodes in the `dataProvider` of the `DataGrid`. As a result, the data grid will have a line for every `screening` tag in the XML, containing the contents of the `dataField` defined in the `DataGridColumn`.

To make this work, you need to put XML files for every date in the combo box in the appropriate place on our web server, but this may not be sufficient. This will work for HTML and .swf files that are hosted on the same domain as the data files, but it won't work in a PDF that is opened on somebody's local machine. The Flash player that runs the Flash application—in a browser, or in a PDF viewer—operates in a secure sandbox. This sandbox will prevent the application from accessing the user's filesystem, and from fetching data from a remote website.

In this case, the Flex application won't be allowed to access the XML files outside the domain to which the application is deployed, unless the owner of the site where the XML files reside allows it. If you open a PDF containing this Flex application locally, you are not on the http://flex.itextpdf.org/ domain, and Adobe Reader will open a dialog box with the following security warning:

> *The document is trying to connect to http://flex.itextpdf.org/crossdomain.xml. If you trust the site, choose Allow. If you do not trust the site, choose Block.*

The next bit of code shows the contents of the crossdomain.xml file that I had to put at the root of the flex.itextpdf.org domain in order to grant access to any Flex application from any domain.

Listing 16.19   crossdomain.xml

```xml
<?xml version="1.0"?>
<!DOCTYPE cross-domain-policy
  SYSTEM "http://www.adobe.com/xml/dtds/cross-domain-policy.dtd">
```

```
<cross-domain-policy>
  <site-control permitted-cross-domain-policies="all"/>
  <allow-access-from domain="*" />
  <allow-http-request-headers-from domain="*" headers="*"/>
</cross-domain-policy>
```

If such a file isn't there, or if it doesn't allow everyone access, the Flex application won't be able to retrieve the data.

Even with the crossdomain.xml file in place, Adobe Reader will show a security warning every time an XML file (for instance, http://flex.itextpdf.org/fff/day_2011-10-12.xml) is fetched, unless you check the Remember My Action for This Site check box.

NOTE Most SWF files that can be found on the market are written to be embedded in HTML files. In theory, you can embed all these files in a PDF document. However, if the SWF files were created using Flex Builder, you may experience problems when zooming in and out, or when printing a page that has a rich media annotation. These problems are caused by the default *scale mode*. To avoid them, you need to change the scale mode as is done in line ❶ in listing 16.17: `stage.scaleMode = StageScaleMode.EXACT_FIT`. This is important if you buy a Flash component that was written using Flex Builder and that was intended for use in HTML. You need to make sure the vendor has taken this into account if you want to use the .swf in a PDF document.

Now that you know how the Flex application was written, let's look at how you can integrate it into a PDF document.

RICH MEDIA ANNOTATIONS

Rich media annotations aren't part of ISO-32000-1. Support for these annotations was added by Adobe in PDF 1.7 extension level 3. In this case, it isn't sufficient to change the version number to 1.7 with `setPdfVersion()`; you also have to set the extension level with the `addDeveloperExtension()` method. You can do this more than once if you're using extensions from different companies.

The method expects an instance of the `PdfDeveloperExtension` class. In listing 16.20, you use the static final object `ADOBE_1_7_EXTENSIONLEVEL3`. This value was created like this:

```
new PdfDeveloperExtension(PdfName.ADBE, PdfWriter.PDF_VERSION_1_7, 3)
```

The first parameter refers to the developing company. The second parameter indicates for which PDF version the extension was written. Finally, you pass in the number of the extension level as an `int`.

Listing 16.20   FestivalCalendar1.java

```
Document document = new Document();
PdfWriter writer
  = PdfWriter.getInstance(document, new FileOutputStream(RESULT));
writer.setPdfVersion(PdfWriter.PDF_VERSION_1_7);          Sets version and
writer.addDeveloperExtension(                             extension level
  PdfDeveloperExtension.ADOBE_1_7_EXTENSIONLEVEL3);
```

```
document.open();
RichMediaAnnotation richMedia
  = new RichMediaAnnotation(writer,
    new Rectangle(36, 400, 559,806));
PdfFileSpecification fs =
  PdfFileSpecification.fileEmbedded(
    writer, RESOURCE, "FestivalCalendar1.swf", null);
PdfIndirectReference asset
  = richMedia.addAsset("FestivalCalendar1.swf", fs);
RichMediaConfiguration configuration
  = new RichMediaConfiguration(PdfName.FLASH);
RichMediaInstance instance
  = new RichMediaInstance(PdfName.FLASH);
RichMediaParams flashVars = new RichMediaParams();
String vars = new String("&day=2011-10-13");
flashVars.setFlashVars(vars);
instance.setParams(flashVars);
instance.setAsset(asset);
configuration.addInstance(instance);
PdfIndirectReference configurationRef
  = richMedia.addConfiguration(configuration);
RichMediaActivation activation = new RichMediaActivation();
activation.setConfiguration(configurationRef);
richMedia.setActivation(activation);
PdfAnnotation richMediaAnnotation = richMedia.createAnnotation();
richMediaAnnotation.setFlags(PdfAnnotation.FLAGS_PRINT);
writer.addAnnotation(richMediaAnnotation);
document.close();
```

- **Creates annotation object**
- **Adds .swf file as asset**
- **Configures RichMedia annotation as Flash app**
- **Sets activation dictionary**

The `RichMediaAnnotation` class isn't a subclass of `PdfAnnotation`, but it can create such an object using the method `createAnnotation()`. The rich media annotation dictionary contains two important entries: a `/RichMediaContent` dictionary and a `/RichMedia-Settings` dictionary. These dictionaries are created internally by iText.

The `RichMediaContent` dictionary consists of the assets, the configuration, and the views:

- *Assets*—These are stored as a name tree with embedded file specifications. You can use the `addAsset()` method to add entries to this name tree.
- *Configuration*—This is an array of `RichMediaConfiguration` objects. Such an object contains an array of `RichMediaInstance` objects.
- *Views*—This is an array of 3D view dictionaries, in case the rich media annotation contains a 3D stream. See listing 16.16.

The `RichMediaConfiguration` dictionary describes a set of instances that are loaded for a given scene configuration. In this example, you use a rich media annotation to embed a Flash application, but you can also use such an annotation for 3D, sound, or video objects.

The constructors of the `RichMediaConfiguration` and `RichMediaInstance` classes accept the following parameters:

- `PdfName._3D`—For 3D objects
- `PdfName.FLASH`—For Flash objects
- `PdfName.SOUND`—For sound objects
- `PdfName.VIDEO`—For video objects

A `RichMediaInstance` dictionary describes a single instance of an asset with settings to populate the artwork of an annotation. In this example, you only have one Flash instance, for which you define `/FlashVars: &day=2011-10-13`. The `day` variable is retrieved in line ❷ of listing 16.17: `Application.application.parameters.day`.

> **NOTE** If you want to reuse the `RichMediaContent` dictionary in more than one rich media annotation, you have to create the first `RichMediaAnnotation` as is done in listing 16.20. You can then get a reference to the `RichMediaContent` dictionary with the `getRichMediaContentReference()` method, and use this reference as an extra parameter for the `RichMediaAnnotation` constructor.

Rich media annotations can be active or inactive. The `RichMediaSettings` dictionary stores conditions and responses that determine when the annotation should be activated and deactivated. iText creates this dictionary automatically, just like the `RichMediaContent` dictionary. It can contain a `RichMediaActivation` dictionary that is set with the method `setActivation()`, and a `RichMediaDeactivation` dictionary set with `setDeactivation()`. Listing 16.20 uses the default activation and deactivation conditions.

The possible conditions for activation—set with `setCondition()`—are:

- `PdfName.XA`—The annotation is explicitly activated by a user action or script; this is the default.
- `PdfName.PO`—The annotation is activated as soon as the page that contains the annotation receives focus as the current page.
- `PdfName.PV`—The annotation is activated as soon as any part of the page that contains the annotation becomes visible.

These are the possible conditions for deactivation—also set with `setCondition()`:

- `PdfName.XD`—The annotation is explicitly deactivated by a user action or script; this is the default.
- `PdfName.PC`—The annotation is deactivated as soon as the page that contains the annotation loses focus as the current page.
- `PdfName.PI`—The annotation is deactivated as soon as the entire page that contains the annotation is no longer visible.

In the `RichMediaActivation` dictionary, you can also add keys to specify the animation, the view, presentation, and scripts.

This first "Flash in PDF" example is cool because you have a PDF document that presents data to the end user that isn't part of the PDF document. I know from experience that the schedule of screenings at a film festival can change at any moment, because the film stock didn't arrive on time or some other reason. By using this Flash application written in Flex, the document can always show the most recent information fetched from the official film festival website.

You could use the same technique to get the most recent items and prices to complete an order form in PDF. To achieve this, you'd need to establish communication between the embedded Flex application and the PDF document.

16.3.4 Establishing communication between Flex and PDF

Figure 16.8 shows a series of widget annotations (PDF), and one rich media annotation (Flash). The sentence, "This is the festival program for 2011-10-14", is shown using a read-only text field. The text is updated using a JavaScript method that is triggered by the rich media annotation. The buttons with the different dates call a `Rich-MediaExecuteAction` that executes an ActionScript method in the Flash application.

This is the festival program for 2011-10-14

| 2011-10-12 | 2011-10-13 | 2011-10-14 | 2011-10-15 | 2011-10-16 | 2011-10-17 | 2011-10-18 | 2011-10-19 |

Time	Location	Duration	Title	Year
20:00:00	CP.2	122	Amélie	2001
22:30:00	CP.2	90	The Pope's Toilet	2007
14:30:00	CP.3	106	Kamchatka	2002
17:00:00	CP.3	90	Princess	2006
20:00:00	CP.3	90	Kopps	2003
22:30:00	CP.3	133	A Very Long Engagement	2004

Figure 16.8   Communication between PDF and Flash

The Flex application, in the next listing, is different from the previous example.

Listing 16.21   FestivalCalendar2.mxml

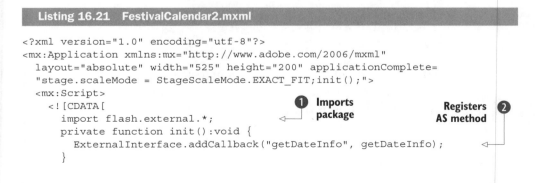

```
<?xml version="1.0" encoding="utf-8"?>
<mx:Application xmlns:mx="http://www.adobe.com/2006/mxml"
  layout="absolute" width="525" height="200" applicationComplete=
  "stage.scaleMode = StageScaleMode.EXACT_FIT;init();">
  <mx:Script>
    <![CDATA[
      import flash.external.*;
      private function init():void {
        ExternalInterface.addCallback("getDateInfo", getDateInfo);
      }
```

❶ Imports package

❷ Registers AS method

```
      private function getDateInfo(day:Object):void {
        screeningsService.url=
          'http://flex.itextpdf.org/fff/day_' + day + '.xml';
        screeningsService.send();
        screeningsDataGrid.invalidateList();
        ExternalInterface.call("showDate", day);
      }
    ]]>
  </mx:Script>
  <mx:HTTPService
    id="screeningsService" resultFormat="e4x" />
  <mx:DataGrid id="screeningsDataGrid"
    dataProvider=
      "{screeningsService.lastResult.screening}"
    width="100%" height="100%">
    <mx:columns>
      <mx:DataGridColumn
        headerText="Time" dataField="time"/>
      <mx:DataGridColumn
        headerText="Location" dataField="location"/>
      <mx:DataGridColumn
        headerText="Duration" dataField="duration"/>
      <mx:DataGridColumn
        headerText="Title" dataField="title"/>
      <mx:DataGridColumn
        headerText="Year" dataField="year"/>
    </mx:columns>
  </mx:DataGrid>
</mx:Application>
```

❸ Calls JS method

HTTP service to fetch XML file

Grid containing screening info

You'll recognize the HTTP service that will get the XML files from http://flex.itext-pdf.org/ and the data grid that visualizes the XML data. You no longer need the combo box and the button, because you're going to change the data from outside the Flex application.

You import the `flash.external.*` package ❶, because you're going to use the `ExternalInterface` object. With the `addCallback()` method ❷, you make the ActionScript method `getDateInfo()` in the Flex application available for external applications. In this method, you call the JavaScript `showDate()` method that is supposed to be present in the PDF document by using the `call()` method ❸.

The `showDate()` JavaScript method in the PDF is very simple:

```
function showDate(txt) {
  this.getField("date").value
    = "This is the festival program for " + txt;
}
```

It gets the text field with the name `date`, and it changes the value of this field so that it corresponds with the date for which the screenings are shown.

The first part of this next listing should look familiar.

Listing 16.22 FestivalCalendar2.java

```java
Document document = new Document();
PdfWriter writer
  = PdfWriter.getInstance(document, new FileOutputStream(RESULT));
writer.setPdfVersion(PdfWriter.PDF_VERSION_1_7);
writer.addDeveloperExtension(
  PdfDeveloperExtension.ADOBE_1_7_EXTENSIONLEVEL3);
document.open();
writer.addJavaScript(Utilities.readFileToString(JS));
RichMediaAnnotation richMedia
  = new RichMediaAnnotation(
    writer, new Rectangle(36, 560, 561, 760));
PdfFileSpecification fs = PdfFileSpecification
  .fileEmbedded(writer, RESOURCE,
    "FestivalCalendar2.swf", null);
PdfIndirectReference asset
  = richMedia.addAsset("FestivalCalendar2.swf", fs);
RichMediaConfiguration configuration
  = new RichMediaConfiguration(PdfName.FLASH);
RichMediaInstance instance
  = new RichMediaInstance(PdfName.FLASH);
instance.setAsset(asset);
configuration.addInstance(instance);
PdfIndirectReference configurationRef
  = richMedia.addConfiguration(configuration);
RichMediaActivation activation
  = new RichMediaActivation();
activation.setConfiguration(configurationRef);
richMedia.setActivation(activation);
PdfAnnotation richMediaAnnotation
  = richMedia.createAnnotation();
richMediaAnnotation.setFlags(PdfAnnotation.FLAGS_PRINT);
writer.addAnnotation(richMediaAnnotation);
String[] days = new String[]{"2011-10-12",
  "2011-10-13", "2011-10-14", "2011-10-15",
  "2011-10-16", "2011-10-17", "2011-10-18",
  "2011-10-19"};
for (int i = 0; i < days.length; i++) {
  Rectangle rect = new Rectangle(
    36 + (65 * i), 765, 100 + (65 * i), 780);
  PushbuttonField button
    = new PushbuttonField(writer, rect, "button" + i);
  button.setBackgroundColor(new GrayColor(0.75f));
  button.setBorderStyle(
    PdfBorderDictionary.STYLE_BEVELED);
  button.setTextColor(GrayColor.GRAYBLACK);
  button.setFontSize(12);
  button.setText(days[i]);
  button.setLayout(
    PushbuttonField.LAYOUT_ICON_LEFT_LABEL_RIGHT);
  button.setScaleIcon(
    PushbuttonField.SCALE_ICON_ALWAYS);
  button.setProportionalIcon(true);
  button.setIconHorizontalAdjustment(0);
  PdfFormField field = button.getField();
```

Adds **JavaScript**

Adds rich media annotation

Adds buttons

```
  RichMediaCommand command = new RichMediaCommand(
    new PdfString("getDateInfo"));
  command.setArguments(new PdfString(days[i]));
  RichMediaExecuteAction action
    = new RichMediaExecuteAction(
      richMediaAnnotation.getIndirectReference(),
      command);
  field.setAction(action);
  writer.addAnnotation(field);
}
TextField text = new TextField(writer,
  new Rectangle(36, 785, 559, 806), "date");
text.setOptions(TextField.READ_ONLY);
writer.addAnnotation(text.getTextField());
document.close();
```

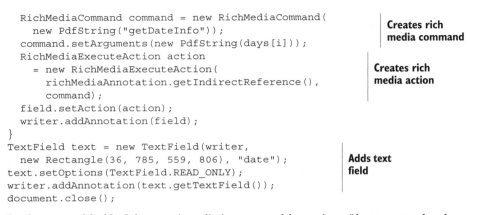

**Creates rich
media command**

**Creates rich
media action**

**Adds text
field**

In the second half of the previous listing, you add a series of buttons to the document, creating a RichMediaExecuteAction for each button. The action will be triggered on the rich media annotation for which you pass the indirect reference. You also pass a RichMediaCommand.

The name of the action is a PDF string that corresponds to the string you used as the parameter of the ExternalInterface.addCallback() method in the Flex application. The argument can be a PdfString, PdfNumber, PdfBoolean, or PdfArray containing those objects.

You also add a text field named date. When you click one of the PDF buttons, the getDateInfo() method will be called, an XML file containing screenings will be fetched from the internet, filling the data grid, and the Flex application will trigger the showDate() JavaScript method to change the value of the date field.

Although this is a very simple example, the techniques that are used can apply to many different types of applications. You could use these techniques to integrate fancy Flash buttons that trigger functions in a PDF file, or you could embed a Flex application to establish client-server communication to retrieve the most recent data. But don't forget that this functionality is very new: it only works with the most recent versions of Adobe Reader!

16.4   *Summary*

In this final chapter, we've looked at different kinds of PDF streams. We started with streams that hold an image or a font and looked at the way iText creates low-level objects that are responsible for writing such a stream to the OutputStream. You also learned how to replace such a stream.

Then we moved on to a type of annotation we encountered in chapter 7: a file attachment annotation. You discovered that there's a difference between file attachments that are added as annotations, and file attachments that are stored at the document level as embedded files. This difference matters if you want to extract files from a PDF document. Files that are embedded at the document level can be organized into a portable collection, aka a portfolio.

Finally, we discussed multimedia files. You added annotations containing a movie file and a 3D stream, and you also used a very new type of annotation that isn't part of ISO-32000 yet.

With a rich media annotation, you were able to integrate a Flash application into a PDF document, and establish communication between the ActionScript in the Flash application and the JavaScript in the PDF document. Those were the last examples of this book.

WHAT YOU'VE LEARNED FROM THIS BOOK

Let's return to the first image in chapter 1 and quickly review everything you've learned. Figure 16.9 shows three main areas.

CREATING PDFS

Chapter 1 provided a short introduction. In chapters 2 and 4 you learned to create PDF documents from scratch using high-level objects. You did the same using low-level functionality in chapters 3 and 5. These first five chapters formed part one of the book.

Essential skills concerning PDF creation were explained in part three. In chapter 9, you learned to create documents on the fly from a web application. We focused on color and images in chapter 10, and on fonts in chapter 11. Chapter 12 was about encrypting and signing documents.

For advanced users, there's also part four, which explains the inner workings of iText and PDF. Chapter 14 will remain especially interesting as a reference for developers who frequently need to add content to a document using low-level methods.

Most of the PDF files in this book were generated using data from a database, but in some cases you converted an XML or an HTML file to PDF. For instance in chapter 9, we talked about using the `HTMLWorker` class to convert HTML snippets; in chapter 11 you converted an XML file containing the word "peace" in many different languages into a PDF document.

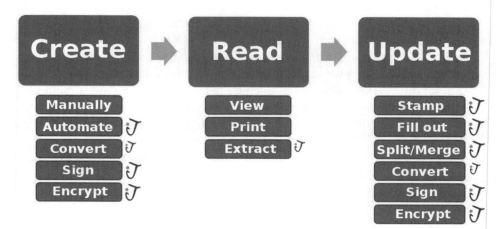

Figure 16.9 Overview of the PDF functionality that was covered

On occasion, we looked at creating a PDF document manually, using Open Office rather than using iText, such as in chapter 6. In chapter 8, you used Adobe Acrobat and LiveCycle Designer. These files were created for the purpose of updating them, and that takes us from the Read block in figure 16.9 to the Update block.

UPDATING PDFS

Part two of this book was titled "Manipulating existing PDF documents." Chapter 6 presented an overview of all the PDF manipulation classes available in iText. You always needed a `PdfReader` instance to access an existing document. You learned how to split and merge PDF documents with `PdfCopy`, `PdfSmartCopy`, `PdfCopyFields`, and even using `PdfImportedPage` objects, but the class you used the most was `PdfStamper`, which was initially written to stamp extra information on an existing document.

In chapter 7, you used `PdfStamper` to add different types of annotations. This functionality is also useful when creating a document from scratch; for instance, to add links that allow the end user to navigate from one page to another, or from one document to another. Along the way, we talked about bookmarks, actions, and destinations.

Chapter 8 was dedicated entirely to forms: you worked with forms built using the AcroForm technology, and with XFA forms. iText has almost complete support for AcroForms, but as soon as you have a form involving the XML Forms Architecture, the possibilities are limited. For instance, iText can't flatten an XFA form (yet).

Signing and encrypting existing PDF documents was discussed in chapter 12. Converting a PDF document to another format turned out to be very difficult, but in some cases, you can extract an XML version of the complete document, or extract plain text from a page.

READING PDFS

iText isn't a PDF viewer, nor can iText be used to print a PDF, but the `PdfReader` class can give you access to the objects that form a PDF document. The different types of objects that are defined in the PDF specification were listed in chapter 13, where you also had a closer look at the root object of a PDF document.

Chapter 14 dealt with the imaging system and the way the content of a page in a PDF document is organized. We continued studying the content stream of a page in chapter 15, looking for ways to add structure. You found out that a PDF can be read out loud if marked content has been added to improve the accessibility of the document. You also learned how to convert a PDF to XML if the PDF was tagged and contains a structure tree. At the end of the chapter, we made a fair attempt at parsing the content of a page to plain text.

Finally, in chapter 16 you learned more about streams. You even wrote a Flex application for use in a PDF document.

This isn't the first book I've written, and based on my previous experience, I know that one can never have enough documentation. But with this book, you have a comprehensible overview of what is possible with PDF in general—the different topics listed in figure 16.9—and with iText in particular—the topics marked with the iText logo.

Sure, writing a book is a lot of work, but I also had a lot of fun writing new material for this second edition: creating the movie database, making my first dynamic PDF using LiveCycle Designer, learning Flex for the sole purpose of creating a PDF containing a rich media annotation, and inventing many other new examples that weren't in the first edition.

I hope you've enjoyed reading this book as much as I enjoyed writing it.

May the source be with you!

appendix A
Bibliography

This appendix contains a list of books, specifications, and presentations for further reading. I'll keep an updated list on the iText site (http://itextpdf.com/), adding new publications by Adobe or standards bodies such as AIIM, ETSI, and ISO.

A.1 Published by Adobe Systems

For more info, see http://www.adobe.com/.

A.1.1 Specifications (PDF documents)

XML Forms Architecture (XFA) Specification version 3.1. November 16, 2009.
Adobe Supplement to the ISO 32000—BaseVersion: 1.7—ExtensionLevel: 5. June 2009.
Understanding the Differences Between Static and Dynamic PDF Forms. July 2008.
Adobe Supplement to the ISO 32000—BaseVersion: 1.7—ExtensionLevel: 3. June 2008.
JavaScript for Acrobat API Reference. April 2007.
Developing Acrobat Applications Using JavaScript. November 2006.
Digital Signature Appearances. October 2006.
PDF Reference, sixth edition—Adobe Portable Document Format Version 1.7. 2006.
XMP specification. September 2005.
Acrobat 7.0 PDF Open Parameters. July 2005.
Warnock, John. *The Camelot Paper.* 1991.

A.1.2 Presentations (PDF documents)

Schellemans, Peter. *PDF Standards & Digital Signatures* (Adobe Benelux Pulse session). 2010.
King, Jim. *The Future of PDF and Flash.* 2007.
King, Jim. *Introduction to the Insides of PDF* (IS&T Archiving Conference). 2005.
Cosimini, Gary. *Acrobat, the Early Years* (keynote, PDF Conference, 2003). 2003.
King, Jim. *Introduction to XML—A Little about PDF.* 2000.
King, Jim. *PDF: A Look Inside.* 1998.

A.2 Published by the Association for Information and Image Management (AIIM)

For more info, see http://www.aiim.org.

Implementation Guide for the Portable Document Format Healthcare (PDF/H)—Best Practices. 2008.

PDF/UA (Universal Accessibility), Draft Meeting Minutes, October 3, 4, 2005.

A.3 Published by the European Telecommunications Standards Institute (ETSI)

For more info, see http://portal.etsi.org/.

Electronic Signatures and Infrastructure (ESI): PDF Advanced Electronic Signature Profiles (in 5 parts).

     [TS 102 778-1] Part 1: PAdES Overview—A Framework Document for PAdES

     [TS 102 778-2] Part 2: PAdES Basic—Profile Based on ISO 32000-1

     [TS 102 778-3] Part 3: PAdES Enhanced—PAdES-BES and PAdES-EPES Profiles

     [TS 102 778-4] Part 4: PAdES Long term—PAdES LTV Profile

     [TS 102 778-5] Part 5: PAdES for XML Content—Profiles for XAdES Signatures

A.4 Published by the International Organization for Standardization (ISO)

For more info, see http://www.iso.org/.

ISO 32000-1:2008, Document management—Portable document format—Part 1: PDF 1.7.

ISO 24517-1:2008, Document management—Engineering document format using PDF—Part 1: Use of PDF 1.6 (PDF/E-1).

ISO 19005, Document management—Electronic document file format for long-term preservation—Part 1: Use of PDF 1.4 (PDF/A-1).

ISO 15930-1 to 8, Graphic technology—Prepress digital data exchange (PDF/X-1a:2001, PDF/X-2, PDF/X-3:2002, PDF/X-1a:2003, PDF/X-2, PDF/X-3:2003, PDF/X-4 and PDF/X-5).

A.5 Other publications

Snyder, Thomas. *Advanced Integrated RPG.* Mc Press, 2010. (Discusses IBM Report Program Generator, with three chapters about iText.)

De Caluwe, Rita. *Vijftig jaar rekencentrum aan de Universiteit Gent.* Academia Press, 2009.

Lowagie, Bruno. *iText in Action: Creating and Manipulating PDF.* Manning, 2007. (The first edition of this book.)

Steward, Sid. *PDF Hacks.* O'Reilly Media, 2004. (About PDF in general, with some outdated examples about using iText.)

appendix B
Useful links

This appendix contains a list of links to interesting sites about iText, PDF, and techniques that were used in this book. For an updated version of this list, visit the iText site (http://itextpdf.com/).

B.1 iText-related links

B.1.1 iText links

iText home page: http://itextpdf.com/
iText at SourceForge:
> http://sourceforge.net/projects/itext/
> http://sourceforge.net/projects/itextsharp/

iText mailing list: itext-questions@lists.sourceforge.net.
> Registration is mandatory: https://lists.sourceforge.net/lists/listinfo/itext-questions

Maven repository: http://maven.itextpdf.com/
SVN repository: http://itext.svn.sourceforge.net/viewvc/itext/
SVN access to the iText source code:
> svn co https://itext.svn.sourceforge.net/svnroot/itext/trunk main

AGPL license: http://www.gnu.org/licenses/agpl-3.0.html
Commercial licenses: sales@itextpdf.com
> Paid consultancy: consultancy@itextpdf.com

B.1.2 iText in Action links

More info about the examples in the book: http://itextpdf.com/examples/
More info about the images in the book: http://www.flickr.com/photos/itextinaction
SVN access to the book examples:
> svn co https://itext.svn.sourceforge.net/svnroot/itext/book book

Extra examples regarding digital signatures:
> http://itextpdf.sourceforge.net/howtosign.html

B.2   PDF-related links

Adobe, JavaScript for Acrobat: http://www.adobe.com/devnet/acrobat/javascript.html

Adobe, PDF Open Parameters:
http://partners.adobe.com/public/developer/en/acrobat/PDFOpenParameters.pdf

Adobe, PDF Reference and Adobe Extensions to the PDF Specification:
http://www.adobe.com/devnet/pdf/pdf_reference.html

Adobe, PDF Reference archives:
http://www.adobe.com/devnet/pdf/pdf_reference_archive.html

Adobe, XML Forms Architecture:
http://partners.adobe.com/public/developer/xml/index_arch.html

Comp.text.pdf newsgroup: http://groups.google.com/group/comp.text.pdf/topics

Planet PDF: http://www.planetpdf.com/

Wikipedia: PDF: http://en.wikipedia.org/wiki/Portable_Document_Format

B.3   Technical links

B.3.1   Tools and products referred to in the book

Adobe Flex: http://www.adobe.com/products/flex/

Apache Ant: http://ant.apache.org/

Apache Batik: http://xmlgraphics.apache.org/batik/

Apache FOP: http://xmlgraphics.apache.org/fop/

Apache Tomcat: http://tomcat.apache.org/

Bouncy Castle Crypto API: http://www.bouncycastle.org/

Eclipse: http://eclipse.org/

Flying Saucer: https://xhtmlrenderer.dev.java.net/

HyperSQL: http://hsqldb.org/

Java: http://java.sun.com/

JavaScript: https://developer.mozilla.org/en/Core_JavaScript_1.5_Reference

JFreeChart: http://www.jfree.org/jfreechart/

B.3.2   Fonts

American Mathematical Society, Type 1 fonts: http://www.ams.org/publications/type1-fonts

Free Font Archives (Luc Devroye): http://cg.scs.carleton.ca/~luc/freefonts.html

Free Fonts: http://www.free-fonts.com/

Gallery of Unicode Fonts: http://www.wazu.jp/

Languagegeek Fonts: http://www.languagegeek.com/font/fontdownload.html

Microsoft Typography: http://www.microsoft.com/typography/

OpenType Naming Tables (section 11.4.1):
http://partners.adobe.com/public/developer/opentype/index_name.html
http://www.microsoft.com/typography/otspec/name.htm

OpenType Q & A: http://www.adobe.com/type/opentype/qna.html

OpenType Specification: http://www.microsoft.com/typography/otspec/

Repository of TrueType Fonts: http://chanae.walon.org/pub/ttf/

Say Peace in all Languages! http://www.columbia.edu/~fdc/pace/

Search Free Fonts: http://www.searchfreefonts.com/

Summer Institute of Linguistics, Computers & Writing Systems: http://scripts.sil.org/

The Unicode Consortium: http://www.unicode.org/

Unicode Fonts for Windows Computers (Alan Wood):
http://www.alanwood.net/unicode/fonts.html

Where Is My Character? http://www.unicode.org/standard/where/

B.3.3 Accessibility

Section 508 (accessibility): http://www.section508.gov/

W3C, Web Content Accessibility Guidelines:
http://www.w3.org/TR/2005/WD-WCAG20-20050630/

B.3.4 Miscellaneous

Adobe, Communication between Flex & JavaScript:
http://cookbooks.adobe.com/post_Communication_between_Flex___
JavaScript-17010.html

Adobe, XMP Developer Center: http://www.adobe.com/devnet/xmp/

ECMA International: http://www.ecma-international.org/

iTextSharp examples: http://kuujinbo.info/iTextInAction2Ed/index.aspx

Oracle, Java Developer Tutorials and Training:
http://java.sun.com/developer/onlineTraining/

World Wide Web Consortium (W3C): http://www.w3.org/

B.4 Other links

B.4.1 Certificate authorities

CAcert: http://www.cacert.org/

GlobalSign: http://www.globalsign.com/

Thawte: http://www.thawte.com/

VeriSign: http://www.verisign.com/

B.4.2 Movie links

Flanders International Film Festival Ghent: http://www.filmfestival.be/

Internet Movie Database (IMDB): http://www.imdb.com/

Java Movie Database (JMDB): http://www.jmdb.de/

Serious efforts have been made to save paper when writing this book. Occasionally, I've printed a chapter I was working on, but I've tried to avoid this as much as possible. I've printed the full manuscript only once to revise it for the final review. Paper is too valuable to waste! See http://www.panda.org/savepaper.

index

RELATED MANNING TITLES

jQuery in Action, Second Edition
by Bear Bibeault and Yehuda Katz

ISBN: 978-1-935182-32-0
488 pages, $44.99
June 2010

C# in Depth, Second Edition
by Jon Skeet

ISBN: 978-1-935182-47-4
500 pages, $49.99
October 2010

Spring in Action, Third Edition
by Craig Walls

ISBN: 978-1-935182-35-1
700 pages, $49.99
January 2011

Struts2 in Action
by Donald Brown, Chad Michael Davis, and
Scott Stanlick

ISBN: 978-1-933988-07-8
424 pages, $44.99
May 2008

For ordering information go to www.manning.com